THE MANAGEMENT OF
HUMAN RESOURCES

THE MANAGEMENT OF HUMAN RESOURCES

David J. Cherrington

Brigham Young University

ALLYN & BACON
A Division of
Simon & Schuster, Inc.

Boston ■ London ■ Toronto ■ Sydney ■ Tokyo ■ Singapore

Series Editor: Jack Peters
Production Administrator: Peter Petraitis
Editorial-Production Service: Barbara Pendergast
Text Designer: Melinda Grosser for *silk*
Cover Administrator: Linda Dickinson
Manufacturing Buyer: Louise Richardson

Library of Congress Cataloging-in-Publication Data

Cherrington, David J.
    The management of human resources / David J. Cherrington.
        p.   cm.
    Includes bibliographical references and index.
    ISBN 0-205-12801-7
    1. Personnel management.   I. Title.
  HF5549.C4466 1991   90-21404
  658.3--dc20   CIP

Copyright © 1991 by Allyn and Bacon
A Division of Simon & Schuster, Inc.
160 Gould Street
Needham Heights, MA 02194

Formerly published under the title *Personnel Management* by Wm. C. Brown, © 1987, 1983.

Printed in the United States of America
10 9 8 7 6 5 4 3 2 1   96 95 94 93 92 91 90

TO MY WIFE, MARILYN, AND MY CHILDREN,
DAVID, NATHAN, JENNIFER, AND JILL

BRIEF CONTENTS

C O N T E N T S

ix

CHAPTER 5 | **Recruitment and Equal Employment Opportunity**   173

CHAPTER 6 | **The Selection Process**   216

CHAPTER 7

Performance Evaluation   269

CHAPTER 8

Principles of Training and Development   311

CHAPTER 9

Training and Development Programs 345

CHAPTER 10

Wage and Salary Administration 383

CHAPTER 14

Grievance and Discipline Procedures 562

CHAPTER 15

Employee Safety and Health 608

APPENDIXES

INDEXES

P R E F A C E

PURPOSE

This text is designed to teach the basic principles of human resource management to a diverse audience of students, including those who are studying to be human resource managers, those preparing to be line managers, and others who simply plan to be part of the work force. This text builds upon the successful foundation of the first and second editions and follows the same primary objectives: to describe the most relevant topics in personnel and human resource management and explain them in a highly readable and interesting manner. The preparation of this revision benefited from the feedback of professors and students who studied the earlier editions, and I am grateful for their insightful comments. I am also grateful for the feedback from dozens of scholars and professional colleagues who participated in the market research study conducted by the publisher to help guide this revision.

The changes in this revision consist of (1) discussing ethics and international HRM—two highly charged emerging topics in human resource management, (2) updating the statistics and research conclusions, (3) explaining the changes in recent legislation, and (4) deleting material that is typically covered in an organizational behavior course. Special efforts have been made to explain recent developments in human resource management, such as employee rights, AIDS, smoking in the workplace, wrongful discharge, the comparable-worth controversy, deferred compensation programs, and employee stock ownership plans (ESOPs). Consistent with the earlier editions, this revision is written in an understandable manner appropriate for both personnel and nonpersonnel majors. In making the text understandable, however, care was taken to avoid deleting or oversimplifying any of the basic principles. The text combines a careful blend of (1) information describing how human resource management is typically performed, (2) research information about the results of behavioral science research studies, (3) prescriptive information explaining how human resource activities ought to be performed, and (4) applied information presenting illustrations of how organizations actually perform their human resource activities.

Another distinctive feature of this text is its balanced treatment of organizational demands and individual interests. The informal employment exchange between the individual and the organization is described in the first section and applied in later chapters to explain how organizational effectiveness and the quality of life are joint goals that must be pursued simultaneously. Human resource activities must be designed to achieve both goals rather than sacrificing one for the other.

SPECIAL FEATURES DESIGNED TO ENHANCE STUDENT LEARNING

Several features of this text were purposely designed to enhance student learning. The following list identifies these features and explains the benefit of each.

Learning objectives. Each chapter begins with a set of learning objectives that are intended as guidelines on how to study the chapter.

Chapter outline. Each chapter contains a chapter outline that previews the text material and helps to keep the information in perspective while it is being read.

Introductory cases. The opening pages of each chapter contain a case study that introduces readers to human resource management problems related to the chapter content.

Exhibits. Each chapter contains several figures, line drawings, and charts that are used to explain or clarify the theoretical concepts.

Chapter summaries. Each chapter contains a summary that helps to organize the content of the chapter and identify the most important information.

Discussion questions. The concluding pages of each chapter contain a set of discussion questions that test the student's understanding of the chapter material and can serve as vehicles for class discussion.

Chapter key terms. Each chapter contains a glossary of key terms and ideas. The key terms summarize the major ideas of each chapter and define vocabulary that may be new to the student.

Concluding cases. The concluding pages of each chapter contain a case that further applies the chapter to a real human resource management problem. Both the introductory cases and the concluding cases refer to real-life problems, although the names of the individuals and organizations have been changed. The situations are condensed and simplified to highlight specific problems and to make them more useful for class discussion.

SUPPLEMENTARY MATERIALS

A *Student Study Guide* has been prepared to accompany this text. The material in this guide provides students with a summary of the key concepts explained in the text and an opportunity to practice and apply what they have learned. Extensive feedback from both teachers and students who have used the study guide indicates that this material is extremely helpful and useful.

The *Student Study Guide* contains fifteen chapters that correspond with the chapters in this text. Each chapter contains four learning aids in which: (1) the content of each chapter is briefly summarized; (2) multiple-choice and true/false questions are provided for students to test their mastery of the material; (3) one or two cases describing human resource problems related to the content of each chapter provide students with an opportunity to develop their skills in diagnosing problems and applying the material they have learned; and (4) experiential exercises or problems are included that require students to interact with other students. Some of the problems are data-based and require specific quantitative answers, while other exercises involve group interactions. These experiential exercises, activities, and projects can be used as either in-class or out-of-class activities to further illustrate the content of each chapter.

ACKNOWLEDGMENTS

As with the development of all texts, this book is a result of the efforts of a great number of people. I would like to express appreciation and give credit where credit is due. Valuable assistance in writing this text came from a number of highly respected colleagues who conscientiously reviewed the manuscript at various stages of completion and suggested improvements. The collective wisdom of the following people helped improve this text:

Razelle Frankl, Glassboro State College

Alan Cabelly, Portland State University

Coy A. Jones, Memphis State University

Thomas G. Pearce, Moorhead State University

Anne C. Cowden, California State University—Sacramento

Various portions of this manuscript have also been reviewed by public affairs directors or staff members in several agencies, including OSHA, AFL-CIO, NLRB, Workmen's Compensation Administration, Social Security Administration, and the Internal Revenue Service. I greatly appreciated their time and advice even though space limitations often forced me to delete or summarize some of their suggestions.

Valuable assistance was rendered by dozens of other individuals, including colleagues at Brigham Young University, corporate officers, personnel directors, supervisors, OSHA inspectors, union leaders, and production workers. Although their enormous contribution would justify naming each of them individually, many asked to remain anonymous. I only hope that the names and places I have substituted in the cases and the other changes I have made to simplify complex situations are acceptable to them.

Typing a lengthy manuscript is always a difficult chore. I appreciate the cheerful service provided by all the secretaries in the Word Processing

Center who not only accomplished the task, but said they enjoyed doing it. I'm especially grateful for the dedicated efforts of two supervisors, Catherine Shumway and Cathleen Cornaby, who were as pleasant in revising the manuscript the third and fourth time as the first time.

The people at Allyn & Bacon Publishers also deserve special thanks. I am impressed with the professional expertise and cheerful cooperation of many employees I have never met, but whose skill and contribution I have admired from afar. I am especially grateful for the assistance of John Peters, who served as a capable developmental editor and not only made significant contributions to the style of the book, but also provided a tremendous motivation to complete the project.

I also express appreciation to two loyal friends of our university, Nyal D. and Bette McMullin, who have contributed time and money to improve the quality of education for our students. I am grateful for their generous financial contribution and the insights and wisdom they share with us.

Last, the personal support of my family and their willingness to make sacrifices while I was writing this text should not go unnoted. All significant accomplishments require a team effort and I am grateful to the other members of my team: Marilyn, David, Nathan, Jennifer, and Jill. And thanks also to some special people: my parents, Jack A. and Virginia F. Cherrington, and my parents-in-law, Dr. Robert H. and Anna M. Daines, whose standards of excellence and constant encouragement will be an inspiration throughout my life.

David J. Cherrington
Nyal D. and Bette McMullin Professor
Brigham Young University

THE MANAGEMENT OF
HUMAN RESOURCES

CHAPTER 1

The Organizational Context of Human Resource Management

After studying this chapter, you should be able to:

1. Explain why human resource management has become increasingly important in the management of modern organizations.
2. Describe the relationship between human resource management and line management.
3. List the major personnel functions.
4. Identify some of the most significant early developments in human resource management.
5. Describe the job of a professional human resource manager and identify some of the major associations.
6. Explain how human resource activities are influenced by the organizational climate.

Chapter Outline

Role of the Human Resource Department
Human Resource Management / Growing Importance of Human Resource Functions / Economic Contribution of Human Resource Management

Human Resource Functions
Relationships Between Human Resource and Line Management / Staffing/Employment / Performance Evaluation / Compensation / Training and Development / Employee Relations / Safety and Health / Personnel Research

Early Developments in Personnel
The Guild System / Changes in the Nature of Work / Scientific Management / Industrial Psychology / Human Relations Movement / Labor unions

The Human Resource Profession
Human Resource Positions / Careers in Human Resource Management /
Professional Human Resource Management Organizations / Personnel Certification

Effects of Organizational Climate on Human Resource Management
Management Style / Presence versus Absence of a Union

International HRM

I N T R O D U C T O R Y   C A S E

"We Don't Have an HR Department"

An article in the *Personnel Administrator* described Nucor Corporation as the most productive steel mill in the world.[1] When students in a human resource management class heard that a Nucor mill was located nearby, they thought it would provide an excellent field trip. One of the student leaders, Rebecca, called to arrange the visit. When she phoned she asked to speak with their human resource manager.

"I'm sorry, we don't have a human resource manager."

"Then could I speak with your personnel director?"

"We don't have a personnel director either."

"Then what do you call that position?"

"I'm sorry, ma'am, but we simply don't have that position."

Assuming they had a special title for the position, Rebecca asked, "Who handles your compensation and benefits?"

"Our benefits are managed by our controller but our compensation is directed by a payroll clerk. Would you like to talk with her?"

"Is she also the one who manages the recruiting, hiring, and performance evaluation?"

"No, those activities are performed by our supervisors. Is there something I could help you with?"

Finally, Rebecca realized that they did not have a human resource manager or a personnel department. Eventually her call was directed to the general manager, who explained how the personnel functions were performed at that steel mill. Although Nucor Steel did not have a human resource manager at each mill, they had a manager of personnel services at the corporate headquarters who was responsible for creating personnel policies and programs for the mills.

The general manager explained that 335 employees worked at that location and all but 55 of them were directly involved in producing steel. These 55 included the supervisors, the clerical support staff, and

2

six vice presidents. Although none of these people had the title human resource manager, they all performed various human resource functions. Wages, salaries, and benefits were distributed by the payroll clerk; health and accident insurance was supervised by an insurance clerk. The supervisors were responsible for most of the remaining personnel functions, including interviewing, hiring, discipline, safety, and training. Recruiting was not assigned to anyone since they had a long waiting list of job applicants and turnover was negligible.

The supervisors received a salary for 52 weeks per year, plus an annual bonus, while production workers received hourly pay plus generous productivity bonuses that were calculated daily and weekly. Everyone also participated in an annual profit-sharing plan. The productivity bonuses generally accounted for over two-thirds of the production workers' pay. Employees who came to work late forfeited their daily production bonus, and if they were absent they lost their weekly production bonus. Consequently, tardiness and absenteeism were not problems at this mill.

Rebecca asked if it would be possible to bring the student group on a field trip to visit the plant.

"I'm sorry, but we cannot accommodate you. It's not that we dislike visitors or want to be secretive, we simply don't have anyone to show you around. We are in the business of producing steel, not guided tours."

Nucor Steel is good at making steel. The top five steel mills in the United States average 347 tons of steel per employee per year, while the top five integrated steel mills in Japan average 480 tons of steel per employee per year. Nucor produces approximately 950 tons of steel per employee per year.[2]

Questions:
1. Most companies with over 300 employees have a human resource manager. How does Nucor Steel get by without one?
2. Since Nucor Steel does not have a human resource manager, and they are so productive, does this suggest that other companies should eliminate or reduce their human resource departments?
3. What would be the advantages and disadvantages of creating a human resource manager position at Nucor Steel? What should be the responsibilities of this position?

ROLE OF THE HUMAN RESOURCE DEPARTMENT

This chapter explains how human resource management contributes to the overall management of an organization by examining the role of the human resource department and why it is necessary to the organization. Since human resource management occurs within the context of an organization, the major purpose of human resource activities is to help the organization function effectively. The major human resource activities include staffing, performance evaluation, training and development, compensation and benefits, employee relations, and safety and health. In an effective organization each of these activities must be performed properly and they must be well coordinated, because a change in one activity will lead to changes in other activities, which will ultimately influence the productivity of the organization. These human re-source activities are described in succeeding chapters of this text.

HUMAN RESOURCE MANAGEMENT

The terms *personnel management* and *human resource management* refer to the same pro-cesses. Human resource management is a modern term that emerged during the 1970s. Its use gradually spread, and in 1989, the American Society for Personnel Administration voted to change its name to the Society for Human Resource Management. Both terms, however, refer to the same thing; the personnel who work for a company represent that company's human resources. Since human resources are an organization's most impor-tant asset, all managers should be vitally concerned with human resource management.

THE GROWING IMPORTANCE OF HUMAN RESOURCE FUNCTIONS

Personnel departments, as they were then called, first appeared in significant numbers during the 1940s. The National Labor Relations Act of 1935 encouraged the creation of labor unions, and organizations thus found themselves involved in collective bargaining, administering labor agreements, and resolving labor grievances. During the following decade, with the onset of World War II, millions of soldiers were recruited to serve in the military, and improved personnel procedures had to be developed to manage such vast numbers. At the same time, new defense industries were created, and, many of them employed large numbers of women who were entering the work force for the first time. The military developed modern selection, training, and evaluation procedures, including tests (used as a cost-effective way to select pilots) and performance evaluations (used to select officers for promotion and to further their career development). Many of these procedures were subsequently adopted by industry.

The early personnel departments were primarily responsible for employee selection, training, record keeping, and collective bargaining. These important activities continue to be part of the personnel/human resource function, but other activities have been added. In recent years human resource departments in many organizations have come to assume a more central role by acting as change masters who clarify the organization's culture and help it adapt to an ever-changing environment.[3] Several factors have contrib-uted to the growing importance of personnel/human resource functions.

ACCOMMODATION TO WORKERS' NEEDS

Workers are demanding that organizations accommodate their personal needs by insti-tuting such programs as flexible work schedules, parental leave, child-care and elder-care assistance, and job sharing. The human resource department plays a central role in establishing and implementing policies designed to reduce the friction between organi-zational demands and family responsibilities.

INCREASED COMPLEXITY OF THE MANAGER'S JOB

Management has become an increasingly complex and demanding job for many reasons, including foreign competition, new technology, expanding scientific information, and rapid change. As a consequence, organizations frequently ask human resource managers for assistance in making strategic business decisions and in matching the distinctive competencies of the firm's human resources to the mission of the organization. Executives need assistance from personnel/human resource departments in matters of recruitment, performance evaluation, compensation, and discipline.

LEGISLATION

The enactment of state and federal laws has contributed enormously to the proliferation and importance of human resource functions. The record-keeping and reporting requirements of the laws are so extensive that to comply with them many human resource departments must work countless hours and often must hire additional staff. Four areas that have been influenced most by legislation include equal employment, compensation, safety, and labor relations. An organization's failure to comply with laws regulating these areas can result in extremely costly back-pay awards, class action suits, and penalties.

CONSISTENCY

Human resource policies help to maintain consistency and equity within an organization. Consistency is particularly important in compensation and promotion decisions. When managers make compensation decisions without consulting the human resources department, the salary structure tends to become very uneven and unfair. Promotion decisions also may be handled unfairly when the human resource department does not coordinate the decisions of individual managers. As organizations have increased in size and complexity and as laws have mandated greater equality in the treatment of employees, the human resource department's role in developing and monitoring consistent policies has become increasingly important.

EXPERTISE

There now exist sophisticated personnel activities that require special expertise. For example, researchers have developed complex procedures for making employee-selection decisions; statistical formulas that combine interviews, test scores, and application-blank information have replaced the subjective interviews traditionally used in making selection decisions. Similarly, many organizations have developed compensation systems with elaborate benefits packages to replace simple hourly pay or piece-rate incentive systems.

COST OF PERSONNEL PROBLEMS

Human resource activities have become increasingly important because of the high cost of personnel problems. As a rule of thumb, managers place their highest priority on controlling their greatest expense. The largest single expense in most organizations is labor cost, which is often considerably higher than necessary because of such personnel problems as absenteeism, tardiness, turnover, and alcoholism.

ECONOMIC CONTRIBUTION OF HUMAN RESOURCE MANAGEMENT

Human resource activities should not be implemented unless they contribute to the accomplishment of organizational goals and to the successful execution of organizational strategies. Therefore, such activities should be evaluated to determine whether they are simply proliferating programs and reports or are making a positive contribution to the economic success of the organization.

Some corporations are not content to view the human resource function as an overhead expense and ask their human resource departments to measure the contribution they make to both employee attitudes and organizational effectiveness. One study attempted to assess the human resource department's contribution in two organizations in the entertainment/recreation industry. This study concluded that the costs of the programs sponsored by the human resource departments could be justified by "hard" data as a result of improved employee attitudes. The study provided empirical support for the subjective beliefs regarding the importance of carefully designed human resource functions.[4]

PERSONNEL OBJECTIVES

Like other management functions, human resource activities should help an organization achieve its objectives. In most instances, this means that human resource activities should be directed toward the accomplishment of the following **human resource objectives**:

Profit/cost containment: In the private sector, the primary objective of a business enterprise is profit, and human resource activities should contribute to an organization's profit level. In the public sector, human resource activities should attempt to contain costs.

Organizational effectiveness: An effective organization must be carefully structured and staffed with competent, highly motivated employees. It also must be able to adapt to a changing environment and be capable of resolving internal conflicts and disagreements.

Service: An important objective for business and government organizations is to provide a useful product or service to society.

Social responsibility: Business organizations are ideally expected to improve the quality of society and to help solve social problems. As a result, many businesses, especially large corporations, have added social responsibility to their corporate objectives and have channeled their resources into such concerns as environmental health programs, inner-city renewal projects, minority training and development programs, and support of the arts.

Quality of work life: Since the quality of life at work profoundly influences the quality of life away from work, many organizations have attempted to improve the quality of life at work by creating flexible work hours, autonomous work teams, job enrichment, and better work environments.

Human resource activities should be evaluated in terms of how they contribute to achieving these five objectives.

HUMAN RESOURCE POLICIES

Human resource policies guide the actions of an organization toward the achievement of its objectives. Whereas an objective tends to specify what is to be done, a policy explains how it is to be done. Therefore, human resource policies refer to standing plans that furnish broad guidelines and direct the thinking of managers about human resource issues. Some of the most common issues treated in human resource policies are: (a) discipline problems, such as absenteeism, tardiness, insubordination, and horseplay; (b) promotions, transfers, and layoffs; (c) compensation, pay increases, and benefits; (d) holidays, vacations, and sick leave; and (e) termination.[5] Human resource policies serve three major purposes:

1. To reassure employees that they will be treated fairly and objectively.
2. To help managers make rapid and consistent decisions.
3. The give managers the confidence to resolve problems and defend their decisions.

To achieve these purposes, human resource policies should be written and available for everyone to examine. Written policies are more authoritative than verbal ones and serve as valuable aids in orienting and training new personnel, in administering disciplinary actions, and in resolving grievance issues. Human resource policies are typically formed under the direction of top-level managers. However, since first-level supervisors are most often involved in administering these policies, input from them is useful in formulating new policies.

Human resource policies are typically explained in employee handbooks, and these manuals have created problems for some employers because they contain "implied promises." For example, such manuals typically call full-time employees "permanent" to distinguish them from temporary or part-time employees. Some courts have construed this to constitute a promise of continued employment, and some employees who have been fired have been reinstated. Because of an increase in the number of wrongful-discharge lawsuits being won by employees, employers are carefully reviewing the language and intent of their human resource policies.[6]

HUMAN RESOURCE FUNCTIONS

Human resource departments are responsible for a variety of company activities. Table 1.1 contains a list of 64 activities and shows what percentage of these activities are performed in most human resource departments, based on a survey of 685 companies.[7] This table also shows whether the human resource department is solely responsible for each activity or whether the responsibility is shared with other departments. Some of the activities are generally not assigned to the human resource department—for example, purchasing, janitorial services, public relations, transportation services, and the library. However, the human resource department often has sole responsibility for many of the other activities, including EEO/affirmative action, insurance benefits administration, exit interviews, outplacement services, worker's compensation, unemployment compensation, wage and salary development, personnel record keeping, employee assistance programs, and attitude surveys. The human resource department frequently shares responsibility for many of these activities with other line or staff areas—even such central human resource activities as recruiting, interviewing, and training.

TABLE 1.1   Personnel activities

Activity	Responsibility for the Activity Is Assigned to:			
	Company Has Activity	P/HR Dept. Only	P/HR and Other Dept(s).	Other Dept(s). Only
Interviewing	99%	37%	61%	2%
Personnel recordkeeping/information systems	99	77	22	1
Vacation/leave processing	99	51	35	14
Insurance benefits administration	99	87	8	5
Orientation/induction	99	61	37	2
Wage/salary adjustment processing	99	77	22	1
Workers' compensation administration	98	73	15	12
Promotion/transfer/separation processing	98	71	28	1
Disciplinary procedures	98	43	55	2
Payroll administration	98	25	25	50
Recruiting	98	73	25	2
Job descriptions	97	62	35	2
Unemployment compensation	97	82	11	7
Wage/salary policy development	97	80	18	2
Performance appraisal, management	97	47	44	8
Performance appraisal, nonmanagement	97	47	45	8
EEO/affirmative action	97	87	11	2
Administrative services	97	15	16	69
Purchasing	95	3	7	90
Maintenance/janitorial services	95	10	5	85
Safety programs/OSHA compliance	95	46	33	20
Job evaluation	94	70	28	2
Security measures	94	22	22	57
Training, nonmanagement	94	21	51	28
Supervisory training	94	48	44	8
Exit interviews	93	86	13	1
Complaint procedures	92	54	44	2
Job analysis	91	75	23	3
Employee communications/publications	91	43	37	21
Award/recognition programs	91	66	29	5
Pension/retirement plan administration	90	73	18	8
Public/media relations	89	17	17	66

Activity	Responsibility for the Activity Is Assigned to:			
	Company Has Activity	P/HR Dept. Only	P/HR and Other Dept(s).	Other Dept(s). Only
Travel/transportation services	89%	9%	14%	77%
Management development	88	49	44	6
Community service	88	30	31	39
Business insurance/risk management	88	12	17	72
Recreation/social programs	86	61	30	9
Tuition aid/scholarships	86	83	12	4
Human resource forecasting/planning	85	58	37	5
Preemployment testing	80	85	12	3
Executive compensation	80	55	26	19
Relocation	75	75	20	5
Office/clerical services	73	16	22	62
Organization development	73	46	44	10
Career planning/development	72	51	45	5
Food service/cafeteria	70	36	6	58
Employee assistance plan/counseling	69	83	14	4
Incentive pay plans	69	50	38	12
College recruiting	67	79	17	4
Productivity/motivation programs	67	26	61	13
Medical services	61	73	12	15
Suggestion systems	60	46	35	19
Health/wellness program	58	78	14	8
Outplacement	58	91	8	1
Attitude surveys	55	81	16	3
Thrift/savings plan administration	53	71	21	8
Preretirement counseling	52	90	4	5
Union/labor relations	50	71	27	2
Library	44	21	9	70
Profit sharing plan administration	39	59	23	18
Flexible benefits plan administration	36	87	11	3
Stock plan administration	33	57	20	23
Flexible spending account administration	29	83	11	6
Child-care center	10	36	9	55

Source: ASPA-BNA Survey No. 52, "Personnel Activities, Budgets, and Staffs: 1987–1988," September 1, 1988.

RELATIONSHIPS BETWEEN HUMAN RESOURCE AND LINE MANAGEMENT

Human resource managers are required to interact constantly with other managers in an organization. These interactions may produce conflict unless the managers have a clear understanding of their relationship and a set of shared expectations about responsibilities and authority.

Most organizations make a distinction between line and staff authority. **Line authority** refers to the right to make decisions and give orders to subordinates regarding production, sales, and finance. Line managers supervise the employees who produce the organization's products and services; they are responsible for making operating decisions, and the units supervised by line managers have the ultimate responsibility for the successful operation of the company.

Staff authority is the responsibility to advise or assist those who possess line authority. Staff members are expected to help line managers accomplish the objectives of the enterprise by providing advice and service when it is requested. However, staff members also have the responsibility to give advice and service even when not requested if they believe such aid is needed. The human resource department is considered a staff department, as are quality control, engineering, and accounting.

Staff personnel typically perform three roles in organizations: (1) the **advisory or counseling role**, (2) the **service role**, and (3) the **control role**.[8]

The advisory or counseling role: In the advisory or counseling role, staff personnel are seen as internal consultants who gather information, diagnose problems, prescribe solutions, and offer assistance and guidance in resolving human resource problems. This relationship between line and staff is similar to that which exists between a professional consultant and a client. It is the responsibility of the human resource manager to give advice regarding staffing, performance evaluation, training programs, and job redesign. In these situations, the human resource department provides input that assists line managers in making decisions.

The service role: In this role, staff personnel perform activities that can be provided more effectively through a centralized staff than through the independent efforts of several different units. These activities are a direct service for line management or for other staff departments. Recruiting, orientation training, record keeping, and reporting duties are examples of the human resource department's service role.

The control role: The human resource department is required to control certain important policies and functions within the organization. This staff role is sometimes called *functional authority*. In performing this role, the human resource department establishes policies and procedures and monitors compliance with them. In exercising this role, the human resource staff members are seen as representatives or agents of top management. Because of legislation, the control role has become increasingly important in the areas of safety, equal employment opportunity, labor relations, and compensation. When the human resource department places hiring quotas on another department to achieve affirmative action goals, it is exercising its control role.

A critical issue in the relationship between line and staff is whether the line managers are required to follow the recommendations of the staff. Traditionally, line managers have had the authority to accept staff advice, modify it, or reject it. In recent years, however, greater authority for certain areas of management has been delegated to staff units. In these areas, accepting staff advice is compulsory for line managers, subject only to appeal to higher authority. The expanded authority of a human resource department is illustrated by the limitations that have been placed on a supervisor's authority to terminate an employee. To protect the organization from expensive wrongful-discharge suits, an employee cannot be terminated until the supervisor has followed the human resource department's termination guidelines.

A poor working relationship can develop between personnel and line managers if both sides do not have shared expectations. Line managers tend to believe that conflict is created because staff personnel (1) tend to assume line authority, (2) do not keep line managers informed, (3) steal credit for success, (4) do not give sound advice, or (5) do not see the whole picture. In essence, line managers may believe that conflicts arise because the human resource staff oversteps its bounds, is noncommunicative, is overrated in terms of its potential contribution, is incapable of giving good advice, or is narrow in scope. On the other hand, staff personnel believe that conflict is created because line managers (1) do not make proper use of staff personnel, (2) resist new ideas, and (3) do not give staff personnel enough authority. To overcome any disagreement, both parties must strive to create shared expectations by emphasizing the objectives of the organization and openly discussing their perceptions of a situation.

The major functions of a human resource department include (1) staffing, (2) performance evaluations, (3) compensation and benefits, (4) training and development, (5) employee relations, (6) safety and health, and (7) personnel research. These functions are necessary for every organization, regardless of size and organizational structure, even though they may not be assigned as responsibilities of a human resource department. For example, a large organization may have a separate safety department, while a small organization may delegate safety responsibilities to a line manager. Nevertheless, safety programs and compliance with the Occupational Safety and Health Act are important to every organization, and in most organizations the human resource department is involved in safety activities.

STAFFING/EMPLOYMENT

Staffing, usually called employment, involves three major activities: human resource planning, recruiting, and selection. Typically, anticipating human resource needs is the responsibility of line managers. As organizations grow in size and complexity, however, line managers come to depend more on the human resource department to gather information regarding the composition of the work force and the skills of present employees. Some human resource departments have developed sophisticated human resource planning systems that assist the organization in coordinating strategic business plans with human resource needs. The use of computers has greatly facilitated the storage of human resource information and the development of projections regarding human resource needs.

Although recruiting is performed primarily by the human resource department, other departments may be involved in providing job descriptions and job specifications to assist the recruiting effort. Also, line managers may be asked to make recruiting visits to college campuses.

In selecting new employees, the human resource department typically screens applicants through interviews, tests, and background investigations, then recommends three or four eligible applicants to the manager or supervisor for a final hiring decision. Because of equal employment opportunity laws and affirmative action requirements, the responsibility of most human resource departments for staffing activities has increased significantly.

PERFORMANCE EVALUATION

The responsibility for evaluating the performance of both managers and nonmanagers is generally shared between the human resource department and other department managers. Department managers and supervisors assume the primary responsibility for evaluating subordinates, since they observe job performance and are best able to make accurate assessments. However, the human resource department is generally responsible for developing effective performance appraisal forms and assessment procedures and for ensuring that performance evaluations are conducted uniformly throughout the organization. To maintain an effective performance evaluation program, the human resource department may need to train supervisors in establishing reasonable performance standards, making accurate assessments, and conducting performance interviews.

COMPENSATION

An effective compensation system is an important factor in preventing excessive turnover and job dissatisfaction. The management of compensation involves the coordinated efforts of the human resource department and operating managers. Typically, line managers are responsible for recommending wage increases, and the human resource department is responsible for developing and maintaining a wage and salary structure. An effective compensation system requires a careful balance between pay and benefits. Pay includes the wages, bonuses, incentives, and profit sharing received by an employee. Benefits are all nonwage items such as medical insurance, life insurance, vacations, and other employee services. Human resource departments try to make certain that employee compensation is competitive with respect to similar organizations, fair in terms of internal equity, legal, and motivating.

TRAINING AND DEVELOPMENT

Most of the training that occurs in organizations is on-the-job training through the coaching and counseling of supervisors. The role of the human resource department is usually that of helping supervisors become better trainers and conducting separate training and development sessions. The human resource department is frequently involved in new-employee orientation training, supervisory-skill training, and various management development activities. The human resource department also may be involved in assessing the training needs of the organization and evaluating the effectiveness of the training programs. In recent years, many organizations have asked their human resource departments to assume responsibility for job redesign and organizational development.[9] These activities often lead to a major restructuring of the organization or to the resolution of major conflicts within the organization.

EMPLOYEE RELATIONS

In unionized organizations, the human resource department takes an active role in negotiating and administering the labor agreement. Gathering information and helping to prepare the company's bargaining position is normally the responsibility of the human resource department prior to negotiations. After an agreement has been negotiated, the human resource department typically instructs supervisors about administering the labor agreement and avoiding excessive grievances. A major responsibility of the human resource department, especially during the organizing campaign, is to ensure that the company avoids unfair labor practices. When a union is present, this activity is often called labor relations or industrial relations.

Human resource departments in nonunion organizations also need to be heavily involved in employee relations. In general, employees do not vote to join a union when their wages are fair and adequate and they believe that management is responsive to their feelings and needs.[10] To maintain nonunion status, human resource departments need to make certain that the employees are treated fairly and that there is a well-defined procedure for resolving complaints. Whether it is unionized or not, every organization needs a clearly defined disciplinary procedure for handling problem employees, plus an effective grievance procedure to protect employees.

SAFETY AND HEALTH

Every organization is required to have an ongoing safety program to eliminate unnecessary accidents and unhealthy conditions. Employees need to be continually reminded of the importance of safety and instructed on how to avoid accidents. An effective safety program can reduce the number of accidents and improve the general health of the work force. It is a major responsibility of most human resource departments to provide safety training, to identify and correct unsafe conditions, and to report accidents and injuries.

PERSONNEL RESEARCH

Countless questions can be asked regarding the attitudes and behaviors of employees and the effectiveness of human resource policies and procedures. Some of the most frequently examined personnel questions concern the causes of absenteeism and tardiness, the appropriateness of recruitment and selection procedures, and the causes of dissatisfaction. Most human resource departments are responsible for collecting and analyzing information that pertains to these problems. The results are used to assess the adequacy of present policies and to suggest necessary changes.

EARLY DEVELOPMENTS IN PERSONNEL

Although personnel/human resource departments as we know them did not generally exist until the 1940s, the activities performed by these departments were not all brand new; in fact, many of the personnel practices and programs that we see today have roots in earlier times.[11] Some of the major historical events in management are shown in Table 1.2.

THE GUILD SYSTEM

The origins of apprenticeship training and trade unions can be traced to the Middle Ages. From the fifteenth through the eighteenth centuries, the **guild system** flourished in Europe. A guild consisted of shop owners in a particular trade who organized to protect their mutual interests. Guilds were essentially employers' organizations that regulated employment in a particular trade primarily by controlling the length of apprenticeship training. An apprentice was someone who studied under the direction of a master craftsman for a period of time. Typically, the length of an apprenticeship was not specified in advance, and in some circumstances the training was extended for many years as a means of restricting the number of people entering the trade. Apprentices were occasionally treated as indentured servants, and some became so disgruntled that they fled from their apprenticeships. Such was the case with Benjamin Franklin, who left his apprenticeship in Boston and fled to Philadelphia as a young man.[12] Sometimes angry craftsmen distributed "wanted" posters offering rewards for the capture and return of runaway apprentices.

After apprentices had completed their training, they became journeymen. Because journeymen lacked the capital to establish their own shops, they were forced to work as employees of other craftsmen. Eventually these employees formed organizations of their own, called *yeomanry guilds*, to protect their interests and to provide mutual assistance. These yeomanry guilds were the forerunners of contemporary trade unions. The labor conflict that occurred at the beginning of the nineteenth century resulted from a dispute between the yeomanry guilds and the craft guilds. When the yeomanry guilds became powerful enough to prevent employers from unilaterally cutting wages, the employers sought the help of the courts to control the trade unions.

CHANGES IN THE NATURE OF WORK

Because of changes in the nature of work, life today is significantly different than it was in the eighteenth, nineteenth, or early twentieth centuries. Knowing how work has changed provides a perspective for seeing how changes in work influence the quality of life.

HANDICRAFT SHOPS

In 1800, about 90 percent of America's workers were farmers who produced most of their own food plus a little extra to buy a few manufactured items. Most of the manufactured items that were not imported were produced in small handicraft shops. Some items, such

TABLE 1.2   Important events in human resource management

Date	Event
1786	Earliest documented strike in America was organized by Philadelphia printers to gain minimum weekly wage of six dollars.
1794	First profit sharing plan in the United States was established by Albert Gallatin at his glass works in Pennsylvania.
1806	The courts entered the arena of labor disputes to declare the Philadelphia cordwainers guild an illegal conspiracy in restraint of trade.
1842	*Commonwealth* v. *Hunt* decision in which the conspiracy doctrine restricting collective bargaining was overturned by the Massachusetts Supreme Court.
1881	Frederick W. Taylor's work in scientific management began at the Midvale Steel Plant.
1883	The U.S. Civil Service Commission was established.
1886	The American Federation of Labor (AFL) was created.
1912	The first minimum wage law was passed in Massachusetts.
1913	The U.S. Department of Labor was created.
1917	First large-scale use of group intelligence tests, the Army Alpha and Beta tests.
1924	The Hawthorne studies were begun at Western Electric Company.
1932	The Norris-LaGuardia Anti-injunction Act was passed.
1935	The National Labor Relations Act (Wagner Act), which gave workers the right to organize and to bargain collectively, was passed.
1935	The Congress of Industrial Organizations (CIO) was created.
1938	The Fair Labor Standards Act, which established a federal minimum wage and overtime beyond 40 hours a week, was passed.
1947	The Labor Management Relations Act (Taft-Hartley Act), which restricted certain union activities, was passed.
1955	The AFL and CIO unions were merged.
1959	The Labor Management Reporting and Disclosure Act (Landrum-Griffin Act), which eliminated improper union activities, was passed.
1963	The Equal Pay Act, which prohibited wage differentials based on sex, was passed.
1964	The Civil Rights Act, which barred discrimination and created the Equal Employment Opportunity Commission (EEOC), was passed.
1970	The Occupational Safety and Health Act, which established safety and health standards and the means of enforcing them, was passed.
1972	The Equal Employment Opportunity Act, an amendment to the Civil Rights Act, which extended the power of the EEOC, was passed.
1974	The Employee Retirement Income Security Act (ERISA), which reformed and regulated private pension systems, was passed.
1978	The Uniform Guidelines on Employee Selection were published by the EEOC.
1984	The Deficit Reduction Act, which changed tax laws and especially encouraged employee stock ownership plans (ESOP), was passed.
1986	The Immigration Reform and Control Act, which creates civil penalties for employers who knowingly hire unauthorized aliens, was passed.
1988	The Employee Polygraph Protection Act, which restricts the use of lie detector tests, was passed.
1988	The Worker Adjustment Retraining and Notification (WARN) Act, which requires companies to give employees advance notice of mass layoffs, was passed.

as clothing, were made by workers in their homes. In this process, called the cottage, or "putting out," system, the workers were essentially subcontractors: the materials were delivered to their cottages, the work was performed in their homes according to their own schedule, the finished or partially finished goods were picked up from their homes, and wages were paid to them.

The typical handicraft shop was owned by a master craftsman or mill proprietor who employed a small number of workers. The typical plant was a room or series of rooms in the craftsman's home or in a small building adjacent to a stream that supplied the power for more complicated manufacturing operations. An example of an early handicraft shop that has been rebuilt is Benjamin Franklin's printing shop in Philadelphia.

THE FACTORY SYSTEM

Between 1820 and 1850, factories began to emerge in America, especially textile factories in the Northeast. One of the most famous ones, located in Lowell, Massachusetts, attracted the attention of many observers in Europe as well as the United States because of its unique social culture and its paternalistic practices. The mill was controlled by the Boston Associates, a group of industrialists who were as interested in developing morality as they were in making a profit. The employees were mostly young women from rural areas who were working temporarily to supplement their families' incomes. They lived in boardinghouses and were expected to follow a strict regimen of moral discipline. Many visitors were impressed with the combination of work, worship, education, and cultural arts that was provided for the "Lowell girls."[13]

Most factories, however, were not as benevolently managed as the Lowell mill. They were wooden structures, located near rivers for power. The lighting, provided by oil lamps, was inadequate, and kerosene, needed to fuel the lamps, created a serious fire hazard. During the winter months, the factories were cold and uncomfortable.[14]

The massive growth of factories and the consequent shift in employment from farm to factory occurred between 1880 and 1920. The production needs generated by World War I caused the number of factory workers to increase significantly in almost all industries: these numbers grew from 2.7 million in 1880, to 4.5 million in 1990, to 8.4 million in 1920.[15]

One of the most significant benefits of the factory system was its contribution to increased productivity. The factory system not only stimulated employment and raised the personal incomes of factory workers, it also dramatically increased the production of basic goods and services, which improved the quality of life. Manufacturing was accomplished through a mass production process in which the work was divided into small, specialized activities. Each activity was assigned to different workers, who could perform the task with little formal training. By 1920, some industries produced more goods than the public could consume; this spurt of industrial efficiency contributed to a high standard of living and an increased disposable income. From 1900 to 1966, productivity (output per employee hour) increased about 3 percent annually, which meant that workers in 1966 could produce as much in two or three hours as their grandparents in 1900 could produce in a twelve-hour day. From 1966 to 1990, however, productivity increases averaged only about 1 percent annually.

HOURS OF EMPLOYMENT

Before 1930, the average workweek usually exceeded 50 hours and occasionally exceeded 80 hours. In 1822, the Philadelphia carpenters complained about the excessively long hours that they were expected to work. Rather than working from sunup to sundown, they wanted their hours cut to twelve hours per day. Before electric lighting became available, some factory work was seasonal, with long hours in the summer and short hours during the winter, but once electrification had spread, most factory jobs demanded very long hours. Men averaged twelve to thirteen working hours, six days a week, until the early 1900s. The average hours of work for women and children during this same period were ten to twelve hours per day, usually six days a week. In the steel industry, two men typically staffed one job around the clock. Each worker averaged twelve hours per shift, seven days a week. The shifts rotated every two weeks, with one man having twenty-

---

HRM in Action

No-Smoking Policy at Pacific Northwest Bell

New personnel policies are more likely to be accepted without resistance if they are carefully designed, if the rationale for them is thoroughly explained, and if the employees have adequate time to change their behavior. In October 1985 Pacific Northwest Bell (PNB) adopted a no-smoking policy that was very well accepted, contrary to the fears of some executives. No grievances were filed by either of the unions representing over 10,000 union members.

Pacific Northwest Bell, with 15,000 employees in over 800 locations, adopted a no-smoking policy at all its facilities for health reasons. Because the company received numerous complaints from nonsmokers, management decided that its informal policy of letting individual work groups establish their own standards was not satisfactory.

In 1983 a Smoking Issues Steering Committee was formed and asked to recommend a policy after investigating other policies and gathering information. The committee included representatives of the unions and management, 30 percent of whom were smokers.

In June 1985 the committee recommended to A.U. Smith, the company president, a simple no-smoking policy that was accepted: "To protect the health of PNB employees there will be no smoking in any company facility." The company offered to pay the full cost of smoking-cessation programs for the employees and their family members. After two years the number of smokers declined from 28 to 20 percent, and about two-thirds of the remaining smokers expressed a desire to quit in the future.

When the policy was announced, the company established two telephone hot lines to answer questions about the policy and provide information about smoking-cessation programs. Four cessation programs were available: behavior modification, aversion therapy, acupuncture, and hypnosis. In the first two years the company paid for 1,741 people to attend one of these programs, and 40 percent of them quit smoking. The people of PNB are pleased with the no-smoking policy and how well it has been accepted, although one executive says that if they were to do it again the company probably would pay for only half the cost of the cessation programs.

Source: "Where There's Smoke," 2nd ed., BNA Special Report, Bureau of National Affairs, 1987, pp. 94–97.

four hours free while the other worked twenty-four consecutive hours.[16] In retail stores such as Carson, Pirie, Scott in Chicago, sales personnel worked 84 hours each week—six fourteen-hour days. Company rules stated that the store was not to be open Sundays except for emergencies. Salesmen were allowed two evenings a week for courting if they had attended Sunday School and one if they had not. Leisure hours after a fourteen-hour workday were to be spent primarily in reading worthwhile books.[17]

An examination of historical records suggests that although most employees were on the job for long periods of time, some did not work hard all of the time. Social customs and religious holidays were introduced to the workplace by the immigrants who comprised most of the workforce in the factories. Extensive drunkenness among many of the first-generation immigrants who were not accustomed to factory life was a serious problem for many employers.[18] Employers frequently complained about excessive time lost from work because of "grog time," "cake time," and "breathing spells."

During the 1930s, the average workweek in most companies was reduced. Henry Ford, reasoning that more leisure time and relatively high wages would increase the demand for cars,[19] took the lead in reducing the workweek in his factories to 40 hours. During the Great Depression, three federal laws helped to standardize the five-day, 40 hour week: the National Industrial Recovery Act of 1933, the Walsh-Healey Public Contracts Act of 1936, and the Fair Labor Standards Act of 1938.

Although in the United States today workweeks longer than 60 hours are typically restricted to workaholics and executives, there are factories outside the United States where laborers toil long hours for little pay. In the People's Republic of China, for instance, some children as young as age 10 are working alongside adults as assemblers in plants with fourteen-hour days, seven-day workweeks, and wages that range from $10 to $31 per month. These working conditions, which seem unbearable to Americans, are quite acceptable to many Asians who want to escape the harsh life on a Chinese farm.[20]

SCIENTIFIC MANAGEMENT

During the latter part of the 1800s, industrial efficiency was significantly increased through **scientific management**. The scientific management movement originated as a result of the studies of Frederick W. Taylor, often called the Father of Scientific Management.[21] Taylor's goals were to identify the best way of performing a job and then to train workers to do the job in that way. Taylor believed that managers were responsible for scientifically studying jobs and for selecting the optimal methods of performing them.

Taylor and some of his contemporaries, such as Frank and Lillian Gilbreth and Henry L. Gantt, significantly influenced the practice of management. Many of the techniques they developed are still used in modern organizations. Taylor and the Gilbreths used time-and-motion studies to analyze the most efficient methods of performing a job. Frank and Lillian Gilbreth pioneered the use of motion pictures as a means of analyzing a task.[22] The scientific study of jobs included careful analyses of the physical motions of the body, the effect of rest pauses, physical surroundings, and various tools and machines. For example, studies indicated the practicality of using small shovels to load heavy materials and large shovels to load lighter materials.

Taylor maintained that workers should be scientifically selected, since certain jobs demanded greater strength or intellectual skills than others. Performance standards were established through time-and-motion studies and then used to train employees and to determine their compensation. Since Taylor believed that workers were motivated by economic incentives, he advocated a differential piece-rate pay system with two rates: workers who produced less than the standard were paid a low piece rate, and those who produced more than the standard were paid a high piece rate. The purpose of the differential piece rate was to encourage slow workers to quit and find employment that was more compatible with their abilities. A rule of thumb in scientific management was that the implementation of a piece-rate incentive plan would increase productivity by at least 25 percent.

Labor unions criticized scientific management, claiming that it made employees work harder, and as a result of this criticism, Taylor was asked to testify before a special Senate subcommittee.[23] Taylor insisted that his piece-rate incentive system, which significantly increased employee earnings, was in the best interests of both the employee and the company. Moreover, his scientific analysis of jobs made the work easier to perform. Many of the principles used in industrial engineering today, such as time-and-motion studies, job evaluation, piece-rate incentives, and Gantt's program evaluation review technique (PERT) planning charts, owe their beginnings to the early scientific management movement.

INDUSTRIAL PSYCHOLOGY

During the early 1900s, several attempts were made to apply knowledge and research from the field of psychology to the management of personnel. One of the most significant early works in **industrial psychology** was Hugo Munsterberg's *The Psychology of Industrial Efficiency*.[24] This book, which was published in 1913, outlined the contributions that psychology could make to the areas of employment testing, training, and industrial efficiency. Munsterberg also described experiments in the development of performance tests and aptitude tests used to select electric railway engineers and telephone operators.

During World War I, psychological testing was significantly advanced by the development of the Army Alpha and Beta tests, which were used for screening applicants for military assignments. A performance evaluation system also was used in the military during World War I. This system was adapted from Walter Dill Scott's Man-to-Man Rating Scale that had been developed for rating salespeople. The procedure involved comparing the performance of salespeople against specific individuals whose performances represented standards at different levels. Walter Dill Scott received acclaim for what is now a classic book on personnel management, and he also was one of the first to question the reliability of employment interviews.[25]

HUMAN RELATIONS MOVEMENT

From 1924 to 1933, Elton Mayo of Harvard University conducted a series of studies at the Hawthorne Works of the Western Electric Company.[26] These **Hawthorne studies** examined the effects of working conditions and group influences on productivity and provided the foundation for the **human relations movement** that was to extend over the next three decades in the field of management.

The first studies were illumination experiments in which the intensity of lighting was varied to examine its influence on worker productivity. The results of these studies indicated that performance improved when lighting was changed—regardless of whether the lighting was increased or decreased. Therefore, the experimenters concluded that productivity had accelerated because the employees had known that their performances were being measured. This phenomenon, in which performance is influenced by the process of observing it, is referred to today as the Hawthorne effect.

Another series of studies, called the relay assembly test room experiments, examined the effects of rest pauses, hours of work, and financial incentives on worker productivity. From these studies the researchers concluded that rest periods, changes in the design of the work, and financial incentives had virtually no effect on productivity and that the important variables were friendly supervision and the influence of the informal work group.

A later study, called the bank wiring room experiment, examined the influence of group norms. Although the men participating in the study were paid a piece-rate incentive and the experiment was conducted during the Depression, when an intense motive to earn money existed, none of the participants produced more than the standard set by the group. This study illustrated the effects of group norms and demonstrated how powerful such norms could be in establishing artificially low levels of performance.

Another segment of the Hawthorne studies consisted of an interviewing program in which employees were questioned about their attitudes toward their jobs and the company. Several thousand employees participated in these interviews, which represented the beginning of nondirective interviewing and counseling.

Although the methodology, results, and conclusions of the Hawthorne studies have been severely criticized in recent years, their enormous influence on management literature and on the development of human resource policies cannot be overlooked.[27] For many years, the results of the Hawthorne studies were used to convince managers that friendly supervision and good human relations had more impact on increasing employee performance than did financial incentives and job design.

LABOR UNIONS

For many years, labor unions fought against employers, politicians, the courts, and even state militias for the right to exist. From 1806, when the courts first became involved in labor disputes, until 1842, a strike by a labor union was considered to be an illegal conspiracy in restraint of trade. After 1842, employees were allowed to form unions and to withhold their labor by striking to demand higher wages. Until 1932, however, strikes were largely ineffective because of court injunctions, yellow-dog contracts, and antitrust legislation. As a result, union organizing activities were characterized by violence and destruction. The efforts of union leaders to establish collective bargaining and the efforts of employers to crush union activities (described in Chapter 13) provided an intense drama in the history of labor, which has been marked by mass protests, riots, the bombing of mines and railroads, and the deaths of laborers, managers, police, and state militiamen.

With the passage of the Anti-injunction Act (Norris-LaGuardia) of 1932 and the National Labor Relations Act (Wagner) of 1935, labor unions obtained legal protection.

These laws gave private employees the right to organize a union and required employers to bargain in good faith with an elected union. Executive orders and state laws have also encouraged government employees as well as teachers and other service workers to form labor organizations to improve their wages, hours, and other conditions of employment. While these legal protections have helped to establish labor unions, they do not guarantee their survival. Labor unions are still struggling to survive. Although unions fought for many years to improve their members' wage levels, the members of several unions voted during the 1980s to accept wage reductions because their jobs were threatened by foreign competition.

THE HUMAN RESOURCE PROFESSION

In recent years, the field of human resource management has become a true profession. A profession is characterized by the existence of a common body of knowledge, standards of ethical conduct, a procedure for certifying members of the profession, and a communication system that allows the exchange of ideas and self-regulation.

The body of knowledge concerning human resource management continues to grow at an enormous rate. Numerous publications contain research reports on human resource topics, case studies describing human resource programs, and articles summarizing the ideas and experiences of human resource people. Some of the major human resource journals are listed in Appendix C at the end of the book.

HUMAN RESOURCE POSITIONS

A small organization with fewer than 60 to 80 employees usually does not need a human resource department or a human resource manager. The functions of recruiting, hiring, training, safety, and performance evaluation (if performance is formally evaluated) are generally discharged by line managers. Compensation decisions are normally made by line managers, and the payroll is handled by the finance officer. As the organization begins to exceed 100 to 200 employees, however, a separate staff position may be required to coordinate the human resource functions.

When the organization becomes too large for one person to handle all of the personnel functions, separate positions are created and placed under the direction of a human resource manager. A typical division of responsibilities for a human resource department would include supervisors in the areas of employment, compensation and benefits, training and development, safety and health, and, if a union is present, labor relations.

Most human resource departments are led by a person with the title of vice president of personnel or director of human resources. A survey of personnel/human resource departments revealed that about 74 percent of the senior human resource executives report to chief executives.[28] The rest usually report to a general executive at the next level. Senior personnel executives are usually **personnel generalists** who possess a broad comprehension of all the human resource functions and how they interact with the other departments in the organization.

The growing importance of human resource management in recent years has led to the creation of **personnel specialists**, especially in large organizations. Figure 1.1 represents an organizational chart for a company that is organized by function. The personnel/human resource department, which is headed by the vice president, reports to the president or chief executive officer just as do the departments of finance, sales, and manufacturing. The major kinds of personnel specialists are shown in Figure 1.2, which illustrates an organizational chart for a large human resource department. In a large corporation, the personnel area may consist of eight departments headed by managers of employment, human resource planning, compensation, benefits and services, training and development, employee (or labor) relations, safety and health, and equal employment opportunity.

An ASPA-BNA survey indicates that the personnel/human resource-staff ratio is about 1 personnel department employee for every 100 employees in a business organization (1:100).[29] Approximately half of the personnel staff are professional/technical employees, and the other half are primarily clerical. In finance organizations, the ratio of personnel staff members to total employment is 1.5:100, slightly higher than the average. In health care organizations, the ratio is 0.6:100, slightly lower than average. For obvious reasons, the size of a human resource department is most directly influenced by the size of an organization. Even though larger organizations have larger human resource departments, the ratio of personnel staff per total number of employees tends to decline as the organization gets larger, as shown in Table 1.3.

The amount of money spent on human resource activities varies dramatically from company to company. The same ASPA/BNA survey revealed that personnel budgets in 1990 varied from $19 to $9,091 per employee, with a median expense of $730 per employee as shown in Table 1.3. Expressed as a percentage of other company costs, the average cost of operating a human resource department is generally about 2.5 percent of the total company payroll and 1.0 percent of the total operating budget, which includes

FIGURE 1.1 An organizational chart for a company organized by function.

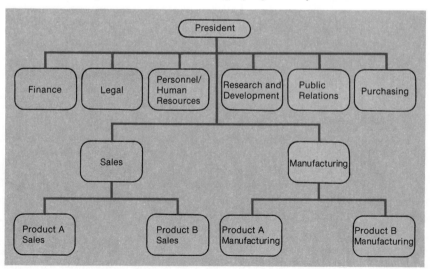

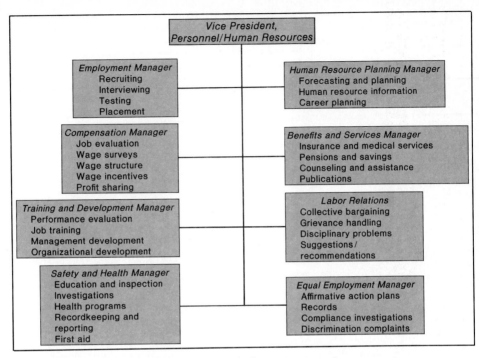

FIGURE 1.2 An organizational chart showing the human resource department.

all operating expenses (such as payroll, energy, plant, and equipment) but excludes nonoperating expenses (such as taxes and payments to investors).

CAREERS IN HUMAN RESOURCE MANAGEMENT

Students who are interested in careers in human resource management should be aware of the opportunities available and how to prepare for them. Although the types of human resource positions vary from company to company, three major types are usually found: (1) general human resource manager/executive, (2) personnel specialist, and (3) supporting position.

General manager/executive: The operating human resource manager is typically a generalist who administers all of the personnel functions and coordinates them with other organizational activities. In very small companies, the human resource director may be someone hired from outside the company or a line officer transferred from another area of the company. In large corporations, the top human resource positions are usually filled by promoting lower-level human resource specialists. However, some companies may select a line manager to be the human resource executive, since line managers have a broad perspective of the company.

Personnel specialists: Personnel specialists are professional and technical people who have special expertise in one of the functional areas of personnel, such as staffing,

TABLE 1.3   Size and expenditures of human resource departments relative to size of company

Size of Company	Total Personnel Staff per 100 Employees	Professional/ Technical Staff per 100 Employees	Personnel Dept. Expenditures per Employee
up to 250	1.8	1.1	$1,235
250–500	1.2	0.8	918
500–1000	0.8	0.5	688
1000–2500	0.8	0.5	569
over 2500	0.6	0.3	415
all companies	1.1	0.6	730

Source: SHRM-BNA Survey No. 54, "Personnel Activities, Budgets, and Staffs: 1989–1990," June 28, 1990.

compensation, employee relations, or training. Multiple levels of skill and responsibility are usually found in each of these functional areas if an organization is large enough. For example, an entry-level position in staffing might entail recruiting and interviewing hourly applicants. From that position, the person might be promoted to manage the employment of professional and managerial applicants. This job could be followed by a promotion to the position that coordinates all staffing activities. The job of personnel specialist is often viewed as a stepping-stone to a higher level human resource position, such as general manager or executive.

Support jobs: About half the positions in a typical human resource department are support jobs such as receptionist, typist, and other clerical positions. These jobs, which involve record keeping, data gathering, and reporting, are usually filled by graduates of high schools or technical colleges. Unless these employees acquire additional training in human resources, however, they are not likely to be promoted to a job such as personnel specialist or general human resource manager/executive.

Students who want to pursue a career in human resource management are advised to select one or two courses that provide a general overview of all the personnel functions and then to take two or three additional courses in a specific functional area. For example, someone interested in staffing might take some in-depth courses in human resource planning, recruiting, interviewing, EEO, tests and measurements, and statistical prediction. Someone interested in labor relations might take additional courses in collective bargaining, labor law, grievance handling, and contract administration.

Career opportunities in human resource management appear promising. The U.S. Department of Labor estimated that by 1986 there were 381,000 jobs for personnel and labor relations specialists, and the outlook through 2000 indicated that the number of new jobs was expected to grow at a rate comparable to that of all occupations.[30] Further-more, the salaries paid to personnel/human resource managers are usually comparable to those of other corporate officers who have similar levels of responsibility and authority, which indicates that in most companies these positions are considered important.

PROFESSIONAL HUMAN RESOURCE MANAGEMENT ORGANIZATIONS

Over a dozen professional personnel/human resource management associations exist in the United States. Many of them are listed in Appendix B at the end of the book.[31] Some of the associations have a very narrow scope and a small membership, and others have a broad scope and a large membership. Most of them publish professional journals and newsletters, and they sponsor annual conventions and other professional meetings where members share information and interact socially. Many associations also maintain place-ment services for members and prepare professional standards of ethical conduct. The associations also encourage research and try to facilitate the sharing of the research findings. These are two of the major professional personnel associations:

> *Society for Human Resource Management (SHRM)*: SHRM, which was originally called the *American Society for Personnel Administration (ASPA)*, was founded in 1948, and is probably the most active professional personnel/human resource association. This association consists primarily of personnel administrators and industrial relations executives in both the public and private sector, and it also has student chapters at many colleges and universities. Through its publications, SHRM informs its mem-bers about the latest developments in personnel, especially legislation and govern-ment agency changes. SHRM has been active in assisting Congress and the courts to understand what changes are needed for more effective personnel/human re-source functions. SHRM also sponsors the Human Resource Certification Institute, which is designed for the professional certification of people in personnel.

> *American Society for Training and Development (ASTD)*: ASTD, which was founded in 1944, is comprised of individuals who are concerned specifically with training and development activities. Its membership largely consists of training directors in busi-ness, education, and government organizations. ASTD also has many student chap-ters on various college and university campuses.

PERSONNEL CERTIFICATION

In 1975, the Society for Human Resource Managers (formerly ASPA) formed an institute to certify individuals who could demonstrate sufficient professional competence. The formation of this institute represented a significant undertaking, since it was an attempt by a professional association to impose internal standards of certification without external pressure. The program, which encourages personnel/human resource professionals to continuously update their knowledge in the field, provides two levels of certification: the basic level and the senior level.

The basic level of certification is called Professional in Human Resources (PHR), and the senior level is called Senior Professional in Human Resources (SPHR). Both levels of

personnel certification require passing an exam and meeting minimum professional experience requirements—four years' experience for the basic level and eight years' for the senior level. A bachelor's degree in personnel/human resource management or social sciences will substitute for two years' experience, and a master's degree is equivalent to three years'. At the senior level, individuals are expected to assume broad policymaking and administrative responsibilities.

The certification exam consists of multiple-choice questions that evaluate the applicant's knowledge of human resource management practices in the six functional areas:

1. Employment, placement, and personnel planning
2. Training and development
3. Compensation and benefits
4. Health, safety, and security
5. Employee and labor relations
6. Management practices

Even though full certification requires minimum experience qualifications, students in personnel, industrial relations, and related fields should consider taking the exam while the information is still fresh in their minds. Many personnel managers resisted the idea of certification when it was first introduced, but certification has since become more generally accepted. In fact, some organizations now accept applications for personnel/human resource positions only from certified individuals.

EFFECTS OF ORGANIZATIONAL CLIMATE ON HUMAN RESOURCE MANAGEMENT

This chapter on the organizational context of human resource management would not be complete without showing how the organizational climate influences human resource management. Several organizational characteristics, such as size and technology, strongly influence personnel activities. In large organizations, for example, the personnel activities tend to be more complex and more highly developed than in small firms. Small organizations simply cannot afford such sophisticated activities as computerized human resource information systems or elaborate employee assistance programs. The two most important characteristics influencing personnel activities are management style and the presence or absence of a union. Each of these characteristics creates a unique organizational climate that significantly alters every personnel function.

MANAGEMENT STYLE

The policies and procedures adopted by a human resource department must be consistent with the policies and procedures followed by other departments in the organization. For example, if a human resource department invites creative ideas and constructive criticism from employees, then managers in every department must be willing to accept comments and criticism without feeling threatened. The level of trust within the organization will have an effect on the performance-appraisal system; that is, on whether employees feel free to participate in identifying their own weaknesses and setting their own goals or whether they feel defensive and threatened in such situations. Virtually every personnel function, including staffing, training, compensation, and employee relations, is significantly influenced by the management philosophy and leadership style within an organization.

A useful model for analyzing organizational climate was developed by Rensis Likert.[32] His model evaluates the company's management style along a continuum that ranges from what he has termed a **System 1** organization to a **System 4** organization. The characteristics used to evaluate the organization include leadership, motivation, communication, decision making, goal setting, and control systems. A System 1 organization is characterized by minimal group loyalty, low performance goals, a lack of motivation to produce, frequent conflict, and feelings of unreasonable pressure. A System 4 organization, on the other hand, is characterized by strong group loyalty and cooperation, high performance goals and motivation to produce, and favorable attitudes toward management. Likert argues that organizations implementing System 4 will have higher sales volumes, higher earnings, and lower costs than those operating within Systems 1, 2, or 3. Moreover, Likert's research has shown that as organizations move from a System 1 or 2 to a System 3 or 4, they become more efficient, reduce their absenteeism and tardiness, and increase their profits.

Personnel/human resource activities in a System 1 organization would be significantly different from those in a System 4 organization. Some of the major differences that may occur are shown in Table 1.4.

PRESENCE VERSUS ABSENCE OF A UNION

Virtually every human resource activity is influenced by the presence of a labor union.[33] Without a union, managers are free to make unilateral decisions regarding human resource policies and practices and other matters. Once employees have voted to organize a union, however, managers must participate in bilateral decision making regarding wages, hours, and other conditions of employment. Management and the union agree to abide by the provisions that they have negotiated in their collective-bargaining agreement. Labor agreements, however, typically regulate more than just wages and hours. Most contain provisions concerning such matters as promotions, layoffs, terminations, the assignment of work, and grievance procedures. When a union is present, the basic goals of the organization—to operate efficiently and to produce a profit—must be modified to accommodate the goals of a union—to protect jobs and to increase wages. Some of the major changes relating to human resource activities that may occur when a union is organized include the following:

> Employees are protected from arbitrary or capricious actions of managers, since their rights are defined by the labor agreement and discipline can occur only after due process.
>
> Recruiting and selection may be done by the union, especially in the construction industry.
>
> Pay levels are negotiated with the union and may contain automatic cost-of-living increases. Wage levels also tend to be higher in union organizations than in non-union organizations.

TABLE 1.4   The influence of organizational climate on personnel/human resource activities

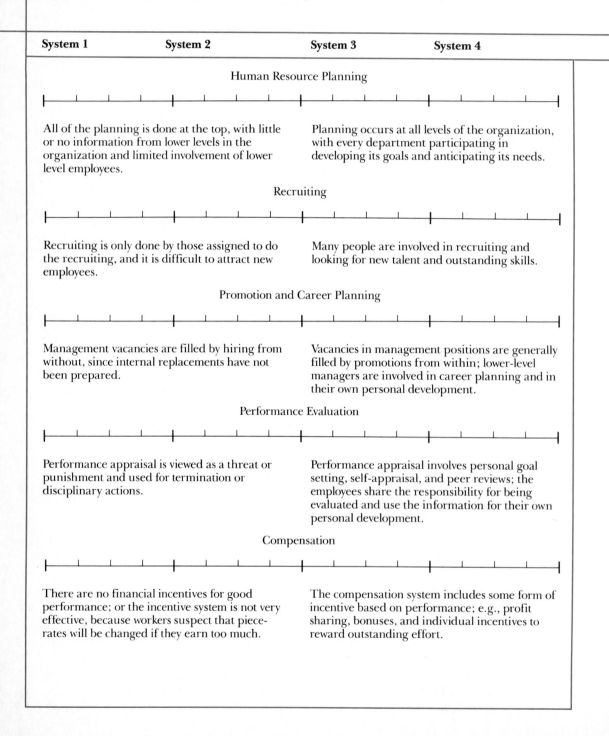

| System 1 | System 2 | System 3 | System 4 |

Human Resource Planning

All of the planning is done at the top, with little or no information from lower levels in the organization and limited involvement of lower level employees.

Planning occurs at all levels of the organization, with every department participating in developing its goals and anticipating its needs.

Recruiting

Recruiting is only done by those assigned to do the recruiting, and it is difficult to attract new employees.

Many people are involved in recruiting and looking for new talent and outstanding skills.

Promotion and Career Planning

Management vacancies are filled by hiring from without, since internal replacements have not been prepared.

Vacancies in management positions are generally filled by promotions from within; lower-level managers are involved in career planning and in their own personal development.

Performance Evaluation

Performance appraisal is viewed as a threat or punishment and used for termination or disciplinary actions.

Performance appraisal involves personal goal setting, self-appraisal, and peer reviews; the employees share the responsibility for being evaluated and use the information for their own personal development.

Compensation

There are no financial incentives for good performance; or the incentive system is not very effective, because workers suspect that piece-rates will be changed if they earn too much.

The compensation system includes some form of incentive based on performance; e.g., profit sharing, bonuses, and individual incentives to reward outstanding effort.

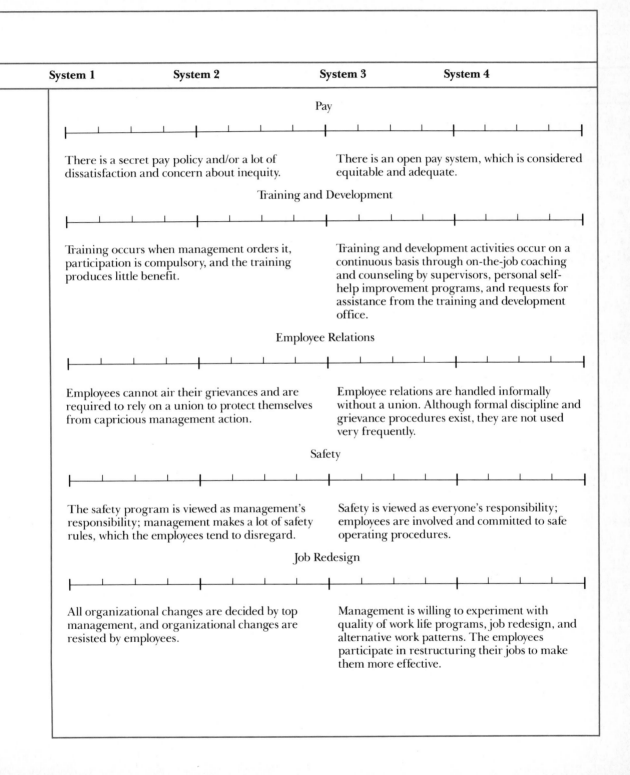

System 1	System 2	System 3	System 4

Pay

There is a secret pay policy and/or a lot of dissatisfaction and concern about inequity.

There is an open pay system, which is considered equitable and adequate.

Training and Development

Training occurs when management orders it, participation is compulsory, and the training produces little benefit.

Training and development activities occur on a continuous basis through on-the-job coaching and counseling by supervisors, personal self-help improvement programs, and requests for assistance from the training and development office.

Employee Relations

Employees cannot air their grievances and are required to rely on a union to protect themselves from capricious management action.

Employee relations are handled informally without a union. Although formal discipline and grievance procedures exist, they are not used very frequently.

Safety

The safety program is viewed as management's responsibility; management makes a lot of safety rules, which the employees tend to disregard.

Safety is viewed as everyone's responsibility; employees are involved and committed to safe operating procedures.

Job Redesign

All organizational changes are decided by top management, and organizational changes are resisted by employees.

Management is willing to experiment with quality of work life programs, job redesign, and alternative work patterns. The employees participate in restructuring their jobs to make them more effective.

HRM in Action

Human Resource Certification

Before they graduate, students who have a serious interest in a human resource management career ought to take the Human Resource Certification exam. Because of the growing number of certified HR managers, the professional status of certification is increasing significantly. Some employers pressure their HR managers to become certified and others indicate in job advertisements that preference will be shown to certified applicants.

Federal Express arranged for its human resource managers to take the certification exam as part of a company training program. On August 21, 1988, ninety-three Federal Express employees from twenty-six cities gathered in Memphis, Tennessee, for two days of intense preparation. Then, on August 23, all of them took the exam.

The exam is a four-hour exam that consists of 250 multiple-choice questions. The following question illustrates the kind of items on the exam:

> Written statements that furnish broad guidelines for making decisions and help managers handle personnel issues are called:
> a. human resource objectives
> b. human resource policies
> c. strategic plans
> d. operational plans

Answer: b. Human resource policies help managers make rapid and consistent decisions by providing guidelines for them to follow.

The exam is offered the first Saturdays in May and December at designated testing centers and at the annual SHRM conference in June. Application forms and other information can be obtained by contacting the Human Resource Certification Institute, 606 North Washington Street, Alexandria, VA 22314, (703) 548-3440. Completed applications must be submitted approximately ten weeks before the test date.

Benefits are negotiated with the union.

The pension program may be managed by the union.

Training programs may be presented by the union, and the union also may establish standards of performance for apprentices, journeymen, and craftsmen. Some collective-bargaining agreements contain provisions for worker retraining, especially in industries where the technology is changing rapidly, such as the aerospace and automotive industries.[34]

Promotions, terminations, layoffs, and callbacks may be based either entirely or in part upon seniority rather than performance.

Production may be stopped by a strike if management and the union cannot successfully negotiate a new labor agreement.

Employees who want to work may be prevented from doing so if the union has called a strike, or employees may be fined by the union for crossing the picket line.

Disciplinary problems and grievances may be handled through formal procedures prescribed in the labor agreement. These procedures usually call for binding arbitration if management and the union cannot resolve the problem. The union also may assist management in administering employee discipline.

In summary, human resource activities do not stand alone; an ideal human resource department cannot be independent of the organization in which it functions. The kinds of activities performed by the human resource department need to be consistent with the climate of the organization, especially the organization's style of management and the presence or absence of a union. The size of the human resource department should be determined by the size of the organization and by the kinds of activities that are needed in the organization. The objectives of the human resource department should be to help the organization function effectively and to contribute to the organization's economic success.

INTERNATIONAL HRM

An examination of the human resource policies and practices in foreign countries provides a valuable perspective for analyzing the effectiveness of what is done in the United States. Practices that are highly effective in one country ought to be carefully examined to determine whether they can be exported elsewhere. It may be that a unique cultural setting is essential for a specific practice to operate effectively. Nevertheless, a careful comparison of international firms can be meaningful and instructive.

An illustration of the lessons that can be learned from international companies is Stephen Carroll's examination of four Asian firms. The four firms he examined were (1) Hissia Tuner Company in Japan, (2) the Chinese Flour Mill in the People's Republic of China, (3) the Mungchi Company, a conglomerate in Taiwan, and (4) the Laegu Bank in the Republic of Korea.

From his analysis of these four companies, Carroll identified eight practices that he recommended U.S. firms consider to help them cope with critical changes presently affecting their operations.

1. *Employment*: Workers should have guaranteed employment.
2. *Training*: Firms should place greater stress on training, and employees should view it as a life-long endeavor.
3. *Appraisal*: Firms should place less emphasis on formal performance evaluations and more emphasis on informal coaching among superiors and subordinates.
4. *Selection*: Firms should take greater care in selecting employees and hire only those who are well-suited to the job.
5. *Motivation*: Firms should supplement reliance on financial incentives with peer-group pressure and appeals to the employee's loyalty and internalization of organizational values.
6. *Supervision*: Line managers should be responsible for managing their own personnel.

7. *Compensation*: Pay should be tied to performance, but the pay differentials between managers and workers should not be exorbitantly wide.
8. *Grievance handling*: Top-level managers should participate actively in processing grievances and complaints.

SUMMARY

A. Human resource management refers to the administration of a firm's human resources. Although all managers are involved in supervising people, the human resource manager has the primary responsibility for coordinating the firm's personnel/human resource activities.

B. In recent years, human resource management has become increasingly important because of state and federal legislation, the complexity of the manager's job, the need for consistency and equity in the treatment of employees, the professional and technical expertise needed to perform personnel activities, and the growing cost of personnel problems.

C. Human resource activities are expected to contribute to the survival and effectiveness of an organization. The human resource department should help the organization achieve its overall objectives, including profit, organizational effectiveness, service, social responsibility, and improving the quality of work life.

D. Human resource managers typically exercise staff authority and are responsible for providing advice and assistance to operating managers who exercise line authority. As staff members, human resource managers may exercise three roles: (1) an advisory or counseling role, (2) a service role, and (3) a control role.

E. The major human resource functions performed in an organization include (1) staffing, (2) performance evaluation, (3) compensation, (4) training and development, (5) employee relations, (6) safety and health, and (7) personnel research.

F. Modern human resource practices have been influenced by some of the early developments in personnel, such as the guild system, changes in the nature of work, scientific management, industrial psychology, the human relations movement, and labor unions.

G. The size of a human resource department is related to the size of the organization. The median ratio is about 1 personnel employee for every 100 employees in the organization (1:100). Approximately half of the personnel staff consists of professional/technical employees and the other half, clerical. The cost of operating a human resource department is approximately 2.5 percent of the total company payroll and 1 percent of the total company operating budget.

H. The professionalism of human resource management has significantly increased in recent years through the publication of personnel journals, the organization of professional personnel/human resource associations, and the development of certification standards to certify members of the profession.

I. Human resource activities are influenced by several characteristics of the organization. Two of the most influential characteristics are the management philosophy and leadership style of the organization and the presence or absence of a labor union.

QUESTIONS

1. In a lecture to students about changes occurring in business, the president of a company described human resource departments as the new power centers. What conditions have contributed to the growing power and influence of human resource departments?

2. If a human resource manager was required to do an elaborate cost-benefit analysis of the department, what kinds of items should he or she list under costs? What should the manager list under benefits?

3. How do human resource policies differ from human resource objectives? What is the value of such policies and why should they be written?

4. How much authority should the human resource department have over line managers? Which issues and activities call for the human resource department to serve in an advisory role, which in a service role, and which in a control role?

5. What are the major personnel functions? Sometimes all these functions are not assigned to the human resource department. Who else might be assigned some of these functions and why?

6. What were the advantages of the factory system? How did it contribute to the quality of life and what were the social costs?

7. Early Americans were very suspicious of leisure time, believing that it contributed to crime and corruption. The average workweek is considerably shorter today than it was in the past. Do you think Americans have more leisure time today, and if so, is it a good thing?

8. Is human resource management a profession in the same sense that medicine and law are professions? Why or why not?

9. What types of careers are available in human resource management? What kinds of entry-level positions are available? What should an individual do to prepare for a career in human resource management?

10. How are human resource activities influenced by the organizational climate? When human resource managers implement programs that have been successful in other organizations, should they expect the programs to be equally successful in their organizations? Why or why not?

KEY TERMS

Advisory or counseling role: Exists when the relationship between the human resource department and the line managers is one of providing advice and counsel and when the authority for deciding what to do is shared.

Control role: Exists when the human resource department has the authority to make decisions regarding personnel policies and procedures that line managers are required to follow.

Guild system: The associations of craftsmen that flourished in medieval Europe.

Hawthorne studies: A series of studies conducted from 1924 to 1933 at the Hawthorne Works of Western Electric that examined how productivity was influenced by rest pauses, financial incentives, friendly supervision, and informal group norms.

Human relations movement: A shift in management thinking, largely as a result of the Hawthorne studies, that emphasized interpersonal relations and the need to consider human needs.

Human resource objectives: The goals or outcomes that human resource activities are expected to achieve.

Human resource policies: Established plans that furnish broad guidelines that direct the thinking of managers about human resource activities and issues.

Industrial psychology: The application of psychological research and theories to human resource management in industry.

Line authority: The authority to make decisions and to direct the performance of subordinates in production, sales, or finance-related activities.

Personnel certification: A procedure for certifying human resource managers as professionals that is based upon passing an exam and satisfying experience requirements.

Personnel generalist: A human resource manager who is required to understand all of the major personnel functions and how they interact with other business functions.

Personnel specialists: Members of a department who specialize in a particular human resource function, such as staffing, compensation, or employee relations.

Scientific management: A major philosophy of management that emphasized performing work in the best way and that pioneered the development of differential piece-rate incentives, time-and-motion studies, and industrial engineering.

Service role: Exists when the human resource department provides assistance to line managers according to their requests.

Staff authority: The right and responsibility to advise and assist those who possess line authority.

System 1:. An organization characterized by a lack of trust in subordinates, a lack of loyalty to the company, low performance goals, and autocratic leadership, decision making, and communication by top management.

System 4: An organization characterized by group loyalty and cooperation, high performance goals, a strong motivation to produce, and favorable attitudes toward management.

C O N C L U D I N G   C A S E

Disputed Authority

Tom Rogers, the field operations manager for Morris Construction Company, stared at the memos in front of him, wondering what he should propose to top management in its monthly planning meeting tomorrow. At the meeting, Tom wants to present a tentative proposal regarding how top management should handle a problem between the personnel department and the crew chiefs that involves more than just a simple personality clash. The two memos before him explain the problem:

To: Tom Rogers

From: Allan Paine, Crew Chief

Regarding: The Takeover by Personnel

Tom, you've got to do something to get the personnel department off our backs. For the past six months it's gotten continually worse and this latest change in hiring has just gone too far. The first thing personnel made us do was fill out a lot of forms to evaluate everyone's performance. Why does personnel need to know how well our people perform? We're the ones who supervise them. When we finally got the forms sent in, personnel said we hadn't done them right and sent them back. Obviously, personnel has no idea what it's like out here and how hard it is to get the supervisors to do a lot of silly paperwork. I finally did the forms myself.

Now personnel thinks they can tell us who we can hire and fire, and we're not about to let that happen. When you work out here in the country, you want to work with people you know and like. We've always handled our own hiring and firing and plan to continue that way. We can do it faster and easier than personnel, plus we get the people we want. We learned a long time ago that friends of the crew members work out as new hires and that strangers do not do well. Why does the personnel department think it can change human nature?

Would you please remind personnel that its job is to serve us, not the other way around. Personnel doesn't make anything; we're the ones who make this company profitable. The company had better remember which people do the building around here. If that mealy-mouthed Romney gets pushy with me again, I'll hit him in the face. You've got to tell him to back off.

To: Tom Rogers, Field Operations Manager

From: Reed Romney, Personnel Director

Regarding: Personnel Programs for Field Crews

As you know, we are attempting to implement a unified personnel management program. However, we are currently experiencing difficulty in enlisting the cooperation of some of the crew chiefs in this effort, and therefore, we are requesting your help in moving the program forward.

The company has decided to centralize all staffing activities. The personnel department will assume the responsibility for recruiting and selecting new employees as they are needed. All your supervisors need to do is complete a requisition form when new personnel are needed. This procedure will allow us to achieve a better mix of minorities and women in several areas where they are severely underrepresented. Furthermore, this procedure will eliminate the favoritism that presently exists in hiring new employees and will allow us to bid for large government contracts.

Also, you will recall that six months ago we instituted a new performance-appraisal program that will be completed annually. In the future all pay increases will be tied to this evaluation, based on guidelines established by the personnel department. We will need your assistance in explaining the procedure to your supervisors. Further instructions will be forthcoming, but for now, please begin to prepare your people for this change.

Questions:

1. What recommendations should Tom propose to top management?
2. Who should be responsible for hiring new employees?
3. What should be the authority of the personnel department regarding hiring, firing, evaluating performance, and regulating pay increases?
4. Is it fair to say that the personnel department does not produce anything and that its only purpose is to serve other departments of the company?

NOTES

1. "Nucor's Ken Iverson on Productivity and Pay," *Personnel Administrator* 31 (October 1986): 46.

2. Ibid., p. 106.

3. Rosabeth Moss Kanter, "Change Masters: Playing a New Game," *Executive Excellence* 5 (January 1988): 8–9.

4. George W. Bohlander and Angelo J. Kinicki, "Where Personnel and Productivity Meet," *Personnel Administrator* 33 (September 1988): 122–30.

5. Thomas M. Hestwood, "Make Policy Manuals Useful and Relevant," *Personnel Journal* 67 (April 1988): 43–46.

6. Roger B. Madsen and Barbara Knudson-Fields, "The Law and Employee-Employer Relationship: Policies and Procedures," *Management Solutions* 32 (January 1987): 38–45.

7. ASPA-BNA Survey No. 52, "Personnel Activities, Budgets and Staffs: 1987–1988," Bulletin to Management (September 1, 1988).

8. Harold Stieglitz, "On Concepts of Corporate Structure," *The Conference Board Record* 11 (February 1974): 7–13.

9. "Anatomy of a Human Resource Executive," *Training* 22 (May 1985): 46.

10. Charles L. Hughes, *Making Unions Unnecessary* (New York: Executive Enterprises, 1975).

11. Cyril C. Ling, *The Management of Personnel Relations: History and Origins* (Homewood, Ill.: Irwin, 1966).

12. L. Jesse Lemish, ed., *Benjamin Franklin: The Autobiography and Other Writings* (New York: Signet Classics, 1961), pp. 33–38.

13. See Herbert G. Gutman, *Work, Culture, and Society in Industrializing America* (New York: Vintage, 1966), pp. 25–30.

14. See Daniel Nelson, *Managers and Workers* (Madison: The University of Wisconsin Press, 1975).

15. Ibid., Chapter 2.

16. Margaret F. Byington, *Homestead: The Households of a Mill Town* (New York: Arno Press, 1910).

17. Company rules published by Carson, Pirie, Scott. Reproduced in Edgar F. Huse and James L. Bowditch, *Be-*

havior in Organizations: A Systems Approach to Managing (Reading, Mass.: Addison-Wesley, 1973), p. 3.

18. Gutman, *Work, Culture, and Society*, pp. 22–25.

19. See Archibald A. Evans, "Work and Leisure, 1919–1969," *International Labor Review* 99 (January 1969): 35–69.

20. Dinah Lee, "Long, Hard Days–at Pennies an Hour," *Business Week* (October 31, 1988): 46–47.

21. Frederick W. Taylor, *The Principles of Scientific Management* (New York: Norton, 1911).

22. Frank B. Gilbreth, Jr., and Ernestine Gilbreth Carey, *Cheaper by the Dozen* (New York: Crowell, 1949).

23. Frederick W. Taylor, *The Principles of Scientific Management and Testimony Before the Special House Committee* (New York: Harper, 1947).

24. Hugo Munsterberg, *The Psychology of Industrial Efficiency* (Boston: Houghton Mifflin, 1913).

25. Walter Dill Scott, "The Scientific Selection of Salesmen," *Advertising and Selling* 25 (1915): 6–6 and 94–96; Walter Dill Scott and R.C. Clothier, *Personnel Management: Principles, Practices and Point of View* (New York: McGraw, 1926).

26. Fritz J. Roethlisberger and William Dickson, *Management and the Worker* (Cambridge: Harvard University Press, 1939).

27. Alex Carey, "The Hawthorne Studies: A Radical Criticism," *American Sociological Review* 32 (June 1967): 403–16; Richard H. Franke and James D. Kaul, "The

Hawthorne Experiments: First Statistical Interpretation," *American Sociological Review* 43 (October 1978): 623–43; Henry A Landsberger, *Hawthorne Revisited* (New York: Cornell University Press, 1958); Delbert Miller and William Form, *Industrial Sociology* (New York: Harper, 1951), pp. 74–83; H.M. Parsons, "What Happened at Hawthorne?" *Science* 183 (March 1974): 922–32.

28. David Stier, "More Use of Human Resource Title," *Resource* 8 (October 1989): 2.

29. SHRM-BNA Survey No. 54, "Personnel Activities, Budgets, and Staffs: 1989–1990," Bulletin to Management (June 28, 1990).

30. U.S. Department of Labor, *Occupational Outlook Handbook, 1988–1989* (Washington, D.C.: Government Printing Office), pp. 38–42.

31. Gale Research Company, *Encyclopedia of Associations* (Detroit, Mich.: Booktower, 1985).

32. Rensis Likert, *The Human Organization* (New York: McGraw Hill, 1967); Rensis Likert, *New Patterns of Management* (New York: McGraw Hill, 1961). "The Profile of Organizational Characteristics" is reported in *The Human Organization*, pp. 197–211.

33. Ali Dastmalchian, Raymond Adamson, and Paul Blyton, "Developing a Measure of Industrial Relations Climate," *Industrial Relations* 41, no. 4 (1986): 851–59.

34. Stephen Deutsch, "Successful Worker Training Programs Help Ease Impact of Technology," *Monthly Labor Review* 110 (November 1987): 14–20.

C H A P T E R 2

The Environmental Context of Human Resource Management

Learning Objectives

After studying this chapter, you should be able to:

1. Identify the major environmental factors that influence human resource management.
2. Describe the major demographic changes occurring in the work force.
3. Describe the effects of economic conditions on human resource management.
4. Identify the major laws and regulations influencing human resource management and explain their main provisions.

Manufacturing in the P.R.C.

The following comments were made by an executive officer of a Hong Kong-based electronics corporation as part of a panel discussion for an international business conference. The panel's topic was "How Can America Compete in an International Economy?"

"My job is president of manufacturing in an international electronics company that employs about 11,000 people. I am responsible for all production activities. Although our electronic products are marketed worldwide, virtually all manufacturing is done in Asian countries, especially Taiwan and Hong Kong. In recent years, however, we have moved an increasing share of our manufacturing into the People's Republic of China (P.R.C.). Although the P.R.C. does not have the infrastructure to support manufacturing like many other countries, the availability of the people and their desire to work more than compensate for things like poor transportation and inadequate utilities.

"I spent a month touring the People's Republic of China, looking for villages where we could establish a production facility. I found several villages well suited for manufacturing, and we moved some of our assembly operations into these places. All we needed was a building we could lease and people we could train as temporary workers.

"To give you one illustration: Let me explain how we produce portable tape recorders and the headsets for listening to them. The component parts for making tape recorders come from various parts of the world and they can be assembled almost anywhere. Once you put the parts in an air-plane and get the plane in the air, they can be delivered anywhere the plane can land. Although we spend a few more dollars on transportation costs by assembling them in the P.R.C., we can save much more by reduced labor costs.

"I contracted with a group of villagers to assemble a specified number of tape recorders. They know they are only temporary workers and their job ends when the contract is filled. I try to time the contracts to avoid interfering with farming. When we train them, we insist on absolutely perfect quality and we usually get it. Consequently, the number of defective products is extremely low. We pay them an hourly wage that is equivalent to $.30 per hour in U.S. currency, and we are not required to pay social security, worker's compensation, unemployment compensation, a pension, or any other employee benefits.

"So you tell me how American manufacturers will ever compete with me in this market. I don't think they can. Our people are happy to work for 30 Hong Kong dollars per day and they will work ten or twelve hours and do top-quality work. Thirty cents an hour isn't much, but our people are happy to get it. Even though we don't pay them benefits, they still want to work for us. They appreciate the money we pay them because it supplements their farming and gives them cash to buy other things. They know there are millions of others who would like to have a job like theirs and so they are very grateful to have a job. They like the company, and they like their job, and they do everything they can to make the company successful. So I don't see how American manufacturers will ever compete with us if their people are not committed to the company, and they don't want to work, and they expect their wages to go higher and higher. There are millions of people in the P.R.C. who would like to have a part-time job in manufacturing to supplement their farming."

Questions:

1. What are the implications for American manufacturing of a large labor force in the People's Republic of China? Are the consequences as dire as this executive portrays?

2. How vulnerable are nonmanufacturing industries, such as service, mining, and construction, to the availability of a large, international labor force?

3. How will the international labor force influence personnel practices, such as wage and salary administration, hiring, turnover, unionization, and training?

Human resource management does not take place in a vacuum; personnel activities are greatly influenced by the environment in which they occur. The purpose of this chapter is to examine the environmental context of human resource management and to identify the major factors that may alter the personnel activities within an organization. Human resource managers have a variety of tools to help them perform their jobs efficiently—such tools include performance evaluations, wage incentives, training programs, recruiting strategies, and selection procedures. Knowing the right tool to use, however, depends on the environment. For example, the proper recruiting method depends on whether there are hundreds of job applicants or none. If the economy is depressed, if unemployment levels are high, or if a competitor has just announced a major layoff, the number of interested applicants will be much greater than if these conditions were reversed.

Human resource managers need to know which environmental factors influence personnel activities, and they need to anticipate changes in these factors. Environmental forecasting is just as important to a human resource manager as weather forecasting is to someone planning a family outing or a company picnic. Although little can be done to change the weather, appropriate activities can be planned to accommodate different weather conditions. Likewise, a human resource manager may be unable to change environmental conditions, but by properly anticipating them, he or she can adapt to the situation. Three major environmental factors that a human resource director must consider are the labor force, economic conditions, and laws and regulations.

THE LABOR FORCE

To meet their staffing requirements, organizations depend on the availability of talent. Significant shifts in the composition of the population have had a profound effect on the composition of the labor force and the supply of labor. Same futurists have predicted that current social trends, especially declining **birthrates** (number of births per 1,000 population), will lead to severe labor shortages in the 1990s.[1] A severe labor shortage would significantly alter all personnel functions, especially recruitment, selection, training, compensation, and employee relations. It is by no means certain, however, that these shortages will occur. Many forces—especially birthrates, participation rates, education, and immigration—influence the size and composition of the labor force. Disasters such as war and disease are possible influences as well.

MEASURING THE LABOR FORCE

The primary agency that collects and publishes information about the labor market is the **Bureau of Labor Statistics (BLS)**, a division of the U.S. Department of Labor. Although state and local government agencies, employer organizations, and private agencies also collect and publish labor market information, the BLS reports are considered the most authoritative and complete.

The statistics published by the BLS are derived from three major employment data series that are published monthly: the Establishment Series, the Insured Unemployment Series, and the **Current Population Survey (CPS)**. The Establishment Series contains information regarding employment, hours, and earning data that are reported monthly and voluntarily to the Bureau of Labor Statistics by various establishments. The Unemployment Series contains information regarding labor turnover and unemployment payments. This information is submitted voluntarily on a monthly basis to the BLS by various state agencies. The Current Population Survey provides information on the number of persons employed, unemployed, or not in the labor force. It also indicates whether workers are full-time or part-time employees and the reasons for working part-time. The statistics reported in the Current Population Survey are compiled through a program of personal interviews conducted monthly by the Bureau of the Census for the BLS. The sample consists of about 55,800 households selected to represent the U.S. population 16 years of age and older. Households are interviewed on a rotating basis so that 75 percent of the sample is the same for any two consecutive months.

To obtain reliable work-force data, the BLS has carefully defined the basic terms that it uses to describe the work force. For example, individuals who are temporarily absent from work because of illness or vacation are still considered *employed*. Individuals who did not work during the survey week but are available for work are termed **unemployed**. The total **civilian labor force** is different from the *total labor force* because of the exclusion of military personnel. *Full-time workers* are separated from *part-time workers* depending on whether they work more or less than 35 hours per week. The major definitions used by the BLS in measuring the labor force are presented in Table 2.1.

The BLS publishes information regarding the labor force in various government reports. Copies of these reports may be obtained from the Government Printing Office, and they are also reprinted in numerous statistical abstracts. One of the most convenient sources of this information is the *Monthly Labor Review*. In the back of each issue of this periodical there is a series of tables that summarize the most recent information.

SIZE AND COMPOSITION

The size and composition of the labor force are shown in Table 2.2. In 1989, the population of the United States was approximately 248 million, and 187 million people were 16 years of age or older and not in a mental or penal institution.[2] This group of 187 million, called the total noninstitutional population, represented those who could work if they wanted to. Sixty-three million people did not enter the labor force—a decision made

Accession rate - avg. # of persons added to a payroll in a given
period per 100 employees

TABLE 2.1   Definition used by the BLS in measuring the labor force

Separation rate - the avg. # of employees dropped from a
payroll per 100 employees

Employed: Persons who (1) worked for pay any time during the week or who worked unpaid for 15 hours or more in a family-operated enterprise, and (2) those who were temporarily absent from their regular jobs because of illness, vacation, industrial dispute, or similar reasons.

Unemployed: Persons who did not work during the survey week but were available for work.

Civilian labor force: All employed or unemployed persons in the civilian noninstitutional population.

Total labor force: The civilian labor force plus military personnel.

Noninstitutional population: All persons 16 years of age and older who are not inmates of penal or mental institutions, sanitariums, or homes for the aged, infirm, or needy.

Not in labor force: Everyone 16 years of age or over not classified as employed or unemployed.

Full-time workers: Those employed at least 35 hours a week.

Part-time workers: Those who work fewer than 35 hours a week.

Productivity: Output per hour of all persons. This index is determined by dividing the gross domestic product in a given period by the total number of employee hours required to produce it.

Participation rate: Percentage of people in a specified age category participating in the labor force.

Discouraged worker - not employed but not included in unemployed
because they stopped looking for a job

for a variety of reasons, such as school, family responsibilities, health problems, and retirement—leaving a work force of 125 million. Therefore, the employment-population rate was 66.6 percent, and approximately 5.1 percent of the labor force was unemployed. To put this figure in context, it compares favorably to an early 1980s unemployment rate of 9.5 percent and a depression-era unemployment rate of almost 25 percent. During the latter half of the 1960s, however, the unemployment rate was less than 4 percent.

Two hundred years ago, approximately 90 percent of the population worked in agriculture. This percentage has steadily declined as a result of new technology and improved methods of farming. In 1989, only 2.8 percent of the work force was required to produce sufficient food for the United States as well as for shipments abroad.

In 1950, 16 million people, or one-third of the work force, worked in manufacturing. By 1989, although the number of people working in manufacturing had increased, the percentage of the labor force working in manufacturing had dropped to 17 percent.

The Bureau of Labor Statistics publishes periodic projections concerning the economic and employment outlook for the coming decade. These estimates, which are derived through the use of an integrated econometric framework and are updated every two years by the BLS, are based on various assumptions regarding the size of the labor force, fiscal policy, productivity growth, unemployment rates, and price changes. Using different assumptions, the BLS provides three projections—high, medium, and low—for each of the economic and employment variables.

Changes in the composition of the work force from 1960 to 1989 are shown in Figure 2.1 along with medium-level projections of expected changes through 2000.[3] The three sectors that have shown the most rapid growth in recent years are wholesale and retail trade, services, and state and local government. The jobs in these three sectors are expected to increase through 2000, especially in the services sector.

TABLE 2.2   Size and composition of the labor force in 1989 (numbers in thousands)

Total noninstitutional population	**187,461**	
Less: Those not in labor force		62,596
Total labor force (66.6% of population)	**124,865**	
Less: Military personnel		1,684
Less: Unemployed (5.0% of labor force)		6,328
Civilian labor force employed	**116,853**	
By industry		
Self-employed	8,508	
Agriculture	3,223	
Mining	714	
Construction	5,513	
Manufacturing	19,785	
Transportation and public utilities	5,723	
Wholesale trade	6,362	
Retail trade	19,631	
Finance, insurance, and real estate	6,743	
Services	26,268	
Government	17,606	
Federal	2,975	
State	4,079	
Local	10,552	
By sex		
Men	64,051	
Women	52,802	
Married men spouse present	40,928	
Married women spouse present	29,412	
Women who maintain families	6,385	
By race		
White	105,798	
Black	13,476	

Source: Bureau of Labor Statistics. Reported in *Monthly Labor Review* 112, No. 4 (1989): 61–67.

AGE AND BIRTHRATES

Fluctuations in birthrates can have an enormous impact on the size and composition of the work force. A change in the death rate would also influence the size of the work force, but this statistic has remained relatively constant for many years, between 8 and 10 deaths per 1,000 population. Because everyone who will be in the total work force for the next twenty years has already been born, human resource managers can examine this demographic information to determine its effects on employment patterns.

The birthrates from 1910 to 1989 are shown in Figure 2.2. During this period, three drastic shifts occurred in U.S. birthrates.[4] The first shift took place during the **birth dearth** of the Depression, when births dropped to about 2.5 million per year from an average of 3 million per year. The **fertility rate**, or the number of children born to the

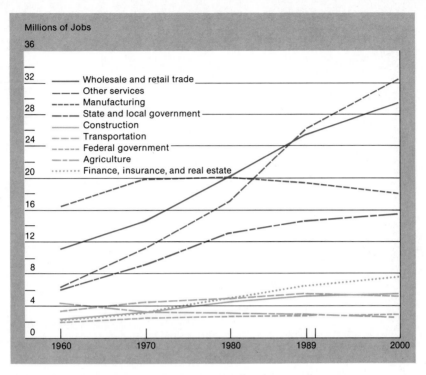

FIGURE 2.1 Employment by major sector: actual and projected.

average woman in her lifetime, dropped close to 2.1, which represents the replacement level that would lead to a stable population. The birthrate, which is the number of births per 1,000 population, declined from 30.1 in 1910 to 18.7 in 1935.

The second shift in the birthrate occurred during the **baby boom** following World War II, when the fertility rate increased to 3.8 and the birthrate increased to 25.0. The third shift occurred during the 1970s, when the birthrate dropped below 15.0. In 1976, the fertility rate fell to 1.76—far below the population-replacement level. Since 1974, fertility rates have remained relatively unchanged at 1.8. If fertility rates in the United States remain low, the predictions by some futurists of severe labor shortages after 1990 might become a reality.

Fluctuations in the birthrate have had an enormous impact on society over the past sixty years and will continue to affect society in years to come. During the 1970s, organizations experienced a relative shortage of people in the 35- to 45-year-old age group due to the low birthrate during the Depression. At the same time, the bulging baby-boom population of people under age 40 first strained hospital facilities and then educational systems. Another consequence of the baby boom is that the average age of the work force will increase. In 1970 the median age was 28, in 1980 it was 30, and by the year 2000 it is expected to be 35.

Society's effort to absorb the baby-boom population has been likened to that of a boa constrictor trying to swallow a melon. Whereas the challenge to society during the 1970s

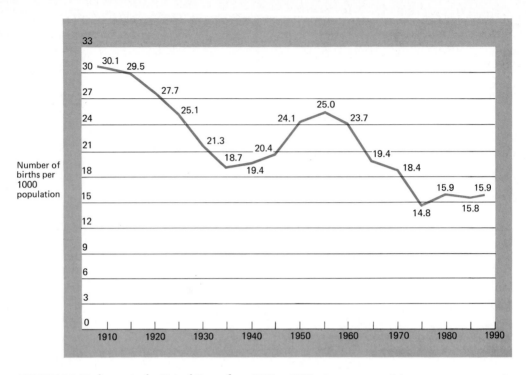

FIGURE 2.2 Birthrates in the United States from 1910 to 1989. *Source:* Bureau of the Census. See *Statistical Abstract of the United States 1990* (Washington, D.C.: U.S. Department of Commerce).

was to provide jobs for "boomers," the challenge during the 1990s will be to provide adequate promotion and management opportunities for these individuals. They are likely to experience difficulty in satisfying their career and income aspirations simply because of the competitive pressures generated by their large numbers. Perhaps the most severe strain on society will occur when this large group retires and expects to receive social security payments funded by the efforts of a smaller work force.

PARTICIPATION RATES

Changes in the **participation rates** over the past fifty years have had an even greater impact on the size of the labor force than changes in birthrates. Participation rate refers to the percentage of people in a specified age category participating in the labor force. Table 2.3 shows the participation rates for selected years. These percentages document some of the powerful social forces that are altering the size and composition of the labor force.

1. Male participation rates have declined, especially for older males. From 1900 to 1989, the percentage of men over 65 years of age who were still working declined from 67 to 15 percent.

TABLE 2.3   Participation rates, by sex and age: 1960 to 1989, and 2000 projections (persons 16 years old and over)

	1960	1970	1980	1985	1900	2000
Total	59.4	60.4	63.8	64.4	66.9	67.0
Male	83.3	79.7	77.4	76.4	76.5	74.7
16–19 years	56.2	56.1	60.5	56.0	62.3	60.2
20–24 years	88.1	83.3	85.9	85.0	84.4	87.5
25–34 years	97.5	96.4	95.2	94.4	93.7	93.6
35–44 years	97.7	96.9	95.5	95.4	95.6	93.9
45–54 years	95.7	94.3	91.2	91.2	91.3	90.1
55–64 years	86.8	83.0	72.1	68.5	65.5	63.2
65 years and older	33.1	26.8	19.0	16.3	14.9	9.9
Female	37.7	43.3	51.5	53.6	58.3	61.5
16–19 years	39.3	44.0	52.9	51.8	56.8	59.5
20–24 years	46.1	57.7	68.9	70.4	78.1	78.4
25–34 years	36.0	45.0	65.5	69.8	78.1	82.3
35–44 years	43.4	51.1	65.5	70.1	78.6	84.2
45–54 years	49.8	54.4	59.9	62.9	67.1	75.4
55–64 years	37.2	43.0	41.3	41.7	41.5	45.8
65 years and older	10.8	9.7	8.1	7.5	7.4	5.4

Source: *Statistical Abstract of the United States 1984, 108th ed.* (Washington, D.C.: U.S. Department of Commerce, 1988), p. 366.

2. Female participation rates have increased in almost every age category, especially for women in the prime working ages (25–54).

The rise in female participation rates is the major variable explaining the remarkable growth of the civilian labor force since 1960. This dramatic rise is illustrated by the statistics presented in Table 2.3 and Figure 2.3. In 1947, when national employment and income statistics were first collected, only 28 percent of the civilian labor force was female. By 1989, the percentage of female workers had risen to 45 percent of the total civilian labor force. According to projections made by the BLS, the female percentage of the labor force should continue to rise until 2000, when it will reach about 47 percent.

The rise in female employment has led to several other significant social changes. Marriage and childbearing have been postponed, and family income has risen due to the growing proportion of two-income families. The large increase in the number of working women has created a need for innovative personnel programs. Approximately 57 percent of all working women are married and living with a working spouse, and another 12 percent maintain a family. Because of family responsibilities, many women have requested some form of alternative work scheduling. Two of the most popular alternative

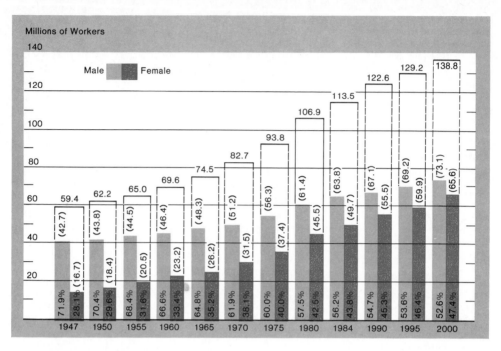

FIGURE 2.3 Civilian labor force, 1947–2000. *Sources:* U.S. Bureau of Labor Statistics. Reported in *Statistical Abstracts of the United States 1980, 101st ed.* (Washington, D.C.: U.S. Department of Commerce), p. 394. Projections by the BLS, Ronald E. Kutscher, "Overview and Implications of the Projections to 2000," *Monthly Labor Review* 110, No. 9 (1987): 3–9.

schedules are flextime and job sharing. Employees on flextime establish their own work hours, subject to certain constraints, and in job sharing, two individuals share one job. To further accommodate family responsibilities, some employers have provided child-care facilities and have granted flexible personal-leave policies so that husbands and wives can stay at home when necessary, such as when a child is sick. Other consequences of the rise in female employment have been increased competition for a limited number of jobs and an unwillingness to accept transfers among those employees who are reluctant to disrupt their spouses' careers.

EDUCATION

There is a general belief that the level of education in the work force is continually rising and that young people entering the work force today are the most highly educated workers of all time. This belief may explain why young workers demand challenging, high-paying jobs and why they are so mobile and uncommitted to organizations. Since 1970, however, educational attainment has reached a plateau.

From 1900 to 1970, the average educational level of the work force steadily increased.[5] In 1940, the median number of school years completed for people over age 25 was only

8.6 years of school; but by 1970, it had increased to 12.1, slightly more than a high school education. Since 1980, it has remained fairly constant at 12.6. These changes reflect the growing importance society attaches to education. Likewise, the percentage of young adults graduating from high school and college has also increased since 1940. From 1940 to 1986, the percentage of young adults who finished four years of high school increased from 38 percent to 86 percent, and the percentage of those with four years of college increased from 6 percent to 22 percent. Since 1970, however, the average educational level of new employees has not continued to increase. In fact, the percentage of 18 year olds who have graduated from high school has declined slightly (from 77 percent in 1970 to 70 percent in 1982), while the percentage of high school graduates going on to college has remained about the same (33 percent). Nevertheless, the overall educational level continues to rise because older workers leaving the labor force tend to have less education than the employees replacing them.

These educational statistics look deceptively impressive and explain why the number of people who are labeled as illiterate—unable to read or write any language—has decreased from 11.3 percent in 1900 to 0.1 percent in 1980. Unfortunately, literacy is usually defined as having completed the fourth grade or answering "yes" to the question "Can you read and write?" These definitions do not accurately indicate how many people are functionally illiterate.[6] In 1982, the Census Bureau administered an English Language Proficiency test to a large sample of adults and found that 13 percent of them could be considered functionally illiterate. Illiteracy appears to be a growing problem, and many organizations have to provide basic education for new employees.

While the average educational levels of new employees are not changing much, the disparity in education is widening. The educated are receiving even more education, while the uneducated obtain even less. New technology, particularly in the areas of electronics and computers, requires extensive education beyond high school for a large percentage of the work force. Unfortunately, many new employees, especially immigrants, have rather low educational levels that limit their job opportunities.

Educational levels have important implications for our ability to provide equal employment opportunities: unequal educational levels impede society's efforts to reduce racial discrimination. A careful analysis of the relationship between education and employment levels reveals that people with more education tend to have higher labor-force-participation rates, lower unemployment levels, and higher earnings. For example, college graduates have a high participation rate of 88 percent and a low unemployment of only 2.7 percent, while the corresponding rates for those who do not finish high school are 65 percent and 12 percent.[7] College graduates hold the majority of managerial and professional jobs. Also, the average money earnings of full-time employees is directly related to educational attainment: college graduates earn about 55 percent more than high school graduates, and those with graduate degrees usually earn more than twice as much as high school graduates. In recent years, important progress has been made toward equalizing educational opportunities. From 1970 to 1982, the percentage of nonwhites enrolled in college increased from 8 percent to 14 percent and the percentage of females increased from 41 percent to 52 percent. Since 1982, however, the percentage of nonwhites enrolled in college has declined slightly, and the percentage of high school graduates who enroll in college is still less for nonwhites than for whites (28 percent vs. 36 percent).

IMMIGRATION

America has always been a land where foreigners from around the world have gathered to live in freedom. During certain periods the immigration rates have been particularly high, especially between 1900 and 1910, when 880,000 immigrants arrived per year. Since 1970, the rate of immigration has again increased significantly. Although legal aliens have generally numbered about 500,000 per year, the actual immigration total probably exceeds 1 million when the number of illegal aliens is considered. In 1980, for example, there were 808,000 immigrants who entered the United States legally and an estimated 500,000 who entered illegally.[8]

The availability of immigrant labor is a significant influence on personnel activities. The influx of immigrants provides a large applicant pool of unskilled labor willing to perform unpleasant jobs for small wages. Difficult economic and political conditions in Central America have pushed millions of Hispanic workers to seek employment in the United States. Political instability in southeast Asia has likewise caused significant numbers of Asians to emigrate. Illegal immigrants now play a major role in the economies of the Southwest, especially California and Texas. Congress has attempted to limit the flow of illegal immigrants into the work force by passing the Immigration Reform and Control Act (IRCA) of 1986. This law was based on the premises that most illegal immigrants were coming to America for economic reasons and that the most effective way to discourage them was to prevent them from holding a job.

The IRCA requires employers to make certain that all job applicants have a legal right to work in the United States, and there are penalties for employers who knowingly hire illegal immigrants. Employers are required to complete an I-9 verification form for all new employees showing proof of their identity and legal right to work. These forms must be retained for the longer of three years or one year after the individual's employment ends. The law provides stiff penalties for employers who hire undocumented workers: up to $1,000 for paper-work errors, up to $10,000 for each illegal alien hired, and prison terms for employers who show a "pattern or practice" of hiring undocumented workers or falsifying documents.[9]

A combination of high birthrates, high participation rates, and immigration has made Hispanics the fastest-growing segment in the U.S. labor force.[10] Hispanic birthrates are higher than the rates for whites and blacks. While the birthrate for blacks has historically been about 50 percent higher than that for whites, the birthrate among Hispanics has been about double the white birthrate. Hispanics also have higher participation rates, usually 3 to 5 percent higher than non-Hispanics, and the participation rates are especially high among Hispanic females. During the 1980s, the Hispanic work force increased four times as fast as the non-Hispanic work force. The BLS projections indicate that this trend will continue through the year 2000, when Hispanics will comprise 10 percent of the U.S. work force, up from 7 percent in 1986. Asian and other race groups are also projected to increase significantly, largely as a result of immigration. These changes in the composition of the labor force will significantly influence hiring practices and affirmative action programs, since 90 percent of the growth in the labor force during the 1990s is expected to be minorities and females.

FOREIGN LABOR FORCE

In 1988, the U.S. population of 248 million represented approximately 4.8 percent of the world population of 5.128 billion people. Over the next century, the population of the United States is expected to increase, but not as rapidly as in most other countries.[11] The birthrate of North America (15.6) is slightly higher than the birthrates of Japan (12) and most European countries (which ranged from 11 to 15), but it is significantly below the birthrates in Africa (45), Latin America (30), and Asia (31). How many of these people will enter the labor force to compete for jobs will depend largely on the economic development and improvements in education in these countries. Table 2.4 shows the populations of the top twenty countries in 1988 and how they are expected to change over the next century as forecasted by the World Bank.

TABLE 2.4   The World's 20 most populous countries: 1988 and 2100

1988			2100		
Rank	Country	Population	Rank	Country	Population
1.	China	1,087,000,000	1.	India	1,631,800,000
2.	India	816,800,000	2.	China	1,571,400,000
3.	USSR	286,000,000	3.	Nigeria	508,800,000
4.	United States	246,100,000	4.	USSR	375,900,000
5.	Indonesia	177,400,000	5.	Indonesia	356,300,000
6.	Brazil	144,400,000	6.	Pakistan	315,800,000
7.	Japan	122,700,000	7.	United States	308,700,000
8.	Nigeria	111,900,000	8.	Bangladesh	297,100,000
9.	Bangladesh	109,500,000	9.	Brazil	293,200,000
10.	Pakistan	107,500,000	10.	Mexico	195,500,000
11.	Mexico	83,500,000	11.	Ethiopia	173,300,000
12.	Vietnam	65,200,000	12.	Vietnam	168,100,000
13.	Philippines	63,200,000	13.	Iran	163,800,000
14.	Germany, West	61,200,000	14.	Zaire	138,900,000
15.	Italy	57,300,000	15.	Japan	127,900,000
16.	United Kingdom	57,100,000	16.	Philippines	125,100,000
17.	France	55,900,000	17.	Tanzania	119,600,000
18.	Thailand	54,700,000	18.	Kenya	116,400,000
19.	Egypt	53,300,000	19.	Burma	111,700,000
20.	Turkey	52,900,000	20.	Egypt	110,500,000

From the *1989 Population Data Sheet* of the Population Reference Bureau, Inc. *Original sources: 1986, Population Reference Bureau, 2100, World Bank.*

Because of different birthrates and participation rates, the labor forces in some foreign countries are growing much faster than in other countries. For example, in 1980 the labor force of South Korea was only slightly larger than Canada (14 vs. 12 million), with both countries having about equal percentages of female workers (39 percent). However, Korea has had a much higher birthrate than Canada (29 vs. 16), resulting in Korea's labor force being 50 percent higher than Canada's labor force a decade later.

Changes in the labor force outside the United States are gradually coming to exert a greater impact on personnel activities than internal changes in the labor force. Techno-logical advances in communication and transportation have made it possible for a man-ufacturing company to locate an assembly operation almost anywhere in the world. Naturally, manufacturing companies want to locate their facilities in places where there is an ample supply of skilled labor willing to produce top-quality products for minimal wages. During the 1980s, many U.S. organizations moved segments of their companies, especially manufacturing, to foreign locations, such as Korea and Taiwan. This trend is likely to continue because many foreign countries have an expanding labor force of people who are willing to work more hours per week at a lower hourly wage than American workers.

TABLE 2.5   International comparison of manufacturing potential

Country	People in Labor Force[a]	Number of Manufacturing Workers[a]	Unemploy-ment Rate	Average Weekly Hours	Average Hourly Compensation[b]	Manufacturing Productivity (1977 = 100)
United States	116,205	19,540	5.0%	34.9	$13.90	132
Canada	12,347	2,097	7.8	32.1	13.58	120
Japan	60,490	12,870	2.3	47.6	13.14	171
England	25,749	5,149	8.4	43.1	10.56	148
Germany	25,782	7,717	8.7	40.3	18.07	130
France	18,210	4,392	7.1	39.1	12.99	139
Sweden	4,399	552	1.6	37.3	16.85	142
Korea	17,123	3,675	2.3	51.9	2.23	—
Israel	1,439	324	5.4	33.0	7.10	—
Hong Kong	2,716	869	1.6	—	2.43	—
Italy	21,103	3,986	12.0	39.0	12.87	158
Spain	11,709	—	19.8	37.6	8.75	—
Australia	7,488	—	6.1	34.4	11.01	—

[a]in thousands
[b]average hourly compensation costs for production workers (wages and benefits) in U.S. dollars
Source: Bulletin of Labour Statistics, 1989-1 (Geneva: International Labour Office) and U.S. Bureau of Labor Statistics.

Table 2.5 shows a comparison among selected countries of the size of the labor market, the number of people in that country working in manufacturing jobs, the average number of hours worked per week, and the average hourly compensation costs for production workers expressed in U.S. dollars. These data explain why foreign competition, especially in Asia, is such a threat to the economies of Europe and North America. During the 1970s, many manufacturers in Europe and the United States felt very threatened as they saw Japanese manufacturers acquiring a sizable market share in such industries as steel, automobiles, and computers. During the 1980s, both American and Japanese manufacturers anxiously watched a repeat of the same drama as manufacturing expanded in Korea, Taiwan, and Singapore. In future years, a similar economic challenge, but possibly more extensive and more intense, will emerge from other countries, especially China and India, as millions of workers acquire the skills and opportunities to enter the worldwide labor force.

ECONOMIC CONDITIONS

Human resource activities are influenced by the overall state of the economy. Interest rates, inflation, fiscal policies, and even the stock market can have a significant impact on human resource activities within an organization. Therefore, human resource managers need to forecast the state of the economy and to anticipate how the economy will affect their activities. Like weather forecasts, economic forecasts are not always accurate; nevertheless, they can be useful for planning. Important economic factors for human resource managers to consider include unemployment levels, inflation, productivity, and foreign competition.

UNEMPLOYMENT

Perhaps the most significant economic factor influencing personnel activities is the unemployment rate. Virtually every personnel activity is influenced in some way by changes in unemployment rates, and some activities, such as recruitment and selection, are altered drastically.

Unemployment rates relate to changes in the gross national product. Rapid growth of the GNP is associated with low levels of unemployment, but as the economy slows down, unemployment goes up. At times, the government has attempted to reduce unemployment, particularly for disadvantaged individuals, by creating temporary jobs. Although government-created jobs temporarily reduce unemployment, they are not a viable long-term solution to high unemployment. Creating new jobs requires a capital investment so that each worker has the necessary resources to produce a useful product or service. The average capital outlay for creating a job is approximately $50,000. However, in certain industries, such as petroleum refining, the capital outlay per job is considerably higher and may exceed $300,000.[12]

Regional unemployment levels are influenced by local economic conditions, particularly plant openings and closings. In a particular local environment, the unemployment level may be significantly different from the overall national level.

Employment levels are influenced by interest rates. When interest rates go up, the cost of capital increases, which reduces the amount of business investment. Therefore, high interest rates tend to reduce employment levels. Employment in the construction and auto industries is especially hurt by high interest rates because consumers use loans to purchase houses and cars.

A labor surplus caused by high unemployment tends to make several personnel functions easier to perform. When there are more workers than jobs, recruiting costs are minimal. Prospective employees readily apply for scarce positions, and employers can choose from a large pool of qualified applicants for each position. Those who are hired during periods of high unemployment tend to be more committed to the company and to quality performance than those who are hired in periods of low unemployment. A labor surplus also tends to discourage employees from pressing for compensation and benefit increases, since employees are aware that other qualified people are available to take their place if their requests are unreasonable. For the same reason, disciplinary problems, absenteeism, and turnover are likely to decrease and equal employment opportunity goals may be easier to reach. Turnover rates and the effects of job dissatisfaction are closely tied to the rate of unemployment. When unemployment rates are high, turnover rates are low because workers are reluctant to leave their jobs, even if they don't like them, to look for better jobs.[13]

During the 1980s, the unemployment rates in the United States ranged from a low of 5.1 percent in 1989 to a high of 9.7 percent in 1982.[14] Although Americans considered these rates high and made many efforts to reduce them, a number of new jobs were created each year and added to the labor force. By contrast, in France, England, and Holland unemployment rates ranged from 10 percent to 13 percent.

In Japan the unemployment rate during the 1980s was generally about 2.5 percent. Japan's low unemployment rate was largely due to a healthy economy and the cultural practice of lifetime employment (*nanko*). Japanese workers expect to work for the same employer until retirement, and employers tend to reduce the length of the workweek rather than terminate employees during slack times. Sweden has also succeeded in maintaining low unemployment rates (between 2 percent and 3 percent). On the other hand, some countries, such as Puerto Rico, Spain, Barbados, and Jamaica, have had unemployment rates that were almost as high as the U.S. Depression rate of 24.9 percent.

INFLATION

Inflation, which has become a fact of life, plays havoc with human resource costs. Managing a compensation program is especially difficult during periods of high inflation. Some multinational corporations with divisions in countries with rampant inflation are required to revise their salary schedules weekly or even daily.

In the United States the annual rate of inflation during the 1980s ranged from 4 percent to 8 percent as measured by changes in the Consumer Price Index.[15] At this rate of inflation, compensation systems must be revised annually to keep wages and salaries competitive, and the value of long-term savings and investments tends to erode. Inflation is disruptive to an economy and can create severe personal inequities if it gets out of control. When compared to other countries, the United States has been relatively successful in controlling inflation. West Germany and Austria, whose rates have been about half the U.S. rate, have controlled inflation even better. But the inflation rates of many other countries have been much greater, especially in Argentina, Brazil, Bolivia, Israel, and Mexico, where prices have sometimes doubled every four to eight months. Runaway inflation creates as much managerial chaos as it does economic chaos, since wages, salaries, budgets, and human resource planning are severely disrupted.

PRODUCTIVITY

Productivity data are compiled by the Bureau of Labor Statistics from information submitted by various establishments.[16] **Productivity** is the total output per hour of all employees. The total output refers to the total gross domestic product, which is the goods and services produced by society. Output per hour of all persons is the gross domestic product divided by the total number of employee hours required to produce the product. From 1939 to 1968, productivity in terms of output per employee hour increased approximately 3 percent per year. From 1968 to 1973, the rate of productivity growth in the private sector was only 2.3 percent, and it was only 0.9 percent between 1973 and 1989.

Several reasons may explain the decline in the productivity growth rate: (1) the influx of inexperienced workers; (2) a decline in capital spending; (3) a large investment in social programs, such as environmental protection and energy conservation, rather than in production; (4) a decline in the work ethics and work habits of employees; and (5) an economic shift away from manufacturing and toward service, where productivity gains are more modest. The BLS estimates that during the 1990s productivity will again increase between 1.9 and 3.1 percent per year, primarily because of technological advances.

Productivity improvements have a major impact on economic prosperity. The standard of living in a country and changes in its real compensation are closely tied to changes in its productivity. Increasing productivity is one sure way a nation can afford to raise wages while remaining competitive in an increasingly global economy. The relationship between productivity, compensation per hour, and real compensation per hour (after adjusting for inflation) is illustrated by the data in Figure 2.4. In the United States, the manufacturing sector has been pushed by foreign competition to achieve significant productivity increases. Since 1980, manufacturing productivity has increased about 3 percent annually, while in the service sector productivity has only been growing at a 0.6 percent annual rate. Most of the industrialized countries have been able to achieve slightly higher productivity increases than the United States, as shown by the data in Table 2.5.

Attempts to influence productivity also influence human resource management. One of the most effective ways to increase productivity is through technological advances. Recent decades have seen technological advances in virtually every aspect of business. Automation has transformed the production and transportation of materials. New power tools, assembly equipment, lift trucks, conveyers, automated material management system, lasers, and alloys have virtually revolutionized production and distribution. The development of jet freight transportation, containerized shipping, pipelines, and super-

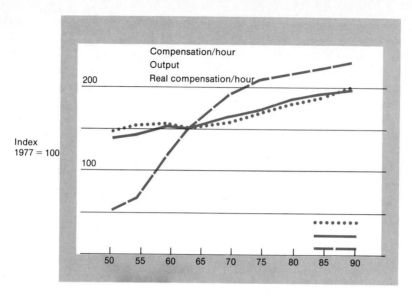

FIGURE 2.4 Productivity.

tankers has changed the way in which raw materials and goods are moved. Computers are drastically changing almost every aspect of an organization's functioning. Computers acquire, store, manipulate, interpret, and display selected information. The processing of information and the solution of complex scientific, engineering, and business problems that would have been impossible only a few years ago are now possible in moments due to computers. Television, fax machines, and the use of microwave and satellite transmission have changed the fundamental patterns of communication in business and government. The use of robots in production activities has changed from fantasy to reality.

The growth of technology and attempts to achieve higher productivity will continue to influence personnel activities in the future. Many jobs will become automated, and as a result, new jobs will be created to build and service the automated equipment. Training and development opportunities will be needed to help employees learn new skills. Striving for greater productivity also will create more favorable attitudes among employees and increase their commitment to pride and craftsmanship.

COMPETITION

Competition occurs in both the public and private sectors. In industry, competition occurs when firms vie for a customer's business. For example, when two gas stations are located at the same intersection, price pressures usually result since motorists generally buy more gas from the station with the lowest prices. Similar pressures also exist among organizations such as hospitals, colleges, and government agencies where there is competition for scarce resources or clients.

Economic pressure through competition can force an organization to change its human resource activities. As competitiveness increases, organizations become less able to offer additional rewards to employees in the form of higher pay and other tangible benefits. In competitive industries, only the highly successful firms are able to offer high wages and benefits and favorable working conditions. Less effective firms may be severely limited in the wages and salaries they can offer, which means they may experience difficulty recruiting and hiring skilled employees. The less successful firms also may not be able to maintain positive worker attitudes, and they may experience higher absenteeism and turnover and more pressure from their employees to organize a union than the successful firms.

Competition between areas within the United States has influenced economic growth patterns. The Federal Reserve Bank of Chicago conducted a statistical study examining the determinants of manufacturing job growth in the nation's 75 largest metropolitan areas over a ten-year period. The analysis suggested that high hourly wages and high unemployment taxes had a detrimental effect on industrial job growth. Manufacturing jobs were more likely to be created or transferred to locations that had lower labor costs, high educational spending per pupil, and greater access to technology.[17]

International competition results in similar job movement, and increased international trade has stimulated foreign competition. Many companies have been forced to close because of their inability to compete successfully with foreign competitors, and many other companies have been struggling to survive. For example, American automakers have faced heavy competition from foreign car manufacturers, especially the Japanese. The American auto companies have criticized the Japanese carmakers for paying substandard wages to their laborers. In turn, the Japanese carmakers have claimed that their employees are the second-highest-paid auto assemblers in the world and have criticized American automakers for paying exorbitant wages and salaries to their employees.

EXTERNAL PUBLICS

The expectations of external publics comprise an influential segment of a firm's economic environment. The most important external publics are a firm's stockholders/owners and customers/clients, and the expectations of these two groups are typically incompatible.

Stockholders/owners expect an organization to be run profitably, using sound management practices. Moreover, they expect all personnel activities to be cost-benefit effective: everything that is done should in some way contribute to the profitability of the organization, including training and development activities, bonuses and benefits, and employee relations programs. For example, stockholders/owners may question the value of programs designed to help employees with alcoholism or financial problems, since such programs do not contribute directly to the profitability of the organization.

Customers/clients, on the other hand, believe that the purpose of an organization is to provide useful products and services for society and also to assume a social responsibility for improving the quality of society. To fulfill its social responsibility, an organization is often expected to recruit and train disadvantaged members of society and to provide a work environment that contributes to the overall quality of life for all employees. Since customers/clients constantly demand high-quality products and competent service, an organization must strive to have a productive and capable work force.

Balancing the demands of these external publics requires a great deal of skill. Human resource managers may be forced to justify the merits of policies and programs in terms of how they will affect future profits. Human resource managers also may be expected to prove that their activities are socially responsible in contributing to the quality of work life for employees.

LAWS AND REGULATIONS

Perhaps the most imposing external factors influencing human resource management are laws and regulations. Many human resource managers respond with feelings of despair to the plethora of legal requirements imposed on them. In addition to numerous state and federal laws, human resource managers also are expected to comply with agency regulations that often involve extensive record keeping and reporting responsibilities.

Although numerous laws and regulations dictate what human resource managers can and cannot do, they should view these requirements as constraints in which they are allowed to operate rather than as procedures that tell them what to do. Within these constraints, human resource managers still have considerable flexibility in designing their human resource practices.

The major federal laws and regulations are introduced in this chapter and described in greater detail in later chapters. Agency regulations and state laws vary too widely to be included here, but these requirements are just as important as federal laws and human resource managers cannot overlook them.

LABOR LAWS

During the 1800s, employees were virtually powerless against employers' arbitrary wage cuts and terminations. In some situations, employees' wages were arbitrarily reduced, even though their rents for company-owned housing remained unchanged. Eventually, employees were allowed to organize unions to protest management actions, and later they were allowed to strike to enforce their demands. These were important gains for labor, but nevertheless, union strikes were ineffective. The balance of power was clearly in the hands of employers, who used court injunctions, yellow-dog contracts, union spies, and even violence to destroy the effectiveness of unions. The major federal laws and executive orders that altered these conditions are listed in Table 2.6.

With the passage of the Railway Labor Act in 1926, Congress declared that labor disputes in the railroad industry should be settled peacefully through collective bargaining between the railroad company and representatives of the railway workers. During the Depression, two other laws were passed to establish collective bargaining as a national policy for all industries. The Norris-LaGuardia Anti-injunction Act of 1932 restricted the use of court injunctions to settle labor disputes. Then, in 1935, the Wagner National Labor Relations Act established the right of workers to organize in companies where a majority of the workers vote in favor of unions. The Wagner Act also created the National Labor Relations Board to oversee union elections and to judge the fairness of labor practices brought to its jurisdiction. These laws created a national policy, which declared

TABLE 2.6   Major labor relations laws

Law	Major Provisions
Railway Labor Act of 1926	Provided for collective bargaining as a means of settling disputes between labor and management in the railroad industry.
Anti-injunction Act (Norris-LaGuardia Act) of 1932	Virtually eliminated the use of court injunctions to settle labor disputes and therefore made yellow-dog contracts legally unenforceable.
National Labor Relations Act (Wagner Act) of 1935	Created the National Labor Relations Board, gave employees the right to organize a union in NLRB supervised elections, and specifically prohibited unfair labor practices by management.
Labor Management Relations Act (Taft-Hartley Act) of 1947	Eliminated unfair labor practices by unions and gave employees the right to refrain from union activity.
Labor Management Reporting and Disclosure Act (Landrum-Griffin Act) of 1959	A labor reform act that required unions to operate democratically and to make information regarding the internal affairs of the union open to the public.
Executive Order No. 10988 of 1962 Executive Order No. 11491 of 1969 Executive Order No. 11616 of 1971 Executive Order No. 11838 of 1975	Gave federal employees the right to organize a union and the right to collective bargaining.

that labor disputes are to be settled peacefully through a process of collective bargaining in which management and the union are required to negotiate in good faith.

During the 1940s, the balance of power shifted in favor of the unions. Unions grew rapidly and wanted to exercise their new power. Many strikes were prevented only because of wartime demands. In 1946, when the war was over, the nation experienced a record number of lost days due to strikes. As a consequence, the Taft-Hartley Act, which amended the National Labor Relations Act, was passed in 1947. This legislation was intended to create a better balance of power by specifying unfair labor practices on the part of both management and labor.

During the 1950s, a congressional investigation revealed serious misuse of union funds and other abuses by union leadership. As a consequence of these revelations, the National Labor Relations Act was amended once again, in 1959, by the Landrum-Griffin Labor Management Reporting and Disclosure Act. This law directed unions to operate using democratic procedures and required that union activities and financial transactions be made public. The provisions of these laws and how they are implemented to reduce labor strife are discussed in greater detail in Chapter 13.

Provisions for organizing a union among public employees have been stipulated by presidential **executive orders**. The first executive order (No. 10988), in 1962, authorized federal employees to bargain collectively with the federal government regarding wages, hours, and conditions of employment. Other executive orders followed, which were designed to establish procedures for resolving labor disputes in the public sector that are similar to those enjoyed by employees in the private sector. The major difference between the rights of public and private employees is that public employees generally do not have the right to strike.

During the 1970s and 1980s, labor unions lost both members and power. Union leaders tried unsuccessfully to obtain passage of federal legislation to increase their economic power, but neither Congress nor the courts supported their initiatives. Congress rejected bills that would have made union strikes more costly to employers, and the federal courts allowed employers facing bankruptcy to terminate their labor agreement. The most serious factor in unions' loss of influence, however, was probably the improvement in labor relations that resulted from labor-management committees, quality of work life programs, and complaint systems that reduced the need for an adversarial union to represent workers' interests. Although union leaders predict a resurgence of union membership and power in the future, others suggest that unions have outlived their usefulness and will become mere social clubs.

COMPENSATION LAWS

Since the early nineteenth century, government has addressed the issue of employees' wages and hours. In 1840, President Martin Van Buren issued an executive order limiting the workday for those employed on federal projects to ten hours. During the next thirty years, most of the heavily industrialized states passed some form of legislation regulating the employment of women and children. During the latter half of the 1800s, several states attempted to limit the workday of all laborers to eight hours. An eight-hour working day was a basic union demand throughout this period, and the eight-hour-day movement was a lively—though unsuccessful—political force.

One reason the eight-hour-day advocates were not successful in obtaining new legislation was that the federal and state governments had difficulty enforcing the laws that had already been passed. Child-labor laws were particularly ineffective. Before 1900, children frequently worked under dangerous and unsanitary conditions, sometimes for as long as eleven or twelve hours a day, six days a week. The states could not effectively enforce their laws because they lacked the cooperation of employers, parents, and even the children. Employers viewed children as a cheap source of labor; parents needed the children's wages; and the children wanted to contribute to the family's earnings.[18] After 1900, several attempts were made to eliminate child labor, either by prohibiting it through federal legislation or by taxing the merchandise produced by it. Legislative attempts, however, either failed or were declared unconstitutional.

Eventually, legislation regulating the wages and hours of employees became a reality. (The major federal compensation laws are listed in Table 2.7). During the Great Depression, several important laws were passed. The objectives of these laws were to expand employment, to compensate workers at levels that would allow them to maintain a reasonable standard of living, and to provide for income continuation during periods of disability, layoff, and retirement. The Davis-Bacon Act, passed in 1931, requires contractors of federal construction projects to pay the prevailing wage of the local geographical area.

TABLE 2.7   Major compensation laws

Laws	Major Provisions
Davis-Bacon Act of 1931	Required federal construction contractors to pay the prevailing wage in the local geographical area.
Social Security Act of 1935	Created the social security program by placing a federal tax on payrolls that would provide retirement and unemployment benefits.
Public Contracts Act (Walsh-Healey Act) of 1936	Required all firms doing business with the federal government, both construction and nonconstruction, to pay wages equivalent to the prevailing wage rate in the local area. Overtime payments were required after 40 hours per week.
Fair Labor Standards Act of 1938	Prohibited the employment of children under age 16 in interstate commerce, and established minimum wages and overtime pay.
Equal Pay Act of 1963	Prohibited discrimination in pay on the basis of sex for jobs that require the same skill, effort, and responsibility.
Employee Retirement Income Security Act (ERISA) of 1974	Regulated the administration, funding, and investment of pension funds, and required the preparation and distribution of annual reports.

Five years later, the coverage of the Davis-Bacon Act was extended to include nonconstruction work. The Walsh-Healey Public Contracts Act, passed in 1936, requires any firm doing business with the federal government to pay wages at least equivalent to the prevailing wages in the area where the firm is located. This act also requires that overtime wages be paid after 40 hours per week.

During the Depression, many people were forced to liquidate their savings, and as a result, large numbers of people, especially older people, were destitute. It was clear that some form of legislative relief for older citizens was necessary, but most people would not accept retiring workers at age 62 and instituting a government dole. Instead, Congress passed the Social Security Act of 1935, a program of forced saving that required workers to set aside part of their incomes to provide pensions after they retired. The payments were only intended to be a supplement to other forms of savings. The benefits were provided for those who retired or for their widows and children under age 18. Amendments to the Social Security Act have provided benefits to disabled workers and health insurance (Medicare) for older people. To pay for these benefits, the funding requirements of the act also have been amended. When the law was first passed, workers were required to pay 1.0 percent of the first $3,000 earned; this meant that the most a worker was required to pay in a given year was $30. In 1990, the funding requirement was 7.65 percent of the first $51,300 earned; thus some workers had to pay over $4,000 per year. The social security tax is a payroll deduction that employers are required to withhold and submit, and employees also are required to pay a matching amount.

In 1938, Congress passed the Fair Labor Standards Act, a law that established minimum wages, overtime pay, and child-labor standards. In 1938, the minimum hourly wage was $0.25, and the legislation applied only to jobs in interstate commerce, which at that time was narrowly defined. By 1991, the minimum wage was $4.25 per hour, and the definition of interstate commerce had become very broadly defined. The law mandated time-and-one-half premium pay for work exceeding 40 hours per week, and this require-ment helped to establish the eight-hour workday standard. Children under the age of 16 (age 18 for dangerous occupations) were prohibited from employment in interstate com-merce jobs, although by 1938 child labor had been virtually eliminated because of the improved quality of education and a growing recognition of its importance. (These requirements will be explained in greater detail in Chapter 12.)

During the 1950s and 1960s, pension funds grew in number and size. Unfortunately, some companies terminated workers before retirement age to avoid paying them a pen-sion, and some retirees were disappointed to learn that the pensions they had been promised were nonexistent because of fraud or mismanagement. Since existing legisla-tion had failed to provide adequate safeguards for pension funds, the Employee Retire-ment Income Security Act (ERISA) of 1974 was passed to protect these funds. ERISA does not require employers to have a pension fund, but if they do, they are expected to comply with elaborate procedures regarding funding, investment, and the disclosure of information. (These requirements will be explained in greater detail in Chapter 12.)

SAFETY AND HEALTH LAWS

Legislation regarding employee safety and health is summarized in Table 2.8. The first series of laws are the workers' compensation laws that provide compensation to injured workers, regardless of who is responsible for the accident. The second type of legislation provides a safe and healthy workplace by eliminating hazards.

During the 1800s, employees were forced to work in unsafe and unsanitary environ-ments, and there was virtually no legislative pressure to reduce accidents or to provide compensation for injuries. During the latter part of the century, many states enacted laws designed to help injured employees bring suit against employers. Most of these laws were patterned after the Employers Liability Act, passed in England in 1880, and were in-tended to eliminate some of the legal defenses that employers had been using to avoid liability for accidents. Most of these laws had almost no effect; injured workers remained virtually powerless to sue employers. The situation changed in 1910, when the New York State Legislature passed a Workmen's Compensation Act (now called Workers' Compen-sation). In the following year, ten more state legislatures adopted workers' compensation acts. By 1948, every state had legislated some form of workers' compensation.[19]

The battle for legislation providing compensation to injured workers was a difficult one. Public sentiment generally supported the idea of compensation, but it questioned the fairness of making employers liable to exorbitant civil suits. In fact, the New York workers' compensation law was declared invalid on March 24, 1911, in a Supreme Court decision for the case of *Ives* v. *South Buffalo Railway Company*. The next day, 145 women

TABLE 2.8   Major laws regarding safety and health

Laws	Provisions
Workers' Compensation Laws (state laws beginning in 1910)	Provided compensation for employees injured on the job regardless of who was responsible for the accident.
Occupational Safety and Health Act of 1970	Created the Occupational Safety and Health Administration (OSHA), which is responsible for providing safety and health standards and for enforcing them through inspections and citations.

employed as machine operators were killed in a fire that destroyed the Triangle Shirtwaist Company in New York City. This holocaust served to focus national attention on the need for some form of worker's compensation. The timing of the Supreme Court's decision was historically significant, because it influenced the type of workers' compensation laws that were subsequently passed in other states.

The basic concept underlying workers' compensation laws is liability without fault, meaning that an injured employee is entitled to a moderate and reasonable amount of compensation, regardless of who causes the accident. Another important concept is that compensation for injured workers is viewed as a basic business expense that should be charged to the employer.

Safety requirements were included in other federal laws (such as the Walsh-Healey Act of 1936 and the McNamara-O'Hara Service Act of 1965) in an effort to reduce industrial accidents. These regulations were superceded, however, by the Occupational Safety and Health Act (OSHAct) of 1970. This act created the Occupational Safety and Health Administration (OSHA), which is responsible for establishing and enforcing health and safety standards. OSHA conducts safety inspections of establishments and issues citations and fines for unsafe working practices. The act also requires employers to maintain records regarding accidents and to submit periodic reports to OSHA.

During the first decade after the passage of OSHAct, employers were extremely critical of the new law and the relationship between employers and OSHA inspectors was usually antagonistic. Many of the safety regulations issued by OSHA were viewed as either picky or excessively technical and the fines imposed by OSHA seemed arbitrary and punitive. During the second decade, however, a much more cooperative relationship emerged, as OSHA refined its regulations, invited employers to participate in public hearings before new regulations were issued, and provided free on-site consultations to help employers know what changes they needed to make. Chapter 15 will describe some of the provisions of OSHAct in greater detail and the kinds of safety programs OSHA requires to provide a safe work environment. Although the frequency of accidents at work has been reduced since OSHAct was passed, too many accidents still occur, creating unnecessary pain, expense, and litigation.

INDIVIDUAL RIGHTS

A basic philosophy in America is that everyone is created equal. Although the authors of the Declaration of Independence did not intend that everyone should remain equal throughout life, they did proclaim that everyone was created equal and should have equal opportunity to life, liberty, and the pursuit of happiness. Equal opportunity is every American's birthright. The American dream is based on the belief that everybody can achieve success if they work hard to earn it; success does not depend on being born into a privileged class. Unfortunately, many Americans have not had equal opportunities for employment. Instead, they have been unfairly treated and discriminated against because of their age, race, religion, sex, or physical handicap. Federal laws have been passed to protect people from these forms of discrimination at work.

RACE DISCRIMINATION

The drive to eliminate racial discrimination has progressed very slowly, and at some points, very painfully. The Civil War highlighted the issue of whether one individual has the right to own another human being. Following the war, two amendments to the Constitution prohibited slavery and provided equal protection for all citizens within state and local governments. Civil rights acts prohibiting racial discrimination and providing all persons the same right to enter into contracts as "white citizens" were passed in 1866, 1870, and 1871.

Although slavery was abolished after the Civil War and civil rights legislation prohibited discrimination, racial prejudice continued. Minorities in America—blacks, Indians, Asians, Hispanics, and other nationalities—have been treated as second-class citizens and systematically excluded from many areas of society. They have been deprived of equal opportunities for employment, housing, education, and even public transportation. The anger and frustration caused by racial discrimination finally erupted in riots and civil disobedience. A significant event occurred December 1, 1955, in Montgomery, Alabama, when Mrs. Rosa Parks, a black department store worker, was arrested for refusing to give her bus seat to a white man. This event precipitated a boycott by blacks of the city buses and created a cohesive group called the Montgomery Improvement Association, which was led by a young minister, Dr. Martin Luther King, Jr. Until he was assassinated in 1968, Dr. King was a major leader in the civil rights movement and was posthumously awarded a Nobel Peace Prize for his dedicated efforts.

Many state and federal laws, executive orders, and social programs have attempted to eliminate racial discrimination. However, the underlying personal prejudice fueling discrimination has been very difficult to change. Some of the major prohibitions against discrimination are presented in Table 2.9. Many additional attempts have also been made (For example, the Railway Labor Act of 1926 and the Wagner National Labor Relations Act of 1935 indirectly prohibited racial discrimination in labor unions by requiring fair representation for all).

Several executive orders were directed toward eliminating racial discrimination. On June 25, 1941, President Franklin D. Roosevelt issued Executive Order 8802, which created the Committee on Fair Employment Practices within the Office of Production Management. The goal of this committee was to eliminate discrimination in federal employment due to race, creed, color, or national origin. Because of the efforts of this committee and the success of the "fair employment practices" provisions that had been

TABLE 2.9   Major laws protecting individual rights

Law	Provision
U.S. Constitution, Thirteenth and Fourteenth Amendments (1865 and 1868)	Prohibited slavery and provided "equal protection" for all citizens in their employment rights provided by state and local governments.
Civil Rights Acts of 1866 and 1870 (based on Thirteenth Amendment)	Prohibited racial discrimination in hiring, placement, and continuation of employment by private employers, unions, and employment agencies.
Civil Rights Act of 1871 (based on Fourteenth Amendment)	Prohibited state and local governments from using state laws to deprive citizens of their equal employment rights.
New York State Fair Employment Practices Act (1945)	New York was the first state to pass a Fair Employment Practices Act. The act was designed to eliminate discrimination due to race, creed, color, or national origin in state employment.
Equal Pay Act of 1963	Required equal pay for men and women who perform substantially equal work.
Title VII, Civil Rights Act of 1964, as amended by the Equal Employment Opportunity Act of 1972	Prohibited employment discrimination based on race, color, religion, sex, or national origin.
Executive Orders 11246 and 11375 (1965)	Prohibited discrimination by federal contractors and subcontractors, and required affirmative action to eliminate prior discrimination.
Age Discrimination in Employment Act (1967), amended in 1975, 1978, and 1986	Prohibited discrimination against individuals over the age of 40.
Vocational Rehabilitation Act of 1973, amended in 1978, and Americans with Disability Act (1990)	Prohibited discrimination based on physical or mental handicaps and required affirmative action by federal contractors and the federal government.
Vietnam Era Veterans Readjustment Act of 1974	Prohibited discrimination against disabled veterans by federal contractors and the federal government, and required affirmative action.
Pregnancy Discrimination Act (1978), amendment to Civil Rights Act	Required disability due to pregnancy to be treated like any other disability for benefits and leave.
Crime Control Act (1968)	Prohibited interception of private communications.
Privacy Protection Act (1974)	Protected dissemination of personal information about public employees.
Fair Credit Reporting Act (1971)	Required applicants to be told if a credit report is made about them and if the report prevented them from being hired.
Polygraph Protection Act (1988)	Limited the use of polygraph exams in employment and surveillance.

established in 1940 to eliminate discrimination in government services, fair employment practices acts were passed in various states, with New York being the first, in 1945. Presidents Truman, Eisenhower, and Kennedy also issued executive orders that established equal employment opportunities within the government and prohibited discrimination in businesses holding government contracts.

The executive order that has had the greatest impact on reducing racial discrimination is Executive Order 11246, which was issued by President Lyndon B. Johnson in 1965. This order, commonly known as **Order Number 4**, prohibits employment discrimination by federal government contractors and subcontractors. Because it was issued during the Vietnam War, when the government was making major purchases, it had immediate results. The order not only prohibits racial discrimination but also requires contractors and their subcontractors to develop written **affirmative action plans** and to establish numerical goals and timetables for achieving them. The guidelines for developing affirmative action plans are discussed in greater detail later in Chapter 5.

In recent years, the most important federal law prohibiting racial discrimination is the Civil Rights Act of 1964. Title VII of this act prohibits discrimination regarding any employment condition, such as hiring, firing, promotion, transfer, compensation, or admission to training programs. Title VII was amended in 1972 by the Equal Employment Opportunity Act. The 1972 amendments strengthened the enforcement of the act and expanded its coverage. Most states also have some kind of equal employment law. Forty-one states and the District of Columbia and Puerto Rico have comprehensive fair employment practices laws similar to the Equal Employment Opportunity Act. These laws have a significant influence on virtually all personnel practices, especially recruiting and hiring new employees. Chapter 5 will explain the Civil Rights Act in greater detail, including the EEOC reporting requirements and the limited exemptions provided in the law for **bona fide occupational qualifications (BFOQs)**. Chapter 5 will also explain the goal-setting and recruiting requirements of affirmative actions plans (AAPs) that government contractors and subcontractors are required to develop and follow.

AGE DISCRIMINATION

While most cultures show respect and veneration for the elderly, the United States is one of the few cultures that tends to attach a stigma to age. Because of so-called "youth worship," middle-aged managers and professionals are often considered more competent than older managers and professionals, and older workers are frequently discriminated against because of their age. Some forms of age discrimination are very visible, such as terminating 60-year-old employees first when there is a reduction in force, and refusing to hire older applicants. Other forms of age discrimination are more subtle, such as not including an older worker on a project team, not listening to the ideas of an older worker in a committee meeting, or demeaning older workers by applying derisive labels (such as "old goat") to them.

Because of these kinds of unfair practices, the Age Discrimination in Employee Act (ADEA) was passed in 1967. The act originally protected job applicants and employees between the ages of 40 and 60. However, subsequent amendments have eliminated the upper age limit and everyone over age 40 is now protected by ADEA. The provisions of this law will be explained in Chapter 14.

GENDER DISCRIMINATION

Prejudice against female employment and laws protecting women are not new. In the early nineteenth century, factory work was viewed as a way for both women and children to increase their personal incomes and escape the arduous rigors of farm work. In fact, however, factory work required long hours under frequently hazardous working conditions. During the late 1800s, the eight-hour movement pushed unsuccessfully for the passage of legislation to restrict working hours for all laborers, especially women and children. By the 1930s, children were finally removed from the sweat shops, as a result of state laws, and women were working fewer hours with mandatory rest pauses. Eliminating the need for women to work in the labor force, thus allowing them to remain at home as mothers and homemakers, was a societal goal that advanced slowly during the 1940s, until the labor shortage of World War II required thousands of women to work in industry to replace the men serving in the military.

During the postwar years, the stereotype of women as mothers and homemakers became widely entrenched. A decade of "togetherness" followed the close of World War II, and women were expected to quit their paid employment and stay home to care for their children. In fact, employment turnover statistics indicated that women were indeed more likely than men to quit, but some of the turnover was undoubtedly caused by the low pay and inadequate challenge associated with the menial jobs they performed as paid employees. Although paid employment is a secondary interest for some women, for others it is a primary career interest, and employment opportunities need to accommodate both groups.[20] Manifestations of sex discrimination have been most frequently observed in five areas.

1. *Hiring*: Women have been typecast into traditionally female jobs, such as secretary, teacher, clerk, teller, flight attendant, and nurse.
2. *Pay*: Women have been paid less than men, a practice that originated when women were viewed as temporary workers earning supplementary income and men were viewed as family breadwinners, who needed a larger income.
3. *Promotion*: Women have often been overlooked for promotions because they are not perceived as having the same long-term career orientation as men, especially if the promotion involves a transfer.
4. *Benefits*: Because of childbirth and child care, women have had different medical benefits and leave policies (such as maternity benefits and mandatory leave following childbirth).
5. *Sexual harassment*: Women have been subjected to a variety of abusive activities that have ranged from sexual assault to verbal harassment.

Protection for women against these types of gender discrimination has been provided primarily by two laws: the Equal Pay Act (1963) and the Civil Rights Act Title VII (1964). The Equal Pay Act, which was adopted as an amendment to the Fair Labor Standards Act, essentially requires equal pay for equal work. Men and women doing the same or substantially similar work requiring equivalent skill, effort, and responsibility must be paid the same. This act and the comparable-worth controversy associated with it will be described in greater detail in Chapter 12.

The Civil Rights Act of 1964 (amended in 1972) prohibits sex discrimination regarding any employment condition, such as hiring, firing, promotion, transfer, compensation, or admission to a training program. This law is also the basis for prohibiting sexual harassment (discussed in Chapter 14). Preferential treatment for either sex, male or female, is strictly prohibited unless there is a bona fide occupational qualification (BFOQ) that justifies it. At first, some employers assumed that sex would be a legitimate BFOQ for many jobs. The beliefs that men are less capable of assembling intricate equipment, that women are less capable of aggressive salesmanship, and that customers would refuse to let members of the "wrong" sex serve them are examples of the obstacles women faced in attempting to obtain nontraditional jobs. The EEOC, however, has narrowly interpreted BFOQs and accepts them only when they are necessary for purposes of (1) authenticity or genuineness (for example, actor), (b) social mores (for example, locker-room attendant or nurse in a labor and delivery room), and (c) physical limitations (for example, wet nurse).[21]

The Civil Rights Act does not protect sexual preference. The federal courts have rejected repeated attempts by homosexuals, transsexuals, and transvestites to shield themselves from unequal treatment by claiming discrimination under Title VII. The EEOC has also concluded that adverse employment actions taken against individuals because of their sexual orientation do not constitute discrimination.[22] The gay rights movement has obtained legislated protection from employment discrimination only at the local level.

PREGNANCY DISCRIMINATION

Gender discrimination against women due to childbirth and maternity leave is prohibited by the Pregnancy Discrimination in Employment Act (1978). This act is an amendment to Title VII of the Civil Rights Act, and it defines discrimination because of sex to include "because of pregnancy, childbirth, or related medical conditions." Therefore, women who are affected by pregnancy, childbirth, or related medical conditions, such as medical complications, abortions, and miscarriages, must be treated the same for all employment-related purposes, including benefits and leave. The act does not require employers to provide medical benefits, but if employers do provide them, the costs of pregnancy must be treated the same as any other type of disability, except in cases of abortion where the life of the mother would not be threatened.

Employers' leave policies must treat pregnancy or childbirth the same as any other type of personal, temporary disability. Female employees who are disabled for these reasons must be allowed to return to the same or a substantially similar job with the employer when their physical condition allows them to do so. Employers may not require pregnant employees to leave or return to their employment within a prescribed number of days. Furthermore, an employer can require a female employee to provide medical certification of her ability to work only if other disabled employees are likewise required to substantiate their physical ability. However, it is not a violation of this act to refuse to hire or to insist on transferring a pregnant or fertile woman who would be unavoidably exposed to substances creating a reproductive hazard.

HANDICAP DISCRIMINATION

In recent years, significant improvements have been made to help handicapped individuals participate actively in the labor force. Most of these improvements have been very slow in coming. The first school for the blind was opened in Baltimore, in 1812. By 1823, additional schools for the blind were available in the Boston area. For those who could not hear, the first school for the deaf was founded in Hartford, in 1817. By 1829, Louis Braille had developed a printing system that allowed the blind to read. However, the amount of literature available in braille has always been inadequate.

The first significant act passed by the U.S. Congress to assist people with disabilities was the Smith-Fees Act of 1920. This act was designed to provide services for the physically handicapped, including vocational training, placement, and counseling. These services were gradually expanded to provide sheltered workshops and institutions to treat the severely disabled and mentally retarded. In 1968, the Architectural Barriers Act was passed, requiring that all federal buildings and facilities be designed architecturally to accommodate the physically handicapped. The next significant act to aid handicapped people was the Vocational Rehabilitation Act of 1973. This act requires all government contractors and subcontractors to develop and pursue affirmative action hiring plans for handicapped persons. This act is enforced by the Office of Federal Contract Compliance Programs (OFCCP) within the Department of Labor.[23] The Americans with Disability Act (1990) requires all employers to make reasonable accommodations to hire handicapped individuals. The definition of handicapped and the protections for handicapped individuals are described in Chapter 14.

PRIVACY PROTECTION

The issue of privacy in the workplace emerged during the 1960s and has been a growing concern since then, because modern technology allows for the storage and retrieval of extensive information. Through background investigations, reference checks, and psychological testing, the privacy of an individual can be so thoroughly invaded that more information can be made public about a person than the person even remembers.

Individual privacy rights are protected to some extent by a combination of state and federal laws. The federal laws are rather narrow in their coverage, and the state laws are not very consistent. Twelve states have some form of privacy rights included in their constitution, and sixteen states have passed a fair credit reporting law largely patterned after the federal law. Twenty-six states have some form of restrictions on the use of polygraphs (lie detectors), but these are largely superseded by a federal restriction on the use of polygraph exams. At the federal level, there are four laws limiting the kinds of information employers can collect and disseminate.

1. *Crime Control Act (1968)*: The Federal Omnibus Crime Control and Safe Streets Act prohibits the deliberate interception of private telephone and oral communications. This law prohibits wire tapping and prevents supervisors from listening to employees' telephone conversations without their permission or knowledge unless it is in conjunction with some business purpose, such as coaching the employees on sales calls. Bugging someone's office with listening devices or intentionally eavesdropping on a conversation between two people in a private location also violate this act.
2. *Privacy Protection Act (1974)*: This law established strict controls for the collection, control, and disclosure of employment-related information on individual employees. However, it applies to government employees and does not require compliance by

private-sector employers except those doing business with the federal government. This act also established a Privacy Protection Study Commission to determine whether private employers should be covered by the act. Although they did not recommend that the law be extended to private employees, the commission proposed procedural guidelines to safeguard employee rights. These guidelines will be discussed in Chapter 4.

3. *Fair Credit Reporting Act (1971)*: This law applies to the collection and dissemination of information about "an employee's character, general reputation, personal characteristics, and mode of living" by a credit reporting agency. This law requires that individuals be notified if an investigation is made of them and whether an adverse decision was made in whole or in part on the basis of the report. Additional provisions of this law will be discussed in Chapter 4.

4. *Employee Polygraph Protection Act (1988)*: Because polygraph exams can be an invasion of personal privacy and their results are not always reliable, the use of the polygraph has been largely prohibited except in cases involving an ongoing investigation of losses suffered by an employer or for purposes of national security. The use of the polygraph for hiring job applicants has also been curtailed, except for jobs that involve the manufacture or distribution of controlled substances or jobs in certain types of security firms.

The violation of workplace privacy rights has become increasingly serious and costly for employers. A review of nearly 100 verdicts against employers in 1986–87 indicated that the average award was about $316,000. Ten years earlier, few court cases were ever decided in favor of the employees.[24] These data emphasize the need for human resource managers to know what constitutes an invasion of privacy and to monitor carefully the collection and dissemination of all information.

WRONGFUL DISCHARGE

Before 1980, employers were generally free to fire employees for good reasons, for bad reasons, and even for immoral reasons, without being guilty of breaking the law. The laws protecting employees from wrongful discharge were limited to requiring employers to abide by collective-bargaining agreements and prohibiting employers from terminating employees who testified against the employer before a government agency, such as OSHA or the NLRB.

This philosophy of hiring whomever you want for as long as you want is called the employment at-will doctrine. At-will employment in essence allows both the employer and the employee the mutual right to terminate the employment relationship at any time for any reason and with or without advance notice to the other.

Although there are no federal laws that specifically address the employment at-will relationship, during the 1980s, the employment at-will doctrine gradually eroded as a variety of tort claims identified various public policy violations leading to wrongful discharge. These changes in the at-will relationship will be discussed further in Chapter 14.

When they consider the many state and federal laws regulating personnel practices, human resource managers often feel overwhelmed by the technical complexity of all these legal requirements. Indeed, the laws are numerous and complex, but they are not designed to destroy organizations or threaten business. They are intended to protect people by creating a safer work environment and eliminating unfair discrimination. These laws were passed in response to specific problems that created a perceived social injustice. Although some court decisions are puzzling, both the laws and how they are applied are usually perceived as reasonable and useful in creating a better quality of work life. Therefore, human resource managers need to know the laws and see that their organizations make good-faith efforts to follow them.

SUMMARY

A. Human resource activities are influenced by the environment in which they occur. Three of the major environmental factors that influence personnel are the labor force, economic conditions, and laws and regulations.

B. The labor force is measured by the Bureau of Labor Statistics (BLS), Department of Labor, primarily through the Current Population Survey (CPS).

C. In 1989, the total labor force consisted of 125 million people, who represented 67 percent of the total noninstitutional population of the United States.

D. The recent growth of the labor force has been due primarily to an increase in female employment. In 1989, women comprised 45 percent of the work force. The female participation rate was 58.3 percent, meaning that over one-half of the available women were in the work force.

E. During the past century, three shifts have occurred in American birthrates: a decline during the Great Depression, an increase following World War II, and another decline during the 1970s. These fluctuations have profoundly influenced the size of the labor market.

F. Human resource activities are affected by changes in economic conditions. When the economy is strong, the gross national product is increasing and unemployment levels are low. These conditions reduce the supply of labor and require human resource managers to be actively involved in recruiting, hiring, and training new employees.

G. Productivity refers to the total output per hour of all employees. Productivity may be increased through training and development and through instilling better work habits in employees. However, new technology is the most important factor increasing productivity.

H. Increased competition generally results in price pressures that may reduce an organization's flexibility in offering compensation and favorable working conditions.

I. Human resource activities are subject to the conflicting demands of stockholders/owners and customers/clients. The first group expects everything to be cost-benefit effective; the latter group expects the organization to provide a service and to assume a social responsibility.

J. Human resource activities are influenced by numerous laws and regulations at both state and local levels. Four of the major areas regulated by federal legislation are labor relations, compensation, safety and health, and equal employment opportunity.

K. All human resource activities are influenced by equal employment opportunity laws and executive orders. The most significant law prohibiting discrimination is the Civil Rights Act of 1964, which prohibits discrimination based on race, color, religion, sex, or national origin.

L. Discrimination has been significantly reduced by executive orders, especially by Executive Order 11246, which requires government contractors and subcontractors to develop written affirmative action programs. These programs direct contractors to employ minorities and females in proportion to the percentage in which each is found in the surrounding labor market.

M. Employees over age 40 are protected from employment discrimination on the basis of age. Pro-motions, demotions, terminations, and other employment decisions must be based on legitimate business-related criteria rather than age.

N. The Civil Rights Act and the Equal Pay Act prohibit gender discrimination regarding hiring, pay, promotion, benefits, and sexual harassment. The Pregnancy Disability Act requires that disabilities due to pregnancy be treated like any other disabilities in terms of benefits and leave policies.

QUESTIONS

1. This chapter has emphasized the idea that human resource activities are influenced by environmental conditions, but are *all* such activities influenced by environmental changes? For example, how is performance evaluation influenced by changes in the environment? Since grades are a form of performance evaluation in colleges, how are grades influenced by the external environment?

2. What methods and sources can a human resources director use to gather information about the labor force and how it will change over the next ten years?

3. The baby boom created a significant increase in the birthrate for several years. How does such a change in the birthrate influence human resource management?

4. From 1947 to 1985, female employment rose from 28 to 45 percent of the civilian labor force. How has this increase in female employment altered human resource activities?

5. What effect does immigration have on human resource activities? What are the advantages and disadvantages of increasing the number of immigrants and of allowing illegal aliens to remain in the United States?

6. How are the human resource activities within an organization influenced by changes in the unemployment levels in the surrounding economy? Which activities are easier to perform when the unemployment levels are high and which are easier to perform when unemployment levels are low?

7. How are human resource activities influenced by customers, clients, and local pressure groups? Should human resource managers try to respond to expectations regarding social responsibility? Why or why not?

8. Most of the major laws governing compensation were passed during the Great Depression in response to specific problems at that time. Are these laws still relevant? Why or why not? If these laws had not been passed earlier, do you think they would be passed today? Explain.

9. Some people believe that civil rights legislation proves that morality can be legislated. Do you agree that racial prejudice has been significantly reduced in recent years, and if so, would you attribute this in whole or in part to the laws that have been passed?

10. In 1964, there was an obvious need for laws prohibiting discrimination. Have federal and state civil rights laws significantly reduced the level of employment discrimination in society? Do you think a time will come when discrimination will be reduced to the point that there will be no need for the EEOC? Why or why not?

11. What are the conditions when sex is considered a bona fide occupational qualification? Do you think the courts have interpreted the law too narrowly and are forcing undesirable changes in social customs? Explain.

12. The EEOC has stated that every organization should have an affirmative action policy as a matter of good employment practice. Why do you agree or disagree with this policy?

KEY TERMS

Affirmative action plans (AAP):. Written plans for recruiting and hiring minorities and females. These plans, which are required of government contractors and subcontractors, must contain goals and timetables for achieving them.

Baby boom:. The period of time following World War II when there was a significant increase in the birthrate in the United States.

Birth dearth:. The decline in the birthrate that occurred during the Great Depression.

Birthrate:. The number of births per 1,000 population.

Bona fide occupational qualifications (BFOQ): Employers are allowed to discriminate on the basis of religion, sex, or national origin only when these attributes are necessary for the operation of their business; that is, when they are bona fide occupational qualifications.

Bureau of Labor Statistics (BLS): An agency in the Department of Labor that collects and publishes information about the labor market.

Civilian labor force: All employed or unemployed persons 16 years of age and older who are not military personnel nor inmates of penal or mental institutions, or homes for the aged, infirm, or needy.

Current Population Survey (CPS): A survey of about 60,000 households that is conducted by the Bureau of Labor Statistics. Personal interviews are conducted monthly to determine participation in the work force, unemployment, and reasons for not working or for only working part-time.

Equal Employment Opportunity Commission (EEOC):. The agency responsible for enforcing Title VII of the 1964 Civil Rights Act as amended by the 1972 Equal Employment Opportunity Act.

Executive orders: Orders issued by the president of the United States. Several executive orders have been influential in reducing discrimination, especially Executive Order 11246, which requires government contractors and subcontractors to adopt affirmative action plans.

Fertility rate: The average number of children born to a woman during her lifetime. The fertility rate of 2.1 represents zero population growth.

Order Number 4: The common name for Executive Order 11246, which requires government contractors to develop affirmative action plans.

Participation rates: The percentage of a particular group, such as males or females, who are participating as employees in the labor force.

Productivity: An index that is calculated by dividing the total output of goods and services produced in society by the total number of employee hours required to produce them.

Unemployed: Persons who are not employed but who are available for work.

C O N C L U D I N G   C A S E

Locating a New Plant

Grimsby Industries, Inc., is a small multinational corporation that manufactures kitchen appliances. For the past ten years, it has successfully marketed its products along the eastern seaboard of the United States and in seven European countries. Top management believes the time has come to expand its markets to the western United States, Mexico, and South America. Within ten years management also hopes to be involved in trade with mainland China.

To meet expansion goals, the company needs additional assembly plants. Top management has decided to build one assembly plant now and another in five years. The big question is where to locate them.

The responsibility for deciding where the new plant should be built has been assigned to the corporate planning staff. Jeff Larson, vice president of human resources for Grimsby, is a member of the corporate planning staff. He has been asked to identify the personnel-related issues regarding the location of the new plant and be prepared to discuss their implications. The company is considering many different locations along the western coast of Canada, the United States, and Mexico. Some countries along the Asian rim of the Pacific also are being considered.

Jeff has been asked to prepare a report summarizing the advantages and disadvantages of alternative locations.

Questions:

1. What factors should be considered in deciding where to locate the new plant?
2. Identify one or two locations and discuss the advantages and disadvantages of building a new plant there.
3. How will the human resource activities at Grimsby Industries likely change when a new plant is at these locations?

NOTES

1. Marvin J. Cetron, Wanda Rocha, and Rebecca Luckins, "Into the 21st Century: Long Term Trends Affecting the United States," *The Futurist* (July–August 1988): 29–40; John Naisbitt and Patricia Aburdene, *Reinventing the Corporation* (New York: Warner, 1985).

2. The data for this section came from statistics compiled by the Bureau of Labor Statistics as published in the *Monthly Labor Review* 112 (April 1989): 61–67.

3. Ronald E. Kutscher, "Projections 2000: Overview and Implication of the Projections to 2000," *Monthly Labor Review* 110, no. 9 (1987): 3–9.

4. The data for this section came from the Bureau of the Census, *Statistical Abstract of the United States 1988, 108th ed.* (Washington D.C.: Government Printing Office): 60–61. See also Manuel D. Plotkin, "Changing Population Patterns," in *The World Almanac and Book of Facts 1979* (New York: Newspaper Enterprise Assoc., 1978), 205–6.

5. The data for this section came from the Bureau of the Census, *Statistical Abstract of the United States 1988, 108th ed.* (Washington D.C.: Government Printing Office): 125, 126, 138, 140.

6. Susan Champlin Taylor, "Adult Literacy—The Numbers Game," *Modern Maturity* (December 1987–January 1988 issue).

7. Ann MacDougal Young, "One-fourth of the Adult Labor Force are College Graduates," *Monthly Labor Review* 108, no. 2 (February 1985): 43–45.

8. Philip L. Martin, "Select Commission Suggests Changes in Immigration Policy: A Review Essay," *Monthly Labor Review* 105, no. 2 (1987): 31–37.

9. Donald L. Rosenthal, *Immigration Reform: A Summary of Employer Obligations under IRCA* (Alexandria, Va.: The American Society for Personnel Administration, 1987); William Odencrantz, Steven T. Nutter, and Josie M. Gonzalez, "The Immigration Reform and Control Act of 1986: Obligations of Employers and Unions," *Industrial Relations Law Journal* 10 (1988): 92–115.

10. Peter Cattan, "The Growing Presence of Hispanics in the U.S. Workforce," *Monthly Labor Review* 111 (August 1988): 9–14.

11. The data for this section came from the Bureau of the Census, *Statistical Abstract of the United States 1988, 108th ed.* (Washington D.C.: Government Printing Office): 798–99; and *Bulletin of Labour Statistics* 1989-1 (Geneva: International Labour Office, 1989).

12. The average capital outlay is calculated by dividing the property, plant, and equipment less accumulated depreciation by the number of employees. According to their published annual reports, the average capital outlay for Exxon Corporation is $535,000, Ford Motor Company is $69,000, and General Mills is $19,000.

13. Geanne M. Carsten and Paul E. Spector, "Unemployment, Job Satisfaction, and Employee Turnover: A Meta-analytic Test of the Muchinsky Model," *Journal of Applied Psychology* 72 (August 1987): 374–81.

14. The data in this paragraph were obtained from various publications of the *Monthly Labor Review* published by the U.S. Department of Labor, and the *Bulletin of Labour Statistics* published by the International Labour Office.

15. The data in this paragraph were obtained from various publications of the *Monthly Labor Review* published by the U.S. Department of Labor, and the *Bulletin of Labour Statistics* published by the International Labour Office.

16. The data for this section were obtained from the Bureau of Labor Statistics as published in various editions of the *Monthly Labor Review*.

17. William A. Testa, "Fishing for Work: The Midwest looks at Possible Job Lures," *Chicago Federal Reserve Letter* 11 (July 1988): 1–3.

18. See Edwin Markham, Benjamin B. Lindsey, and George Creel, *Children in Bondage* (New York: Hearsts' International Library Company, 1914); Florence Kelley, "Obstacles to the Enforcement of Child Labor Legislation," *Annals of the American Academy of Political and Social Science* (January 1907).

19. Walter F. Dodd, *Administration of Workers Compensation* (New York: The Commonwealth Fund, 1936).

20. Felice N. Schwartz, "Management Women and the New Facts of Life," *Harvard Business Review* (January–February 1989): 65–76.

21. Barry A. Hartstein, "EEO Issues in the Health-Care Field: A Roundup of Recent Developments," *Employee Relations Law Journal* 12 (Autumn 1986): 241–61.

22. Sabrina M. Wrenn, "Gay Rights and Workplace Discrimination," *Personnel Journal* 67 (October 1988): 91–102.

23. Michael J. Album, "Affirmative Action and the Handicapped," *Employment Relations Today* 15 (Summer 1988): 99–106.

24. Gary S. Marx, "Workplace Privacy: Big Brother Beware," *Bobbin* 29 (June 1988): 40, 43.

C H A P T E R 3

Human Resource Programs: Improving the Quality of Life at Work

Alternative Patterns of Work

Flextime / Permanent Part-time / Job Sharing / Compressed
Workweek / Telecommuting

Job Redesign

Job Specialization versus Job Enrichment / Job-enrichment Programs

Quality of Work Life Programs

Autonomous Work Teams / Quality Circles / Representation on the Board of
Directors / Labor-Management Committees / Employee Ownership /
Organizational Development

Evaluating HR Programs

Satisfaction / Absenteeism and Turnover / Personnel Audits / Human
Resource Accounting

International HRM

Work Values / Work Groups / Hours of Work

INTRODUCTORY CASE

Complex Scheduling

The chemical department of the Davis County refinery has a serious personnel shortage. The department should normally be staffed with twenty-six full-time employees. But for the past two weeks it has limped along with only twelve full-time employees and three former employees who are helping temporarily. The supervisor, Kevin Jackson, knows that something must be done soon about the shortage of workers.

Everyone has to work overtime to accomplish the necessary work. Some even have to work sixteen-hour shifts almost every day, and these employees are threatening to quit if the situation does not improve. Efforts to recruit new employees have not been successful, largely because of the working hours. Since the refinery operates around the clock, each employee works on one of the three rotating shifts: day shift, swing shift, or night shift. Every week the entire work force rotates to a different shift.

Kevin would like to reschedule the working hours in the chemical department. He thinks some of the former employees would return to work if they could choose their own hours. Many former employees in the chemical department are women who quit because their responsibilities at home interfered with the demands of eight-hour rotating shifts. Many want to work only four to six hours, and none of them wants to change shifts every week. Only two positions have to be staffed around the clock. Kevin thinks he could easily schedule those jobs and still allow the other employees to schedule their work hours at their own convenience.

The problem is that the refinery has a policy that all employees must be part of the rotating shifts. This policy was adopted to eliminate favoritism in the scheduling of work assignments. Kevin agrees that favoritism is not good; however, he is more concerned about finding capable replacements and thinks the policy should not apply to his department. The top managers are skeptical about Kevin's plan because they doubt that it will attract many former employees, and they think the scheduling will be too confusing with so many people coming and going at odd hours. But most importantly, if some have to work rotating shifts, top management argues that it is only fair that everyone work a rotating schedule.

Questions:

1. What arguments would you use to persuade top management to change the rotating-shift policy? How would you defend your recommendations?
2. What are the effects of rotating shifts on the quality of employees' lives?

EMPLOYEE EXPECTATIONS

Human resource management focuses on how people are treated on the job, including how they are hired, promoted, evaluated, paid, trained, and terminated. Human resource management serves both the organization and the individual. Effective human resource activities are designed to provide a well-trained and motivated work force that will achieve the organization's goals. People expect to be treated fairly and with dignity and respect. Individuals do not exist solely to serve the organization; organizations are created for the benefit of people. Another major purpose of human resource management is to protect individuals and enhance the quality of life at work. This chapter describes some of the most popular quality of work life programs.

EMPLOYMENT EXCHANGE

When people decide to work for an organization, they enter into a voluntary agreement called an **employment exchange**: they agree to work in exchange for the wages, benefits, and other rewards the employer provides. The voluntary nature of this employment exchange and the expectations of each party represent a very important foundation for all human resource activities and other management actions.

Since the abolition of slavery following the Civil War, Americans have been committed to the principle that individuals cannot be held in servitude. Thus, organizations must compete for employees, and the ability to attract and retain individuals is a major factor in the survival of any organization. An organization that is unable to attract new members will eventually fail. Business organizations usually rely on monetary incentives to attract labor. Political parties, religious organizations, and other voluntary associations must generally rely on incentives other than money to attract members. One notable exception to the "attract-or-perish" rule is provided by the military, which has the legal right to use a draft to recruit personnel. During the Vietnam War, for example, a random lottery was used to draft young men into the military services. No other organization can draft people into employment, however. In all cases other than the military, individuals must choose to join the organizations that hire them.

INDUCEMENTS-CONTRIBUTIONS BALANCE

An employment exchange occurs when individuals are willing to trade their labor for rewards and when an organization is wiling to exchange rewards for labor. In this employment exchange, called an **inducements-contributions balance**,[1] the inducements individuals receive for working must be balanced with the contributions they make to the organization. A state of equilibrium, or balance, is achieved if the inducements are essentially equal to the contributions.

Inducements are the rewards that accrue to individuals from working. One of the most important inducements is money in the form of wages, salaries, and benefits; no matter how desirable a job may be, it will be rejected if it does not provide an employee with an adequate income. Other inducements include satisfying work that creates feelings of fulfillment and involvement, congenial coworkers, the opportunity to provide service to others and to society, the opportunity for self-expression, and economic security.

Contributions are the things individuals offer the organization, such as effort, skill, knowledge, and ideas. The essential contributions that enable an organization to survive include: dependable attendance, dependable performance, and spontaneous and innovative behaviors.[2] Dependable attendance means staying with the organization; employees must be at work when they are expected to be there, and they also must be on time. Dependable performance refers to the quantity and quality of employees' work. Employees must perform their jobs well enough to satisfy the needs of the organization. Spontaneous and innovative behaviors are those contributions to organizational effectiveness that are above and beyond the formal job description. Examples of these behaviors include cooperative acts that help the organization operate smoothly, creative suggestions, self-training for additional responsibility, acts that are protective of the organization, and conduct that creates a positive climate and a pleasant work environment.

Employees will be willing to participate in the employment exchange only as long as the inducements are greater than or equal to the contributions they are asked to make. Likewise, the organization will be willing to support the employment exchange only as long as the employees' contributions are greater than or equal to the rewards offered by the organization. This inducements-contributions balance is illustrated in Figure 3.1. When either party believes the situation is out of balance, the employment contract may be terminated.

Managers should remember that the inducements-contributions balance is based on the subjective perceptions of individuals. The relative value of money, satisfying work, and other inducements is evaluated on an individual basis. Employees working in identical situations will not necessarily evaluate the inducements equally. Moreover, two employees may not feel the same about their contributions even though they are performing identical jobs. How employees evaluate their inducements and contributions is largely determined by their personal values and the relative importance of alternative activities. Working for an organization may be very costly to an employee who places a higher value on leisure and other activities than on working. For example, employees who are typically satisfied with the inducements they receive from working may be very dissatisfied with

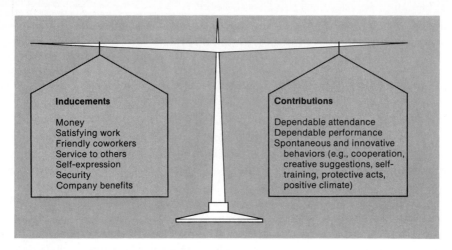

Inducements

Money
Satisfying work
Friendly coworkers
Service to others
Self-expression
Security
Company benefits

Contributions

Dependable attendance
Dependable performance
Spontaneous and innovative
    behaviors (e.g., cooperation,
    creative suggestions, self-
    training, protective acts,
    positive climate)

FIGURE 3.1 Inducements-contributions balance.

the same inducements on the day their softball team plays for the city championship if work prevents them from attending the game. In this situation, the cost of the employee's contribution has increased dramatically because of a highly valued alternative activity. Unless the company offers different rewards or penalties the employees might miss work to play their game.

INDIVIDUALS VERSUS ORGANIZATIONS

An employment exchange is not always terminated the moment it becomes imbalanced. Sometimes the inequity results in individuals abusing the organization or in the organization abusing individuals. This abuse may be intentional (on either side), but it also may occur by happenstance.

ABUSE OF ORGANIZATIONS

Abusive actions toward an organization may take the form of employee theft or fraud. In retail stores, for example, theft is measured in terms of inventory shrinkage—the reduction in the amount of merchandise that stores ought to have versus what they actually have. Ten percent of this loss is attributed to clerical errors and 30 percent is attributed to shoplifting. The remaining 60 percent is attributed to theft by the store's own employees.[3] Employee theft occurs at all levels in an organization, with some of the major fraud being committed by top-level managers.[4]

A much more subtle and perhaps costlier form of abuse occurs when employees are paid for work that is not performed. This type of abuse assumes many forms, such as loafing on the job, coming late to work, taking extra personal time or lengthy coffee breaks, abusing sick leave, and performing careless or sloppy work.[5] Employees often get away with these types of careless performance because they are protected by work rules in a labor agreement or because the organization has not developed adequate human resource procedures for evaluating and correcting such problems.

ABUSE OF INDIVIDUALS

Organizations also have the power to abuse individuals. In power struggles over wages, benefits, and working conditions, the odds are clearly on the side of the organization. Although discontented individuals are free to leave an organization, the consequences of terminating employment are clearly more costly to the individual than to the organization. The loss of a job to an employee is more catastrophic than the loss of an employee to an organization.

Unless there exists an actual or an implied contract, employers are generally free to dismiss their employees for good reasons, bad reasons, or even reasons that are morally wrong without being guilty of breaking the law. Employees who belong to labor unions sometimes enjoy a measure of protection against arbitrary management decisions, but over three-quarters of the employees in America are not union members. Although the Bill of Rights guarantees certain freedoms to American citizens, employees in organizations do not enjoy many of these rights. For example, freedom of speech is sometimes constrained by company regulations that prohibit employees from complaining to people outside the company.[6] Employees who violate these regulations can be fired, even if their criticisms are legitimate. The rights of privacy and security guaranteed by the Bill of Rights are often not extended to employees at work. Although employees' homes are protected from arbitrary search and seizure, their lockers, desks, and files at work can be inspected without a search warrant.

In some situations employees are faced with moral dilemmas because their jobs require them to perform unethical or illegal acts. Even relatively minor episodes, such as a secretary having to tell people that a manager is out when the manager is really in, can create an uncomfortable situation for the secretary who may feel forced to compromise his or her personal integrity.

Organizational abuse may also be unintentional. Organizations do not have a heart or soul and the devotion and sacrifices of employees under one administration may be ignored and forgotten by new leaders. An emotionally hazardous situation occurs when employees transfer responsibility for their actions and decisions to the organization. For example, employees in large and powerful organizations are sometimes seduced into believing that the organization's goals are inherently right, that "someone" in top management is looking after them and that they should just quietly serve the organization. As employees respond to real or imagined job pressures, marriages are broken, family relationships are destroyed, physical health deteriorates, and emotional health is threatened. Another common problem is that employees develop a distorted concept of authority. When a person is promoted to a high-level position, the promotion somehow seems to bestow upon that person an aura of moral superiority, innate goodness, or any other virtuous quality. As a result, employees tend not to question the decisions of upper-level managers and they give too much credence to managers' opinions.

A partial solution to organizational abuse is to change the structure and processes of organizations in order to eliminate improper and unfair treatment. But more practically, individuals should be taught how to protect themselves from organizational influences. While organizations can be improved to make them safer for people, the major efforts of human resource managers should be directed toward helping people learn to protect themselves from both intentional and unintentional organizational abuse. Protecting employees and helping them grow and achieve fulfillment is a basic ethical concern in human resource management.

EMPLOYEE RIGHTS

Employee rights are practices that are judged to be inherently right and proper. Employers cannot give employee rights to employees nor can they take them away. Some employee rights are guaranteed by the Constitution, the Bill of Rights, or federal legislation. Legislation, however, is not necessary to establish employee rights; the absence of law does not mean the absence of rights. Lying to employees or verbally insulting them is morally wrong even though specific legislation prohibiting these acts does not exist. Increasingly, however, acts that are considered immoral are also becoming illegal.

The concept that workers possess certain inalienable rights and that these rights should not be abridged by an organization is becoming generally understood. Most Americans agree that workers should not have to forfeit their personal rights to work for an organization. Although organizations have basic requirements that are essential for them to operate effectively, these requirements need to be balanced carefully against the rights of individuals.[7]

Most of the laws that guarantee employee rights are summarized in Chapter 2. In addition to these legislated protections, however, employees have come to expect additional rights that, for the most part, can be viewed as an extension of these laws. For example, the Civil Rights Act prohibits employers from using race, religion, sex, or national origin as the basis for making personnel decisions. But it does not go a step further and mandate that all personnel decisions be based on performance-related criteria unique to each job. Employers are still free to hire on a random basis, a first-come basis, or any other basis as long as it is unrelated to age, race, religion, sex, or national origin. Nevertheless, job applicants have come to expect equal access to job openings, and if they are denied a job they expect the employer to have an objective, performance-related justification for offering the job to someone else. Explanations like "We liked the other person better," or "The other person was here at the right time," are often viewed as pretexts for discrimination.

The consequence of the evolution of employee rights is that employees now expect organizations to observe the following unwritten rules:

1. All employment decisions regarding hiring, promotion, pay increases, training opportunities, and terminations should be based on objective, performance-related criteria rather than on subjective biases or personal whims. This means that employment decisions should be more than just color-blind—they should be based on job-related criteria.
2. Each employee should be treated as a person of worth with dignity and respect rather than as an object that can be physically, sexually, or verbally abused. Employees should not be subjected to acts that are unwelcome or intimidating.
3. Disciplinary actions and criticisms should only occur for good cause, and the employee should have the right to due process before any punitive actions are taken. ("Good cause" and "due process" are explained in Chapter 14.)

4. Employees should be terminated from their jobs only if the jobs are eliminated or if they are clearly unable to perform them. Personal whims and personality clashes are not valid reasons for termination.
5. Performance should be evaluated fairly and objectively against clearly defined standards; the evaluation should not be influenced by subjective biases or irrelevant personality traits.
6. Employees should be fairly and equitably paid for the work they do based on the requirements of the job, how well they perform, and the knowledge, skills, and abilities they bring to the job. One person should not be paid more than another unless there is a legitimate, job-related reason for it.
7. Employees should be taught how to perform their jobs, and they deserve accurate and timely feedback on their performance.
8. Employees should have a safe and healthy work environment free from unnecessary hazards or harmful substances, and they should be informed about anything that could cause future health problems.
9. An employee's personal health and family responsibilities have a higher priority than organizational responsibilities; therefore, the organization should make reasonable accommodation to help employees handle personal problems and family emergencies.
10. The organization should not invade the personal privacy of employees, and only relevant, job-related information should be disseminated within the organization. Nothing should be disseminated outside the organization unless the employee authorizes it or the outside party has a legitimate need to know.

CAREER-DEVELOPMENT PROGRAMS

A career is the sequence of work-related experiences individuals acquire during the span of their work lives. A career is an individual concept, because each person has a unique sequence of work-related experiences. An individual can have a career with one organization or with many. A career is not the same as a profession, since both professionals and nonprofessionals have careers. An individual may follow a very well-defined career path—for example, accountants and lawyers join an accounting or law firm and progress systematically from junior to senior partner—or they may have a very disorganized career, characterized by sporadic changes from one organization to another or by moves into different occupations.

BENEFITS OF CAREER PLANNING

Many organizations try to improve the quality of life at work by helping employees plan their careers. Through career counseling, organizations hope to help employees avoid the frustration, anxiety, and mid-life crisis that can occur when employees do not believe they are progressing toward their career aspirations. Career development refers to helping individuals plan their future careers within the organization. The objectives of career development are to help individuals achieve maximum self-development and also to help the organization achieve its objectives.

INDIVIDUAL BENEFITS

For the individual, the most immediate benefits of career development include a better job, more money, increased responsibility, greater mobility, and the acquisition of skills that improve productivity. Career development also provides less tangible benefits for individuals, such as increased satisfaction, the development of a career orientation rather than a job orientation, increased involvement in work, greater exposure and visibility to top management, a better understanding of what is expected, and a broader knowledge of additional areas of career interest.[8] The employees who are most likely to benefit from career-development activities are those who hold positive work attitudes and who plan to seek fulfilling work within one organization.

ORGANIZATIONAL BENEFITS

Through the development of competent employees, organizations are better able to identify future managers and prepare them to achieve organizational goals. By developing competent replacement managers, an organization is able to practice promotion from within, which increases the level of motivation for aspiring managers.

Occasionally, supervisors build an effective work team and do not want to break it up, which results in the hoarding of qualified people. This practice is usually detrimental to both the organization and the employees because it creates overqualified employees who become frustrated. Career-development programs tend to reduce both the hoarding problem and the frustration that results from being overqualified for a job.

Employees who remain in the same position for an extended period typically become obsolete either because of a lack of training or a lack of motivation to remain current. Career planning helps to prevent the problems of obsolescence by providing employee training, by moving employees into different jobs, and by stimulating employees' desires to make valuable contributions to the organization and society.

Finally, an organization that conscientiously tries to help employees plan their careers can benefit directly through lower turnover and personnel costs.[9] In general, career activities and programs lead to increased individual and organizational efficiency.

CAREER STAGES

Several models have been developed to describe the career stages through which individuals progress. Creating useful career-development programs requires an understanding of career stages and the interests relevant to each stage. Most of these models suggest that careers evolve through at least four major stages: exploration, establishment, maintenance, and decline.[10]

In the *exploration stage*, adolescents and young adults are still trying to develop their occupational images from the mass media and personal observations. As they assess their talents and limitations and develop their self-images of what they might be, their occupational choices are gradually formed.

The *establishment stage* consists of finding a first job and settling into it. This early stage in an individual's career includes the anxiety of the recruiting and selection process, the dilemma of choosing between competing job offers, and the uncertainty of being rejected or accepted by a new supervisor and coworkers. This stage is longer for individ-

HRM in Action

Mobil Oil Company Reduces Employee Relocation

Employees who survived the Great Depression and World War II were generally happy to do whatever their employer asked them to do. If they were asked to relocate they usually did it without complaining even if it meant moving across the country. Promotions often involved relocation and refusing a promotion was simply unthinkable. But, times have changed. Promotions are not always accepted, and many employees would rather change jobs than relocate.

Mobil Oil Company surveyed its employees regarding the impact of family life on career decisions and found an increasing number of both male and female professionals who were unwilling to relocate because of family considerations. The most surprising finding was that a higher percentage of male than female professionals refused to relocate (27 to 19 percent). Relocation has traditionally been viewed as a greater problem for women than men, but Mobil's survey found that the employees most resistant to relocation were white males in their forties. The most commonly cited reason for refusing to relocate was children's education. Mobil projects, based on its survey, that the number of employees refusing to relocate will continue to increase over the next decade.

As a result of its survey, Mobil is changing its corporate structure and revising its relocation policy. To reduce the need for relocation, Mobil will centralize many of its operations around three or four "hub" locations. This restructuring will allow many employees to change jobs and accept promotions without having to relocate.

When relocation cannot be avoided, Mobil will help to relocate a working spouse and provide a child-care referral service. When assignments are less than two years in length, Mobil will pay a housing and transportation subsidy to allow employees to commute to work rather than relocate.

Source: Christine Klingberg, "More Employees Choosing Family Over Career," *HR News*, 8 (April 1990), p. 9.

uals who skip from job to job. As part of the establishment stage, young employees are required to resolve conflicts between family and work in order to find a comfortable level of accommodation. They also are required to form a career strategy of how to succeed, such as through working hard, finding mentors, conforming to the organization, or joining a union. If their future prospects do not look positive, they may need to leave the organization or turn to a union or other sources of strength to protect themselves from unfair treatment.

The *maintenance stage* occurs when individuals are in their mid and late careers. During this period they are given more responsible and important assignments and are expected to achieve their highest levels of productivity. Whereas earlier career stages are characterized by learning what to do, the maintenance stage is characterized by teaching others—coaching and mentoring new employees. Individuals at this stage must develop greater acceptance of themselves and others, more concern with teaching others and passing on their wisdom (at home as well as at work), and new avenues of self-expression and opportunities for self-improvement off the job (such as civic or religious activities).

Individuals in the *decline stage* are required to make preparations for formal retirement. They must learn to accept reduced roles with less responsibility and learn to manage less-structured lives. At this stage (physical and emotional health permitting), individuals typically develop new activities and responsibilities, combined with increased leisure pursuits.

DEVELOPMENTAL PROGRAMS

Many organizations provide a broad assortment of activities to help employees manage their careers (see Table 3.1). Most of these career-development programs refer to human resource activities that are described in later chapters.[11]

MENTORING

Some organizations assign an experienced employee to serve as a mentor for new employees. Effective mentors teach their protégés valuable job skills, help them develop a network of contacts, and, most importantly, provide emotional support and encouragement. Although mentoring is usually a valuable career-development activity, a mentoring relationship can be very destructive if the protégé becomes overly dependent, if the mentor resists freeing the protégé, and if jealousy or romantic interests enter the relationship. Although mixed-gender matches have been utilized effectively, they can also be the most destructive.[12]

CAREER COUNSELING

Most organizations provide some form of career counseling on various occasions: during employment interviews when employees are first hired, during employees' annual performance-evaluation interviews, and as a part of the special career counseling that is provided for high-potential employees. Career counseling typically occurs as part of the day-to-day relationship between a supervisor and a subordinate. Moreover, some organizations provide special career counseling by conducting psychological assessments of employees and helping them to interpret their individual results.

CAREER PATHING

Career pathing refers to identifying a sequence of jobs through which individuals can expect to progress toward higher levels in management. Some organizations try to provide job-progression plans for all new employees, while others identify possible job changes only for high-potential employees who are being groomed for upper-level management positions. In some organizations, a committee reviews the strengths and weaknesses of each manager and then develops a five-year career plan for each. Some technical specialists want to advance their careers, but they do not want to move into management. To provide upward mobility for those people without removing them from their technical specialty, organizations have created **dual career ladders**. While movement up the managerial ladder means greater power and decision-making authority, movement up the technical ladder means greater autonomy in practicing the profession.[13]

TABLE 3.1   Career-development programs

1. **Mentoring**

   Assigning an experienced employee to help a new or inexperienced employee

2. **Career Counseling**

   During the employment interview
   During the performance evaluation
   Psychological assessment
   Coaching and development by supervisors

3. **Career Pathing**

   Job progression plans for new employees
   Job moves for high-potential employees
   Annual review of managers by a committee
   Dual career ladders

4. **Human Resource Planning**

   Succession planning and replacement charts
   Development and using a computerized human resource information system

5. **Career Information Systems**

   Job-posting and bidding systems
   Announcement boards

6. **Management and Supervisory Development**

   Special programs, conferences, and seminars
   Job rotation
   In-house management training

7. **Training**

   Technical-skills training
   Intern programs
   Tuition reimbursement
   In-house supervisory training

8. **Programs for Special Groups**

   Preretirement counseling
   Career counseling for women and minorities
   Refresher courses for mid-career managers
   Out-placement programs
   Minority indoctrination and orientation programs

HUMAN RESOURCE PLANNING

Organizations that have formal human resource planning systems typically have succession plans that identify potential replacements for each manager and supervisor. Succession planning is sometimes facilitated by the use of a computerized human resource information system that describes each employee's skills and abilities.

CAREER INFORMATION SYSTEMS

To help individuals plan their careers, organizations try to provide additional information on career opportunities through job posting and bidding systems.

MANAGEMENT AND SUPERVISORY DEVELOPMENT

Management and supervisory development programs are major responsibilities of most human resource departments. These programs, which may include both on-the-job and off-the-job training activities, are described in detail in Chapter 9.

HRM in Action

Career Planning at Chrysler First, Inc.

A task force at Chrysler First, Inc., discovered that many people at all levels of the company were not adequately trained to accept advancement. This failure was attributed to two factors: (1) supervisors were not helping their employees develop their potential, and (2) the company did not have a central direction for coordinating the developmental efforts of employees. A special advisory committee was assigned to resolve these problems by creating and implementing a corporate-wide human resource plan. The plan they implemented contained three elements that were centrally coordinated and budgeted. These three elements formed the foundation of Chrysler's career-planning efforts.

1. Recruiting and hiring were improved by assistance from the home office in coordinating visits to schools, developing newspaper ads, and creating a new, videotaped training program for hiring.
2. Career planning was improved by having all managers complete a needs-assessment form that forced them to explore the career aspirations of their employees and to identify the developmental activities needed by these people to achieve their career goals.
3. A company-wide succession plan was created covering anticipated changes for the next five years. Future managerial requirements were projected both in quantitative and qualitative terms to serve as a guide for appraising possible candidates and identifying developmental needs.

The career-development plant at Chrysler First, Inc., was well-received by employees at all levels and it greatly improved the attitudes of supervisors toward the importance of training activities. Effective forms also were created to assist in gathering relevant information and these forms contributed to the success of the program.

Source: Paul Egelhauf, "A Human Resources Plan: Chrysler First Develops Employee Career Paths," *Credit*, Vol. 14 (May/June 1988), pp. 36–39.

JOB TRAINING

Basic job-instruction training is probably the most common form of career development because all employees need at least some job training and basic orientation instructions. Both management development and job training can occur on and off the job, and both are major human resource activities.

PROGRAMS FOR SPECIAL GROUPS

Some organizations provide unique training programs to help special groups manage their careers. Examples include preretirement counseling for employees soon to retire, career counseling for women and minorities, and special orientation programs for minorities and employees being relocated.[14]

Supervisors ought to be trained in career counseling so they can help employees by providing counseling and coaching, performance appraisal and feedback, and mutual goal setting. Although supervisors probably have more impact on employees' careers than any other people within an organization, they often are reluctant to get too involved in career discussions because of a lack of experience and skill. Employees are ultimately responsible for managing their own careers; however, supervisors play an important role in evaluating employees' performances and in suggesting future possibilities for them.[15]

The human resource department should not attempt to replace the supervisor, nor can it expect to provide individual career counseling for all employees. The role of the human resource department in career planning is to: (1) train supervisors so they can provide individual counseling; (2) ensure that supervisors and employees meet periodically to discuss employees' career plans and progress; (3) provide information about career opportunities elsewhere in the organization that supervisors and managers may not know about; and (4) provide special guidance and assistance when a supervisor's expertise is inadequate. Human resource departments need to provide realistic career information to help employees determine whether their goals are realistic and to help employees prepare for future opportunities.

ETHICAL ISSUES OF CAREER DEVELOPMENT

Who should be responsible for career development? Individuals differ in how well they plan their careers. Some develop elaborate career plans with specific timetables, while others do essentially no planning at all. During the last three or four weeks of spring semester, college placement offices are typically flooded with students who have failed to plan what they want to do after graduation. Some students, however, do an excellent job of managing their careers; they know what they want to pursue and arrange their educational training to prepare them for those careers. Long before graduation they conduct an aggressive job search to find which organizations offer the best opportunities to fulfill their career aspirations.

The responsibility for career planning belongs to each individual. Finding a job does not just happen; individuals have to make it happen. Every individual should be responsible for managing his or her career, regardless of economic factors that influence the supply and demand of labor. Finding a good job involves a careful process of assessing one's abilities and interests, becoming aware of job opportunities, preparing an effective resumé, locating job openings, interviewing with prospective employers, and then assessing the job offers. Each of these activities takes time. An individual should begin to find a job before graduation or before leaving a job.

An ethical issue that is seldom addressed is whether it is right for society or for organizations to induce people to alter their career choices. When individuals select a career should they try to please themselves, or should their selection make a "social statement"? How much pressure should be exerted on people to choose nontraditional careers? Should men and women be encouraged to choose careers in fields historically dominated by the opposite sex in an effort to eliminate sex stereotypes in jobs? Should advertisements regarding particular blue- and white-collar jobs be targeted at particular ethnic groups? Social influences affect people's career decisions. Should this influence be encouraged or discouraged?

Career stereotypes can limit an organization's ability to attract and retain new employees and can influence the effectiveness of human resource programs. Before a recruiter tries to sell a job opening, the applicants may have already decided that they are not willing to consider it. Training and development programs, opportunities for promotion, and job-redesign projects may ultimately fail because individuals feel their career goals are inconsistent with these plans. In fact, some organizations have found that the occupational interests of minorities and females can present serious obstacles to achieving their affirmative action goals. A classic illustration occurred when American Telephone and Telegraph was required to employ women in outside crafts jobs and found this task more difficult to execute than the company anticipated. In order to achieve its goals, the company had to launch an aggressive educational program in high schools and technical colleges to convince women that outside crafts jobs were a legitimate female occupation.

Another ethical issue concerns making career decisions for people without input from them. Job-rotation, transfer, and even relocation decisions are sometimes made without telling employees how these changes are steps in a career path. Several rising stars may be groomed for one position but to prevent disappointment none of them are told. Is it right to have several compete when only one can reach the top?

Too often career success focuses exclusively on promotion. Career programs should focus on career development rather than just advancement. Advancement opportunities are often limited; there is simply not room for every employee at the top of an organization. However, all employees can develop their skills and make better contributions in their present jobs. Job satisfaction and personal fulfillment come from knowing how to perform a job well.

ALTERNATIVE PATTERNS OF WORK

Many employees think the most significant improvement in the quality of life at work is greater flexibility in scheduling when they work. Since the Great Depression, the typical workweek for most employees has been a five-day, 40-hour week. Numerous exceptions to the standard workweek have always existed, particularly in the farming and transportation industries, but during the 1980s, novel changes were made to the typical workweek. Five of the most popular alternatives to the standard workweek include flextime, permanent part-time, job sharing, the compressed workweek, and telecommuting.

These five alternative patterns of work have both advantages and disadvantages. They are not universally desirable to all workers, and they are not feasible for some jobs. But the fact that they are being implemented in so many companies indicates the concern top managers have for improving the quality of life at work. These alternatives contribute to the quality of life because they are more consistent with the unique circumstances of workers and the nonwork demands of their lives.

FLEXTIME

Flexible working hours, or **flextime**, is an attractive alternative to the standard workweek. For many years, professionals, managers, salespeople, and the self-employed have had considerable freedom in setting their own hours of work. Flextime extends this privilege to clerical, production, and other service workers. Flextime, as a formal innovation, was started in Germany in 1967 and spread rapidly to America. Under flexible work hours, employees choose when they arrive at work and sometimes when they depart, subject to limits set by management. Usually the organization establishes a **core period** when all employees are expected to be at work and allows flexible hours at both ends of the working day. Three typical flextime schedules are illustrated in Figure 3.2.

Flextime cannot be extended to all employees because of the demands of certain jobs. Jobs that require continuous coverage, such as those of receptionist, switchboard operator, and bus driver, make flextime inappropriate unless employees cover these jobs during their core hours and perform other discretionary activities during their flexible hours. Assembly-line jobs and other activities that require interdependence with other employees also are not appropriate for flextime. Some of the major advantages and disadvantages of flextime are presented in Table 3.2

Flextime is widespread in most European countries, and the same expansion is expected in America.[16] Studies on the effects of flextime have produced generally favorable results. Almost all changes to flextime have created more favorable job attitudes. Employees say that flextime makes them feel more trusted, and they report higher levels of job satisfaction. The effects of flextime on productivity are not as clear. Most studies have indicated that flextime either increases productivity or has no effect. However, these studies generally relied on the perceptions of employees regarding their performance rather than on objective measures of productivity. Nevertheless, very few companies that have tried flextime have reported undesirable results.[17]

Since most executives enjoy the luxury of setting their own hours of work, they usually feel inclined to allow their employees to have the same privilege when possible. However, most employees do not make extensive use of flextime when the option is offered to them. Even on jobs where flextime is appropriate and employees are free to set their own work hours, companies find that employees tend to follow the standard workday and generally vary their starting times by fewer than plus or minus thirty minutes. The typical response of most employees is to start work a few minutes earlier. But even if employees do not use flextime much, they like having the option of flexible hours.

PERMANENT PART-TIME

Part-time employment has been defined by the Bureau of Labor Statistics as a job consisting of less than 35 hours per week. The distinction between full-time and part-

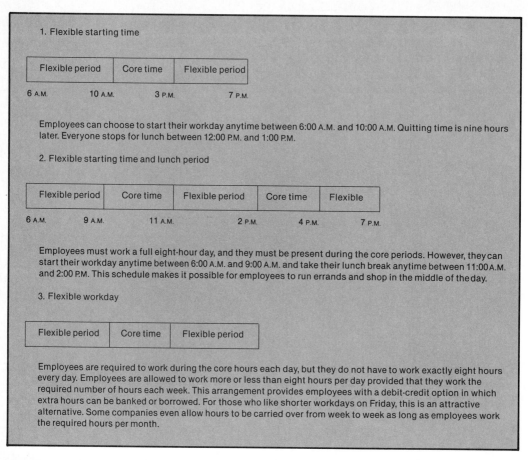

1. Flexible starting time

Flexible period	Core time	Flexible period

6 A.M.   10 A.M.   3 P.M.   7 P.M.

Employees can choose to start their workday anytime between 6:00 A.M. and 10:00 A.M. Quitting time is nine hours later. Everyone stops for lunch between 12:00 P.M. and 1:00 P.M.

2. Flexible starting time and lunch period

Flexible period	Core time	Flexible period	Core time	Flexible

6 A.M.   9 A.M.   11 A.M.   2 P.M.   4 P.M.   7 P.M.

Employees must work a full eight-hour day, and they must be present during the core periods. However, they can start their workday anytime between 6:00 A.M. and 9:00 A.M. and take their lunch break anytime between 11:00 A.M. and 2:00 P.M. This schedule makes it possible for employees to run errands and shop in the middle of the day.

3. Flexible workday

Flexible period	Core time	Flexible period

Employees are required to work during the core hours each day, but they do not have to work exactly eight hours every day. Employees are allowed to work more or less than eight hours per day provided that they work the required number of hours each week. This arrangement provides employees with a debit-credit option in which extra hours can be banked or borrowed. For those who like shorter workdays on Friday, this is an attractive alternative. Some companies even allow hours to be carried over from week to week as long as employees work the required hours per month.

FIGURE 3.2 Three flextime schedules.

time employment has served several useful purposes in analyzing the underutilization of the work force and the transition of new employees from temporary to permanent employment. Until recent years, part-time employment was considered temporary work; a part-time worker was thought of as an individual who was involuntarily working less than a full-time job. The 35-hour cutoff has been questioned in recent years because a growing percentage of the work force has begun to work less than 35 hours per week. Many part-time employees do not consider themselves temporary; working less than 35 hours per week is a permanent position for them. Since 1970, the growth in part-time jobs has been twice the rate of that in full-time work.

One of the reasons for the growth in **permanent part-time** employment is that it fits the needs of people who prefer working shorter hours. Mothers who have children at home and older employees who have less stamina are two groups who especially prefer part-time employment. For many people, having a job that allows them to work shorter hours makes the difference between having a job versus no job at all.

Additional part-time positions would likely increase the size of the work force. Many individuals who are unable to work full-time could probably be attracted to work part-time if more part-time jobs were available. Other advantages of part-time employment include (1) greater job satisfaction for those who need to work but do not want to work full-time, and (2) greater flexibility in hiring employees to meet erratic work requirements.[18]

The major disadvantages of part-time employment are that it creates additional administrative and scheduling difficulties and it increases benefits costs. These problems also occur in job sharing.

JOB SHARING

A variation of permanent part-time employment is **job sharing**. Here, a full-time position is divided into two part-time positions, and the duties and responsibilities of the job are assigned to two separate employees. In some cases, the job functions of the two individuals may be distinctly different since each may be responsible for separate activities. Accountability for the total job may be divided between the two sharers, or both may assume equal and full accountability. Job sharing usually involves a splitting of the responsibilities and the accountability between the sharers. When both part-time employees are held responsible for the whole job, it is sometimes called "job pairing."

TABLE 3.2   Advantages and disadvantages of flextime

Advantages	Disadvantages
1. Tardiness is virtually eliminated since employees are not tardy unless they miss the core hours.	1. Communication problems increase since employees frequently need to communicate during the flexible hours.
2. Absenteeism is reduced, especially the one-day absences caused by employees deciding to miss work rather than come to work late.	2. Keeping attendance records can become a problem. Employees do not like time clocks, but some tend to misrepresent their hours when they are on their own.
3. It is easier to schedule personal appointments and personal time.	3. If administrative decisions need to be made throughout the day, providing supervision for twelve to fifteen hours a day can become a problem.
4. Employees can schedule their work to match their biorhythm or internal clock. Some people work best early in the day, and others work better late in the day.	4. Legislation presents some obstacles to the use of flextime since overtime pay is required for certain jobs that exceed the standard workweek.
5. It reduces traffic congestion and creates less stress on getting to work on time.	5. Utility costs may be higher with flextime because of longer operating hours.
6. It provides greater flexibility in handling uneven workloads.	
7. It provides increased customer service because the company is open longer.	

▌ HRM in Action

Flexible Careers for Mothers: A step forward or a step backward?

In a *Harvard Business Review* article, Felice N. Schwartz described two career paths for women and explained why working mothers need greater flexibility in structuring their careers. This article was very controversial because it said that women cost more to employ than men and it encouraged companies to identify which women will follow the fast track as opposed to those who will detour through the nursery and to treat them differently.

Schwartz described two kinds of career paths for women. One career path is for "primary career women" who either don't have children or are willing to allow others to raise their children. These women expect to be and ought to be treated like men who want to pursue an executive career. Creating a career path for these women who are headed for the top requires (1) identifying them early, (2) giving them the same developmental opportunities and responsibilities as talented men, (3) accepting them as valued members of the management team, and (4) recognizing that their environment is more difficult than that of their male peers and reducing these stresses when possible.

The other career path, called the "mommy track," is for "career-and-family" women who want to pursue serious careers while participating actively in the rearing of their children. These women, who represent a majority of working females, are willing to temporarily trade some career growth and compensation for the freedom from having to work long hours and weekends. The greatest need for these women is flexible scheduling to accommodate family responsibilities. Part-time employment and job sharing are especially valuable because they allow mothers to return to the work force earlier without being too exhausted physically or emotionally to care for their newborn infants. Returning to work part-time enables them to maintain responsibility for critical aspects of their jobs, keeps them in touch with changes in the workplace, reduces stress and fatigue, and eliminates the need for paid maternity leave.

The greatest criticism against defining a separate career path for career-and-family women is the fear that it will be used by employers to stereotype women and set back efforts to eliminate sex discrimination. Schwartz argues, however, that multiple career paths for women should be viewed as an opportunity, not a roadlock, especially because the labor shortage makes female employment so important to organizations. She believes women need more career options consistent with their personal values and circumstances. She is in favor of greater flexibility at work so women can pursue their chosen careers.

Sources: Felice N. Schwartz, "Management Women and the New Facts of Life," *Harvard Business Review* (January–February 1989), pp. 65–76; Cindy Skrzycki, "Mommy Track Author Answers Her Critics," *The Washington Post*, March 19, 1989.

The initial interest in job sharing was expressed by female professionals who were interested in maintaining a better balance between their career and family responsibilities. Two successful job-sharing experiments in the mid 1960s, one with social workers and the other with teachers, stimulated considerable interest in this work arrangement. Approximately 80 percent of job sharers are females.

An example of job sharing is a husband and wife team who share one teaching position in the history department of a university. He teaches American history classes, his specialty, and she teaches Asian history classes, her specialty. Together, their combined teaching loads, committee assignments, and salary are equivalent to one position.

Job sharing has been tried successfully in many different jobs, including clerical and office positions, elementary school teachers, district attorneys, librarians, and various production level jobs. In many instances, job sharing has been initiated by two individuals who submitted a proposal to split a job in response to a job opening. Two mothers, for example, prepared a proposal to split the job of an elementary school teacher. They convinced the school district that their combined efforts and unique contributions were superior to what was offered by any of the alternative full-time applicants for the job.

Some of the major advantages of job sharing include the following:[19]

1. Productivity is usually higher because two people sharing one job have higher levels of energy and enthusiasm than one full-time person. In an early study of job sharing among social workers, it was found that half-time social workers handled 89 percent as many cases as full-time workers.[20] Other studies also have reported greater productivity for job sharers; however, most of the evidence relies on subjective measures of performance.

2. Increased flexibility in scheduling work assignments allows for better coverage of peak periods.

3. Reduced absenteeism and turnover have resulted from job sharing. One of the major causes of absenteeism is the need for more personal time than a 40-hour workweek allows. Job sharing not only provides more personal time but also provides the option of trading hours between partners during times of crisis or illness. Reduced turnover rates are probably an indication that part-time employment is more consistent with the personal needs of employees as they try to balance competing responsibilities and interests.

4. Job training is improved by job sharing. When one member of a team quits, the remaining partner can provide on-the-job training for the new employee. The remaining partner also provides continuity during the transition period.

5. Better employment options are provided through job sharing for people who cannot perform a full-time job. Job sharing provides greater employment opportunities not only for parents but also for individuals who are older, handicapped, or disabled. Part-time employment in the form of job sharing may provide meaningful employment to people who might otherwise be unable to work full-time.

Job sharing also has certain disadvantages. The most serious problem is the allocation of benefits. Generally, benefits are prorated to each according to the percentage of the job that each performs. If they want full benefits, job sharers are sometimes allowed to pay the additional costs themselves. Job sharers are usually surprised at the costs of benefits and sometimes prefer to take fewer benefits. However, a growing percentage of companies are providing full benefits for part-time employees. Other disadvantages of job sharing stem from the fact that employing twice as many people requires greater supervision, additional paperwork, and added communication problems. These problems are usually not very serious, however, if the partners work well together. Most job sharers say that a cooperative working relationship between them is a prerequisite for a successful team. Another problem that has to be resolved in a job-sharing situation is how a team should be promoted, fired, or evaluated. If one member is fired or promoted, what happens to the partner? Can two people sharing the job of a university professor submit combined resumes and expect to be promoted?

COMPRESSED WORKWEEK

A **compressed workweek** consists of scheduling a full-time job in fewer than five working days per week. The most typical compressed workweek consists of four workdays of ten hours each per week. This alternative is usually referred to as the 4/40 alternative. A workweek that is compressed even further consists of three twelve-hour days. However, this 3/36 alternative has not been very popular.

The idea of a compressed workweek was considered exciting when it was first tried in a few companies. Working a couple of extra hours each day did not seem like much of an added burden since many employees frequently worked overtime anyway. The trade-off was a free day with no work. The compressed workweek was typically scheduled to free either a Friday or a Monday to provide an extended weekend.

The advantages of a compressed workweek include the following:

1. It reduces the time and costs of commuting to work.
2. It increases the leisure time of employees.
3. It creates greater job satisfaction and morale for employees who like it.
4. It reduces the set-up and clean-up costs on certain jobs.

The disadvantages of a compressed workweek usually outweigh the advantages. The early proponents of the compressed workweek expected it to increase productivity and lead to higher quality work. The results have suggested just the opposite. Working more than eight hours per day generally creates increased fatigue. An extended schedule of ten-hour days (beyond two or three weeks) often results in less total productivity during a ten-hour day than during a regular eight-hour day. Heavy physical or taxing mental work is generally not suited to a compressed workweek schedule. Accidents and safety violations also are likely to increase with a compressed workweek schedule because of fatigue and carelessness.[21]

The compressed workweek is not popular with some employees. Even though workers' initial responses to a compressed schedule are usually favorable, many dislike it after a short time. This schedule is not convenient for working mothers who want a steady daily routine that enables them to handle family responsibilities, or for older employees who are prone to fatigue, or for young employees who do not want long work schedules to interfere with their social lives. A compressed workweek appears to be most suitable for middle-aged males, especially those who want to hold a second job. Compressed workweeks usually lead to increased moonlighting.

Compressed workweeks are best-suited for jobs where the responsibility to initiate action comes from the job itself rather than from the worker. Security guards, hospital nurses, and refinery workers who monitor dials are examples of jobs where actions are made in response to a job demand. These jobs are better suited for compressed workweeks than physically tiring jobs that require the worker to initiate action, such as most construction jobs.[22]

TELECOMMUTING

One way to significantly alter the quality of life at work is to allow employees to work at home. Technological advances in computer networks, phonemail systems, and facsimile machines have made it possible for many jobs to be performed at home more effectively and efficiently than at the office. Working at home eliminates the disadvantages of lengthy commutes to work and reduces the number of unnecessary interruptions.

Working at home or at a satellite office and communicating with the home office by phone, usually with a computer terminal, is called "**telecommuting**," or "teleworking." Some companies have found that telecommuting is advantageous to both the employees and the company. Some managers of employees who work at home report that these workers actually work more hours, significantly improve their productivity, and are easier to manage. For example, DuPont Company's Wilmington, Delaware, office has over 1,000 sales representatives and managers telecommuting. The company reports that the administrative workload of each sales representative has been reduced and morale, communication, and information turnaround have been improved.[23]

The disadvantage of telecommuting is the lack of person-to-person communication and the loss of benefits that come from such encounters. Face-to-face conversations satisfy affiliation needs and help employees feel part of a group. Creative ideas and improved work procedures occasionally come from such casual conversations.

JOB REDESIGN

Another valuable intervention for improving the quality of life is job redesign. The kind of job an individual performs has a great influence on that person's life. Job satisfaction and satisfaction with life in general are influenced by the demands of a job and how consistent these demands are with the abilities and interests of the individual. Sometimes very simple job changes can make a big difference to the job holder.

The professional disciplines that study job redesign include industrial psychology, human factors engineering, and ergonomics. **Ergonomics**, sometimes called biotechnology, is that aspect of technology concerned with the application of biology and engineering factors to problems relating to the mutual adjustment of people and machines. Professionals in ergonomics are concerned with the adaptation of technology to the betterment of productive efficiency and human life.

The two major strategies of job redesign are job specialization (sometimes called job simplification) and job enrichment. These two strategies are almost exact opposites. Job specialization simplifies a job by reducing the number of elements performed by the worker. Job enrichment makes a job more complex by combining elements or by increasing the job holder's level of responsibility.

JOB SPECIALIZATION VERSUS JOB ENRICHMENT

The job-specialization versus job-enrichment controversy has a long history. One of the major themes of the industrial revolution was task specialization: complex jobs were divided into separate tasks and assigned to separate individuals. Indeed, the history of the industrial revolution was the history of task specialization. Assembly-line manufacturing is often viewed as the epitome of highly specialized jobs.

Many good reasons have been proposed to explain why task specialization increases efficiency. Through specialization, a worker becomes more proficient in a narrow job and gives greater attention to the minute elements of the task. Training time is dramatically reduced since the worker only has to master a small segment of the job. Specialized tools and machines can be designed to significantly increase performance. Less time is wasted going from one activity to the next. Training is reduced since each employee needs to learn only one specialized task. Specialization also increases management's flexibility in making job assignments, and workers are allowed greater mobility in their jobs.

The problem with task specialization is that highly specialized jobs sometimes cause workers to feel alienated. They are expected to behave like machines. They do not see the final product, and they never have the satisfaction of pointing to a finished product and saying, "I made that myself." Job enrichment is designed to counter feelings of alienation and to produce greater motivation. Even though enriched jobs may be less efficient, proponents of job enrichment argue that increased motivation more than compensates for the loss in efficiency. Job enrichment has also been viewed as the solution to many other problems. Indeed, job enrichment has been proposed as the primary cure for such diverse forms of worker discontent as job dissatisfaction, labor grievances, careless work, alcoholism, and drug abuse.

Job enrichment is not the same as job enlargement. Job enlargement consists of making a job larger in scope by adding more of the same kinds of elements. An example of job enlargement would be to allow a sewing machine operator to sew both sleeves on a shirt rather than just one. Another example would be to allow an assembler to solder both the red wires and the black wires rather than just the black ones. Job enlargement primarily increases the length of the work cycle; that is, it takes a longer time to do each repetitive activity since the cycle contains more elements. Job enlargement may add a little variety to a job, but not much, since it usually involves just more of the same type of tasks.

JOB-ENRICHMENT PROGRAMS

Job enrichment on an assembly line would probably allow workers to determine their own pace (within limits), to serve as their own inspectors by giving them responsibility for quality control, to repair their own mistakes, to be responsible for their own machine setup and repair, and to select their own work procedures. Basically, job enrichment consists of modifying the job to increase any of the following variables.

1. *Skill variety*: The degree to which a job allows workers to develop and use their skills and to avoid the monotony of performing the same task repeatedly.
2. *Task identity*: The degree to which a task consists of a whole or complete unit of work as opposed to a small, specialized, repetitive act.
3. *Task significance*: The degree to which a task has a significant impact on the organization, the community, or the lives of other people.
4. *Autonomy*: The degree to which workers are free of the direct influence of a supervisor and can exercise discretion in scheduling their work and deciding how it will be done.

5. *Feedback*: The degree to which workers obtain evaluative information about their performance in the normal course of doing their jobs.[24]

Skill variety, task identity, and task significance contribute to the meaningfulness of a job, but whether an activity is meaningful or meaningless also depends on an employee's personal values. Some people (such as some school teachers) think their jobs are meaningless even though they contain extensive variety, identity, and significance. Greater autonomy tends to develop a greater feeling of personal responsibility. Feedback provides knowledge of results. The best form of feedback is usually from the job itself rather than from a supervisor. Letting workers know how well they produce is like letting chefs taste what they cook.

Numerous job-enrichment programs have been used to make work more interesting and motivating. Some of the most popular programs include the following:

1. Combining tasks to eliminate highly specialized jobs and to make larger work modules (called horizontal loading).
2. Forming natural work units—teams of workers—in which each person feels a part of the team and in which certain jobs can be rotated among team members.
3. Establishing client relationships so that workers know who uses the product or service they produce and how the client feels about their work.
4. Giving workers greater authority and discretion by allowing them to perform functions previously reserved for higher levels of management (called vertical loading).
5. Opening feedback channels so that information about the quality of performance goes directly to the employee performing the job.

One of the benefits of job enrichment is that it can create a more flexible work force if employees are trained to perform several jobs. This practice of training workers to perform a variety of tasks, called **multiskilling**, allows employers to adjust to unstable staffing needs by redeploying existing workers. This concept has been used by retail stores, auto assembly plants, and steel mills to improve speed and efficiency by dispensing with rigid work classifications. Wages and pay increases are often based on the number of jobs the workers learn to perform.[25]

QUALITY OF WORK LIFE PROGRAMS

Quality of work life (QWL) programs refer generally to any programs that are implemented to change the traditional methods of working. Job-enrichment programs and the alternative patterns of work discussed earlier are considered examples of quality of work life programs. Some QWL programs, such as autonomous work teams, are dramatic departures from the traditional methods of doing business. Other QWL programs, such as quality circles, are not entirely new. The major component that all QWL programs have in common is that they seek to improve the quality of life by creating better jobs.

Almost all QWL programs share four common goals:

1. They attempt to create a democratic organization where everyone has a voice in deciding issues that influence their lives.

2. They try to share the financial rewards of the organization so that everyone benefits from greater cooperation, high productivity, and increased profitability.
3. They seek to create greater job security by increasing organizational vitality and
   furthering employee rights.
4. They try to enhance individual development by establishing conditions that contribute to personal growth and adjustment.

The major QWL programs discussed in this section include (1) autonomous work
teams, (2) quality circles, (3) representation on the board of directors, (4) labor-management committees, (5) employee ownership of the company, and (6) organizational development. Research evaluating the potential benefits of these QWL programs has focused
primarily on the effects of participation and ownership on various dependent measures,
such as satisfaction, productivity, profitability, cooperation, and survival. A review of this
research presents very mixed results. The success of any given QWL program depends
largely on the kind of participation, the degree of ownership, and many other situational
factors. Many QWL programs have been highly successful, while the best that can be
said of others is that they created a little excitement for a while.[26]

AUTONOMOUS WORK TEAMS

An **autonomous work team** consists of a small group of workers, usually fewer than
fifteen or twenty in number, who are responsible for performing a series of jobs. The
group is directed by its own informal leadership rather than through a layer of supervisors. Members of a team are free to rotate jobs as they choose. Someone may perform
the same repetitive job day after day, while someone else may shift from one job to
another or even build a complete unit alone. Some groups handle their own human
resource functions, such as hiring new people, evaluating each other's performance, and
determining each member's pay increase.

Several companies have eliminated the traditional assembly line and have changed
to a production system based on autonomous work teams. The two most widely known
experiments in autonomous work teams are the Swedish car companies Volvo and SAAB.
Each company tried to outdo the other in its attempts to introduce a radical alternative
to the traditional assembly line. Volvo, for example, built an entirely new assembly plant
in Kalmar, Sweden, in which assembly lines were replaced with work stations for each
autonomous group. Partially completed cars were moved from station to station on small
electric carts.[27]

Other companies in both Europe and America have expanded the use of autonomous
teams. Some companies (such as Signetics and Proctor and Gamble) prefer to use the
label of semiautonomous work teams to emphasize the fact that the teams are still subject
to the direction of management and must comply with company personnel policies.
Although the results of using work teams are not spectacular and some employees
transfer out of them, most companies report favorable results.

QUALITY CIRCLES

The term **quality circle** comes primarily from Japan and describes the process used by
many Japanese firms to involve employees in work-redesign experiments. A quality circle

consists of a group of workers who meet periodically to discuss methods of increasing productivity. Participation in the group discussion is voluntary, and most employees choose to be involved. The group meets regularly, typically one hour each week, usually on company time. The discussions are led by a supervisor or a group facilitator. The purposes of the meeting are to identify and diagnose problems, to explore alternative solutions, and to recommend the best solution. The members of the group are encouraged to discuss only the problems they can do something about. Problems out of their control are referred elsewhere.[28]

The reports on quality circles show three major benefits. First, the creative suggestions usually produce greater productivity in terms of both quantity and quality. Second, quality circles improve communication within the group, between groups, and with upper levels of management. Third, quality circles enhance the level of morale and increase employees' commitment to their work and satisfaction with the company.

REPRESENTATION ON THE BOARD OF DIRECTORS

Many companies, especially in Europe, have placed production workers on boards of directors. These members are elected by the work force to represent the workers' interests. In many European companies, this practice is mandated by a national law. In Sweden, for example, a national law requires all corporations with more than 100 people on the payroll to have worker representatives on their boards. West German companies adopted this practice many years ago to minimize labor disputes, and it appears to have been effective since the number of lost days due to strikes has been reduced. In some American companies, such as Eastern Airlines and Chrysler, worker representatives were placed on the board of directors as part of the negotiated "give-backs" that reduced wages.

The reason for placing production workers on boards of directors is to assure that the interests of the workers are considered. During a board's deliberations, when decisions of tremendous economic importance to the employees are being made, the board members can be reminded of the employees' interests by the employees' representative to the board.[29] Having worker representation on a board, however, is no guarantee of survival or profitability. Serious financial problems have not disappeared because the interests of employees are represented in board decisions. Productivity appears to be unchanged, although one study of fifty retail cooperatives in England reported very small productivity increases that ranged from .78 to 1.4 percent.[30]

LABOR-MANAGEMENT COMMITTEES

To reduce conflict and to create a more cooperative climate, some unions and companies have formed committees with representatives from both sides. Such committees are not intended to replace the traditional collective bargaining function, and they must be careful not to interfere in the collective bargaining process. Their purposes are to resolve conflicts between management and union and to help both to survive. Many labor-management committees have originated in response to severe economic threats, such as an economic depression, a plant closing, declining markets, or intense foreign competition. Effective programs have evolved in many different kinds of industries, most having been created in response to specific economic needs.

Until recently, labor-management committees have been rare. Managers have had low expectations of the workers' willingness or ability to make contributions. They also have feared that workers' participation would reduce managerial prestige and authority and add to the strength of the union. Meanwhile, unions have been concerned about the effects of productivity gains on job opportunities and fearful that cooperation would weaken their bargaining power. The Federal Mediation and Conciliation Service has encouraged unions and managers to organize joint committees. The efforts of these committees should reduce grievances, improve union-management relations, and reduce the impact of industrial disputes.[31]

EMPLOYEE OWNERSHIP

A "revolutionary" method for creating greater involvement and participation is for the employees to buy the company and operate it themselves. This form of peaceful takeover by employees has occurred frequently in recent years in an effort to reverse the trend of plant closings, especially in the Northeast. Most takeovers occur shortly after a plant closing has been announced. The employees band together and buy the company. These takeovers usually require extensive financial assistance because the employees are not able to raise sufficient capital on their own. Financial assistance usually is obtained from a union or through community interest groups.[32]

Employee ownership is not a new idea. During the mid-1800s, it was popular in the form of worker cooperatives. Many union leaders and social reformers thought that worker cooperatives were the answer to the industrial problems of the time. Several cooperatives were started, but very few survived for long. At that time, the major problem in starting a cooperative was collecting enough money from the workers to provide sufficient plant, equipment, and working capital. After the cooperative had been started, the major problem again was finances. The goal was for all workers to share in the ownership of the cooperative, preferably on an equal basis. But trouble surfaced when new members were added and old members left. New workers did not have sufficient capital to buy into the cooperative, and old members could not get their money out.

Employee ownership today takes two major forms. One form is for employees to own shares in the company, the same as if they were ordinary shareholders in a joint-stock company. The Jeanette Sheet Glass Corporation, near Pittsburgh, is an example of a company in which the employees own the company's stock. The workers became owners by each buying twenty shares of stock at $100 a share. This money was used to buy the company. The employees hold the stock in the company, although they are free to trade their shares.[33]

Another form of employee ownership is where the employees own shares through a trust, called an employee stock ownership trust (ESOT). Money is either paid or loaned to the trust, and the trust buys the company. The shares in the trust are owned by the employees who bought them. The employee owners in the trust are entitled to dispose of their stock at market value once it has been distributed to them. Unlike a profit-sharing or a pension trust, an ownership trust must invest "primarily" in the stock of the company. An example of a company that was purchased with an employee stock ownership trust is the South Bend Lathe Company. When the company's closing was announced, an ESOT was established by a group of managers, lawyers, and bankers. Loans were obtained for the trust from the city and from banking interests. In the first few years of operation under employee ownership, the company's profitability increased substantially, allowing the trust to repay some of its loans ahead of schedule.[34]

Increased profitability from employee ownership is typical. A review of 389 companies in which a large portion of the stock was directly owned by employees indicated that employee-owned companies generally have higher profit ratios. Employees seem to have greater motivation when they own the company for which they work.[35]

A problem with employee ownership through an ESOT, however, is that the employees do not have voting rights. (Voting privileges are only allowed in the first method, where employees own direct shares in the company.) Not being able to vote means that employees are less likely to have representatives on the board of directors or to be involved in making important administrative decisions. The lack of participation became a problem for the employee owners of the South Bend Lathe Company. Even though they owned the company, they did not control it, and on one occasion the workers went on strike against the company they owned.

ORGANIZATIONAL DEVELOPMENT

Organizational development refers to a series of planned, systematic changes introduced into an ongoing organization. These changes are typically referred to as *interventions*. The purpose of the change is to improve the effectiveness of the organization. Organizational development, abbreviated OD, includes a wide range of change activities that may be targeted toward individuals, groups, or the entire organization. Regardless of the target, the purposes of OD are to create organizational self-renewal and to avoid organizational decay, obsolescence, and rigidity.

Most OD interventions are only a loosely defined sequence of activities that must be adapted to the situation. Although an OD facilitator is usually involved in structuring and guiding the intervention activities, the facilitator does not have to be an external management consultant. Many companies have their own organizational development specialists within the human resource department, and therefore, their OD interventions are directed by their own internal change agents.

Interpersonal interventions are directed primarily toward individual learning, insight, and skill building. They are designed to improve the effectiveness of individuals and to contribute to personal growth and adjustment. One of the most popular interventions for improving interpersonal skills is sensitivity training, also called **T-group training** and sensing meetings. **Sensitivity training** basically consists of unstructured group discussions by small, face-to-face groups of not more than ten to twelve persons. The focus of the discussions is on the here and now as opposed to what has happened in the past. The here and now consists mostly of the feelings and emotions experienced by the group members. Group members share their perceptions of each other; they describe the attributes that they admire in one another and what irritates them.

The OD interventions that receive the most attention are those that focus on group functioning. Effective teams help the members of the group satisfy their own personal needs while eliciting their cooperation to achieve the group's goals. Successful group interventions usually require the involvement of all group members. One of the most popular group interventions is a team-building meeting, which is a group discussion that diagnoses the group's strengths and weaknesses, clarifies its goals, and makes the necessary changes to create an effective and cohesive group. Most team-building meetings involve getting the work group together for an extended block of time (one to three days) away from the workplace. The group identifies the important problems, usually with the help of a consultant or an outside facilitator. As these problems are discussed, alternative solutions are developed and evaluated. The outcome of the meeting should be a carefully planned procedure that identifies the action steps and specifies who will do what and when. This plan should be a realistic solution acceptable to all group members.[36]

Two of the most widely known organizational interventions are survey feedback and structural change. When survey feedback is used as an OD intervention, everyone in the organization completes a questionnaire. The data are then shared with everyone in the company. Each group is the first to receive a report on its own group attitudes. The data are used to identify problems and as an aid in diagnosing the organization. During the feedback session, the groups engage in problem-solving activities to correct problems and to increase organizational effectiveness.

Perhaps the easiest change to make in an organization is a change in the organizational structure. Structural changes are changes in the hierarchical reporting relationships. Such changes often have an enormous and relatively permanent impact on individual behavior and organizational functioning. Structural changes are often suggested as part of the problem solving and action planning of other OD interventions.

Some examples of structural changes include moving a job from one department to another, reducing a supervisor's span of control, dividing a large department into two smaller departments, transferring an entire department to a new division (such as taking security out of the human resources department and assigning it to the operations division), creating a new department to centralize a particular function (such as creating a word-processing center rather than allowing managers to have personal secretaries), and reorganizing an entire organization along different lines (such as eliminating the purchasing, mixing, baking, and packaging departments of a cookie company and assigning these functions to new departments organized according to specific products).

EVALUATING HR PROGRAMS

Over the years, human resource managers have been encouraged to implement a variety of innovative programs to improve organizational effectiveness and the quality of work life. Although some programs have endured the test of time, others were brief fads. For example, the fads of the 1950s included management by objectives, quantitative management, job enrichment, and Theory Y. The 1960s brought sensitivity training, managerial-grid training, and personality testing. The 1970s saw zero-based budgeting and Theory Z, and the 1980s saw intrepreneuring, one-minute managing, and reviving the corporate culture.[37]

New programs need to be evaluated to assess whether they produce desirable results. Human resource managers ought to play a major role in this evaluation since they have access to most of the relevant information. In addition to measuring productivity, the traditional measures for evaluating organizational changes are employee satisfaction, absenteeism, and turnover.

SATISFACTION

Monitoring job satisfaction is important to both behavioral scientists and human resource managers. The effects of many management decisions are examined with respect to their impact on job satisfaction. Positive job attitudes are generally viewed as an important indication of how well things are going, and they are also viewed as a legitimate "end state," worthy of pursuing for their own sake.

Individuals differ in how they respond to the conditions of work. While some employees may be highly satisfied with a particular job, other employees may find the same conditions extremely dissatisfying. An important issue surrounding every human resource activity is how it will influence job satisfaction. Will satisfaction increase or decrease as a result of a different recruiting strategy, a better benefit package, a new training program, or some other change in human resource practices? Low morale contributes to labor problems, attempts to organize labor unions, excessive turnover, labor grievances, and a negative organizational climate.

Grievances, absenteeism, and turnover are frequently used as indirect measures of employee satisfaction. While these variables are usually related, they are also influenced by other economic forces. The best ways to measure satisfaction are either to interview employees or ask them to complete a questionnaire. Paper-and-pencil questionnaires, which can also be administered by computer, are the most popular methods of measuring satisfaction because they are relatively short, they can be administered to large numbers of employees simultaneously, and the responses can be compared across jobs and across companies to diagnose problems. Figure 3.3 illustrates two popular formats for measuring satisfaction: semantic differential scales and Likert scales.

Studies of job satisfaction have determined that job attitudes are influenced most by the qualitative aspects of the job. Good pay policies and practices generally create positive satisfaction with pay. Supervisors who are fair, considerate, and competent generally create positive feelings of satisfaction with supervision. However, job satisfaction also is related to other variables not directly associated with the job, such as age, sex, and work values. Older workers, for example, usually report greater job satisfaction than younger workers, even when both age groups are performing similar jobs. Employees who have a strong work ethic also report greater job satisfaction than those who reject the work ethic.[38] Satisfaction with a job is apparently influenced by the kinds of values and expectations that employees bring with them to the job.

Satisfaction on the job is also influenced by what happens to employees off the job. Just as work influences a person's satisfaction with life in general, so too does the quality of life away from work influence satisfaction with work.[39] The frustrations and difficulties people face in their personal lives have contributed to the general decline in job satisfaction throughout the work force. A comparison of the attitudes of working Americans from 1973 to 1979 by the Roper Organization showed a significant decline in all facets of job satisfaction, including satisfaction with coworkers, supervision, benefits, income, hours worked, and the job itself. This decline was attributed to three factors: the retire-

Semantic Differential Scales
ME AT WORK—HOW I FEEL MOST OF THE TIME

	Extremely	Quite	Slightly	Neutral	Slightly	Quite	Extremely	
APPRECIATED	1	2	3	4	5	6	7	UNAPPRECIATED
EFFICIENT	1	2	3	4	5	6	7	INEFFICIENT
PENALIZED	1	2	3	4	5	6	7	REWARDED
SATISFIED	1	2	3	4	5	6	7	DISSATISFIED
UNPRODUCTIVE	1	2	3	4	5	6	7	PRODUCTIVE
ENCOURAGED	1	2	3	4	5	6	7	DISCOURAGED
INEFFECTIVE	1	2	3	4	5	6	7	EFFECTIVE
VALUABLE	1	2	3	4	5	6	7	WORTHLESS

Likert Scales

	Strongly Disagree				Strongly Agree
1. Considering everything about the company, I am very well satisfied with it.	1	2	3	4	5
2. Top management is not very interested in the feelings of employees.	1	2	3	4	5
3. This company is a better place to work than most other companies.	1	2	3	4	5
4. My job is a real drag; I hate coming to work.	1	2	3	4	5

FIGURE 3.3 Illustration of two methods for measuring job satisfaction.

ment of employees who had experienced the Depression, the employment shift from large to small firms, and the dramatic increase in the proportion of working women. Women tended to express less satisfaction than men because of inferior jobs, restricted opportunities for promotion, and lower income than men and because family dynamics place greater strains on women.[40]

ABSENTEEISM AND TURNOVER

Absenteeism and turnover are often used as indications of organizational effectiveness. Absenteeism is missing work temporarily. Turnover occurs when employees leave permanently. Many factors besides poor morale influence absenteeism and turnover. Frustration and conflict are created by conditions away from work as well as conditions on the job. When absenteeism and turnover statistics rise, managers need to evaluate the situation and determine whether the rise is caused by aggravating conditions at work. If so, the high costs of absenteeism and turnover are a good justification for improving the workplace.

To diagnose these problems carefully a distinction should be made between two types of absenteeism and turnover, voluntary and involuntary. **Voluntary absenteeism and turnover** occur when employees have a choice of working or not working and they intentionally decide to miss work or quit.[41] **Involuntary absenteeism and turnover** occur when employees miss work or are terminated for reasons beyond their control. Two examples of involuntary turnover are layoffs, when the organization terminates employees because they are no longer needed, and dismissals, when employees are terminated due to incompetence or unacceptable behavior. Some examples of involuntary absenteeism are health problems, the death or serious illness of a family member, transportation problems, and bad weather.

Although the distinction between voluntary and involuntary causes is helpful in diagnosing absenteeism, the definition of what is voluntary versus involuntary is not entirely clear. When is a problem beyond a person's control? Major surgery and serious illnesses may force employees to be absent, but some return to work much sooner than others. Some football players have appendectomies and return only a few days later to play a game. When their cars are broken down, some employees miss several days of work, while others take public transportation, ride a bike, or walk several miles to get to work. For some employees, a heavy snowstorm means getting up an hour earlier to get to work on time; for others, it means sleeping in. Consequently, it is difficult to decide when an absence is truly involuntary or when the employee should have taken an aspirin and gone back to work. Most managers believe that job satisfaction and motivation can make a big difference in situations such as those described.

MEASURING ABSENTEEISM

Developing a meaningful measure of absenteeism is difficult because of the problem of distinguishing between voluntary and involuntary absences. Another problem is that absenteeism figures can be seriously distorted by extended illnesses. The **job-absence-rate** formula used by most companies and accepted by the Bureau of National Affairs (BNA) in its quarterly survey is

$$\text{Job-absence rate} = \frac{\text{Number of worker-days lost through job absences during the month} \times 100}{(\text{Average number of employees}) \times (\text{Number of workdays})}$$

To obtain comparable data from all companies, the BNA asks companies to exclude absences of less than one day (tardiness) and to count only the first four days of long-term absences. Consequently, the BNA's job-absence rate understates the actual amount of missed work and makes no distinction between voluntary and involuntary absences.

The median monthly job-absence rates of 233 companies for 1989 are reported in Figure 3.4. The absence rates vary substantially between companies of different size: larger companies tend to have higher absence rates than smaller companies. The absence rates also vary greatly among companies, regardless of size. In September 1989, for example, the median job-absence rate was 1.8, but one company had an absence rate of .02 percent while another had an absence rate of 7.0 percent.[42]

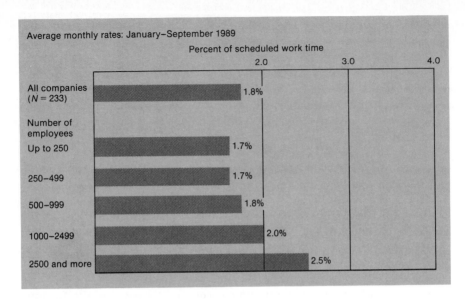

FIGURE 3.4 BNA's job-absence report.

Some have suggested that another useful measure would be an *absenteeism-frequency* measure. This measure would show the number of absences (regardless of duration) per month or per year. A long absence would only count as one absence, the same as a short absence. Absenteeism-frequency measures would help in identifying the causes of absenteeism. The need for a careful analysis of absenteeism is illustrated by the results of a study concerning 610 employees of a General Motors division located in Scotland. Absenteeism records were examined for a six-year period. The average number of days that employees had been absent was three days per year, or eighteen days over the six-year period. However, these averages did not tell the complete story, since there were wide variations in the amounts of individual absenteeism. Some employees had perfect attendance records for the entire six years while others had missed over 600 days of work.[43]

MEASURING TURNOVER

An analysis of absenteeism and turnover statistics shows that these two factors are highly correlated. When absenteeism rates are high, turnover rates also are likely to be high. Apparently absenteeism and turnover are not alternative ways of expressing dissatisfaction; they are both caused by many of the same factors. As working conditions become undesirable, employees may first start to miss a few days and then leave permanently.

To help companies analyze their turnover rates, the Bureau of National Affairs collects turnover data in its regular survey. These data concern monthly turnover rates and are reported on a quarterly basis. The procedure for calculating turnover rates is

$$\text{Monthly turnover rates} = \frac{\text{Number of separations during month} \times 100}{\text{Average number of employees on payroll during month}}.$$

The number of separations includes all permanent separations except those who have been laid off. Persons who have been laid off are excluded from the calculations entirely. Therefore, the BNA's report is primarily a measure of how many people have quit or have been dismissed. The monthly turnover rates of 341 companies for 1989 are shown in Figure 3.5. These data illustrate a typical trend: smaller companies tend to have higher turnover rates than larger companies. The variation among companies is considerable: some companies reported no turnover while others reported monthly turnover rates that exceeded 10 percent.

CAUSES OF TURNOVER

Because turnover can be so costly, organizations need to reduce it to acceptable levels. But maintaining a zero turnover rate is unrealistic and even undesirable. A certain amount of turnover is necessary and desirable as employees develop new skills and advance to higher levels of responsibility. Turnover rates are generally quite high in college communities because many employees are students or spouses of students. After obtaining their degrees, the graduates leave the communities for better-paying and more challenging jobs.

The two variables most significantly related to turnover are job dissatisfaction and economic conditions. The highest turnover levels are found in companies or divisions of companies where employees report the greatest dissatisfaction. Consequently, most explanations of turnover maintain that employees leave their jobs when alternative jobs that better satisfy their needs become available. Therefore, turnover levels are generally high in companies with poor working conditions, undesirable jobs, wage inequities, and restricted opportunities for advancement. To reduce abnormally high turnover levels, companies must improve the quality of the work environment. For example, a field

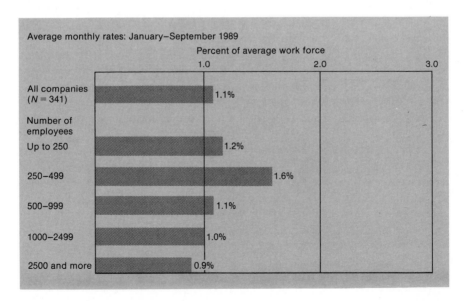

FIGURE 3.5 BNA's job-turnover report.

experiment involving 350 clerical employees found that improved pay and promotion policies reduced the turnover level from over 30 percent to 18 percent the first year and to 12 percent the next year.[44] Another field study compared the attitudes of sales people who stayed with those who left. Those who left rated the company lower as a good place to work and thought their futures were less secure than those who stayed.[45]

Turnover rates are strongly influenced by economic conditions. When the economy is depressed and unemployment levels go up, turnover in most companies goes down. An analysis of fluctuations in average turnover and unemployment over a period of several years shows an inverse relationship. Apparently high unemployment levels reduce the perceived and real opportunities of changing to another job. Employees are reluctant to leave one job unless they know another job is available. Companies cannot control economic conditions or unemployment levels. Consequently, their turnover levels may fluctuate widely regardless of other actions they may take. These fluctuations make it difficult to assess the effectiveness of other changes designed to reduce turnover.

Another variable influencing turnover that is outside the control of an employer is family unity and support. Employees who have higher levels of work-family conflict are more likely to leave the company. People who come from unstable families have difficulty leaving their personal problems at home, and they are sometimes forced to change employment to accommodate family pressures. On the other hand, people who have extended family ties in the community, such as parents, children, and relatives, have better attendance records and less turnover.[46]

PERSONNEL AUDITS

A **personnel audit** evaluates the effectiveness of the human resource department.[47] How well do the policies and programs sponsored by the human resource department meet the needs of the employees and the company? A systematic audit of the department can answer this question, particularly if it includes an objective evaluation of performance and candid feedback from line managers.

The first step in an audit, as shown in Figure 3.6, is to clarify the objectives of the audit and to define the responsibilities of the department. Ambiguous responsibilities and uncertain objectives will become apparent at this point. Is the department responsible for safety? Who is responsible for scheduling campus recruiting interviews? The outcome of this step should be a comprehensive list of the department's responsibilities and objectives.

The second step is to collect data from people both inside and outside the department on how well they think the department is performing. Two methods of assessing the department are illustrated in Figure 3.7. One method is a subjective assessment using five-point scales on which managers rate the effectiveness of the major human resource responsibilities. The second method consists of assessing whether the department is or is not performing a list of critical activities at a specified level of competence. The checklist method requires greater time and effort to create measurable standards, but it has the advantage of being more precise. The subjective-assessment method simply lists all of the major responsibilities and asks those completing the questionnaire to use their own standards for evaluating the department.

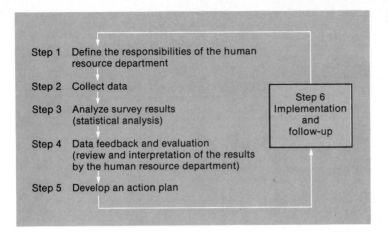

FIGURE 3.6 Personnel audit process.

When the data are analyzed in step 3 of Figure 3.6, the strengths and weaknesses of the department will be identified. The attitudes of people inside and outside the department ought to be analyzed separately to provide greater meaning when the data are fed back to the department in step 4. If those responsible for administering the audit successfully elicited the cooperation of those who completed the survey, the results will provide useful information for redesigning and altering the department in steps 5 and 6.

HUMAN RESOURCE ACCOUNTING

Human resource accounting represents one of the most aggressive attempts to estimate the economic contribution of human resource activities. Human resource accounting refers to the process of identifying and measuring data about human resources and communicating this information to interested parties, especially investors and managers. Rensis Likert drew attention to the economic value of human assets by asking executives this question: "If you woke up tomorrow and had all of your plant and equipment, all of your machines, and all of your physical resources, but you didn't have any people, how long would it take you and how much would it cost to replace your entire work force?"[48] Replacing an entire work force would be an extremely difficult, if not impossible, task to accomplish.

Human resource accounting information is especially valuable for managers of service firms where people are the key assets of the firm, such as public accounting firms, management consulting firms, and sports teams. Managers typically receive extensive information concerning the firm's financial resources, but relatively little information about its human resources. Therefore, human resource accounting is an attempt to provide information that will help managers make accurate decisions about recruiting, hiring, training, supervising, evaluating, developing, and replacing personnel. Studies have shown that human resource accounting information has influenced managers making layoff decisions and has altered the investment decisions of investors.[49]

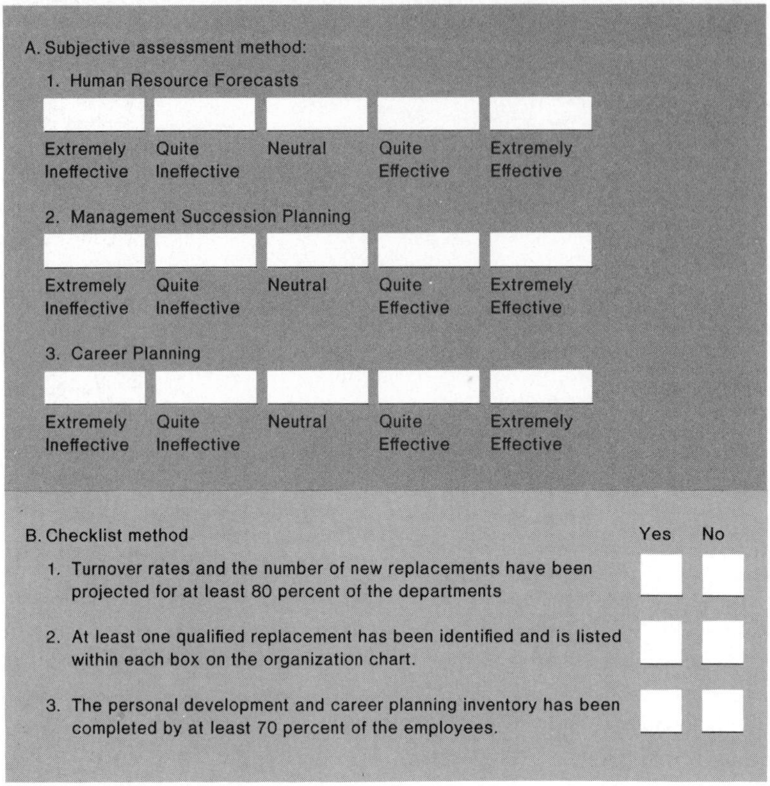

A. Subjective assessment method:

1. Human Resource Forecasts

Extremely Ineffective	Quite Ineffective	Neutral	Quite Effective	Extremely Effective

2. Management Succession Planning

Extremely Ineffective	Quite Ineffective	Neutral	Quite Effective	Extremely Effective

3. Career Planning

Extremely Ineffective	Quite Ineffective	Neutral	Quite Effective	Extremely Effective

B. Checklist method

	Yes	No
1. Turnover rates and the number of new replacements have been projected for at least 80 percent of the departments	☐	☐
2. At least one qualified replacement has been identified and is listed within each box on the organization chart.	☐	☐
3. The personal development and career planning inventory has been completed by at least 70 percent of the employees.	☐	☐

FIGURE 3.7 Two methods of assessing the human resource department.

Several human resource measures have been proposed to help managers make better-informed decisions. The development and reporting of multiple measures has been recommended to provide a broad perspective of the value of human resources. Three of the most frequently recommended measures include outlay costs, replacement costs, and human resource value.[50]

1. *Outlay cost*: The **outlay cost** is also referred to as the historical acquisition cost. This measure represents the value of "human capital" and includes all of the costs associated with recruiting, selecting, training, and developing employees for a firm. It has been suggested that these costs should be capitalized and treated the same way as costs for capital equipment, which are depreciated over the expected useful life of the assets.

2. *Replacement cost*: The **replacement cost** is an estimate of how much it would cost to replace a firm's existing human resources. Included in this estimate is the cost of recruiting, hiring, training, and developing replacements who could perform at the same level of proficiency as the firm's present employees. The total replacement value includes not only the current replacement costs but also the opportunity costs of lost income that would be incurred while the replacements were developing the same level of proficiency as existing employees.

3. *Human resource value*: The **human resource value** represents the expected contribution to the firm's net income for individuals at each level in the firm. This value is estimated by calculating the net present value of each person based on the person's expected future services and probability of staying with the firm.

The purpose of human resource accounting is to improve the quality of financial decisions affecting personnel activities. Better methods of evaluating the value of human resources are needed because of the distortion that occurs when conventional accounting practices are used. For example, conventional accounting practices treat a company's training and development expense as a cost that reduces the company's profit. Therefore, training and development appears to be an unnecessary cost. However, managers might have a different attitude about the value of training and development activities if they were treated as capital expenditures that increase the productive capacity of their assets in the same way that money spent to overhaul a piece of equipment or to renovate a building is treated as a capital expenditure and depreciated over the asset's useful life.

Human resource accounting measures can affect how personnel activities are evaluated. Short-term pressure to increase productivity may produce an immediate increase in profitability, but this short-term result may be achieved at the sacrifice of long-term profitability. On the other hand, the development of personnel systems and the creation of an effective management team require outlays of time and money that reduce the short-term profit. Conventional accounting methods understate income during periods of human asset building and overstate income in periods of human resource liquidation.

In spite of their value, human resource measures have been developed and used by very few companies. The Human Resource Accounting Committee of the American Accounting Association has recommended that human resource measures be used for internal decision making and also be reported to external parties in a company's annual report.[51] This recommendation, however, has largely gone unheeded. Nevertheless, the value of this information can be seen by considering the data in Table 3.3, which show the acquisition and development costs of one corporation that hired a total of ninety-six managers.[52] The costs are listed separately for first-line supervisors, middle managers, and high-level managers. These numbers show the actual replacement costs for hiring new mangers. The costs are significantly greater than most mangers would normally expect.

INTERNATIONAL HRM

WORK VALUES

The inducements-contributions balance for Soviet workers has changed significantly since 1930, providing a valuable comparison between American and Soviet employment patterns and an interesting analysis of worker motivation. When the communist ideology of the Stalin era was formed in the 1930s, it was believed that Soviet citizens were motivated to work by three factors: first, and above all, by a devotion to communism and the motherland; second, by fear of punishment for violations of labor discipline; and third, by the "material" (financial) incentives.[53]

TABLE 3.3   Human resource accounting average replacement costs for three levels of managers

	First-line Supervisor	Middle-level Manager	High-level Manager
Acquisition cost			
Recruiting and selection costs	$2,280	$7,600	$25,840
Hiring costs	760	6,460	13,300
Development cost			
Formal training and orientation	190	1,900	3,800
On-the-job training	3,420	11,400	19,380
Familiarization	7,220	25,460	38,760
Individual development	760	5,320	7,600
Total	$14,630	$58,140	$108,680

Source: The data for this table have been adjusted for inflation (1990 = 380) from the 1967 data reported by R. Lee Brummet, Eric G. Flamholtz, and William C. Pyle, "Human Resource Accounting: A Tool to Increase Managerial Effectiveness," *Management Accounting* (August 1969): 13.

Under Stalin's leadership a "statute of discipline" was established which imposed administrative discipline for violations of labor rules. Workers received severe punishment for such small infractions as tardiness to work or leaving the job without permission. This statute was abolished after Stalin's death in 1953, and gradually the harsh labor laws were relaxed.

During the 1950s and 1960s, Soviet leaders tried unsuccessfully to motivate workers by appealing to their devotion to the communist ideology rather than "material incentives." During this period labor leaders were dismayed by the high labor turnover and migration, which they interpreted as evidence of a lack of worker loyalty and inadequate job commitment. Over 600 studies by Soviet sociologists produced similar conclusions that turnover and migration occurred for material reasons, such as more money, better jobs, and improved family circumstances.

During the 1970s, Soviet sociologists examined the relationship between job satisfaction and productivity and for a brief period they claimed that improved working conditions would lead to greater productivity. Further research, however, failed to confirm this relationship, and they eventually concluded that wage incentives had a larger impact on productivity than previously acknowledged.

The focus of Soviet sociology during the 1980s turned to the work ethics of workers in an attempt to understand why some workers were conscientious and responsible while others were negligent. Researchers found that positive or negative attitudes toward work were deeply rooted in family influences and passed from one generation to the next. As Soviet sociologists began to describe the "good and bad workers," prominent Soviet politicians such as Mikhail Gorbachev and Yuri Andropov adopted the same labels as they talked about the labor force. Alcoholism, absenteeism, and careless work were serious problems among a growing segment of Soviet workers. Gorbachev drew attention to this issue by pleading for greater "social justice" to halt the exploitation of committed workers by a growing group of negligent ones. As the Soviet sociology of work evolved from ideology to pragmatism, corresponding changes in Soviet policies were manifested in greater openness and individual autonomy.

WORK GROUPS

Although the democratic reforms in Eastern Europe and the Soviet Union were surprising to many Western observers, these political changes were entirely consistent with the labor reforms that occurred in those countries during the preceding decade. By 1980 most of the communist countries had initiated work teams, called "brigades," that were similar to the autonomous work teams in Western countries, especially Sweden. The decade of the 1980s witnessed a dramatic increase in the number of workers who were members of brigades, especially in the Soviet Union, Cuba, Czechoslovakia, and Hungary. By the end of 1982, for example, the brigade movement in Czechoslovakia had over 200,000 work groups with about 3 million workers.[54]

The major driving forces behind the spread of the brigade movement were increased labor productivity and material incentives. Studies by the Scientific Research Institute of Labor in Moscow reported that the brigades improved all economic indicators, which pleased the party leaders, and they also contributed to increased wages, which pleased the workers.[55] The success of the brigades largely came from (1) decentralized leadership that allowed brigade leaders to make production decisions and (2) "material incentives" in the form of individual and group financial incentives that significantly increased worker motivation. Worker enthusiasm and improved productivity forced communist leaders to redefine many socialist philosophies regarding the compensation for labor and the distribution of wealth. Socialist ideologies moved clearly toward a pay-for-performance policy. Members of a brigade received an individual wage that could not be less than the minimum wage, plus a bonus that was based on the group's productivity and allocated according to a "coefficient of labor participation" (CLP). This coefficient was determined by brigade leaders in consultation with the brigade council, and it was used to reward each worker based on that member's contribution to the collective results.

In Hungary, some brigades were almost separate organizations and served as outside contractors. These units, called VGMKs, had remarkable autonomy and were responsible for organizing and regulating themselves, selecting members, and monitoring their own costs and quality. The success of these work groups and the perception that they embody socialist ideals suggests that work teams will become increasingly popular in the Soviet Union and Eastern Europe.

HOURS OF WORK

Although a 40-hour week has been fairly standard in the United States since the Depression, the hours of work in other countries have not been as standardized and in some countries they are changing. Policies also vary on the length of vacations and whether vacations are paid.

In England the average workweek is about 38 hours and it has not changed much in the past two decades. British workers log about 1,600 hours annually. The length of the annual paid vacation has increased, however. Three-fourths of all British workers have over five weeks of vacation and some even have six weeks. The Trade Union Congress in England has argued for reduced work hours by calling for 35 hours of work per week, six weeks annual vacation, and early retirement at age 60.

In West Germany a five-day workweek, six weeks of annual vacation, and 1,600 hours of annual work are recognized standards. The German trade unions are also attempting to mandate a reduction in work hours, similar to the legislative changes requested by the French unions. In France, 38.5 hours of work per week is officially recognized by law. Actual annual working hours in France average about 1,550 hours.

The workweek in Asian countries is much longer than the European workweek, but it is also declining. During the 1980s some Korean factory workers worked 10 to 12 hours daily all but two days of the year. However, the average workweek in Korea during the decade dropped from 56 to 52 hours. Similarly, the workweek in Singapore declined from 44 to 42 hours as additional companies eliminated the standard practice of working Saturday morning.

By 1990 Rengo (Japanese Private Sector Trade Union Congress) had succeeded in reducing the official number of annual working hours in Japan below 2,000 to 1,994, but the actual working hours averaged 2,160 because of overtime. For a variety of reasons, the Japanese workers work long workweeks. The number of annual weekend days off was officially 84 days, plus 18 days of paid vacation, for a total of 102 days off. But even though they were offered 18 days of paid vacation, they only used an average of 10.6 days. The Japanese workweek will continue to decline as additional companies adopt a five-day workweek as a standard labor practice.[56]

SUMMARY

A. To survive, an organization must be able to attract new employees and keep them.

B. An employment exchange occurs when an organization and its employees reach an informal agreement in which the inducements provided by the organization are equivalent to the contributions made by the employees.

C. Individuals sometimes abuse organizations through theft, careless work, and laziness. On the other hand, organizations sometimes abuse individuals by infringing on their personal rights and by creating an overwhelming influence on their values and attitudes.

D. Individuals expect to be treated fairly, and they have come to expect certain conditions as employee rights even though these rights have not been guar-

anteed by federal legislation. These rights include protection against unfair treatment, discrimination, harassment, and threatening conditions of work.

E. Career planning is important for individuals who desire meaningful employment. Individuals should be responsible for their own career planning and not assume that organizations will direct their careers.

F. Individuals typically go through four stages of career development in their working lives: exploration, establishment, maintenance, and decline.

G. The most prominent forms of career-development activities found in organizations include career counseling, career pathing, human resource planning, career information systems, management and supervisory development, training, and programs for special groups such as minorities or employees who are preparing for retirement.

H. There are five major alternatives to the standard five-day, 40-hour week: flextime, permanent part-time, job sharing, compressed workweek, and telecommuting. Flextime refers to a schedule where workers set their own starting time subject to certain constraints. Permanent part-time refers to treating a part-time job of less than 35 hours per week as a permanent job. Job sharing consists of allowing two employees to perform one full-time position. The compressed workweek alternative involves working longer hours per day but fewer days per week, such as the 4/40 plan of working four 10-hour days each week. Telecommuting allows employees to work at home. Each of these alternatives has advantages and disadvantages but the advantages outweigh the disadvantages for all but the compressed workweek.

I. Job enrichment is a potentially valuable method of increasing satisfaction and productivity. Job enrichment is the opposite of job specialization. Since job specialization has contributed greatly to increased productivity, job-enrichment programs should carefully avoid destroying the productive efficiency of specialization.

J. Job enlargement consists of adding several elements to enlarge a task. Job enrichment consists of giving the job holder greater skill variety, task identity, task significance, autonomy, and feedback. Increases in satisfaction and productivity are more likely to result from job enrichment than from job enlargement. Some of the most popular job-enrichment programs include horizontal and vertical loading, forming natural work units, establishing client relations, and opening feedback channels.

K. Quality of work life programs are changes in the traditional methods of work to improve the quality of life. QWL programs have four common goals: (1) more democratic participation of all employees, (2) sharing of the financial rewards of the organization, (3) greater job security, and (4) greater personal development. Some of the major QWL programs include autonomous work teams, quality circles, representation on the board of directors, labor-management committees, and employee ownership.

L. Organizational development (OD) refers to a series of planned changes to improve organizational effectiveness. It assumes that employees want to contribute to the goals of their organization and that group interaction can be improved to assist members in accomplishing these goals.

M. OD interventions generally focus on creating change in a specific target area. Sensitivity training is a popular interpersonal intervention, team-building meetings are a popular group intervention. A conflict-resolution meeting is a popular inter-group intervention, and organizational interventions include survey feedback and structural change.

N. Human resource programs ought to be carefully evaluated by human resource managers. The traditional measures of effectiveness include job satisfaction, absenteeism, and turnover. The best way to measure job satisfaction is to use a written questionnaire.

O. Absenteeism and turnover are influenced by numerous factors, especially economic conditions and job satisfaction. To keep absenteeism and turnover at acceptable levels, managers need to establish good working conditions and fair and equitable wages. To know what acceptable levels of absenteeism and turnover are, managers should distinguish between voluntary and involuntary reasons for missing work and collect accurate data measuring the seriousness of the problem.

P. Personnel audits evaluate the effectiveness of the human resource department by asking members both inside and outside the department to rate the department's performance on each of its major objectives and responsibilities.

Q. Human resource accounting consists of measuring data about human resources and communicating this information to interested parties, especially stockholders and investors. The three most popular human resource measures are outlay costs, which include all of the costs associated with recruiting, selecting, and training the present employees; replacement costs, which estimate how much it would cost to replace a firm's existing employees; and human resource value, which measures the expected contribution employees will make to the firm's future income.

QUESTIONS

1. Except for the military, which has the potential to draft new recruits, organizations must rely upon their own resources to attract new employees. What can an organization do if it begins to lose its membership? What happens if it fails?

2. What are the most important inducements a bank has to offer its employees? What are the inducements offered by a college or university?

3. Is it possible for both an organization and an individual to feel that the inducements-contributions balance is weighted in favor of each? Why or why not?

4. How do individuals abuse organizations and how do organizations abuse people?

5. What are the consequences of inadequate career planning? What should be the role of the human resource department in providing career-development activities?

6. Which jobs are particularly well suited for flextime, permanent part-time, job sharing, compressed workweek, and telecommuting? What are some jobs that are poorly suited to each of these alternative patterns of work?

7. What changes would you recommend for enriching the job of a teaching assistant who grades exams and papers?

8. What are the advantages of autonomous work teams? Can a work group really be free of the influence and control of management? What constraints are necessary?

9. How are quality circles different from a regular employee-suggestion system?

10. Should labor-management committees get involved in discussions about the labor agreement that is normally negotiated at the bargaining table? Why or why not?

11. If organizations are collections of people, why can't you change an organization by simply changing each individual?

12. What is the value of human resource accounting measures? How could this information help managers or investors make better decisions?

KEY TERMS

Autonomous work team: A group of workers that is largely self-managed and only loosely directed by management. The group collectively decides who will perform which job and members typically rotate from job to job.

Career pathing: The development of a sequential series of career activities that an individual might pursue during his or her career.

Compressed workweek:. An alternative work schedule in which employees work fewer days per week by working more hours on the days they work. The most typical compressed workweek schedule is four 10-hour days, called the 4/40 plan.

Contributions: The behaviors an individual is willing to contribute to an organization, such as dependable attendance, dependable performance, and spontaneous and innovative behaviors.

Core period: The period of time when employees on flexible work hours must be at work.

Dual career ladders: A separate career track for technical specialists who advance within their profession.

Employment exchange: An agreement in which an individual agrees to provide labor in exchange for rewards offered by an organization.

Ergonomics: The application of technology and engineering to human abilities, interests, and feelings. Sometimes called biotechnology, it considers the mutual adjustment of people and machines in improving organizational effectiveness.

Flextime: An alternative work schedule that allows employees to set their own work hours subject to specific contraints, such as requiring them to work a specific number of hours per day or per week and to be at work during a core period.

Human resource value: The expected financial contribution to a firm's net income for individuals at various levels in the firm.

Inducements-contributions balance: The balance achieved in an employment exchange where the rewards offered by an organization are roughly equivalent to the contributions that an employee is required to make.

Involuntary absenteeism and turnover:. Absenteeism or turnover that is caused by forces beyond the control of employees.

Job-absence rate: The rate of absenteeism defined by the Bureau of National Affairs as the number of worker-days lost through job absences during the month multiplied by 100, divided by the product of the average number of employees times the number of workdays.

Job sharing: A work arrangement whereby two workers split one job. Each worker is responsible for his or her share of the job. They split the salary, the benefits, and the responsibilities.

Multiskilling: The practice of training workers to perform a variety of tasks.

Outlay cost: A human resource accounting measure that represents the costs of recruiting, selecting, and training the present employees.

Permanent part-time: A work arrangement permitting employees to work less than 35 hours per week. This arrangement is considered a permanent rather than a temporary part-time job.

Personnel audit: An evaluation of how well the human resource department is performing its responsibilities and objectives.

Quality circle: An organizational improvement strategy that involves work groups meeting periodically, usually one hour per week, to discuss ways to improve productivity.

Replacement cost: A human resource accounting measure that estimates how much it would cost to replace a firm's existing employees in current dollars.

Sensitivity training:. An unstructured group discussion in which members of the group share their perceptions and feelings about each other and what is happening in the organization. Such a discussion is designed to create greater self-awareness and sensitivity to other individuals and to group processes.

Telecommuting:. An alternative pattern of work where employees work at home and communicate with the home office electronically by computer, telephone, or facsimile.

T-group:. T-group (*T* for *training*) is another name for sensitivity training.

Voluntary absenteeism and turnover:. Absenteeism and turnover that result from a personal choice of the employee.

C O N C L U D I N G   C A S E

Unwanted Promotions

The following comments were made by the vice-president of operations of a major West Coast steel mill:

> The steel industry in America is really suffering and our company is hurting just as badly as any of the rest. For the past few years we've blamed our troubles on foreign steel imports and cried to Washington for help. The government hasn't been very sympathetic; they don't believe there is enough dumping of subsidized steel [by other countries] to justify controlling it. We've tried to convince them that foreign steel dumping is

> going to destroy American steel, and we really believe it. But our most serious problem is not foreign steel dumping; our most serious problems are our own internal labor problems.

> The greatest threat to the future of our company right now is our inability to promote capable employees into responsible positions. We have all kinds of promotion opportunities in our higher labor grades and we're having to fill some of them with unqualified people because the qualified people will not accept them.

At first we thought the reason so many employees turned down promotions was because they did not want to change from union to management. That might be a factor sometimes, but most of the promotions are within the union jobs and they still refuse them. We also considered the pay differentials because we knew some union members earned more than their supervisors. Although we found a few problems, most of the promotions provided rather substantial wage incentives.

Last week we asked one fellow if he would like to be promoted to an operator's job. We thought he would be an excellent operator, and it was the fourth time we had asked him. Each time he said no. Just for my own curiosity, I went out to visit him and asked why he refused the promotion.

His answer was quite disturbing. He said he had no desire for a promotion; all it would mean is more headaches and worry. He didn't want a job with a lot of responsibility because then he wouldn't feel free to call in sick whenever he wanted a day off. In his present job as a laborer he could get away with being absent occasionally. But if he agreed to be an operator, he would feel obligated to be at work each day. He realized that the operator's job was still in the union and that it paid almost four dollars more per hour. But he said both he and his wife worked, and he didn't want more money as much as he wanted more leisure time to play with his "toys" (a camper and two trail bikes). "Frankly," he said, "I don't like to work. I'd quit working right now if I had enough money. But since I don't, I have to put in my time."

Questions:

1. How credible is this executive's assessment of why the employee refused the promotion? What are other possible explanations why employees might refuse promotions?
2. Is the promotion problem really as serious as the vice-president of operations seems to think it is? Why or why not?
3. What can companies do about the problem of employees not accepting promotions?

NOTES

1. James G. March and Herbert A. Simon, *Organizations* (New York: Wiley, 1966), Chapter 4; see also Cherlyn Skromme Granrose and James D. Portwood, "Matching Individual Career Plans and Organizational Career Management," *Academy of Management Journal* 30 (December 1987): 699–720.

2. Daniel Katz and Robert L. Kahn, *The Social Psychology of Organizations*, Second Edition (New York: Wiley, 1978), Chapter 13.

3. R. A. Rupe, "Formula for Loss Prevention," *Retail Control* (March 1980): 2–15; see also "The Seventh Annual Survey of Security and Loss Prevention," *An Ounce of Prevention* (New York: National Mass Retailing Institute and Arthur Young and Company, 1985), pp. 22–43.

4. W. Steve Albrecht, Marshall B. Romney, David J. Cherrington, I. Reed Payne, and Allan J. Roe, *How to Detect and Prevent Business Fraud* (Englewood Cliffs, NJ: Prentice-Hall, 1982).

5. Paul Scelsi, "Time Is Money-Lots of it," *Management World* 17 (November/December, 1988): 19–20.

6. David W. Ewing, *Freedom Inside the Organization* (New York: MacGraw-Hill, 1977), p. 7.

7. Daniel W. Kendall, "Rights Across the Waters," *Personnel Administrator* 33 (March 1988), 58–61.

8. Urs E. Gattiker and Laurie Larwood, "Predictors for Managers' Career Mobility, Success, and Satisfaction," *Human Relations* 41 (August 1988): 569–91; Dennis C. Sweeney, Dean Haller, and Frederick Sale, Jr., "Individually Controlled Career Counseling," *Training and Development Journal* 41 (August 1987): 58–61.

9. Jerry W. Gilley, "Career Development as a Partnership," *Personnel Administrator* 33 (April 1988): 62–68; Glenn J. Gooding, "Career Moves—for the Employee, for the Organization," *Personnel* 65 (April 1988): 112–16.

10. John VanMaanen and Edgar Schein, "Career Development," *Improving Life At Work*, Eds., J. Richard Hackman and J. Lloyd Suttle (Santa Monica, Calif.: Goodyear, 1977); William L. Cron, "Industrial Salesperson Development: A Career Stages Perspective," *Journal of Marketing* 48 (Fall 1984): 41–52; William L. Cron, Alan Dubinsky, and Ronald E. Michaels, "The Influence of Career Stages on Components of Salesperson Motivation," *Journal of Marketing* 52 (January 1988): 78–92; William L. Cron and John W. Slocum, Jr., "Career Stages Approach to Managing the Sales Force," *Journal of Consumer Marketing* 3 (Fall 1986): 11–20; Peggy Simonsen, "Concepts of Career Development," *Training and Development Journal* 40 (November 1986): 70–74.

11. Lorraine M. Carulli, Cheryl L. Noroian, and Cindy Levine, "Employee-driven Career Development," *Personnel Administrator* 34 (March 1989): 66–70; Joan P. Klubnik, "Putting Together a Career Development Program," *Management Solutions* 33 (January 1988): 31–36; Sandy B. Leibowitz, "Designing Career Development Systems: Principles and Practices," *Human Resource Planning* 10 (Number 4, 1987): 195–207; Steven Slavenski, "Career Development: A Systems Approach," *Training and Development Journal* 41 (February 1987): 56–60.

12. Raymond A. Noe, "An Investigation of the Determinants of Successful Assigned Mentoring Relationships," *Personnel Psychology* 41 (Autumn 1988): 457–78; James D. Portwood and Cherlyn Skromme Granrose, "Organizational Career Management Programs: What's Available? What's Effective?" *Human Resource Planning* 9 (September 1986): 107–19.

13. Barbara Moses, "Giving Employees a Future," *Training and Development Journal* 41 (December 1987): 25–28.

14. James E. Harris, "Moving Managers Internationally: The Care and Feeding of Ex-Patriots," *Human Resource Planning* 12, no. 1 (1989): 49–53; Stephan A. Laser, "Career Development in a Changing Environment," *Journal of Managerial Psychology* 3, no. 2 (1988): 23–25.

15. Neil A. Strout, "The Manager's Role in Staff Development," *Training* 25 (August 1988): 47–51.

16. Frances Williams, "Flexible Working Hours," *European Trends* 4 (1986): 59–62.

17. Edward J. Harrick, Gene R. Vanek, and Joseph F. Michlitsch, "Alternative Work Schedules, Productivity, Leave Usage, and Employee Attitudes: A Field Study," *Public Personnel Management* 15 (Summer 1986): 159–69; Richard E. Kopelman, "Alternative Work Schedules and Productivity: A Review of the Evidence," *National Productivity Review* 5 (Spring 1986): 150–65; Jean B. McGuire and Joseph R. Liro, "Flexible Work Schedules, Work Attitudes, and Perceptions of Productivity," *Public Personnel Management* 15 (Spring 1986): 65–73.

18. Carl S. Greenwald and Judith Liss, "Part-time Workers Can Bring Higher Productivity," *Harvard Business Review* 51 (September–October 1973): 20–22; Hermine Zegat Levine, "Alternative Work Schedules: Do They Meet Workforce Needs?" *Personnel* 64 (February 1987); 57–62.

19. Patricia Leighton, "Bridging the Skills Shortage: Job Sharing," *Industrial Society* (December 1988): 21–23; David Clutterbuck, "Why a Job Shared is Not a Job Halved," *International Management* 35 (October 1979): 45–47; Gretl S. Meier, *Job Sharing: A New Pattern for Quality of Work Life* (Kalamazoo, Mich.: W.E. Upjohn Institute for Employment Research, 1978).

20. Greenwald and Liss, "Part-time Workers."

21. "Effect of Scheduled Overtime," in *Coming to Grips with Some Major Problems in the Construction Industry* (New York: Business Roundtable Report, 1974): 1–14; Randall B. Dunham, John L. Pierce, and Maria B. Castenada, "Alternative Work Schedules: Two Field Quasi-experiments," *Personnel Psychology* 40 (Summer 1987): 215–42.

22. Sandy Gould, "12-Hour-Shift Plant Schedule Improves Operator Productivity," *Power Engineering* 92 (November 1988): 38–39.

23. Lad Kuzela, "Sandy's Working At Home Today," *Industry Week* 233 (June 1, 1988): 34–35.

24. J. Richard Hackman and Greg R. Oldham, "Motivation Through the Design of Work: Test of a Theory," *Organizational Behavior and Human Performance* 16 (1967): 250–79; J. Richard Hackman, Greg R. Oldham, Robert Janson, and Kenneth Purdy, "A New Strategy for Job Enrichment," *California Management Review* 17 (Summer 1975): 57–71; and Greg R. Oldham, "Job Characteristics and Internal Motivation: The Moderating Effect of Interpersonal and Individual Variables," *Human Relations* 29, no. 6 (1976): 559–69.

25. Norm Alster, "What Flexible Workers Can Do," *Fortune* 119 (February 13, 1989): 62–66.

26. Gervase R. Bush, "Temporary or Permanent Middle-Management Groups?—Correlates with Attitudes in QWL Changes Projects," *Group and Organization Studies* 12 (March 1987): 23–37; Michael A. Conte and Jan Svejnar, "Productivity Affects of Worker Participation in Management, Profit-Sharing, Worker Ownership of Assets and Unionization in U.S. Firms," *International Journal of Industrial Organization* 6 (March 1988): 139–51; Colin Hales, "Quality of Working Life, Job Redesign and Participation in a Service Industry: A Rose By Any Other Name?" *Service Industries* 7 (July 1987): 253–73; David R. Kamerschen, Robert J. Hall, and David A. Dilts, "Ownership and Management of the Firm: Another Look," *Business and Society* 25 (Spring 1986): 8–14; Katherine J. Klein, "Employee Stock Ownership and Employee Attitudes: A

Test of Three Models," *Journal of Applied Psychology* 72 (May 1987): 319–32; Katherine J. Klein and Rosalie J. Hall, "Correlates of Employee Satisfaction with Stock Ownership: Who Likes an ESOP Most?" *Journal of Applied Psychology* 73 (November 1988): 630–38; David Nachmias, "The Quality of Worklife in the Federal Bureaucracy: Conceptualization and Measurement," *American Review of Public Administration* 18 (June 1988): 165–73; Patrick Michael Rooney, "Worker Participation in Employee-Owned Firms," *Journal of Economic Issues* 22 (June 1988): 451–58; Robert P. Steel and Russell F. Lloyd, "Cognitive, Affective, and Behavioral Outcomes of Participation in Quality Circles: Conceptual and Empirical Findings," *Journal of Applied Behavioral Science* 24, no. 1 (1988): 1–17; James W. Thacker and Mitchell W. Fields, "Union Involvement in Quality-Of-Worklife Efforts: A Longitudinal Investigation," *Personnel Psychology* 40 (Spring 1987): 97–111.

27. The experiments at Volvo and SAAB and many other QWL experiments are described in Paul Dickson, *The Future of the Workplace* (New York: Weybright and Talley, 1975).

28. John Kersell, "Public Sector Teams in Canada: Evaluating Quality Teamwork," *Journal for Quality and Participation* 11 (June 1988): 28–30.

29. John Hoerr, "Blue Collars in the Boardroom: Putting Business First," *Business Week* (December 14, 1987): 126, 128; Robert N. Stern, "Participation by Representation: Workers on Boards of Directors in the United States and Abroad," *Work and Occupations* 15 (November 1988): 396–422.

30. Derek O. Jones, "The Productivity Effects of Worker Directors and Financial Participation by Employees in the Firm: The Case of British Retail Cooperatives," *Industrial and Labor Relations Review* 41 (October 1987): 79-92.

31. Gervase R. Bush, "Developing Cooperative Labor-Management Relations in Unionized Factories: A Multiple Case Study of Quality Circle and Parallel Organizations Within Joint Quality of Worklife Projects," *Journal of Applied Behavioral Science* 24, no. 2 (1988): 128–50; John L. Cotton, David A. Vollrath, and Kirk L. Froggatt, Mark L. Lengnick-Hall, and Kenneth R. Jennings, "Employee Participation: Diverse Forms and Different Outcomes," *Academy of Management Review* 13 (January 1988): 8–22.

32. Avner Ben-Ner, "Comparative Empirical Observations on Worker-Owned and Capitalist Firms," *International Journal of Industrial Organization* 6 (March 1988): 7–31; Robert J. Paul, Yar M. Ebadi, and David A. Dilts, "Commitment in Employee-Owned Firms: Involvement or Entrapment?" *Quarterly Journal of Business and Economics* 26 (Autumn 1987): 81–99.

33. Warner Woodworth, "The Emergence of Economic Democracy in the United States," *Economic Analysis and Workers' Self Management* 15 (1981): 207–18.

34. I. Ross, "What Happens When Employees Buy the Company," *Fortune* (June 2, 1980): 108–11.

35. Michael Conte and Arnold S. Tannenbaum, "Employee-Owned Companies: Is the Difference Measurable?" *Monthly Labor Review* 101 (July 1978): 23–28.

36. William G. Dyer, *Team Building: Issues and Alternatives*, 2nd edition (Reading: Mass.: Addison-Wesley, 1987).

37. John A. Byrne, "Business Fads: What's In—And Out," *Business Week* (January 20, 1986): 52–60.

38. Amos Drory and Boas Shamir, "Effects of Organizational and Life Variables on Job Satisfaction and Burnout," *Group and Organization Studies* 13 (December 1988): 441–55.

39. "Job Satisfaction Hits Fifteen Year Low: New Era for Working America?" *The Public Pulse* (March 1989): 1–3.

40. A. H. Brayfield and W. H. Crockett, "Employee Attitudes and Employee Performance," *Psychological Bulletin* 52 (1955): 396–424.

41. Michael A. Abelson, "Examination of Avoidable and Unavoidable Turnover," *Journal of Applied Psychology* 72 (August 1987): 382–86; Kenneth Teel and Sal M. Kukalis, "Is Voluntary Turnover Really Voluntary?" *Personnel Journal* 67 (November 1988): 80–84.

42. "BNA's Quarterly Report on Job Absence and Turnover, 3rd Quarter 1989," December 14, 1989.

43. Hilde Behrend and Stuart Pocock, "Absence and the Individual: A Six-Year Study in One Organization," *International Labor Review* (November–December 1976): 311–27.

44. Charles L. Hulin, "Job Satisfaction and Turnover in a Female Clerical Population," *Journal of Applied Psychology* 50 (1966): 280–85; Charles L. Hulin, "Effect of Changes in Job Satisfaction Levels on Employee Turnover," *Journal of Applied Psychology* 52 (1968): 122–26.

45. Edward F. Fern, Ramon A. Avila and Dhruv Grewal, "Sales Force Turnover: Those Who Left and Those Who Stayed," *Industrial Marketing Management* 18 (February 1989): 1–9.

46. Mary A. Blegen, Charles W. Mueller, and James L. Price, "Measurement of Kinship Responsibility for Organizational Research," *Journal of Applied Psychology* 73 (August 1988): 402–409; Linda K. Good, Grovalynn F. Sisler, and James W. Gentry, "Antecedents of Turnover Intentions Among Retail Management Personnel," *Journal of Retailing* 64 (Fall 1988): 295–314.

47. John A. Hooper, "A Strategy for Increasing the Human Resource Department's Effectiveness," *The Personnel Administrator* 29 (June 1984): 141–50.

48. Quoted from the film "Management of Human Assets," produced by BNA Films, 1967. See also Rensis Likert, *The Human Organization* (New York: McGraw-Hill, 1967).

49. Henry L. Dahl, "Measuring the Human ROI," *Management Review* (January 1979): 44–50; Sue A. Ebersberger, "Human Resources Accounting: Can We Afford It?" *Training and Development Journal* (August 1981): 37–40; Ferdinand A. Gul, "Relationship of Dogmatism and Confidence in the Evaluation of Accounting Information," *Psychological Reports* 52 (1983): 475–78; Bruce G. Meyers and Hugh M. Shane, "Human Resources Accounting for Managerial Decision: A Capital Budgeting Approach," *Personnel Administrator* 29 (January 1984): 29–35: Sherman R. Roser, "A Practical Approach to the Use of Human Resource Accounting," *Managerial Planning* (September/October 1983): 35–39.

50. Eric G. Flamholtz, Gerald D. Searfoss, and Russell Coff, "Developing Human Resource Accounting as a Human Resource Decision Support System," *Accounting Horizons* 2 (September 1988): 1–9; R. Lee Brummet, Eric G. Flamholtz, and William C. Pyle, "Human Resource Accounting: A Tool to Increase Managerial Effectiveness," *Management Accounting* (August 1969): 12–15.

51. Human Resource Accounting Committee, "Report of the Committee on Human Resource Accounting," *The Accounting Review* 48 (Supplement 1973): 169–85.

52. R. Lee Brummet, Eric G. Flamholtz, and William C. Pyle, "Human Resource Accounting: A Tool to Increase Managerial Effectiveness," *Management Accounting* (August 1969): 12–15.

53. Vladimir Shlapentokh, "Evolution in the Soviet Sociology of Work: From Ideology to Pragmatism," *Work and 'Occupations* 14 (August 1987): 410–33; Paul R. Gregory and Janet E. Kohlhase, "The Earnings of Soviet Workers: Evidence from the Soviet Interview Project," *Review of Economics and Statistics* 70, (February 1988): 23–35; H. Stephen Gardner, "The Sluggish Soviet Economy," *Baylor Business Review* 3 (Winter 1985): 9–13.

54. Lajos Hethy, "New Developments in Collective Forms of Work Organization and Socialist Countries," *International Labor Review* 125 (November–December 1986): 659–674; Alexis Codina Jimenez, "Worker Incentives in Cuba," *World Development* 15, No. 1 (1987): 127–38; Andrew Zimbalist, "Incentives and Planning in Cuba," *American Research Review* 14, No. 1 (1989): 65–93.

55. Lajos Hethy, "New Developments in Collective Forms in Socialist Countries."

56. "Shorter Working Hours Says Union Leader," *Productivity in Japan* 2 (Summer 1989): 3–5.

Job Analysis, Human Resource Planning, and Privacy Protection

Learning Objectives

After studying this chapter, you should be able to:

1. Explain how human resource planning provides a foundation for recruitment and selection.
2. Describe the interaction between business planning and human resource planning.
3. Explain how job descriptions and job specifications are developed and used.
4. Explain how jobs are described in the *Dictionary of Occupational Titles*.
5. Identify the kinds of information that should be contained in a human resource information system, and explain where it comes from and how it can be used.
6. Describe the major methods of long-term forecasting and explain how long-term forecasts interact with short-term forecasts.
7. List the major causes of turnover.
8. Explain the alternative methods of dealing with a surplus of labor.
9. Illustrate how replacement charts are used in succession planning.
10. Identify the laws that protect the privacy of employees and explain their restrictions on the collection and dissemination of information.

Chapter Outline

Human Resource Planning Process
Staffing Model / Interaction Between Business Planning and Human Resource Planning

Job Analysis
Job Descriptions and Job Specifications / Uses of Job Analysis / Job Identification / Job-analysis Methods

Analysis of Present Employees

Categorizing Jobs / Human Resource Information Systems / Sources of
Employee Information

Forecasting Employment Needs

Short-term Forecasting / Long-term Forecasting

Projected Staffing Requirements

Net Projections / Turnover Analysis / Surplus Personnel / Management
Succession and Development / Corporate Restructuring

Privacy Protection

Ethical Issues in HRP / Legal Protections

International HRM

I N T R O D U C T O R Y   C A S E

Uncoordinated Employment

The need for human resource planning is illustrated by the hiring and layoff problems of Collings Construction Company. The company employs about 1,200 workers. The central office staff consists of 60 employees, and the rest of the employees are assigned to construction projects supervised by project managers. The project managers are fairly autonomous and do most of their own hiring and firing.

The hiring of technical and professional employees is handled by Bruce Cole, who is also responsible for college relations. When a project manager needs a professional or technical employee, Bruce recruits two or three likely candidates and lets the project manager make the final decision. Collings Construction Company does not have a central human resource planning office, and the project managers make no effort to coordinate their hiring and firing. During the past two years, Bruce has observed some serious problems that a human resource planning system could have prevented.

Last October, the manager of Project A requested three MBA graduates with construction experience. Bruce explained to the project manager that October was not a good time to recruit new MBA graduates. Because the graduates were needed, however, Bruce recruited until he filled the three positions. The qualifications of all three recruits were marginal, and their academic records were mediocre. Only one of them had previous construction experience.

In November, the manager of Project B laid off twenty-three employees, including four electrical engineers who has been with the company for many years. Bruce questioned the decision, but the manager claimed that with the completion of the present projects there was nothing for these electrical engineers to do. The engineers were given six months' severance pay from the company, and they were eligible to collect unemployment compensation. Two months after the engineers had been laid off, the manager of Project C requested two electrical engineers for a new project. Bruce immediately tried to rehire the former employees, but was disappointed to learn that they had already accepted employment with other companies.

In examining the situation, Bruce discovered that the same problem was occurring in skilled jobs. Skilled workers laid off by one project manager were frequently hired by another project manager. Bruce also discovered that to avoid shortages, managers would sometimes retain surplus skilled

workers while other managers were having people in the same trade work overtime to satisfy labor needs.

When the company was small, the staffing problems were not so serious, but now that the company has over 1,200 employees, the problems have become significant.

Questions:

1. How would a comprehensive human resource planning system help Collings Construction Company? What features would such a system need?
2. Why is a human resource planning system more valuable when economic conditions are unstable?

THE HUMAN RESOURCE PLANNING PROCESS

Personnel planning is usually called human resource planning to emphasize the idea that planning for a firm's human resources is as important as planning for its capital and financial resources. Managers have always been very concerned about planning for their capital and financial resource needs, but only recently have they become equally concerned about planning for their human resource needs.

STAFFING MODEL

Although human resource planning has a major impact on organizational effectiveness, its importance is often overlooked. The human resource planning process precedes recruitment and selection activities and provides the foundation for personnel staffing, as shown in Figure 4.1. Before new employees are recruited, someone needs to decide what kinds of employees are needed and how many, and to correlate this decision with the organization's strategic business plans. To reach its long-term goals, an organization must have the proper mix of employees with the necessary skills and background. Hiring new employees should be based on the projected staffing requirements: if the projection indicates a demand for new employees, recruiting activities should be initiated; if it indicates a surplus of personnel, early retirements, layoffs, or other actions may be necessary.

LINE VERSUS STAFF RESPONSIBILITY

The responsibility for developing and implementing a human resource plan generally belongs to both line managers and staff specialists. Line managers are primarily responsible for business planning, including long-range, middle-range, and short-range plan-

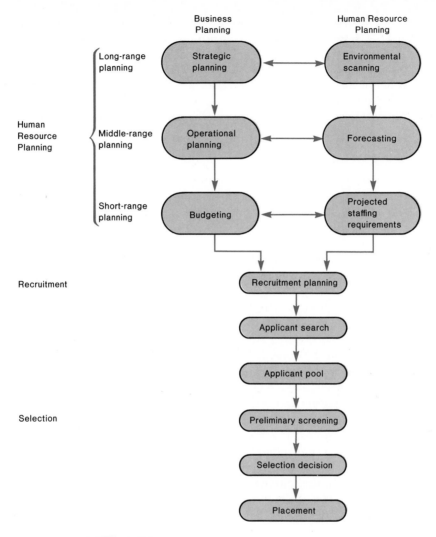

FIGURE 4.1 Staffing Model.

ning. Although staff specialists may help to establish the business plans, they usually serve in an advisory capacity only.

Top management generally assumes full responsibility for long-range planning and major responsibility for middle-range planning. Long-range planning involves directing the destiny of an organization by establishing a corporate philosophy and an organizational mission. Middle-range planning consists of defining the goals and objectives that an organization will pursue during the next two to five years. Short-range planning consists of developing yearly budgets, performance goals, and annual operating plans. Managers at all levels ought to be involved in short-range planning, especially supervisors and unit managers.

Once business plans have been established, human resource specialists generally develop and maintain a human resource planning system. An organization with a human resource planning system typically has a human resource planning manager or analyst who reports to the human resource executive. The human resource planning manager is responsible for maintaining the information and systems necessary for human resource planning. This responsibility includes analyzing changes in the labor force, forecasting the human resources needed to achieve the business objectives, and maintaining information about present employees.

NEED FOR A SYSTEM

A formal human resource planning system is not essential in a small organization. Until an organization has more than two or three hundred employees, human resource planning activities can generally be accomplished by one or two top executives. When there are fewer than two hundred employees in an organization, the top executives generally know all of the supervisors and managers, can predict when they are likely to leave, and can even name the most likely replacements. Unless the positions change rapidly, one individual should be able to remember this information with the aid of an organizational chart and a few notes.

As organizations become larger, however, a more sophisticated human resource planning system is needed. A simple system that relies on someone's memory might be adequate with a couple hundred employees, but when there are 200,000 employees, an organization must have a formal, well-developed system. In an extremely large organization the efforts of many people must be combined to produce a unified product. Forms must be developed to obtain the relevant information, and numerous individuals, including supervisors, managers, and corporate planners, must be involved in providing this information. A system also must be designed to process the information, since several individuals must be involved in collecting and synthesizing it. Decision rules need to be established so that each individual knows when a specific piece of information calls for an action plan and where the action plan needs to be sent. Information about training needs should be sent to the training and development office; projected staffing requirements should be relayed to the recruiting office; an analysis of the forecasted employment levels should be submitted to top management; and an analysis of replacement needs should be sent to the managers who will be involved in making the replacement decisions. The vehicles that are typically used to integrate these activities are the annual performance-evaluation process and the compensation system. These activities require managers to complete the relevant forms and process the necessary information to create career paths, succession plans, and other human resource plans.[1]

A human resource planning system should only be as sophisticated as the situation warrants. Planning forms and questionnaires should only ask for necessary information and, where possible, the processing of the paperwork should be simplified to avoid a paper-shuffling jungle. Unless the planning system is structured efficiently, it could cost more in time and effort than it is worth.

STAGES OF DEVELOPMENT

A highly sophisticated planning system cannot be designed and implemented all at once. It takes time and experience to design a system that will fit an organization's needs and be accepted by organizational leaders. In the early stages of human resource planning, the employment forecasts are highly subjective and informal. As the system matures, however, the forecasting process becomes more elaborate, using formal methods of statistical estimation and computers to analyze and store the information.

Human resource planning systems vary in their level of complexity and sophistication. Four kinds of systems can be identified that correspond with different stages of development.[2] These four stages are listed in Table 4.1. In Stage I, human resource forecasts are highly informal and subjective. Managers establish organizational goals and discuss the human resource needs that will be required to achieve these goals in the short run. In Stage II, human resource needs are forecast for the coming year, usually in a rather simple way, using "rules of thumb" or past experience. These forecasts are communicated to other managers in the organization, and at the same time information is obtained identifying the talents of individuals and their interests in promotion. In Stage

---

TABLE 4.1 Stages of human resource development

Stage I
- Managers discuss goals and plans and try to estimate the numbers of people they will need in the short-term.
- Highly informal and subjective.

Stage II
- The annual planning and budgeting process includes an assessment of labor needs.
- The quantity and quality of talent needs are specified as far out in the future as possible.
- Management succession and the readiness of successors is analyzed.

Stage III
- Computer-generated analyses are used to examine causes of problems and future trends regarding supply and demand of talent.
- Computers are used to relieve managers of forecasting routine tasks such as vacancies or turnover.
- Career paths and career progress are analyzed using computer data files.
- Current data on the skills and interests of employees are maintained in a computerized human resource information system.

State IV
- On-line modeling and simulation of talent needs, flows, and costs are used to aid in a continuing process of updating projected needs, staffing plans, career opportunities, and program plans.
- Simulated forecasts with varying assumptions provide the best possible current information for managerial decisions.
- Economic, employment, and social data are exchanged with other companies and with the government.

III, future human resource needs are forecast with the aid of a computer and sophisticated forecasting models. Employees are assisted in mapping their career paths and in planning for their futures. Stage IV involves a continuous process of developing future forecasts of employment needs. The career interests of individuals are disseminated both within the organization and among other organizations to help employees find an ideal occupation.

In some organizations a simple Stage I model involving informal discussions may be adequate. For them, a more elaborate system may be too costly and not productive. On the other hand, organizations such as American Telephone and Telegraph (AT&T), International Business Machines (IBM), and the United States Military need and already have personnel planning systems that approach the sophistication of Stage IV.[3] Each organization needs to determine its ideal human resource planning system. Conceptually, every organization could have a totally integrated, complete, and highly functional human resource planning system, but an elaborate system may be more costly and time consuming than the needs of an organization warrant.

INTERACTION BETWEEN BUSINESS PLANNING AND HUMAN RESOURCE PLANNING

Human resource planning should not occur in isolation. The size of an organization's work force, including its occupational mix, should be based on its business plans. In every organization someone should ask, "How many of which types of employees will be required to achieve our organizational goals?" As shown in Figure 4.2, three levels of human resource planning need to occur, with each of the three levels interacting with a corresponding level of business planning.[4]

LONG-RANGE PLANNING

To survive more than the next year or two, organizations must engage in long-range **strategic planning**. Top executives need to formulate a corporate philosophy that identifies what an organization is about, what it expects to do, and why it exists. The organizational mission needs to be examined to determine what useful products or services the organization should produce. In addition, the strategic planning should include a careful analysis of the strengths and weaknesses of the organization. Does the organization have a competitive advantage in its products or services that it should pursue in the future? Are there serious weaknesses that will injure or destroy the organization in the long run?

The strategic planning also should involve a long-range analysis of employment. This analysis, which is called **environmental scanning**, consists of a careful review of the composition of the labor force, including demographic changes, social and cultural changes, changes in the labor supply, and changes in laws and regulatory agencies. Each of these changes could have a significant influence on the availability of personnel, as described in Chapter 2. An organization cannot achieve its long-range strategic goals without the necessary personnel, and if the long-range planning indicates that the necessary personnel will not be available, the strategic plans may need to be modified.

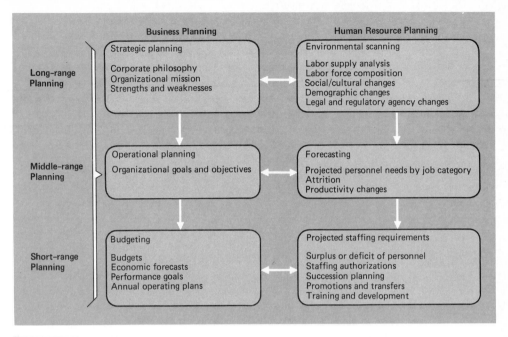

FIGURE 4.2 Interaction between business planning and human resource planning.

MIDDLE-RANGE PLANNING

Middle-range business planning consists of formulating the specific organizational goals and objectives that the organization expects to achieve within the next two to five years. These plans may be stated in terms of sales, the number of units produced, or some other index of business activity.

Achieving these goals and objectives requires the proper mix of personnel. Middle-range human resource planning involves forecasting how many employees will be needed within each job category to achieve the business goals. Since some of the present work force will leave due to turnover, the attrition rate must be estimated and included in the calculations. Productivity changes also must be forecast, since changes in productivity will influence the employment needs. Some of the most popular forecasting methods are explained later in this chapter.

SHORT-RANGE PLANNING

In the short run, business planning typically involves developing budgets, or annual operating plans. Most organizations probably do some form of short-term business planning even if they do not have elaborate long-range business plans, since short-term business planning is important for the economic success and survival of most organizations. Many studies in the accounting literature have demonstrated the importance of budgets and economic forecasts.[5] These planning tools help to coordinate the activities within the organization and to guide the activities of individual employees as they work toward profitable outcomes.

Short-range planning often overlooks the human resource requirements. Budgets and economic forecasts are frequently developed without a careful analysis of whether the human resources will be available to achieve them. The major responsibility for projecting human resource needs belongs to each operating officer. Supervisors and managers should anticipate the numbers of employees and the kinds of skills and training needed to achieve the business objectives. If more employees will be needed, staffing authorizations should be prepared and sent to the people responsible for recruiting. On the other hand, if a surplus of employees is forecast, administrators must decide how the work force should be reduced. The short-range human resource plan also should include an analysis of promotions and transfers, which is called **succession planning**, and should project whether these changes will necessitate additional training and development activities.

Short-range plans typically have a great influence on the day-to-day activities of an organization. Although long-range plans provide an important sense of direction by pointing the organization in the direction it will move, they generally do not have much impact until they are translated into specific short-range plans. Some organizations maintain five- to ten-year forecasts. In those cases, plans and forecasts are revised and updated annually so that the organization always has a five-year plan and separate yearly plans leading toward its long-range objectives.

JOB ANALYSIS

One of the first steps in developing a human resource planning system is to perform a job analysis and develop a set of clearly defined job descriptions and job specifications. **Job analysis** refers to the study of jobs within an organization. It consists of analyzing the activities that an employee performs; the tools, equipment, and work aids that the employee uses; and the working conditions under which the activities are performed. Job-analysis information is important for human resource planning and for many other human resource functions as well.

Job analysis as described in this chapter should not be confused with job evaluation, which is described in Chapter 10. A job analysis focuses on what the job holder does and the skills needed to do it. A job evaluation, on the other hand, focuses on how much money the job holder should be paid for performing the job.

A *job* consists of a group of activities performed by an employee. Several employees may perform the same job, but each employee has a separate *position*. For example, an organization with 500 employees has 500 positions, but it may have only 140 different jobs that these 500 employees perform.

JOB DESCRIPTIONS AND JOB SPECIFICATIONS

Job analyses are typically performed on three occasions: (1) when the organization is first started and the job-analysis program is initiated for the first time; (2) when a new job is created; and (3) when a job is changed significantly as a result of new methods, new procedures, or new technology. Two products may result from a job analysis: a job description and a job specification.

JOB DESCRIPTIONS

Job descriptions form the foundation for a human resource planning system. A **job description** provides information concerning the duties and responsibilities contained in a job. Such a description should consist of accurate, concise statements that indicate what the employees do, how they do it, and the conditions under which they do it. The major items included in a job description are the following.

1. *Identification*: Job title, job number, and department. May also include date of analysis, reporting relationships, number of employees holding the job, and pay grade.
2. *Job summary*: A general summary of the major responsibilities and components that make the job different from others.
3. *Duties and responsibilities*: Clear and precise statements of the major tasks, duties, and responsibilities performed. May include the percentage of time devoted to each duty, working conditions and potential hazards, supervisory responsibilities, and machines and equipment used.

The job description should be concise, and action verbs should be used to describe the specific activity of each major duty. For example, vague words and phrases such as "handles," "manages," and "is responsible for" should generally be replaced by specific action verbs. The outputs of the job should be described in quantitative terms whenever possible; such things as how many, what quality, and how fast should be specified. The components of the job should be listed in order of importance and the time that is devoted to each should be noted.

JOB SPECIFICATIONS

A **job specification** identifies the minimum acceptable qualifications required for an employee to perform the job adequately. The information contained in a job specification typically falls into one of three categories: (1) general qualification requirements, such as experience and training; (2) educational requirements, including high school, university, or vocational education; and (3) knowledge, skills, and ability.

A job specification should include only qualifications that are clearly related to acceptable job performance. Superfluous requirements that are not essential to performing the job, especially unnecessary educational requirements, discriminate against minority groups and are prohibited by equal employment opportunity laws.[6]

There is a trend toward writing broader job descriptions and job specifications to accommodate technological innovations. For example, just-in-time manufacturing increases profitability by eliminating large inventories of parts and having them produced as they are needed. But just-in-time manufacturing requires workers to perform a broader variety of tasks to accommodate the fluctuating workload. Consequently, broader job descriptions must be written to include all that the workers may be required to do. Likewise, autonomous work teams and job-enrichment programs require workers to perform a broader variety of tasks, and these ought to be included in the job description.[7]

USES OF JOB ANALYSIS

Job analysis is performed for many reasons.[8] The information provided in job descriptions and job specifications is used in numerous human resource functions. As outlined in Figure 4.3, some of the major uses of job analysis information include the following.

Personnel planning: Used to develop the job categories.

Recruiting: Used to describe job openings and to advertise new positions.

Selection: Used to identify the skills and activities that serve as the criteria for deciding which candidates to select.

Orientation: Used to tell employees what activities they must perform.

Evaluation: Used to identify the standards and performance objectives against which employees are evaluated.

Compensation: Used to evaluate job worth and to aid in developing a wage structure.

Training: Used to conduct a training-needs assessment by identifying the activities that employees ought to be able to perform.

Discipline: Used to identify standards of acceptable performance that employees are expected to achieve.

Safety: Used to identify safe working procedures so that unsafe activities can either be changed or discontinued.

Job redesign: Used to analyze the characteristics of a job that need to be changed in job-redesign projects.

JOB IDENTIFICATION

When writing a job description, every job should be clearly labeled with a unique title. Although organizations are free to label jobs however they choose, the use of common terms by all organizations for **job identification** has certain advantages, especially for recruiting, selection, compensation, and training. For example, if an organization needs a pipefitter, using the label pipefitter in recruiting ads is more sensible than using a unique job title such as Class H Laborer.

The United States Department of Labor has developed a classification scheme for identifying jobs. It has grouped similar jobs together in occupational categories, and all of these jobs are described in a massive publication called the **Dictionary of Occupational Titles (DOT)**.[9] The DOT was first published in 1939 and has been updated in 1949, 1965, and 1977. The Department of Labor periodically issues supplements to the DOT to describe new occupations resulting from new technology and to update occupations that have changed. Over 20,000 occupations are described in the DOT. Each occupation has a unique job title and occupational code number.

Each occupational definition in the DOT consists of six basic parts that always appear in this order:

1. The occupational code number
2. The occupational title
3. The industry designation

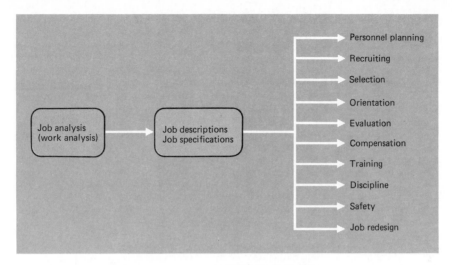

FIGURE 4.3 Impact of job analysis on human resource activities.

4. Alternative titles, if any
5. The body of the definition
   a. lead statement
   b. task element statements
   c. "may items"
6. Undefined related titles, if any

The DOT definition of a cloth printer is illustrated in Figure 4.4. The occupational code number of a cloth printer is 652.382-010. Each set of three digits that comprise the nine-digit code number has a specific purpose or meaning that differentiates this job from all others. The initial set of three digits identifies a particular occupational group. Each occupation is clustered into one of nine broad categories, and it is one of these categories that is identified by the first digit. The nine primary occupational categories are:

0/1 professional, technical, and managerial occupations
  2. clerical and sales occupations
  3. service occupations
  4. agricultural, fishery, forestry, and related occupations
  5. processing occupations
  6. machine trades occupations
  7. bench work occupations
  8. structural work occupations
  9. miscellaneous occupations

The second and third digits of the DOT occupational code divide the occupations into further subcategories. The middle set of three digits describes the kinds of activities the worker performs in relation to data, people, and things (as shown in Table 4.2), and the

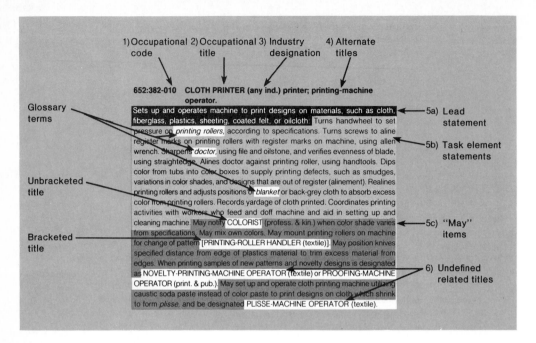

FIGURE 4.4 Parts of a DOT job definition.   Source: *Dictionary of Occupational Titles, 4th ed.* (Washington, D.C.: Department of Labor, 1977), p. xvi.

last set of three digits indicates the alphabetical order of titles within the six-digit code groups. Therefore, the full nine-digit number provides a unique code for each occupation. These nine-digit codes, which are suitable for computerized human resource information systems, facilitate comparisons of job descriptions among companies.

Italicized words in the DOT job definitions refer to technical terms or special uses of terms that are not ordinarily found in a standard dictionary. The precise meaning of these words can be found in the DOT glossary. The definitions also include both bracketed and unbracketed labels of other occupations. An unbracketed title designates occupations that have frequent working relationships with the occupation being defined. Bracketed titles indicate that the workers in the occupation being described may perform some of the duties of the bracketed occupation as part of their regular duties.

JOB-ANALYSIS METHODS

Describing what people really do in a job is difficult. Descriptions of work activities and requirements must be based on data, and data have to be provided by people. Even the employees who are performing a given job may not totally understand the activities, time allocations, or requirements involved in their work. Managers, peers, and other observers are likely to be less accurate than workers in describing the job, since even direct observations may be influenced by the subjective perceptions of the observers. Moreover, time logs and other self-reports by workers inevitably involve the condensation of diverse work activities and are influenced by the workers' subjective perceptions.

Rather than describing reality, job analysis frequently reports perceptions of what the individuals plan to do or what managers think the individuals ought to do. Such job descriptions are sometimes more useful than those based on actual observations when they are used for training or evaluation, since it is more important to know what the employees ought to do than what they are actually doing.

Four methods can be used to gather job-analysis information: observations, interviews, questionnaires, and employee recordings. None of these methods is superior for all situations; each has advantages and disadvantages. A job analyst can rely on any one of these methods or a combination of them in gathering information to describe a job. An integrated job analysis using a combination of observations, interviews, and questionnaires is generally considered best.[10]

OBSERVATIONS

To analyze a job, observers may watch an individual work and then record a brief description of the activities performed. Using observers to gather information, however, can create an unrealistic situation, since employees may behave differently when they know they are being observed. This problem is especially severe when employees know that a job description will be used for determining their wage levels. Employees, hoping to raise their jobs to higher pay levels, may add unnecessary, time-consuming actions to make their jobs appear difficult. Videotapes or films of workers as they perform can sometimes provide more accurate information than direct observations. One study, however, found that it didn't make any difference whether high producers or low producers were used as the source of job-analysis information. The high performers, the low performers, and the supervisors all rated the jobs similarly in terms of the knowledge, skills, and abilities required to perform the jobs.[11]

TABLE 4.2   DOT codes for worker functions

DATA (4th Digit)	People (5th Digit)	Things (6th Digit)
0 Synthesizing	0 Monitoring	0 Setting-up
1 Coordinating	1 Negotiating	1 Precision working
2 Analyzing	2 Instructing	2 Operating-controlling
3 Compiling	3 Supervising	3 Driving-operating
4 Computing	4 Diverting	4 Manipulating
5 Copying	5 Persuading	5 Tending
6 Comparing	6 Speaking-signaling	6 Feeding-off bearing
	7 Serving	7 Handing
	8 Taking instructions-Helping	

Source: Dictionary of Occupational Titles, 4th ed. (Washington, D.C.: Department of Labor, 1977), p. xviii.

Another problem with using observation is that some jobs cannot be easily observed. Jobs that primarily involve thinking and problem-solving activities, such as professional and technical occupations, may not provide much overt behavior to observe.

A specific method of job analysis that uses observation is called **functional job analysis**.[12] This method of analyzing the functions of a job was developed during the 1930s to assist the Department of Labor in developing the *Dictionary of Occupational Titles*. Functional job analysis classifies jobs in terms of three basic functions—data, people, and things. Each functional dimension is coded in terms of level of complexity and degree of importance. Functional job analysis also provides information regarding career ladders, including the kinds of training and development experiences that are necessary for advancement. This job-analysis method tends to be costly because it requires a trained analyst, and it is not very applicable to managerial and professional positions.

INTERVIEWS

Job-analysis information can be obtained by interviewing the job incumbent as well as his or her supervisor. Interview information is particularly valuable for professional and technical jobs that mainly involve thinking and problem solving.

QUESTIONNAIRES

A convenient method for obtaining job-analysis information is to ask employees and/or their supervisors to describe a job by answering a questionnaire. A questionnaire may be tailored specifically to the activities of a given organization, or it may be a published questionnaire containing activity checklists. Although a questionnaire that is tailored to a particular organization tends to have high initial cost, it does have the advantage of probing in great detail into the various aspects of work in a specific situation. Published activity checklists tend to be inexpensive, but they capture only the broad dimensions of each job.[13]

One of the major advantages of using questionnaires is that the information garnered is quantitative in nature and can be easily updated as the jobs change. A typical questionnaire contains two sections. The first section asks the worker to describe the kinds of experiences, qualifications, and attitudes needed to perform the job. The second section contains a detailed list of many activities, and the individuals are asked to describe which activities apply to their job and the importance of each activity or the percentage of time spent performing it.

One of the best-known job-analysis questionnaires is the **Position Analysis Questionnaire (PAQ)**, developed by Ernest McCormick and his associates at Purdue University.[14] The PAQ is a checklist of 195 job elements that measure the following six major categories of each job.

1. *Information input*: Where and how does the worker get the information used in performing the job?
2. *Mental processes*: What reasoning, decision-making, planning, and information-processing activities are involved in performing the job?
3. *Work output*: What physical activities does the worker perform, and what tools or devices are used?

4. *Relationships with other persons*: What relationships with other people are required in performing the job?
5. *Job context*: In what physical and social contexts is the work performed?
6. *Other job characteristics*: What activities, conditions, or characteristics other than those described above are relevant to the job?

Individuals completing the PAQ use a code to describe the job on each of the 195 items (see Table 4.3). This information can then be further analyzed to classify the job into other job dimensions, and it allows for a comparison of jobs across occupational groups. Because the questionnaire is standardized and applies to so many different jobs, the information is useful in making salary comparisons, such as between occupations, between companies, and between males and females.

Although the PAQ has been recommended as a useful instrument for describing all jobs, the evidence indicates that it is not as useful on some jobs and that naive raters are not sufficiently reliable. Nevertheless, research on the PAQ indicates that it is a reliable instrument in the hands of experienced analysts, and the PAQ dimensions are highly related to the actual job components.[15]

EMPLOYEE RECORDINGS

Descriptive job information can be obtained by asking employees to maintain written records of what they do. Such a record may be in the form of a time log or a daily diary. Written descriptions of activities that are recorded shortly after they occur typically

---

TABLE 4.3   One item from the PAQ (Position Analysis Questionnaire)

MENTAL PROCESSES

S   Reasoning in problem solving (indicate, using the code below, the level of reasoning that is required of the worker in applying knowledge, experience, and judgment to problems)

Code Level of Reasoning in Problem Solving

1. **Very limited** (use of common sense to carry out simple or relatively uninvolved instructions; for example, hand assembler, mixing machine operator)
2. **Limited** (use of some training and/or experience to select from a limited number of solutions the most appropriate action or procedure in performing the job; for example, salesperson, electrician apprentice, library assistant)
3. **Intermediate** (use of relevant principles to solve practical problems and to deal with a variety of concrete variables in situations where only limited standardization exists; for example, many supervisors, technicians)
4. **Substantial** (use of logic or scientific thinking to define problems, collect information, establish facts, and draw valid conclusions; for example, petroleum engineer, personnel director, manager of a "chain" store)
5. **Very substantial** (use of principles of logical or scientific thinking to solve a wide range of intellectual and practical problems; for example, research chemist, nuclear physicist, corporate president, or manager of a large branch or plant)

HRM in Action

The Coast Guard's Description of a Machinery Technician

Job descriptions in the Coast Guard may be used for many purposes, including salary determination, job redesign, performance evaluation, training-needs assessment, and orientation training. Consequently, the Coast Guard wanted to develop a rigorous job-analysis program that would produce better job descriptions than brief one- or two-page reports.

The job-analysis method developed by the Coast Guard relies on a panel of experts to produce a list of job tasks that are used to form a questionnaire. This method was used to describe the job of machinery technician. A panel of nine experts who had worked as machinery technicians was asked to make an exhaustive list of all the job tasks performed by machinery technicians. Each task was written on a separate index card, and by the time they finished they had generated approximately 10,000 cards. This stack of task statements was then reduced to 1,503 items that were included in a questionnaire. The items in the questionnaire included statements such as "operate multimeter," "operate armature test growler," and "inspect battery."

The questionnaire was then sent to over 3,000 job incumbents, and they were asked to check which tasks they performed in their present job. For each task they checked they were also expected to indicate the relative length of time they spend performing the task and the amount of training that should be devoted to the task.

The information from these questionnaires was reviewed by job analysts who interpreted it with input from the training managers. They then used the data to review personnel resources, training, and advancement qualifications for the entire occupation. Although this method provided the Coast Guard with a comprehensive analysis of a machinery technician's job, it is a very time-consuming method that may have limited applicability in other organizations.

Source: Jerrold Markowitz, "Managing the Job Analysis Process," *Training and Development Journal* 41 (August 1989): 64–66.

provide different kinds of information than reconstructions through memory at a later date. Immediate reports of activities not only contain greater detail than reconstructions but they also tend to emphasize specific problems that occurred and personal feelings of satisfaction or frustration. Time logs may be especially useful in helping job incumbents analyze where their time actually goes and what activities they actually perform each day. However, keeping such records requires a commitment on the part of the employees, and employees often feel that written records are undesirable intrusions.

ANALYSIS OF PRESENT EMPLOYEES

The next step in developing a human resource planning system is to analyze the organization's present work force. How many employees are working for the organization? What jobs do they perform? How many employees are in each job category? Information also must be collected about the skills and characteristics of each employee. In a small organization, collecting information about the present work force is not a difficult task.

In a large organization, computers are needed to handle the enormous mass of information. For the information to be useful, a system must efficiently collect and organize it, keep it current, and have it immediately available.

CATEGORIZING JOBS

Forecasts of human resource needs are usually made for job categories. A company with 1,000 employees would have 1,000 positions, one for each employee, but only 200 or 300 different jobs and only 10 or 15 job categories. The jobs need to be grouped into a limited number of job categories, since trying to forecast and plan for each separate job would be a cumbersome task. Three criteria should be used to group jobs into similar categories:

1. The specific skill preparation and educational requirements needed to perform the job
2. The degree of responsibility and location of the job in the organizational hierarchy
3. The nature of the activities performed

The job of tax accountant, for example, would be very similar to that of a cost accountant and an internal auditor. These accounting positions also would be somewhat similar to the job of financial analyst. However, other office jobs, such as file clerk or inventory-control clerk, would not be similar to either accountant job. Categorizing all of these jobs as office jobs would overlook some of the important differences among them.

In classifying the jobs within an organization, a balance needs to be achieved between having too many job categories and too few. Having too many categories could result in an unwieldy condition characterized by too much useless detail (such as hiring 1.2 receptionists when employment increases by 20 percent). And if too few job categories have been established, important differences among jobs may be overlooked, and the planning system would not be as useful.

A useful method for classifying jobs is to adopt the EEOC's nine major job categories.[16] Since organizations are required to submit EEO reports, the reporting burden can be reduced if the company's job categories coincide with the EEOC's job categories. The EEOC's nine major job categories include: (1) officials and managers, (2) professionals, (3) technicians, (4) sales workers, (5) office and clerical, (6) crafts workers, (7) operatives, (8) laborers, and (9) service workers. In the instruction booklet that explains how to prepare the EEO reports, general definitions of the jobs in each category are produced.

If an organization uses the EEOC's job categories, it may need to develop subcategories to accommodate its unique situation. For example, an engineering firm may need to identify different kinds of engineers, such as civil engineers, electrical engineers, and chemical engineers. Likewise, an insurance company may need to identify several categories of office and clerical employees.

HUMAN RESOURCE INFORMATION SYSTEMS

The development of an effective planning system requires an inventory of the people working for the organization; this collection of information is called a **human resource**

information system (HRIS). Human resource information systems are designed to help managers make more effective decisions. If information is not relevant to the strategic business plans of an organization or if it is an invasion of personal privacy, it should not be included in the HRIS. A carefully designed HRIS that is current and reliable can assist managers in many ways.[17] The major uses of an HRIS include the following.

1. *Personnel planning*: To anticipate replacements and promotions.
2. *EEO reports*: To know how many employees of each sex and race are employed in each job category.
3. *Compensation reports*: To obtain information regarding how much each employee is paid, the overall compensation costs, and the financial costs of pay increases and other compensation changes.
4. *Personnel research*: To conduct research into such problems as turnover and absenteeism, or to discover the most productive places to look for new recruits.
5. *Training-needs assessment*: To analyze the performances of individuals and to determine which employees need further training.

One of the major purposes of collecting information on employees is to make staffing and promotion decisions. For example, a construction company considering a project in Mexico might want to know how many of its employees speak Spanish and if there is a potential project manager who has an MBA degree, who has experience in construction, and who also speaks Spanish.

Human resource information systems should also be designed to facilitate the reporting requirements of the EEOC. The Civil Rights Act requires all employers to keep records that could indicate whether unlawful employment practices have been committed. This information is submitted in annual reports to the EEOC, which also has the authority to request additional information regarding an employer's employment practices. The EEOC is primarily interested in knowing whether the percentage of minority employees in each job category within an organization is comparable to the percentage of employees in the external labor market. If the percentages are roughly comparable in each job category, the EEOC generally does not look for further evidence of discrimination. A computerized HRIS could quickly indicate how many employees of each race and sex are employed in each job category.

The following information is typically useful in an employee profile: (1) present job category or current position; (2) skills, including areas of knowledge and experience; (3) educational level, including degrees and certificates; (4) geographical location and geographical preference (if the corporation is geographically decentralized; (5) length of service; (6) retirement plans; (7) time in present position; (8) potential for development and interest in promotion; (9) wage and salary history; (10) performance rating and supervisory evaluations; (11) attendance record; and (12) disciplinary actions. For research and EEOC reporting purposes, and HRIS should also contain information about each employee's age, race, religion, sex, national origin, marital status, and number of dependents, but this information should not be illegally used for selection, promotion, training, compensation, or evaluation.

Two types of inventories are frequently used to collect and assemble employee information: a management inventory and a skills inventory. A **management inventory** contains information that relates specifically to managers. It is used to describe not only the employees who are presently serving as managers but also those employees who have the potential of being promoted into management-level positions. Management inventories describe the employees' work histories, their strengths and weaknesses, their promotion potential, and their career goals. This information is typically described in detail in the management inventory and summarized on a replacement chart.

HRM in Action

Skills Inventory at IBM

Since IBM is a leader in computers, it is only natural that their Havant, England, plant would have an excellent human resource information system. Their Personal Skills Inventory Database (PSID) was created in 1985—and one of its outstanding features is that it allows employees to enter their own data. Since over 80 percent of the Havant work force receive and send mail electronically, a system was created for each employee to create and update his or her own file in the PSID.

From a series of screens, the employees are asked to provide information about their job title, qualifications, language capability, professional institute membership, work experience, external activities, and fields in which they would like to work in the future. Employees can update their personal data whenever they wish, but they are encouraged to do so whenever they change jobs and to review it at least annually.

Employees are asked to describe all of their skills using five basic skill categories. Within each category, the employees describe their skills using a free format limited only by the length of the available field. This system avoids the need for a lengthy codebook, since the data are stored in a natural language form. When a search of the data is made, a software program is used that allows the data to be searched using any string of characters.

The IBM Havant plant has about 1,800 full-time employees who can be classified into about 200 specific job titles. Since IBM has a policy of continuous employment, the company makes extensive use of information from the PSID to move people between departments, reassign employees to other locations, retrain employees, update their current skills, and decide when external hiring is necessary. The PSID has also been used for other unique purposes, such as to find female graduates to give career talks in local schools, engineers with disk file experience, and people with qualifications in nursing and first aid.

The data in the PSID are carefully protected. All data in the PSID database are encrypted so that unauthorized access would not result in any intelligible information. A series of updated passwords and filenames are used to control who has access to the data.

Source: Gary Winsor, "How High Tech Helped Uncover Hidden Talents," *Personnel Management* 20 (March 1988): 48–51.

A **skills inventory** describes the skills and knowledge of employees, and is mainly used for making placement and promotion decisions. Each organization should identify the critical skills that are needed to make it effective and compile an inventory of which employees have which skills. This inventory should include everything that might be useful and is job-related. For example, musical talents may be valuable to a nursing home and a list should be made of which employees sing, lead music, play the piano, or perform

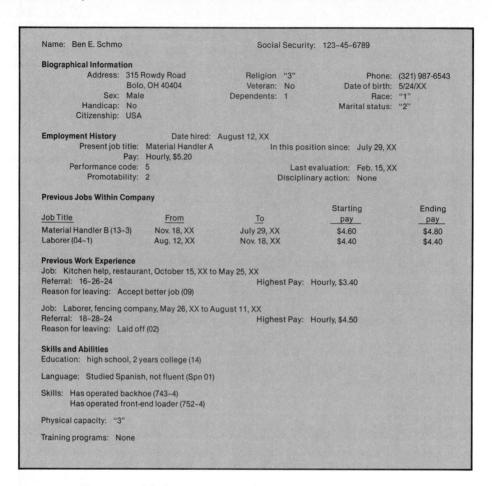

FIGURE 4.5 Illustration of the human resource information in the HRIS on each employee.

other musical instruments. With the growing application of computers, most organizations would do well to know which employees have their own personal computers and what skills they possess. The trend toward international business has made language skills increasingly valuable. Many hospitals, for example, maintain a current inventory of which employees speak which languages so they can assist as needed in translating for patients or visitors.

Skill inventories can be used to foster growth and prevent employee stagnation. The process used to create the inventory can itself be developmental for the job incumbents and their supervisors, since it involves summarizing the employees' past development, assessing the strength of these skills, and discussing the employees' aspirations and training needs. The motivation to sharpen present skills or learn new ones is strengthened.[18]

Several methods are available for developing an HRIS. The traditional method was to develop individual files and store them in file cabinets. In recent years, however, computerized data files have replaced file cabinets because they can store more information in less space and the data can be quickly retrieved and updated. Figure 4.5 illustrates the kind of information that can be stored about each employee. The numbers and codes assist in retrieving the information. For example, if a request were made for a list of all employees who can operate a backhoe, this employee would be included on that list. Significant technological advancements continue to make computers more convenient and useful, and various software packages have been developed. The trend is toward small, portable computers that can store massive amounts of easily retrievable information. For example, if information has been properly entered, a manager can ask the computer to list all employees who have graduate degrees in business, speak Spanish, and have previous construction experience. The ability to obtain this form of fast, reliable, and informative human resource data greatly facilitates human resource planning.

SOURCES OF EMPLOYEE INFORMATION

To develop a comprehensive HRIS, information must be obtained from many different sources. Special forms and questionnaires can be developed for collecting the information, but if the forms create unnecessary paperwork, the system can lose much of its effectiveness. Therefore, before developing special forms to collect HRIS information, organizations should consider using the sources that are already available to them, such as application blanks, performance evaluations, personnel-change notices, disciplinary-action reports, and payroll data.

APPLICATION BLANKS

Virtually every organization uses an application blank as part of its hiring process. The application blank ought to be designed in part to collect the information needed for a human resource information system. This information includes educational level, skills, and other pertinent biographical data. Some organizations prefer to keep their initial application blanks simple, asking only for information that will help them decide whether an applicant is a desirable job candidate. After a candidate is selected for employment, he or she is then asked to complete a second form that requests more detailed information for the HRIS.

PERFORMANCE EVALUATIONS

Because some information changes every year, an HRIS needs to be updated periodically to be useful. Important information that should be updated includes employees' skills and talents, present levels of performance, and potential for growth. Although this information can be obtained from performance-evaluation forms, there are problems in collecting and storing this information. The organization needs valid information for making long-range planning decisions regarding individuals who have the potential for promotion, but if this information is available to the employees, the information tends to be less valid. Supervisors may be unwilling to make negative judgments that might in some way harm the careers of their immediate subordinates. On the other hand, keeping the ratings secret may create tension in the organization because employees know that the ratings exist and wonder how they have been evaluated. The situation is further complicated by the privacy laws that prohibit organizations from divulging certain information that may be necessary for legitimate business reasons.[19]

PERSONNEL-CHANGE NOTICES

Since personnel changes occur throughout the year, this type of information needs to be updated more frequently than annually. Many organizations have developed a simple form called a personnel-change notice that supervisors are required to complete and forward to the human resource office. Usually, a supervisor indicates on the form the changes that have been made in an employee's status, such as a transfer, termination, promotion, or upgrading of job duties.

DISCIPLINARY ACTIONS

Information regarding formal disciplinary action also may be included in the HRIS. Some organizations use special forms for reporting this information to the employee, to a union representative, and to the human resource office. When this information is received in the human resource office, it can be added to the employee's personnel file.

PAYROLL DATA

Human resource information systems sometimes contain each employee's salary history, including base pay, percentage increases for each year, and any bonuses and special awards that have been given. This information may be part of the data provided through the performance-evaluation form. However, some organizations prefer to use a separate form for submitting recommendations for pay increases and bonuses. In organizations that do not have a comprehensive HRIS, the payroll system can represent a convenient starting point for the development of an HRIS. Many firms have computer-based payroll administration systems, and others use time-sharing or computer service firms for processing payrolls. These payroll systems typically include some of the basic employee data that can serve as the foundation for a human resource information system. The payroll system could be expanded to include other relevant data, or a separate system could be established and interfaced with the payroll system to provide the additional data required.

FORECASTING EMPLOYMENT NEEDS

After an organization's present work force has been analyzed, the next step in developing a human resource planning system is to forecast future employment needs. This requires an analysis of the demand for labor that answers these three questions: (1) What employees will be needed in the future? (2) What kinds of skills and talents will the employees need? and (3) When will the new employees be needed? This type of information is necessary for planning human resource management actions.

Forecasting employment needs is more of an applied art than a science. Even though many sophisticated forecasting techniques have been developed, in practice forecasting is usually informal, highly judgmental, and subjective. The accuracy of employment forecasts is related to the length of time they cover, with short-term forecasts tending to be much more precise and accurate than long-term forecasts. In developing an employment forecast, the forecaster is required to make various assumptions about economic conditions and the future of the organization. While it might be safe to assume that economic conditions a year from now will be much the same as at present, the assumption of "no change" is not a very sound assumption for long-term planning. Over a long period of time, economic conditions and organizational objectives tend to change dramatically.

Forecasting is more accurate in organizations that have stable environments. If the demand for an organization's products is steady and if the technology for producing these products does not change much over time, the employment forecasts for this organization can be quite accurate. However, employment forecasts are usually more valuable for an organization in a volatile environment, even if the forecasts are not as accurate as those for an organization operating within a stable environment. In organizations where new technologies or operating processes are frequently introduced, some form of forecasting and planning is essential. Plans for adequate staffing are particularly critical in an organization that has a rapidly expanding technology, an unstable environment that needs to be anticipated, or a heavy reliance upon managerial, professional, and technical talent.

Employment forecasting does not have to produce exact estimates of future employment needs in order to be useful. The forecasting process itself, apart from the numbers that result, facilitates the planning process. Requiring managers to think about the future and to anticipate the kinds of events that might occur is a useful process even though the events that do occur may be quite different from those anticipated. Having a forecast that is wrong is usually better than having no forecast at all, since an incorrect forecast can be modified as conditions change and new assumptions become necessary. The value of a forecast should be judged not so much by how close it was to the actual needs, but by the degree to which it caused managers to think about and anticipate future situations.

Forecasting employment needs involves two quite different time periods: short-term forecasting and long-term forecasting. These two periods differ in terms of the methods used for forecasting, their impact on an organization, and the people responsible for the forecasts. A survey of the forecasting practices among 83 firms indicated that most of them used multiple forecasting methods to develop both short-term and long-term forecasts and that their major motive was to avoid layoffs.[20]

SHORT-TERM FORECASTING

Short-term forecasting typically refers to predicting employment demands for a one-year period. However, short-term forecasts may be as long as two years for oil and steel companies and as short as three to six months for construction companies or contract aerospace engineering firms. The responsibility for short-term forecasting usually belongs to the immediate supervisors and unit managers.

BUDGETING

In many organizations, short-term employment forecasting is accomplished through the process of budgeting. Managers are expected to identify the kinds of resources that they will need for the coming business period. If they will need additional personnel to fill new positions demanded by their unit's objectives, then this information should be included in their budgets. The budget represents a plan of future business activity that includes financial and capital resources as well as human needs. Although managers are often irritated by the time required to develop a budget, this time is usually very well spent and can have an enormous impact on the success and effectiveness of their units.

The quality of short-term forecasts is heavily influenced by a manager's ability to make accurate estimates. Although the forecasts are largely judgmental, various techniques have been developed to facilitate short-term forecasting. Some managers use rules of thumb for determining their staffing needs, such as having three technicians assigned to each repair crew or two sales clerks assigned to each cash register. Other managers base their staffing estimates on comparisons with similar units in other organizations.

Most business organizations rely on a "bottom-up" method of short-term forecasting in which unit managers identify their employment needs; however, an alternative method is a "top-down" approach. The top-down approach occurs when top managers place constraints either in terms of budget allocations or number of employees and then require unit managers to plan their objectives given these constraints. This type of forecasting has become increasingly popular in government agencies in recent years. Declining tax revenues have forced some governmental units to impose ceilings on spending, thereby forcing managers to decide which activities they can pursue, given the limits. In this situation the number of employees who can be hired determines how much work will be done, rather than having the amount of work determine how many employees to hire. Hence, the number of employees is constrained by available income.

WORK-LOAD ANALYSIS

The most accurate method of short-term forecasting is to use information about the actual work content based on job analyses of the work that needs to be accomplished. This type of short-term forecasting, often called **work-load analysis**, involves the use of ratios or standard staffing guidelines to identify personnel needs. The work-load analysis identifies both the number of employees and the kinds of employees required to achieve the organizational goals. The first step is to identify how much output the organization expects to achieve. This is then translated into the number of employee hours in each job category that will be required to achieve it. If the level of output is expected to change, the change in employment can be estimated by calculating how many employee hours will be needed. For example, a company that manufactures water beds and expects to increase sales by 20 percent in the coming year needs to analyze which activities will be influenced by the increase. Although the increased production level may not require additional clerical and managerial positions, the number of production jobs will probably need to be increased. If it takes 2,000 employee hours per week of production time to produce the present number of water beds, then it would require 2,400 employee hours per week of production time to achieve a 20 percent increase. This increase of 400 employee hours per week would require ten additional production workers, assuming that each worker works a 40-hour week. A similar analysis must also be made for other activities influenced by the increasing demand for water beds.

A work-load analysis is shown in Table 4.4. The table illustrates the short-term forecasting of a school district for the kindergarten through sixth-grade classes. The school district has a policy that sets eighteen students as the ideal size for a kindergarten

TABLE 4.4 Short-term forecasting for a school district

Grade	Ideal Teacher-Student Ratio	Student-Enrollment (Projected)		Teachers (Projected)	
		Current Year	Next Year	Current Year	Next Year
Kindergarten	1:18	962	960	54	54
First	1:20	914	962	46	48
Second	1:22	896	914	41	42
Third	1:24	945	896	40	37
Fourth	1:26	1,021	945	39	36
Fifth	1:28	968	1,021	35	38
Sixth	1:30	943	968	31	32
	Total	6,649	6,666	286	287

class, increasing to thirty students for a sixth-grade class. Since the number of students is not expected to change much as a result of families moving in and out of the district, the number of teachers needed for the next year can be forecasted quite accurately. The totals at the bottom of the table indicate that there will be very little change in the student enrollment from this year to the next year. There also will be very little change in the number of teachers—only one new teacher will be needed. However, several internal changes are needed in the teaching staff. The number of third- and forth-grade teachers must be reduced, while the number of positions in the other grades will have to be increased. By identifying the problem early, the school administrators may be able to minimize some of the conflict caused by resistance to change.

Some hospitals use a patient acuity system that is a form of work-load analysis to measure the amount of care patients will need and to plan for adequate staff. Law offices also use a work-load analysis to determine how many legal assistants to hire. Legal assistants are not as expensive as lawyers and can perform many of the tasks lawyers would otherwise need to do.[21]

An important consideration in both short-term and long-term forecasting is whether productivity will change; greater productivity per employee could reduce the demand for labor. Productivity changes due to experience and training can be forecast with some degree of confidence based on previous experience with present employees. However, productivity improvements due to technological changes are much more difficult to forecast, since managers do not know in advance whether new technological break-throughs will be made. Regardless of how secure managers may feel in forecasting productivity changes, they should at least consider the possibility that productivity might change and anticipate how such a change might influence the demand for labor.

LONG-TERM FORECASTING

Long-term forecasts typically cover a time frame of two to ten years and are typically adjusted each year on a rolling basis. For example, the four-year forecast becomes the three-year forecast and a new four-year forecast is developed. The sophistication of long-range forecasting varies greatly from company to company. Some organizations attempt to identify how many employees in each job category will be needed to satisfy their strategic plans for the next several years. Other organizations only try to forecast the total number of people in the major divisions. Still other organizations are content to identify some of the major social changes that may occur and try to maintain an awareness of the environmental and technological changes that could influence their future human resource needs.

All long-term forecasts should be based on strategic business plans. Until someone has identified what an organization expects to be doing and the level of its business activity, forecasting how many employees will be needed is a futile exercise. However, once the projected level of business activity has been identified, several methods of forecasting long-term employment demands can be used, such as unit demand, expert opinion, trend projections, probabilistic models, and Markov analysis.

UNIT DEMAND

The **unit-demand** method of long-term forecasting is an extension of the short-term forecasting method previously described. This method requires managers to know what business activity will be performed by their units in future years and how many personnel will be needed year by year to achieve their business objectives. After this information has been obtained from each unit manager, it is aggregated to form an overall forecast for the organization.

Using unit-demand forecasting, Japan's major air carriers forecasted a serious pilot shortage during the 1990s. For example, Japan Air Lines found that 60 captains would retire yearly in the latter half of the 1990s and radical traffic expansions would probably exacerbate the shortage. By anticipating the problem, however, the airlines have an opportunity to recruit and train adequate replacements.[22]

One of the advantages of unit-demand forecasting is that unit managers typically have very accurate information regarding the effects of increasing production on the need for additional personnel. For example, doubling the production of a department does not necessarily mean that twice as many employees will be needed. The unit manager is in the best position to know how many new positions will be needed to achieve the additional level of output.

One of the major disadvantages of unit-demand forecasting is that collecting the data requires the cooperation of a large number of people. Furthermore, the information sometimes cannot be aggregated conveniently because each unit manager may have used slightly different assumptions.

EXPERT OPINION

Long-term employment needs can be forecast from the subjective estimates of experts. **Expert opinions** may come from a group or from a single individual, such as the human resource director or a long-range planning specialist. This form of forecasting is considered to be the least sophisticated approach to employment planning. Experts typically base their judgments on their own intuition or past experience, the opinions of others, or the economic and social conditions they observe.

One way to achieve confidence in the estimates of experts is to combine the opinions of many experts. Three methods for combining this information include pooling, group consensus, and the Delphi technique. The estimates can be *pooled* by asking the experts to submit their individual opinions and then simply averaging their estimates. A second method is to bring the experts together in a group discussion and ask them to achieve a *consensus*. Research on group decision making suggests that the group consensus will probably be more accurate than pooling the separate estimates.[23] A third method is to use the **Delphi technique**, which consists of experts responding to a series of questionnaires or interviews, providing their best estimates of the future.[24] This information is collected by a person called an intermediary who summarizes it and then submits a report to the experts. If any expert's views are not consistent with the rest of the group, that expert is asked to justify why he or she thinks differently. This information is then collected by the intermediary and circulated to all the experts in written reports. Written reports are used, rather than face-to-face discussion, because the reports are more convenient and less biased. They allow the experts to privately consider each other's opinions or justifications and consider whether they want to change their own estimates. After several iterations, the experts are expected to move toward a consensus.

TREND PROJECTIONS

Trend projections are based on the relationship between a factor related to employment and the employment level itself. For example, in many organizations employment needs are related to the levels of sales or production. If such a relationship exists, the human resource planner can use the forecasted levels of sales or production to estimate how many employees in each job category will be needed.

Some form of informal trend projection is typically involved in the two techniques described previously—unit demand and expert opinion. In unit-demand forecasting, managers often try to make informal estimates of their employment needs based on anticipated levels of business activity. Likewise, expert estimates are usually based on a subjective judgment of how many employees will be required to fill the demands for an organization's products.

Identifying the most appropriate factor related to employment is a critical step in making trend projections. Sales levels may be the most appropriate factor for predicting employment levels in many organizations, although manufacturing firms may find that their employment levels are more closely associated with the number of units produced. The nature of an organization's business must be considered in determining the most significant factor related to employment. For example, airlines may discover that their employment levels are most closely related to numbers of flights, whereas nursing homes usually find that their employment levels are closely related to numbers of patients.

Successful identification of the best factor involves a careful historical analysis of employment levels and the volume of business activity. Figure 4.6 illustrates a historical analysis of the volume of business activity with the number of employees in a given job category for a ten-year period. Although the points do not fall exactly on a straight

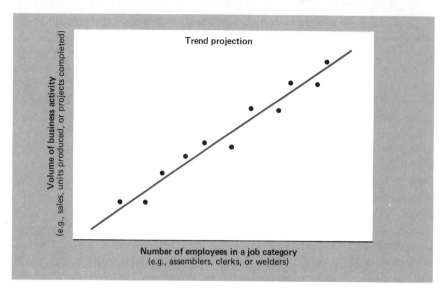

FIGURE 4.6 Correlating employment levels with the volume of business activity.

line, the graph clearly indicates that a fairly good correlation exists between the volume of business activity and the number of employees.

The historical information shown in Figure 4.6 can be used in several ways to develop trend projections. One method is a simple long-run trend analysis. If the organization's volume of business activity for the next five years is expected to continue at the same rate as the previous ten years, a simple linear extrapolation can be made to show the volume of business for each of the five years being forecast. Since employment levels are correlated with the volume of business activity, this linear extrapolation also would indicate how many employees in each job category will be needed.

A more sophisticated way to use the historical information shown in Figure 4.6 is to do a regression analysis, which is a statistical technique for showing the quantitative relationships between variables. A regression analysis is an ideal procedure for estimating the number of employees in each job category based on the volume of business activity.

Since the employment levels for nursing homes usually are related to numbers of patients, regression analysis is a useful method of forecasting future employment levels for nursing homes. An analysis of historical information relating to one nursing home produced these formulas showing employment levels:

$$\text{Nursing aides/orderlies} = 8 + .40 \text{ patients}$$
$$\text{Nurses (LPNs and RNs)} = 3 + .15 \text{ patients}$$
$$\text{Kitchen employees} = 1 + .20 \text{ patients}$$

These regression equations allow the nursing home director to forecast employment needs as the nursing home expands. At the present time the nursing home has eighty patients. Caring for these patients requires forty nursing aides and orderlies, fifteen nurses, and seventeen kitchen workers. Within the next year the nursing home expects to add another twenty patients. To accommodate these additional patients, the nursing home will need to hire eight additional nursing aides and orderlies, three additional nurses, and four additional kitchen employees.

Many hospitals use a sophisticated form of regression analysis to forecast their employment needs. Rather than using forecasts based on the number of patients, however, hospitals use forecasts based on the projected kinds of health care activities that will be performed. Through an extensive analysis of historical information, a hospital identifies standard performance rates for how long it takes to perform various activities, such as feeding patients, delivering a child, performing an appendectomy, and doing laboratory tests. Projections are then made concerning how many operations, laboratory tests, and other activities will be conducted at the hospital during a period of time. When these projections are combined with the performance rates that have been established, the hospital is able to identify how many employees will be needed in each area. Although the hospital may overestimate the number of appendectomies that will be done and underestimate how long each childbirth might require, the projections and time standards allow the hospital to at least make an initial estimate of employment needs. This information also provides an index of the productivity of the hospital. For example, the hospital administrator would be interested to know why the time required to perform a given operation frequently takes longer than the performance standards indicate.

PROBABILISTIC MODELS

A **probabilistic model** is a long-term forecast of employment needs that uses probabilities of future events to estimate future employment levels. A computer simulation that models the business environment of an organization can be designed to describe how the organization might look in the future depending on alternative decisions and economic conditions. The simulation can show the effects of each decision on human resources as well as on business outcomes, such as prices, sales, and profits. If the relationships among the variables within the model accurately describe the interactions that actually occur within the organization, then the simulation can be used to examine possible future employment needs. Assumptions made about the future can be fed into the computer to discover their probable consequences. The advantage of using a computer simulation as opposed to a subjective model is that the computer allows simultaneous examination of many organizational and economic factors, such as sales, gross national product, discretionary income, unemployment rates, and other market conditions.

All forecasts of future employment needs are only estimates, although forecasts generally become increasingly accurate as additional variables are considered. However, the cost of simultaneously considering numerous factors may be more than the forecast is worth. Forecasting should be practical, and the additional accuracy gained from considering more variables may not be worth the cost in time or effort. In some situations anything more than a simple estimate may not justify the expense.

MARKOV ANALYSIS

Markov analysis is a simple form of probabilistic forecasting. In Markov analysis, the movement of employees among different job classifications can be forecast based on past movement. Markov analysis can be used not only to forecast movement of employees from one job category to another but also movement that might occur among organizational units, among organizational levels, among different locations, or among salary classes.[25]

An illustration of a Markov analysis is shown in Figure 4.7, which examines the movement of personnel among four job categories. The upper matrix in the figure shows the data of the period used to establish the transition probabilities. For example, 400 employees were in Job A at the beginning of the year, and of these 400 employees, 60 percent remained in Job A, 10 percent transferred to Job B, 10 percent transferred to Job C, 10 percent transferred to Job D, and 10 percent terminated employment. There were 360 employees in Job B at the beginning of the year, and of these 360 employees, 70 percent stayed in Job B, 10 percent transferred to Job A, and 20 percent terminated. As a result of the terminations and transfers between Jobs A, B, and C, 356 people were in Job A at the end of the year. Similar calculations indicate how many people will be in Jobs B, C, and D at the end of the year.

After the transition probabilities have been determined, they can be used to forecast employment changes in future years. The lower matrix in Figure 4.7 shows how the probabilities can be used to analyze what will likely happen to the initial staffing levels and to determine the forecasted levels at year end.

For Markov analysis to be successful, there must be many employees in each job category and a fairly stable situation. If any job category has fewer than fifty employees, Markov analysis is generally not very useful. Likewise, if the transition probabilities are not stable or if the categories are changed through job redesign, Markov analysis loses its usefulness.

PROJECTED STAFFING REQUIREMENTS

After an organization's present work force has been analyzed and future employment needs have been forecast, a careful analysis must be made of the changes that need to occur in the employment levels in each job category. This analysis involves a comparison of the supply and demand for labor as well as an assessment of how many employees will leave due to attrition.

NET PROJECTIONS

When the present supply of labor is compared with the current employment demands, one of three conditions may be obvious. First, the number of employees may equal the number of available positions. Second, there may be more employees than available positions, creating a surplus of labor. Third, there could be more positions than people to fill them, the most likely possibility.

The projected supply and demand of labor for each forecasted year should be calculated and carefully examined. Table 4.5 shows a simple five-year personnel forecast for three job categories. These projections assume different turnover rates for each of the three job categories, but the rates remain constant throughout the five years. The forecast also assumes a constant 8 percent annual growth rate. The calculations shown in Table 4.5 indicate that a total replacement of four supervisors will be required during

Period used to establish transition probabilities

Initial staffing levels beginning of year

A 400	B 360	C 250	D 640		
.6 240	.1 36	.2 50	.0 0	A 326	
.1 40	.7 252	.0 0	.1 64	B 356	
.1 40	.0 0	.4 100	.1 64	C 204	Net staffing levels at year end
.1 40	.0 0	.1 25	.7 448	D 513	
.1 40	.2 72	.3 75	.1 64	Out (turnover)	

Using the probabilities to forecast subsequent years

Initial staffing levels beginning of year

A 420	B 380	C 260	D 660		
.6 252	.1 38	.2 52	.0 0	A 342	
.1 42	.7 266	.0 0	.1 66	B 374	Forecasted levels
.1 42	.0 0	.4 104	.1 66	C 212	
.1 42	.0 0	.1 26	.7 462	D 530	
.1 42	.2 76	.3 78	.1 66	Out (turnover)	

FIGURE 4.7 Markov analysis of personnel flows for four jobs.

the first year since two supervisors will be lost due to turnover and the creation of two new supervisory positions will be necessary. However, the greatest replacement needs will occur among sales personnel: 54 of the 150 sales personnel will leave due to turnover and the creation of 12 new sales positions will be necessary, making a total of 66 replacements for the first year.

If assumptions regarding an organization's growth and turnover are accurate, the organization can forecast its projected employment needs for the next five years. This simple forecast is easy to construct, since it assumes that most of the present conditions will continue into the future. If an assessment of the relevant factors suggests that the

TABLE 4.5   Five-year personnel forecast

	Supervisors	Office/Clerical	Sales
Present work force	24	66	150
Turnover[a]	2	15	54
New positions created[b]	2	5	12
Total replacements (year 1)	4	20	66
Projected work force			
Start of year 2	26	71	162
Turnover	2	16	58
New positions created	2	6	13
Total replacements (year 2)	4	22	71
Projected work force			
Start of year 3	28	77	175
Turnover	2	17	63
New positions created	2	6	14
Total replacements (year 3)	4	23	77
Projected work force			
Start of year 4	30	83	189
Turnover	2	18	68
New positions created	2	7	15
Total replacements (year 4)	4	25	83
Projected work force			
Start of year 5	32	90	204
Turnover	3	20	73
New positions created	3	7	16
Total replacements (year 5)	6	27	89
Work force at end of year 5	35	97	220

[a]Turnover projections: supervisors = 8%; office/clerical = 22%; and sales personnel = 36%.
[b]Assumes an 8% growth rate.

assumptions need to be changed, the forecast can be altered and made more sophisticated. For example, if top management anticipates launching an aggressive sales campaign, the projected 8 percent annual growth rate may need to be increased to reflect the anticipated changes. On the other hand, if they anticipate an economic recession, the annual growth rate may need to be reduced. An economic recession could also be expected to have a profound impact on turnover rates. As unemployment levels rise, turnover rates in organizations generally tend to decline dramatically. Although a simple five-year forecast may be slightly inaccurate, it can help an organization plan for the future. The major benefit of such a forecast is realized when the information regarding human resource needs becomes translated into action plans influencing other areas of the organization.

TURNOVER ANALYSIS

The accuracy of employment forecasts depends heavily on the accuracy of turnover forecasts, as was illustrated in Table 4.5. Knowing how many employees are expected to leave is as important as knowing how many new positions will be created.

Two processes are involved in estimating turnover levels: collecting historical information and analyzing economic trends. For most organizations, the turnover rates of previous years are the best indicators of future turnover. Consequently, an organization should collect historical information on the turnover levels for each year and analyze how they have changed. Separate turnover statistics should be computed for each job category, since turnover rates vary among different job categories. As the turnover rates are analyzed, particular care should be taken to assess the effects of internal and external economic conditions. As unemployment levels in the external labor market change, an organization's turnover rates typically fluctuate inversely.

When analyzing turnover, the reasons for leaving must be identified. Turnover may be caused by any of these reasons: (1) retirement, (2) death or disability, (3) layoffs, (4) discharge or termination, (5) quits, and (6) promotions within the company to another division. Although the turnover numbers may be quantitatively the same regardless of the reason, a significant qualitative difference exists among the reasons for turnover.[26]

Little can be done about turnover caused by retirement. Although some organizations try to encourage early or delayed retirement, they generally are limited in the degree to which they can influence retirement decisions.

Turnover caused by layoffs and discharge, however, is largely at the discretion of the organization. High turnover rates created by extensive layoffs can be reduced by careful employment planning and long-range business forecasting. Employees are usually discharged either for disciplinary reasons or because of incompetent performance. If an organization's turnover levels are high because many employees are being discharged, the organization may need to improve both its selection procedures and its management by providing better training and supervision.

Employees usually quit when they have better job offers or when they dislike their present jobs. If several people quit because of unpleasant working conditions, the work environment needs to be examined and improved. However, not much can be done to eliminate competing alternatives from other organizations.

Promotions and transfers within an organization do not constitute a real form of turnover. Although promoted employees must still be replaced, most managers are proud to see their subordinates find better opportunities within the company.

SURPLUS PERSONNEL

Occasionally, projected staffing requirements indicate a surplus of personnel. This situation can be much more painful to managers than having inadequate personnel, since it is usually more difficult to reduce the size of the work force than to increase it. The primary methods for reducing the number of personnel include layoffs, attrition, reduced hours, and early retirements.

LAYOFFS

The most direct method of reducing the number of personnel is through layoffs. The employees who are to be laid off are typically given advance notice, such as two weeks for production workers or one or two months for managerial and professional employees. Since layoffs typically produce a great deal of anxiety, the employees to be laid off should be named as soon as possible. In a union organization layoff decisions are typically based on seniority as specified in the labor agreement. In a nonunion organization layoff decisions may be based on a combination of seniority, ability, and informal politics. At the time they are laid off, employees should be informed about any plans for calling them back to work at a later date. This information allows the laid-off employees to plan for the future.

ATTRITION

Attrition, sometimes called restrictive hiring, refers to reducing the number of personnel by failing to replace individuals who leave. If enough advance planning has been done, an organization may avoid layoffs simply through attrition; only those replacements that are absolutely essential to the organization are made. For example, IBM Corporation relied heavily on attrition to reduce a serious overstaffing problem. Due to a serious slump in computer sales, IBM was forced to reduce employment, and over a three-year period its work force was reduced by 16,000 employees without layoffs through attrition and early retirement.[27]

REDUCED HOURS

If the labor surplus appears to be a short-term problem, many organizations prefer to reduce the number of hours each employee works and keep all of the employees. Instead of continuing a 40-hour workweek, management may decide to cut each employee's wages and hours by a fixed percentage.

EARLY RETIREMENTS

If an organization has a number of employees who are nearing retirement age, it may be able to reduce its work force by encouraging older employees to take early retirement. To encourage early retirement, however, an organization must frequently offer financial incentives that may offset the savings that might have been accrued by reducing the work force.

MANAGEMENT SUCCESSION AND DEVELOPMENT

Succession planning refers to the process of deciding how management vacancies will be filled. If a top manager retires, the position can be filled either by hiring someone from outside the organization or by promoting someone from within. Hiring from outside may bring fresh ideas into the organization and may not disrupt the organizational chart as much as promoting from within; however, promotions from within can serve as valuable motivational incentives for lower-level managers. One change in an upper-level management position may necessitate numerous changes at lower levels. Developing a succession plan to fill all of these vacancies is sometimes a difficult task, especially in large organizations.

The traditional approach to succession planning has been for managers to groom their own replacements. This process is not necessarily the best developmental experience, however. Managers frequently need more extensive training experiences than their mentors can provide. Especially important are developmental job assignments where managers receive special training by serving as managers of other departments.

Succession planning represents a major step in linking together development of the present work force with short-term forecasts. Since succession planning consists of identifying future management replacements and developing them for their new assignments, this activity is largely a line-management responsibility. The human resource staff can facilitate the process by developing the appropriate forms and helping line managers to complete them, but the line managers are ultimately responsible for the decisions that are made. The major activities involved in succession planning include the following.

1. The information about managerial candidates should be carefully considered, including such factors as career progress, experience, education, and future career interests. An assessment of the career interests of prospective managers is especially important, since the organization cannot assume that everyone is interested in being promoted to a managerial position, particularly if relocation is required. Knowing whether a candidate desires to be promoted is as important as knowing that the person has the ability to become a good manager.

2. The performances of prospective managers need to be assessed to determine whether they already are promotable or, if not, what developmental experiences they need to prepare for advancement. Their performances should be evaluated against established goals and standards.

3. The requirements for each position need to be determined. A position profile identifying the activities that must be performed by a manager should be prepared.

4. The responsible managers at each level in the organization should conduct a thorough review and discussion of the foregoing information. The discussion should focus on identifying the most likely replacements for each management position, particularly those positions that are likely to be vacated in the near future. If a replacement is not prepared to fill a vacancy immediately, the kinds of training experiences that the replacement needs should be identified in the discussion.

5. Developmental activities should be initiated to accomplish the identified needs. Promising candidates may be moved into developmental activities, such as temporary assignments, special projects, or formal training programs.[28]

The managerial review and discussion represent the heart of succession planning. The human resource staff may help by providing information for these decisions, but the operating managers are in the best position to develop the future succession plans.

Replacement planning has been formalized in some organizations with the aid of replacement charts. Figure 4.8 illustrates a portion of such a chart. The **replacement chart** is a detailed organizational chart that is designed to provide a quick picture of the key management positions, their relationships, and the availability of replacements. For example, Figure 4.8 indicates that a vacancy will soon occur in the store manager's

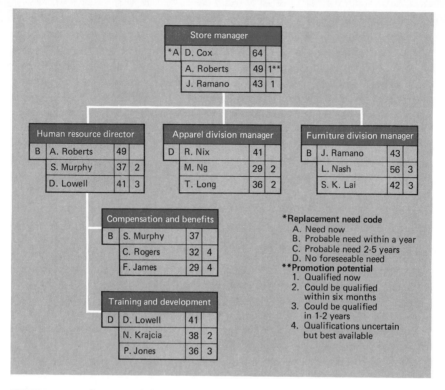

FIGURE 4.8 Replacement chart.

position and that the two possible candidates for this position are the human resource director and the furniture division manager. Since the human resource director is the most likely replacement for the store manager, it is important that replacements for the human resource director be carefully considered.

A detailed position-replacement chart is shown in Figure 4.9. In completing this form, managers are forced to carefully consider not only the abilities of each replacement but also the specific training experience that a replacement needs before filling a vacancy.

Succession planning is useful to the extent that it contributes to the development of new managers and facilitates the promotion process. If promotion decisions continue to be made based on subjective, ill-defined criteria, then the planning process has lost much of its effectiveness. Succession planning is a waste of time if it results only in static charts. The objective of succession planning is not to create added paperwork but to provide for developmental experiences in preparing managers to fill potential vacancies.

CORPORATE RESTRUCTURING

Human resource departments have had to respond to many kinds of corporate restructuring that have forced them to alter their personnel activities and respond to some difficult interpersonal problems. A survey of human resource executives indicated that

80 percent of them were involved in some form of corporate restructuring during the latter half of the 1980s.[29] The most common kinds of restructuring were downsizing, acquisitions, mergers, leveraged buyouts, divestitures, relocations, and plant closings. Some of these transactions were simply buy and sell actions by Wall Street investors with no operational changes; however, most restructuring was intended to streamline the corporation and make it more profitable.

FIGURE 4.9 Detailed position replacement chart.

Position: Personnel director   Date: July 1, 19XX

Incumbent: A. Roberts   Age: 49   Overall Performance Rating: 9

Present Salary: $46,500   Years in this Position: 6

Replacement Need: B   (Probably next January)

Comments: A. Roberts may be promoted to replace D. Cox within the next year.

Most Qualified Replacement: S. Murphy   Age: 37

Title: Compensation and benefits director   Salary: $39,000

Years in this Position: 2   Years with Company: 11

Promotion Potential: 2   Could be qualified in 3-6 months

Overall Performance Rating: 8

Training Needed: Needs to learn how to prepare the personnel budget and how to control expenditures.

Second Most Qualified Replacement: D. Lowell   Age: 41

Title: Training and development director   Salary: $38,400

Years in this Position: 6   Years with Company: 12

Promotion Potential: 3   Could be qualified in 1-2 years

Overall Performance Rating: 7

Training Needed: Needs some experience in labor relations and college recruiting.

▌ **HRM in Action**

The Human Toll of an LBO

During the 1980s leveraged buyouts, or LBOs, were used extensively to generate profits by transferring corporate ownership, thanks largely to the rise in junk-bond financing. While LBOs have been praised for transforming flabby, obsolete corporations into lean, efficient ones, they have also been criticized for eliminating jobs and damaging people's lives.

In a leveraged buyout, a small group of investors that usually includes senior management borrows heavily to buy a company from public shareholders and make it a private corporation. The heavy debt must be repaid either by selling some of the assets or by streamlining operations to make it highly profitable. Both strategies usually result in a loss of jobs, but the owners and investors usually realize a sizable return on their investment.

The Safeway LBO is often cited as an example of a very profitable buyout. In 1986, Safeway faced a hostile takeover by corporate raiders Herbert and Robert Haft. Safeway decided instead to sell the publicly held company to a group of buyout specialists, Kohlberg, Kravis, Roberts and Company (KKR). When the shareholders sold their stock they received 82 percent more than the stock was trading at three months earlier and the top-management team made $25 million on the sale of their shares. For putting together the buyout, three investment banks received $65 million, law and accounting firms were paid another $25 million, and KKR charged Safeway $60 million in advisory fees. KKR put down an initial $175 million to buy the controlling interest in Safeway, which four years later was valued at $800 million.

Not everyone benefited from this financial coup, however. The buyout had a devastating effect on the lives of many former employees. Over 63,000 managers and workers were terminated from Safeway through store sales or layoffs. Those who were rehired generally took a 30 to 50 percent cut in pay and many could only find part-time employment. Many others, especially those in the Dallas area, remained unemployed for an extended time and suffered both financially and psychologically.

Human suffering is difficult to quantify, but the president of Safeway's credit union in Dallas estimated that 80 percent of the people in that division were devastated by the layoff. Many homes and cars were repossessed. A *Wall Street Journal* article described specific cases of divorce, alcoholism, and suicide attributed to the layoff. James White, a Safeway trucker for nearly thirty years in Dallas, is an example. One year after the layoff, while still unemployed, he told his wife he loved her and went into the bathroom, locked the door, and shot himself in the head with a hunting rifle.

Source: Susan C. Faludi, "Safeway LBO Yields Vast Profits but Exacts a Heavy Human Toll," *Wall Street Journal*, May 16, 1990, A1.

ACQUISITIONS AND MERGERS

After an acquisition or merger, the human resource department should expect to play an important role in making a smooth transition. The efficiency that comes from a unified sense of direction and purpose requires that the human resource functions of the two previously separate units be combined into one consistent policy. Many human resource activities are influenced by an acquisition or merger.

- *Job redesign*: Duplicate functions and unnecessary tasks need to be eliminated.
- *Staffing*: Decisions about who does what need to be made and unneeded people are redeployed or terminated.
- *Performance evaluation*: The best performers need to be identified and kept, otherwise the decisions about who stays will be based on seniority.
- *Incentives*: Severance pay is provided for those who leave and incentive systems are created for those who stay.
- *Pay and benefits*: The pay systems and benefit programs for the separate units will need to be joined into one coherent package.
- *Work scheduling*: The hours of work may need to be readjusted due to forced transfers, reduced workweeks, and job sharing.[30]

DOWNSIZING

Economic forces may compel an organization to cut its operating costs and reduce the size of its work force. This process, called downsizing, can be very disruptive to operations and painful to employees. Some CEOs delay making cuts until the company's survival is threatened, and then they become almost brutal and ruthless in their reductions. A merger of two companies often involves layoffs, especially of mid-level managers, because of duplicate functions. During the 1980s, approximately 100,000 to 150,000 managers per year lost their jobs due to downsizing and mergers.[31] Alternatives to downsizing include reduced hours, job sharing, and wage cuts, but these measures are typically used in conjunction with layoffs. When the need for downsizing is clear, executives are encouraged to make a single, deep reduction in personnel to avoid repeated reductions.[32]

Employees who are laid off face the trauma of finding another job. The surviving employees also face the trauma of uncertainty and change. If employee loyalty is to be preserved, surviving employees need to know why and how decisions in personnel changes will be made. Organizations that observe the following strategy guidelines are able to minimize the loss of loyalty.

1. Be honest and straightforward about the real issue and make certain the appropriate individuals take the consequences.
2. Explain the available courses of action and why the option selected was most appropriate.
3. Make cuts consistent with historical performance criteria.
4. Create a program to help terminated employees find new employment and deal with feelings of rejection.
5. Communicate openly and put central ideas in writing to make them clear.
6. Establish and communicate the strategies being implemented to prevent layoffs from happening again.
7. Establish contingency funds and employee participation to minimize the need for distrust.[33]

Some companies provide outplacement services for laid-off employees, usually through an outside consulting firm. These services may include personal counseling, assistance in preparing a resumé, coaching in how to interview for a job, information about job openings, and job retraining to develop new skills. The focus of these activities is to help laid-off employees find a new job, but they also play an important role in reducing stress and preventing alcoholism, family abuse, and suicide.[34]

While management wants to cut costs by reducing employment, they want to retain their best employees. Ironically, however, the best employees are most likely to find another job or be recruited away. Unless an organization has a good performance-evaluation system and financial incentives to reward good performance, it will probably lose some of the employees it most wants to keep.

PRIVACY PROTECTION

ETHICAL ISSUES IN HUMAN RESOURCE PLANNING

Since human resource planning involves steering the careers of people, it necessarily raises several ethical issues. Although most employees do not seem particularly concerned about these issues, human resource managers need to be sensitive to them anyway.

The process of forecasting employment needs means that decisions are being made about the future careers of employees. Should they be told about these plans and how their careers might be affected? Human resource planning occasionally involves job rotations and transfers to prepare employees for advancement, and these events can be terribly disruptive to the personal lives of those involved. But since these plans are not certain, and more people are trained than can be promoted, how can companies avoid creating false expectations among those not promoted?

When an employment forecast indicates that employees will be terminated, how soon should they be told? More advance notice provides employees with greater opportunities to find alternative employment, but in some employees it tends to destroy enthusiasm to the point that they become totally unproductive. Many employers resist giving advance notice for fear of disrupting the workplace. Experience has shown, however, that the sooner employees know, the better their transition to a new job. Congress has decided that a plant closing has ethical implications for the employees and the local community, and in 1988 it passed the Worker Adjustment and Retraining Notification Act.[35] This law requires companies with 100 or more full-time employees to give 60-day advance notice of layoffs or plant closings that affect large numbers of workers. Notice is required for layoffs that are scheduled to last more than six months if they affect 50 or more employees. Downsizing an organization therefore may have both ethical and legal implications.

Collecting personal information about employees and storing it in a human resource information system involves at least three ethical issues: (1) Should the employees have any control over the data collection and how it is obtained? (2) Should employees have access to their own files and the right to challenge or correct what is in them? and (3) Who should have access to this information?

The most troublesome issue regarding the development of a human resource information system is that of privacy protection. The desire for personal privacy conflicts with an organization's need to collect information and act upon it. Individuals do not like having information about their private lives available to just anyone who is curious; they want to have control over who is able to examine such personal information as medical histories, test scores, salaries, performance evaluations, and biographical data. The issue of privacy protection is not whether personal data should be totally eliminated but how much control individuals should have in deciding what information can be included in their files and who can be allowed to examine it.[36] The concern for privacy protection has increased in recent years because of technological advances in electronic data processing and a growing distrust of social institutions. Computerized systems containing thousands of pieces of information on numerous individuals can make this information readily available for public observation.

Although most people think employers should totally avoid meddling in their employees' private lives, there are good reasons why employers sometimes need to intrude. Managers have been forced to deal with some critical social problems, such as illegal drug use, smoking, and AIDS, because they affect job performance and the safety or rights of other employees. Furthermore, accident rates and health insurance costs are related to the employees' manner of living. Consequently, corporate wellness programs are often just one step away from controlling off-the-job habits. In some cases, employers have a legitimate need to know; nevertheless, they should resist the temptation to interfere in workers' private lives or to obtain irrelevant personal information.[37]

LEGAL PROTECTIONS

CRIME CONTROL ACT

Although the Crime Control and Safe Streets Act of 1968 largely focuses on issues outside the organization, its limitations on wiretapping are relevant to workplace privacy. This federal law prohibits the deliberate interception of private telephone and oral conversations. Supervisors and other coworkers are not allowed to listen to employees' personal conversations without their permission or knowledge unless there is a legitimate business need for it, such as coaching a new sales representative. This law also prohibits putting a secret listening device in an employee's office ("bugging") or even eavesdropping on private conversations unless they occur in public locations.

The case of *Watkins* v. *L. M. Berry & Company* (1983) illustrates the privacy protection provided by the Crime Control Act.[38] The Company had a policy allowing supervisors to routinely monitor sales calls on an extension phone. In this case the supervisor overheard an employee discuss her intention to take another job during a personal call to another person. The court decided that while the unintentional interception of a personal conversation does not violate the act (if the listener hangs up when it is clear that the call is personal and does not use what was overheard against the employee), in this case the supervisor went beyond these bounds and in so doing violated the employee's privacy rights. Employers can limit or even prohibit personal calls (except in emergencies) during working hours, but they may not eavesdrop on them.

FAIR CREDIT REPORTING ACT

Privacy protection is provided by a combination of federal and state legislation and voluntary compliance. The Fair Credit Reporting Act was passed in 1970 to offer protection to individuals against negative credit reports containing false or misleading information. The act applies to employers who purchase "consumer reports" from "consumer-reporting agencies." These consumer reports may contain information regarding an individual's credit standing, character, reputation, personal characteristics, and mode of living. The law allows employers to use this information for employment purposes, but requires the employers to inform applicants that an investigative report has been requested within three days of the request. The law also restricts the information that can be included in the reports and the uses to which the reports can be applied. For example, information over seven years old (fourteen years for bankruptcies) cannot be included in the reports. Under certain circumstances the consumer has the right to know that a report is being made and has a chance to challenge any incorrect or misleading information.

If an individual is denied employment or promotion on the basis of a credit report, either in whole or in part, the employer is required to inform the individual of the name and address of the consumer-reporting agency. However, the employer does not have to tell the individual what was in the report. An employer also is not required to report information obtained in connection with employment or promotion for which the employee has not specifically "applied." Nor does the law require an employer to disclose information obtained from sources other than a consumer-reporting agency. Consequently, the Fair Credit Reporting Act is very limited in its ability to protect the privacy of employees.

PRIVACY ACT

The Privacy Act of 1974 was passed to protect the privacy of individuals employed in government agencies or by government contractors. This act essentially prohibits an agency from disclosing records about individuals. While the Privacy Act restricts what government agencies can release, the Freedom of Information Act requires government agencies to release certain information to anyone who asks for it. The Freedom of Information Act requires government agencies to provide information about the agency (how it is organized and what it does) and allows individuals, employers, and unions to request copies of government documents. However, the Freedom of Information Act specifically exempts the disclosure of personal information that could constitute an unwarranted invasion of personal privacy, such as performance evaluations and medical reports.

Under the Privacy Act of 1974, a Privacy Protection Study Commission was established to examine the need for further legal protection of employee privacy. The commission conducted extensive hearings on the problems of employee privacy and submitted a massive report.[39] It recognized the fine line between protecting employees from unwarranted invasions of personal privacy and the employers' interests in being able to make informed decisions. As a result of its hearings, the commission established three general policy goals: (1) to minimize intrusiveness, (2) to maximize fairness, and (3) to create legitimate expectations of confidentiality.

Minimizing intrusiveness largely refers to the process of collecting information. When information is obtained, individuals should be informed of the need for and potential use of the information at the time it is requested to enable them to make an informed decision about whether to disclose the information.

Maximizing fairness refers to the way confidential information is used. The information that is used must be accurate, timely, complete, relevant, and used according to a general notion of fairness.

Creating legitimate expectations of confidentiality refers to the process of disseminating information. Confidentiality limits need to be placed on the recordkeeper's freedom to make voluntary disclosures of information to third parties.

The Privacy Commission also recommended five basic procedural rights for employees:

1. *Notice.* Employees should be kept informed about the kinds of information kept by employers and how such information is used.
2. *Authorization.* The collection of information about employees from third-party sources should require specific authorization by the employees.
3. *Access.* Employees should be able to see and obtain copies of information about them kept by employers.
4. *Correction.* Employees should be able to challenge the accuracy, timeliness, or completeness of information kept about them by the employers and be able to either correct it or add a statement of dispute to the record.
5. *Confidentiality.* Disclosure of information about employees to third parties should generally require the employees' authorization.

The Privacy Commission recommended that these procedural rights be implemented through voluntary employer compliance rather than through federal legislation. The voluntary compliance was proposed on an experimental basis to ascertain whether employers would undertake changes providing greater privacy protection for employees. Some organizations, such as IBM, have done an excellent job in adopting privacy-protection policies and practices.[40] Most organizations, however, have disregarded the commission's recommendations. A study conducted by the chairman of the Privacy Commission indicated that 64 percent of the companies surveyed did not have privacy-protection programs.[41] However, privacy protection does not seem to be of great concern to most employees. When questioned in opinion surveys about improper disclosure of employment records by their employers, 76 percent of the employees answered that they thought it was unlikely. Only 7 percent thought it was very likely.[42]

California became the first state to pass an employee privacy law in 1976. Since then several other states have enacted legislation providing for some form of employee privacy protection, but inconsistencies exist among these laws, particularly regarding their coverage of medical records and health information.

Even though the Privacy Commission recommended voluntary employer compliance, it left open the possibility of federal legislation to protect the privacy of employment records if the voluntary approach should fail. Some observers expect that a federal privacy-protection law will eventually be passed because of the inconsistencies resulting from the passage of state laws.[43]

INTERNATIONAL HRM

Job descriptions are used by companies throughout the world for essentially the same purposes as they are used in the United States. Some European firms even use standardized questionnaires similar to the Position Analysis Questionnaire to assist in the development of job descriptions. Compensation systems everywhere are typically tied to the demands of the job as described in a job description. Even in socialist countries, such as Cuba, which experimented with paying workers on factors unrelated to the job they performed, were forced to abandon that system and return to using job descriptions to help them make pay decisions.

Human resource planning seems to depend more on the sophistication of the multinational corporation than the economic development or culture of the host country. Some multinational organizations have elaborate human resource planning systems that they use wherever they have a plant. In its United Kingdom plant, for example, Nissan has implemented some very sophisticated computerized personnel systems for human resource planning and other personnel functions.

Nissan established a plant in the United Kingdom in 1984, and over the next four years it installed eighteen computerized human resource systems. These computerized systems, which operate on eight different software programs, include such programs as human resource planning, human resource information systems, safety statistics, organization charts, absence-monitoring, management development, and recruitment control. Nissan's computerized systems would be considered advanced in any country. As human resource professionals acquire greater computer skills and more software is developed, other countries and more corporations will achieve similar levels of sophistication in their human resource functions.[44]

Privacy protection is a concept unique to the Western free world. Workers in communist countries have had no control over the kinds of personal information collected about them or who should have access to it. The basic procedural rights recommended by the Privacy Commission, such as authorization, access, and confidentiality, are foreign concepts to most communist workers.

SUMMARY

A. Human resource planning provides a foundation for personnel staffing activities. Recruitment and selection are based on human resource plans.

B. Human resource planning activities need to be carefully integrated with business plans. Long-range strategic business plans need to be correlated with environmental scanning to estimate whether appropriate numbers of employees with the proper skills will be available for future plans. Middle-range business planning should provide adequate employment forecasts so that an organization can plan ahead to provide the human resources needed to achieve its goals and objectives. Short-range budgets and annual operating plans should identify the employment needs for the coming year to achieve the business plans.

C. Job analysis refers to the studies that are performed to obtain job descriptions and job specifications. Job descriptions provide information concerning the duties and responsibilities contained in jobs. Job specifications identify the minimum acceptable qualifications of the employees who perform the jobs.

D. Job descriptions and job specifications are used for many different personnel functions, especially performance evaluation, compensation, training, and discipline. An exhaustive list of job descriptions is contained in the *Dictionary of Occupational Titles*.

E. Four methods for gathering job-analysis information are (1) observations, (2) interviews, (3) questionnaires, and (4) employee recordings.

F. One of the first steps in developing a human resource planning system is to analyze the jobs presently performed and the employees who perform them.

G. The jobs within an organization need to be categorized into major job categories, which are then subcategorized as necessary to form meaningful job categories.

H. A profile should be made on each employee. The profile should include information about the employee's skills and talents, potential for development, desire for promotion, present job, and other relevant information for human resource planning. All the employee profiles comprise a human resource information system, which is most useful when it can be stored on a computer for ready access and analysis.

I. Supervisors and unit managers are typically responsible for short-term forecasting. The most accurate method of short-term forecasting is called work-load analysis, which is based on estimates of the number of employee hours required to produce a product.

J. Long-term forecasting is the responsibility of both line managers and staff specialists. Line managers are typically responsible for identifying the projected levels of business activity. Staff specialists share in the responsibility of translating these business goals into human resource needs.

K. Long-term forecasting methods include (1) unit demand, (2) expert opinion, (3) trend projections, (4) probabilistic models, and (5) Markov analysis. Expert opinion is probably the least sophisticated approach to employment planning. The most sophisticated approach is to develop a probabilistic model that simulates the business and its environment. Trend projections that associate employment with levels of business activity are sufficiently sophisticated for most organizations.

L. The present work force can be compared with the forecasted employment needs to determine the number of new positions. The number of new positions plus an estimate of the losses due to turnover equals the number of new employees who must be hired.

M. Turnover levels typically are estimated by examining historical turnover information and by altering this information on the basis of current economic conditions, especially unemployment levels.

N. If net employment projections indicate a surplus of personnel, the number of employees can be reduced by (1) layoffs, (2) attrition, (3) reduced hours, and (4) early retirement.

O. Succession planning refers to the process of deciding how management vacancies will be filled. Succession plans significantly influence individual career planning and facilitate the development of managers.

P. Privacy-protection laws place legal constraints on the information that can be stored and used in a human resource planning system. The Fair Credit Reporting Act of 1970 and the Privacy Act of 1974 place moderate restrictions on information that can be contained within personnel files and how it can be released. However, private employers are expected, through voluntary compliance, to adopt procedural rights assuring privacy protection for employees.

QUESTIONS

1. A small manufacturing company with twenty employees does not need a sophisticated human resource planning system, but if the organization gets larger, the need for a system will arise. What conditions would indicate the necessity of developing a formal human resource planning system?

2. What type of interaction needs to occur between business planning and human resource planning?

3. Which job-analysis methods would you recommend for developing a job description of a computer programmer? Would observations alone be adequate? Why or why not?

4. Why are job categories rather than separate jobs used in the development of a human resource planning system? Would a human resource planning system that forecasted employment levels in each separate job be superior to a system that was based on job categories? Why or why not?

5. Should employees be responsible for keeping their profiles current? Explain your viewpoint.

6. Should employees be allowed to examine all the information in their profiles, including performance measures? Why or why not?

7. How do changes in productivity influence the demand for labor? How can changes in productivity be forecasted or anticipated?

8. What methods would you use to forecast the number of students who will be enrolled in the college of business over the next ten years?

9. Why is it important to know the causes of turnover?

10. If an organization had a surplus of personnel, would you recommend that layoffs or reduced hours be used to immediately reduce the work force? Explain the reasons for your recommenda-tion. What would be the effects of both strategies on the attitudes of employees?

11. If an organization has an outstanding all-star, this person is frequently listed as a probable replacement in many places on a replacement chart. What problems are created when one person is listed frequently on a replacement chart? What limitations would you recommend?

12. What is the process whereby succession plans get translated into developmental activities, such as training programs and new job assignments?

13. Should employees have access to all of the information kept by the employer about them? Do you think that the accuracy or completeness of the information would be influenced by making it accessible to the employees? Explain.

KEY TERMS

Attrition: A reduction in the number of personnel caused by failing to replace people who leave.

Delphi technique: A group decision-making process in which the group members do not interact in a face-to-face situation. Information from each individual is collected separately, integrated, and sent back to the group members who are then asked if they would like to revise their opinions. An intermediary coordinates the process.

DOT (Dictionary of Occupational Titles): This dictionary consists of over 20,000 job descriptions compiled by the Department of Labor. The jobs are organized according to occupational categories.

Environmental scanning: An examination of demographic and social forces influencing the long-term composition of the labor force and the future availability of employees.

Expert opinion: A method of long-term forecasting that is based on the subjective estimates of experts.

Functional job analysis: A method of analyzing jobs by observing them. Each job is analyzed according to "worker functions," which refer to the interaction of the worker with respect to data, people, and things. The interactions are classified according to a set of categories for each function. The analysis also includes information regarding career ladders and the kinds of training and development experiences that are needed for each job.

HRIS (Human resource information system): An integrated system of employee information that is usually computerized.

Job analysis:. The analysis of jobs within a company that produces a job description or a job specification.

Job description:. The description of the duties, responsibilities, working conditions, and reporting relationships contained in a job.

Job identification: A label or occupational code number associated with each job. Each job in the *Dictionary of Occupational Titles* has a unique nine-digit identification number.

Job specification: A list of the minimum acceptable qualifications that an employee must possess to perform a job adequately.

Management inventory: An employee profile of managers or potential managers that describes their present managerial position, potential for advancement, and interest in promotions.

Markov analysis: A method of long-term forecasting in which probabilities of movement among job categories in one period are used to forecast movement in a later period.

PAQ (Position Analysis Questionnaire): A standardized questionnaire containing 195 items that are used in a job analysis to create a job description.

Probabilistic model: A long-term forecasting method that uses probabilities of future events to estimate future employment levels. A simulation is a sophisticated probabilistic model.

Replacement chart: An organizational chart showing the employees who hold various positions and their most likely replacements.

Skills inventory: A profile that describes the skills and talents of each employee.

Strategic planning: Long-term business planning that focuses on corporate philosophy and organizational mission and determines what types of products or services the organization will provide in the long run.

Succession planning: The process of planning for replacements and designing developmental activities to make certain that the replacements will be qualified when they are needed.

Trend projections: A method of long-range forecasting in which employment levels are associated with levels of business activity. Trend projections include simple linear extrapolations as well as more sophisticated techniques of regression analysis.

Unit demand: A long-range forecasting method that is based on the estimates of each unit manager. These estimates are aggregated to identify the overall needs.

Work-load analysis: A method of short-term forecasting in which the number of employees is identified by computing how many employee hours will be needed to produce the output that the organization expects to achieve.

C O N C L U D I N G   C A S E

Fast-track Failure

For over fifteen years, Central Bank Corporation has used a special job-rotation program to identify and train future corporate leaders. The employees in this program represent the potential stars of the corporation and are known as "fast-track trainees." Since the top corporate leaders are the only ones who know which employees have been designated as fast-track trainees, the employees have to guess which of their peers are destined for the top by observing who is promoted most rapidly. Fast-track trainees receive new assignments frequently to give them a broad exposure to the corporation and a general administrative orientation. The frequency of promotion is often used as an index of a trainee's success and potential. The top 20 percent of each incoming group of managers are identified as fast-track trainees, which means that an enormous number of managers are constantly being promoted.

Within the past two years the fast-track program has come under attack, especially by the managing director of banking services. In a memo to the corporate human resource office, she criticized the frequent promotions and proposed that the corporation adopt a fixed policy that a person cannot be promoted until he or she has served in the same position for at least three years. Her memo recounted that when the fast-track program was first started the shining stars were only supposed to be promoted every three years. The average stay in a given position now is only fourteen to eighteen months, and the fast-track trainees continually pressure their superiors to be promoted even sooner so that they will appear more successful than their peers.

According to the managing director of banking services, the frequent promotions have caused these problems:

1. Fast-track trainees have developed a short-term orientation and focus only on projects and products that lead to dramatic results in the shortest time possible. Long-term projects that build the company are never considered.
2. The rapid turnover has created a lack of continuity in direction and structure. New managers blame all problems on their predecessors, reorganize their departments, and then move on.
3. Fast-track trainees are overly concerned with visibility and insist on keeping control of important projects and presentations to top management even when these responsibilities should be delegated to their subordinates.
4. Because fast-track trainees are promoted so rapidly in management positions, they lose contact with their specialties and areas of technical expertise.

The managing director of banking services concluded her memo by threating to adopt a three-year transfer policy in her division even if it was not adopted as a general corporate policy. Although the threat was never implemented, rumors concerning the threat were circulated, and managers now refuse promotions into the banking services division. The corporate personnel office can no longer ignore the issue, and the provision of some kind of statement is currently under consideration.

Questions:

1. Should the fast-track program be eliminated entirely?
2. Should a minimum time for promotions be specified, and if so, what should be the minimum?
3. Should employees be told whether they have been designated as fast-track trainees?
4. Should a smaller percentage of employees than the current 20 percent be designated as fast-track trainees?

NOTES

1. Robert J. Sahl, "Get It Together! Integrating the HR Department," *Personnel* 66 (February 1985): 39–45.

2. James W. Walker, "Evaluating the Effectiveness of Human Resource Planning Applications," *Human Resource Management* 13, no. 1 (Spring 1974): 19–27.

3. Michael D. Hawkins, "Micros and Mainframes: Emerging Systems to Support HRP's Newer Roles," *Human Resource Planning* 11, no. 2 (1988): 133–49; Peter D. Weddle, "Capturing the Benefits of High Technology," *Personnel Administrator* 11 (June 1986): 107–18.

4. Cynthia A. Lengnick-Hall and Mark L. Lengnick-Hall, "Strategic Human Resources Management: A Review of the Literature and a Proposed Typology," *Academy of Management Review* 13, (July 1988): 454–70; Andrew O. Manzini, "Integrating Human Resource Planning and Development: The Unification of Strategic, Operational, and Human Resource Planning Systems," *Human Resource Planning* 11, no. 2 (1988): 79–94.

5. J. Ronon and J. L. Livingstone, "An Expectancy Theory Approach to the Motivational Impact of Budgets," *Accounting Review* 50, (October 1975): 671–85.

6. *Willie S. Griggs et al.* v. *Duke Power Company*, 401 U.S. 424 (1971).

7. Stephanie Tailby and Peter Turnbull, "Learning to Manage Just-in-Time," *Personnel Management* 19 (January 1987): 16–19.

8. Philip C. Grant, "What Use Is the Job Description?" *Personnel Journal* 67 (February 1988): 44–53.

9. *Dictionary of Occupational Titles*, 4th ed. (Washington, D.C.: Department of Labor, 1977).

10. Hubert S. Field and Robert D. Gatewood, "Matching Talent with the Task," *Personnel Administrator* 32 (April 1987): 113–26; Carl Swope and Jack Lemonik, "New Task Analysis Methodology: The Corporate CAT Scan," *Journal of Compensation and Benefits* 22 (May/June 1987): 350–54; John G. Veres III, Maryanne Lahey, and Ricki Buckley, "A Practical Rationale for Using Multi-method Job Analyses," *Public Personnel Management* 16 (Summer 1987): 153–57.

11. Patrick R. Conley and Paul R. Sackett, "The Effects of Using High- v. Low-Performing Job Incumbents as sources of Job-Analysis Information," *Journal of Applied Psychology* 72 (August 1987): 434–37.

12. Sidney A. Fine, "Functional Job Analysis: An Approach to a Technology for Manpower Planning," *Personnel Journal* (November 1974): 813–18.

13. Samuel B. Green and Thomas Stutzman, "An Evaluation of Methods to Select Respondents to Structured Job Analysis Questionnaires," *Personnel Psychology* 39 (Autumn 1986): 643–64.

14. Ernest J. McCormick, "A Study of Job Characteristics and Job Dimensions as Based on the Position Analysis Questionnaire," *Journal of Applied Psychology* 57 (August 1972): 347–68.

15. Stephanie K. Butler and Robert J. Harvey, "A Comparison of Holistic v. Decomposed Rating on Position Analysis Questionnaire Work Dimensions," *Personnel Psychology* 41 (Winter 1988); 761–71; Robert C. Carter and Robert J. Biersner, "Job Requirements Derived from the Position Analysis Questionnaire and Validated Using Military Aptitude Test Scores," *Journal of Occupational Psychology* 60 (December 1987): 311–21; Angelo S. DeNisi, Edwin T. Cornelius III, and Allyn G. Slencoe, "Further Investigation of Common Knowledge Effects on Job Analysis Ratings," *Journal of Applied Psychology* 72 (May 1987): 262–68; Lee Friedman and Robert J. Harvey, "Can Raters with Reduced Job Descriptive Information Provide Accurate Position Analysis Questionnaire (PAQ) Ratings?" *Personnel Psychology* 39 (Winter 1986): 779–89.

16. These nine job categories are described in the EEOC publications such as the instructions for completing the EEO-1 report that employers are required to submit.

17. John Lawrie, "Skill Inventories: Pack for the Future," *Personnel Journal* 66 (March 1987): 127–30; Joe Pasqualetto, "Evaluating the Future of HRIS," *Personnel Journal* 67 (August 1988): 82–86.

18. John Lawrie, "Skill Inventories: A Developmental Process," *Personnel Journal* 66 (October 1987); 108–10; Harry H. Washing and Kurt W. Boveington, "How Useful Are Skills Inventories?" *Personnel* 63 (June 1987): 13–19.

19. Susan D. Manos, "Human Resource Decisions—Better Evaluations, More Computerization," *Data Management* 25 (February 1987): 32–34.

20. Jack Fiorito, Thomas H. Stone, and Charles R. Greer, "Factors Affecting Choice of Human Resource Forecasting Techniques," *Human Resource Planning* 8, No. 1 (1985): 1–17.

21. Linda Dmytryk, "When to Hire a Lawyer; When to Hire a Legal Assistant," *Legal Assistant Today* 6 (September/October 1988): 32–34; Letty R. Piper, "Patient Acuity Systems and Productivity," *Topics in Health Care Financing* 15 (Spring 1989): 43–53.

22. "Japanese Carriers Speed Up Air Crew Hiring, Training to Avoid Shortfall," *Aviation Week and Space Technology* 128 (June 13, 1988): 143.

23. Marvin D. Dunnette, John Campbell, and Kay Jaastad, "The Effect of Group Participation on Brainstorming Effectiveness for Two Industrial Samples," *Journal of Applied Psychology* 47 (1963): 30–37; Ernest J. Hall, Jane S. Mouton, and Robert R. Blake, "Group Problem Solving Effectiveness Under Conditions of Pooling Versus Interaction," *The Journal of Social Psychology* 59 (1963): 147–57.

24. Andre L. Delbecq, Andrew H. Van de Ven, and David H. Gustafson, *Group Techniques for Program Planning* (Glenview, Ill.: Scott Foresman, 1975): Chapter 4; Daniel J. Couger, "Key Human Resource Issues in IS in the 1990s: Views of IS Executives versus Human Resource Executives," *Information and Management* 14 (April 1988): 161–74.

25. Thomas P. Bechet and William R. Maki, "Modeling and Forecasting Focusing on People as a Strategic Resource," *Human Resource Planning* 10 (1987): 209–17; Allen S. Lee and George E. Biles, "A Microcomputer Model for Human Resource Planning," *Human Resource Planning* 11 (1988): 293–315; Richard J. Niehaus, "Models for Human Resource Decisions," *Human Resource Planning* 11, no. 2 (1988): 95–107.

26. Tim R. V. Davis and Fred Luthans, "Organizational Exit: Understanding and Managing Voluntary Departures," *Personnel Review* 17, no. 4 (1988): 22–28.

27. Jeoff Lewis, "Big Changes at Big Blue," *Business Week* (February 15, 1988): 92–98.

28. Richard Hansen and Richard H. Wexler, "Effective Succession Planning," *Employment Relations Today* 15 (Spring 1988): 19–24.

29. "Corporate Restructuring: 1989 ASPA/CCH Survey," (June 27, 1989): 2.

30. Ibid., pp. 3–10.

31. Susan R. Sanderson and Lawrence Schein, "Sizing Up the Down-Sizing Era," *Across the Board* 23 (November 1986): 14–23.

32. David R. Bywaters, "Managing During Down-Sizing," *Executive Excellence* 5, (July 1988): 13–14; Jospeh T. McCune, Richard W. Beatty, and Raymond V. Montagno, "Down-Sizing: Practices in Manufacturing Firms," *Human Resource Management* 27 (Summer 1988): 145–61; Kirkland Ropp, "Down-Sizing Strategies," *Personnel Administrator* 32, (February 1987): 61–64.

33. Ken Metejka and Bill Presutti, "Rebuilding the Survivor's Loyalty," *Management Decision* 26, no. 6 (1988): 56–57.

34. Stephan L. Guinn, "Outplacement Programs: Separating Myth from Reality," *Training and Development Journal* 42 (August 1988): 48–49.

35. *Plant Closings: The Complete Resource Guide, a BNA Special Report* (Washington D.C.: The Bureau of National Affairs, 1988).

36. James M. Jenks, "Protecting Privacy Rights," *Personnel Journal* 66 (September 1987): 123–32.

37. John A. Murphy, "Whose Business Is it? Your Job and Your Privacy," *Vital Speeches* 55 (December 15, 1988): 146–49; Barry Newman, "Expanded Employee Rights Increase Liability Exposure," *Journal of Compensation and Benefits* 4 (January/February 1989): 204–8.

38. *Watkins* v. *L.M. Berry and Company*, 1983, 704 52d 577.

39. Privacy Protection Study Commission, "Personal Privacy in an Information Society" (Washington D.C., Superintendent of Documents, 1977), especially pp. 236–73.

40. "Respecting Employee Privacy," *Business Week* (January 11, 1982): 130–31.

41. David F. Linowes, chairman of the Privacy Commission, statement in "The Department of Labor Hearings on Workplace Privacy," Federal Register 44, no. 57537 (1979).

42. Louis Harris and Associates, Inc., *The Dimensions of Privacy: A National Opinion Research Survey of Attitudes Toward Privacy* (1979).

43. Thomas E. Reinert, Jr., "Federal Protection of Employment Record Privacy," *Harvard Journal on Legislation* 18, no. 1 (Winter 1981): 207–58.

44. Brian Carolin and Alastair Evans, "Computers as a Strategic Personnel Tool," *Personnel Management* 26 (July 1988): 40–43.

Recruitment and Equal Employment Opportunity

Learning Objectives

After studying this chapter, you should be able to:

1. Describe the recruiting process and explain how yield ratios are used in planning recruiting activities.
2. Identify the issues involved in developing a recruiting strategy.
3. Explain the advantages and disadvantages of internal and external recruiting.
4. List the major sources of internal and external recruiting.
5. Identify which recruiting methods are usually best for recruiting blue-collar, clerical, professional/technical, and managerial employees.
6. Identify four alternatives to recruiting and evaluate them.
7. Describe the legal constraints that equal employment opportunity laws impose on recruiting.
8. Describe what an affirmative action plan is and explain the issue of reverse discrimination.

Chapter Outline

Alternatives to Recruiting

Overtime / Temporary Help / Subcontracting / Employee Leasing / Ethical Issues in Hiring Part-time and Temporary Employees

Equal Employment Opportunity

Civil Rights Act, Title VII / Affirmative Action / Illegal Preemployment Inquiries

International HRM

I N T R O D U C T O R Y   C A S E

Campus Recruiting

Every Wednesday morning on the campus of Virginia Tech University during the recruiting season a curious drama unfolds as students anticipate life after school, hopefully with a high starting salary at a major company.[1] A similar drama occurs at other American universities as graduating students compete for job openings.

At dawn each Wednesday morning students begin forming a line outside the placement office hoping to get an "open-slot" interview with a corporate recruiter. Although these students have worked hard, many of them do not have the outstanding credentials that companies are seeking, such as a 3.5 grade-point average or above.

Although some schools use a lottery, a computer-matching, or a bidding system to schedule interviews, many schools permit prescreening by employers, which allows them to skim top candidates from resumes sent to them through the placement office. Students, usually those with lower grade-point averages, are then allowed to schedule an interview if open slots are still available. These are the students who begin forming a line outside the college placement offices in the early morning hours, sometimes in the cold and snow.

Getting an interview, however, is no guarantee of getting a job, and most students "catch many bullets" (rejection letters) that they use to decorate their walls.

In a typical year, between 500 and 600 corporate, educational, and government recruiting teams will visit Virginia Tech and conduct approximately 17,000 interviews. The graduating seniors will submit an average of twenty resumes and letters requesting interviews and over three-fourths of these 80,000 requests will be denied. But if they survive the interview, they still need to compete with students from other schools. Large companies recruit nationwide at up to 100 universities like Virginia Tech.

Questions:

1. Is this an efficient way for students to find employment or for employers to find new employees? How could the process be improved?
2. Is too much emphasis placed on grade-point averages? Should companies prescreen applicants and, if so, what information other than GPA should they use in their prescreening?
3. How involved should the faculty be in recommending students?

RECRUITING PROCESS

Recruiting refers to the process of attracting potential job applicants from the external labor force. Every organization must be able to attract a sufficient number of job candidates who have the abilities and aptitudes needed to help the organization achieve its objectives. An effective employee-selection procedure is limited by the effectiveness of the recruiting process. Outstanding job candidates cannot be selected if they are not included in the applicant pool. The recruiting process also interacts with other human resource functions, especially performance evaluation, compensation, training and development, and employee relations, as illustrated in Figure 5.1.

Recruiting activities do not occur until someone in the organization has decided what kind of employees are needed and how many. The recruitment process, which is

FIGURE 5.1 Interaction between recruitment and other human resource functions.

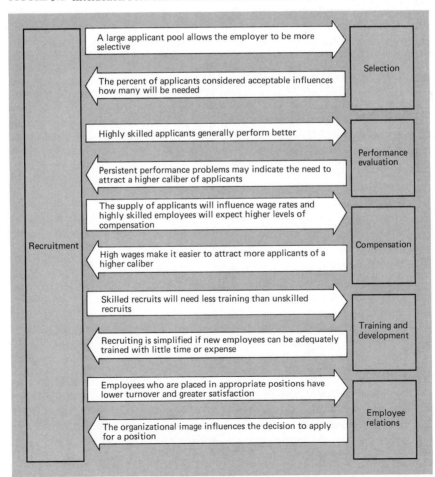

illustrated in Figure 5.2, basically consists of: (1) developing a recruiting plan, (2) formulating a recruiting strategy, (3) searching for job applicants, (4) screening those who are obviously unfit, and (5) maintaining an applicant pool.

RECRUITMENT PLANNING

Recruitment is typically a human resource function. A survey of 245 firms indicated that the responsibility for advertising job openings and screening applicants was centralized in the human resource department in 82 percent of the firms.[2] Top management may be involved in formulating general recruiting policies, such as determining where to recruit, deciding how much to spend, and specifying the organization's affirmative action goals. Line managers typically are not involved in the recruiting process, except when they are asked to make special recruiting trips. However, line managers are usually involved in interviewing applicants who have been screened and they usually make the final decision. The human resource department is largely responsible for most recruiting activities—it recommends policy to top management, develops the strategies and procedures for advertising job openings, collects information from prospective job applicants, and screens this information to form an applicant pool. The human resource department also is responsible for evaluating the recruiting process to identify the most effective recruiting procedures.

Recruiting activities are mainly controlled by the employee requisitions sent to the human resource department. These **employee requisitions** are formal authorizations to fill positions. Line managers are responsible for submitting employee requisitions as the final step in the human resource planning process. An employee requisition should specify the type of job the new employee will perform and the qualifications necessary to perform the job successfully. These job descriptions and job specifications are very important to the recruiting process. The human resource department must rely on the job description to advertise the job opening. The job specification helps the human resource department identify the skills and abilities needed by job applicants.

In planning recruiting activities, an organization needs to know how many applicants must be recruited. Since some applicants may not be satisfactory and others may not accept job offers, an organization must recruit more applicants than it expects to hire. **Yield ratios** are important tools in helping organizations decide how many employees to recruit for each job opening. These ratios express the relationship between the number of people at one step of the recruiting process relative to the number of people who will move to the next step. The yield ratios for a major oil company are presented in Figure 5.3.[3] This figure describes the experience of the company in its college recruiting efforts. The yield ratio of interviews to invitations is 6:1, the yield ratio of invitations to offers is 5:1, and the yield ratio of offers to acceptances is 2:1. The overall yield ratio is 60:1, which means that 60 college students are interviewed for every person who accepts a position. According to these ratios, 21,600 students must be interviewed to obtain 360 new hires from college campuses. A recruiting agency for a business journal reports that it interviews 100 applicants to fill one editorial position, for a yield ratio of 100:1.[4]

Another factor influencing recruitment planning is an organization's equal employment opportunity and affirmative action goals. If the organization has a history of discrimination against minorities and females, special recruiting efforts may be required

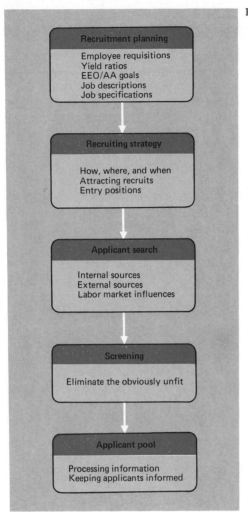

FIGURE 5.2 The recruitment process.

to correct this imbalance. The Equal Employment Opportunity Commission, sometimes backed by court decrees, may require an organization to revise its recruiting practices and establish hiring quotas to correct prior discriminatory practices. An organization ought to voluntarily examine its posture on hiring members of protected classes. As explained later, the EEOC recommends that affirmative action plans be established even though government contractors and subcontractors are the only organizations actually required to do this.

RECRUITING STRATEGY

After an organization has identified how many people it needs to recruit, a specific strategy must be developed to identify how the employees will be recruited, where they

HRM in Action

Recruitment Planning in Public Accounting

Eric Flamholtz has developed a recruitment planning method to help public accounting firms anticipate how many new recruits they will need to staff their organization. Public accounting firms have well-defined job levels, and they can use historical information to estimate the probabilities of how many professionals will stay at each level, how many will be promoted to the next level, and how many will leave.

One of the offices of Touche Ross & Company, a major accounting firm, used Flamholtz's model to decide how many accountants should be recruited to fill the anticipated vacancies at the "audit senior" level. The job progression in the audit area goes from accounting (level 1), to semi-senior (level 2), to senior (level 3), to supervisor (level 4), to manager (level 5), to partner (level 6).

The formula showing how many new recruits will be needed is:

New hires $= (A + L)H$, where:

L = The number of people at a given level who are expected to leave.

A = The number of additional positions that need to be created at a given level to accommodate growth.

H = The number of people that need to be hired at level 1 to gain one person at the higher level.

The office of Touche Ross had 20 audit seniors and needed to know how many new recruits to hire. Their records indicated that each year 25 percent of their seniors left the company and 35 percent were promoted to supervisor. Therefore, they could expect 5 to leave and 7 to be promoted, for a total of 12 leaving ($L = 12$). The firm expects to grow at a 10 percent annual growth rate and it normally takes three years for new recruits to advance to the level of senior. This growth rate means that 7 new positions will need to be filled in three years, but the firm should recruit them now ($A = 7$). Only 65 percent of new hires are eventually promoted to senior; therefore, the ratio is 1:15 ($H = 1.5$).

Inserting these numbers into the formula tells the firm that it should hire 29 new recruits this year to anticipate its future staffing needs.

$(12 + 7)1.5 = 29$ new hires

Source: Eric G. Flamholtz, D. Gerald Searfoss, and Russell Coff, "Developing Human Resource Accounting as a Human Resource Decision Support System," *Accounting Horizons* 2 (September 1988): 1–9.

will come from, and when they should be recruited. Numerous methods are available for helping the human resource department decide how to find job applicants. Private employment agencies, help-wanted posters, and newspaper advertising are some of the most popular methods for attracting recruits. These and other methods will be discussed in more detail later.

WHERE TO RECRUIT

Organizations need to recruit in areas where they have the greatest probability of achieving success. Although the local labor market is the best place to initiate recruiting

6 : 1
Interviews to invitations
5 : 1
Invitations to offers
2 : 1
Offers to acceptances

Overall yield ratio = 60 : 1

To obtain 360 new hires from college campuses, 21,600 students need to be interviewed, 3,600 students need to be invited to visit the company, and 720 offers need to be made.

FIGURE 5.3 Yield ratios: Mobil Oil Company.

efforts, regional or national recruiting may be necessary for certain positions. The relevant labor market for recruiting blue-collar and clerical employees is typically the local labor market. The labor market for technical employees is a regional market, while managerial and professional employees have a national or regional market. Some companies rely heavily on college campus recruiting; other companies, such as Hewlett-Packard, make special recruiting trips to locations where other companies are reducing their staffs.[5] Specific characteristics of geographical areas dictate the most appropriate places to recruit. For example, a number of people are opposed to moving to New York City and would not apply for jobs there. However, many people who live in New York City have very strong feelings about the city and would not want to live elsewhere.

In deciding where to recruit, two considerations are important. First, an organization should identify the prime labor markets from which potential applicants can be obtained. For example, an organization is most likely to find highly skilled applicants in areas with high unemployment levels. Second, an organization should analyze its own work force and identify the sources of its best employees. An organization may discover that most of its outstanding employees tend to come from one particular source, such as a particular university program, a vocational school, or a private employment agency. However, overuse of one recruiting source increases the potential of systemic discrimination, since a certain race or sex may be underrepresented.

ATTRACTING RECRUITS

A major component of an organization's recruiting strategy is how it plans to attract job applicants. An organization may have difficulty attracting the people it wants, especially highly skilled employees in highly competitive markets. To strengthen its recruiting efforts, the organization must decide what enticements it has to offer. Recruitment should be concerned with two simultaneous issues: securing people and ensuring that they will remain. Organizations frequently overlook the second issue and do not pay adequate attention to keeping their employees satisfied.

When an organization is recruiting job applicants, it is forced to walk a fine line between conveying a positive image and conveying an unrealistic image. Recruiters often fear that if they "tell it like it is," no one will be interested in applying for a position. However, when recruiters paint only a one-sided, positive view of an organization, new recruits often undergo reality shock because of unmet expectations, disillusionment, surprise, anxiety, and other feelings of not being fully prepared for the day-to-day activities and problems of the work environment.

Reality shock can be reduced by providing job applicants with realistic views of what an organization is like and the kind of working conditions that will be experienced on the job. Research has shown that when new recruits are given realistic information about a job, (1) no decrease occurs in the number of people who apply for the job, and (2) a significant reduction in turnover rates is realized.

One study concerning the effects of realistic job previews involved eighty female applicants for the job of telephone operator at Southern New England Telephone Company.[8] The applicants were assigned to either an experimental or a control group. The control group saw a traditional film that showed typical situations that operators encounter on the job and implied that their work was exciting, important, challenging, and satisfying. The experimental group saw a realistic film that showed the same situations as the traditional film, but also portrayed the position as easily learned and routine, as offering little chance for socializing, and as a job where employees were closely supervised, often criticized for mistakes, and seldom praised for good performance. Neither film had any effect on acceptance rates; seventy-eight of the eighty applicants accepted the job. However, the realistic films influenced the applicants' job expectations. The expectations of both groups declined, but the expectations of the group that had viewed the traditional film fell much more sharply than those of the group that had seen the realistic film. Probably because of disillusionment and unfulfilled expectations, the traditional group had a lower level of job satisfaction than the realistic group. After three

---

HRM in Action

Burger King™ Uses PR Firm to Hire Teens

Like most industries that rely heavily on teenage employees, Burger King has had difficulty finding enough employees to staff their fast-food restaurants. BBD Enterprises, operator of 23 Burger King restaurants in western Michigan, asked a public relations firm to help them identify why employees were leaving, to diagnose the needs of potential employees, and to develop a recruiting strategy to attract these people.

From the analysis, the PR firm decided that mothers and teens were the most promising groups of stable hires and they recommended two programs to attract them: free day care for the children of mothers and tuition reimbursement for teens. Free day care was advertised as the equivalent of getting a $1.50 an hour raise, but the company only had to provide this benefit to a select group for whom they were able to negotiate a group rate. Thus the cost of day care was much less than a pay raise would have cost, yet it succeeded in attracting many additional recruits.

The tuition-reimbursement program attracted 200 high school and college students. This program consisted of a $2,500 tuition reimbursement to workers who stay on the job two years or more.

Source: Meryl Davis, "Labor Shortage Woes," *Public Relations Journal* 44 (November 1988): 24–29, 59.

months, the turnover in the traditional group was 50 percent, whereas the turnover in the realistic group was 38 percent.[6]

Several other studies also have indicated that when a company attempts to communicate realistic expectations to recruits, the result is lower turnover among those who are hired.[7] Furthermore, a company's success in recruiting employees does not seem to be hurt by divulging honest information.

In developing recruiting strategies, organizations must consider what enticements can be offered to new recruits. Some employers assume that new applicants are attracted by high wages, and therefore they offer high starting salaries to entice employees. If employees are attracted by high starting salaries, this is an effective procedure; otherwise, it is an expensive practice.

ENTRY POSITIONS

Another recruiting-strategy decision that must be made is where the entry-level positions should be within an organizational hierarchy. Most organizations typically have two major starting positions. One entry-level position is at the very bottom of an organization. A new employee may be hired to fill an operative or production job with the possibility of eventual promotion to the job of first-line supervisor. The second entry-level position is typically in a lower level of management, such as first- or second-level supervision, or in a staff department. Individuals hired into these positions are considered to have potential for advancement into upper levels of management. The career paths for each entry-level position must be considered during recruitment. Some job applicants may be eliminated, not because they lack the necessary skills for an entry-level position, but because they do not have the abilities and skills to be promoted into higher career paths.

The entry-level positions in the retail industry illustrate these two entry points. Most of the people hired by a retail store are hired as sales associates, cashiers, or stockers. These people may eventually be promoted to department manager and possibly to higher levels of management. Most retail executives, however, start as department managers or staff assistants and are promoted into store management. Very few top retail executives started as sales associates and advanced to the top within the same company.

EFFECTIVE RECRUITERS

The success of a company's recruiting activities is probably influenced more by the competence of the recruiter than by any other single factor. In the eyes of a job applicant, the recruiter represents the company, and as a representative of the company, the recruiter is viewed as an example of the kind of people the organization employs and wants in the future. Since a recruiter normally has only thirty minutes per interview, the recruiter must be organized to allow sufficient time to become acquainted with the applicant, to create a favorable impression about the company, and to explain the kinds of job opportunities the company has to offer. Conducting twelve to sixteen personal interviews each day can be an exhausting experience, since the recruiter is expected to respond to each applicant with an attitude of enthusiasm and interest. A recruiter has to repeat the same information over and over, and therefore must work hard to make the information sound new and exciting in each interview.

Several studies have examined the characteristics of effective college recruiters. The following characteristics appear to be the most important:

1. *Interest and concern for the person as an individual.* Several studies have found that college students feel most positively about a recruitment interview when they believe that they are being interviewed by someone who is appreciative and interested in them as people. When asked to list the flaws of recruiters, students typically cite a lack of interest in the applicant as the major flaw.
2. *Enthusiasm.* Students are generally more attracted to recruiters who are enthusiastic, who make the job opportunity sound inviting, and who depict the company as a good place to work.
3. *Age of the recruiter.* Students prefer middle-aged recruiters who are between 35 and 55 years old. Students generally indicate that recruiters over age 55 do not understand them and that those under 30 lack status and prestige.
4. *Time to talk and listen.* Students are critical of recruiters who dominate the interview time with lengthy descriptions of the company's history and information about the number of employees, the products, assets, sales, and pensions. Students believe that the purpose of an interview is to both gather information and give information, and they want to talk about half the time.
5. *Comfortable rapport.* Students do not want to be embarrassed or put on the spot by a recruiter. They dislike stressful interviews and questions that make them feel defensive. Students want to be evaluated for their accomplishments and resent being asked too many personal questions about social class, parents, or their personal lives.[8]

To help college recruiters develop the ability to conduct effective interviews, training programs have been developed by the College Placement Council, the American Management Association, and other organizations affiliated with college recruiting. Most college recruiters are skilled interviewers who have been carefully trained. Unfortunately, an organization does not always have enough professional recruiters to visit all the campuses scheduled for interviews, and operating managers may be asked to assist in recruitment by visiting their alma maters. Armed with an interview schedule, a stack of blank reports, and assorted company brochures, these managers try to learn how to interview through on-the-job training.

APPLICANT SEARCH

Once the recruiting plans and strategies have been developed, the actual recruiting activities take place. The applicant search may involve traditional recruiting methods, such as newspaper ads and help-wanted posters. With a little creativity, however, novel methods can be used to attract highly qualified applicants. But whatever the method of search used, an important issue in recruiting job applicants is deciding whether a particular position should be filled by promoting someone from within the organization or by hiring someone from outside.

INTERNAL VERSUS EXTERNAL RECRUITING

Vacancies in upper-level management positions can be filled either by hiring people from outside the organization or by promoting lower-level managers. Both strategies have advantages and disadvantages. A major advantage of a **promotion-from-within** policy is its positive effect on employee motivation. Knowing that they have opportunities to be promoted tends to motivate their performance, to increase their satisfaction with the company, and to solidify their feelings of loyalty toward the company. Moreover, the wealth of information that is generally available about present employees minimizes the likelihood that a poor placement decision will be made. Employees who are promoted into higher-level positions also are knowledgeable about the organization, and thus little time is lost in orienting them to their new positions.

The major disadvantage of a promotion-from-within policy is that it creates narrowness of thinking, a condition sometimes referred to as "inbreeding." A promotion-from-within policy also requires a strong management development program to prepare managerial candidates to assume greater responsibility. Such training activities, however, do not solve the problem of "company thinking."

The major advantage of external hiring is that new people bring new ideas and new insights into an organization. They also are able to make changes in the organization without having to please constituent groups. However, some risk is involved in hiring someone from outside the organization, since the person's skills and abilities have not been assessed on a firsthand basis. Hiring someone from outside the organization also involves an opportunity cost because of the loss of time that occurs while the individual is becoming oriented to the new job. Moreover, if external hiring occurs frequently, the present employees may become dissatisfied because they have no opportunities for advancement.

Finally, if the new recruit was working for a competitor and signed a noncompete agreement, the former employer may sue both the employee and the new employer, especially if the individual possessed trade secrets or other valuable information. The courts have been especially prone to declare unfair competition when a large number of employees simultaneously defect to a new company.[9] The advantages and disadvantages of promotion from within versus external hiring are summarized in Table 5.1.

LABOR-MARKET INFLUENCES

The recruiting process is influenced by labor-market conditions. When the economy is growing rapidly and unemployment levels are very low, recruiting is extremely difficult. Recruiters, especially on college campuses, have to compete aggressively for job applicants. However, when the economy is stagnant and unemployment levels are high, organizations can obtain a large applicant pool with very little effort. During the 1970s and 1980s, most companies could recruit from a large labor pool of high-caliber entry-level workers. By 1990, however, the labor force was not expanding as rapidly, due to reduced birthrates and changing demographics, and recruiting was much more difficult. To remain competitive when recruiting is difficult, employers need to alter their tactics by such means as looking beyond the traditional sources of recruits, using temporary employees, and eliminating jobs through technology.[10]

TABLE 5.1   Promotion from within versus external hiring

Promotion from Within

Advantages	Disadvantages
Provides greater motivation for good performance	Creates a narrowing of thinking and stale ideas
Provides greater promotion opportunities for present employees	Creates political infighting and pressures to compete
Provides better opportunity to assess abilities	Requires a strong management development program
Improves morale and organizational loyalty	
Enables employee to perform job with little lost time	

External Hiring

Advantages	Disadvantages
Provides new ideas and new insights	Loss of time due to adjustment
Allows employee to make changes without having to please constituent groups	Destroys incentive of present employees to strive for promotions
Does not change the present organizational hierarchy as much	No information is available about the individual's ability to fit with the rest of the organization
	Potential law suit if new employee signed a noncompete agreement with a competitor

OCCUPATIONAL CHOICE

The effectiveness of a recruiting strategy is heavily influenced by personal choice. Occupational preferences place severe limitations on the ability of a recruiter to attract applicants to jobs. A recruiter cannot hope to attract applicants for jobs that are inconsistent with the individuals' basic occupational preferences. An aggressive recruiting strategy might produce short-term results in enticing people to explore new jobs, but if the new jobs do not fit recruits' career goals, they will leave the organization.

Occupational choices are influenced by such variables as socioeconomic status, sex, educational attainments, and personal interests. The high correlation between occupational level and social background raises important issues about the equality of educational and employment opportunities. The data indicate that children born to parents with little formal education who perform unskilled work are likely to remain at the same occupational level.[11] The social-background factors created by parents, peers, and significant others tend to impede an individual's opportunities to move into higher occupational levels. Therefore, although recruiting efforts may be directed toward moving people into higher occupational levels, they have little chance of succeeding against the overwhelming influence of social-background forces.

SCREENING

As applicants apply for job openings, the organization screens them to eliminate those who are obviously unqualified. Great care must be exercised to prevent applicants from being disqualified for improper reasons. The reasons for disqualification should be legitimate business reasons. Some examples of legitimate reasons include inadequate educational preparation or degrees, lack of the necessary professional certificates, or lack of previous experience and training. The purpose of screening is to help both the organization and the applicants who are not qualified. A great deal of time and effort can be wasted processing the applications of individuals who are obviously unqualified. Moreover, the individuals are better off knowing immediately that they are unqualified so that they can pursue other employment options.

APPLICANT POOL

The applicant pool consists of individuals who have expressed an interest in pursing a job opening and who might be feasible candidates for the position. As applications are received, the organization should process the information and organize it so that it can be readily examined. If an immediate selection decision is not anticipated, the organization should keep the applicants informed about the status of their applications. If any of the applicants accept employment elsewhere and no longer want to keep their applications active, the organization should remove these applications from the applicant pool.

EVALUATION

An organization must periodically evaluate its recruiting process to determine whether the process can be improved and costs reduced. The following issues should be examined during an evaluation:

Are the yield ratios acceptable, and if not, can they be improved? An organization can significantly reduce its recruiting costs by achieving a favorable yield ratio. The savings can be illustrated by evaluating the information presented in Figure 15.3. If the ratio of interviews to invitations, which is 6:1, could be reduced to 4:1 by more effective recruiting methods, the overall yield ratio would be reduced from 60:1 to 40:1. This improved ratio would reduce the number of college student interviews from 21,600 to 14,400.

Are the recruiting advertisements effective? The effectiveness of the various advertising methods should be evaluated to identify which are the most effective and whether they are attracting the quality of recruits needed.

Are the recruiting efforts consistent with the equal employment opportunity and affirmative action goals of the company? The kinds of people who are being attracted into the organization should be examined to determine whether the percentages of minority and female applicants are comparable to the surrounding work force or whether higher goals should be set to correct imbalances.

Are the procedures for collecting and storing applicant information designed to avoid unnecessary inconvenience? The applicant pool should contain only individuals who are viable candidates for a position.

Are the criteria used for screening applicants appropriate? Applicants who are obviously unqualified should immediately be eliminated from the applicant pool, but the criteria used for making this decision should be carefully examined to make certain that viable candidates are not being arbitrarily eliminated.

What is the organization's image, and can it entice people to accept employment? If the organization is having difficulty attracting qualified applicants, both its image and the kinds of opportunities and benefits it offers to prospective employees should be evaluated. Some organizations, such as the United States Army, have decided that they need to create a more favorable organizational image to attract more recruits.

INTERNAL RECRUITING SOURCES

When job vacancies exist, the first place that an organization should look for replacements is within itself. An organization's present employees generally feel that they deserve the opportunity to be promoted to higher-level positions because of their service and commitment to the organization. Moreover, the organization has had opportunities to examine the track records of its present employees and to estimate which of them would be successful. Also, recruiting among present employees is generally less expensive than recruiting from outside the organization. The major forms of internal recruiting include: (1) promotion from within, (2) job posting and bidding, and (3) contacts and referrals.

PROMOTION FROM WITHIN

Promoting entry-level employees to more responsible positions is one of the best ways to fill job vacancies and an important reason why a company should have a human resource planning system. An organization that has a human resource planning system uses succession plans and replacement charts to identify and prepare individuals for upper-level positions. An effective promotion-from-within policy requires companies to hire entry-level employees who may be overqualified for their initial job but capable of being trained for more responsible positions. Skills inventories are useful in identifying individuals who have the potential for advancement. An individual's desire to be promoted can be assessed in a performance-appraisal review, and this information can then be used to place the individual in training and development activities. A promotion-from-within policy is intrinsic to career development and human resource planning. As was noted earlier, a promotion-from-within policy can stimulate great motivation among employees, and this motivation is often accompanied by a general improvement in employee morale.

JOB POSTING AND BIDDING

An organization that does not have a human resource planning system and does not know which employees want to be considered for promotion can use a job posting-and-bidding system. In a **job-posting** system, the organization notifies its present employees about job openings through the use of bulletin boards, company publications, or personal letters. The purpose of job posting is to communicate the fact that job openings exist. **Job bidding** allows individuals who believe they have the required qualifications to apply for the available jobs. An effective job-posting-and-bidding system involves the following six guidelines:

1. Jobs should be posted in prominent places or advertised in such a way that interested employees are likely to see them.
2. All permanent promotions and transfer opportunities should be posted.
3. Job openings should be posted for at least one week prior to recruiting from outside the organization.
4. A job specification should be included with the listing so that employees can judge whether they possess the necessary abilities and skills.
5. The eligibility rules and criteria for deciding how the job will be filled should be clarified. For example, an applicant should know whether the decision will be based on seniority, performance, or a combination of seniority and performance, and if he or she must fulfill minimum length-of-service requirements in his or her present job before applying for a transfer.
6. Once the decision is made, all applicants should be informed about the decision.[12]

Job-posting systems generally work quite well. A survey of 245 firms by the Bureau of National Affairs indicated that about 76 percent of the responding organizations used a job-posting system. For example, the Bank of Virginia instituted a job-posting system in which its employees were allowed to bid on promotional opportunities by completing applications and having them signed by their immediate supervisors.[13] Employees were allowed to bid for only one job at a time, and they were not allowed to bid for a new job unless they had served at least six months in their present position. The program was accepted very well by managers, who actually encouraged capable subordinates to pursue positions outside their departments. After several years of using the program, the bank reported that no staff members had left the company as a result of being turned down for promotions. It also noted that no additional personnel staff were required to administer the job-posting program. The bank posts an average of 2.5 jobs per week, and about 18 percent of the staff members who have bid for these jobs have been successful in obtaining them.

CONTACTS AND REFERRALS

Before going outside to recruit new employees, many organizations ask present employees to encourage friends or relatives to apply for job openings. The BNA survey indicated that 91 percent of the firms relied on their own workers to refer potential employees to the firm.[14] Contacts and referrals from present employees are valuable sources of job recruits. A survey of the job-search behavior of 1,500 men found that 23 percent of the white males and 29 percent of the black males had found their first jobs through friends and that 31 percent of both races had found their jobs through the aid of family members.[15] Since the surroundings of people at work are such an important part of job satisfaction and satisfaction with life in general, employees like to refer their friends and relatives and help them find employment where they can work together. Some organizations have even offered cash bonuses to employees who have referred successful recruits. One company in the aerospace industry that was having difficulty recruiting sufficient engineers offered a bonus of $500 to any employee who referred someone who was hired and stayed with the organization for six months.[16]

Employee referrals are relatively inexpensive and usually produce quick responses. However, some organizations are concerned about problems that result from hiring friends of employees. For example, the practice of hiring friends and relatives increases the likelihood of **nepotism**, favoritism shown to friends and relatives. Hiring friends and relatives also is more likely to create cliques, causing some individuals to feel excluded from informal group associations. Since friends and relatives tend to be of the same race and sex as present employees, relying on contacts and referrals for finding new employees also can create an inability to achieve equal employment opportunity and affirmative action goals.

EXTERNAL RECRUITING SOURCES

A broad variety of methods are available for external recruiting. An organization should carefully assess the kinds of positions it wants to fill and select the recruiting methods that are likely to produce the best results. The methods used in recruiting professional employees are significantly different from those used in recruiting clerical and sales personnel.

DIRECT APPLICATIONS: WALK-INS AND WRITE-INS

Because of an organization's favorable location or reputation, it may be able to obtain a large applicant pool from individuals who voluntarily submit applications for employment. Some companies have a constant flow of applications for employment, and these voluntary walk-ins and write-ins are an inexpensive source of recruits. Although direct applications are not good sources for recruiting top-level executives, they do provide some organizations with all the candidates they need for clerical and blue-collar jobs. The number of unsolicited applications that an organization receives is largely determined by its reputation as a good place to work. Companies that are perceived as model employers often receive hundreds of unsolicited applications weekly.

PUBLIC EMPLOYMENT AGENCIES

Public employment agencies were created by the Wagner-Peyser Act of 1933, which provided for a "national system of employment offices for men, women, and juniors." Public employment agencies are operated by each state under the general direction of the U.S. Training and Employment Service (USTES). USTES sets national policies and establishes common reporting requirements for the state employment services. These public employment agencies are generally called **Job Service** offices, and most large cities have them.

Job Service offices are funded by the contributions that employers make to state unemployment insurance funds. Part of the money that employers are required to pay for unemployment insurance (.7 percent of each employee's pay up to a base amount) is sent back to the state employment agencies by the federal government. The Social Security Act provides that workers who are laid off must register with the state employment agencies to be eligible for unemployment benefits. Since unemployment insurance benefits are supposed to be available only to laid-off individuals who are seeking employment, these individuals provide a roster of potential job seekers for organizations looking for job applicants. Job Service provides a wide range of benefits to job seekers, including job placement, unemployment insurance, labor-market information, testing, employer consultation, training programs, and individual counseling. Some of the state agencies do an excellent job in helping people to prepare for and find jobs. The state agencies also are required to provide special services for military veterans and minority-group members.

Job Service has been criticized by both employers and job seekers. Employers have complained that Job Service is so intent on placing minorities, veterans, and the handicapped that it fails to screen job applicants adequately. Job seekers complain that the Job Service's activities are primarily oriented to clerical work, blue-collar jobs, and other unskilled positions. Job Service has attempted to respond to these criticisms by improving its service and increasing its information about professional, technical, and highly skilled jobs. For example, Job Service has installed a computer-matching system that contains information about people applying for work as well as information about jobs available. Job Service is generally able to provide rapid information to both individuals who are seeking employment and employers who are seeking job applicants.

PRIVATE EMPLOYMENT AGENCIES

Private employment agencies are business organizations that specialize in helping employers find applicants to fill job openings. These employment agencies are business organizations that produce profits from their recruiting activities. They perform many recruiting and selecting functions for employers, such as obtaining application-blank information, conducting screening interviews, and recommending highly qualified applicants. Although private agencies are involved in filling virtually every kind of position, the survey by the BNA of 245 firms indicated that they are more likely to be used to find managerial (60 percent) and professional employees (58 percent) than for sales (44 percent), office (28 percent), or production workers (11 percent).[17]

Private employment agencies can provide a valuable service in bringing together compatible job seekers and organizations. Some private employment agencies have been operating for many years and have developed outstanding reputations for their services. Many of the outstanding agencies have national data bases regarding job openings and applicants, and as a result, these agencies can rapidly provide information to job seekers and employers. An important consideration in using private employment agencies is the cost of their services. The fee charged by a private employment agency is typically between 10 and 20 percent of a first year's salary, and this fee is normally assessed to the party that is being served. If an employer requests job applicants, the employer typically pays the fee. If an individual asks for assistance in obtaining employment, the fee is assessed to him or her. Individuals should be very cautious about signing a contract with a private employment agency. They should examine the contract and consider the costs and benefits as carefully as if they were signing a contract to make a major purchase or loan. Sometimes agencies are able to help individuals find ideal jobs for which they are uniquely qualified, and then the agencies' fees are more than offset by the high salaries received by those hired. At other times, however, agencies do not do anything more than what individuals could have done for themselves. This is particularly true for local agencies, which simply check the same local recruiting sources that are available to the applicant.

Many private employment agencies are able to tailor their services to the specific needs of their clients. For example, some agencies specialize in particular employment areas, such as engineering, human resources, or computer programming. For an organization, the benefit of using a private employment agency increases as the agency gains familiarity with the specific needs of the organization, knowledge that enables the agency to more effectively screen potential employees.

EXECUTIVE SEARCH FIRMS

Executive search firms, sometimes called "headhunters," are specialized forms of private employment agencies that place top-level executives and experienced professionals. If an organization decides to go outside to fill an upper-level management position, it may ask an executive search firm to find potential candidates. Since the candidates are usually working as managers for competitors, the organization's use of an executive search firm to identify the candidates helps the organization avoid accusations of pirating by its competitors.[18]

The recruiting activities of an executive search firm usually are more aggressive than those of a private employment agency. Executive search firms often visit their clients' headquarters to interview members of management. The purpose of these interviews is to gather information concerning the goals and objectives of the organization and the job qualifications required of the new executive. This information aids the executive search firm in reviewing potential candidates and in recommending those best qualified for a selection decision. Like the fee of a private employment agency, the fee charged by an executive search firm is substantial. The fee is approximately 25 percent of an executive's annual salary, or between $15,000 and $50,000 or more.[19]

SCHOOLS AND COLLEGES

Educational institutions are excellent sources of young applicants with varying amounts of formal training and relatively little full-time work experience. High schools are excellent sources of employees for jobs that require very little skill, such as some blue-collar jobs, clerical jobs, and jobs in the retail industry. Vocational schools are generally excellent sources of applicants for the skilled trades and technical positions. Colleges and universities are good sources for supervisory, managerial, and professional positions.

Some organizations have developed special agreements with educational institutions whereby students are provided with specialized training. While they are in school, the students know they are preparing to work for a particular organization, although there is no obligation on the part of either to accept or offer employment after graduation. These arrangements typically benefit the student, the school, and the company: the student's education is relevant to getting a job, the education offered by the school is practical and applicable to a company's needs, and the company often contributes financially to the school. The special case of college recruiting will be discussed later.

PROFESSIONAL ASSOCIATIONS

Professional associations and trade organizations provide a valuable service in bringing together professionals and professional job openings. Most professional organizations have newsletters, annual meetings, and trade publications that advertise job openings. The annual meetings of these associations are good occasions for professionals to learn about available job openings and for employers to interview potential applicants.

MILITARY SERVICE

All branches of the United States military provide extensive training in a broad range of areas. New recruits continually join the military services and obtain training in many different skills. After they are discharged from the military, these individuals represent a valuable source of applicants, particularly for those organizations that need employees possessing the skills taught in the military.

UNIONS

Labor unions provide an informal employment service for members who move from one employer to another. In some industries, especially construction and maritime, the relationship is much more formal and the union serves as an intermediary between the employer and the labor force through a union hiring hall. In construction, for example, contractors send a written employment request to a local union official, who then dispatches applications from a list of eligible union members, providing each with a referral card to be presented to the union steward on arrival at the job site. While it provides employers with an important employment service, the hiring hall is also a major source of union power. At times unions have abused this power by creating artificial labor shortages to inflate wage levels, manipulating referral lists to provide preferential hiring, and withholding services to out-of-town employers to help local employers maintain a monopoly.[20]

THE HANDICAPPED

While many employers are somewhat reluctant to hire the handicapped for fear of encountering higher insurance rates, poor attendance, and low productivity, a study of the Urban Institute revealed these consequences to be incorrect. Another study found that supervisors were equally satisfied with the work performance of handicapped and non-handicapped employees. Thus, handicapped people represent a potentially valuable source of applicants who have largely been overlooked. Employers need to know that in general handicapped workers have fewer industrial accidents, less turnover, and better attitudes than nonhandicapped workers, and employing them has no effect on the cost of medical insurance or workers' compensation rates. In fact, the majority of workplace accommodations cost less than $500.[21] A number of mechanical and technological devices have been developed to allow the physically impaired to perform many jobs successfully that previously were impossible for them. Employers ought to perform a careful case-by-case analysis to determine whether a job can be modified to fit the capabilities of a handicapped person.

FORMER EMPLOYEES

A frequently overlooked source of new employees is the pool of former employees who have been laid off or who have quit. Some union contracts require that employees who have been laid off be rehired before new employees can be hired for the same positions. Since the former employees are already trained and are familiar with company policies, rehiring them is usually in the best interests of the company.

Many employees quit for temporary reasons but would like to be considered for employment at a later date. This situation occurs frequently with female employees. Many women choose to leave the work force during their childbearing years but want to return when their children are in school. Organizations should retain personnel files on these individuals, and as job openings occur in the future, the possibility of reemploying them could be explored. For example, many women trained as nurses are not actively employed in their profession. Nevertheless, they maintain their certification with the expectation that at some future point they may decide to reenter the work force.[22]

ADVERTISEMENTS IN THE MEDIA

Organizations can use a variety of media to advertise job openings. The most common medium used is the help-wanted section in the daily newspaper. Other popular media include help-wanted signs placed on storefronts, billboards, subway and bus posters, and spot announcements on radio and television. The major considerations in using any type of advertising are the cost and reaching the appropriate clientele. Newspapers tend to be the cheapest method of advertising, whereas television is generally the most expensive. In some situations, however, television commercials have been used not only to advertise job openings but also to create public awareness of the company and a favorable image in the minds of the present employees. Newspaper ads can be used effectively to recruit applicants for almost any job, including top management, if they are placed in the right newspaper. For example, a small international company with headquarters located in a very rural area advertised for a new CEO in the *Wall Street Journal* and received over 600 applications.

The effectiveness of advertising via various media can be evaluated by using the same form of cost-benefit analysis that is used to assess other marketing advertisements. This research requires that special care be exercised when the media are selected and when the ads are prepared and presented. Information must be collected to permit analysis of the effectiveness of each medium used for advertising.

In preparing advertisements for the media, special care must also be exercised to avoid violating equal employment opportunity requirements. Advertisements should not indicate a preference for a particular age, race, religion, national origin, or sex; nevertheless, an analysis of over 39,000 ads found that 2.7 percent of them were blatantly illegal.[23] Research studies have examined the extent to which recruitment advertising fosters discrimination in employment. The results of one study found that sex-biased advertising did indeed discourage members of one sex from applying for a job designed to be performed by members of the other sex.[24]

SPECIAL-EVENT RECRUITING

Many different kinds of special events—for example, job fairs, open houses, and hospitality suites at professional meetings—have been used successfully to attract potential employees. A job fair is usually organized by a placement agency, such as a college placement office, which widely advertises the event in order to attract a large number of job seekers for employment interviews. The placement agency arranges to have recruiters from several organizations in one place at one time for the job seekers to visit. Some organizations sponsor open houses at their headquarters and invite prospective employees to visit and learn about the kinds of products produced and the jobs available. These open houses are especially effective if they are held on holidays and weekends when college students are home from school and when employees of other companies are free to look for other jobs. Some organizations have hospitality suites at professional meetings and conventions to attract professionals.

Special-event recruiting is especially useful for small organizations that are not very well known. Many small-company employers believe that special-event recruiting not only helps to attract qualified applicants but also improves the organizational image held by both the public and the present employees.

Resumé sharing is another recruiting strategy that has helped recruiters, especially in the insurance industry. A network of human resource professionals can decide to create a pool of qualified applicants and share information about them. The primary purpose of starting a resumé-referral network is to get more people into the selection process for companies to consider. However, it also creates a more efficient outlet for candidates. Therefore, resumé sharing reduces recruiting costs and makes the process more convenient for both parties.[25]

SUMMER INTERNSHIPS

Hiring college students to work as student interns during the summer is typically viewed as a training activity rather than as a recruiting activity. However, organizations that sponsor internship programs have found that such programs represent an excellent means of recruiting outstanding employees. Internship opportunities for college students are growing because of the successful experiences organizations have had with them. Most internship opportunities are arranged by a human resource officer in an organization who works with a placement officer in a college or university. The human resource officer develops the internship opportunities by working with line managers to identify specific activities that college students could perform during the summer months. The college placement officer, sometimes called a cooperative education director, advertises the internship opportunities and screens interested students for the company. Studies in cooperative education have shown that a high percentage of interns return to work full-time for the sponsoring company.[26]

CHOOSING A RECRUITING METHOD

The recruiting methods discussed in this chapter present a wide range of possibilities for attracting new employees. Other methods also are useful, depending on the creativity of the personnel specialists.

In deciding which recruiting method to use, the human resource department should consider two factors: how many recruits are needed and which positions need to be filled. If an organization needs to recruit many new applicants, it should select a recruiting method that offers great visibility, such as a corporate open house. Since different recruiting methods will appeal to different segments of society, the method chosen should have the greatest appeal to the individuals most likely to apply for a specific position. Table 5.2 describes which recruiting methods are most applicable for attracting

TABLE 5.2   Choosing a recruiting method

	Blue-collar	Office/ Clerical	Professional/ Technical	Executive/ Managerial
1. Promotion from within	*	*	*	*
2. Job posting and bidding	*	*	*	
3. Contacts and referrals	*	*	*	—
4. Direct applications	*	*	*	
5. Public employment agency	*	*	—	
6. Private employment agency	*	*	*	*
7. Executive search firm			—	*
8. Schools and colleges		*	*	*
9. Professional associations			*	*
10. Military service	—	—	*	
11. Unions	*	—		
12. Former employees		*	*	—
13. Media advertisements	*	*	—	
14. Special events			*	—
15. Summer interns		—	*	
16. Temporary help	*	*		

*A good recruiting method.
—A possible recruiting method.

applicants from each of four categories: blue-collar, office and clerical, professional and technical, and executive and managerial. Some methods, such as promotions from within and private employment agencies, are useful for finding applicants for any type of job. Other recruiting methods, such as executive search firms, are relevant only for finding a particular type of applicant.[27]

COLLEGE RECRUITING PROCESS

The recruiting that occurs on college campuses has important consequences for companies, students, and colleges. Many organizations rely on college recruiting to fill professional, technical, and managerial positions. Students also have a large stake in the college recruiting process because they need help in matching their career interests with job opportunities. Colleges and universities are concerned about the success of college recruiting, too, because they depend upon it not only as a means of finding jobs for their graduates but also as a way of discovering what changes in their curriculums may be necessary to meet the needs of organizations.

Students should be aware of the college recruiting process, and long before graduation, they should contact the placement office and plan their job-seeking strategies. The college recruiting process is illustrated in Figure 5.4. The typical fall recruiting season for most universities is during the months of October and November, and spring recruiting occurs during February and March. However, the process actually begins long before

FIGURE 5.4 College recruiting process.

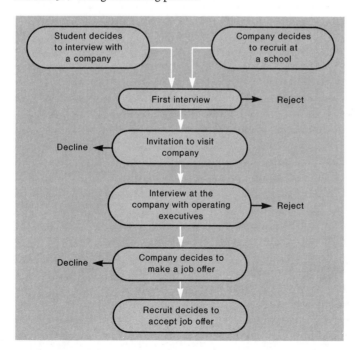

a college recruiter visits a campus. Many decisions already have been made regarding the need for job applicants and the places from which they should come. Some organizations maintain elaborate records showing how successful they have been in attracting applicants from the different universities and how successful these applicants have been as new employees. The decision to send a college recruiter to a particular campus is often based on a careful cost-benefit analysis, since an organization stands to benefit the most by sending its recruiter to a campus that has the highest probability of providing outstanding job applicants.

College placement directors are continually trying to attract new organizations to recruit on their campuses. In some situations the visit of a college recruiter is the result of a lengthy campaign involving letter writing, phone calls, and company visits by placement officers trying to impress company representatives with the qualifications of their students. Students are usually unaware of how much effort the college placement office has to put into attracting company recruiters.

The college placement office serves as a labor-market exchange by providing opportunities for students and employers to meet and explore employment possibilities. The placement office advertises visits by company recruiters through bulletin boards, student newspapers, mailings, and sometimes even personal phone calls. Students who are interested in job possibilities with a particular company can schedule an interview and often receive brochures and other information about the company. Some company recruiters expect the placement officers to save them time by screening the student applicants.

Recruiting interviews are typically scheduled every thirty minutes and occur in small interview rooms. Sometimes students think the interviews are too mechanical. They complain that the recruiters do not give them the attention and interest that they desire and are overly concerned about obtaining specific information. The students' complaints are often valid. Recruiters often interview as many as sixteen applicants per day, and to help them remember the interviewees, they usually complete a report on each. A recruiter may try to complete a report during an interview or at least make adequate notes to complete the report later. Realizing how exhausting a day of interviewing can be, some students try to schedule interviews early in the morning.

After the recruiter returns to the company, all of the interviews are evaluated, and the most promising applicants are invited to visit the company. The purpose of the visit is to gather further information about the applicant and to convince the applicant that the company is a good place to work. The applicant is interviewed by potential supervisors and executives and may be given a series of psychological tests. The costs of the recruiting trip usually are paid by the company, and occasionally the applicant's spouse is also invited as a guest of the company. The interview trip is an important part of the decision-making process, since the organization must determine whether a job offer should be made to the applicant and the applicant must decide whether to accept if an offer is made. If an organization decides to hire an applicant, it will make a job offer either during the company visit or shortly thereafter by mail or phone. The applicant may then negotiate with the company regarding salary and benefits. Most applicants prefer having competing job offers so that they can compare such factors as salary, benefits, job responsibilities, and opportunities for growth and development.

The strategy used for finding a job varies from student to student. Some students conduct very aggressive campaigns, gathering information from many organizations and obtaining numerous job offers. Other students wait until the week before graduation and then begin to ask, "What do I do now?" Students searching for jobs may be characterized as maximizers, satisficers, and validators.[28]

1. *Maximizers*: Students who are **maximizers** have the most aggressive job-search behavior. They assume that the labor market is large, diversified, and disorganized and that whether they get good jobs or bad jobs depends on their search behavior. Consequently, these individuals collect information from many organizations, have many job interviews, get as many offers as they can, and rationally choose the best offers based on their career goals. Most of these individuals have previous work experience that has prepared them for conducting an aggressive job search.
2. *Satisficers*: Students who are **satisficers** either have no job choice or do not feel a choice is important. Because of insecurity, they may accept the first job offered to them. Because of inexperience, they may not be aware of the opportunities available in other organizations.
3. *Validators*: Students who are **validators** are not willing to accept their first job offer without gathering additional information, but neither are they willing to conduct aggressive job searches to find alternative offers. A validator typically gets one offer—his or her favorite—then gets one more offer just to make sure the favorite was a good one, and finally takes the favorite one.

One study that examined the effectiveness of each of the three job strategies found that students who followed the maximizer choice pattern received higher salary offers, held their first jobs longer, and had higher levels of job satisfaction.

ETHICAL ISSUES IN RECRUITING

As part of the college recruiting process, students often face some difficult issues that have ethical implications. Some of the most frequent dilemmas students face include the following.

1. Should students accept a company's invitation for an on-site visit if they know they are not going to work for that company? This depends on how sure the students are. If they are absolutely certain they would never work for a particular company then it is deceptive to let this company spend money entertaining them. But if there is a possible chance they might change their minds and they are willing to seriously consider a job offer, then it is not wrong to give the company a chance.

2. If students accept a job offer from Company A and Company B makes them a better offer, is it all right to reverse their decision? Although many students think it is not illegal, and therefore not wrong, they should consider the issue more carefully. An honorable person would consider a verbal agreement as binding as a legal contract that can only be broken with the mutual consent of both parties. Therefore, students ought to discuss their agreement with Company A; the company may release them from it, hold them to it, or match Company B's offer. Students should remember that Company A may be unable to offer the position to the next candidate since other candidates may have been told that the position was filled.

3. Is it wrong for applicants to have multiple offers and play one company against another to increase their starting salary? If this is perceived as a negotiating ploy (and if it is, it will probably be perceived that way), it could work against an applicant by creating antagonism and a loss of respect. However, there is nothing wrong with applicants having multiple offers and letting one company know that they don't plan to accept its offer because they have better offers. The company may appreciate knowing the situation and may want to make a more competitive offer. A person's starting salary doesn't just affect his or her paycheck, it also has an effect on his or her perceived competence and subsequent career advancement.

4. Should applicants expect the company to pay for an on-site visit and, if so, is it all right to go first class? Who pays for the trip needs to be clarified when the invitation is extended. If the trip is more than a short distance, the company normally offers to pay for reasonable expenses. Although it may be reasonable for the job applicants to live a little better on an expense account than they could on a tight student budget, unnecessary expenses are still inappropriate. Students have to decide for themselves where they will draw the line.

ALTERNATIVES TO RECRUITING

Some employers have experimented with flexible staffing and creative scheduling to solve their employment needs in a tight labor market. Staffing alternatives have included developing a pool of people who can be on-call as needed, hiring people who work only during peak hours, telecommuting on a home computer attached to the office, and permanent part-time work. These options often appeal to people who do not want a full-time position.[29] When an organization decides to add personnel to its staff, it makes a significant financial investment. Recruitment and selection costs are high, especially for professional, technical, and managerial employees. After new employees are hired, other costs besides their salaries must be considered. For example, the costs of benefits are usually more than 30 percent of the payroll. Furthermore, once employees are placed on the payroll, removing them may be difficult, even if their performance is below standard. Consequently, before an organization decides to recruit new employees it ought to consider the feasibility of other alternatives. Four alternatives to recruiting are overtime, temporary help, subcontracting, and employee leasing.

OVERTIME

When organizations experience short-term pressures to complete a contract or meet a production goal, the most common solution is overtime. By using overtime, organizations can avoid the incremental costs of recruiting and hiring additional employees for a short time. The organization is able to obtain higher levels of production without having to increase the size of its work force. Moreover, many employees, especially younger ones, who often have heavy financial debts, like to work overtime because in many industries they receive premium pay.

Although overtime is a useful way for an organization to increase its production for a short period of time, the long-term consequences of overtime are very undesirable. Studies on the effects of overtime have reached these conclusions:

1. As the number of overtime hours increases, more scheduled work time is lost through absenteeism.
2. As overtime hours increase, the frequency and severity of injuries increase also.
3. As the hours of work increase above eight hours per day or 48 hours per week, three hours of work are required to produce two additional hours of output; or, if the work is heavy, two hours of work are required to produce one hour of additional output.
4. If continuous overtime is scheduled, the time will come when the total weekly production on overtime will be less than the total production would have been if a 40-hour week had been maintained.[30]

In general, the evidence suggests that overtime is not an effective alternative to hiring new employees except in very limited circumstances and for a very short period of time. One study examined the effects of scheduled overtime on construction projects and found that working more hours only increased the amount of work performed during the first eight weeks for those working 50-hour weeks, or nine weeks for those working 60-hour weeks.[31] After eight or nine weeks of continuous overtime, the amount of work completed is actually less than with a 40-hour week.

TEMPORARY HELP

Another alternative to recruiting new employees is to use a temporary help service. Many temporary help agencies specialize in supplying employees who can fill the needs of local companies. Other temporary help agencies are located nationwide.

The use of temporary employees is widespread; a survey of 174 firms found that 91 percent of them used temporary services, mostly for clerical, financial, and accounting positions. Some corporations have even hired temporary executives and CEOs as part of a corporate restructuring to assist in a turnaround situation or to prepare a division for sale.[32]

On any given work day, the labor force includes approximately 1 million temporary employees. Most companies use temporaries for emergency fill-ins or to cover peak periods. There is a growing trend toward hiring temporary workers on a long-term basis, and sometimes they are promoted to permanent positions.[33]

One of the major advantages of using temporary help services is that an organization does not have to provide benefits or train new employees. The organization also has the flexibility of requesting temporary services only when they are needed, thereby avoiding the issue of laying off employees during slack times. One disadvantage of using temporary help services is that temporary employees do not feel the same degree of loyalty and commitment to the organization as permanent employees. Another problem is that in spite of their specialized training, temporary employees lack specific information about the company and general company procedures.

SUBCONTRACTING

A third alternative to recruiting new employees is subcontracting work to another organization. An organization loses some of its control over work that is subcontracted, but if the subcontractor is dependable and produces high-quality work at a reasonable cost, subcontracting may be beneficial. The decision to use subcontracting should be based on a careful cost-benefit analysis of the situation. Organizations that use subcontractors often do so because the subcontractors have greater expertise in producing a specialized product or service than the organizations themselves. For example, many hospitals subcontract their cleaning services to ServiceMaster, a separate organization that specializes in cleaning.

EMPLOYEE LEASING

A fourth alternative to recruiting new employees is to lease them from an employee leasing company. This method is similar to a temporary help agency but the employees are not temporary. The employees are actually employed by the leasing company and it performs all the human resource functions.

The 1982 Tax Equity and Fiscal Responsibility Act (TEFRA) officially recognized the practice of employee leasing and it has been growing ever since. Companies are allowed to exclude leased employees from their pension plans if the leasing company includes them in its pension plan. Employee leasing involves a company firing all or part of its employees and then immediately contracting with a leasing firm for the same employees after the leasing firm employs them. This arrangement is well suited for firms with fifty or fewer employees and for nonprofit organizations. The leasing firm essentially replaces the company's human resource department and handles all hiring and firing, scheduling of vacation and sick time, administration of benefits, maintenance of personnel records, and payroll.

The advantage of leasing is that it relieves the company of the burdensome costs and administrative tasks associated with providing the full range of personnel services. The leased employees are able to participate in a pension plan and receive other employee benefits. Although leasing is less expensive than hiring temporary employees, executives worry about relinquishing control. Many executives believe quality, safety, and a commitment to excellence are more likely to be found in permanent, internal employees.[34]

ETHICAL ISSUES IN HIRING PART-TIME AND TEMPORARY EMPLOYEES

One of the advantages of using part-time and temporary workers is that in most cases they do not receive any employee benefits. Is this good or bad? Employers and temporary agencies justify this policy by claiming that: (1) the workers do not need benefits because they are usually covered by their parent's or spouse's benefits; (2) benefits coverage is not important to them since they don't plan to keep the job very long; and (3) the record keeping and reporting involved in providing benefits coverage would be very cumbersome because of the rapid turnover.

Since some temporaries actually hold permanent jobs, however, not providing benefits has the effect of cheapening the work force with undesirable consequences to workers and their families. Some of the proposals for preventing this kind of "employee abuse" include: (1) limiting the time a worker can be considered temporary; (2) requiring employers to provide medical insurance and pension coverage for all temporaries; (3) establishing ratios of temporary and full-time employees to limit the use of temporaries; and (4) requiring temporary agencies to provide benefits coverage.[35] So far, Congress has not required employers to provide medical insurance or pensions for either part-time or full-time employees. Whether they should pass such legislation depends in part on the ethical issue of whether employees have a right to receive employee benefits. This issue is discussed further in Chapter 12.

EQUAL EMPLOYMENT OPPORTUNITY

One of the most sensitive issues in recruiting and hiring new employees is providing equal employment opportunity for all job applicants, regardless of their age, race, religion, sex, or national origin. For many years, human resource managers became increasingly sophisticated in selecting job applicants who had the highest probability of being outstanding performers. As expected, the best performers were usually the people who had the most work experience and the best educational preparation. Unfortunately, minority citizens were often deprived of equal opportunities for experience and education. Therefore, as people with good educational backgrounds and previous work experience were screened into organizations, people who did not fit these achievement-oriented stereotypes were screened out.

Finally, in 1964, Congress decreed that employment opportunities should not be denied to anyone because of that person's race, religion, sex, or national origin. The Civil Rights Act and subsequent executive orders have attempted to guarantee equal employment opportunities for everyone.

CIVIL RIGHTS ACT, TITLE VII

The need for federal civil rights legislation is obvious when the economic conditions of blacks and whites in the early 1960s are compared. The unemployment levels for black adults were twice as high as those for white adults, and unemployment levels for black teenagers were three times higher than those for white teenagers. Although blacks comprised only about 10 percent of the labor force in the early 1960s, they represented about 20 percent of the total unemployment and nearly 30 percent of the long-term unemployment. The job opportunities available for blacks were typically low-level jobs that provided substandard incomes. Blacks were over three times as likely as whites to be unskilled laborers, while whites were over three times as likely as blacks to be in professional or managerial positions. In 1962, the average family income for blacks was only $3,000, or 52 percent of the family income for whites. Furthermore, the income disparity between black and white families was increasing: in 1952, the black family income had been 57 percent of the white family income.

Although Senate filibusters stalled the passage of civil rights legislation for several years, the Civil Rights Act was finally passed in 1964. Title VII of this act (as amended) prohibits discrimination in employment on the basis of race, color, religion, sex, or national origin. The law applies to employers with fifteen or more employees, employment agencies, labor organizations, state and local governments, and educational institutions.

> Sec. 703. (a) It shall be an unlawful employment practice for an employer—
> 1. to fail or refuse to hire or to discharge any individual, or otherwise to discriminate against any individual with respect to his compensation, terms, conditions, or privileges of employment, because of such individual's race, color, religion, sex, or national origin; or
> 2. to limit, segregate, or classify his employees or applicants for employment in any way which would deprive or tend to deprive any individual of employment opportunities or otherwise adversely affect his status as an employee, because of such individual's race, color, religion, sex, or national origin.

The act expressly prohibits any advertisements or any recruiting activities that indicate a preference based on race, color, religion, sex, or national origin unless such preference is related to a bona fide occupational qualification for employment. Under the provisions of the act, a human resource activity is illegal if it has a **disparate impact** on the composition of a company's work force. A human resource activity is said to have a disparate impact if the operation of that activity tends to significantly reduce the numbers of minorities or females who are employed in any job category. The act also established the **Equal Employment Opportunity Commission**, and it outlined the procedures that the commission should follow to prevent unlawful employment practices. Furthermore, the act requires employers to compile and keep records that can be used to determine whether unlawful employment practices have been or are being committed.

EQUAL EMPLOYMENT OPPORTUNITY COMMISSION (EEOC)

The jurisdiction of the EEOC has been broadened since it was first created by Title VII of the Civil Rights Act of 1964. The EEOC was originally charged with the responsibility of preventing unlawful employment practices through informal methods of conciliation and persuasion. In 1972, Congress gave the EEOC the power to bring lawsuits against employers in the federal courts on behalf of an aggrieved person or a class of aggrieved persons. In 1978, an executive order further extended the authority of the EEOC to include the enforcement responsibilities of the Civil Service Commission, the Wage and Hour Division of the Department of Labor, and the Equal Employment Opportunity Coordinating Counsel (EEOCC). This reorganization plan gave the EEOC responsibility not only for preventing discrimination based on race, color, religion, sex, and national origin, but also for preventing discrimination based on age and on physical or mental handicaps.

The EEOC does not have the same authority as other federal agencies to issue directly enforceable orders. However, the EEOC has issued a *Guidebook for Employers on Affirmative Action and Equal Employment* and also "Uniform Guidelines for Employee Selection Procedures." In two major court decisions, the Supreme Court has indicated that "great deference" should be shown toward the EEOC's guidelines.[36] The EEOC also has issued guidelines on sex discrimination and other procedural regulations. For example, an employer with 100 or more employees is required to submit an EEO-1 report to the EEOC. This report indicates how many workers of each sex and race are employed in nine different job categories. For reporting purposes, race is divided into five categories (COINS):

C   Caucasians/whites

O   Orientals/Asians, including Pacific Islanders

I   American Indians, including Eskimos and Aleuts

N   Negroes/blacks

S   Hispanics and Spanish surnamed

When discrimination charges are brought to the EEOC, it conducts an investigation to determine whether they are legitimate. EEOC inspectors have the power to obtain many kinds of information from the employer even though the information may seem irrelevant to the charges that have been made and even though it may be costly and difficult to collect. For example, if a Hispanic female who was fired for insubordination charged that she was terminated because her employer did not want to promote her, the EEOC may request more information than just that relevant to this particular case. The inspector might request a complete census of each job category by race and sex, a record of all promotions and transfers over the past several years, and a record of all disciplinary actions and the bases for them over the past several years. These requests for information can be enforced with a court order if an employer resists providing them.

When an EEOC investigation determines that a charge of discrimination is justifiable, it attempts to resolve the problem through a process called **conciliation**. Conciliation refers to an out-of-court settlement between the employer and the EEOC. Most discrimination charges are settled by conciliation agreements. If the EEOC and the employer are unable to reach an agreement, the case can be prosecuted in a federal district court either by the EEOC or by the aggrieved individual. If either party appeals the decision of the federal district court, the appeal is generally heard by a three-judge panel of a federal court of appeals. The case can be further appealed to a larger group of appeals court judges and eventually taken to the U.S. Supreme Court. The EEOC wins a surprisingly small percent of the discrimination cases that are taken to court, mainly because employers are unwilling to take a case to court unless they feel quite confident of winning. Discrimination charges usually require a long time to be resolved and are very expensive, regardless of whether they are processed in the courts or resolved through conciliation agreements. If an employer is found guilty of discrimination, the court decrees can call for drastic remedies. These remedies may include back-pay, hiring quotas, reinstatement of employees, immediate promotion of employees, elimination of testing programs, or the creation of special recruitment and training programs.

BONA FIDE OCCUPATIONAL QUALIFICATIONS (BFOQ)

Section 703 (e) of the Civil Rights Act states that it is not unlawful for an employer to discriminate on the basis of religion, sex, or national origin if such an attribute is a "**bona fide occupational qualification** reasonably necessary to the normal operation of that particular business or enterprise." Race is never a legitimate BFOQ. The concept of *business necessity* has been narrowly defined by the courts. When a practice is found to have a discriminatory effect, it can be justified only by showing that it is necessary to the safe and efficient operation of the business, that it effectively carries out the purpose it is supposed to serve, and that there are no alternative policies or practices that would serve the same purpose with less discriminatory impact.

An employer who discriminates on the basis of religion, sex, or national origin must be able to demonstrate that the attribute in question is a BFOQ necessary to the normal operation of his or her organization. Many employers initially assumed that sex was a BFOQ that would make women ineligible for strenuous jobs and males ineligible for traditional female jobs such as airline flight attendants. Employers were concerned that customers might object when jobs were performed by members of the nontraditional sex. However, the courts have refused to view tradition as establishing a BFOQ. The few times when sex has been held to be a legitimate BFOQ include: (1) in order to satisfy basic social mores about modesty, such as the case of a locker-room attendant; (2) when a position demands a particular sex for aesthetic authenticity, as in the case of a fashion model or movie actor; and (3) when one sex is by definition unequipped to do the work, as in the case of a wet nurse.

AFFIRMATIVE ACTION

While Title VII is intended to prohibit discrimination on the basis of race, color, religion, sex, or national origin, Executive Order 11246 states that employers who hold federal contracts or subcontracts are required to do more than just not discriminate. According to the order, such employers are required to develop written affirmative action plans that establish goals and timetables to achieve equal opportunity. This executive order applies to all government contractors and their subcontractors that have fifty or more employees and $50,000 or more in government contracts. Since 1974, the EEOC has also encouraged other employers to take positive, affirmative actions beyond neutral nondiscriminatory recruiting and hiring to correct imbalances in the percentage of employed minorities and females.

The affirmative action plans of federal contractors are reviewed by the **Office of Federal Contract Compliance Programs (OFCCP)** from the Department of Labor. The OFCCP enforces not only Executive Order 11246 but also laws covering the employment of veterans and the handicapped, since federal contractors are required to have affirmative action plans covering these groups, too.

Preparing an affirmative action plan as required by Executive Order 11246 requires collecting extensive information, and it usually requires a great deal of top-management time. Eight steps (see Table 5.3) are involved in the development of a plan.[37] The primary objectives are to communicate clearly the message that a company is an equal opportunity employer and to make certain that all human resource decisions are consistent with that message. One of the most difficult steps in developing a plan is gathering data that identify areas of underutilization. An area of underutilization is a job category that has fewer minority or female employees than would reasonably be expected by their presence in the relevant labor market outside the organization.

Assessing the underutilization of minorities and females is difficult because the employer has to survey the labor area to determine: (1) the percentage of each minority group, including females, in the total population; (2) the percentage of each minority group in the work force; (3) the extent of unemployment for minorities and females;

TABLE 5.3   Procedure for developing an affirmative action plan

---

1. The employer is required to issue a written equal employment policy and affirmative action commitment. The policy statement should be issued by the chief executive officer and should be publicized both within and outside the organization.

2. A top-level official should be appointed as the affirmative action officer. The responsibility and authority for implementing the program are delegated to this office.

3. The affirmative action program must be publicized both internally and externally. All employees should be informed of the company's equal employment policies through newsletters, publications, meetings, reports, bulletins, and posters. The statement that the company is an equal opportunity employer must also be advertised externally to all appropriate media, including public and private employment agencies, educational institutions, subcontractors, vendors, and suppliers. This statement should be supported by pictures and advertising showing minorities and women in nonstereotyped jobs.

4. The organization is required to survey and analyze the employment of minorities and females by department and by job classification. This survey of minority and female employees should identify all areas of underutilization.

5. The employer must develop goals and timetables for increasing the percentage of females and minorities in every job category in which they are underutilized. The organization should have a long-range goal of attaining equal representation of minorities and females in each job classification in "reasonable" relation to the overall labor-force participation of such groups. The long-range goals should be supported by intermediate annual targets indicating the progress the organization expects to make each year.

6. The employer must develop and implement specific programs to eliminate discriminatory barriers and achieve its goals. The barriers that need to be examined include recruiting and selection procedures, promotions and transfers, wage and salary structure, benefits, layoffs and recalls, discharges, and disciplinary actions.

7. The employer is required to establish an internal audit and reporting system to monitor and evaluate progress in each aspect of the affirmative action program.

8. The employer is expected to develop supportive in-house and community programs, such as supervisory training, personal counseling, transportation, day-care centers, and housing.

---

(4) the availability of minorities and females with the required skills; and (5) the availability of promotable and transferable females and minorities in the employer's work force. Most employers discover that determining the availability of women and minorities for various jobs is difficult because statistics listing individuals with the requisite skills who are willing to accept the jobs are virtually nonexistent. Consequently, the development of an affirmative action plan is an arduous and time-consuming activity.

Almost every human resource function must be carefully evaluated to determine whether it systematically discriminates against minorities and females. This form of discrimination is referred to as **systemic discrimination**, meaning that the human resource systems and how they operate tend to exclude protected groups. The OFCCP requires employers to have written affirmative action plans available for review and audit. However, the reviews by the OFCCP are quite infrequent, usually no more than once every two years.

▌ **HRM in Action**

Immigration Law Causes Employment Discrimination

In March 1990 the General Accounting Office released the results of a study showing that the immigration law had caused widespread discrimination against applicants of foreign appearance or accent, especially Hispanics and Asians. The GAO surveyed a random sample of 9,491 employers and found that 19 percent discriminated on the basis of physical appearance or accent. Nine percent hired only native-born citizens.

Although the immigration law prohibits discrimination, the severe sanctions for hiring illegal immigrants have caused employers to be extra cautious in their hiring practices. The discrimination is most pronounced in areas with the largest Hispanic and Asian populations. To reduce discrimination, some legislators are recommending that the employer sanctions be repealed.

In 1986 Congress passed the Immigration Reform and Control Act, which contains severe penalties for employers who hire illegal immigrants. Employers who violate the law can be fined up to $10,000 and jailed for six months. All job applicants are expected to demonstrate that they have a legal right to hold a job, and employers are required to maintain accurate documentation.

After three years of enforcing the law, the United States Immigration Service reported that it had assessed $17 million in fines for 3,500 cases of hiring illegal aliens and 36,000 cases of failing to complete and maintain the proper paperwork. The Immigration and Naturalization Service requires employers to have a completed I-9 form for each employee.

Source: Paul M. Barrett, "Immigration Law Found to Promote Bias by Employers," *Wall Street Journal*, March 30, 1990; "A National Identity Card?" *Wall Street Journal*, April 3, 1990, A22.

The annual goals and timetables that move an organization toward its long-range employment objectives represent a powerful driving force behind an affirmative action plan. For several years the EEOC refused to admit that affirmative action plans created "hiring quotas." Nevertheless, to achieve their goals and timetables, employers often found it necessary to hire only members of a specific race or sex.

REVERSE DISCRIMINATION

Many white males have complained that affirmative action plans have made them the victims of "**reverse discrimination**," but so far, the courts have not been very sympathetic to such charges. In one case (*Regents of the University of California* v. *Bakke*, 1978), the Supreme Court ordered a medical school to accept a white male applicant who had higher entrance-test scores than some of the minorities who had been admitted to fill the 15 positions reserved for minorities in a class of 100. The Supreme Court said that its decision applied only to this specific case and should not be interpreted very broadly. In a later case (*Steel Workers* v. *Webber*, 1979), the Supreme Court ruled against a white male who was trying to get into a training program. The training program had been jointly designed by the company and the union expressly to help the company achieve its affirmative action goals, and 50 percent of the positions had been reserved for minority trainees. The Supreme Court issued a broad ruling that endorsed special programs for achieving affirmative action goals and said that the preferential treatment these programs provided for minorities was consistent with the intent of Congress in creating civil rights legislation.[38]

Since 1979, the Supreme Court has issued numerous opinions in support of race-conscious or sex-conscious affirmative action programs when they are designed to correct a manifest imbalance. Employers are allowed to give preferential treatment to minorities and females through an affirmative action plan, providing the rights of other workers are not "unnecessarily trammeled," such as by violating a negotiated seniority agreement when making layoffs or promotions.[39] The Supreme Court's endorsement of voluntary affirmative action plans is illustrated by the cases summarized in Table 5.4.

ILLEGAL PREEMPLOYMENT INQUIRIES

Recruiting announcements, employment application forms, and preemployment interviews are the traditional instruments that have been used to eliminate unqualified persons at an early stage of the employment process. Unfortunately, these methods often have been used in a way that arbitrarily restricts or denies employment opportunities to women and members of minority groups. The law, interpreted through court rulings and EEOC decisions, prohibits the use of recruiting methods that disproportionately eliminate members of minority groups or of one sex unless the methods are valid predictors of successful job performance or can be justified by business necessity. Title VII

TABLE 5.4   Supreme Court decisions regarding affirmative action plans

1978	*University of California Regents* v. *Bakke*—Court strikes down, 5–4, medical school admissions plan that favored minorities, but upholds, 5–4, race as one factor in admissions.
1979	*Steelworkers* v. *Webber*—Court upholds, 5–2, a voluntary affirmative action plan for crafts training at Kaiser Aluminum & Chemical Corp. plants.
1980	*Fullilove* v. *Klutznick*—Court upholds, 6–3, Congress's decision to set aside a portion of public works funds for minority business.
1984	*Wygant* v. *Jackson Board of Education*—Court rules, 5–4, that the Constitution bars Jackson, Michigan, from laying off white teachers with more seniority than blacks who remain at work.
1986	*Local 93* v. *City of Cleveland*—Court approves, 6–3, a plan of promotions for firefighters using a 1:1 ratio to increase the number of minorities in upper-level jobs.
1986	*Local 28* v. *EEOC*—Court rules, 5–4, that a federal court properly set a goal of 29 percent minority membership in a Sheet Metal Workers local and made the union pay for training.
1987	*U.S.* v. *Paradise*—Court upholds, 5–4, a 1:1 ratio for promoting black state troopers in Alabama, saying the Constitution doesn't prohibit this corrective action.
1987	*Johnson* v. *Transportation Agency*—Court rules, 6–3, that public employers, as well as private, may voluntarily implement affirmative action to correct sex discrimination.
1989	*City of Richmond* v. *J.A. Croson Co.*—Court rules, 6–3, that a plan requiring 30 percent of construction contracts be performed by minority businesses is unlawful when no prior history of discrimination has been shown.

expressly prohibits discrimination on the basis of race, color, religion, sex, or national origin. Some of the state fair employment practice laws also prohibit requesting information that could indirectly reveal race, religion, or national origin, such as former name, previous residence, names of relatives, place of birth, citizenship, education, or color of eyes and hair. Most of these state laws are more restrictive than the federal law in limiting preemployment inquiries, and recruiters need to be familiar with the laws of the states in which they recruit. The EEOC cautions against obtaining the following kinds of information unless an employer can demonstrate a business necessity.

1. *Height and Weight.*
2. *Marital status, number of children, and provisions for child care.* The Supreme Court has ruled that an employer may not have different hiring policies for men and women with preschool children.
3. *Educational level*: Unless evidence exists that a specific educational level is significantly related to successful job performance, this information should not be requested since a high rate of minorities tend to be disqualified on this basis.[40]
4. *English language skill.* Unless skill in the English language is required of the work, it should not be assessed since minority groups could be discriminated against on this basis.
5. *Names of friends or relatives working for the employer*: Information about friends or relatives working for an employer is not relevant to an applicant's competence and could be used to reduce or eliminate opportunities for minorities and women.
6. *Arrest records*: Making personnel decisions on the basis of arrest records involving no subsequent convictions could have a disproportionate effect on minorities because members of some minority groups are arrested more frequently than whites.
7. *Conviction records*: Federal courts have held that a conviction for a felony or misdemeanor may not in and by itself lawfully constitute an absolute bar to employment and that an employer should give fair consideration to the relationship between a conviction and the applicant's fitness for a particular job.[41] The courts' decisions indicate that conviction records should be used as bases for rejection only if their number, nature, and recency indicate that the applicant is unsuitable for the position. If an inquiry is made concerning an applicant's record of convictions, it should be accompanied by a statement that the conviction record will not necessarily be a bar to employment and that factors such as age at the time of offense, seriousness and nature of the violation, and rehabilitation will be taken into account.
8. *Discharge from military service*: Employers should not, as a matter of policy, reject applicants with less than honorable discharges from military service. According to the Department of Defense, minority service members receive a higher proportion of undesirable discharges than whites. An applicant's military service record should be used to decide whether further investigation is warranted, but it should not be used as a basis for summarily rejecting the applicant. Since an organization's request for military service information may discourage minority workers from applying for positions, such questions should be avoided unless business necessity can be shown. As with conviction records, a question regarding military service should be accompanied by a statement that a discharge indicating other than honorable service is not

an absolute bar to employment and that other factors also will influence the hiring decision.

9. *Citizenship*: The law clearly protects all individuals, both citizens and noncitizens residing in the United States, against discrimination on the basis of race, color, religion, sex or national origin.

10. *Economic status*: Rejecting applicants because of poor credit ratings can have a disparate impact on minority groups, and hence, questions about economic status have been found unlawful by the EEOC unless business necessity can be proven. This includes inquiries regarding bankruptcy, car ownership, rental or ownership of a house, length of residence at an address, or past garnishment of wages.

11. *Availability for work on weekends or holidays*: While questions relating to availability for work on weekends or holidays are not automatically considered violations of the law, employers and unions should attempt to accommodate the religious beliefs of employees and applicants unless to do so would cause undue economic hardship.

Although the preceding information is not to be used in making an employment decision, some of it may be needed for legitimate business purposes. For example, employers need such information as marital status, number and ages of children, and age of the employee for benefits, insurance, reporting requirements, and other business purposes. The EEOC recommends that this information be obtained after the selection decision has been made.[42]

Although the EEOC guidelines and state laws restrict employers from asking certain questions, it is important to remember that discrimination does not occur because of the questions that are asked nor is it prevented by avoiding these questions. Discrimination is a function of how people are treated, not what they are asked. A recruiter who is prejudiced has countless ways of determining age, race, and sex without asking.

Regarding sex discrimination, however, it is interesting to note that one study found no evidence of either direct or indirect sex discrimination among recruiters on college campuses. Using a large sample of corporate recruiters this study examined (1) the perceived similarity of the applicant to the recruiter, (2) the interpersonal attraction of the recruiter for the applicant, (3) the sex of the applicant, and (4) both subjective and objective evaluations of the applicant's qualifications. While the recruiter's subjective evaluations were unrelated to the sex of the applicants, they were greatly influenced by whether they liked the applicants and whether they saw them as similar to themselves.[43]

INTERNATIONAL HRM

At most American universities, graduating students compete vigorously to be included on the interview schedules of their placement offices. Because there are more graduates than good jobs the major American companies can be selective in which students they choose to interview. In Japan, the supply and demand situation is reversed and companies compete aggressively for graduating students. Japanese companies have traditionally wanted to hire more college graduates than they have been able to recruit.

As early as 1953, while Japan was still engaged in its postwar reconstruction, efforts were made to regulate the college recruiting process to protect students from being coerced to make a life-time decision before their senior year. The Ministry of Education issued guidelines that prohibited introducing students to companies before their senior year, but these guidelines were often ignored during the economic expansion of the 1960s. The new system, which originated in 1986, prevents companies from interviewing graduates before September 5 and formal job offers cannot be extended until October 1.

In spite of these protections, however, students are subjected to intense pressures during the annual recruiting season. Students complain about the strong-arm tactics used by some companies to prevent them from seeing competitors during this season. Many of the top students at Tokyo University claimed that they were virtually kidnapped and held under house arrest by some companies. Some were shipped abroad on visits to overseas subsidiaries or on trips to popular resorts such as California's Disneyland.

An emergency phone-in system allows students to report "acts of persecution," and during one recruiting season 474 calls were received involving complaints against 154 companies. The calls included 95 cases of "daily detainment," where students were allowed to go home at night but forced to visit companies for extended periods of up to ten hours per day, and 131 cases of overnight detention, either at the company's headquarters or at resorts or rest houses outside Tokyo. The abuses are believed to be much more widespread than were reported, since most students are too shy or too polite to resist offers of trips.[44]

SUMMARY

A. In planning their recruiting activities, organizations need to know how many applicants to recruit. Yield ratios facilitate recruitment planning by expressing a relationship between the number of people at one step of the recruiting process relative to the number of people who will move to the next step.

B. Recruiters need to balance their enthusiasm for selling the organization with realistic recruiting information. When recruiters impart realistic information about a job, the number of applicants does not decrease, and reduction in turnover occurs.

C. Vacancies in management positions can be filled by external recruiting or by promotions from within. Promoting from within is generally the best policy because of its effect on employee motivation and satisfaction. However, external recruiting produces new ideas and new methods.

D. The major sources of internal recruiting include promotions from within, job posting and bidding, and contacts and referrals.

E. The major external recruiting sources include direct applications, public and private employment agencies, executive search firms, schools and colleges, professional associations, military service, unions, former employees, advertisements in the media, special-event recruiting, and summer internships.

F. Some private employment agencies are very helpful in recruiting new employees. However, they are generally quite expensive. The Job Service is a free, public employment agency that should be used more frequently by employers.

G. Advertising through the media represents one of the most common recruiting practices. Newspaper advertisements tend to be the least expensive, while television advertising is generally the most expensive.

H. College placement offices perform a valuable service in bringing employers and students together. Students are able to learn about job openings and interview with company representatives. The most promising students are invited for company visits and may receive job offers.

I. In finding a job, some students are maximizers who examine many possibilities; some are satisficers who accept the first offers they receive; and some are validators who only look far enough to confirm their favorite job offers.

J. Four alternatives to recruiting are overtime, temporary help, subcontracting, and employee leasing. Although overtime is used frequently to avoid hiring additional employees, the evidence shows that prolonged overtime increases labor costs and decreases productivity.

K. The Civil Rights Act, Title VII, was passed in 1964 (amended in 1972) to prohibit discrimination against people because of their race, religion, sex, or national origin. This law is enforced by the Equal Employment Opportunity Commission (EEOC), which tries to eliminate discriminatory practices by conciliation or prosecution in the federal courts.

L. An employer may discriminate on the basis of religion, sex, or national origin only if such an attribute is a bona fide occupational qualification reasonably necessary to the normal operation of the business.

M. Federal contractors and subcontractors are required to create and implement an affirmative action plan for hiring minorities and females proportionate to their representation in the external labor market. The Office of Federal Contract Compliance Programs (OFCCP) reviews these plans and disqualifies contractors that fail to achieve their affirmative action goals. Because companies have shown preferential treatment for minorities and females to satisfy their affirmative action goals, some white males claim that they are the victims of reverse discrimination. Nevertheless, the courts have generally endorsed affirmative action plans, provided the rights of others are not seriously damaged.

N. To avoid employment practices that have a disparate effect on protected groups, organizations must carefully review their recruiting methods, employment applications, and preemployment interviews. Unless an employer can demonstrate a business necessity for the following information, the EEOC cautions against its use: height and weight requirements, marital status, number of children, provisions for child care, educational requirements, English language usage, friends or relatives working for the employer, arrest records, conviction records, discharge from military service, citizenship, and economic status.

QUESTIONS

1. What is the relationship between recruiting and other human resource functions?

2. What are the comparative advantages and disadvantages of external recruiting versus promotion from within?

3. What issues would you consider before signing an agreement with a private employment agency to help you find a job?

4. What are the reasons why an organization may not want to list its name in a recruiting ad?

5. Rather than following a standard form of job advertising, should an organization consider using unique ads that are "cute" and "funny"?

6. What can an organization do to increase the number of direct applications through walk-ins or write-ins? Should an organization even try to increase direct applications?

7. What recruiting methods would you recommend for a construction company planning to build a major project in an isolated wilderness area? Where should the construction company recruit, and what sort of enticements could it offer?

8. The EEOC has stated that every organization should have an affirmative action policy as a matter of good employment practice. Why do you agree or disagree with this policy?

KEY TERMS

Bona fide occupational qualifications (BFOQ): Employers are allowed to discriminate on the basis of religion, sex, or national origin only when these attributes are necessary for the operation of their businesses; that is, when they are bona fide occupational qualifications.

Conciliation: An informal process of agreement used by the Equal Employment Opportunity Commission for resolving charges of discrimination.

Disparate impact: To have the effect of discriminating. A recruitment or selection procedure is said to have a disparate impact on a particular race or sex if the operation of that activity tends to significantly reduce the number of minorities and females who are accepted for employment.

Employee requisition: An authorization to recruit a new employee to fill a job opening.

Equal Employment Opportunity Commission (EEOC): The EEOC is a government agency created by the Civil Rights Act (1964) responsible for enforcing Title VII of the Civil Rights Act, the Age Discrimination in Employment Act of 1967, the Equal Pay Act of 1963, and Section 501 of the Rehabilitation Act of 1973.

Headhunters: Private employment agencies that search for individuals who are able to assume positions of leadership for client organizations.

Job bidding: An internal recruiting process that allows employees who believe they have the necessary qualifications to apply for a job that has become vacant.

Job posting: An internal recruiting process in which job vacancies are advertised to present employees. The employees who want to be considered for the job vacancy are allowed to bid for it by completing an application.

Job Service: Public employment agencies operated by each state under the general direction of the federal government. Job Service provides job placement, training, counseling, and testing as free services to those who use it, and it is funded by a portion of the unemployment compensation benefits.

Maximizer: An individual who launches an aggressive campaign to obtain numerous job offers and then selects the best one.

Nepotism: Employment practices that are considered unfair because they show favoritism to friends or relatives.

Office of Federal Contract Compliance Programs (OFCCP): The OFCCP is a government agency in the Department of Labor that reviews the affirmative action programs of government contractors and monitors their compliance.

Promotion from within: An internal recruiting method in which vacancies in management positions are filled by promoting lower-level managers.

Reverse discrimination: Where preferential treatment is shown to females and minorities, often to achieve an affirmative action goal.

Satisficer: An individual who accepts the first job offer received either because of inadequate experience or lack of self-confidence.

Systemic discrimination: Employment discrimination that results from the normal operation of human resource systems, especially the procedures used for hiring, promoting, compensating, and training employees. Because these practices can create a disparate effect on the employment of minorities and females, EEO laws require their elimination.

Validator: An individual who conducts a very limited job search. A validator looks only long enough to confirm his or her decision to accept the favorite offer.

Yield ratios:. Ratios that show the number of applicants at one stage of the recruiting process who move to the next stage. These ratios provide valuable information for recruitment planning.

C O N C L U D I N G   C A S E

Physical Fitness or Systemic Discrimination?

Since engineering has been a male-dominated profession, Patricia Davis was very pleased when she landed an engineering job with the Streuling Scientific Company. Patricia had done well in graduate school, and she antici-pated being respected as a competent professional within the company. She was especially pleased that she would be working with another female engineer, Chris Lauritz, who had been employed at Streuling for four years.

Chris tried to caution Patricia about being too optimistic about her job expectations. Although Chris also had joined the company with excellent academic qualifications, she had never been promoted or received challenging job assignments. Instead, she had been treated like a second-class citizen. When a broken water pipe had flooded the floor, Chris had been expected to mop up, although some of the male engineers had helped initially. At social events Chris had always been asked to coordinate the refreshments.

Pat resolved that she would not allow anyone to treat her as a second-class citizen. Instead, she would insist on being treated as a professional who was equal to the fifty-one men in the engineering department. After a short time, however, Pat realized that she was not being treated as an equal by the male engineers. The men were friendly and cordial and she was treated with respect. If she had questions, the men were willing to assist and they seemed to be genuinely interested in helping her do the work. But she continued to be treated as an outsider and could not seem to achieve acceptance into the inner circle.

At first Pat decided that being accepted was only a matter of time. But gradually she became aware that the real root of the problem was the athletic club. All of the male engineers were members of a men's athletic club located one block away from the office. The company paid the club's membership fees for the men as part of their company benefits and allowed female members to join another health club of their choosing.

Most of the men visited the athletic club regularly to participate in various sports, especially jogging, swimming, and racquet-

ball. Since the athletic club served inexpensive meals, the men typically ate lunch there together three days a week after exercising. Even the men who did not exercise usually attended the luncheons. Most of the noontime discussions concerned politics and sports, but occasionally significant departmental issues were discussed.

When Pat realized how important the athletic club gatherings were to achieving group acceptance and to being treated as an equal, she wrote a memo to the company president, asking that Streuling discontinue paying the club memberships. Pat believed that both she and Chris would be systematically excluded as long as they could not participate in the athletic club activities.

When the men heard about Pat's memo, some regarded it as a joke, some were irate and made snide comments, and others simply said that the whole situation was unfortunate. Most of the men stated that they would pay their own membership fees if the company discontinued paying them.

The president of the company was sympathetic to Pat's memo and wanted to deal with the problem. He did not think the problem would disappear by eliminating club membership as a company benefit, but he could suggest no other alternatives, either. As a result, Pat has investigated the possibility of taking the issue to the EEOC as a case of systemic discrimination.

Questions:
1. Would you recommend that Pat try to involve the EEOC in this case? Why or why not?
2. What would be the probable consequences if Pat pursued this issue?
3. What actions should the president of the company take to resolve the problem?

NOTES

1. Gerri Hirshey, "Desperately Seeking Employment," *The Washington Post Magazine* (January 3, 1988): 20–29.

2. "Recruiting and Selection Procedures," Personnel Policies Forum, The Bureau of National Affairs, Survey No. 146, May 1988.

3. R. Martin, "Recruiter Revisited," *The Wall Street Journal*, April 10, 1972.

4. Jan Jaben, "Help Wanted: Business Editors," *Folio: The Magazine for Magazine Management* 17 (November 1988): 46–47.

5. Barbara LaBarbara, "Recruiting and Interviewing: The Trump Card of the Personnel Game," *Supervision* 49 (December 1988): 14–16.

6. John P. Wanous, "Tell it Like it Is at Realistic Job Previews," *Personnel* 52, no. 4 (1975): 50–60.

7. Bruce M. Meglino, Angelo S. DeNisi, Stuart A. Young-blood, and Kevin J. Williams, "Effects of Realistic Job Previews: A Comparison Using an Enhancement and a Reduction Preview," *Journal of Applied Psychology* 73 (May 1988): 259–66; Marcia P. Miceli, "Effects of Realistic Job Previews on Newcomer Affect and Behavior: An Operant Perspective," *Journal of Organizational Behavior Management* 8 (Spring/Summer 1986): 73–88; Steven L. Premack and John P. Wanous, "A Meta-Analysis of Realistic Job Preview Experiments," *Journal of Applied Psychology* 70 (November 1985): 706–19; Mary K. Suszko and James A. Breaugh, "The Effects of Realistic Job Previews on Applicant Self Selection and Employee Turnover, Satisfaction, and Coping Ability," *Journal of Management* 12 (Winter 1986): 513–23.

8. William F. Glueck, "Decision Making: Organization Choice," *Personnel Psychology* (Spring 1974): 77–93; William F. Glueck, "How Recruiters Influence Job Choices on Campus," *Personnel* (March–April 1971): 46–52; Donald P. Rogers and Michael Z. Sincoff, "Favorable Impression Characteristics of the Recruitment Interviewer," *Personnel Psychology* 31 (Autumn 1978): 495–504.

9. Linda D. McGill, "Hiring a Competitor's Employee: Assessing the Risks," *Employment Relations Today* 15 (Autumn 1988): 191–98.

10. Ronni Sandroff, "What Managers Need to Know about the Hiring Crisis of the '90s," *Working Woman* 14 (February 1989): 92–94; Katherine E. Smith, "Creative Recruiting," *Folio, The Magazine for Magazine Management* 18 (February 1989): 149–51.

11. Douglas T. Hall, *Careers in Organizations* (Pacific Palisades, Calif.: Goodyear, 1976), Chapter 2.

12. See Dave Dahl and Patrick Pinto, "Job Posting: An Industry Survey," *Personnel Journal* (January 1977): 40–42.

13. "Recruiting and Selection Procedures," Personnel Policies Forum, The Bureau of National Affairs, Survey 146 (May 1988): 5.

14. Ibid.

15. Michael Ornstein, *Entry Into the American Labor Force* (New York: Academic, 1976), pp. 53–56.

16. Glenn Rifkin, "Recruiting in MIS: Facing Up to Hire Stakes," *Computer World* 23 (February 13, 1989): 1, 99–101; Emanuel Weintraub, "Competition for Labor: Deal With it Now," *Bobbin* 29 (May 1988): 20–24.

17. "Recruiting and Selection Procedures," Personnel Policies Forum, p. 8.

18. Kathy Gevlin, "Bank Headhunters: Kings of the Recruitment Jungle," *Bankers Monthly* 106 (January 1989): 71–74; Johnston F. Hughes, "Don't Search, Research," *Personnel Journal* 68 (February 1989): 83, 85.

19. Norman E. VanMaldegiam, "Executive Pursuit," *Personnel Administrator* 33 (September 1988): 96–98.

20. "The Hiring Hall in the Construction Industry," in *Coming to Grips with Some Major Problems in the Construction Industry*, a Business Round Table report (1974), 15–23.

21. Michael R. Carrell and William T. Heavrin, Jr., "The 'Handi-Capable' Employee: An Untapped Resource," *Personnel* 64 (August 1987): 40–45; Joseph D. Levesque, *People in Organizations* (Sacramento, Ca.: American Chamber of Commerce Publishers): I.5.157.

22. Roger D. Neathawk, Susan E. Dubuque, and Carolyn A. Kronk, "Nurses' Evaluation of Recruitment and Retention," *Nursing Management* 19 (December 1988): 38–45; Marion Turner, "Getting Members Back on the Career Path," *Accountancy* 102 (December 1988): 19–20.

23. John P. Kohl and David P. Stephens, "Wanted: Recruitment Advertising that Doesn't Discriminate," *Personnel* 66 (February 1989): 18–26.

24. Sandra Bem and Daryl Bem, "Does Sex-Biased Job Advertising 'Aid and Abet' Sex Discrimination?" *Journal of Applied Psychology* 57 (1973): 6–18.

25. Guy M. Pulley and James C. Seigler III, "Resume Sharing: Business Working with Business," *Managers Magazine* 63 (December 1988): 17–18.

26. Ralph W. Tyler, "Introduction to the Study: Conclusions and Recommendations," in *Work-Study College Programs*, eds., James W. Wilson and Edward H. Lyons (New York: Harper, 1961).

27. Morton E. Grossman and Margaret Magnus, "Hire Spending," *Personnel Journal* 68 (February 1989): 73–76.

28. William F. Glueck, *Personnel: A Diagnostic Approach*, *rev. ed.* (Dallas, Tex.: Business Publications, Inc., 1978), pp. 171–72.

29. Leslie Stackel, "The Flexible Workplace," *Employment Relations Today* 14 (Summer 1987): 189–97.

30. Andrew G. Smith, "Increasing Onsite Production," *AACE Transactions* (1988): K.4.1–K.4.14.

31. "Effect of Scheduled Overtime on Construction Projects," in *Coming to Grips with Some Major Problems in the Construction Industry*, a Business Round Table report (1974), 1–14; see also Dwight A. Zink, "The Measured Mile: Proving Construction Inefficiency Costs," *Cost Engineering* 29 (April 1986): 19–21.

32. L. Lincoln Eldredge, "The Executive 'Temp': Do You Need Help at the Top?" *Canadian Manager* 13 (September 1988): 15–16; Allan Halcrow, "Temporary Services Warm to the Business Climate," *Personnel* 67 (October 1988): 84–89

33. Samuel R. Sacco, "Temporary Employees Meet Needs of Business," *Office* 107 (May 1988); 37–40; Jack L. Simonetti, Nick Nykodym, and Louella M. Sell, "Temporary Employees, a Permanent Boon?" *Personnel* 65 (August 1988): 50–56.

34. George Munchus III, "Employees Leasing: Benefits and Threats," *Personnel* 65 (July 1988): 56–61; Joani Nelson-Horchler, "The Trouble with Temps," *Industry Week* 235 (December 14, 1987): 53–57.

35. Ellen Bravo, "Part-Time and Temporary Employees Are not Given Any of the Benefits Pie," *Business and Health* 5 (April 1988): 60–61.

36. *Willie S. Griggs et al.* v. *Duke Power Company*, 401 U.S. 424 (1971); *Albemarle Paper Company* v. *Joseph P. Moody et. al.*, 422 U.S. 405 (1975).

37. *Affirmative Action and Equal Employment: A Guidebook for Employers, Vol. 1* (Washington D.C.: U.S. Equal Employment Opportunity Commission, 1974).

38. *Regents of the University of California* v. *Bakke*, 438 U.S. 265 (1978); *Steelworkers* v. *Webber*, 433 U.S. 193 (1979).

39. Lawrence S. Kleiman and Robert H. Faley, "Voluntary Affirmative Action and Preferential Treatment: Legal and Research Implications," *Personnel Psychology* 41 (August 1988): 481–96; Nancy Kubasek and Andrea M. Giapetro, "Moving Forward on Reverse Discrimination," *Business and Society Review* (Winter 1987): 57–61; Carol D. Rasnic, "The Supreme Court and Affirmative Action: An Evolving Standard for Compounded Confusion?" *Employee Relations Law Journal* 14 (Autumn 1988): 175–90.

40. *Griggs* v. *Duke Power Company*, 401 U.S. 424 1981.

41. *Carter* v. *Gallagher*, 1952 F.2d 315 (C.A. 8, 1971); *Green* v. *Missouri Pacific R.R. Co.*, 523 F.2d 1290 (C.A, 8, 1975).

42. Preemployment Inquiries (Washington, D.C.: Equal Employment Opportunity Commission).

43. Laura M. Graves and Gary N. Powell, "An Investigation of Sex Discrimination in Recruiters' Evaluations of Actual Applicants," *Journal of Applied Psychology* 73 (February 1988): 20–29.

44. Charles Smith, "Get 'em Young, Boss: Japanese Companies Use Heavy Hand Tactics to Recruit Graduates," *Far Eastern Economic Review* 141 (September 22, 1988): 74.

The Selection Process

After studying this chapter, you should be able to:

1. Explain the basic principles of selection.
2. Describe the steps that might be included in a selection process.
3. Describe the concept of reliability and explain how the reliability of a measuring instrument can be estimated.
4. Describe the concept of validity and explain how to test the validity of a selection procedure.
5. Explain how application blanks can be used in the selection process.
6. Describe the types of employment interviews and discuss the purposes and limitations of interviewing.
7. Describe the major kinds of personnel tests and when each test might be useful.
8. Describe assessment centers and explain how they can be used to select managers.
9. Explain how selection information can be used to make a selection decision.

Chapter Outline

Employee Selection
Basic Principles of Selection / Selection Process

Reliability
The Issue of Reliability / Operational Definitions

Validity
The Issue of Validity / Operational Definitions / Legal Requirements

Application Blanks
Use of Application Blanks / Weighted Application Blanks

Employment Interviews
Purpose of Interviews / Types of Interviews / Reliability and Validity of Interviews

Personnel Tests

Test Selection / Types of Tests / Ethical Issues of Selection

Assessment Centers

Assessment Activities / Reliability and Validity of Assessment Centers

Making a Selection Decision

Expectancy Charts / Usefulness of a Predictor / Selection Errors / Self-selection / Orientation and Probation

International HRM

I N T R O D U C T O R Y   C A S E

Negligent Hiring versus Invasion of Privacy

A security guard for Pinkerton's, Inc., participated as a co-conspirator in the theft of $200,000 in gold from Welsh Manufacturing Company. Welsh sued Pinkerton's in a jury trial claiming that Pinkerton's had failed to adequately research the guard's background. In court, Pinkerton's showed that it had contacted the guard's high school principal, a supervisor at a hospital where he had previously worked, and his superior officer in the Navy. These references were generally positive, although no specific comments were made about the guard's honesty or trustworthiness. Pinkerton's also checked and found no criminal convictions in Rhode Island, where he worked.

The jury ruled that Pinkerton's was guilty of negligent hiring and its decision was upheld by the Rhode Island Supreme Court. For sensitive jobs, the court ruled that employers must do an aggressive background search, even if the initial information is positive and does not arouse suspicions.[1]

In a similar case of negligent hiring, American Airlines was sued in U.S. District Court by a woman who was bitten by a boarding agent. The woman did not have a boarding pass and the boarding agent bit her hand during a skirmish as he tried to prevent her from entering a plane in Chicago. She requested that the agent be tested for the AIDS virus, and when he tested positive she sued claiming that American Airlines knew or should have known about his medical condition and violent tendencies.[2]

Questions:

1. Suppose Pinkerton's learned that the applicant had cheated on one test in school fifteen years ago. Should he be disqualified for employment as a guard? What if he was an ex-convict? What kinds of jobs should ex-convicts be allowed to hold?

2. When investigating an applicant's background, where do you draw the line between invasion of privacy versus avoiding negligent hiring? Should a company inquire whether an applicant has AIDS, is diabetic, has a violent temper, uses drugs, or stole from previous employers?

EMPLOYEE SELECTION

Except in small organizations, the human resource department assumes major responsibility for personnel selection. The personnel department normally reduces the field of applicants to three or four possible candidates. Line managers then interview these candidates and make their selection. Selection decisions can be made in a variety of ways. Some procedures amount to nothing more than simple random choice, while others involve careful, informed decisions. If twelve individuals apply for four typing jobs, the positions could be filled by a simple random process, such as hiring the first four applicants, hiring every third applicant, or writing their names on pieces of paper and drawing the first four out of a hat. A careful employer could make an informed decision by choosing the four applicants who have the most experience or who type the fastest.

Because employee selection is so important to organizational effectiveness, organizations ought to make careful, informed choices. These decisions should be based on relevant information that is not too costly or time consuming to collect. The major procedures for collecting and using information to make informed selection decisions are explained in this chapter.

BASIC PRINCIPLES OF SELECTION

The process of making an informed hiring decision depends largely on two basic principles of selection. The first principle is that *past behavior is the best predictor of future behavior*. Knowing what an individual has done in the past is the best indication of what the individual is likely to do in the future. This principle is not deterministic; an employee who has been outstanding in previous jobs may be only mediocre in a new position. A student who did very poorly as a freshman can change and have an outstanding sophomore year. Knowing what people have done in their past is not an absolutely accurate indication of what they will do in the future. Nevertheless, in making selection decisions it is best to assume that past behavior is the best predictor of how an individual will perform in the future. The selection decision is similar to that faced by a baseball manager who has to determine which batter to send to the plate in the final inning of a playoff game. If the manager has the option of sending several players to the plate, he or she will probably send the batter with the highest season batting average. A batter with a .400 average has a higher probability of getting a hit than a batter with only a .200 average. Although the possibility always exists that either batter could get a hit or that either could strike out, the player with the highest batting average has demonstrated that he or she has the highest probability of getting a hit.

The second basic principle of employee selection is that *the organization should collect as much reliable and valid data as is economically feasible and then use it to select the best applicants*. Reliable data refers to information that is repeatable and consistent. Valid data refers to information that indicates how well employees will perform their jobs. In some situations, very little information needs to be collected regardless of its reliability and validity. For example, detailed information is unnecessary when a job is simple and can be performed by almost any applicant or when the cost of making a bad hiring decision is negligible. However, as jobs become increasingly difficult to staff with competent employees and as the costs of making a poor hiring decision increase, the collection of reliable and valid information becomes very important. The selection of good managers is especially important, and some organizations have prospective managers spend several days in assessment center activities from which reliable and valid information can be obtained.

SELECTION PROCESS

The selection process is a sequential procedure involving some or all of the steps illustrated in Figure 6.1. Each step in the process is typically treated as a hurdle that systematically screens the number of employees advancing to the next step. To survive the process and be placed in the job, an applicant must successfully pass each hurdle. Most organizations reject undesirable applicants at each step of the process to reduce the burden of keeping track of a number of applicants, but some organizations have all applicants go through the entire selection process, waiting until the end to choose the best candidate. Each step in the selection process should be designed to obtain specific, useful information for making a hiring decision.

FIGURE 6.1 Selection process.

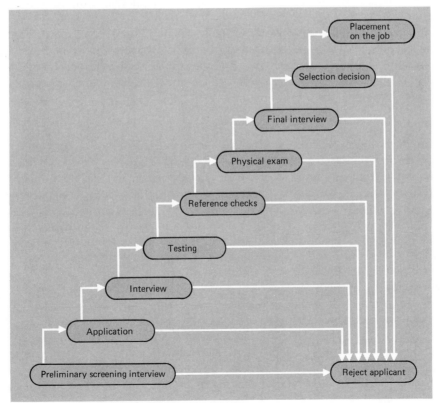

PRELIMINARY SCREENING INTERVIEWS

The first step in the selection process is a preliminary screening interview that typically occurs as part of the recruiting process. Individuals who are obviously not qualified for the job opening should be immediately eliminated from the applicant pool. However, the criteria for deciding that someone is unqualified need to be established carefully. Arbitrary standards that have no relationship to an individual's ability to perform the job should not be used to disqualify an applicant. It is especially important that age, race, religion, sex, and national origin not be used as the criteria for disqualifying job applicants.

The most frequently cited reason for rejecting applicants at this first stage is that they lack the education, training, or experience necessary for performing the job. Any of these are legitimate disqualifications if they are related to job performance. Individuals who do not have the required knowledge, skills, abilities, educational certificates, or academic training ought to be immediately removed from the applicant pool and notified that they are not being considered for employment.

APPLICATION BLANKS

Completing an application blank is a basic part of the selection process in almost every organization; all but the smallest organizations have job seekers complete an application blank or some other biographical data form. The primary purpose of an application blank is to provide meaningful employment information that helps employers make accurate hiring decisions.

A carefully designed application blank can be a useful selection tool that is both reliable and valid. Such an application blank is typically referred to as a **weighted application blank**, a **biodata form**, or a **biographical-information blank**. The process for developing a weighted application blank as a valid selection tool is described in detail in a later section.

INTERVIEWS

Employment interviews are used by virtually every organization to hire employees at all job levels, and they are very influential. The results of a survey conducted by the Bureau of National Affairs indicated that 56 percent of the participating companies believed that interviews were the most important aspect of the selection procedure and that 90 percent had more confidence in interviews than any other sources of information.[3]

Unfortunately, research evidence does not support the value of employment interviews. Interviews are conducted by individuals who have different orientations, different levels of competence, and different perceptual biases. The interview process generally is not consistent—each interview is conducted differently depending on what is said—and the evaluations of the interviewer are essentially random observations. Although interviewers may believe their conclusions are the most important step in the decision process, research shows that interview data are generally neither reliable nor valid.[4]

Some types of interviews are more useful than others. Structured interviews, for example, are usually more reliable than unstructured interviews. Furthermore, selection interviews are used for more than just selection purposes. The purposes of a selection interview and the procedures for developing a patterned interview are described in a later section.

EMPLOYMENT TESTING

Personnel testing is a valuable way to measure individual characteristics. Hundreds of tests have been developed to measure numerous dimensions of human behavior; these include paper-and-pencil tests, performance tests, performance simulations, graphology, and honesty tests. The tests measure mental abilities, physical abilities, knowledge, skills, personality, interests, temperaments, and other attitudes and behaviors.

A description of these tests and how they can be used in personnel selection is presented in a later section.

REFERENCE CHECKS

Before employers make a selection decision, they should investigate the backgrounds of prospective employees. These background investigations usually are referred to as reference checks and may include an investigation of previous employment, educational credentials, criminal activities, credit records, and general character. Many organizations, including graduate schools, ask applicants to provide letters of recommendation from former employers and acquaintances. These letters of recommendation generally constitute the most useless form of reference check, since applicants do not ask someone to write a letter unless they are certain that the person will make a favorable evaluation. Since letters of recommendation generally represent a very biased form of information, employers usually disregard such letters unless they contain negative information. The value of letters of recommendation also has decreased in recent years because of a growing concern among employers that they could be sued for reporting adverse information. To protect themselves from potential law suits, many employers simply confirm the individual's employment, the dates of employment, and salary information.[5]

A reliable means of obtaining information about an applicant's previous employment history is to phone the applicant's previous employer and request a reference. While a letter of recommendation may simply say that an individual is creative and brilliant, a phone call affords the opportunity to ask the employer how the individual demonstrated creativity and brilliance.[6]

Another way in which employers can check the backgrounds of prospective employees is to buy investigative reports from a credit reporting agency or private investigative agency. Such agencies specialize in gathering information about applicants for employment, life insurance, and financial credit. Four of the largest credit reporting agencies are Equifax, American Service Bureau, Hooper Holmes, and Dunn and Bradstreet. Metropolitan areas also have smaller credit reporting agencies. When employers request an investigative report, they can specify the length of time to be covered in the report. For example, Equifax produces investigative reports that typically go back one year, five years, or ten years. A five-year report generally costs about fifty or sixty dollars and includes information obtained from an applicant's past employers, neighbors, and business associates. The information usually concerns an applicant's length of service with previous employers, a salary history, reasons for termination of employment, eligibility for rehire, and other information about the applicant's general reputation, living habits, credit records, criminal records, health, and driving habits. This information is collected by field representatives who are employed in over 1,700 regional offices located throughout the United States and Canada. The Fair Credit Reporting Act (discussed in Chapter 4) requires that an individual be notified when he or she is being investigated and when his or her application is rejected either in part or in full because of the investigative report. An applicant also is allowed to challenge incorrect information and have it changed.

In some situations, an employer may find it useful to examine an applicant's criminal record. Court records are open to the public, and information can be obtained that indicates whether an applicant has been tried for a crime and either convicted or acquitted. Because of the Privacy and Security Act (1976), however, police records are not open to the public.

Employers need to know whether an applicant's background indicates that the applicant has a propensity for abusive behavior. An appellate court in Florida has ruled that an employer can be held liable for injuries committed by its employees if the company failed to investigate the applicant's criminal record and medical history. As part of an emerging legal trend, firms are now being held responsible for their employees' wrong doing, even if the crimes have no connection with the workers' jobs. Injured parties have been successfully advancing the legal theory of **negligent hiring**, claiming that employers knew, or should have known, that their employees were dangerous.[7]

Although reference checks are costly and inconvenient, they are increasingly important because there appears to be a growing tendency for applicants to misrepresent information on their resumés and applications. Some impostors have been fired for employee theft multiple times from different stores, and a simple reference check would have indicated these people were poor hiring risks. Some cases have even been found in which impostors changed their names and obtained graduation certificates, grade transcripts, and other supporting documents to pretend they were someone else.

PHYSICAL EXAMS

Some organizations require applicants to obtain physical examinations, particularly if a job requires heavy physical exertion. Other organizations, especially hospitals and food service concerns, depend on physical examinations to eliminate applicants with communicable diseases. However, many organizations that require a physical exam do not use the information for selection purposes as much as for protection from excessive worker compensation claims that could be related to an individual's preemployment health record.

Physical examinations have not proven very reliable for predicting future medical problems. A careful physical exam may be useful for diagnosing existing medical problems, but it is not particularly useful in forecasting future medical difficulties. A carefully designed medical questionnaire is probably just as accurate as a physical exam in predicting future medical problems and far less costly.[8] An even better strategy is for an organization to devise a preventive health maintenance program that teaches employees how to avoid medical problems.

FINAL INTERVIEW

Before a selection decision is made, an applicant may be processed through an additional interview with a member of the human resource staff. The purpose of this interview is to integrate all of the information that has been collected during the selection process and to clarify information that is inconsistent or missing.

An applicant's final interview is typically held with the line manager or supervisor to whom the selected applicant will report. This interview usually occurs after the human resource office has narrowed the selection decision to three or four candidates. Although the human resource office may indicate its choice of an applicant, the ultimate hiring decision is left to the line manager. Since managers usually select the person that they like the most and think they would enjoy working with, the final interviews essentially comprise a personality contest.

SELECTION DECISION

After all of the information is collected, a selection decision is made, and the new employee is placed on the job. Three methods are typically used for making selection decisions: (1) clinical judgment, (2) weighted composite, and (3) multiple cutoff. **Clinical judgment** refers to the informal process of examining the information about each individual and making a subjective decision about the most desirable applicant to hire. The **weighted-composite** procedure involves weighing the information and statistically combining it into a composite score. The applicant with the highest composite score is hired. **Multiple cutoff** consists of a sequential process in which applicants are required to achieve satisfactory levels at each successive step. Illustrations of each of these methods are presented in later sections.

RELIABILITY

Reliability refers to consistency of measurement or repeatability. A selection instrument, such as a test, is said to be reliable if individuals obtain essentially the same scores each time they take the test. An achievement test, for example, is said to be reliable if the same person's scores do not vary greatly when the test is taken several times. The higher a measuring instrument's reliability, the greater the confidence that can be placed in the instrument.

THE ISSUE OF RELIABILITY

The issue of reliability has been considered extensively with respect to personnel testing. Test publishers include evidence of reliability in the examiner's manuals and in advertisements about the tests. However, more than just personnel testing is at issue. The reliability of every selection-measuring instrument should be examined, including application blanks, interviews, reference checks, and physical exams. The issue of reliability also is important for other human resource functions, especially performance evaluations. If a supervisor cannot reliably evaluate the performance of a subordinate, the evaluation should not be used for human resource decisions such as firing, promoting, or granting pay increases.

Reliability is an important issue in employee selection because it serves as a limiting constraint on validity. If a measuring instrument is not reliable, it cannot be valid; unreliable information cannot be used to predict performance on the job.[9] Unreliable data are essentially capricious random numbers that do not really measure anything. These are some of the major reasons why selection information may be unreliable:

1. The selection instrument may be ambiguous and unclear. For example, items on an application blank may not be specific, questions in an interview may not be clear, and test questions that are ambiguous may lead to random responses that do not measure a consistent, repeatable personality characteristic.
2. The person using the measuring instrument may not have a clear perception of the behavior being measured or a well-defined standard to use as a basis for making the evaluation.
3. The behavior being evaluated may be an unstable phenomenon that changes from time to time, such as personal feelings, rather than a stable personality characteristic.

Reliability is not the same as accuracy. The measuring instrument may be reliable and still not be accurate. For example, a cloth measuring tape may stretch over time and not provide an accurate measurement of length. However, the tape could still be termed a very reliable measuring instrument because it produces the same measurements time after time.

OPERATIONAL DEFINITIONS

The reliability of a measuring instrument is estimated by different kinds of tests. These testing procedures are referred to as *operational definitions*, since the reliability is defined by specifying the operation used to estimate the reliability. The four operational definitions of reliability include: (1) test-retest reliability, (2) alternate-forms reliability, (3) split-halves reliability, and (4) conspect reliability.

TEST-RETEST RELIABILITY

One of the most obvious ways to test the reliability of a measuring instrument is to use the same measure twice on the same sample of people and determine if the second measures are similar to the first. This procedure is called **test-retest reliability**, or *coefficient of stability*.[10] If the measuring instrument is reliable, the individual's score on the second measurement should be essentially the same as that obtained on the first measurement. The test-retest reliability of most selection instruments can be examined quite easily. For example, the reliability of employment tests and application blanks can be checked by administering the instruments when the applicants first apply and then asking the applicants to complete the same instruments again one week later. If the responses are essentially the same, the instruments would be considered reliable. The reliability of interviews and reference checks also can be examined by repeating them to determine if the same evaluations were made both times.

When the test-retest reliability of an instrument is examined, an important consideration is how much time should elapse between the first and second measurement. A useful rule is that enough time should pass so that the individuals do not remember the responses they made the first time, but not so much time that the characteristic being measured has an opportunity to change. A one-week interval is probably sufficient for testing the reliability of application blanks, interviews, and some personnel tests. However, a two- or three-month interval may be necessary for testing the reliability of a mental-ability test.

ALTERNATE-FORMS RELIABILITY

The reliability of a measuring instrument can be estimated by developing an alternate form of the instrument and then correlating the responses of a sample of people to both forms. Many test publishers, for example, develop two or more forms of the same test. Both Form A and Form B of the same test can be given to a group of applicants, and the scores can be compared to see if the two scores for each individual are essentially the same. Although the tests are not identical, the number of questions and the nature of the items are essentially equivalent. If the scores are highly correlated, the test is said to be a reliable instrument. **Alternate-forms reliability**, which is sometimes called the *coefficient of equivalence*, avoids the problem of having to decide how long to wait to readminister the second form.[11] Both Form A and Form B can be administered at the same testing session.

An illustration of alternate forms reliability is presented in Table 6.1, which shows the scores on Form A and Form B of a mental-ability test for twenty-five individuals. The test publisher advertises that Form A and Form B are equivalent measures of mental ability and the high correlation coefficient of .92 supports this claim.

SPLIT-HALVES RELIABILITY

Another method of estimating the reliability of a measuring instrument is to split the instrument in half, forming two separate scores, and then to correlate the scores for each individual to determine if comparable scores have been obtained. This **split-halves reliability** method is similar to alternate-forms reliability except that one test is divided into two parts rather than developing two alternate tests. The split-half method, which is sometimes called the *coefficient of internal consistency,* can only be used if the test is measuring a single dimension.[12] The two halves must theoretically be measuring the same personal characteristic to be meaningful.

CONSPECT RELIABILITY

Two people observing the same behavior may or may not evaluate it the same. The degree of consistency between the scores assigned by two different observers is referred to as **conspect reliability**, or interrater reliability. Conspect reliability is especially important in assessing the reliability of interviews and performance evaluations. If two interviewers talk with a group of individuals and independently evaluate them, their evaluations are said to have high conspect reliability if they agree. Unfortunately, the conspect reliabilities of interviews and performance evaluations are often low.[13]

VALIDITY

Selection information should be both reliable and valid. Information collected on a job applicant should be consistent and useful in predicting whether the applicant will be a successful performer on the job.

TABLE 6.1   Estimating the reliability of a mental-ability test using the alternate-forms method:
Form A and Form B (N = 25 students)

Students	X Form A	Y Form B	X²	Y²	XY
1	18	17	324	289	306
2	19	17	361	289	323
3	30	28	900	784	840
4	26	25	676	625	650
5	19	22	361	484	418
6	23	22	529	484	506
7	28	25	784	625	700
8	24	27	576	729	648
9	19	17	361	289	323
10	18	20	324	400	360
11	22	23	484	529	506
12	31	31	961	961	961
13	26	25	676	625	650
14	24	26	576	676	624
15	17	18	289	324	306
16	19	21	361	441	399
17	20	17	400	289	340
18	23	23	529	529	529
19	28	29	784	841	812
20	30	31	900	961	930
21	32	33	1,024	1,089	1,056
22	21	22	441	484	462
23	20	18	400	324	360
24	25	23	625	529	575
25	26	25	676	625	650
Totals (Σ) =	588	585	14,322	14,225	14,234

$$r_{xy} = \frac{N(\Sigma XY) - (\Sigma X)(\Sigma Y)}{\sqrt{N\Sigma X^2 - (\Sigma X)^2}\ \sqrt{N\Sigma Y^2 - (\Sigma Y)^2}} = \frac{(25)(14,234) - (588)(585)}{\sqrt{(25)(14,322) - 588^2}\ \sqrt{(25)(14,255) - 585^2}}$$

$r = .92$

THE ISSUE OF VALIDITY

The term *validity* is used in a number of ways, especially in experimental research. In personnel testing, validity refers to the extent to which a *predictor* variable is correlated with a *criterion* variable. *Predictor* variables refer to all the kinds of information that are collected as part of the employment process, such as application blank data, interview data, test scores, personal references, and physical exam data. A *criterion* variable refers to a measure of job performance, such as a measure of productivity, absenteeism, tardiness, supervisory evaluations, or any other information that indicates the degree of success on the job.

The validity of a predictor is evaluated by looking at the relationship between the predictor and a criterion. Typically, this examination involves computing a correlation coefficient between the two variables. A correlation coefficient is a number between +1.0 and −1.0 that indicates the degree of relationship between the two variables. The correlation coefficient of +.92 in Table 6.1 indicates a strong positive correlation between Form A and Form B. Although correlation coefficients assessing reliability should be greater than .70, validity coefficients very seldom exceed .50. In fact, validity coefficients in the .30s and low .40s are generally considered quite acceptable. Correlation coefficients close to .00 indicate that no relationship exists between the two variables. Negative correlation coefficients are just as meaningful as positive correlations. Negative correlations simply mean that low predictor scores are associated with high criteria scores. Therefore, a negative correlation of −.42 is just as useful as a positive correlation of .42, and most personnel specialists would think that both correlations are "quite good."

A positive correlation coefficient is illustrated in Figure 6.2, which shows the relationship between typing speed and supervisor performance ratings. The correlation coefficient of .48 indicates that the employees who have the highest typing speeds receive

FIGURE 6.2 Illustration of positive correlation coefficient between typing speed and performance ratings.

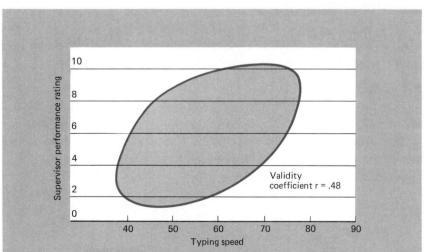

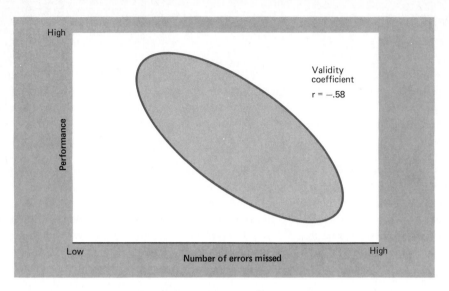

FIGURE 6.3 Illustration of negative correlation coefficient between number of errors-missed in a perfor-mance test and later performance on the job.

the highest performance ratings by their supervisors. A negative correlation coefficient is illustrated in Figure 6.3, which shows the relationship between the performance scores of a group of inspectors and the number of errors they missed in a performance test. Each of the inspectors examined a batch of materials in which a known number of defects were included. The inspectors who missed the most errors had the lowest performance ratings. A correlation coefficient of −.58 was observed between the predictor and the criterion.

OPERATIONAL DEFINITIONS

The five methods for evaluating the validity of a selection procedure are (1) predictive validity, (2) concurrent validity, (3) content validity, (4) construct validity, and (5) synthetic validity.

PREDICTIVE VALIDITY

The procedure used for determining **predictive validity** is shown in Figure 6.4. Here the predictor information is obtained on job applicants at the time they apply for employment, but hiring decisions should not be based on this information. After all new employees have been oriented and trained, the criteria data (performance measures) are obtained. A correlation coefficient is then computed between the predictor data and the criteria data. If the validity coefficient is significantly greater than zero, the predictor is considered valid and it can now be used to select the best employees. This procedure also is called the "follow-up" method of validation since subsequent performance is evaluated and used to assess the soundness of the selection procedure. Predictive validity is the most valuable kind of validity information since the method used to collect the predictor data is identical to the way the data will be collected in the future. Furthermore, evidence suggests that predictive validity persists over time, regardless of the effects of training and experience, at least with ability tests. Individuals who are successfully predicted to be good performers immediately continue to be good performers several years later.[14]

CONCURRENT VALIDITY

Sometimes an employer does not want to wait until after an orientation and training period to validate the selection procedure. Moreover, unless an employer is hiring many new employees, he or she may have to wait a long time to obtain a sample size large enough to conduct a predictive-validity study. In these situations, an alternative procedure would be to conduct a **concurrent-validity** study, which is sometimes called the "present-employee" method. As illustrated in Figure 6.4, this method involves collecting the predictor data and the criteria data on a sample of present employees and then correlating them to determine if a relationship exists.

There is no necessary relationship between concurrent- and predictive-validity studies. However, if a concurrent-validity study produces a significant correlation, the personnel specialist can be optimistic that subsequent predictive-validity studies will also. The results of a concurrent-validity study are generally a conservative estimate of what would be obtained using a predictive-validity study. The present employees represent a restricted range of potential individuals, since those employees who were unsuccessful have already quit or been fired. Correlation coefficients are smaller when there is a restriction in the range of responses.

Predictive and concurrent validity are referred to as **criterion-related validity**. In the *Uniform Guidelines on Employee Selection Procedures* (1978), employers are asked by the EEOC to provide evidence of criterion-related validity.[15] The guidelines call for empirical data demonstrating that the selection procedure is predictive of or significantly corre-

FIGURE 6.4 Comparison of predictive validation and concurrent validation.

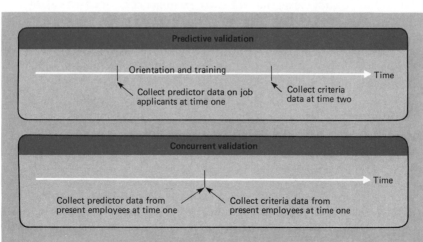

lated with important elements of job performance. However, the EEOC also will accept other evidence of validity.

CONTENT VALIDITY

Content validity refers to the perceived similarity between the predictor information and the nature of the job. Content validity is a matter of judgment—not empirical correlation—and is sometimes referred to as "face validity" to indicate that validity is inferred by subjectively assessing whether the predictor "looks as if" it is related to job performance. Perhaps the best illustration of content validity is a typing test as a predictor of secretarial performance. A typing test measures the same kind of behavior that is performed by a typist who spends eight hours a day typing. Therefore, it seems rational to assume that individuals who have high scores on a typing test would be good typists.

The EEOC is willing to accept a content-validity study as long as the employer can show that the content of the selection procedure is representative of important aspects of performance on the job for which the candidates are to be evaluated. However, the EEOC states that a content-validity strategy is not appropriate for demonstrating the validity of selection procedures that measure traits or constructs such as intelligence, aptitude, personality, common sense, judgment, and leadership. Content validity also is not an appropriate strategy when the selection procedure involves knowledge, skills, and ability which employees are expected to achieve on the job. In short, to claim that a predictor has content validity, the burden of proof is on the employer to demonstrate the similarity between the predictor and job performance.

CONSTRUCT VALIDITY

A construct is a concept (or word) that refers to the relationship between events and objects; it is not something we can see directly, but we think it exists anyway. Some prominent psychological constructs include intelligence, aggressiveness, need for achievement, and honesty.

Construct validity refers to whether an instrument that purports to measure a psychological construct is actually measuring what it claims to be measuring. Does a test that claims to be an IQ test really measure intelligence? Construct validity is determined by showing that a test is highly correlated with other known tests measuring the same thing or by showing through a series of studies that the test scores actually predict how people will behave. For example, if an IQ test has construct validity, people with high scores should be able to solve more puzzles and do other things requiring intelligence than people with low scores.

Construct validity is difficult to establish, but it is accepted by the EEOC if there is sufficient research evidence to show that the test is a valid measure of a construct and if a job analysis determines that this construct is a critical job duty or essential for successful performance.

SYNTHETIC VALIDITY

To perform a criterion-related validity study requires at least twelve to fifteen people in each job category, and fifty or more would be desirable. Because this type of study would be useless for an organization that may have only two or three people in some jobs, a

▌ **HRM in Action**

Validating a Reading Test

Since reading is such an important ability for both learning and performing a job, a project was undertaken to select and validate a reading test for civil service employees. The first step in this project was to interview groups of employees to assess the reading-level requirements of the training manuals, city codes, and guidebooks they needed to read. The study concluded that the average readability requirements were at the eleventh-grade reading level with the minimum proficiency being the ninth-grade reading level. It found that reading was especially important in training and concluded that trainees with inadequate reading skills could not adequately compensate for their deficiency.

The next step was to find a professionally-developed reading test that was reliable and reasonably priced. The test selected was the ABLE Level III Reading Test, a one-hour test that had been standardized with adult groups that included minority individuals.

The validation of the reading test relied on a *content-validity* study. Since the interviews had documented the importance of reading skills, the ABLE test was closely examined to make certain that it had strong face validity as a test of reading ability. A criterion-related validity study, was not done, however.

Two groups were used to check the test for adverse impact, one group of sixty-four present employees and another group of seventy job applicants. The results indicated that race was significantly related to the test scores: white job incumbents had the highest average score of 50.3, while male minority applicants averaged only 38.1.

Although the median test score for the ninth-grade level was 38, the cutoff score was set at 31 to adjust for measurement error. At that score, only 72 percent of male minority applicants, compared with 98 percent of white applicants would pass the test. Since 72 percent is less than four-fifths of 98 percent, it can be said that this test has an adverse impact on minority male applicants. Nevertheless, this test was recommended for use because (1) other minority and gender groups had acceptance rates above the four-fifths level, (2) the test was judged to be a valid predictor of job performance, and (3) none of the other fifteen tests under consideration was expected to have less adverse impact. This project illustrates the difficulty of finding a valid predictor that satisfies the EEOC's *Uniform Guidelines*.

Source: Rosemarie J. Park, René V. Dawis, Elizabeth K. Rengel, and Rebecca L. Storlie, "The Selection and Validation of a Reading Test To Be Used with Civil Service Employees," *Public Personnel Management*, Vol. 14, No. 3 (Fall 1985), pp. 275–284.

validation procedure has been designed especially for small organizations. Called **synthetic validity**, this procedure is sometimes referred to as *validation by parts*.[16]

Synthetic validity involves: (1) developing a battery of tests measuring various aptitudes, (2) conducting a job analysis to identify which jobs require which aptitudes, and (3) validating each test in the battery by combining the jobs that require that aptitude. For example, an organization may find that several jobs involve creative judgment, and therefore, a valid predictor of creative judgment would be an adaptability-test score. Another group of jobs may involve computations with numbers, and a valid predictor of this skill would be the number score on an aptitude test. Other tests in the test battery may be useful in predicting other job components, such as leadership, customer relations, and sales ability. In essence, synthetic validity is in part a combination of content and criterion-related validities. After judgments have been made about the components of each job, jobs requiring similar components are combined to validate a particular set of predictors.

An excellent illustration of synthetic validity is the Validity Generalization (VG) program developed by the Job Service using the General Aptitude Test Battery (GATB). This test measures nine basic abilities, as described in Table 6.2, and the scores are combined to form three composite scores: cognitive, perceptual, and psychomotor. The Job Service has identified five job families that use different combinations of these

---

HRM in Action

Using Validity Generalization to Select Sewing-Machine Operators

The U.S. Employment Service (USES) has been using the General Aptitude Test Battery (GATB) for fifty years to help employers select successful job applicants. A recent development in the use of the GATB is the Validity Generalization (VG) Program, where composite scores are used to predict performance for jobs assigned to one of five job families. The GATB consists of twelve timed tests—eight paper-and-pencil tests and four apparatus tests. Each part involves performing familiar tasks, such as arithmetic computations, name comparisons, reasoning, pegboard drills, and word interpretations. These tests measure nine aptitudes that are combined to form three composite scores: cognitive, perceptual, and psychomotor.

The VG program was tested with a large multiplant manufacturer of casual wear garments to see how well the GATB could reduce the costs of hiring sewing-machine operators. The job of sewing-machine operator was selected because of the large numbers of operators and the availability of both subjective and objective performance data. The sewing-machine operators job was determined to fall into Job Family 5, requiring 54 percent psychomotor ability and 44 percent cognitive ability.

GATB test scores were obtained on a sample of 571 newly hired operators along with monthly performance measures for a six-month period. The turnover rate of these new employees was high (51 percent). Since the GATB produces a percentile score for each person, the sample was divided into four quartile groups based on their scores.

The results indicated that both the objective productivity rates and the subjective supervisor ratings were higher on average for groups in higher quartiles. For example, after six months the first quartile earned an average of $3.83 per hour, while the fourth quartile earned an average of $4.59 per hour. The overall supervisor ratings on a five-point scale (1 = low, 5 = high) were 3.0 and 3.5, respectively. Turnover was also higher among those in quartile 1 than quartile 4 (53 percent versus 37 percent).

It was estimated that if the Job Family 5 scores were used in hiring sewing-machine operators, the increased productivity would result in a $519 annual savings per hire. Additional savings could also be derived from reduced turnover and lower training costs.

Source: K. Dow Scott, Robert M. Madigan, and Diana L. Deadrick, "Selecting the Right Employee," *Personnel Administrator*, Vol. 33 (December 1988), pp. 86–91.

TABLE 6.2 Aptitudes measured by the General Aptitude Test Battery

Cognitive

G — General learning ability The ability to "catch on" or understand instruction and underlying principles; the ability to reason and make judgments. Closely related to doing well in school.

V — Verbal aptitude The ability to understand the meaning of words and ideas associated with them, and to use them effectively. The ability to comprehend language, to understand relationships between words, and to understand meanings of whole sentences and paragraphs. The ability to present information or ideas clearly.

N — Numerical aptitude The ability to perform arithmetic operations quickly and accurately.

Perceptual

S — Spatial aptitude The ability to think visually of geometric forms and to comprehend the two-dimensional representation of three-dimensional objects. The ability to recognize the relationships resulting from the movement of objects in space.

P — Form perception The ability to perceive pertinent detail in objects or in pictorial or graphic material. The ability to make visual comparisons and discriminations and see slight differences in shapes and shadings of figures and widths and lengths of lines.

Q — Clerical perception The ability to perceive pertinent detail in verbal or tabular material. The ability to observe differences in copy, to proofread words and numbers, and to avoid perceptual errors in arithmetic computation.

Psychomotor

K — Motor coordination The ability to coordinate the eyes and hands or fingers rapidly and accurately in making precise movements with speed. The ability to make a movement response accurately and swiftly. Probably related to reaction time.

F — Finger dexterity The ability to move the fingers, and manipulate small objects with the fingers, rapidly and accurately.

M — Manual dexterity The ability to move the hands easily and skillfully. The ability to work with the hands in placing and turning motions.

composite scores, and every job can be assigned to one of these five job families based on a job analysis. A sewing-machine operator's job, for example, is a semiskilled job in Job Family 5 that requires 44 percent cognitive ability and 56 percent psychomotor ability.

For many years, validity was believed to be situationally specific to the job and the organization. Each organization was expected to conduct a separate validity study on the selection procedures it used for each job. However, an analysis of hundreds of validity studies has indicated that tests that consistently predict success for a few jobs of similar complexity can be used to predict success in related occupations within the same job family. In other words, the results can be generalized. The concept of applying the validity of specific tests based on a few jobs to a larger group of related and equally complex jobs is known as **validity generalization**.[17]

LEGAL REQUIREMENTS

Regulations governing the validation of selection procedures are stated in the *Uniform Guidelines on Employee Selection Procedures* that was issued in 1978 by four federal agencies—the Equal Employment Opportunity Commission, the Civil Service Commission, the Department of Labor, and the Department of Justice. The uniform guidelines apply not only to tests but also to other selection procedures that are used as a basis for any employment or promotion decision. Employers should be prepared to show that all of the steps in their selection procedures are valid, including recruiting practices, preliminary screening interviews, application blanks, interviews, tests, and reference checks.[18] However, the guidelines do not require employers to conduct validity studies of selection procedures where no **adverse impact** results. Adverse impact is defined by the EEOC according to the "**four-fifths rule**." This rule states that there is evidence of adverse impact (i.e., discrimination) whenever the selection rate for any race, sex, or ethnic group is less than four-fifths (or 80 percent) of the rate for the group with the highest selection rate. For example, if an organization hires 50 percent of all Asians who apply for work, the selection rate for Asians is .50. Eighty percent of .50 is .40. If the selection rate for any other ethnic or minority group is less than .40 (assuming that the .50 rate for Asians is the highest), this will generally be regarded as evidence of adverse impact.

The types of validity evidence acceptable to the EEOC are the five types specified previously. Although content validity is acceptable when an employer provides clear evidence supporting it, the EEOC prefers a criterion-related validity study. Correlation coefficients demonstrating validity need to be statistically significant. The EEOC adopts the .05 level of statistical significance, which means that there are only 5 chances in 100 of obtaining a correlation this high when there really is no relationship.

Unfortunately, the use of valid cognitive-ability tests clashes with society's efforts to provide racial equality, since the mean scores for some ethnic groups are lower than for others. During the 1960s, the EEOC claimed that these differences were created by culturally biased ability tests, and it called for better tests that were free from bias. Empirical evidence over the past two decades, however, indicates that the differences cannot be explained by cultural bias. The differences in ability test scores are directly related to differences in academic achievement and job performance. The differences in test scores reflect real differences in developed ability. If these differences result from poverty and hardship, they will vanish as poverty and hardships are eliminated. Until then, cognitive-ability tests will create an adverse impact, and better tests, being more reliable, will have slightly more adverse impact.[19] To reduce the adverse impact of the GATB, adjustments are made in the scores of minority groups, even though these adjustments compromise the validity of the test.[20]

APPLICATION BLANKS

Almost every organization uses an application blank of one kind or another. Although application blanks have the potential of being valuable selection tools, very few are designed to provide the kind of reliable and valid information needed for a selection decision.

USE OF APPLICATION BLANKS

The primary purpose of an application blank is to provide reliable and valid selection information, but as a selection tool, the typical application blank is only partially successful. Although an application blank can be used to eliminate applicants who are obviously unqualified, it is very seldom useful in making fine discriminations between the best-qualified applicants. Nevertheless, an application blank can facilitate the selection process in other ways. First, it can serve as the basis for the employment interview. Interviewers can examine an application blank and clarify information such as time lapses, discrepancies in dates, and significant contributions and experiences of the applicant; however, interviewers should not use it as a "crutch" to carry the discussion. Application blanks also provide names, dates, and places that are subject to verification for reference checks. Application blanks provide information for personnel records too. In fact, most application blanks are primarily designed to obtain such information as vital statistics, social security numbers, addresses, and names of those to notify in case of emergency.

LENGTH

Application blanks vary in length. Some may be as short as one side of a 3-by-5-inch card and ask only for name, address, telephone, and social security number. Others may be considerably longer. For example, the application blank for certain government jobs is a seventeen-page form, 8-by-10½ inches in size. The application for the Barnum and Bailey Clown College is also a lengthy form that requires applicants not only to provide an enormous amount of biographical information but also to answer multiple-choice questions and to provide original jokes. This application blank essentially represents a combination of a biographical-information form and a personnel test.

CONTENT

Applicants typically are required to provide four different kinds of information on application blanks: (1) vital statistics, such as name, address, phone number, and social security number; (2) educational background, including schools attended, degrees obtained, and dates of enrollment; (3) work history, including former employers over the past five to ten years, jobs held, salaries, and reasons for leaving; and (4) background experiences, such as professional associations, hobbies, interests, and civic involvement. In addition, applicants are usually required to sign the application in order to certify that the information is correct, to give the employer permission to investigate its accuracy, and to acknowledge that falsifying information is grounds for dismissal.

RELIABILITY AND VALIDITY

Application blanks are generally very reliable. The test-retest reliability of application blanks is extraordinarily high since applicants can easily report the same kinds of information both times. Studies comparing application-blank information with other sources of information, such as records of previous employers, indicate that little distortion occurs, especially for easily verified information.[21]

Application blanks generally are not very valid, however, because they are not designed to identify outstanding performers. To be a valid selection instrument, an application blank must request information about an applicant's previous background that can be used to predict the applicant's future performance. Carefully designed application blanks have proven to be very valid predictors of success in certain jobs.[22] Inventories of biographical information, for example, have sometimes been more effective than other instruments for the prediction of supervision and sales success. Biographical information also has been used quite extensively in the selection of officer candidates in the military, and such information has even been found to be a good predictor of turnover among office workers.[23] Some of the most valid application blanks are called weighted application blanks, biodata forms, or biographical information blanks.

Some applications contain open-ended questions intended to obtain a sample of the applicant's handwriting. Handwriting analysis, called **graphology**, can be used to study an individual's personality and is especially popular in some European countries, such as Germany, France, and Holland. It has been reported that as many as 3,000 firms in the United States use graphology in some form, particularly for selection and promotion.[24] Handwriting analysis is surprisingly reliable. Skilled graphologists make almost identical evaluations when analyzing samples of writing on different occasions or when analyzing two samples of an individual's handwriting. However, the validity of graphology is questionable. Personality traits measured by handwriting analysis are not similar to personality traits measured by personality tests. Furthermore, most studies have failed to find a relationship between handwriting and job performance.[25]

LIMITATIONS

Although an application blank can be a very reliable and valid selection tool, it does have limitations. An application blank is an impersonal selection procedure, and no written form can ever substitute for the direct personal contact of a company representative. A second limitation is that an application blank only asks for a limited amount of information; individuals who have unique backgrounds and experiences may have difficulty describing what they have done on a given form. A third limitation is that an application blank elicits biased information. The information on an application blank represents only what the applicant wants the organization to know, which usually means that unfavorable information is omitted. A fourth limitation is that the information is strictly objective and fails to explain an individual's motives and situational constraints. Application blanks tell the "what" of an individual's background but not the "how" or the "why" that may be more important. A fifth limitation is that an application blank is interpreted by people, and therefore its interpretation is subject to observer biases.

Some organizations have attempted to reduce the amount of providing a detailed analysis of how specific information on an appl interpreted. For example, one organization provided these six ex breaks in education: (1) economic necessity, (2) the individual lac (3) the individual was a slow maturing person, (4) personal procra and family pressures, (6) no appreciation of academic training. The vided similar lists of potential inferences for other application-blank responses and instructed the evaluator to examine all of the information and to develop a *clinical judgment* of the job applicant based on recurring behavior problems.

Since most people seldom use more than six or seven pieces of information in making decisions, the best method for evaluating an application is a weighted application-blank procedure. Weighted application blanks attempt to reduce the degree of subjectivity by substituting a weighted-composite score for a clinical judgment.

WEIGHTED APPLICATION BLANKS

A weighted application blank is a convenient selection tool that eliminates much of the customary bias in selection procedures. Specific information from the application blank is used to derive a score for each applicant, which indicates whether the applicant will be a successful performer or not. Separate procedures, in which different pieces of information are combined to form separate scores, can be used to predict how well applicants might perform on different jobs.

A weighted application blank is developed by correlating each piece of information from the application blank with a performance criterion such as productivity or supervisor evaluations. Although sophisticated procedures can be developed using regression analysis, a very simple yet useful procedure is illustrated in Table 6.3. This procedure consists of following these seven steps.

1. *Choose performance criterion*: The performance criterion is usually some measure of job success, such as productivity or superior evaluations; however, weighted application blanks also can be developed to predict such things as employee theft and turnover statistics.
2. *Identify criterion groups.* Employees are classified as either high or low performers. It is recommended that at least seventy-five employees be in each group. Of these seventy-five employees, fifty are placed in a "weighting" group and twenty-five are placed in a "holdout" group that is used to confirm the weights after they are developed.
3. *Select application-blank items to be analyzed*: The application blank should be designed to collect information that might be useful in predicting successful job performers. Each piece of information from the application blank is analyzed to determine whether it is a useful predictor. Questions that do not predict job performance or serve any other useful purpose are dropped from the application blank.
4. *Divide item into specific response categories*: This step is illustrated in Table 6.3, where educational background is divided into four categories: eight to eleven years of education, a high school diploma, two years of college, or a college degree. The

TABLE 6.3 How the weights are determined in a weighted application blank

Educational Background	Number of Employees in Each Group		Percentage of Employees in Each Group		Difference in Percentages	Assigned Weights
	High-performance Group	Low-performance Group	High-performance Group	Low-performance Group		
8–11 years	2	18	10%	90%	−80%	−2
High school diploma	9	11	45%	55%	−10%	0
2 years college	14	6	70%	30%	+40%	+1
College degree	19	1	95%	5%	+90%	+2

categories should be meaningful and clear so that everyone scores the application blank similarly. Some items may have only two categories, such as military service versus no military service.

5. *Determine item weights*: The item weights are determined by comparing the percentages of employees who are in the high- and low-performance groups. If the responses to an item show a significant difference between the proportions of those who are high performers and those who are low performers, then that item is weighted in the scoring of the application blank. In Table 6.3, applicants receive two points if they have a college degree, one point if they have completed two years of college, no points for a high school diploma, and lose two points if they have not finished high school.

6. *Confirm weights using hold-out groups*: After the weights have been developed using the employees in the weighting groups, the weighting procedure is applied to the hold-out groups to determine if the scores of the high-performance group are significantly greater than the scores of the low-performance group. If the weights are useful predictors, the high-performance group should have significantly higher scores than the low group.

7. *Establish cut-off scores*: A decision must be made on how high an applicant's score must be before the applicant can be hired or advanced to the next step of the selection process. Applicants with scores that are too low are rejected from the selection process.[26]

A weighted application blank allows a recruiter to score an applicant's responses very rapidly and to determine whether the applicant should be considered further for employment. Reviews of validation studies indicate that the weighted application blank is often a highly valid predictor of both job performance and length of service. Relative to other predictors, the weighted application blank is one of the most valid selection devices. Separate application-blank information should be validated for each specific job.

EMPLOYMENT INTERVIEWS

The major purpose of an employment interview is to gather information for making a selection decision. But very few interviews achieve this goal. Employment interviews are generally unreliable and, therefore, do not provide valid information. However, other reasons exist for conducting employment interviews besides gathering information. Furthermore, carefully developed interview schedules can make it possible to achieve acceptable levels of reliability and gather valid information.

PURPOSE OF INTERVIEWS

Interviews are conducted for several purposes, including the following:

1. *To obtain information about the applicant.* Since the information obtained via other selection tools may be incomplete or unclear, an interview provides an opportunity for factual information to be clarified and interpreted.
2. *To sell the company.* The employment interview provides an excellent opportunity for the interviewer to convince the applicant that the organization is a good place to work. Interviewers should not "oversell" the organization, but they can provide a realistic picture of the organization's advantages and disadvantages and still provide a positive explanation of why they have chosen to work for the company.
3. *To provide information about the organization.* During the interview, general information about the company—its services, policies, and job opportunities—should be explained to the applicant. Often the interviewer finds it necessary to direct the applicant toward the kinds of opportunities within the company for which he or she is suited.
4. *To establish friendship.* If nothing else, the interview should represent a friendly, interpersonal exchange. When the interviewer and the applicant conclude the interview, both should leave with the feeling that they are personal friends. As noted in Chapter 5, personal contacts can greatly influence applicants' decisions regarding job offers.

TYPES OF INTERVIEWS

An interview is simply an interaction between two or more individuals in which information is usually exchanged through questions and answers. This interaction may occur in several different ways; interviews vary in the amount of structure and advance preparation built into their design.

PATTERNED INTERVIEW

The most highly structured type of interview is the **patterned interview** in which the interviewer prepares a list of questions in advance and does not deviate from it. In its most structured form, the patterned interview contains both the questions asked by the interviewer and a list of the applicant's possible responses. The interviewer simply asks the questions and checks the response given by the applicant. In a patterned interview, for example, the interviewer would never ask such a question as "How do you feel about working in the food service industry?" Instead, the interviewer would read aloud a question and its possible responses:

Which of the following describes your feelings about working in the food service industry?

    _____ I don't expect to enjoy it.

    _____ I guess it's OK.

    _____ I think I will like it.

    _____ It should be a lot of fun.

    _____ I know I'll really enjoy it a lot.

The applicant would then be expected to select one of the five multiple-choice answers.

Although patterned interview questions are frequently used for research purposes, most employment interview questions are not as highly structured. A highly structured interview is very restrictive and allows little opportunity for either the interviewer or the applicant to qualify or elaborate on the information being obtained. To the applicant, a highly structured interview is almost like talking to a tape recorder or completing an application form. In fact, companies may want to consider taping the questions or including them on an application blank to avoid the costly expense of interviewing unless the interview also serves other purposes.

SEMISTRUCTURED INTERVIEW

In the **semistructured interview**, only the major questions are prepared in advance. Although these questions are used to guide the interview, the interviewer also can probe into areas that seem to merit further investigation. This approach combines enough structure to facilitate the exchange of factual information with adequate freedom to develop insights.

A typical interviewer's rating form is shown in Figure 6.5. This interview form was designed to evaluate college graduates applying for a management training program. To rate the applicants on each of the dimensions, the interviewers prepared a series of general questions to ask, such as:

What are your future vocational plans?

Why did you choose your particular field of work?

What courses did you like best and least, and why?

What do you hope to be doing ten years from now?

Depending on an applicant's answers to these questions, the interviewer could then probe deeper into the applicant's characteristics and qualifications. Most employment interviews would be considered semistructured.

Two popular interviewing programs that use semistructured interviews are called situational interviewing and targeted-selection interviews. Situational interviewing con-

Applicant's name _____   Date _____
Rater's name _____
University _____

	Poor		Average		Outstanding	

1. Intelligence. The capacity to learn by experi-
   ence and adapt to new situations successfully.   1 2 3 4 5 6 7

2. Self-confidence. Strong assurance of one's
   ability to perform.   1 2 3 4 5 6 7

3. Effective verbal expression. Ability to express
   ideas and concepts clearly and concisely.   1 2 3 4 5 6 7

4. Sociability. Ability to relate with and interact
   with others.   1 2 3 4 5 6 7

5. Maturity. Good sound judgment; ability to make
   decisions and act on them.   1 2 3 4 5 6 7

6. Appearance. Overall physical presentation, including grooming and dress.   1 2 3 4 5 6 7

7. Ambition or drive. Goal-directed personal energy that is behaviorally oriented.   1 2 3 4 5 6 7

8. Interest level. General enthusiasm as evidenced
   by personal involvement in interview.   1 2 3 4 5 6 7

9. Dependability. Ability to win trust of others
   through dedication to his/her responsibilities.   1 2 3 4 5 6 7

10. Loyalty. Personal commitment to the people
    and organizations with which the interviewee is
    affiliated.   1 2 3 4 5 6 7

11. Persistence. Determination to follow through
    with tasks initiated.   1 2 3 4 5 6 7

12. Overall recommendation   Definitely   Weak   Good   Definitely
    to hire.   not hire   potential   potential   hire

                              1   2   3   4   5   6   7

Are there any indications that this person's background should be
checked more extensively, such as unexplained gaps in education or
employment, excessive absences due to illness, disloyalty to former
employers, or excessive personal obligations or indebtedness?

Yes _____ No _____

Rank: _____ of _____ interviewed

FIGURE 6.5 Interviewer's rating form.

sists of asking job candidates to respond to a series of hypothetical situations by deciding what actions and solutions they actually would perform on the job. The applicant's responses are evaluated against preset criteria. Both the hypothetical situations and the criteria for evaluating them are derived from a detailed job analysis that identifies essential characteristics and skills. Situational interviewing has proved effective in predicting the immediate and future potential of sales associates and public relations agents.[27]

Targeted-selection interviews also rely on a careful job analysis to identify the critical job requirements (target dimensions) for each position. However, target interviews assume that past behavior is the best predictor of future behavior, and the questions focus on what the person has done in previous situations. The questions are carefully structured to allow the interviewer to extrapolate from previous experience when rating the applicant on the critical target dimensions for that position. Evidence indicates that targeted-selection interviews are more reliable and valid than regular semistructured interviews.

NONDIRECTIVE INTERVIEW

A **nondirective interview** also is called an unstructured interview because the interviewer does not plan the course of the interview in advance. The interviewer may prepare a few general questions to get the interview started, but the applicant is allowed to determine the course of discussion. Some of the broad general questions that an interviewer might ask include these:

Tell me about yourself.

What are your future vocational plans?

Tell me about your experiences on your last job.

What school activities have you participated in, and which did you enjoy the most?

How do you spend your time, and what are your hobbies?

Once the individual begins to respond to the interviewer's general question, the interviewer continues to encourage the individual to talk by nodding and by such statements as "Yes," "Mm-hmm," "Go on," and "Can you tell me more?" This process is built on the assumption that an individual will talk about things that are personally important if given the opportunity and encouragement to do so.

To conduct a successful nondirective interview, the interviewer should listen carefully and not argue, interrupt, or change the subject abruptly. The interviewer should ask questions sparingly, allow pauses in the conversation, and occasionally rephrase responses to encourage the individual to say more.

For many years, nondirective interviewing has been recommended for personal counseling. It is especially recommended as a technique for identifying factors that cause frustration or anxiety in the lives of employees. Although the nondirective interview is a valuable counseling technique, its use as a selection tool is highly questionable because of the lack of reliability in drawing inferences about the applicants.

STRESS INTERVIEW

Most interview situations involve a certain amount of stress simply because the applicants know they are being evaluated. Occasionally, interviewers intentionally create additional stress and justify doing so by claiming that they want to know how applicants can respond under pressure since stress is an important part of the job. Rarely, however, is the stress created in an interview similar to the stress found on a job, and knowing how an applicant responds to a **stress interview** is seldom a valid predictor of successful job performance. Fortunately, most interviewers try to avoid stress interviews because they believe such interviews are worthless, unpleasant, and partially unethical, even if the applicants are debriefed at the end.[28]

Stress can be created in an interview in several ways, such as by several interviewers rapidly firing questions at the applicant, by verbal attacks on the character and responses of the applicant, or by questions challenging the applicant's self-concept in areas of personal uncertainty. Stress interviews were developed during World War II as a technique for selecting military espionage personnel. Their use as a standard part of the selection process is not encouraged.

GROUP INTERVIEW

A **group interview** allows an interviewer not only to collect information from several applicants simultaneously but also to avoid having to repeat the same information about the company to each individual applicant. Sometimes group interviews involve asking the group to discuss an issue or to solve a problem. This technique is frequently used in assessment centers, described in a later section.

BOARD INTERVIEW

A type of interview commonly used by government agencies, the military, and some universities is the **board interview**. It involves the use of a panel of interviewers to question and observe a single candidate. This technique is particularly useful in situations where an applicant's nomination for a position must be approved and voted upon by several people. Rather than the candidate rushing from office to office for several exhausting interviews, all the interviewers can be brought together so that the applicant can respond to all their questions during a single time period.[29]

RELIABILITY AND VALIDITY OF INTERVIEWS

Although the employment interview is used extensively as a selection tool and many personnel specialists believe that interview information is the most important aspect of the selection procedure, the reliability and validity of interview information is highly questionable. Numerous studies have examined the reliability and validity of employment interviews, and in general, the following conclusions have emerged:

1. Interrater reliability is typically quite low. Two interviewers interviewing a group of applicants generally do not agree on their evaluations.
2. Intrarater reliability may be fairly high, depending on the competence of the interviewer and whether the interview is highly structured or not.

3. Although interviewers are not able to consistently evaluate most personal characteristics, higher reliabilities are usually obtained on characteristics that are directly observable, such as appearance, verbal fluency, sociability, and (surprisingly) intelligence.
4. Structured interviews are more reliable than those that are less structured.
5. Some carefully structured interviews have been found to be reasonably valid. However, the validation of interviews is lower than other predictors, especially ability tests and biodata forms.[30]
6. Because of its lack of reliability, most interview information is not a valid predictor of job performance, although a few exceptions have been found.[31]

In short, the evidence indicates that although the interview may serve some important functions, it is not a very useful selection tool for predicting outstanding performers. This lack of reliability should not be too surprising to anyone who carefully considers the interview process. Even structured interviews are characterized by an emormous amount of variability. The interviewer's behavior varies from interview to interview, based on moods, feelings, and physical conditions. The responses of applicants also may change from time to time, depending on their moods, feelings, and physical conditions. The responses that are made during an interview represent only a small part of the possible behavior of both the interviewer and the interviewee. Everyone has probably experienced conversations where everything seemed to "click" and other times when nothing did.

The evaluations of interviewers also are influenced by other aspects of the interview situation,[32] particularly by contrast effects. In such situations, an evaluation of one applicant is partially influenced by the previous applicant. For example, an applicant of average qualifications will be rated lower if he or she is preceded by an outstanding applicant. Evaluations also are influenced by an interviewer's stereotype of an "ideal employee," and each interviewer may have a different stereotype of the ideal. Interviewers tend to make their evaluations very quickly, based on their first impressions. Within the first two or three minutes of an interview, most interviewers form fairly firm opinions that are typically changed only by significant information to the contrary. An interview frequently involves a search for negative rather than positive information, and interviewers are more influenced by a small amount of negative information than by large amounts of positive data. Finally, the interview process is occasionally used as an opportunity to discriminate against minorities and females who may be underrated when applying for management positions that have traditionally been dominated by white males.

PERSONNEL TESTS

Carefully selected personnel tests can significantly improve the selection process for many jobs. Following the successful use of testing in the military during World War II, many organizations began to use personnel tests in their selection process. Testing increased dramatically during the 1950s and 1960s as many organizations required all job applicants to complete lengthy batteries of personality tests and interest inventories. By 1970, however, it became clear that some of these tests were eliminating a large proportion of minorities from jobs for which the tests were not valid. In one significant

Supreme Court case, *Griggs* v. *Duke Power Company*, the issue concerned a company policy that required employees to have a high school diploma and to pass two professionally developed personnel tests in order to be promoted from the labor department to higher levels in the company.[33] Because of their inferior educational backgrounds, many black employees failed the tests. When the company was asked to defend its policy, it was unable to prove that passing the tests was relevant to successful job performance. Therefore, the Supreme Court ruled that selection procedures such as tests that exclude a dispropor- tionate number of minority employees are illegal when the employer cannot demonstrate that the procedures are related to the safe and efficient operation of the company. In short, such tests must be valid. Since the tests used by Duke Power Company were not valid and eliminated minorities from higher-level jobs, the Supreme Court declared that the use of these tests was illegal.

After the ruling in the *Griggs* case in 1971, personnel testing dramatically declined. Most companies did not know whether their tests were valid, and rather than validate them, simply eliminated them from their selection procedures. The EEOC's attack on personnel testing was unfortunate since test information is often the most reliable and valid information garnered during the selection procedure. Rather than dropping their testing programs, the employers should have validated them. Reliable and valid tests are not illegal.

Although personnel testing declined after 1971, it has since recovered. A 1988 survey of 167 companies found that 84 percent used some form of personnel test to assist in making employment decisions. The most popular selection tests were those used to de- termine secretarial and clerical skills (83 percent).[34] Some organizations do not use tests because they believe that validating them requires extensive time and money. This belief is unfortunate since tests can be validated with little time and expense and without the services of a full-time consulting psychologist. Professionally developed personnel tests generally have high reliabilities and the validities are acceptable for carefully selected tests.

TEST SELECTION

A personnel test is an objective and standardized measure of such human characteristics as aptitudes, interests, abilities, and personalities. Test results measure how much of a given characteristic individuals possess relative to other individuals. If the characteristics being measured are important to successful job performance, personnel tests represent a valuable selection device.

Like other selection devices, personnel tests should be used to select applicants for a specific job. Deciding which tests to use to predict performance on a given job requires a careful job analysis. Someone who knows each job very well or who has examined the job descriptions and job specifications should identify the abilities and aptitudes essential for effective job performance. Thus, the necessary skills for a secretarial position might be the ability to type, to take shorthand, and to work cooperatively with others. Once the critical skills and abilities have been identified, personnel tests can be examined to iden- tify those that predict these characteristics. Whether the initial selection of a set of tests is a good or bad decision will ultimately be confirmed by the validity studies.

Deciding which test to use can be difficult. Over 2,000 tests are listed in the catalogs of test publishers in the United States. Two of the most extensive bibliographies of commercially available tests are *Tests in Print, Volumes 1 and 2* and *The Mental Measurements Yearbook*.[35] These volumes contain alphabetical lists of various tests arranged under different topics. Each test is briefly described, including what the test measures, how to obtain a specimen set, how long it takes to administer the test, how much the test costs, and what articles and books describe reliability and validity studies on the test. Personnel specialists who believe that a particular test might improve their selection process can obtain specimen sets to examine. A specimen set typically includes a test manual, a copy of the test, an answer sheet, and a scoring key. The test manual provides information about the construction of the test, its recommended use, reliability and validity studies that concern it, and instructions for administering and scoring it. If the scoring procedure is time-consuming or very complex, the completed tests often may be returned to the test publisher for scoring.

Employers may develop their own tests if they do not want to rely on the products of test publishers. However, the difficulties involved in developing a reliable and valid test generally discourage most from undertaking such a task. The exceptions are job-knowledge and job-sample tests, which can be constructed quite easily. If a personnel specialist clearly understands the information that employees need to know, a *job-knowledge test* can be constructed to measure whether job applicants know what they need to know to perform the job well. A *job-sample test*, also called a *job-tryout test*, consists of a small, well-defined portion of the actual job. Applicants are asked to perform this job sample, and their behavior is observed to see how well they do. Job-knowledge tests and job-sample tests typically possess good content validity.

TYPES OF TESTS

Tests can be classified in many different ways. One way is by individual or group—an individual test must be administered to only one person at a time, but a group test may be administered to many people at once. Another classification is based on the format of the test: in a paper-and-pencil test the candidates read a test booklet and mark an answer sheet, but in a performance test candidates actually perform a particular behavior. The best way to describe the different kinds of tests is to classify them according to what they measure.

ACHIEVEMENT TESTS

Numerous published tests are available that measure how much individuals have achieved or learned. These achievement tests are used extensively in education to assess how much students have learned relative to each other and relative to their year in school. Achievement tests also are available for evaluating how much individuals know about a particular trade. These exams are typically referred to as written trade tests. For example, the Purdue Test for Machinists and Machine Operators evaluates how much applicants know about hand tools, lathe machines, milling machines, and other machine tools. The test contains multiple-choice questions such as this one: "One of the best bearing metals contains antimony, tin, and copper. This metal is called: (a) bronze, (b) brass, (b) babbitt, (d) lead."

Many organizations have been successful in validating achievement tests for specific jobs, especially when the achievement test measures information that is essential for favorable job performance. For example, if an organization needs to hire plumbers and several applicants claim to have previous experience in plumbing, a written trade test on plumbing might be useful.

APTITUDE AND ABILITY TESTS

Rather than measuring what already has been learned, aptitude tests measure the capacity for learning. Aptitude and ability tests are typically used to indicate which individuals will learn best during training and which will perform best after they have been trained. Although there are hundreds of ability tests, most of them can be grouped into three major categories: mental abilities, mechanical abilities, and psychomotor abilities.

In the mental-abilities category are tests of intelligence (I.Q.), verbal reasoning, word fluency, perceptual speed, and similar characteristics. Some examples of typical test items for measuring these abilities are shown in Table 6.4. Mechanical aptitude refers to an individual's ability to recognize mechanical relationships and to visualize internal movement in a mechanical system. The correlation of mechanical aptitude with mental aptitude indicates that mechanical aptitude is partially correlated with mental ability but that a specific mechanical ability also is associated with the ability to visualize a mechanical system. Psychomotor ability refers to an individual's skill in making various body movements. Some of the specific psychomotor abilities that have been identified and tested include (1) control precision, (2) multilimb coordination, (3) reaction time, (4) speed of arm movements, (5) manual dexterity, and (6) finger dexterity. These appear to be specific abilities that are largely unrelated to each other and are not related to mental abilities.

Aptitude and ability tests are frequently combined into a test battery and then used to predict different jobs within organizations. Many organizations have been successful in validating various parts of their test batteries to predict successful performers on various jobs. One of the most extensively used test batteries is the General Aptitude Test

---

TABLE 6.4 Sample items on a mental ability test

A. If 6 pencils cost 30¢, how much will 11 pencils cost? _____

B. Which does not belong? _____
     1. violin   2. guitar   3. trumpet   4. harp   5. piano

C. What is the next number in this series? _____
     6   8   11   15   ?

D. Looking in the mirror in front of you it appears that the clock behind _____
you indicates the time is 4:35. What time is it?

E. Seven years ago Sam was three times as old as Jim, but now he is only _____
twice as old. How old is Jim now?

Battery (GATB) developed and used by the United States Employment Service. This test is available to employers. The Job Service will administer the test to potential applicants and provide information showing the extensive validity studies that have been performed for predicting various types of jobs.

PERSONALITY TESTS AND INTEREST INVENTORIES

Personality tests are used extensively in psychological research for diagnosing mental disorders. Interest inventories primarily help individuals make career decisions. Before the ruling in the *Griggs* case in 1971, these tests also were used extensively to measure individual motivation and to predict how genuine an individual's desire was to have a particular job.

The personality tests most frequently used by organizations were the Minnesota Multiphasic Personality Inventory (MMPI) and the California Psychological Inventory (CPI). These tests are lengthy and numerous scoring keys have been developed to predict dozens of different kinds of mental disorders or personality profiles.

Two of the most widely used interest inventories are the Strong Vocational Interest Blank (SVIB) and the Kuder Vocational Preference Record. The Strong Vocational Interest Blank compares an individual's likes and dislikes with the responses made by thousands of other individuals and indicates how consistent the individual's interests are with those of people in various professions. Although interest inventories are useful for diagnostic and counseling purposes, most organizations have found that the validity coefficients of these instruments are generally low and close to zero.[36]

HONESTY TESTS

Special tests have been constructed to measure the orientation of individuals toward the issues of honesty and personal integrity. Honesty tests are the most frequently used psychological tests in industry. These tests contain questions regarding such situations as whether a person who has taken company merchandise should be trusted in another job that involves handling company money or whether taking damaged goods without permission from a company is acceptable if the merchandise would be disposed of otherwise. An individual's responses to the test statements indicate the individual's attitudes toward theft, embezzlement, and dishonest practices. Several studies have indicated that these attitudes are good predictors of a previous history of theft and of future dishonest acts.[37]

Extensive research has shown that some of these instruments not only produce reliable information that validly predicts dishonest behavior but that they also are free from biases of age, race, and sex.[38] These honesty tests represent a valuable selection tool for choosing employees who will occupy positions that involve handling company money.

DRUG TESTING

The statistics on drug use document how serious the problem is and why companies need to be involved in curtailing the use of illegal drugs. The financial costs to employers of drug-related illnesses, absences, health care premiums, lost productivity, and accidents were estimated in 1986 to exceed $100 billion. In an effort to reduce drug use in the workplace, many employers, including about one-third of the Fortune 500 companies, are using drug testing to screen job applicants and, in some cases, current employees.[39]

Drug-testing programs have been controversial because some people claim that testing violates their personal rights, that it is an invasion of personal privacy, that the tests are unreliable, and that drug use off the job does not impair job performance. On the other hand, employers may be liable for the improper acts of employees who use drugs if they knew or should have known that an employee's condition, propensity, or history created a serious risk and they failed to take precautions. Therefore, the decisions of an employer can be challenged for either acting or failing to act against drug users. These competing forces require employers to use caution in designing legal and defensible drug-testing programs.

As a general rule, all employers, both public and private, can legally require job applicants to pass a drug test as a condition of employment if the testing program is non-discriminatory. According to the courts, applicants do not have a vested right to a job that warrants protection. Therefore, employers are not obliged to hire applicants who use illegal drugs and applicants who refuse to take a drug test may be disqualified from employment. However, some drug-testing programs for current employees, especially public employees, have been restricted and these restrictions are discussed in Chapter 14.

Although the reliability of drug tests has been questioned, the real issue is how to use the results. The most common tests for screening urine samples for evidence of substance abuse rely on a methodology known as "immuno-assay technique." The leading manufacturers of immuno-assay tests claim they are 99 percent accurate, but warn that a positive result should be confirmed by another, more elaborate and costly test of the same sample. If the second test confirms the presence of an illegal substance, the applicant is usually rejected even though there is a slight possibility that the person tested positive to marijuana because of the passive inhalation of a friend's marijuana smoke. Current employees could be given a chance to explain their positive results and offered rehabilitation, but applicants who test positive are typically removed from the applicant pool.[40]

ETHICAL ISSUES OF SELECTION

Personnel testing has been criticized on moral and ethical grounds; however, most of this criticism also applies to other selection procedures.

FAKING

One criticism of personnel tests is that test-takers can intentionally give false responses and provide misleading information. In fact, one critic who claims that personnel testing is immoral has written a book that explains how to beat personality tests.[41] He recommends that test-takers answer test questions as if they were a successful, stable Horatio Alger, rather than answer truthfully.

Aptitude, ability, and achievement tests generally cannot be faked. But faking can affect the results of personality tests and interest inventories even though they typically contain built-in scales to assess the honesty of responses. Honesty tests use complex scoring formulas to detect faking and inconsistent answers by applicants who try to fake.

Faking represents just as serious a problem in interviewing and application information as it does in personnel testing. Because applicants want to look good, they may exaggerate their desirable qualities to the point of serious misrepresentation. Some employers are suspicious of all information unless it can be confirmed through a second source.

Job applicants should think twice before providing false or misleading information. Many organizations will automatically terminate anyone who provides false information on an application blank, even if the person has been an outstanding employee. Furthermore, if individuals lie to get jobs for which they are unqualified, they may be very uncomfortable when faced with continual failure on the job day after day.

PRESSURE TO CONFORM

Some critics of personnel testing say that it creates "square Americans," and, indeed, Americans do undergo enormous pressure to conform to social standards. In reality, however, the pressures to conform are created not by personnel tests or other selection devices, but by the "criteria of performance," especially supervisors' evaluations and other procedures used to determine rewards.[42]

INVASION OF PRIVACY

Another criticism of personnel testing is that it is a wanton invasion of an individual's private thoughts. Interviews and application blanks also threaten the privacy of the individual when they request information about an applicant's private life. In fact, almost every interpersonal interaction involves at least a casual evaluation of individual character and personality.

Throughout the employment process, both the applicant and the interviewer are engaged in a process of mutual assessment, and therefore, the possibility of an invasion of privacy is always present. However, there is a general rule governing this situation: it is a clear invasion of privacy for an applicant to be asked to reveal details of thought or emotion that are not relevant to performance on the job. Ethically, personnel tests and interviews should not be used to satisfy the curiosity of a personnel specialist; they should be used to make predictions of future performance.

PREDICTION ERROR

A final criticism of personnel testing is that it involves a statistical prediction in which applicants who may be outstanding performers may be rejected because of low test scores. Because tests are not perfectly reliable and valid, some job applicants are inappropriately rejected. The possibility of a prediction error seems to violate personal rights; citizens are innocent until proven guilty, but they can be rejected from employment because the odds are against hiring them.

Although prediction error is unfortunate, the consequences of not using any predictors should be considered. A random hiring process or any other arbitrary procedure would create even more serious consequences for the individuals, the organization, and society. Even though outstanding applicants are occasionally eliminated by a valid selection procedure, the number of errors is less than would occur if a random hiring process were used.

ASSESSMENT CENTERS

An **assessment center** is one of the most powerful methods for identifying management potential. It is typically used when a group of applicants is being considered for hiring or promotion into management positions. These applicants participate in a series of activities that usually occur over a period of two or three days. The participants are evaluated on each activity by a group of trained assessors who unobtrusively observe their performance. After the participants have been observed in many different activities, the evaluators discuss their observations and try to achieve a consensus decision regarding the evaluation of each participant.

Although the assessment-center technique was first used by the military during World War II, the pioneering work in its development was done by American Telephone and Telegraph.[43] Most assessment centers today are patterned after AT&T's assessment technique, which involves clinical interviews, projective tests, work samples, paper-and-pencil tests, and participation in group problems and leaderless group discussions.

ASSESSMENT ACTIVITIES

Over time, assessment centers have generally been excellent predictors of job performance because the activities included in them are usually designed to replicate the activities and responsibilities of the actual job. These activities are also structured to provide opportunities for the assessors to observe the participants in a broad range of behavior. A variety of activities may be included in an assessment center, although the center's specific content may vary from organization to organization.[44]

IN-BASKET EXERCISE

A typical in-basket exercise is a two-hour activity in which participants are expected to read and respond to a series of memos and other correspondence. The instructions generally indicate that the participants are to imagine that they are assuming the managerial position of someone who has quit or died, that they are at the office on a Saturday morning, and that they have two hours to review the correspondence before leaving town for a week. The results of this exercise are evaluated to determine how well the participants can understand a work environment and make careful managerial decisions in a short time.

GROUP DISCUSSION

The participants in an assessment center typically participate in one or more group discussions. To simulate a work-group situation, a group leader may be appointed. At other times, the group may be required to lead itself without the benefit of an appointed leader. In this type of situation, the observers watch carefully to see which participant will try to lead the group and how the members respond to leadership attempts. Some group situations may involve cooperative brainstorming, while others may involve competition in which the participants make proposals and try to convince the group to allocate scarce resources for their own ideas. To illustrate, the group may be asked to assume that it is a scholarship committee and that each member of the committee represents a student requesting financial aid. Since the committee cannot fund all grant requests, the group must decide how to allocate the money among the students represented by the group members.

INDIVIDUAL TESTS

The participants in an assessment center may be asked to complete various personnel tests. The test battery may be a combination of intelligence tests, personality tests, aptitude tests, and tests measuring attitudes about management and supervision. If the tests are lengthy, the participants frequently are asked to complete them before coming to the assessment center. Additional time also may be needed for scoring the tests so that the information is available to the assessors at the conclusion of the assessment-center activities.

INTERVIEWS

Assessment-center participants typically are involved in at least one interview with one or more assessors. The focus of the interview is largely on career development and planning. In some situations, a biographical form that has been completed ahead of time by the participant may be used as the basis of the interview. Interview topics usually include educational background, extracurricular activities, expectations for the future, and personal interests and hobbies.

BUSINESS GAMES

Assessment centers typically include some type of business games, video exercises, or computer simulations, such as those that involve solving manufacturing problems or performing experiential exercises. The game instructions usually simulate real-life situations and require the participants to engage in role playing and group decision making.

RELIABILITY AND VALIDITY OF ASSESSMENT CENTERS

After each activity, each participant is evaluated by each of the assessors. At the conclusion of the assessment center, the assessors combine their evaluations and try to reach a consensus regarding the competence of each participant and his or her potential for development. Multiple assessors and concensus decision making tend to produce higher reliabilities and validities for assessment-center data than for typical selection procedures.

Numerous studies have examined both the reliability and validity of the assessment-center technique.[45] Reliability is generally quite high because the assessors are trained to observe and respond to similar types of behaviors and because assessment-center rating forms often request assessors to evaluate participants on specific observable behaviors. Validity coefficients predicting future management behavior frequently reach .60, which is remarkably high. In fact, the validity coefficients are sometimes so high that one has to wonder if the assessment-center conclusions do not become self-fulfilling prophecies in which the subsequent performances of managers are heavily influenced by what was said about them in the assessment-center reports.

Many organizations have found that assessment centers represent not only a useful means for selecting managers but also a valuable training method. At the conclusion of an assessment center, the participants receive feedback on their strengths and weaknesses from the observers. For example, after completing the in-basket exercise, the participants are told which of their decisions were bad and which might have been effective solutions. An additional benefit of the assessment-center technique that has been discovered by many organizations is that the assessment center is especially useful for teaching the assessors about the important dimensions of supervisory behavior and how to observe them.

In designing an assessment center, or any selection process, human resource specialists should realize that some predictors are much better than others and should be weighted much more heavily. An analysis of hundreds of validity studies indicates that mental ability and aptitude tests have consistently been excellent predictors of many jobs using a variety of different criteria.[46] Biographical-information forms and job-sample tests have also produced fairly respectable validity coefficients, while interviews and academic achievement have generally produced rather disappointing correlations. One analysis comparing the average validities of eleven predictors of entry-level jobs is shown in Table 6.5. The criterion used in these studies was supervisor ratings.

According to the averages in Table 6.5, the mean validity of using an ability test alone is .53, and the mean validity of using an interview alone is .14. By using an ability test and an interview together it is possible to raise the validity from .53 to .55, but only if the interview measures something more than the ability test and if the interview is weighted

TABLE 6.5   Mean validities of various predictors for entry-level jobs where the criterion is supervisor ratings

Predictor	Validity	Correlations
Mental ability/aptitude	.53	425
Job sample/tryout	.44	20
Biographical inventory	.37	12
Reference check-background investigation	.26	10
Experience/work history	.18	425
Interview	.14	10
Training and experience ratings	.13	65
Academic achievement (GPA)	.11	11
Education, (number of years)	.10	425
Interest inventory	.10	3
Age	−.01	425

Source: John E. Hunter and Ronda F. Hunter, "Validity and Utility of Alternative Predictors of Job Performance," *Psychological Bulletin,* Vol. 96 (1984), pp. 72–98.

one-fourteenth as much as the ability test (the predictors should be weighted proportionate to the square of the validity coefficients, i.e., $.53^2:14^2$). Of course, the validity of a specific selection process may be quite different than these averages.

MAKING A SELECTION DECISION

After all information about the applications has been collected, three methods can be used for making the hiring decision: (1) clinical judgments, (2) weighted composites, and (3) multiple cutoffs. When a great deal of information has been collected, clinical judgments are inefficient. Most individuals only consider three or four factors when making a decision, and therefore clinical judgments entail much wasted effort when more information is collected than can be used.[47]

The use of a weighted composite avoids this loss of information. Organizations that use the weighted composite keep all applicants in the selection process until data have been obtained on each predictor. This information is then weighted and combined into a composite score, and those with the highest composite scores are hired.

The multiple-cutoff procedure has the advantage of reducing the size of the applicant pool at each step. Organizations that use the **multiple-cutoff** procedure systematically eliminate applicants who do not achieve satisfactory scores on each predictor.

Both weighted-composite and multiple-cutoff procedures are used by universities in determining admittance of undergraduate and graduate students. Some universities establish a minimum composite score as an admission requirement. The students' grade-point averages, test scores, class ranks, and recommendations are combined to form their composite scores, and those who have composite scores above the minimum are admitted to the universities. Other universities establish a minimum cutoff score on each predictor, and reject applicants who are below the cutoff on any specific factor.

The weighted-composite method allows applicants to compensate for a low score on one predictor with a high score on another. For example, some students with low grade-point averages are admitted to an MBA program because their scores on the Graduate Management Admissions Test are very high. A multiple cutoff would have eliminated students with low grades regardless of their test scores. Using a multiple-cutoff procedure is recommended anytime a particular ability is absolutely crucial to job performance. For example, good eyesight would be an essential attribute for a driving instructor.

EXPECTANCY CHARTS

Expectancy charts provide a method for interpreting test scores in terms of the probability of successful performance. Each bar on an expectancy chart shows what percentage of the employees in a given predictor category are successful. Valid predictors typically produce expectancy charts with long bars for high predictor scores and short bars for low predictor scores as illustrated in Figure 6.6. Although expectancy charts show the same information that is reported by a validity coefficient, expectancy charts are more useful in counseling employees since most employees do not understand correlation coefficients. The expectancy charts in Figures 6.6 and 6.7 are derived from Table 6.6.

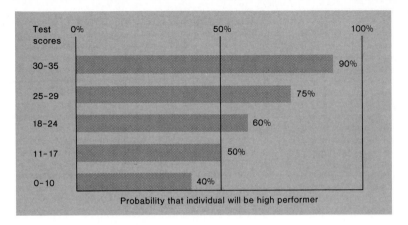

FIGURE 6.6 An individual expectancy chart.

Figure 6.6 is called an individual expectancy chart since it shows the probability of an individual employee being a high performer depending upon his or her test score.

Figure 6.7 is an institutional expectancy chart, which is similar to an individual expectancy chart except that it shows the proportion of employees who would be considered high performers given different cutoff scores for the test. Each bar on an institutional expectancy chart shows what proportion of the new employees would be high performers if the company only accepted applicants who scored at that cutoff point or higher.

USEFULNESS OF A PREDICTOR

The usefulness of a predictor is determined by how well it contributes to hiring successful employees. If an extremely high proportion of employees achieve success even when they

TABLE 6.6	Expectancy table			
Test Scores	No. of High Performers	No. of Low Performers	Percentage Who Were High Performers	Cumulative Percentage of High Performers
30–35	18	2	90	90
25–29	15	5	75	82.5
18–24	12	8	60	75
11–17	10	10	50	69
0–10	8	12	40	63

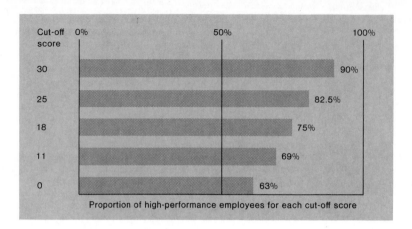

FIGURE 6.7 An institutional expectancy chart.

have been hired at random, an elaborate selection procedure would be worthless. However, if only a small proportion of randomly selected employees achieve success, then a careful selection procedure would be valuable, especially if the position is important. For example, an elaborate selection procedure for hiring a landscaping crew would be unnecessary since most applicants could probably handle a rake and a shovel. However, the selection of someone who could capably operate a backhoe or other heavy equipment should involve a careful selection procedure.

In any situation, the costs of using a predictor should be weighed against the benefits expected from it. The costs, which include the interviewer's time, printing application forms, and buying and scoring personnel tests, are usually easy to compute through standard cost accounting procedures. However, the benefits are usually difficult to estimate. The benefits obtained from using a new predictor are determined by three factors: the selection ratio, the validity coefficient, and the base rate of success.

Selection ratio: The **selection ratio** is defined by the formula:

$$\text{selection ratio} = \frac{\text{number of applicants hired}}{\text{total number of applicants}}.$$

The selection ratio indicates how many applicants are hired for the job. If everyone who applies is hired, the selection ratio is 1.00. However, if only one out of five applicants is hired, the selection ratio is .20. As noted in Chapter 5, the selection ratio is heavily influenced by the recruiting strategy. A poor recruiting strategy may result in a high selection ratio, since most of the applicants will need to be hired even though they have low probabilities of being outstanding performers.

Validity coefficient: The **validity coefficient** is the correlation coefficient between the predictor and the criteria. A correlation coefficient of 0 indicates that no relationship exists between the two variables. However, as the correlation coefficient approaches ± 1.00, the relationship between the two variables becomes stronger. A high correlation means that the predictor will be useful in identifying outstanding performers.

Base rate of success: The **base rate of success** refers to the percentage of employees that would be considered successful if they were hired at random without the use of the new predictor. A very high base rate of success indicates that a high percentage of the employees will be successful without the use of the new predictor.

A convenient way to remember the three factors that influence the usefulness of a predictor is illustrated in Figure 6.8. The selection ratio determines where the vertical line is drawn. As the selection ratio decreases, the vertical line is moved further to the right, and the organization can be more selective in its hiring decisions. The base rate of success determines where the horizontal line is placed. As a smaller percentage of job applicants is considered successful, the horizontal line is raised to a higher level. The validity coefficient is illustrated by the ellipse. As the shape of the ellipse becomes longer and narrower, approaching a straight line, the validity coefficient approaches 1.00.

A series of tables have been designed to show how the three factors can be combined to determine the improvement in the percentage of successful employees. Examples of these tables, which are called Taylor-Russell tables, are presented in Table 6.7.[48] The tables illustrate two different base rates of success, three different selection ratios, and four validity correlations. Table A, for example, shows that the base rate of successful

FIGURE 6.8 Assessing the usefulness of a predictor.

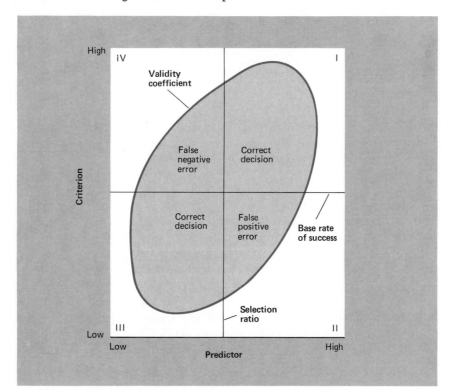

TABLE 6.7   The improvement in the percentage of successful employees given different selection ratios, validity coefficients, and base rates

A. Base Rate = 30%

Validity	Selection ratio		
r	.20	.50	.80
.00	.30	.30	.30
.20	.40	.36	.32
.40	.51	.41	.34
.60	.64	.47	.36

B. Base Rate = 70%

Validity	Selection ratio		
r	.20	.50	.80
.00	.70	.70	.70
.20	.79	.76	.73
.40	.88	.81	.75
.60	.95	.87	.79

Source: From H. C. Taylor and J. T. Russell, "The Relationship of Validity Coefficients to the Practical Effectiveness of Tests in Selection: Discussion and Tables," *Journal of Applied Psychology* 23 (1939): 565–78.

performance will rise from 30 to 64 percent with a selection ratio of .20 and a validity coefficient of .60. The Taylor-Russell tables assist a human resource specialist in identifying the probable improvement that should be expected from the use of a new predictor.

SELECTION ERRORS

The process of making a selection decision involves a probability situation in which the decision-maker attempts to make the best decision given the available information. In making selection decisions, two kinds of errors may occur: false positive errors and false negative errors, as illustrated in Figure 6.8. A **false positive** error is shown in Quadrant II. This error represents individuals whose predictor scores were sufficiently high to merit hiring but whose performances were unsatisfactory. They are called false positives because a positive hiring decision was made based on their predictor scores. The individuals in Quadrant IV represent a **false negative** error. These individuals would have been successful performers if they had been hired, but because of their low predictor scores, they were not hired. The individuals in Quadrant I and Quadrant III represent a correct decision—those who were hired are successful performers and those who were not hired would have been unsuccessful performers.

As can be seen in Figure 6.8, the number of errors is influenced by the validity coefficient, the base rate of success, and the selection ratio. The costs of making bad selection errors, especially false positive errors, need to be weighed against the costs of additional recruiting expenses (which would influence the validity coefficient). Therefore, reducing the costs of selection requires a careful analysis involving several different factors of time, money, and personnel procedures.

SELF-SELECTION

Although this chapter has emphasized the employer's selection procedure, it is important to remember that staffing decisions are a two-way decision-making process. The organization decides which applicants it wants to hire, and the applicants decide which organization they want to join. Job applicants ought to play an influential role in deciding whom to hire since they are the best source of information about themselves. Only they have observed themselves in a variety of situations. Only they can predict best how well they will do in the future. Most importantly, the applicants are in the best position to assess the important factors of interest in the job and motivation to succeed. This information must come from the applicants since they are the ones who determine their commitment, motivation, and dedication to the job and organization. The applicants know their own strengths and weaknesses better than the organization will know them.

To become genuinely involved in the selection process, applicants need to receive complete information about the jobs they may perform. The more they understand the nature of the job, the job requirements, the working conditions, and their peer-group associations, the more accurately they can assess whether the job is for them. After they know more about the job, the applicants may decide they do not want it. One organization plagued by high turnover decided to include a tour of its plant before the final selection decisions were made. The company found that when qualified applicants were given a plant tour and observed others performing the jobs for which they were being considered, 30 percent withdrew their names from further considerations.[49] Having accurate information and knowing what to expect before accepting a job tends to increase applicants' feelings of responsibility and commitment to stay on the job and perform dependably if they are hired. Moreover, if new employees have been forewarned about what to expect on the job, they are not as likely to view quitting as a means of coping with unpleasant parts of the job.

ORIENTATION AND PROBATION

Appropriate information about a job is especially important to new employees. The first few days of employment are critical. How employees are treated on their first day can color their attitudes and affect their success on a job. New-employee orientations are frequently handled ineptly. Most individuals are able to tell at least one good "war story" about how poorly they were treated their first day on a new job. The employees who usually receive the poorest orientation are young, part-time employees—those who are most in need of a good orientation program.

Carefully designed orientation training fulfills the following objectives:

1. Reduces employee turnover
2. Reduces anxiety and hazing
3. Creates positive work values
4. Reduces start-up costs
5. Saves time of supervisors and coworkers

Orientation programs should not contain a lot of detailed information, such as extensive facts and figures about the company history, sales volume, production figures, company benefits, and company policies. When employees are flooded with a massive amount of "very important for you to remember" information they tend to disregard most of it as being unimportant. In designing an orientation program, the following questions should be considered:

1. What information do new employees need to know about their immediate environment to make them comfortable?
2. What impression and impact does the organization want to make on new employees the first day?
3. What key policies and procedures must new employees understand the first day so that mistakes will not be made the second day?
4. What can be done to help new employees begin to know their fellow employees without feeling overwhelmed?
5. What special things, such as desks and work areas, are needed to make new employees feel physically comfortable, welcome, and secure?
6. What job-related tasks can new employees learn the first day to provide them with a sense of accomplishment?
7. What positive experiences can new employees be provided that will give them something to talk about to the "folks at home"?

Many organizations use a probationary period during the initial period of employment to help new employees and also to protect the organization. During this probationary period the new employees receive special counsel and encouragement to help them develop the skills and abilities to perform adequately. At the end of the probationary period, they receive performance feedback from supervisors or others who have observed them.[50]

Probationary periods also are designed to protect the organization from making a bad hiring decision, especially in a union organization. Probationary periods are typically specified for a period of time such as thirty, sixty, or ninety days. During this period an employee can be terminated with little or no justification. Most labor contracts do not require a new employee to join the union until after the probationary period. During the probationary period, a new employee is not protected by the labor agreement, and the employer has an opportunity to assess whether the new employee is likely to be a successful performer.

INTERNATIONAL HRM

The employee-selection procedures used in other countries are as varied as the procedures found in the United States. In general, however, most European and Asian employers place much more emphasis on educational testing and academic performance in deciding whom to hire. In Singapore, Hong Kong, and Japan, for example, individuals are subjected to extensive testing from preschool through adulthood. The results of these tests determine the kind of academic preparation students receive, which students will be allowed to go on to college, and what kind of company and job opportunities they will eventually have.

Although the Asian people are very test-oriented, they are accustomed to knowledge-based testing, not performance-based evaluations. Performance evaluations and results-oriented testing are largely incompatible with the group-oriented culture, especially in Japan. Consequently, assessment centers are seldom found in Japan.

One Japanese firm, Wacoal Corporation, conducted a pioneering effort to install an assessment center and found that the evaluation process had to be revised to make it acceptable to the Japanese culture.[51] Because Japanese managers tend to avoid performance-based evaluations, the evaluation instruments had to be far more structured than customary. The assessors used a structured, multiple-choice behavioral-evaluation form to describe the participants' actions. This method required the assessors to *describe* what they observed rather than *evaluate* the effectiveness of what they saw. The evaluations were mechanically derived later from the descriptions—specific points were awarded for specific behaviors that were accumulated for an overall point total for each skill. This information was then combined with self-assessment data to make career-planning and promotion decisions.

Assessment centers appear to be more popular in European firms than in Asian firms. The apprehension about individual evaluation is not a great problem among European workers. In the United Kingdom, for example, assessment centers are regarded as one of the most accurate and credible methods for assessing an individual's ability. British firms have access to a large variety of off-the-shelf assessment materials and standardized evaluation instruments. These materials are readily available, but they are not as useful as task-related exercises based on actual job tasks.[52] The disadvantage of task-related exercises is that they require more time and money to develop.

SUMMARY

A. Selection decisions should be based on reliable and valid information. A formal hiring procedure is especially desirable when only a small percentage of the applicants is likely to perform successfully. On the other hand, a very casual and informal selection decision is acceptable when virtually every candidate could successfully perform the job.

B. The best predictor of future behavior is knowing what an individual has done in his or her past.

C. These steps may be included in the selection process used by a company: (1) preliminary screening interviews, (2) application blanks, (3) interviews, (4) employment tests, (5) reference checks, (6) physical exams, (7) final interviews, (8) placement.

D. Reliability refers to the repeatability or consistency of measurement. The reliability of all measures should be assessed to make certain that they represent repeatable and consistent information.

E. Four operational definitions of reliability are test-retest reliability, alternate forms reliability, split-halves reliability, and conspect reliability.

F. Selection procedures should be valid. Validity refers to the relationship between the predictor information and performance on the job. Selection information that indicates which applicants will be the highest performers is said to be valid information.

G. Five methods for evaluating the validity of a selection procedure include predictive validity, concurrent validity, content validity, construct validity, and synthetic validity.

H. If a selection procedure produces an adverse impact on minorities, females, or other protected groups, the Equal Employment Opportunity Commission requires the employer to provide evidence showing that the selection procedure is valid at the .05 level of statistical significance.

I. Virtually every organization requires applicants to complete an application blank, biodata form, or biographical information blank. This information is typically reliable, but its validity depends on the kind of information obtained and how it is evaluated. Some weighted application blanks and biodata forms have proved to be very successful predictors of job performance.

J. Interviews are included in the selection process of almost every organization, and many recruiters claim that interviews provide the most helpful information for making a selection decision. Interviews also serve other purposes, such as selling the organization and counseling job applicants. However, research evidence indicates that employment interviews generally are not reliable and therefore are not valid predictors of job performance. Patterned interviews, though, are usually more reliable than unstructured interviews.

K. Personnel tests generally are reliable predictors of individual characteristics and represent a valuable selection tool if these characteristics are essential to performing a job. The thousands of tests that are available include achievement tests, aptitude tests, personality tests, interest inventories, and tests measuring personal integrity.

L. Assessment centers are sometimes used to select applicants for management positions. Those attending an assessment center typically participate in group and individual activities. Observers evaluate the behavior and performance of each participant.

M. Three methods can be used for making a selection decision after the information about the applicants has been collected: a clinical judgment, a weighted composite, or a multiple-cutoff procedure.

N. The value of a selection procedure is determined by how well it improves the selection of good employees. The three factors that influence the effectiveness of a selection procedure are the selection ratio, the validity coefficient, and the base rate of success.

O. After new employees have been hired, a carefully designed orientation program is needed to reduce turnover and anxiety and to help the employees adjust to their new environment. An effective orientation program should explain what new employees need to know immediately, create a favorable impression of the organization, and promote positive expectations on the part of new employees.

QUESTIONS

1. What factors in the environment influence the selection of personnel?

2. Is past behavior always a good predictor of future behavior? Why or why not?

3. What is reliability? How can the reliability of a measuring instrument be assessed?

4. What is validity? What methods can be used to assess the validity of a selection procedure?

5. If a selection procedure is not creating an adverse impact on employment decisions, is there any reason why an employer should validate the procedure anyway?

6. Why are employment interviews so unreliable? What can be done to increase the reliability of an interview?

7. What are the different types of interviews and when would each be useful?

8. How would you decide which tests to include in a test battery? How could you learn which tests are available, and how could you check to make sure you had selected good tests?

9. What are job-knowledge tests and job-sample tests? How are they constructed?

10. What are the differences between aptitude and achievement tests? When would you want to use each kind of test?

11. What kinds of selection information would be considered an invasion of privacy?

12. What is an assessment center, and why is it so useful in selecting managers? Could an assessment center also be useful for filling other positions? Which ones?

13. What are the advantages and disadvantages of using clinical judgment, a weighted composite, or a multiple-cutoff procedure for making a selection decision?

14. What is an expectancy chart and how is it used?

15. Describe the three factors that determine the usefulness of a selection procedure. Explain the interaction between these three factors.

16. Should organizations rely on the self-selection process and allow applicants to decide whether they are suitable for a job? What should an organization do to obtain applicant involvement in the selection procedure?

KEY TERMS

Adverse impact: A selection procedure is said to have an adverse impact if the percentages of any minority or sex group are less than four-fifths of the selection rate for the highest group.

Alternate-forms reliability: A method of testing the reliability of an instrument by using two alternate (or equivalent) forms of that instrument.

Assessment center: A selection procedure primarily used for selecting managers in which candidates participate in individual and group exercises and are evaluated by observers.

Base rate of success: The percentage of employees who would normally be considered successful without the use of a given selection procedure.

Biodata form: An application blank containing extensive biographical information that can be used as a selection instrument.

Biographical-information blank: A special application blank that is used to collect extensive information on an applicant's previous experiences and background.

Board interview: An interview format in which one applicant is interviewed by a group of interviewers at one time.

Clinical judgment: An informal method of subjectively combining information to arrive at a selection decision.

Concurrent validity: A method of testing the validity of a selection procedure, sometimes called the present-employee method, in which the predictor and criteria data are collected simultaneously from a group of present employees.

Conspect reliability: The degree of agreement between two evaluators.

Construct validity: A type of validity that assesses whether a measuring instrument actually measures the psychological construct or trait it purports to measure.

Content validity: A subjective assessment of whether the content measured by a selection procedure is similar to the critical requirements of performing the job. Sometimes referred to as face validity.

Criterion-related validity: A validity study, either predictive or concurrent, in which the predictor data are statistically correlated with the criteria of performance.

Expectancy charts: Bar charts showing the probability of being a successful performer for various categories of predictor scores.

False negatives: Individuals who are subject to a selection error. These individuals were not hired because of low predictor scores but would have been outstanding performers.

False positives: Individuals for whom a selection error occurred. These individuals obtained sufficiently high predictor scores to be hired, but they are poor performers.

Four-fifths rule: The guideline used by the EEOC to determine whether a selection procedure has an adverse impact on selection. A selection procedure is biased if the selection rate for any ethnic group is less than four-fifths of the selection rate for any other ethnic group.

Graphology: Handwriting analysis.

Group interview: A method of conducting interviews in which one person interviews a group of applicants at one time.

Multiple cutoff: A sequential selection procedure that eliminates individuals who do not achieve satisfactory scores on each step in the procedure.

Negligent hiring: A legal theory that makes employers liable for the abusive acts of employees if the employer knew or should have known about the employees' propensity for such conduct.

Nondirective interview: An unstructured interview in which the interviewer allows the interviewee to discuss whatever he or she wishes to discuss.

Patterned interview: A structured interview in which the interviewer asks a series of predetermined questions.

Predictive validity: A method of testing the validity of a selection procedure, also called the follow-up method, in which the predictor information on a group of applicants is statistically correlated with performance data that are collected after the applicants have been hired and trained.

Reliability: Repeatability or consistency of measurement.

Selection ratio: The percentage of individuals hired relative to the total number of applicants.

Semistructured interview: An interview in which the interviewer determines the major questions beforehand, but allows sufficient flexibility to probe into other areas as needed to evaluate an applicant's personality.

Split-halves reliability: A method of assessing the reliability of an instrument by splitting the instrument into two parts and determining if the applicants obtain similar scores on both halves.

Stress interview: A method of interviewing in which the interviewee is subjected to intentionally created stress to observe how well he or she performs in that situation.

Synthetic validity: A method of testing the validity of a selection procedure by combining jobs that require similar abilities and by separately validating the specific predictors intended to measure those abilities.

Test-retest reliability: A method of assessing the reliability of a measuring instrument by testing and retesting the same population with the instrument and then correlating each individual's first and second scores.

Validity coefficient: The correlation coefficient showing the relationship between a predictor and a criterion.

Validity generalization: Using the validity evidence based on a few jobs to infer that the same tests would be valid for other related jobs.

Weighted application blank: An application blank containing valid information that can be weighted, used to form a composite score, and then used for making a selection decision.

Weighted composite: A method of making a selection decision by statistically combining the predictor data about each applicant and selecting applicants with the highest composite scores.

C O N C L U D I N G   C A S E

Test Scores versus Letters of Recommendation

Marlin Porter, the hiring officer for Davis Electronics Company, quickly realized the dilemma he faced as he reviewed the application file of Jody Williams. Jody had applied for a position in the filament department, and several openings in that department still remained. However, Marlin was unsure whether Jody would be able to learn the job and do it well.

Jody's application indicated that she was a recent high school graduate who had never held a full-time job. Her best recommendation was a letter from Phil Robbins, the general superintendent for Davis Electronics. Phil described Jody as an excellent worker, a dedicated person, and "the kind of person our company ought to employ." Jody had been a babysitter for the Robbins family and lived on the same street.

Although Jody's application and letters of recommendation were very positive, Marlin doubted that she would succeed in the filament department because of her low test scores. To work in that department, all candidates were expected to achieve satisfac-

tory scores on tests of eye-hand coordination and finger dexterity. Jody's scores on both tests were well below the normal cutoff levels and indicated that her chances of surviving the thirty-day probationary training were less than 20 in 100.

Jody probably would be a very pleasant and cooperative employee and hiring her would please Phil Robbins. But could she do the job?

Questions:

1. Should Marlin disregard the test scores and hire Jody?
2. Should Phil Robbins's recommendation be disregarded or discredited because he is an officer in the company or because he is a neighbor to Jody?
3. Would it be kinder to Jody to hire her or not hire her?

NOTES

1. *Welsh Manufacturing, Division of Textron Inc.* v. *Pinkerton's, Inc.*, 474 A.2d 436 (R.I. 1984).

2. Larry Reibstein, "Firms Face Lawsuits for Hiring People Who Then Commit Crimes," *Wall Street Journal* (April 30, 1987): 29.

3. Bureau of National Affairs, *Personnel Policies Forum*, Survey No. 114 (September 1976).

4. James J. Asher, "Reliability of a Novel Format for the Selection Interview," *Psychological Reports* 26 (1970): 451–56; Michael M. Burgess, Virginia Calkins, and James M. Richards, "The Structured Interview: A Selection Device," *Psychological Reports* 31 (1972): 867–77; Herbert Heneman et al., "Interviewer Validity as a Function of Interview Structure, Biographical Data, and Interviewee Order," *Journal of Applied Psychology* 60 (1975): 748–53; Eugene Mayfield, "The Selection Interview—A Reevaluation of Published Research," *Personnel Psychology* (Autumn 1964): 239–60; Donald P. Schwab and Herbert Heneman III, "Relationship Between Interview Structure and Interviewer Reliability in an Employment Situation," *Journal of Applied Psychology* 53 (1969): 214–17; Lynn Ulrich and Don Trumbo, "The Selection Interview Since 1949," *Psychological Bulletin* 63 (February 1965): 110–16; Michael J. Cam-

pion, Elliot D. Pursell, and Barbara K. Brown, "Structured Interviewing: Raising the Psychometric Properties of the Employment Interview," *Personnel Psychology* 41 (Spring 1988): 25–42.

5. David Nye, "Speak No Evil About Former Employees," *Across the Board* 25 (November 1988): 24–36; Andrew J. Templer and James W. Thacker, "Credible Letters of Reference: How You Read Them Is Important," *Journal of Managerial Psychology* 3, no. 1 (1988): 22–26.

6. Erwin S. Stanton, "Fast-and-Easy Reference Checking by Telephone," *Personnel Journal* 57 (November 1988): 123–30.

7. Jane Easter Banis, "Your Worker's Crime May Make You Pay," *Nation's Business* 76 (December 1988): 38–39.

8. A. J. Erdmann et al., "Health Questionnaire Use in Industrial Medical Department," *Industrial Medicine and Surgery* 22 (1953); E. P. Luongo, "The Preplacement Physical Examination in Industry—Its Values," *Archives of Environmental Health* 5 (1962): 358–64; *Time*, January 10, 1977.

9. Robert Guion, *Personnel Testing* (New York: McGraw-Hill, 1965), Chapter 2.

10. *Ibid.*

11. *Ibid*.

12. *Ibid*.

13. Anne S. Tsui and Patricia Ohlott, "Multiple Assessment of Managerial Effectiveness: Interrater Agreement and Consensus in Effectiveness Models," *Personnel Psychology* 41 (Winter 1988): 779–803.

14. Frank L. Schmidt, John E. Hunter, Alice N. Outerbridge, and Stephen Goff, "Joint Relation of Experience and Ability with Job Performance: Test of Three Hypotheses," *Journal of Applied Psychology* 73 (February 1988): 46–57.

15. "Uniform Guidelines on Employee Selection Procedures," *Federal Register* 43, 166 (August 25, 1978, Part IV): 290–313.

16. Guion, *Personnel Testing*, 169–74.

17. John E. Hunter and Ronda F. Hunter, "Validity and Utility of Alternative Predictors of Job Performance," *Psychological Bulletin* 96, no.1 (1984): 72–98.

18. Chris Lee, "Testing Makes a Comeback," *Training* 25 (December 1988): 49–59.

19. Frank L. Schmidt and John E. Hunter, "Employment Testing: Old Theories and New Research Findings," *American Psychologist* 36 (1981): 1128–37; Frank L. Schmidt and John E. Hunter, "The Future of Criterion-Related Validity," *Personnel Psychology* 33 (1980): 41–60; Laurence S. Kleiman and Robert H. Faley, "The Implications of Professional and Legal Guidelines for Court Decisions Involving Criterion-Related Validity: A Review and Analysis," *Personnel Psychology* 38 (Winter 1985): 803–33.

20. Robert M. Madigan, K. Dow Scott, Diana L. Deadrick, and Jil A. Stoddard, "Employment Testing: The U.S. Job Service Is Spearheading a Revolution," *Personnel Administrator* 31 (September 1986): 102–112.

21. W. F. Cascio, "Accuracy of Verifiable Biographical Information Blank Responses," *Journal of Applied Psychology* 60 (1975): 767–70.

22. James J. Asher, "The Biographical Item: Can It Be Improved?" *Personnel Psychology* 25 (1972): 251–69; William Owens, "Background Data," in *Handbook of Industrial and Organizational Psychology*, ed. Marvin Dunnette (Chicago: Rand McNally, 1976); C. Harold Stone and Floyd L. Ruch, "Selection, Interviewing, and Testing," in *Staffing, Policies, and Strategies*, vol. 1, eds. Dale Yoder and Herbert G. Heneman, Jr. (Washington D.C.: Bureau of National Affairs, Inc.), pp. 129–33. For evidence suggesting that application blanks have been overvalued, see Donald P. Schwab and R. L. Oliver, "Predicting Tenure with Biographical Data: Exhuming Varied Evidence," *Personnel Psychology* 27 (1974): 125–28.

23. The Examiner's Manuals for two instruments created by Richardson, Henry, and Bellows report an average validity coefficient of .40 for the Supervisory Profile Record (SPR) based on data from 39 organizations and a validity coefficient also of .40 for the Management Profile Record (MPR) based on data from 11 organizations. Russell J. Drakeley, Peter Herriot, and Alan Jones, "Biographical Data, Training Success, and Turnover," *Journal of Occupational Psychology* 61 (June 1988): 145–52; Myron Gable, Charles J. Hollon, and Frank Dangello, "Predicting Voluntary Managerial Trainee Turnover in a Large Retailing Organization from Information on an Employment Application Blank," *Journal of Retailing* 60 (Winter 1984): 43–63.

24. David L. Kurtz, Patrick C. Fleenor, Louis E. Boone, and Virginia M. Rider, "CEO: A Handwriting Analysis," *Business Horizons* 32 (January/February 1989): 41–43; Susan M. Taylor and Kathryn K. Sackheim, "Graphology," *Personnel Administrator* 33 (May 1988): 71–76.

25. Gershon Ben-Shakhar, Maya Bar-Hillel, Yoram Bilu, Edor Ben-Abba, and Anat Flug, "Can Graphology Predict Occupational Success? Two Empircal Studies and Some Methodological Ruminations," *Journal of Applied Psychology* 71 (November 1986): 645–53; David J. Cherrington, "Predicting the Performance of Middle Managers From Handwriting Analysis," Working Paper Series (Provo, Utah, Graduate School of Management, Brigham Young University, 1976); C L. Hull and R. P. Montgomery, "Experimental Investigation of Certain Alleged Relations Between Character and Handwriting," *Psychological Review* 26 (1919): 63–74; L. W. Ference, "Dental Student's Selection Through Handwriting Analysis (Ph.D. Diss., University of Southern California, 1970); Cited in *Dissertation Abstracts International*, vol. 31 (7-B. 1971), 4378-79; S. M. Zdep and H. B. Weaver, "The Graphoanalytical Approach to Selecting Life Insurance Salesmen," *Journal of Applied Psychology* 51 (1967): 295–99; Brian Lynch, "Graphology: Towards a Hand-picked Workforce," *Personnel Management* (March 1985): 14–18.

26. George W. England, *Development and Use of Weighted Application Blanks, rev. ed.* (Minneapolis: University of Minnesota, Industrial Relations Center, 1971).

27. Michel Syrett, "Recruitment: Survival of the Fittest," *Director* 41 (April 1988): 117–19; Jeff A. Weekley and Joseph A. Gier, "Reliability and Validity of the Situational Interview for a Sales Position," *Journal of Applied Psychology* 72 (August 1987): 484–87.

28. Carol J. Reitz, "Be Steps Ahead of Other Candidates," *Legal Assistant Today* 5 (March/April 1988): 24–26, 84–86.

29. Herman M. Smith, "When a Board Hires . . . Making Committee Hiring Work," *Business Quarterly* 92 (Summer 1987): 28–31.

30. Michael A. Campion, Elliott D. Purcell, and Barbara K. Brown, "Structured Interviewing: Raising the Psychometric Properties of the Employment Interview," *Personnel Psychology* 41 (Spring 1988): 25–42; Willi H. Wiesner and Steven F. Cronshaw, "A Meta-Analytic Investigation of the Impact of Interview Format and Degree of Structure on the Validity of the Employment Interview," *Journal of Occupational Psychology* 61 (December 1988): 275–90.

31. Richard D. Arvey, Howard E. Miller, Richard Gould, and Phillip Burch, "Interview Validity for Selecting Sales Clerks," *Personnel Psychology* 40 (Spring 1987): 1-12; R.E. Carlson, P. W. Thayer, E. C. Mayfield, and D. A. Paterson, "Improvements in the Selection Interview," *Personnel Journal* 50 (1971): 268–75; Frank Landy, "The Validity of the Interview in Police Officer Selection," *Journal of Applied Psychology* 61, no. 2 (1976): 193–98; Eugene Mayfield, "The Selection Interview—A Re-Evaluation of Published Research," *Personnel Psychology* (Autumn 1964): 239–60; E. C. Webster, *Decision Making in the Employment Interview* (Montreal: Eagle Press, 1964); O. R. Wright, "Summary of Research on the Employment Interview Since 1964," *Personnel Psychology* 22 (1969): 391–413.

32. *Ibid.*; S. W. Constantin, "An Investigation of Information Favorability in the Employment Interview," *Journal of Applied Psychology* 61, no. 6 (1976): 743–49; Marvin Okanes and Harvey Tschirgi, "Impact of the Face-to-Face Interview on Prior Judgments of a Candidate," *Proceedings*, Mid-West Academy of Management, April 1977; N. Schmitt, "Social and Situational Determinants of Interview Decisions: Implications for the Employment Interview," *Personnel Psychology* 29 (1976): 79–101; Robert Wareing and Janet Stockdale, "Decision Making in the Promotion Interview: An Empircal Study," *Personnel Review* 16, no. 4 (1987): 26–32.

33. *Willie S. Griggs et al.* v. *Duke Power Company*, 401 U.S. 424 (1971).

34. "Most Employers Test New Job Candidates, ASPA Survey Shows." *Resource* (June 1988): 2.

35. Oscar K. Buros, ed., *Tests in Print, vol. 2* (Highland Park, N.J.: Gryphon Press, 1974); Oscar K. Buros, ed., *The Eighth Mental Measurements Yearbook, vols. 1 and 2* (Highland Park, N.J.: Gryphon Press, 1978).

36. Ramon A. Avila and Edward F. Fern, "The Selling Situation as a Moderator of the Personality-Sales Performance Relationship: An Empirical Investigation," *Journal of Personal Selling and Sales Management* 6 (November 1986): 53–63; G. Gough, "Personality and Personality Assessment," in *Handbook of Industrial and Organizational Psychology*, ed. Marvin Dunnette (Chicago: Rand McNally, 1976); Robert M. Guion and R. F. Gottier, "Validity of Personality Measures in Personnel Selection," *Personnel Psychology* 18 (1965): 135–64; A. K. Korman, "The Prediction

of Managerial Performance: A Review," *Personnel Psychology* 21 (1968): 295–322.

37. Karen M. Evans and Randall Brown, "Reducing Recruitment Risk Through Pre-Employment Testing," *Personnel* 65 (September 1988): 55–64; Linda A. Goldinger, *Honesty and Integrity Testing: A Practical Guide*, (Impress, 1989).

38. Philip Ash, "Screening Employment Applicants for Attitudes Towards Theft," *Journal of Applied Psychology* 55 (1971): 161–64; Philip Ash, "Predicting Dishonesty with the Reid Report," *Journal of the American Polygraph Association* 5 (June 1975): 139–53; Philip Ash, "Convicted Felon's Attitudes Towards Theft," *Criminal Justice and Behavior* 1, no. 1 (March 1974): 1–8; William Terris, "Attitudinal Correlates of Employee Integrity: Theft Related Admissions Made in Preemployment Polygraph Examinations," presented at the American Psychological Association Annual Meetings, Montreal, Canada, 1978.

39. Joseph D. Levesque, *People in Organizations*, (Sacramento, Calif.: American Chamber of Commerce Publishers, 1989): II.1.13-24; Lawrence Z. Lorber and J. Robert Kirk, "Fear Itself, a Legal and Personnel Analysis of Drug Testing, AIDS, Secondary Smoke, VTDs" (ASPA Foundation, 1987); Carlton E. Turner, "Drug Testing: A Step-By-Step Approach," *Business and Health* 6 (July 1988): 10–14.

40. "Drug Testing in the Workplace: What are the Legal Problems?" *Journal of American Insurance* 64, no. 2 (1988): 5–6; William H. Wagel, "A Drug Screening Policy That Safeguards Employees' Rights," *Personnel* 66 (February 1988): 10–11.

41. Martin L. Gross, *The Brain Watchers* (New York: Random House, 1962); Marten Lasden, "The Trouble with Testing," *Training* 22, no. 5 (1985): 79–86.

42. Robert M. Guion, *Personnel Testing* (New York: McGraw-Hill, 1965), pp. 371–77.

43. Douglas W. Bray and Donald L. Grant, "The Assessment Center in the Measurement of Potential for Business Management," *Psychological Monographs* 80, whole no. 625 (1966); Douglas W. Bray, Richard J. Campbell, and Donald L. Grant, *Formative Years in Business* (New York: John Wiley, 1974).

44. For a description of assessment centers see J. L. Moses and W. C. Byham, eds., *Applying the Assessment Center Method* (Elmwood, N.Y.: Pergamon, 1977); R. B. Finkle, "Managerial Assessment Centers," in *Handbook of Industrial and Organizational Psychology*, ed. Marvin D. Dunnette (Chicago: Rand McNally, 1976); Jeffery S. Schippmann, Garry L. Hughes, and Erich P. Prien, "Raise Assessment Standards," *Personnel Journal* 67 (July 1988): 68–79; Ron Zemke, "Using Assessment Centers to Measure Management Potential," *Training/HRD* 17 (March 1980): 23–31.

45. Rob Feltham, "Assessment Centre Decision Making: Judgemental vs. Mechanical," *Journal of Occupational Psychology* 61 (September 1988): 237–41; Rob Feltham, "Validity of a Police Assessment Centre: A 1–19 Year Follow-Up," *Journal of Occupational Psychology* 61 (June 1988): 121–44; Barbara B. Gaugler, Douglas B. Rosenthal, George C. Thornton III, and Cynthia Bentson, "Meta-Analysis of Assessment Center Validity," *Journal of Applied Psychology* 72 (August 1987): 493–511; S. D. Norton, "The Empirical and Content Validity of Assessment Centers vs. Traditional Methods for Predicting Managerial Success," *Academy of Management Review* 2 (1977): 442–53.

46. John E. Hunter and Ronda F. Hunter, "Validity and Utility of Alternative Predictors of Job Performance," *Psychological Bulletin* 96, no.1 (1984): 72–98.

47. Wayne F. Cascio, Ralph A. Alexander, and Gerald V. Barrett, "Setting Cutoff Scores: Legal, Psychometric and Professional Issues and Guidelines," *Personnel Psychology* 41 (Spring 1988): 1–24.

48. H. E. Taylor and J. T. Russell, "The Relationship of Validity Coefficients to the Practical Effectiveness of Tests in Selection: Discussion and Tables," *Journal of Applied Psychology* 23 (1939): 565–78.

49. Edward L. Sherman, "Turnover Cut One-Third by Seven-Step Program," *Personnel Journal* 37 (January 1975): 296–97.

50. Milan Moravec and Kevin Wheeler, "Speed New Hires into Success," *Personnel Journal* 68 (March 1989): 74–75; Darrel W. Ray, "Important Impressions: You Only Get One Chance to Influence a New Employee," *Management World* 17 (March/April 1988): 34–35.

51. Craig Taylor and Fredric Frank, "Assessment Centers in Japan," *Training and Development Journal* 42 (February 1988): 54–57.

52. Peter Goodge, "Task-Based Assessment," *Journal of European Industrial Training*" 12, no.6 (1988): 22–27.

Performance Evaluation

Learning Objectives

After studying this chapter, you should be able to:

1. Identify the major criticisms of performance evaluation.
2. Explain the objectives of performance evaluations and when formal evaluations are better than informal evaluations.
3. Identify the important dimensions of performance that ought to be evaluated.
4. Describe several performance-evaluation methods and explain the advantages and disadvantages of each.
5. Explain the difference between a contributions appraisal and a personal-development appraisal.
6. Describe the characteristics of a good performance-evaluation interview.
7. Discuss how performance information ought to be used in an organization.
8. Describe management by objectives and explain how it is both a philosophy of management and a performance-evaluation program.

Chapter Outline

Role of Performance Evaluation
Objectives of Performance Evaluations / The Ethics of Evaluation / Personal Accountability / Criticisms of Performance Evaluations / Training for Evaluators / Formal and Informal Evaluations

Performance Criteria
Criteria of Performance / Outcomes versus Behaviors / Dimensions of Performance / Sources of Data

Evaluation Procedures
Classification Procedures / Ranking Procedures / Graphic Rating Scales / Critical Incidents / Weighted Checklists / Behaviorally Anchored Rating Scales (BARS) / Forced-choice Procedures

I N T R O D U C T O R Y   C A S E

The Strict Evaluator

Mark Poulsen is upset about his recent performance review. Of a possible fifty-four points, he only received a total of thirty-eight. This score is the sum of the ratings his supervisor gave him on six dimensions. Each dimension uses a nine-point scale, with one point equaling a low evaluation and nine points equaling a high evaluation. An average rating for each dimension is five, making thirty an average score on all six dimensions. Mark's score of thirty-eight is above average, but lower than Mark thinks it should be.

Mark has worked for the HiLand Food Company for twelve years. For the first nine years, Mark's job performance was consistently rated outstanding. However, for the past three years, Mark's performance has been rated only a little above average. According to Mark, his performance-review scores have been low during the past three years because his supervisor gives unreasonably low ratings. Eric Weber was assigned as Mark's supervisor three years ago.

On attendance, Eric gave Mark a rating of seven. Other supervisors always have rated Mark a nine on attendance, and Mark believes he still deserves a nine. Both Eric and Mark agree that Mark was never absent last year and that he was tardy for work only once. Mark argues that his attendance record is outstanding and that he deserves a rating of nine. Eric believes that seven is a good rating.

Mark has similar objections concerning his ratings on the other dimensions. Eric rated Mark a six on quantity, quality, initiative, and job knowledge and gave him an overall performance rating of seven. Mark thinks that he should have received at least an eight on each of these five dimensions.

Eric says that he tries to evaluate his subordinates objectively, and he refuses to change Mark's ratings. Mark claims that any other supervisor would have evaluated him at least ten points higher. He feels very disappointed about his low evaluation because he knows it will mean a minimal pay increase and that it will hurt his chances for promotion.

Questions:

1. To what extent is Eric being unfair? Is it possible that Mark has inflated expectations? Why do most people expect higher evaluations than they receive?

2. What is wrong with this performance evaluation process and what can be done to improve it?

3. If Mark and Eric were members of different ethnic or religious groups, how could the problems with the performance appraisal process be separated from allegations of discrimination?

ROLE OF PERFORMANCE EVALUATION

This chapter examines the process of evaluating employee performance. Many names are used to describe this process, such as merit rating, performance review, performance appraisal, and employee appraisal. The label used in this text is performance evaluation.

Discussions about performance evaluation involve both practical considerations regarding how it should be done as well as philosophical considerations regarding why it should be done. These considerations are related, since a dysfunctional evaluation process discourages managers from wanting to evaluate performance while the need for accurate performance data demands that an acceptable process be developed.

OBJECTIVES OF PERFORMANCE EVALUATIONS

Performance-evaluation programs serve at least five important organizational functions. The first role of performance evaluation is to *guide human resource actions*, such as hiring, firing, and promoting. Just as performance information is needed to validate selection procedures, some form of performance data is required for making rational decisions on promotions and terminations. Without this information, personnel actions have to be made randomly or by subjective impressions. An organization that makes careful, defensible decisions based on good performance data will be protecting itself as well as its employees. Since it is illegal to make personnel decisions on the basis of race, religion, sex, national origin, or age, an organization must have performance data to defend its decisions to hire, fire, promote, and grant pay increases. Therefore, performance data are needed not only to make personnel decisions but also to defend them.[1]

The second role of performance evaluation is to *reward* employees. The principle of appropriate reinforcement (described in Chapter 11) suggests that reinforcement (money, status, promotions, recognition) should be based on performance. Without performance data, everyone has to be rewarded equally or rewards have to be distributed randomly or subjectively—conditions that the recipients perceive as inequitable. Performance appraisals also may provide intrinsic rewards, since outstanding performers receive positive recognition of their efforts.

The third role of performance evaluation is to provide individuals with information for their own *personal development*. Individuals need feedback on performance to help them improve. Accurate and timely performance feedback facilitates the learning of new behavior. Furthermore, most individuals want to know how well they are doing and where they need to improve.

The fourth role of performance evaluation is to *identify training needs* for the organization. A well-designed performance-evaluation system informs the organization which individuals or departments could benefit from training. It also aids in establishing the abilities and skills needed for each job and in setting minimum performance levels.

The fifth role of performance evaluation is to *integrate human resource planning* and coordinate other personnel functions. Performance appraisals provide the basis for an integrated human resource system. As noted in Chapter 4, performance evaluations form the foundation of a human resource planning system that assembles and integrates information regarding new positions to be created, the skills of present employees, their potential for development, and the developmental experiences they need.

THE ETHICS OF EVALUATION

Numerous ethical issues are associated with performance evaluations because of how the information is used. Performance information may lead to unethical treatment of employees even though the evaluations are accurate. Although managers are encouraged to use performance data when they make human resource decisions, and the use of objective performance data provides the best legal defense, it does not automatically follow that these decisions will always be morally correct. Moral behavior is not defined by organizational effectiveness, nor by what will contribute to the greatest efficiency. For example, when a layer of management is eliminated because of a merger or acquisition, the managers with the lowest performance ratings are usually terminated.[2] Although this appears to be the most fair policy, it is still possible that several dedicated, loyal, long-term employees could be displaced through no fault of their own by employees with slightly higher ratings. Because their evaluations were slightly lower than others' does not automatically mean that terminating them is morally justified.

The use of performance information is also ethically questionable when negative feedback serves to destroy the self-esteem and self-confidence of marginal performers. Just because they are not doing as well as others does not mean they are not trying or that they deserve to be criticized. And even though they need feedback to improve, the feedback can be personally destructive.

Human resource decisions must be made, and using objective performance evaluations usually contributes to more rational and defensible decision making. But all managers need to go a step further and consider the impact of their decisions; they should not assume that a decision is morally justified just because it was based on performance data. The following sections will discuss the ambiguities associated with the concept of performance and the criticisms that surround the measurement process. But even when these ambiguities and criticisms are resolved, the potential for using the information unethically still remains.

PERSONAL ACCOUNTABILITY

Performance evaluation is a basic part of the employment exchange described in Chapter 3. The employer agrees to compensate employees for their work and the employees agree to work in exchange for the compensation. Both sides must fulfill their parts of the agreement for the employment exchange to continue. Just as the employees can be expected to evaluate the adequacy of their pay, so too should the employer be expected to evaluate the adequacy of performance. If the employees think their pay is satisfactory, they probably will stay with the company; if it is unsatisfactory, they probably will leave or organize a union to demand higher wages. If the employees' performance is considered adequate, the employer usually tries to keep them; if their performance is inadequate, they may be terminated. Most employees agree that poor performers ought to be terminated and that outstanding performers deserve to be promoted and receive pay increases.

According to the employment exchange, employees are accountable for their performance. The concept of personal accountability refers to the responsibility and obligation that each employee accepts. When employees accept job assignments, they should feel a sense of responsibility for doing them well and expect to have their performance evaluated at some point.

Surveys of different companies indicate that performance evaluation is done in virtually every type of organization. Most surveys indicate that over 90 percent of both large and small companies have formal performance-evaluation programs and about half of these companies have separate programs to evaluate different employee groups, such as production, office and clerical, professional and technical, and supervisors. Nonunion companies are slightly more likely to have a formal evaluation program than union companies.[3] Nevertheless, even in highly unionized industries, performance evaluations generally are part of the employment exchange and are used to decide which employees will be promoted or fired.

CRITICISMS OF PERFORMANCE EVALUATIONS

The performance-evaluation process has been severely criticized, and the criticisms have prompted some managers to abandon performance evaluation as a useless and perhaps harmful practice. Some of the major criticisms of performance evaluations include the following:

1. *Individual threat.* Many people, especially poor performers and people who dislike work, simply dislike being evaluated. Such individuals are basically opposed to having anyone conduct any sort of evaluation of their performance. The evaluation process threatens their self-esteem, and they feel worse about themselves after the evaluation interview.[4] The irony of evaluation is that poor performers who are most in need of performance feedback to help them improve are the most threatened and therefore the most resistant to accepting the feedback.

2. *Threat to supervisors.* Some supervisors do not like to evaluate their subordinates and feel threatened by having to explain their evaluations. These supervisors argue that evaluating their subordinates places them in a position of role conflict by forcing them to be judge, coach, and friend at the same time. Many supervisors do not have the interpersonal skills needed to handle evaluation interviews.[5]

3. *Defining performance.* In many instances *performance* is difficult to define, especially for jobs that do not produce a physical product. Managers provide leadership, engineers create new ideas, and trainers present information. But these products cannot be meaningfully quantified, and, consequently, there is disagreement concerning what should actually be evaluated.[6]

4. *Halo effect.* Sometimes one positive or negative characteristic about a person strongly influences all other attitudes about that person. This is known as the **halo effect**.[7]

5. *Leniency-strictness effect.* Some evaluators tend to give mostly favorable ratings to each employee, while others tend to evaluate the same performance levels much more unfavorably, thus creating a **leniency-strictness effect**.

6. *Central-tendency effect.* Some evaluators create the **central-tendency effect** by giving all average ratings to avoid "sticking their necks out" by identifying marginal or outstanding performance.

7. *Interrater reliability.* Two evaluators observing the same behavior may disagree and give different ratings. As a result of low **interrater reliability**, employees receiving low performance evaluations could argue that their low ratings did not result from poor performance, since another supervisor might have evaluated them higher.

8. *Sequencing effect.* The evaluation of one individual's performance may be influenced by the relative performance of the preceding individual, creating what is called the **sequencing effect**. Thus, an individual might receive a favorable evaluation when following a poor performer and an unfavorable evaluation when following an outstanding performer.

9. *Zero-sum problem.* In some performance appraisal systems the number of above-average ratings has to be balanced by an equal number of below-average ratings. Such systems create a **zero-sum problem**, since some individuals are forced to receive low ratings in spite of how well they have actually performed.

10. *Numbers fetish.* An excessive focus is sometimes placed on numbers. An evaluator who has a **numbers fetish** will show an undue regard for the accuracy of numbers and small differences between them, even those that measure relatively unquantifiable dimensions of the job.

11. *Recency effect.* Recent events tend to have an unusually strong influence on performance evaluations. Because of the **recency effect**, an individual's good work for a whole year may be ignored as a result of one negative incident occurring just prior to the performance review.

12. *Biased subjective evaluations.* Some evaluations are largely subjective and rest almost entirely on the impressions of supervisors. Studies on perceptual bias show that evaluations may be influenced by many factors. In one study, for example, evaluators who were told that certain workers had been hospitalized for severe depression rated these disabled workers more favorably than nondisabled workers.[9] Supervisor evaluations tend to be clearly biased by the degree of perceived and actual similarity between the supervisor and the subordinate; subordinates who are perceived as similar receive better evaluations.[10] Supervisors also tend to be biased by gender, showing a pro-male bias, although supervisors who have worked for female managers tend to show less gender bias.[11] Bias has even been attributed to participation in the hiring process; employees are rated more favorably by supervisors who played a role in hiring them.[12] Because subjective evaluations are so prone to discrimination against protected groups, the courts have not been willing to accept evaluation procedures that allow "unfettered subjective judgment." In some instances, organizations have been required to establish objective, formal guidelines for evaluation, promotion, and transfer.[13]

All of these criticisms represent legitimate problems that need to be addressed. But most importantly, the criticisms need to be treated as problems that can be resolved, rather than as insurmountable obstacles.

TRAINING FOR EVALUATORS

Since most of the problems with performance evaluation are indicative of poor supervisory skills, most of them can be overcome by proper training of evaluators. One of the major reasons that supervisors dislike evaluating performance is that it makes them feel insecure and uncertain. They are unsure of their evaluations and are uncomfortable discussing the evaluations with their subordinates.

The ability to evaluate performance is a critical administrative skill. To be a good supervisor or manager, a person must be a competent evaluator. The following are necessary for making good performance evaluations:

1. The evaluator must know the job responsibilities of each subordinate.
2. The evaluator must have accurate information about each subordinate's performance.
3. The evaluator must have a standard by which to judge the adequacy of each subordinate's performance.
4. The evaluator must be able to communicate the evaluations to the subordinates and explain the basis on which they were made.

Many supervisors feel uncomfortable as evaluators because they do not have a standard to help them judge whether performance is good or bad. They do not know whether their ratings are "too hard," "too easy," or "too concentrated in the middle." In these situations, supervisors tend to give higher and higher ratings until the evaluations become so inflated that they have little meaning. Another reason why supervisors may give inflated ratings is to avoid giving negative feedback. Giving high evaluations eliminates most hassles. Unfortunately, the lives of many performance-evaluation programs have been cut short because inflated ratings have destroyed their usefulness.[14]

Evidence has shown that the problem of inflated ratings can be reduced through supervisory training, although some efforts have not been very successful.[15] About 60 percent of companies provide specific performance-evaluation training for appraisers to reduce the problem of bias.[16] When the U.S. Forest Service installed a new performance-evaluation program, it provided training and feedback for both employees and supervisors.[17] As part of the training, supervisors observed and evaluated the behavior of typical

■ **HRM in Action**

Employee Attitudes about Evaluation

The Minnesota Department of Transportation conducted a survey of its performance-appraisal process among 1,800 employees. The Department expected most employees to accept the process as a necessary managerial function, but it did not expect them to like it. To its surprise, 40 to 60 percent of the employees expressed satisfaction with the process. Yet, even though the majority of employees responded favorably, they were not in favor of formal evaluations more frequently than once a year. Instead, they expressed a preference for frequent informal evaluations in the form of day-to-day comments by supervisors regarding their expectations and disappointments.

One important conclusion that emerged from the survey was the value of self-appraisal. The study clearly found that the majority of employees wanted the opportunity to evaluate themselves. About 60 percent of the employees stated that self-appraisal was one of the central purposes of a performance evaluation, and a similar number indicated that they had, in fact, been given the opportunity for self-appraisal in their last formal session.

The value of self-appraisal was evident in some of the comments made by employees:

"I definitely would like the chance to rate myself. Also, I want more input to the direction of where my position is heading."

"It was too automatic a process. No input on my part. The supervisor does not understand many aspects of my job and does not seem to want to learn."

In summary, this survey illustrates a growing acceptance among employees of a formal performance-evaluation process. It also clearly illustrates the desire for more informal feedback from supervisors and a greater desire to participate in the evaluation process.

Source: Jim Laumeyer and Tim Beebe, "Employees and Their Appraisal," *Personnel Administrator* 33 (December 1988): 76–80.

employees and then compared their ratings with each other and with the "correct" answers. Being able to compare and to discuss their ratings helped the supervisors develop a common standard of performance.

Developing the interpersonal and communications skills needed to give performance feedback takes time and experience. Two of the best methods for helping supervisors gain these skills are role playing and behavior modeling. As explained in Chapter 9, these methods teach supervisors what to do in an interview and demonstrate specific behaviors they can imitate.[18]

To minimize the problem of inflated evaluations, some organizations have used forced distributions, forced-choice rating scales, and ranking procedures. Other organizations simply design a new form every few years. The problem, however, is not the form; the problem is incompetent evaluators. Therefore, the solution is that supervisors must be trained to make competent evaluations. No evaluation form will compensate for incompetent evaluators. Only experience and training can create competent evaluators and minimize the problems associated with performance evaluations.

FORMAL AND INFORMAL EVALUATIONS

Performance evaluations occur whether or not a formal evaluation program exists. The demands to hire, fire, promote, and compensate all necessitate some form of evaluation. Supervisors have always evaluated their subordinates and formed impressions about each employee's worth to the company. These informal evaluations have been just as important in influencing personnel decisions as evaluations made in a more formal manner. The advantage of an informal evaluation system is that it does not take as much time to design and administer as a formal program. Small organizations usually prefer an informal system and seem to function reasonably well with it.

The advantage of a formal evaluation program is that it is more unbiased, defensible, and open to inspection than an informal program. Employees are able to examine their evaluations and review their performances. Supervisors can compare their ratings of subordinates with those of other supervisors to check for consistency. Moreover, since the criteria used to evaluate performance are specified in advance, the tendency to give biased evaluations is reduced. Numerous court decisions (*Albemarle Paper Co.* v. *Moody; Wade* v. *Mississippi Cooperative Extension Service; Brito* v. *Zia Co.*) have required performance-evaluation programs to be administered in a way that does not discriminate against minority employees. Other court decisions (*Rowe* v. *General Motors Corp.; Baxter* v. *Savannah Sugar Refining Corporation*) have required some companies to establish formal evaluation programs to avoid discrimination in promotions. The courts have not required small organizations with fewer than thirty to fifty employees to have formal evaluation procedures. But even in small companies the informal performance evaluations must be based on informed judgments that do not create an adverse impact.[19]

PERFORMANCE CRITERIA

Deciding what to evaluate is one of the most difficult aspects of developing a performance-evaluation system. Until someone has actually tried to design a performance-evaluation system, it is hard to appreciate the difficulty involved.

CRITERIA OF PERFORMANCE

Deciding what to evaluate is, in part, a value judgment. The personal values of the individuals who design the evaluation system will be reflected in it. Most people agree that quantity and quality of performance are important dimensions to evaluate, but there is less agreement about traits such as appearance, initiative, and enthusiasm. Performance standards may be unique to each supervisor, and it is not uncommon for different supervisors to use different criteria for assessing each job.[20]

Whatever is measured in the evaluation influences the employees' behavior. When employees know they will be evaluated on certain dimensions, they usually behave in the way expected to obtain high performance ratings. For example, the commanding officer of a group of military clerk-typists designed a performance-evaluation form that measured several traits, including "orderliness." The officers who conducted the evaluations defined orderliness in terms of how clear and uncluttered the clerk-typists kept their desks. The clerk-typists responded by removing everything from the tops of their desks and keeping it in their desk drawers. Although this procedure was inefficient and the volume of work dramatically declined, the clerk-typists obtained high performance evaluations.[21]

The example of the clerk-typists illustrates why it is so important to measure only the most important dimensions of performance. Three criteria should be considered during the construction of performance evaluations:

1. **Relevance**. Performance evaluations should measure whatever is related to the objectives of the job. Ideally, everything that is related to the "ultimate success" of the employee should be measured, and nothing that is important should be left out. Therefore, the relevant performance dimensions are determined by the duties and responsibilities contained in the job description.
2. **Reliability**. The performance-evaluation procedure should produce consistent and repeatable evaluations. If the same behavior is evaluated differently by the same rater at different times, or even by different raters at the same time, then an evaluation is not reliable.
3. **Freedom from contamination**. Evaluations should measure each employee's performance without being contaminated by factors that an employee cannot control, such as economic conditions, material shortages, or poor equipment. The purpose of an evaluation is to assess an employee's performance, not extraneous factors.

OUTCOMES VERSUS BEHAVIORS

In deciding what to evaluate, an important issue is whether to focus on outcomes (results) or behaviors (activities). For example, the performance evaluation of a seamstress could focus on the number of items correctly sewn per hour or it could focus on the behaviors required to produce the product, such as cutting, sewing, and hemming. Department managers could be evaluated on the basis of the productivity of their departments (outcomes) or according to their administrative abilities (behaviors).

When asked which is most important, most people say outcomes are more important than behaviors; they are interested in measuring results. Most performance evaluations, however, especially evaluations of managers and supervisors, generally focus on behaviors rather than results. The behaviors evaluated include decision making, planning, organizing, delegating, communicating, motivating, and problem solving.[23] Behaviors are measured rather than outcomes because managers' outcomes are hard to identify and making comparisons between managers' outcomes is difficult. Another reason is that managers' outcomes are contaminated by outside factors, such as economic conditions, which they cannot be expected to control. Managers' behaviors, on the other hand, are less contaminated and therefore can be more easily evaluated and compared.

There are some important advantages to evaluating outcomes, however. The major advantage is that when outcomes are evaluated, the focus of attention shifts toward producing specific results. The primary objective of all employees ought to be to produce results, not behaviors. Unfortunately, some employees perform many of the right behaviors and still fail to produce results. This situation can be illustrated by examining the behaviors of a student who is writing a research paper. The right behaviors include finding references, reading articles, making notes, and studying the materials. A student can perform all of these activities very well and still not achieve the desired result—getting the paper written.

A potential problem with evaluating outcomes exclusively is that the outcomes can sometimes be achieved by unethical or undesirable means. By exerting excessive pressure on subordinates, for example, supervisors usually can increase performance. But over an extended period of time, excessive pressure can lead to turnover, dissatisfaction, and dishonesty. When managing people, the way it is done (behaviors) is just as important as the results (outcomes).

In summary, there are both advantages and disadvantages to focusing exclusively on either outcomes or behaviors. Both outcomes and behaviors are appropriate for performance evaluation, depending on the intended use. If the evaluations are to be used for compensation systems and other personnel actions, their focus should be on outcomes, but if they are to be used primarily for personal development, they should focus largely on behaviors. Perhaps a single performance evaluation cannot satisfy both of these functions simultaneously, and these functions should be evaluated with different forms at different times.

DIMENSIONS OF PERFORMANCE

Perhaps the most serious error that can be committed while deciding what to evaluate is to assume that performance is unidimensional—that is, that all individuals are high producers, low producers, or something in between. One scale can never adequately describe the variation in the performance of all employees. There are numerous dimensions of performance, many of which are unrelated. Thus, an individual may rank very high on one dimension and lower on several others. In fact, some dimensions, such as quantity and quality, may be inversely related.[24]

The relationships among different performance measures were examined in a study concerning 975 nonsupervisory employees of a delivery firm having twenty-seven offices. The employees were evaluated on five measures of performance: productivity, accidents, unexcused absences, errors, and overall performance. The first four measures were objective quantities taken from company records, but overall performance was a subjective judgment of the office managers. The results indicated that none of the measures were highly correlated; all five measures essentially evaluated different dimensions of performance. This study shows the complexity of performance and illustrates why a single, unidimensional scale is grossly inadequate.[25]

For an organization to function effectively, people must be induced to enter and remain with the organization, they must perform their role assignments in a dependable fashion, and they must contribute spontaneous and innovative behaviors that go beyond their formal task assignments.[26] Each of these three basic types of behavior ought to be included in a performance appraisal.

ATTRACTING AND HOLDING PEOPLE IN THE ORGANIZATION

The first requirement of any organization is to attract a sufficient number of personnel into the organization and to hold them there for some minimum length of time. This means that for an organization to function effectively, it must minimize turnover, absenteeism, and tardiness. In evaluating performance, therefore, absenteeism, tardiness, and length of service should be considered.

DEPENDABLE TASK ACCOMPLISHMENT

It is not enough for organizational members simply to report to work. For an organization to be effective, it must obtain dependable task accomplishment from its members. In other words, minimal levels of quantity and quality of performance must be achieved.

For some tasks, evaluating the quantity and quality of performance is a simple process of counting the number of items produced and the number of errors or defects. For other tasks, however, especially those performed by managers, measuring quantity and quality requires subjective ratings. These dimensions can be adequately evaluated if the organization has developed subjective rating scales that are reliable.

SPONTANEOUS AND INNOVATIVE BEHAVIORS

In addition to the formal task requirements, numerous other employee behaviors profoundly influence the effectiveness of an organization. These activities, called **spontaneous and innovative behaviors**, cannot be built into the formal task requirements. Since an organization cannot foresee all contingencies within its operations, its effectiveness is influenced by the willingness of its employees to perform spontaneous and innovative behaviors. Some of the most important of these behaviors include: (1) cooperation, the extent to which an individual will come to the aid of coworkers and assist them in achieving the organization's goals; (2) protective acts, the extent to which employees will go out of their way to remove hazards or eliminate threats to the organization; (3) constructive ideas, the extent to which employees will contribute constructive and creative ideas to improve the organization; (4) self-training, the extent to which employees will engage in self-training programs to help the organization fill its ever-present need for better-trained personnel; and (5) favorable attitudes, the extent to which employees strive to develop favorable attitudes about the organization among themselves, the customers, and the public, thus facilitating recruitment, retention, and sales.

SOURCES OF DATA

Several sources of data are available to reliably measure various aspects of performance. These sources can be classified into three major categories: production data, personnel data, and judgments of others.

PRODUCTION DATA

Production data evaluate the degree of dependable task accomplishment by measuring quantity and quality of performance. Examples of production data are number of units produced per hour, percentage of errors, dollar volume of sales, profit, return on investment, number of people supervised, number of students taught, and number of new insurance policies sold. Production data are usually considered the best measures of performance because they are directly observable; they can be counted, so everyone agrees on their measurement. Production data also appear to measure exactly what performance evaluations are supposed to measure. As a consequence, production data are often overvalued and used to the exclusion of other useful performance information.

The prevalence of technology allows employers to monitor the performance of employees and collect extensive production data. Some companies monitor customers' telephone calls to determine the quality of customer service provided by employees, and then use this information to implement incentive programs to motivate employees. Monitoring through video display terminals (VDTs) enables employers to know how many tasks were completed by each employee, the amount of time spent on each task, the time spent between tasks, and the time each employee spent away from the terminal. Some groups, including some labor unions and labor associations, are opposed to electronic monitoring. They claim that monitoring violates employees' rights of privacy and creates stressful working conditions that can lead to health problems. Human resource managers and executives defend the practice of monitoring because it helps to ensure that employees are doing an adequate job and the information provides valuable performance data. Groups opposed to monitoring have asked Congress to pass regulations to protect employees, such as requiring an audible beep whenever a call is being monitored.[27]

Jobs that produce services rather than physical products need to be evaluated on the basis of indirect rather than direct measures of performance. Personnel trainers, for example, are expected to train employees and therefore should ideally be evaluated according to the quantity and quality of their training. Since training cannot be measured directly, however, indirect measures are used as potential indices of performance. For example, a trainer could be evaluated by: (1) number of training programs conducted during the year; (2) total number of participants in the training programs; (3) improvement in the participants' scores on standard achievement tests or other tests covering the content of the training; (4) ratings by the participants of how well they enjoyed the training; (5) increases in the profitability of departments that were trained compared with those not trained; and (6) amount of grievances, absenteeism, and tardiness in the departments that were trained compared with those not trained. Because these measures are influenced by many factors besides the quantity and quality of the training, they need to be examined carefully and compared against historical information. Historical information can provide a useful perspective for analyzing current productivity data.

PERSONNEL DATA

Personnel data refer to the information found in an individual's personnel file. Examples of personnel data are absenteeism, tardiness, years of service, time in training to develop competence, training programs completed, and critical incidents. A well-designed human resource department should have an established system for collecting and analyzing these data. Except for critical incidents, these data are directly observable and can be reliably measured.

JUDGMENTS OF OTHERS

While production and personnel data are sometimes difficult to obtain, the judgments of others are always available. Furthermore, since many of the spontaneous and innovative behaviors so important to organizational effectiveness can only be assessed by the judgments of others, such judgments *ought* to be obtained for every evaluation. The best procedure for obtaining the judgments of others depends on the purpose of the performance appraisal.

EVALUATION PROCEDURES

Some of the most popular methods for evaluating performance include: (1) classification procedures; (2) ranking procedures; (3) graphic rating scales; (4) critical incidents; (5) weighted checklists; (6) behaviorally anchored rating scales (BARS) and behavioral observation scales (BOS); and (7) forced-choice procedures.

CLASSIFICATION PROCEDURES

Classification procedures are the easiest and quickest evaluation procedures to use, but they also are the most unreliable and biased, unless they are carefully developed and closely monitored. Classification procedures simply categorize individuals into one of several categories, such as high, low, outstanding, superior, excellent, good, average, fair, or poor.

Some argue that it is not possible to effectively use more than three categories when classifying employees: about 10 percent of an average group are poor performers, another 10 percent are outstanding, and the remaining 80 percent are average. Some even suggest that performance evaluation and feedback reviews may not be necessary for the middle group.[28]

Classification procedures usually evaluate an individual's overall performance and require the evaluator to combine the various aspects of individual performance into an overall composite. However, individuals also can be classified on specific dimensions, such as quantity of work, quality of work, and cooperativeness, as shown in Figure 7.1.

FIGURE 7.1 A classification procedure evaluating four dimensions.

Name: ______________________ Date: ____________

Supervisor: ______________________ Department: ____________

	Outstanding	Excellent	Good	Fair	Poor
1. Quantity of work	____	____	____	____	____
2. Quality of work	____	____	____	____	____
3. Cooperativeness	____	____	____	____	____
4. Overall performance	____	____	____	____	____

Comments:

The major problem with classification procedures is the difficulty of defining each category. Each evaluator may have a different definition of fair, good, and excellent, and as a result, supervisors tend to give inflated ratings. The military provides a good example of this tendency: because one way to destroy a new officer's chances for advancement is to rate him or her less than outstanding on any one characteristic, most officers are rated outstanding. A Merit Systems Protection Board study of rating inflation among federal government employees found that fewer than 1 percent were rated "unacceptable" or "minimally acceptable," while 46 percent were rated "fully acceptable," 36 percent were rated "exceeds fully acceptable," and 17 percent were rated "outstanding."[29]

To avoid inflated ratings, some organizations have placed quotas on the number of favorable ratings that an evaluator can assign. Another precaution is a policy that requires the ratings to be kept secret in hopes that less pressure on the evaluators will produce more accurate evaluations. Both of these modifications tend to produce negative consequences in the form of distrust, a lack of cooperation, and destructive competitiveness.

The best solution is to establish general guidelines showing how a "typical" distribution should look. For example, a useful guideline is to specify that only 5 percent of a typical group of employees should be rated outstanding, 20 percent superior, and so forth. Studies also have shown that the quality of the ratings generally improves when the evaluators are trained in rating, when they interact with other evaluators, and when they know they will have to defend their ratings.[30]

Placing quotas on the number of individuals who can be put in each category is called **forced distribution**. In some instances, the distribution is constructed to force equal numbers of employees into each category. However, the "normal distribution" (from statistics) is a better method than an equal forced distribution because it allows a larger percentage of the sample to be placed in the middle categories. A popular method of forcing superiors to classify employees along a normal distribution is the *card-stacking method*. Here, each employee's name is written on a separate card. The evaluator places 30 percent of the cards into the top end and 30 percent of the cards into the low end. Then one-third of each of the high and low groups are selected to be the very best and the very poorest. Thus, the distribution is divided into five categories with the following percentages: 10 percent, 20 percent, 40 percent, 20 percent, and 10 percent.

RANKING PROCEDURES

The objective of ranking procedures is to order a group of employees from highest to lowest along some dimension, usually overall performance. There are three different methods for rank ordering a group of employees: straight ranking, alternate ranking, and paired comparisons.

Straight ranking consists of asking an evaluator to consider all the individuals in a group, to identify the best employee, and to rank that employee number one. The second best employee is then ranked number two, the third best employee is ranked number three, and so on through the entire group. This procedure is a natural one for most evaluators, since most people are accustomed to ranking objects and people on an informal basis in daily life.

In **alternate ranking** the evaluator is given the list of individuals to be ranked and is asked to identify the very best employee and the very poorest employee among those listed. These two names are then removed from the list and placed at opposite ends of another list. The evaluator then identifies the best employee and the poorest employee among those remaining on the first list, and these names are removed from that list and placed on the other. Since the people in the middle of the list are usually the most difficult to rank, this method allows the evaluator to consider a shortened list of names when ranking the most difficult part of the group.

Paired comparisons consists of asking an evaluator to consider only two individuals at one time and to decide which of the two is better. Then another pair of names is presented to the evaluator for another evaluation. This process continues until each individual in the group has been paired with every other member of the group. An employee's position in the final ranking is determined by the number of times that employee is chosen over the other employees. A simple method of paired comparison is to have each pair of names written on separate cards and then to present the evaluator with one card at a time. The evaluator simply circles the best employee. Another method that entails less time and paperwork involves listing the name of each employee down the left side of a chart and also across the top to form a matrix, as shown in Figure 7.2. The evaluator considers each pair of names in half of the matrix and indicates the best performer.

Obviously, the paired-comparison procedure may involve a large number of comparisons as the size of the group expands. The formula for computing the number of paired comparisons in a group is $N(N - 1)/2$, with N being the number of employees in the group. A group of twenty employees would require $(20)(19)/2$, or 190 comparisons.

The advantage of using the paired-comparison procedure for ranking a group of employees is that it is very simple and uncomplicated. Also, a crude idea of the reliability of the ranking can be obtained by looking at the number of intransitive relationships. An example of an intransitive relationship is when A is rated better than B, and B is rated better than C, but C is rated better than A. Intransitive relationships generally mean either that the three individuals are essentially equal in performance or that the evaluator was careless.

FIGURE 7.2 Paired-comparison matrix for performance appraisal.

		Ann A.	Bob B.	Char C.	Duong D.
Ann A.	A		A B	A C	A D
Bob B.	B			B C	B D
Char C.	C				C D
Duong D.	D				

Ranking procedures are not subject to the problems of central tendency, leniency-strictness, and halo effect, but, they do have certain disadvantages. A group of employees is usually ranked only once on a scale of overall performance that does not adequately describe the complexity of each employee's performance, and some employees have to be ranked low regardless of how good they are. Ranking procedures do not reward cooperation and group cohesiveness; in fact, they often lead to dysfunctional personal discussions about the relative merits of each group member.

GRAPHIC RATING SCALES

Graphic rating scales are the most frequently used procedure for evaluating performance.[31] Graphic rating scales appear in numerous forms and are used to evaluate both performance-related characteristics and personality characteristics. Two steps are involved in these scales: selecting the characteristics and scaling the characteristics.

SELECTING THE CHARACTERISTICS

For hourly paid workers, typical characteristics include quantity of work, quality of work, cooperativeness, job knowledge, dependability, initiative, creativity, and overall performance. For management personnel, typical characteristics include leadership, communication, decision making, planning, delegation, consideration, initiative, creativity, mental ability, and job knowledge. To both of these lists some of the characteristics of appearance, intelligence, dominance, aggressiveness, achievement-orientation, attitude, attendance, punctuality, and neatness are occasionally added.[32] An illustration of a graphic rating scale is presented in Figure 7.3

Employers are generally free to select any characteristics they desire, although they are prohibited by law from selecting characteristics related to labor-union participation, race, color, religion, sex, or national origin. The selection of characteristics should be made primarily on the basis of which characteristics are related intuitively or empirically to organizational effectiveness. Basic personality characteristics that are difficult to change, such as intelligence, dominance, and aggressiveness, should usually be omitted. Personality characteristics (other than mental ability) are usually not related to organizational effectiveness.[33] The critical-incidents technique, described later, is one of the best methods for selecting the most appropriate characteristics.

A performance-evaluation procedure called *rated ranking* combines a ranking procedure and a rating process. The employees are first ranked, usually by an alternative-ranking procedure, and then each employee is rated on selected scales. The initial ranking imposes limits on the subsequent ratings, since individuals who receive low rankings should also receive lower ratings than those ranked higher. The rated-ranking procedure appears to reduce problems of subjective bias, halo effect, leniency-strictness, central tendency, and unreliability.[34]

SCALING THE CHARACTERISTICS

Rating scales can use either a continuous or discrete scale for each item. A continuous scale means that the evaluator can choose any point between the two extremes for rating an individual. A discrete scale requires an evaluator to use one of a specified number of categories. Examples of several types of scales are shown in Figure 7.4. Discrete scales usually have at least three points and sometimes more than thirty points. The optimal

1. Amount of work	5	4	3	2	1
2. Quality of work	5	4	3	2	1
3. Dependability	5	4	3	2	1
4. Judgment	5	4	3	2	1
5. Comprehension	5	4	3	2	1
6. Attitude	5	4	3	2	1
7. Cooperation	5	4	3	2	1
8. Capacity and ambition for future growth	5	4	3	2	1
9. Overall job accomplishment	5	4	3	2	1

5	4	3	2	1
Outstanding	Superior	At expected level	Below expected level	Marginal
Top 5%	10%	70%	10%	Bottom 5%

FIGURE 7.3 A graphic rating scale.

number of categories is about seven, although experienced evaluators sometimes prefer as many as ten.

The comments used to describe the points along a scale can be quite useful. The best descriptions are behaviorally anchored descriptions that tell the evaluator what behavior describes each point. The Civil Service Reform Act of 1978 emphasizes the importance of using behavioral descriptions to accurately assess the performance of employees. Behaviorally anchored rating scales are described later.

The advantages of using graphic scales are that they are easy to understand, fairly simple to develop, and convenient to use. They can be conveniently scored and are amenable to numerous statistical computations. They also permit a ready comparison of scores that presumably reveal the merit or value of every employee.

The problems arising from the use of rating scales usually are a result of selecting inappropriate characteristics, incorrectly scaling them, or incorrectly combining the scores into a total. As mentioned earlier, an illusion of precision exists when definite numbers are assigned to a supervisor's opinions. There is also the possibility that a high score on one characteristic can compensate for a low score on another. It would be a serious mistake, for example, to allow an employee to compensate for poor ratings on quantity and quality of work with good ratings on appearance and attitude. If the ratings on various characteristics are combined into a total score, the relative importance of each characteristic must be examined and possibly weighted.

CRITICAL INCIDENTS

One of the best techniques for identifying the most important dimensions of a job is the **critical-incidents** method.[35] The critical requirements of a job are those behaviors that make the difference between doing the job competently or incompetently. As the term implies, critical incidents are simply descriptions by qualified observers of behaviors that are especially effective or ineffective. Such incidents are actual behavioral accounts recorded as stories or anecdotes. They are obtained from supervisors, subordinates, peers, or anyone close to the jobs being studied. Sometimes supervisors are asked to take time at the end of each week to describe briefly the behaviors of their subordinates, particularly noting any favorable or unfavorable incidents.

The following descriptions by a partner in a public accounting firm of ways in which two members of the firm had performed very effectively are illustrations of critical incidents.

> While auditing a health care entity, the auditor picked up an error in the accounting system that saved the organization a considerable sum. The organization had not been allocating food service costs to patient costs. The auditor suggested an alternative procedure that resulted in partial reimbursement through federal and state medicare. The savings for the organization were significant.

> This auditor was reviewing the agency payable account for a company with a computerized accounting system. The system was inefficient and did not have adequate controls to handle three significant problems. After these problems were pointed out to the corporate controller, a revised accounting system was instituted that resulted in significant savings.

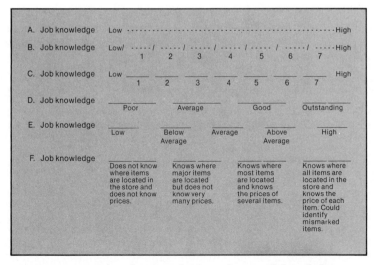

FIGURE 7.4 Examples of rating scales for evaluating job knowledge.

These two statements suggest that one of the critical behaviors of effective public accountants is to make creative suggestions that help clients redesign their accounting procedures and save money. Characteristics that might be associated with this behavior include technical competence, insightful application of accounting practices, and problem solving.

The use of critical incidents in performance evaluation involves two steps. The first step is to identify which categories of behavior are related to effective performance. This is accomplished by obtaining numerous descriptions of effective and ineffective behaviors, usually from supervisors. The contents of these incidents are analyzed, and the incidents are abstracted or reduced to a smaller number of behavioral categories. In a study of U.S. Air Force officer-executives, for example, nearly 3,000 incidents were collected and abstracted into six major categories.[36]

The second step involves giving each evaluator a list of the general categories to use in evaluating performance, along with sample behaviors that describe each category. The evaluator is then expected to record any positive or negative incidents that occur pertaining to the general categories. This procedure is sometimes referred to as the **free-form essay**. The critical incidents are simply described and placed in an individual's personnel file. This information can be very helpful in coaching and developing subordinates. It also can aid in developing year-end appraisals that accurately reflect an individual's performance for the entire year.

WEIGHTED CHECKLISTS

The critical incident method can provide information that is useful in the development of other performance appraisal procedures. A weighted checklist can be developed by obtaining a number of statements about employee performance from the critical incident descriptions. After a comprehensive list of these statements has been obtained, a group of judges—either supervisors or job incumbents—evaluate each statement on a zero to ten scale regarding its favorability and contribution to organizational effectiveness. When the judges do not agree on the favorability of a statement, it is eliminated. The items on which the judges agree are then weighted on the basis of the average scores assigned by the judges.

Returning to the example of the public accountants, a panel of judges assigned these weights to statements taken from the critical incidents:

(9.4) Continually looks for superior accounting procedures to save money for clients.

(7.9) Is inquisitive and thoroughly examines problems.

(7.4) Learns new areas of public accounting eagerly and rapidly.

(4.1) Accepts all assignments from his or her superior without question.

In using the weighted-checklist procedure, an evaluator is given the list of statements without the assigned weights and is asked to indicate which statements best describe an employee's behavior. The score for the employee is the average of the favorability ratings of the statements used to describe him or her. Thus, if statements with low favorability ratings are used to describe an employee, that individual would receive a low evaluation score.

Weighted checklists are good performance-evaluation procedures when they have been well developed. Because the statements refer to observable behaviors rather than to subjective perceptions, most of the biases and problems mentioned at the beginning of this chapter are avoided or minimized.

The major disadvantages of weighted checklists are the time and effort required to develop them and the time required to complete them. Unless the jobs are fairly stable and there are several employees performing the same job, the advantages of using weighted checklists are offset by the time and effort required to develop them.

BEHAVIORALLY ANCHORED RATINGS SCALES (BARS)

The critical-incident method also contributes to the development of **behaviorally anchored ratings scales (BARS)**. Behaviorally anchored rating scales are about the same as graphic rating scales except that the scales are described more accurately by specific behaviors. The use of critical incidents helps to overcome the two major problems of graphic rating scales: the selection of characteristics and their scaling. Since critical incidents are descriptions of especially effective or ineffective behaviors, the best characteristics to include in an evaluation are those identified by the critical-incidents method.[37]

The problems of scaling each characteristic can be largely overcome by using behavioral descriptions obtained via the same process as weighted-checklist items. Discrete scales can relate each step to specific behavioral descriptions. An example of a behaviorally anchored rating scale is shown in Figure 7.5.

The major advantages of BARS are that: (1) they are less biased than other rating scales; (2) their characteristics are more carefully selected; and (3) they inspire agreement among evaluators, since they evaluate observable behavior rather than subjective perceptions. Most of the research evidence indicates that BARS are superior to regular graphic rating scales because they are more reliable, less ambiguous, and less biased.[38] The disadvantages are the time and effort required to develop these scales. Furthermore, since BARS focus on behaviors, rather than outcomes, managers would probably want to combine BARS with a results-oriented appraisal, such as management by objectives.[39]

A newer rating method similar to BARS is called **behavioral observation scales (BOS)**. An advantage this method has over BARS is that it asks the rater only to evaluate the frequency of behavior rather than the level of performance. The evaluator simply records the number of times various behaviors were observed—always, frequently, occasionally, seldom, or never—without deciding whether they were good or bad. The scores for each employee are obtained by assigning a numerical value to the frequency judgments and possibly weighing some behaviors greater than others. The scores are then summed and translated to an overall appraisal score. Like BARS, one of the chief merits of BOS is its value in providing personal feedback to employees.[40] Another important benefit is the contribution BOS makes to improved productivity through individual goal setting. One study found that the use of BOS led to significantly higher levels of three goal-setting attributes: goal clarity, goal acceptance, and goal commitment.[41]

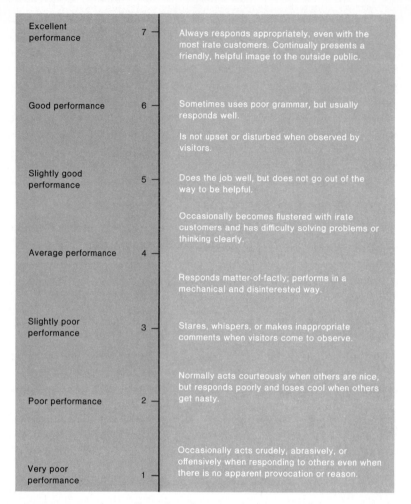

Excellent performance	7	Always responds appropriately, even with the most irate customers. Continually presents a friendly, helpful image to the outside public.
Good performance	6	Sometimes uses poor grammar, but usually responds well.
		Is not upset or disturbed when observed by visitors.
Slightly good performance	5	Does the job well, but does not go out of the way to be helpful.
		Occasionally becomes flustered with irate customers and has difficulty solving problems or thinking clearly.
Average performance	4	
		Responds matter-of-factly; performs in a mechanical and disinterested way.
Slightly poor performance	3	Stares, whispers, or makes inappropriate comments when visitors come to observe.
Poor performance	2	Normally acts courteously when others are nice, but responds poorly and loses cool when others get nasty.
Very poor performance	1	Occasionally acts crudely, abrasively, or offensively when responding to others even when there is no apparent provocation or reason.

FIGURE 7.5 Behaviorally anchored rating scale: Contact with customers or clients.

FORCED-CHOICE PROCEDURES

The **forced-choice technique** of rating was developed at the close of World War II by a group of industrial psychologists who were evaluating the performance of officers in the army. Since that time, this method also has been used in industry.

The rating form consists of a number of statements arranged in pairs, as shown in Figure 7.6. For each pair the evaluator must check the one statement that is most descriptive of the performance of the person, or for negative statements, the statement that is least descriptive. The pairs of statements are so designed that both statements appear equally favorable (or equally unfavorable), but one statement is actually more descriptive of an outstanding (or poor) performer. In other words, the statements in each pair have equal social desirability but unequal discriminability. The actual value or weighing of the statements is kept secret from the evaluators to prevent deliberate bias on their part. The evaluators cannot slant the rating to make the final scores appear in any desired way; the evaluators are essentially reporters who check the statements that best describe an individual's behavior. The scoring of the statements is done in the personnel office.

Experiments comparing the forced-choice technique with other rating-scale procedures have shown that less bias is evident in the forced-choice method than in other methods. The forced-choice method also seems to allow greater objectivity than most other methods.[42] The principal disadvantage is that the development of a forced-choice scale requires a great deal of time and skill. Unless there are many employees performing a stable job, the effort is not justified. Forced-choice evaluations also are difficult for supervisors to discuss with subordinates, because the supervisors themselves do not know how the items are scored.

EVALUATION PROCESS

Other issues concerning the evaluation process relate to: (1) who should evaluate performance; (2) when the evaluation should occur; and (3) how the information should be shared with employees.

WHO SHOULD EVALUATE PERFORMANCE?

In most performance-evaluation procedures, the immediate superior is responsible for evaluating an employee's performance. Although supervisors should have the primary responsibility, others should be included in the procedure too. These others could be

FIGURE 7.6 Illustration of a forced-choice evaluation procedure.

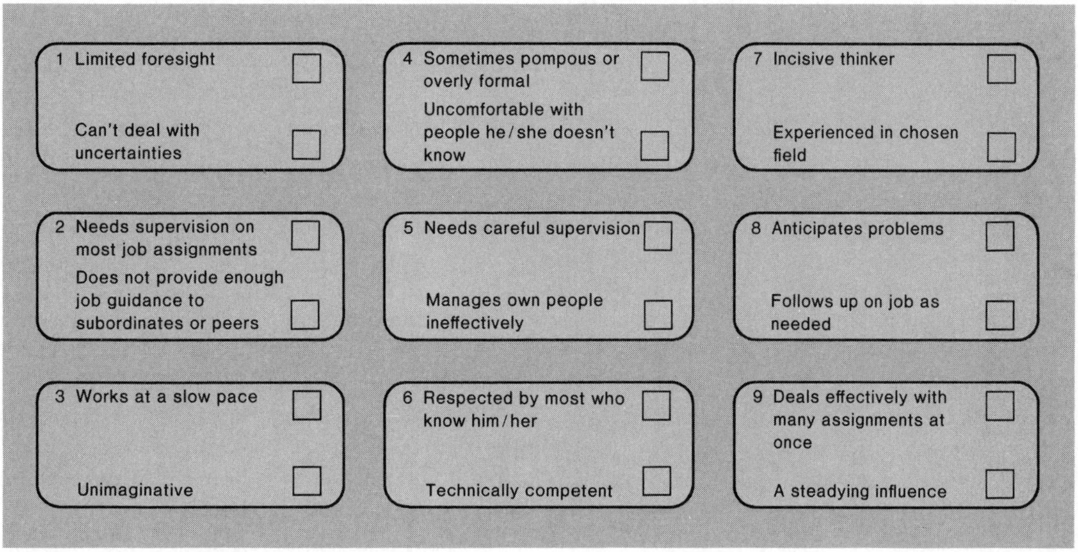

subordinates, peers, the employee being evaluated, and clients or customers. As a general rule, performance appraisals are more accurate and useful when the evaluations come from sources closest to the person being rated. To make quality evaluations, assessors need to have appropriate knowledge and adequate opportunity to observe the types of performance being assessed.

SUPERVISORS

The hierarchical arrangement of formal authority in most organizations gives the supervisor the legitimate responsibility to evaluate subordinates. In most instances there is a shared expectation between both parties that the superior has both the right and the obligation to evaluate performance. To behave otherwise would seem unnatural and inappropriate. Furthermore, since supervisors administer the rewards and punishments, they should be responsible for evaluating performance.

SUBORDINATES

Although evaluations of superiors by subordinates might seem backward, they can be useful in some circumstances. Subordinates are being asked more frequently to evaluate corporate officers in what are sometimes called upward appraisals, or subordinate appraisals, and this information may be used to decide pay increases and promotions.[43] Subordinates possess unique information about superiors that ought to be included in the evaluation process. Subordinates have to live with the leadership of a superior, and they know better than anyone else whether the leadership is good or bad. The kind of influence that superiors exert on subordinates is an important dimension of their performance.

One of the most valuable uses of subordinate ratings is for personal development. Subordinates can provide a valuable profile of managerial effectiveness, and their comments are especially useful when they contradict a manager's self-evaluation. When subordinates unanimously disagree with a manager's self-evaluation, the manager usually becomes tremendously motivated to reexamine his or her leadership style and to consider changing it.[44]

Two other benefits of evaluations by subordinates are that they equalize the power differentials in organizations and make the workplace more democratic and responsive to human needs. Power equalization increases the flow of communication and improves coordination and planning. In the traditional situation, only the supervisor is able to evaluate subordinates and say, for example, they are lazy and will not respond to work orders. But when subordinate evaluations are used, the subordinates are able to explain that sometimes the supervisor's work orders are so garbled and confusing they do not know what to do.[45]

Subordinate evaluations of superiors have certain limitations. Subordinates can only evaluate what they observe, and they generally evaluate their superiors based on their interactions with them. This means that supervisors are primarily evaluated on the basis of consideration rather than organizational effectiveness. Some administrative decisions are not popular, and a desire to please subordinates could cause managers to make bad decisions. Subordinate evaluations also have the potential of undermining the legitimate authority of superiors and of reducing their organizational effectiveness. For a two-way evaluation process to function effectively, both superiors and subordinates must have adequate maturity to make responsible evaluations and to accept feedback from one another.

PEERS

In some situations, the most knowledgeable and capable evaluators are an employee's peers. Coworkers are sometimes in a better position than their supervisor to evaluate each other's performance. Research on peer evaluations has found them to be predictive of success and correlated with both objective and subjective ratings of success in numerous situations. A review of many studies examining the use of peer ratings in the military services found that peer ratings were more valid predictors of leadership performance than ratings by superiors. Peer ratings also have yielded good reliability and validity.[46]

The conditions required for good peer appraisals are: (1) a high level of interpersonal trust; (2) a noncompetitive reward system; and (3) opportunities for peers to observe each other's performances. When these conditions are not met, the use of peer appraisals is severely restricted. Peer appraisals are most frequently used among professional and technical employees in organizations where the conditions just listed are met. The use of peer appraisals has the potential for increasing the interaction and coordination between peers.[47]

SELF

People are always evaluating themselves. The question is how formally and systematically these self-evaluations should be recorded and acted upon. In recent years a decline in authoritarian leadership has contributed to an increase in self-evaluations in both large and small companies. Some of the arguments in favor of self-evaluation are that self-evaluation results in: (1) more satisfying and constructive evaluation interviews; (2) less defensiveness regarding the evaluation process; and (3) improved job performance through greater commitment to organizational goals.[48]

On the other hand, the arguments opposing self-evaluations center on the fact that low agreement usually exists between self- and supervisory evaluations.[49] Because of the systematic biases and distortions that can appear, self-evaluations have to be used very carefully. Self-evaluations are very valuable for personal development and the identification of training needs, but they are not useful for evaluative purposes. Asking employees to evaluate themselves for purposes of promotions or pay increases is like asking students to grade themselves. It puts individuals in the awkward and uncomfortable situation of trying to guess how biased everyone else will be in rating themselves.

CLIENTS

As a general rule, anyone who is in a position to observe the behaviors or outcomes of an individual should be included in the evaluation process. According to this principle, there are occasions when clients and customers ought to be asked for their observations. For example, the use of student evaluations of teachers is increasing because students are the consumers of the teacher's product and are in the best position to decide such issues as how interesting the class is, how clearly the ideas are explained, and how much interest and concern are shown to them. On the other hand, the students are probably not capable of deciding whether the course content is current or if more relevant material should be included.

WHEN SHOULD PERFORMANCE BE EVALUATED?

Performance evaluations ought to occur at the conclusion of a typical work cycle. Public accountants, for example, are usually evaluated at the conclusion of a major audit. School teachers are evaluated at the end of a school year or at the end of a semester. Learning theory suggests that frequent performance feedback helps learners improve their performance. Frequent appraisals, for instance, tend to reduce the impact of appraisal errors, to provide more timely data for taking corrective action, and to help appraisers feel more confident of their appraisals.[50] However, formal evaluation of performance is often inconvenient. Instead, supervisors should provide informal feedback often, soon after the behavior occurs, and then summarize evaluations in a formal review once or twice a year. If the work cycle is continuous, a performance review should be scheduled at periodic times, but at least once a year.

Because supervisors complain about having to act as judge and coach simultaneously in evaluating performance and claim that these two roles are incompatible, two separate evaluations should occur. One evaluation—the contributions appraisal—should focus on outcomes and evaluate results, and the other—the personal-development appraisal— should focus on behaviors and personal development.[51]

CONTRIBUTIONS APPRAISAL

In the evaluative role of performance evaluation, the focus is on past performance with the objective of improving future performance through effective reward contingencies. This evaluation is called a **contributions appraisal** because it concentrates on what the employee has contributed to the company: what the employee's objectives and responsibilities were and how well they were achieved. The contributions appraisal is usually a confrontational interview. The role of the evaluator is to judge and evaluate, while the role of the employee is to be either passive or defensive. Employees should come to a contributions appraisal prepared to explain what they have contributed to the organization and why they deserve a pay increase or promotion.

PERSONAL-DEVELOPMENT APPRAISAL

The developmental aspect of performance appraisal is quite different from the evaluative aspect. Whereas the atmosphere of a contributions appraisal is confrontational, that of a **personal-development appraisal** is supportive. The focus of the developmental appraisal is on improving future performance through self-learning and growth, with the evaluator offering guidance, help, and counsel along with accurate performance feedback. The role of the employee is active involvement in self-analysis and learning. The personal-development appraisal is an important part of a human resource planning system. The employee's interests in advancement and promotion should be assessed and developmental experiences should be arranged for those interested in advancing.

Clearly, the developmental appraisal and the contributions appraisal are incompatible and need to be conducted at separate times. Some corporations separate the evaluations by six months. After the end of the year, usually in January, employees are evaluated on how well they performed relative to their stated objectives. These evaluations are used to determine bonuses and pay increases. The other evaluation usually occurs in July and is designed to examine employees' managerial and administrative skills, including potential for development. This information is used primarily for replacement planning and analysis of training needs.

EVALUATION INTERVIEWS

Performance-evaluation interviews can be uncomfortable for both superiors and subordinates. The difficulties managers experience include explaining poor performance to marginal employees, providing feedback to poor performers who think they are doing a good job, and trying to find something fresh to say about a long-time employee's performance.[52] These interviews are especially threatening to insecure supervisors and new employees. Some supervisors tend to postpone interviews indefinitely, which means that the employees do not receive adequate feedback on their performance. And if the interview is handled poorly, feelings of disappointment, anger, and resentment may result. Rather than increasing performance and improving personal development, poor evaluation interviews can destroy initiative and create feelings of defeat and despair.

The effectiveness of evaluation interviews will be enhanced if managers and subordinates follow some simple guidelines.

1. Evaluators should develop their own style so they feel comfortable in an interview. If an interview makes the evaluator feel uncomfortable, the employee being evaluated probably will feel uncomfortable too. An evaluator should not try to copy someone else or follow a rigid format if it does not feel comfortable and natural.

2. Both parties should carefully prepare for the interview beforehand. Employees should review their performance and assemble their own information documenting how well they have done. Evaluators should gather relevant information about each employee's past performance and compare it against the objectives for the period. Lack of preparation for the interview by either party is an obvious indication of disregard and disinterest.

3. The evaluator should clarify the purpose of the interview at the very beginning. The employee should know whether it is a disciplinary session, a contributions appraisal, or a personal-development appraisal. In particular, the employee should understand the possible consequences of the interview so that he or she can prepare appropriate responses. For example, an employee's responses during a contributions appraisal can appropriately be a bit guarded and defensive. But in a personal-development appraisal, such responses would greatly reduce the effectiveness of the interview.

4. Neither party should dominate the discussion. The superior should take the lead in initiating the discussion, but the employee should be encouraged to express opinions. The superior should budget time so that the employee has approximately half the time to discuss the evaluation.

5. The most popular format for the interview is the "sandwich" format—criticism sandwiched between compliments. The rationale for the **sandwich-interview** format is that positive comments made at the beginning and end of the interview create a positive experience. The opening compliments should put the employee at ease for the interview. The closing compliments should leave the employee feeling good about the interview and motivated to do better.

6. An alternative format is the problem-recognition and future-planning format. This approach is very direct and to the point. The supervisor begins by saying, "There are __ problems I'd like to talk with you about: __ , __, and __ ." Each problem is briefly identified at the beginning before the supervisor discusses the problems in detail. An employee immediately knows what the "charges" are and does not sit in uncertainty waiting for the next bomb to fall. After the problems have been discussed by both superior and subordinate, the discussion focuses on accomplishments for which the employee deserves recognition. The superior should describe specific actions deserving recognition and be as complimentary as the behavior merits. The interview should not end until the superior and subordinate have discussed plans for future performance. Future goals and objectives should be clarified, and plans for personal development and performance improvement should be discussed.

Employees should be encouraged to take an active role in the performance-evaluation process. Most employees wait until their superior initiates action and schedules an interview. Then they sit through the interview feeling as though they are being "chewed out," manipulated, or run over. Instead, employees should take an active role by anticipating their evaluations, collecting data about their performance, scheduling interviews with their superior, taking the lead in interviews to discuss their strengths and weaknesses, and asking for feedback. This active role makes the evaluation process a dramatically different experience for subordinates. Rather than dreading interviews, the subordinates are consciously planning for them and anticipating the experience.

The evaluation interview should focus on behaviors and results rather than on personality factors. Accurate feedback can help an employee change his or her behavior and achieve better results. However, discussions about personality characteristics are usually dysfunctional. Because personality factors are poorly defined and value laden, discussing them usually causes bad feelings and creates unnecessary conflict. Personality changes are difficult to achieve and are usually not necessary anyway. When a supervisor thinks a change in personality is needed, what the supervisor is actually concerned about are certain behaviors caused by the employee's personality. To correct such problems, the supervisor should describe the improper behaviors and help the employee change his or her behavior. If a personality change is indeed required, feedback about the specific behavior that needs to be changed is still the best approach to changing personality.

Some have suggested that appraisal interviews should include only the outstanding and poor performers, while the middle group should be excluded. Not only are the ones in the middle more difficult to evaluate, but it appears that telling people they are average is dysfunctional. Most people resent being labeled as average when they think they are members of an above-average group. In support of this position is the finding that employees report a significant drop in organizational commitment when they are told that their performance is satisfactory, but below average.[53]

USING PERFORMANCE INFORMATION

The purpose of the evaluation should be to provide information for making important decisions. All too often, however, the formal evaluation procedure occurs in isolation. The information gained from the evaluation is buried in file cabinets, and decisions are then based on informal evaluations and subjective impressions instead. Some decisions, such as pay increases and personal-development programs, should be part of the performance-evaluation process. Other decisions, such as promotions, are usually made at different times, but performance information should be considered when these decisions are made.

PAY INCREASES AND INCENTIVE COMPENSATION

In organizations where pay increases are based on performance, the performance-evaluation period is a convenient time to recommend a pay increase. If all members of a work group are evaluated at about the same time, the supervisor usually makes the pay-increase recommendations as soon as everyone has been evaluated. When subordinates are evaluated at scattered times, such as on their date-of-hire anniversaries, supervisors usually recommend a pay increase according to guidelines provided by the human resource office.

Tying pay increases to performance evaluations has become increasingly popular, especially when performance can be assessed against defined job objectives. These pay-for-performance programs have been introduced in both public and private organizations for both managerial and nonmanagerial employees.[54]

PERSONAL DEVELOPMENT AND TRAINING

Personal-development decisions ought to occur as part of the performance evaluation. During the evaluation, the kinds of training and learning experiences an employee needs for personal development should be examined. An employee should discuss the future and indicate interests in learning new skills and developing different talents. This is a good time for an employee to request special training programs or academic courses. If the organization has a replacement chart, the superior and employee should discuss which positions the employee can anticipate attaining and which coworkers could replace the employee.

DISCIPLINARY ACTIONS AND PERFORMANCE IMPROVEMENT

When the performance of an employee is not adequate, the causes of poor performance need to be carefully analyzed. If the cause is a lack of motivation and effort, a performance-improvement plan with specific measurable goals and objectives should be developed. If the employee refuses to accept or follow the plan, disciplinary actions can be taken.

PROMOTIONS

The two most important criteria for making promotion decisions are seniority and merit. Union employees usually prefer to base promotions on a strict seniority system to preserve union security. Nonunion employees, especially managers, think promotions should be based primarily on merit. Both of these criteria are considered appropriate, and they are used in varying degrees for real promotions and quasipromotions. A real promotion involves a new job with additional responsibilities. A quasipromotion is primarily a change in title only, such as the promotion of an assistant professor to associate professor, a priest to archpriest, or an accountant to senior accountant.

If promotions are based on merit, formal performance evaluations should play an important role in promotion decisions. The evidence indicates, however, that formal evaluations are not used as often in promotion decisions as they should be.[55] A study of the promotions of Roman Catholic priests found that the decisions were based almost entirely on seniority ranking, even though many priests wanted to include merit as a criterion.[56] Rank advancements of university professors also are based almost exclusively on seniority, even though most universities claim that their rank advancements are based on teaching and research performance.[57] When professors are recommended for promotion, most departments send extensive performance information to the review committee. All of this information gives the appearance that the promotions are based on performance, but actually, professors usually have to wait a specified number of years before they can be recommended for promotion, regardless of performance. And when actual decisions are made, they often are based more on departmental politics and personal friendships than on performance.

Even in business organizations, formal performance evaluations are probably used less often in promotion decisions than most business leaders think. In a lab experiment, fifteen line managers were asked to rank the importance of various sources of information that they preferred to use in making a promotion decision.[58] They ranked formal performance evaluations very high and said they would use this information. But when the managers proceeded to make simulated promotion decisions during the experiment, they largely disregarded the performance information. A survey of seventy-one top managers in thirteen corporations found similar results.[59] Informal evaluations and personal knowledge were used more frequently than formal evaluations in the consensus decision making of the committees that selected top managers. Personal favoritism was not a significant factor. But for younger executives to reach the top, they had to be discovered early, receive broad experience, and become visible to top management by means of precocious successes. Formal performance evaluations were not completely ignored, but they did not seem to be as important in promotion decisions as informal evaluations.

The American military probably has the most aggressive programs for using formal evaluations in promotion decisions. The performance evaluations and personnel files of potential officers are sent to a special decision-making committee called the Promotion Board. This board consists of high-ranking officers who are specially selected and trained to make promotion decisions. They review thousands of evaluations and make their decisions according to clearly specified criteria from the Pentagon. A typical officer being reviewed is evaluated at least nine times by various board members and may be evaluated as many as fifteen times. Because promotion decisions are based entirely on the information included in the formal evaluation and personnel file, it is easy to understand why military personnel are so concerned about their performance reviews and why the pressure to give inflated evaluations is so intense.

The elaborate system used by the military would not be cost-benefit effective for most organizations. Although promotions, pay increases, and other personnel actions should be based on performance evaluations, every organization does not need a highly sophisticated, formal performance-evaluation procedure. Small companies with fewer than fifty employees may not need anything more than a simple, informal evaluation procedure. But as organizations become larger, the benefits of a formal evaluation procedure increase.

RESULTS-ORIENTED EVALUATIONS—MBO

Recent shifts in management theory and practice have led to increased individual accountability through a results-oriented approach to performance evaluation. Less emphasis is placed on the activities that employees ought to perform, and more emphasis is placed on the results expected of employees. Many labels have been attached to these results-oriented evaluations; the most popular label is **management by objectives (MBO)**.[60]

A PHILOSOPHY OF MANAGEMENT

MBO is applied not only as a performance-evaluation procedure but also as a general management philosophy.[61] It is not a prescribed procedure for managers to follow or a cookbook approach to managing. Moreover, there is no one best way to manage by objectives. Each program must be adapted to the needs and circumstances of the specific organization.

MBO is primarily a philosophy of management that espouses a positive, proactive way of managing rather than a reactive way. The focus is on: (1) predicting and shaping the future of the organization by developing long-range organizational objectives and strategic plans; (2) accomplishing results rather than performing activities; (3) improving both individual competence and organizational effectiveness; and (4) increasing the participation and involvement of employees in the affairs of the organization.

MBO also is a process consisting of a series of integrated management functions: (1) the development of clear, precise organizational objectives; (2) the formulation of coordinated individual objectives designed to achieve the overall organizational objectives; (3) the systematic measurement and review of performance; and (4) taking corrective actions when needed to achieve the planned objectives.

Peter Drucker is credited with first publicizing MBO in his 1954 book, *The Practice of Management*.[62] Drucker noted the advantages of managing managers by "objectives" rather than by "drives." The advantages are that each manager from the highest level to the lowest level has clear objectives that reflect and support the objectives of higher-level management. All managers participate in the goal-setting process and then exercise "self-control" over their own performance; that is, they monitor their own performance and take corrective actions when necessary. To do this, their performance is measured and compared with their objectives. The measurements need not be rigidly quantitative or exact, but they must be clear and rational.

THREE PHASES OF MBO

Getting an effective MBO program started in an organization requires a great deal of coordination and planning. The implementation of a program typically occurs in three phases.[63] In Phase 1, the performances of managers are evaluated. The emphasis is on developing measurable objectives. In this phase, MBO is administered almost exclusively by the human resource department. At this stage, the program usually receives only moderate support from top management, and line managers usually are even less enthusiastic because the program not only takes time but also involves paperwork.[64] Still, Phase 1 MBO programs generally are moderately successful, because they tend to clarify responsibilities and focus on achieving results.

In Phase 2, MBO programs are integrated into an organization's planning and control processes. Greater involvement and support are obtained from both top management and line managers, and the MBO program becomes tied to the organization's planning and budgeting cycle. Training and developing subordinates is emphasized.

Phase 3 is a fully implemented MBO system. In this phase, all of the major organizational functions and key management processes are integrated in a logical and consistent manner. These functions and processes include performance evaluations, budgeting and financial planning, the development of strategic plans and overall goals, staffing, compensation, human resource development, and management training and development. The emphasis is on teamwork and flexibility in establishing goals and plans, frequent performance reviews, and achieving individual growth and development.

PRINCIPLES OF MBO

MBO has been described in numerous books and articles. Most of these descriptions indicate that MBO can be basically defined by four principles: goal setting, delegation, feedback reviews, and evaluation.

GOAL SETTING

The most distinctive characteristic of MBO is the formulation of tangible, measurable, and verifiable objectives in key areas of performance. Everyone in the organization should be involved in goal setting, but since corporate planning is generally the responsibility of top management, MBO programs will fail without its active support.

Once the central mission and long-range plans of an organization have been formulated, the **cascading process** begins. Departmental and individual objectives are derived from organizational goals that cascade downward through the organization. Briefly described, the long-range goals become the basis for formulating short-range objectives, from which the objectives for each major division and subunit are then obtained. These objectives must fit together to achieve the overall organizational objectives. This cascading process continues through successively lower levels in the organization until all employees know their objectives and understand how they combine to achieve the organization's overall goals.[65]

DELEGATION

In MBO programs, delegation is characterized by its focus on results rather than on activities. The reason for delegating results rather than activities is to increase personal responsibility. When a supervisor tells a subordinate which activities to perform, the supervisor is still responsible for the final result. Personal accountability arises from delegating the results.

Effective delegation requires the superior to carefully decide what results need to be delegated and to whom. At the time the results are delegated, a "contract" is established between the superior and the subordinate. The contract is not a formal or legal document; it is a psychological contract. It does not need to be written, but having some written record for review purposes may be helpful to both the supervisor and the subordinate. This record should specify the results expected of the subordinate in sufficient detail so that at a later date both supervisor and subordinate will be able to agree on how well the results have been achieved.

FEEDBACK REVIEWS

Periodic reviews should be scheduled to evaluate progress and to provide assistance, if needed. However, if assistance is given, the subordinate should not feel released from the responsibility of achieving the results. If the review is conducted properly, the subordinate will still retain the responsibility for the results. Periodic reviews need to be expected by the subordinate so that no suspicion exists that a review has been necessitated by poor performance. The subordinate should assume the responsibility of evaluating his or her own progress. The role of the superior should be to ask questions that will guide the subordinate is assessing his or her own progress. If significant differences of opinion occur concerning the progress being made, these differences need to be resolved, and, if necessary, a new contract should be established.

Written feedback in the form of budget reports and other performance indicators should be provided as frequently as possible if the reports are meaningful, if they are not too costly to prepare in terms of time or money, and if the individual is not already inundated with numerous reports. Frequent reports can help an employee monitor personal performance and can serve as a form of reinforcement.

EVALUATION

If the contract between a superior and a subordinate was carefully constructed and periodic reviews were held, then the final evaluation should be a positive experience, and the subordinate's success should be recognized and rewarded. But even if the subordinate was not successful, the final evaluation does not have to be anxiety-ridden and confrontational. If the previous steps were followed, the atmosphere should be one of compatible problem solving. The failure should come as no surprise if the periodic reviews were conducted properly, and the evaluation discussion should concern the possible causes of failure and alternative solutions. The causes might be unrealistic objectives, inadequate resources, or a lack of personal effort or skill. If the superior chooses to retain the subordinate, a new contract is established. This contract, like the previous one, not only specifies the results to be achieved by a certain date with periodic reviews, but also provides for additional resources, greater opportunities for training, or whatever else is necessary to achieve success.

RESEARCH ON MBO

Since the early 1950s, hundreds of organizations have introduced MBO, and the effectiveness of these programs has been reported in numerous research studies. MBO generally seems to produce positive changes in performance and behavior.[66] Managers working under MBO programs are more likely to take specific actions to improve performance, and MBO seems to produce more positive job attitudes. However, the evidence that MBO produces solid productivity improvements is generally weak. MBO has been criticized for creating excessive paperwork, especially when it is first initiated. However, this problem is reduced somewhat after managers become familiar with the forms.

Research on MBO is hindered because each company has a slightly different MBO program. Consequently, the best evidence supporting the value of MBO comes from research concerning goal setting, performance feedback, participation, delegation, budgeting, and reinforcement, which are the major processes that combine to form an MBO program. Extensive research has been conducted on these processes, and from this research, some conclusions can be drawn about the value of MBO. Many studies have demonstrated the value of goal setting and have shown that setting specific objectives can greatly increase performance and change behavior.[67] Performance feedback is an important component of learning, and studies have indicated that specific performance feedback greatly facilitates learning new behavior and changing old behavior. The effects of participation depend on the norms and cohesiveness of the group. If the group is a cohesive one, and if it supports the goals of the organization, then greater participation tends to increase the performance and morale of the group.[68] Delegating authority for specific tasks and having managers develop their own budgets and live within them are motivating experiences if they are properly handled. The evidence shows that if the budgets are realistic and if managers are rewarded for achieving them, the usual result is high levels of satisfaction and performance.[69] Although this evidence does not conclusively prove that all MBO programs will be successful, it at least suggests that they should succeed if they are properly adapted to specific situations.

INTERNATIONAL HRM

Evaluating the performance of subordinates and conducting feedback interviews is a monumental challenge for most supervisors. Cross-cultural situations make the evaluation process even more difficult. People raised in different cultures give and receive feedback in ways that may differ significantly from the way managers and employees raised in the United States do.

The Asian cultures, especially the Japanese, emphasize loyalty to the company and a commitment to the group. Employees perceive themselves as members of a team, and they succeed as the team succeeds. This group approach to work is quite unlike the individualism found in the United States, and it means that individual feedback, even positive recognition, may create problems, especially if it occurs in public.[70] An American manager assigned to supervise an international division in Japan made the mistake of publicly recognizing one of the employees for her outstanding work. The compliments seriously embarrassed the employee. She declined to accept the small gift recognizing her performance, and two weeks later she asked to be transferred to a new work group. It is not uncommon for people raised in an Asian culture to display little or no emotion when they are paid a compliment, and they tend to deny that they have done anything worthy of special recognition.

Business in the Hispanic cultures, especially in Mexico, tends to be more relaxed and easygoing than in the United States.[71] Consequently, a Mexican employee being evaluated with direct, businesslike efficiency by a U.S. manager could feel threatened by the manager's manner and may respond defensively. Hispanic cultures place a high priority on personal relationships; business will get done when the time is right. Before the performance review focuses on performance, a Hispanic employee expects the evaluator to engage in a personal conversation and to be well acquainted with the person and the person's family.

Even the European cultures seem to differ from ours in their attitude toward performance feedback. Although the differences may be small, at least two studies have concluded that the performance of U.S. workers is influenced more by feedback than the performance of English workers is. U.S. workers who expect and accept feedback exhibited a stronger relationship between the amount of feedback they received and their performance improvement than did English workers, who were more indifferent to feedback.[72]

SUMMARY

A. Performance evaluations serve several different objectives: (1) to guide personnel actions, such as hiring, firing, and promoting; (2) to reinforce behavior through pay increases and other rewards; (3) to aid personal development; (4) to identify training needs; and (5) to integrate the human resource functions, particularly human resource planning.

B. As part of the employment exchange, employees are expected to perform their jobs in exchange for compensation and other rewards. Employees expect to be paid fairly, and the organization expects dependable performance. Employees should evaluate their pay, and the organization should evaluate the employees' performance. Performance evaluation is part of the personal accountability that employees should accept as part of the employment exchange.

C. Performance evaluations have been criticized because of their susceptibility to various forms of bias and because they are frequently conducted by incompetent supervisors. Experience and training can help supervisors do a better job of evaluating performance. Minimizing performance-evaluation problems depends more on training than on developing a new form. No form or procedure can compensate for incompetence or a lack of supervisory ability.

D. The question of whether performance should be evaluated is not a serious consideration, since performance has always been evaluated and always will be. The question is whether the evaluations will be formal or informal. Formal evaluations are generally less biased, more open to observation, and more defensible than informal, subjective evaluations.

E. Performance evaluations should assess the important dimensions of performance, and the evaluations should be relevant, reliable, and free of contamination. Both results and behaviors are legitimate dimensions to evaluate, depending on the purpose of the evaluation.

F. The major kinds of data used in evaluating performance include production data, personnel data, and the judgments of others. All three sources of information are important.

G. The major procedures for evaluating performance include: (1) classification procedures; (2) ranking procedures; (3) graphic rating scales; (4) critical-incident procedures; (5) weighted checklists; (6) behaviorally anchored rating scales; and (7) forced-choice procedures. Each procedure has its advantages and disadvantages. Selection of a procedure should be based in part on the purpose of the evaluation.

H. Anyone who can reliably observe and evaluate an employee's performance should participate in the evaluation process, including superiors, peers, clients or customers, subordinates, and self. However, an employee's immediate superior should assume the responsibility for collecting, integrating, and summarizing all relevant information and for giving feedback to the employee.

I. Because performance evaluations serve two distinctly different and sometimes contradictory purposes, two separate evaluations are recommended. A contributions appraisal is a confrontational evaluation of what an employee has contributed to the organization. A personal-development appraisal is a collaborative, problem-solving evaluation designed to help an employee develop talents and skills.

J. An evaluation interview should be carefully planned: both parties should know what to expect, and both parties should participate equally in the discussion. Negative information should be concisely summarized at the beginning so the employee will know immediately what criticisms will be discussed.

K. Performance evaluations should be used as the basis for granting pay increases, for developing training programs, for administering disciplinary actions, and for promotions. Often, however, managers rely more on informal evaluations than on formal evaluations in making these decisions.

L. Management by objectives (MBO) is a results-oriented form of evaluating performance. It also is a philosophy of management that focuses on developing long-range organizational goals, translating these goals into specific objectives for every employee, delegating to each employee the responsibility and authority to act, evaluating the accomplishment of the objectives, and allowing all members of the organization to participate in the decision making and control of the organization. MBO is usually implemented in an organization as a performance-evaluation procedure built on setting goals and objectives. Gradually, the MBO program encompasses other management functions, such as strategic planning, compensation, training, and human resource planning.

QUESTIONS

1. Many employees dislike performance evaluations. Many students dislike grades. What would happen if teachers quit giving grades? What if everyone received the same grade? What if everyone received an A?

2. What difference does it make to you in terms of effort and learning to take a course on a pass-fail basis rather than on a grade basis?

3. The performance-evaluation form used at an oil refinery for employees who mostly watch gauges measures these nine dimensions: quantity, quality, job knowledge, attitude, appearance, initiative, leadership, motivation, and presence of mind. How would you rate these performance measures in terms of their relevance, reliability, and freedom from contamination?

4. How would you respond to an executive who said, "I do not want any personality factors on the company's performance evaluation. I only want to measure quantity and quality. It's results we're after!"

5. Suppose a group of engineers was evaluated using a simple ranking procedure from 1 to 18, and this ranking was used for both pay increases and personal development. What effect do you think this procedure would have on group morale, personal development, cooperation among group members, and interpersonal relationships?

6. How is MBO both a performance-evaluation procedure and a philosophy of management?

7. Some managers complain that MBO does not make good jobs out of bad jobs, that it is only a management gimmick to increase production, that it is a new whip to create more pressure, and that it only results in a lot of useless paper shuffling. Is MBO based on sound principles of management, and does research evidence support these principles?

8. Is involving someone else besides the immediate superior a realistic approach to evaluating performance? Could students grade each other? Should student evaluations determine the promotions and pay increases of teachers?

9. How would you discuss negative information with an employee if you were a supervisor? How would you want your supervisor to handle negative information if you were the employee?

10. What changes would you recommend for solving the problem of grade inflation at colleges and universities?

KEY TERMS

Alternate ranking: An evaluation procedure in which employees are ranked by identifying the best and worst employees on a list. These names are then removed from the list, and the best and worst of the remaining names are identified. The procedure continues until everyone on the list has been ranked.

BARS (Behaviorally anchored rating scales): A form of graphic rating scales where the scales are accompanied by specific behavioral descriptions.

BOS (Behavioral observation scales): A performance-evaluation method that consists of reporting how frequently certain behaviors are observed.

Cascading process: The procedure used in MBO programs whereby top corporate goals are translated into goals for each successively lower level in the organization until everyone has a specific goal and the accomplishment of the individual goals will lead to the accomplishment of the organizational goals.

Central-tendency effect: The tendency for an evaluator to give average ratings to all employees.

Classification procedure: An evaluation procedure in which employees are simply placed in different categories describing their overall performance.

Contributions appraisal: A confrontational performance evaluation that focuses on how well the employees have reached their objectives and what they have contributed to the organization.

Critical incidents: Essay descriptions of especially good or bad responses by employees to their jobs. These descriptions are useful in identifying the important dimensions of successful performance.

Forced-choice technique: An evaluation procedure that contains pairs of items, all sounding equally desirable, even though only one item in each pair is actually descriptive of an outstanding performer.

Forced distribution: An evaluation procedure that requires the evaluator to classify employees according to a predetermined percentage in each category.

Freedom from contamination: A criterion for good performance data. The data should be a direct reflection of an employee's performance and not influenced by outside factors such as other people, organizational policies, or the economy.

Free-form essay: An evaluation procedure in which the evaluator writes an open essay describing an employee's performance.

Graphic rating scales: An evaluation procedure consisting of specified dimensions of performance and a scale for each dimension to evaluate the employee's behavior.

Halo effect: A form of evaluation bias in which one attribute influences the evaluation of other traits.

Interrater reliability: The degree of consistency between two evaluators who have evaluated the same employee.

Leniency-strictness effect: A form of evaluation bias whereby evaluators tend to rate everyone especially high or low.

MBO (Management by objectives): Philosophy of management that reflects a positive, proactive way of managing.

Numbers fetish: The tendency to overemphasize numbers and to assume that they are more exact and precise than can be legitimately assumed from their subjective derivation.

Paired comparisons: An evaluation procedure that ranks employees by comparing each employee with every other employee.

Personal-development appraisal: A supportive performance evaluation that focuses on helping an employee develop skills and talents.

Recency effect: A form of evaluation bias in which recent events are weighted more heavily in the mind of the evaluator than distant events.

Relevance: A criterion of good performance data. The data must measure information that is closely associated with the "ultimate success" of the job.

Reliability: A criterion of good performance data. The dimensions of performance must be sufficiently clear and unambiguous so that evaluators can make consistent and repeatable evaluations.

Sandwich interviews: A format for a performance evaluation interview in which negative comments are sandwiched between positive comments at the beginning and end of the interview.

Sequencing effect: A form of evaluation bias whereby an employee's ratings are influenced by a relative comparison with the previous employee.

Spontaneous and innovative behaviors: Behaviors that are important for organizational effectiveness but are not typically considered part of an employee's formal job description, such as cooperative actions, creative suggestions, and protective acts.

Zero-sum problem: A form of evaluation bias whereby employee evaluations must fit a specified average or total. For someone to be rated high, someone else must be rated low.

CONCLUDING CASE

Promoting the Best-Qualified

The Burrito Barn Company has twenty-eight fast-food outlets located in the Southwest. Most of the company's employees are young people still in school who work part-time at the minimum-wage rate. Each spring some of the part-time employees are promoted to full-time employees. They receive significantly higher pay and assume supervisory responsibilities. The promotions are decided by each outlet manager, who recommends two or three of the "best-qualified" part-time employees for training to be team supervisors. The training is provided by Alberto Mendiola, the manager of outlet operations for the company, who designed the training program and presents it himself.

Marie Ortega, the personnel manager, has been very impressed with the results of Alberto's two-day supervisor training course, and she has appreciated his initiative in organizing it and presenting it. This year, however, there is a problem. After the promotions were announced, three Asian employees came to Marie to ask why they were

not on the list. They noted that of the seventy-three part-time employees who are being promoted, almost 80 percent are Hispanic and none of them are Asian. Yet only 45 percent of the part-time workers are Hispanic, whereas 20 percent are Asian. The three employees told Marie they had already contacted the EEOC and been told that their complaint is legitimate.

When Marie questioned Alberto about the promotion decisions, he justified them by saying that the managers had been instructed to select the "best qualified." He also reminded her that each employee is evaluated on the company's performance-evaluation form and that it is not discriminatory to base promotion decisions on performance.

The performance-evaluation form is a simple graphic rating scale that measures work habits, attitude, appearance, punctuality, and overall performance. To learn how effectively the form is being used, Marie called some of the outlet managers. She was dismayed to learn that the form is used in only about half the outlets and that even where it is used the managers generally do not refer to it before deciding whom to recommend for promotion. The managers said they do not need to look at this data to decide who is best qualified. Marie also talked to some of the employees who were being promoted and became even further disturbed when they said that their managers could not have recommended their promotions based on performance because their

managers did not work with them and therefore had little opportunity to observe their performances.

Questions:

1. When the EEOC contacts Marie, how can she justify the company's promotion system?
2. Is the system really fair?
3. Is the performance-evaluation process satisfactory?
4. What does Marie need to change?

NOTES

1. Robert W. Goddard, "Is Your Appraisal System Headed for Court?" *Personnel Journal* 68 (January 1988): 114–18.

2. Roy Serpa, "The Often Overlooked Ethical Aspect of Mergers," *Journal of Business Ethics* 7 (May 1988): 359–62.

3. Alan H. Locher and Kenneth S. Teel, "Appraisal Trends," *Personnel Journal* 67 (September 1988): 139–45; Bureau of National Affairs, "Performance Appraisal Programs," *Personnel Policies Forum*, No. 135 (February 1983).

4. Charles Waldo, "Do Performance Appraisals Really Improve Performance?" *Supervision* 49 (November 1988): 3–4.

5. Mo Cayer, Dominic J. DiMattia, and Janis Wingrove, "Conquering Evaluation Fear," *Personnel Administrator* 33 (June 1988): 97–107.

6. William A. Ruch and Thomas E. Hendrick, "A Model for Professional Productivity: Evaluating Purchasing Performance," *National Productivity Review* 7 (Autumn 1988): 285–97.

7. Robert C. Sinclair, "Mood Categorization Breadth and Performance Appraisal: The Effects of Order on Information Acquisition and Affective State on Halo, Accuracy, Information Retrieval and Evaluations," *Organizational Behavior and Human Decision Processes* 42 (August 1988): 22–46.

8. Paul H. Thompson and Gene W. Dalton, "Performance Appraisal: Managers Beware," *Harvard Business Review* (January–February 1970): 149–57.

9. Joseph M. Czajka and Angelo S. DeNisi, "Effects of Emotional Disability and Clear Performance Standards on Performance Ratings," *Academy of Management Journal* 31 (June 1988): 394–404.

10. Daniel B. Turban and Allan P. Jones, "Supervisor-Subordinate Similarity: Types, Affects, and Mechanisms," *Journal of Applied Psychology* 73 (May 1988): 226–34.

11. Asya Pazy, "The Persistence of Pro-Male Bias Despite Identical Information Regarding Causes of Success," *Organizational Behavior and Human Decision Process* 38 (December 1986): 366–77.

12. F. David Schoorman, "Escalation Bias in Performance Appraisals: An Unintended Consequence of Supervisor Participation in Hiring Decisions," *Journal of Applied Psychology* 73 (February 1988): 58–62.

13. *EEOC v. duPont*, 445 F. Suppl. 223, 249 (D. Del. 1977); See Patricia Lineneberger and Timothy J. Keaveny, "Performance Appraisal Standards Used by the Courts," *The Personnel Administrator* 26, no. 5 (May 1981): 89–94; Robert W. Goddard, "Is Your Appraisal System Headed for Court?" *Personnel Journal* 68 (January 1988): 114–18.

14. Beverly Geber, "The Hidden Agenda of Performance Appraisals," *Training* 25 (June 1988): 42–47.

15. Beverly Dugan, "Effects of Assessor Training on Information Use," *Journal of Applied Psychology* 73 (November 1988): 743–48; Jerry W. Hedge and Michael J. Kavanagh, "Improving the Accuracy of Performance Evaluations: Comparison of Three Methods of Performance Appraisor Training," *Journal of Applied Psychology* 73 (February 1988): 68–73; Elaine D. Pulakos, "The Development of Training Programs to Increase Accuracy with Different Rating Tasks," *Organizational Behavior and Human Decision Processes* 38 (August 1986): 76–91.

16. Alan H. Locher and Kenneth S. Teel, "Appraisal Trends," *Personnel Journal* 67 (September 1988): 139–45.

17. Richard L. Prather, "Extending the Life of Performance Appraisal Systems," *Personnel Journal* 53, no. 10 (October 1974): 739–43. See also, Wayne K. Kirchner and Donald J. Reisberg, "Differences Between Better and Less-Effective Supervisors in Appraisal of Subordinates," *Personnel Psychology* 15, no. 3 (Autumn 1962): 295–302.

18. Ronald R. Sims, "Training Supervisors in Employee Performance Appraisals," *Journal of European and Industrial Training* 12, no. 8 (1988): 26–31.

19. *Baxter* v. *Savannah Sugar Refining Corp.*, 495 F2d 437 (1974); *Brito* v. *Zia Co.*, 478, F2d, 1200 (1973); *Albemarle Paper Co.* v. *Moody*, 95 SCt 2362 (1974); *Rowe* v. *General Motors Corp.* 457 F2d 348 (1972); *Wade* v. *Mississippi Cooperative Extension Service;* 528 F2d 508 (1976). See also *Jenkins* v. *Caddo-Bossies Assn.*, 570 F.2d 1227, 1228 (5th Civ. 1978); *Taylor* v. *Weaver Oil & Gas Corp.*, 18 FEP Cases 23, 31 (S.D. Tex. 1978).

20. George A. Marcoulides and Bryant R. Mills, "Employee Performance Appraisals: A New Technique," *View of Public Personnel Administration* 8 (Summer 1988): 105–13.

21. Personal communication from the commanding officer.

22. Robert L. Thorndike, *Personnel Selection: Test and Measurement Techniques* (New York: Wiley, 1949); Robert Guion, *Personnel Testing* (New York: McGraw Hill, 1965), p. 113; James A. Buford, Jr., Bettye B. Burkhalter, and Grover T. Jacobs, "Link Job Descriptions to Performance Appraisals," *Personnel Journal* 67 (June 1988): 132–40.

23. John P. Campbell, Marvin D. Dunnette, Edward L. Lawler, and Karl E. Weick, *Managerial Behavior, Performance, and Effectiveness* (New York: McGraw Hill, 1970), Chapters 5–7.

24. Barry R. Nathan and Ralph A. Alexander, "A Comparison of Criteria for Test Validation: A Meta-Analytic Investigation," *Personnel Psychology* 41 (Autumn 1988): 517–35.

25. Stanley E. Seashore, B.P. Indik, and B.S. Georgopolos, "Relationships Among Criteria of Job Performance," *Journal of Applied Psychology* 44, no. 3 (June 1960): 195–202.

26. Daniel Katz and Robert Kahn, *The Social Psychology of Organizations* (New York: Wiley, 1966, rev. 1978), Chapter 12.

27. Joseph E. Collins, "OTA Report On Electronic Monitoring," *Data Management* 25 (December 1987): 7–8; Don Nichols, "Monitoring Employees: When Measurement Goes Too Far," *Incentive Marketing* 161 (December 1987): 27–30, 92–93; Peter A. Susser, "Electronic Monitoring in the Private Sector: How Closely Should Employers Supervise Their Workers," *Employee Relations Law Journal* 13 (Spring 1988): 575–98.

28. Richard Girard, "Is There A Need for Performance Appraisals?" *Personnel Journal* 67 (August 1988): 89–90; William M. Fox, "Improving Performance Appraisal Systems," *National Productivity Review* 7 (Winter 1987–88): 20–27.

29. Judith Havemann, "Worker Appraisals: On The High Side," *Washington Post* (July 21, 1988): A21.

30. Richard L. Prather, "Extending the Life of Performance Appraisal Systems," *Personnel Journal* 53 (October 1974): 734–43.

31. Bureau of National Affairs, "Performance Appraisal Programs" (Washington DC: BNA) PPF Survey No. 135, February 1983.

32. Campbell et al., *Managerial Behavior*, Chapters 5–9.

33. Campbell et al., *Managerial Behavior*, Chapter 6.

34. John B. Miner, "Development and Application of the Rated Ranking Technique in Performance Appraisal," *Journal of Occupational Psychology* 61 (December 1988): 291–305.

35. J. C. Flanagan, "The Critical Incidents Technique," *Psychological Bulletin* 51 (1954): 327–58.

36. J. C. Flanagan, "Defining the Requirements of the Executive's Job," *Personnel* 28 (1951): 28–35.

37. Charles A. Rarick and Gerald Baxter, "Behaviorally Anchored Rating Scales (BARS): An Effective Performance Appraisal Approach," *Advanced Management Journal* 51 (Winter 1986): 36–39; "Behaviorally Anchored Rating Scales: A Method for Effective Management," *Small Business Report* 11 (February 1986): 71–77.

38. Philip G. Benson, Ronald M. Buckley, and Sid Hall, "The Impact of Rating Scale Format on Rater Accuracy: An Evaluation of the Mixed Standards Scale," *Journal of Management* 14 (September 1988): 415–23; John P. Campbell, R. Darvey, Marvin D. Dunnette, and L.V. Hellervik, "The Development and Evaluation of Behaviorally Based Rating Scales," *Journal of Applied Psychology* 57, no. 1 (1973); L. Foglie, Charles L. Hulin, and Milton R. Blood, "Development of First Level Behavioral Job Criteria," *Journal of Applied Psychology* 55 (1971): 3–8; Donald P. Schwab, Herbert G. Heneman, and T. A. DeCotis, "Behaviorally Anchored Rating Scales: A Review of the Literature," *Personnel Psychology* 28, no. 4 (Winter 1975): 549–62; Patricia C. Smith and L. M. Kendall, "Retranslation of Expectations: An Approach to the Construction of Unambiguous Anchors for Rating Scales," *Journal of Applied Psychology* 47 (1963): 149–55.

39. Peter J. Pecora and Jeff Hunter, "Performance Appraisal in Child Welfare: Comparing the MBO and BARS Methods," *Administration in Social Work* 12, no. 1 (1988): 55–72. See also Luis R. Gomez-Mejia, "Evaluating Employee Performance: Does the Appraisal Instrument Make a Difference?" *Journal of Organizational Behavior Management* 9, no. 2 (1988): 155–72.

40. Gary P. Latham, C. H. Fay, and L. M. Saari, "The Development of Behavioral Observation Scales for Appraising the Performance of Foremen," *Personnel Psychology* 32 (1979): 299–311.

41. Anaron Tziner and Richard Kopelman, "Effects of Rating Format on Goal-Setting Dimensions: A Field Experiment," *Journal of Applied Psychology* 73 (May 1988): 323–26.

42. Lee W. Cozan, "Forced-Choice: Better Than Other Rating Methods?" *Personnel* 36, no. 3 (May–June 1955): 80–83; Donald E. Sisson, "Forced Choice: The New Army Rating," *Personnel Psychology* 1, no. 3 (Autumn 1948): 365–81.

43. Lisa Crumrine, "Subordinate Appraisals," *Credit Union Executive* 28 (Summer 1988): 18–20.

44. Harry Levinson, "How They Rate the Boss," *Across the Board* 24 (June 1987): 53–57; William G. Dyer, "Management Profiling: A Disparity Model for Developing Motivation for Change," presented at the New Technology in Organization Development Conference-ASTD, New Orleans, February 18, 1974.

45. Joani Nelson-Horchlar, "Performance Appraisals," *Industry Week* 237 (September 19, 1988): 61–63.

46. Glenn M. McEvoy, Paul. F. Buller, and Steven R. Rognaar, "A Jury of One's Peers," *Personnel Administrator* 33 (May 1988): 94–101; E. P. Hollander, "Buddy Ratings: Military Research and Industrial Implications," *Personnel Psychology* 7, no. 3 (Autumn 1954): 385–93; E. P. Hollander, "Peer Nominations as a Predictor of the Pass-Fail Criterion in Naval Air Training," *Journal of Applied Psychology* 38 (1954): 150–53; Harry E. Roadman, "An Industrial Use of Peer Ratings," *Journal of Applied Psychology* 48, no. 4 (1964): 211–14; William P. Ferris and Peter W. Hess, "Peer Evaluation of Student Interaction in Organization Behavior and Other Courses," *The Organizational Behavior Teaching Review* 9, no. 4 (1984–85): 74–82.

47. Juliene M. Morath, "The Clinical Nurse Specialist: Evaluation Issues," *Nursing Management* 19 (March 1988): 72–80.

48. MaryBeth DeGregorio and Cynthia D. Fisher, "Providing Performance Feedback: Reactions to Alternate Methods," *Journal of Management* 14 (December 1988): 605–16; Jiing-Lin Farn, James D. Werbel, and Arthur G. Bedeian, "An Empirical Investigation of Self-Appraisal-Based Performance Evaluation," *Personnel Psychology* 41 (Spring 1988): 141–56; John W. Lowrie, "Your Performance: Appraise It Yourself!" *Personnel* 66 (January 1989): 21–23.

49. George C. Thornton, "The Relationship Between Supervisory and Self-Appraisals of Executive Performance," *Personnel Psychology* (Winter 1968): 441–55. See also Glen A. Bassett and Herbert H. Meyer, "Performance Appraisal Based on Self-Review," *Personnel Psychology* 21 (Winter 1968): 421–30.

50. Francine Alexander, "Performance Appraisals," *Small Business Reports* 14 (March 1989): 20–29.

51. Donald J. Campbell and Cynthia Lee, "Self-Appraisal in Performance Evaluation: Development vs. Evaluation," *Academy of Management Review* 13 (April 1988): 302–14.

52. Barbara LaBarbara, "Performance Appraisals: Management's Yardstick," *Supervision* 49 (August 1988): 14–19.

53. William M. Fox, "Improving Performance Appraisal Systems," *National Productivity Review* 7 (Winter 1987–88): 20–27; Jon L. Pearce and Lyman W. Porter, "Employee Responses to Formal Performance Appraisal Feedback," *Journal of Applied Psychology* 71 (May 1986): 211–18.

54. Alan Fowler, "New Directions in Performance Pay," *Personnel Management* 20 (November 1988): 30–34.

55. Robert Wareing and Janet Stockdale, "Decision-Making in the Promotion Interview: An Empirical Study," *Personnel Review* 16, no. 4 (1987): 26–32.

56. Douglas Hall and Benjamin Schneider, *Organizational Climates and Careers: The Work Lives of Priests* (New York: Academic Press, 1974), pp. 30–31, 98–102.

57. Marvin Jolson, "Criteria for Promotion and Tenure," *Academy of Management Journal* 17, no. 1 (1974): 149–54; David Katz, "Faculty Salaries, Promotions, and Productivity at a Large University," *American Economic Review* (June 1973): 469–77.

58. Ronald Taylor, "Preferences of Industrial Managers for Information Sources in Making Promotion Decisions," *Journal of Applied Psychology* 60, no. 2 (1975): 269–72.

59. Albert Glickman, *Top Management Development and Succession* (New York: Macmillan-Arkville, 1968).

60. Stephen J. Carroll and Henry L. Tosi, *Management By Objectives: Applications and Research* (New York: Macmillan, 1973); George L. Morrisey, *Management by Objectives and Results* (Reading, Mass.: Addison-Wesley, 1970); George S. Odiorne, *Management by Objectives: A System of Managerial Leadership* (New York: Pitman, 1965); Peter F. Drucker, *Managing for Results* (New York: Harper, 1964).

61. Carroll and Tosi, *Management by Objectives*; Morrisey, *Management by Objectives: Results*; Odiorne, *A System of Managerial Leadership*, Anthony P. Raia, *Managing by Objectives* (Glenview, Ill.: Scott, Foresman, 1974); Edward C. Schleh, *Management by Results* (New York: McGraw-Hill, 1961).

62. Peter F. Drucker, *The Practice of Management* (New York: Harper, 1954).

63. Raia, *Managing by Objectives.*

64. Jeffrey S. Kane and Kimberly A. Freeman, "MBO and Performance Appraisal: A Mixture That's Not a Solution, Part I," *Personnel* 63 (December 1986): 26–36.

65. Robert D. Pritchard, Philip L. Roth, Steven D. Jones, Patricia J. Galgay, and Margaret D. Watson, "Designing a Goal-Setting System to Enhance Performance: A Practical Guide," *Organizational Dynamics* 17 (Summer 1988): 69–78.

66. Dennis Daley, "Performance Appraisal and Organizational Success: Public Employee Perceptions in an MBO-Based Appraisal System," *Review of Public Personnel Administration* 9 (Fall 1988): 17–27.

67. James E. Svatko, "Simplifying the Performance Appraisal," *Small Business Reports* 14 (March 1989): 30–33; Judith F. Bryan and Edwin H. Locke, "Goal Setting as a Means of Increasing Motivation," *Journal of Applied Psychology* 51 (1967): 274–77; Edwin A. Locke, "Toward a Theory of Task Motivation and Incentives," *Organizational Behavior and Human Performance* 3 (1968): 157–89; A. C. Stedry and Emanual Kay, "The Effect of Goal Difficulty on Performance: A Field Experiment," *Behavioral Science* 11 (1966): 459–70.

68. Lester Coch and John R. P. French, Jr., "Overcoming Resistance to Change," *Human Relations* 1 (1948): 512–32; John R. P. French, Joachim Israel, Jr., and Dagfinn As, "An Experiment on Participation in a Norwegian Factory," *Human Relations* 13 (1960): 1–13; John R. P. French, Eman-

ual Kay, and Herbert H. Meyer, "Participation and the Appraisal System" *Human Relations* 19 (1966): 3–19.

69. John P. Singleton, Ephraim R. McLean, and Edward N. Altman, "Measuring Information Systems Performance: Experience with the Management by Result System at Security Pacific Bank," *MIS Quarterly* 12 (June 1988): 325–37; David J. Cherrington and J. Owen Cherrington, "Budgets, Performance, and Appraisal," *Business Horizons* 17 (December 1974): 35–44; Y. Ijiri, J. D. Kinard, and F. B. Putney, "An Integrated Evaluation System for Budget Forecasting and Operating Performance with a Classified Budgeting Bibliography," *Journal of Accounting Research* 6, no. 1 (Spring 1968): 1–28; J. Ronon and J. L. Livingstone, "An Expectancy Theory Approach to the Motivational Impacts of Budgets," *Accounting Review* 50 (October 1975): 671–85.

70. Louis A. Allen, "Working Better with Japanese Managers," *Management Review* 77 (November 1988): 55–56.

71. James B. Stull, "Giving Feedback to Foreign-Born Employees," *Management Solutions* 33 (July 1988): 42–45.

72. P. Christopher Earley, "Trust, Perceived Importance of Praise and Criticism, and Work Performance: An Examination of Feedback in the United States and England," *Journal of Management* 12 (Winter 1986): 457–73. See also Clive Morton, "Bringing Manager and Managed Together," *Industrial Society* (September 1988): 26–27.

Principles of Training and Development

Learning Objectives

After studying this chapter, you should be able to:

1. Explain the difference between training and education and how both processes are important to training and development programs.
2. Describe a systems model for training and development, and explain how training interacts with other human resource functions.
3. Describe the kinds of information that are important for assessing training needs.
4. Describe the components of good behavioral objectives for training, and write a behavioral objective that contains each of these components.
5. Describe social cognitive theory, and explain how it differs from operant conditioning.
6. List the major principles of learning, and explain how they influence the rate of learning.
7. Identify the different levels of learning, and explain the conditions that facilitate each type of learning.

Chapter Outline

Role of Training and Development
Training versus Education / Kinds of Training / Benefits of Training

The Systems Approach to Training and Development
Relevant Considerations / A Systems Model for Training / Assessing Training Needs / Behavioral Objectives

Theories of Learning
Operant Conditioning / Social Cognitive Theory / Adult Learning Theory

Principles of Learning
Stimulus: Meaningful Organization of Materials / Response: Practice and Repetition / Motivation: Reinforcement and Active Participation / Feedback: Knowledge of Results / Transfer of Training / Learning Curves / Forgetting

Levels of Learning

Motor Response / Rote Learning / Learning Ideas / Value Internalization

International HRM

I N T R O D U C T O R Y   C A S E

Getting Trainees off Plateaus

Jolene's, Inc., manufactures women's clothing. The sewing machines they use have the capacity to run about five times faster than an ordinary home sewing machine. Each week the company conducts a training program for between eight and twelve new operators that consists of four days of instruction and practice in a training room. The operators are paid a piece-rate incentive plus a training bonus to encourage them while they are learning. The training bonus starts at $2.50 per hour and is reduced by $.25 each week.

After four days of training the operators start in actual production and within sixty days they are expected to be producing at least 80 percent of standard. About 50 percent of the new operators are able to achieve that level of proficiency without much difficulty. About 15 percent discover that they lack the necessary skills or temperament and quit.

A critical point in the training is when the operators reach 55 to 60 percent of standard because most of them hit a plateau at that point. About 10 percent of the new operators never exceed this plateau and are terminated after twelve weeks. The length of time other operators spend on this plateau seems to vary dramatically.

The training director thinks the problem of the plateau is that the operators never get the feel of the machines going fast and do not feel the rhythm of coordinating their hands and feet. Since they are too concerned about making errors that they will be required to repair, the production manager has proposed paying them to spend an afternoon practicing on scrap pieces of cloth to get the feel of their hands and feet operating simultaneously with the machines going full speed.

The production manager objects to the idea of practicing on scrap pieces because she believes the practice will encourage carelessness and reinforce bad habits. Furthermore, she thinks paying the operators for sewing scrap pieces is an unnecessary expense. She thinks the plateau problem is a lack of motivation and recommends reducing the time employees receive a training bonus.

Questions:

1. What effect do you think the two strategies proposed by the training director and production manager will have on productivity and employee attitudes?
2. What causes learning plateaus when acquiring new skills?
3. What can a trainer or a learner do to shorten or eliminate a learning plateau?

ROLE OF TRAINING AND DEVELOPMENT

Training and development are important activities in all aspects of life. Virtually everything people do has been learned. Each day people are faced with new situations and are forced to respond appropriately to them. This applies to young children learning to walk and talk, to students learning to spell or do calculus, to employees learning to run a new machine, or to managers learning to communicate effectively.

Training and development are important activities in all organizations, large and small. Every organization, regardless of size, needs to have well-trained employees who are prepared to perform their jobs. Approximately 3 million new employees enter the work force each year and need to be trained. Even those who have been trained in professional and technical fields require orientation training to help them understand their specific roles in an organization. Present employees also need training. Because of the rapidly expanding technology and the growth of new knowledge, there is a need for continual retraining of experienced workers to perform new and changed jobs.

In previous years, much of the responsibility for providing training and education was assumed by the schools. In recent years, however, business organizations have begun to assume a larger share of the responsibility for providing both specific job training and general education. The growth of training and development activities in organizations is evidenced by the amount of money that is spent on these activities.

The training and development expenditures by businesses are conservatively estimated to be roughly equivalent to the total cost of higher education. And when informal training is included, which consists of unbudgeted on-the-job training, the total training cost is almost as great as the cost of all formal education.[1]

TRAINING VERSUS EDUCATION

The terms training, development, education, and learning all refer to a similar process. It is the process that enables people to acquire new knowledge, to learn skills, and to perform behaviors in a new way. Although training and education are similar, a distinction usually is made between them. **Training** refers to the acquisition of specific skills or knowledge. Training programs attempt to teach trainees how to perform particular activities or a specific job. *Development* usually refers to improving the intellectual or emotional abilities needed to do a better job. **Education**, on the other hand, is much more general and attempts to provide students with general knowledge that can be applied in many different settings.

To illustrate the differences, teaching an employee how to use a specific computer program that has already been written to produce a computerized payroll is an example of training, but teaching an employee how to program a computer using basic computer language is an example of education. Specific instruction on how to produce a payroll helps the employee perform a specific activity, but learning how to use a computer language helps the employee obtain general skills that can be applied to many different situations.

Another distinction between training and education concerns their effects on the range of responses. Training tends to narrow the range of responses so that all employees who have been trained will make the same response in a specific situation. Education, on the other hand, tends to broaden the range of responses so that individuals who have obtained a general education will respond to a particular situation in a variety of different ways.

Although we usually associate education with formal schooling, it is also an important part of the learning that occurs in business. Many of the training and development programs in industry combine both education and training. Management development programs, in particular, try to teach general knowledge that managers can apply in a variety of situations. The trend for many years has been to provide more general education in training and development programs. This trend probably will continue because the growing complexity of society requires employees who can think for themselves and adapt to new situations.

KINDS OF TRAINING

Training is a complex topic to study because there are many different kinds of training activities. To understand the role of training, it is important to appreciate the different kinds of training and the purpose of each. Teaching managers how to make effective decisions, for example, is significantly different from teaching a sewing machine operator how to sew pockets. The major kinds of training programs include the following:

1. *Orienting and informing employees.* The purpose of this training is to disseminate information and to provide direction and new knowledge. This training includes telling new employees about the company's benefit program, calling sales representatives together to explain a new product line, or explaining a new organizational structure to the work force. Orientation training is described in Chapter 9.

2. *Skill development.* Many situations call for new skills to be learned. New employees must acquire the skills needed to perform their jobs, and experienced employees need to acquire new skills when their jobs are changed or when new equipment is introduced.

3. *Safety training.* This training is designed to prevent accidents and is required by law. Employees should never be allowed to perform any tasks until they know how to perform them safely. In industries where hazardous materials are used, the Occupational Safety and Health Act requires specific training that explains why the materials are hazardous and how to use them safely. In some situations this training must be repeated annually. Safety training is discussed further in Chapter 15.

4. *Professional and technical education.* The purpose of this training is to avoid professional and technical obsolescence. Because of the rapid expansion of new knowledge, professional and technical employees must be retrained periodically. This training might involve imparting knowledge that has recently been discovered or it might concern a related field of professional expertise. Some professions, including law, accounting, medicine, and dentistry, require their members to obtain continuous education and training to practice their profession. Accredited human resource professionals are required to demonstrate what they have done to upgrade their knowledge to be reaccredited every three years.

5. *Supervisory and managerial training.* Supervisors and managers need training in how to make administrative decisions and how to work with people. This training involves such topics as decision making, communication, problem solving, and motivation.

Because so many different kinds of training exist, training specialists need to carefully determine the training needs of the organization.

BENEFITS OF TRAINING

Training plays a large part in determining the effectiveness and efficiency of an organization. A successful training and development program will achieve the following benefits:

1. Improve the quality and quantity of productivity.
2. Reduce the learning time required for employees to reach acceptable standards of performance.
3. Create more favorable attitudes, loyalty, and cooperation.
4. Satisfy human resource planning requirements.
5. Reduce the number and cost of accidents.
6. Help employees in their personal development and advancement.

These benefits assist both the individual and the organization. An effective training program is an important aid in career planning and is often viewed as a cure for organizational ills. When productivity is low, when absenteeism and turnover are high, and when employees express dissatisfaction, many managers think the obvious solution is a company-wide training program. Unfortunately, the benefits of training are sometimes overestimated. Training programs do not cure all organizational problems, although they certainly have the potential to improve many situations if they are conducted properly.

THE SYSTEMS APPROACH TO TRAINING AND DEVELOPMENT

Training activities do not occur in isolation; they are related to and influenced by other human resource functions, especially staffing, performance evaluation, compensation, and employee relations (as illustrated in Figure 8.1). Consequently, training activities should be designed and evaluated in view of the demands of the overall organization. An analysis of training and how it interacts with other organizational activities is called a systems approach to training.

RELEVANT CONSIDERATIONS

In designing and presenting a training program, planners should consider the following questions.

1. *Why should an organization sponsor a training and development program?* Before a training program is presented, someone should ask, "Why should this training be presented?" Companies decide to sponsor training programs for a variety of reasons, both good and bad. One bad reason is because the competition is doing it and managers think they will fall behind unless they conduct the same training. Another bad reason is because it is

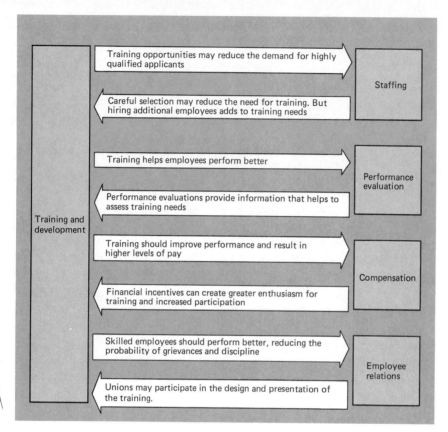

FIGURE 8.1 Training and development.

popular. Some training programs, like management fads, are highly advertised, and management buys them because they seem like the "latest thing." Other training programs are conducted because of real or perceived pressure from government agencies, especially the EEOC and OSHA. The best reason, of course, for conducting a training program is because it contributes to the organization's goals and objectives and meets defined needs.

2. *What types of training and development should be offered?* Since training is supposed to make an organization more effective, the appropriate type of training is that which improves employee performance. Training programs that are designed merely to present interesting information are generally a waste of time and money. Training programs that attempt to change basic personality traits are also inappropriate. Basic personality changes are difficult to obtain, and training programs designed to change personalities or leadership styles are generally ineffective and highly questionable.

3. *Who gets trained?* The obvious answer to this question should be the individuals who need training. The evidence indicates, however, that the individuals who are most in need of training typically do not receive it. In one study, for example, the activities of

1,247 young men were observed over a four-year period. Only one out of seven individuals was selected for training during this period of time. The companies tended to select those men with the best educational backgrounds, who came from the highest socioeconomic groups. In essence, those who already had the most training were selected for additional training, and as a result, the gap between the trained and untrained widened.[2] Other surveys have shown similar results. The individuals who have the highest skill levels are the ones selected for further training, while disadvantaged employees, minorities, and individuals with low skill levels are the ones who either choose not to participate in training programs or are not selected by their companies.[3]

4. *Who will supply the training and development?* Should the training be provided in-house by the human resource department or by external sources such as consultants? The preparation of in-house training programs requires an investment of time and effort, and many organizations lack the expertise to provide the kind of technical training that is needed. However, external training programs frequently are much more expensive than internal ones.

5. *How are training and development evaluated?* Most training programs are evaluated very informally: participants are asked how much they enjoyed the experience. These subjective impressions largely ignore the basic reasons for presenting the training. Instead, a careful evaluation should be made based on the objectives of the training and the goals of the organization. Training evaluation is discussed further in Chapter 9.

A SYSTEMS MODEL FOR TRAINING

A model showing how training programs should be developed and implemented is presented in Figure 8.2. This figure illustrates the three phases of training: (1) an assessment phase, (2) a training and development phase, and (3) an evaluation phase.[4]

In the assessment phase, the need for training and development is examined, as well as the resources available to provide the training both within the organization and in the external environment. The assessment should include a consideration of who should be trained, what sort of training they will need, and how such training will benefit the organization. The objectives of the training program are derived from the assessment. These objectives play a vital role in both the development of the training program and its subsequent evaluation.

In the training and development phase, the training is designed and presented. The training should contain activities and learning experiences that will satisfy the objectives established in the assessment phase. Many different training activities, including both on-the-job and off-the-job activities, can be used, depending on the objectives of the training. A description of various on-the-job and off-the-job training techniques is presented in Chapter 9.

After the training has been conducted, the evaluation occurs. The first step in evaluating the success of a training program is deciding what the evaluation criteria are. These criteria should be based on the initial objectives of the training. For example, was the purpose of the training to disseminate new information, to change certain behaviors, to acquire new skills, or to change specific attitudes? Once the criteria have been established, the trainees can be evaluated to determine whether the training was successful.

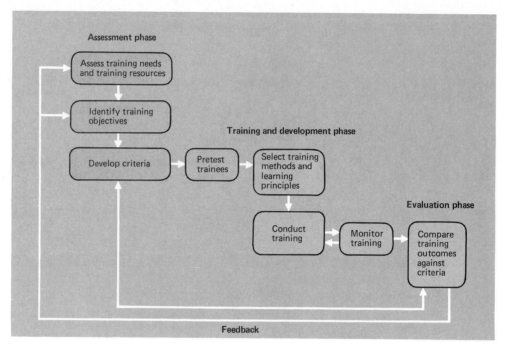

FIGURE 8.2 A systems model for training.

The evaluation also should assess whether the learning that occurred in the training program transferred to the actual job situation.

The feedback arrow at the bottom of Figure 8.2 emphasizes the idea that training should be ongoing. Training does not have a definite beginning and end; it is an ongoing process of assessing needs, presenting programs, and evaluating results to determine whether organizational needs have been satisfied. Because it is an ongoing process, the degree to which a training program has met its objectives cannot really be assessed at one particular point in time. Instead, the effects of training have to be viewed in terms of their short-term and long-term implications.

ASSESSING TRAINING NEEDS

Training programs are intended to correct performance deficiencies. A performance deficiency refers to a discrepancy between the actual behavior and the behavior that is desired. If an employee is not performing at the expected level, a performance discrepancy exists. Training programs are usually proposed as solutions to such discrepancies; however, all performance deficiencies are not necessarily caused by inadequate training. Performance problems may be caused by a variety of problems, including a lack of ability, insufficient effort, an inefficient organizational or task structure, and inadequate job knowledge. A need for training is indicated only if the performance deficiency is caused by inadequate job knowledge.

The development of a sound training program requires a systematic approach to gathering and interpreting data and the training needs. A good assessment of training needs should include an analysis of: (1) the organization's goals, (2) the skills needed by the work force to accomplish these goals, and (3) the strengths and weaknesses of the current work force. A careful analysis of these three issues will provide a training manager with the necessary information to design effective training activities that will eliminate performance deficiencies. The analyses that the training manager should perform are organizational analysis, operational analysis, and personnel analysis.[5]

ORGANIZATIONAL ANALYSIS

An **organizational analysis** is an examination of the kinds of problems that an organization is experiencing and where they are located within the organization. The specific areas of the organization that need to be examined are organizational-effective indices, personnel succession planning, and the organizational climate.

1. Organizational-effectiveness indices are such measures as labor costs, production efficiency, quality, machine maintenance, accidents, turnover, and absenteeism. Although these measures can be influenced by many different forces, the organization should consider the possibility that they are influenced by inadequate training.
2. Personnel succession planning is a consideration of the job openings that presently exist in an organization, the openings that are likely to occur in the future, and how these positions might be filled. If positions are to be filled from within, training will be needed to prepare employees for promotion. If positions are to be filled by hiring from without, the organization will need to make a careful analysis of the labor market and the likelihood of finding qualified replacements.
3. Organizational-climate analysis refers to an examination of the feelings, opinions, beliefs, and attitudes that members of an organization have about the organization. An organizational climate that contains many negative feelings may indicate a need for skill training to help employees perform their jobs more effectively or orientation training to clarify misunderstandings.

The organizational climate needs to be consistent with the kind of training that is presented. A training program that attempts to develop behaviors that are inconsistent with the organizational climate will not be successful. For example, when supervisors receive human relations training that attempts to create a participative leadership style, the training will create problems if the organizational climate does not support it. If this is the situation, the supervisors' new behaviors will not be accepted when they return to their jobs.

OPERATIONAL ANALYSIS

An **operational analysis** identifies the kinds of skills and behaviors required of the incumbents of a given job and the standards of performance that must be met. An operational analysis largely relies on the ability of an expert to identify the appropriate behaviors and the quantity and quality of these behaviors required to perform in a job.

An operational analysis is somewhat similar to a job analysis except it is employee-centered, not job-centered; it focuses on what an employee must do to perform a job. The value of an operational analysis is that it not only specifies the training objectives but also indicates what will be the criteria for judging the effectiveness of training.

PERSONNEL ANALYSIS

The objective of a **personnel analysis** is to examine how well individual employees are performing their jobs. Training should be provided for those who need it. Assigning all employees to a training program, regardless of their skill levels, is a waste of organizational resources and creates an unpleasant situation for employees who do not need training. A personnel analysis requires a careful examination of each individual's skills and abilities. Each person should be examined individually to identify deficiencies that could be corrected through training.

Data on training needs can be obtained through discussion with supervisors and work groups and by reviewing performance evaluations and succession plans. A training-needs-assessment questionnaire can also provide useful information to assist in designing cost-effective training programs. Special questionnaires have been developed to assess the training needs of supervisors and managers.[6]

BEHAVIORAL OBJECTIVES

The final step in conducting a training-needs analysis is to translate the needs into **behavioral objectives.** When the training needs are assessed, the trainer should try to present the results in behavioral terms. The needs analysis should include the specific results desired from training, and the criteria for evaluating the outcomes of the training activities should be specified in advance. Determining training needs in terms of the specific behaviors that the learners are expected to acquire is not easy. Managers rarely think in behavioral terms and usually require assistance in formulating training outcomes in such terms.

The following list is an illustration of poor behavioral objectives.

As a result of completing this course managers will increase their effectiveness in learning how:

1. To think like a manager in identifying personal and company goals.
2. To sharpen their oral and written communication skills.
3. To learn the art of making sound decisions.
4. To discover proven methods for planning and organizing.
5. To be more productive using time-management techniques.

The problem with these objectives is that they fail to specify what terminal behaviors the trainees should display at the end of the training program. They describe topics and concepts rather than behaviors. For example, rather than indicating that the supervisors will become "sensitive to the feelings of others," a behavioral objective would state: "In reprimanding employees, supervisors will direct their remarks to the employees' behaviors rather than criticize the employees personally." Being sensitive to others is a personality trait of a supervisor, not a behavioral objective.

A good behavioral objective possesses three basic attributes. First, the objective is described in specific behavioral terms, using an active verb such as *to make, to construct, to adjust, to describe,* or *to list.* For example, there is an important difference between saying that a trainee will *know* how to manage time and saying that the trainee will *make a list* of things that need to be done, *assign a priority* to each item, *make an agenda* for committee meetings, and *schedule quiet time* to study important issues.

Second, a good behavioral objective specifies the standard of performance. The standard of performance should be expressed in terms of number, degree, and accuracy.

Third, a good behavioral objective specifies the relevant constraints and time limitations for performing the behavior. For example: The trainee will be able to enter numeric data on a computer keyboard at the rate of 200 strokes per minute, with less than 1 percent errors for a period of twelve minutes.

The following list of objectives for a safety-training program for a supervisor is an example of good behavioral objectives.

> After completing the safety training, supervisors should be able to do the following without referring to the safety manual:
>
> 1. List, within five minutes, all of the hazardous materials that are present in the workplace.
> 2. Identify, within five minutes, the maximum exposure limits to all of the hazardous materials in their department and at least 80 percent of the materials outside their department.
> 3. Teach subordinates how to use all materials safely so they do not exceed the maximum exposure limits.
> 4. Explain the physiological effects of the hazardous materials they and their subordinates handle, using proper medical terminology.
> 5. Identify, in both their early and mature stages, the symptoms that result from excessive exposure to these hazardous materials.

THEORIES OF LEARNING

Learning refers to a relatively permanent change in behavior that occurs as a result of experience or practice. Two of the major theories explaining how this process occurs are operant conditioning and social cognitive theory. Although there are important differences in how these two theories view cognitive thought processes, both emphasize the importance of reinforcement in changing behavior and both postulate similar conditions to facilitate learning. A working knowledge of both theories is essential for understanding the principles of learning and for designing an effective training program. A separate theory has also been proposed to explain adult learning. This theory contributes to our understanding of the conditions that facilitate learning even though the same conditions seem to apply to learners of all ages.

OPERANT CONDITIONING

Operant conditioning theory developed during the 1940s and 1950s as a result of B. F. Skinner's research on animals, particularly pigeons and rats.[7] The behavior of animals was observed in a controlled environment where the variables that influenced their behavior could be isolated and examined. Extensive research has extended the principles of operant conditioning to humans and helps us understand human behavior. Operant conditioning focuses strictly on observable behavior rather than on motives, feelings, and other internal processes.

In operant conditioning, behavior is analyzed as a series of responses performed by an organism, either animal or human. Learning consists of getting the organism to make a particular response or series of responses when the appropriate stimulus is presented. Some responses are simple, such as typing and some assembly-line work, while other response patterns are complex, such as solving a calculus equation or supervising a work group. To change an organism's behavior or to motivate it to learn a new response, the trainer identifies the desired response and selectively reinforces it. The response must be compatible with the physical abilities of the organism. Rats cannot be trained to fly, and managers cannot be trained to be in two places at the same time or to make their days twenty-six hours long.

If the organism already knows how to make the correct response but needs to learn when to do it, training consists of creating the stimulus environment, getting the organism to make the correct response, and then reinforcing it. This process is diagrammed as

$$S \longrightarrow R \quad\text{————— Reinforcement}$$

In the diagram, S represents the stimulus environment, and R, the response. An illustration of this training situation would be learning to type, which is basically learning when to push the right keys. The most important part of the stimulus environment should be the manuscript to be typed. When trainees make the correct response, they should be reinforced to strengthen the association between the stimulus and the response. The reinforcement could be verbal praise from an instructor or the feedback that tells trainees they have made the correct response.

When the organism does not already know how to make the correct response, two important processes are involved in training: chaining and shaping. **Chaining** consists of combining a series of simple responses into a complex response pattern. Changing a flat tire, for example, is not a single response but a combination of several responses. Each response changes the stimulus environment and serves as a cue for the next response. For example, raising the car becomes the stimulus for loosening the lug nuts. Only the final response is reinforced. Chaining can be diagrammed in this way:

$$S_1 \rightarrow R_1 \rightarrow S_2 \rightarrow R_2 \rightarrow S_3 \rightarrow R_3 \rightarrow S_n \rightarrow R_n \quad\text{——Reinforcement}$$

During the initial stages of training, each stimulus-response association is reinforced to strengthen the association and to provide feedback about performance. As training continues, the reinforcements are gradually withheld from the responses in the middle of the chain, and eventually the entire series of responses must be successfully performed before reinforcement occurs.

Shaping refers to the process of acquiring a unique response by reinforcing closer and closer approximations of it. This process is also called the **method of successive approximations.** During the early stages of learning, any response that remotely resembles the correct response is reinforced. However, as training continues, only the responses that most closely approximate the correct response are reinforced. The process of shaping is used extensively in animal training, such as in teaching porpoises to sing, ducks to play the piano, and chickens to play poker. Anyone who has watched trained animals perform in places like Sea World™ or Sea Life Park™ has seen what can be accomplished through shaping. The process of shaping also occurs in human learning, especially in the development of skills, such as in learning to shoot a jump shot, to ice skate, to dance, and to operate a machine.

SOCIAL COGNITIVE THEORY

Social cognitive theory developed primarily from the research of Albert Bandura and others who recognized the need to consider cognitive thought processes in understanding human behavior.[8] Social cognitive theory also developed in part as a reaction against operant conditioning's refusal to consider thinking processes or any other psychological functions that could not be openly observed. Social cognitive theory is also called social learning theory, the title first used by Bandura.

According to social cognitive theory, behavior is influenced by the consequences of the behavior. Responses that are rewarded are more likely to occur in the future, while responses that are punished probably will be terminated. This basic proposition that behavior is influenced by its consequence is central to both operant conditioning and social cognitive theory.

Although both operant conditioning and social cognitive theory maintain that individuals are controlled by the environment, they have different views of the nature and degree of this control. According to operant conditioning, behavior is environmentally determined. The environment contains both the cues for responding as well as the reinforcement; if the environment is changed, the behavior of individuals will change. Although this description is a bit oversimplified, it illustrates why the possibility of cultural engineering and the consequent loss of freedom and dignity are important issues.

According to social cognitive theory, behavior is influenced by the environment, but at the same time, the environment is influenced by an individual's behavior. Here, the environment, behavior, and personal factors, such as skills, values, and physical limitations, interact to influence each other. This interaction is called **reciprocal determinism**.

Another important difference between operant conditioning and social cognitive theory concerns the analysis of thought processes. Social cognitive theory emphasizes the importance of vicarious learning, symbolic thinking, and self-regulatory processes in understanding human behavior. **Vicarious learning**, also called **imitative learning**, refers to the process of learning by observing others—watching how they behave and seeing the consequences that they experience from their behavior. An enormous amount of human learning occurs through observational learning. By observing other people perform complex behaviors, individuals learn quickly and sometimes with very few errors how to perform the same behaviors. Imitative learning is especially superior to trial-and-error learning when mistakes can produce costly or even fatal consequences. When teaching a child to swim, an adolescent to drive a car, or a novice medical student to perform surgery, a trainer cannot rely on trail-and-error learning or simply wait to reinforce correct responses.

The benefits of seeing a model perform a training task were demonstrated in a study of 145 adults who volunteered to spend three hours learning a computer spreadsheet software program. The adults were assigned to either a tutorial or a modeling training program. In the tutorial training, the participants were given diskettes containing step-by-step interactive instructions that they could use in a self-paced training session. In the modeling session, the participants observed a videotape of a middle-aged man demonstrating the use of the software. The tape was stopped during the presentation to allow the participants to practice the procedure. A test at the end of the training indicated that those in the modeling condition had learned significantly more than those in the tutorial condition.[9] Seeing a model perform a learning task appears to help trainees visualize what they are trying to learn and makes learning more relevant and motivating.

In **symbolic learning** the use of symbols, either as words, pictures, or mental images, greatly facilitates learning. Humans are able to use symbols to represent events, to analyze conscious experiences, to communicate with others at any distance in time and space, to imagine, to create, to plan, and to engage in purposeful action. Learning statistics, for example, relies heavily on Arabic and Greek letters as symbols of complex mathematical functions. The use of symbols also contributes to the effectiveness of imitative learning. When a model is present, the trainee can observe the model and immediately try to reproduce the same behavior. But when a model is absent, the trainee must rely on symbols such as mental images, verbal statements, or written descriptions to reproduce the behavior. Without symbols, humans would be unable to engage in reflective thought or meaningful planning. Even conducting a careful analysis of the present environment requires the use of symbols to represent objects, events, and relationships. According to social cognitive theory, symbolic activities cannot be ignored in understanding human behavior.

Another distinguishing feature of social theory is its recognition and analysis of the *self-regulatory* capacities of humans. People are able to effectively control their own behavior by arranging environmental rewards, generating cognitive supports, and producing consequences for their own actions. For example, a student who is dissatisfied with his or her poor academic performance because study time is frittered away talking to friends and participating in student activities can decide to do something about it. The student can find a quiet place to study, remove all distracting materials such as magazines and newspapers, record the hours spent each day in studying, set daily study goals, and give a friend six dollars that can only be returned at the rate of one dollar per day if each day's goals are met. Although individual behavior is influenced by the reinforcers that exist in the environment, individuals have the ability to change their environment both physically and psychologically. Social cognitive theory explains how individuals can monitor and regulate their own behavior. One study examined absenteeism among employees who had been taught self-regulatory skills of assessing problems, setting goals to overcome problems, and rewarding and punishing themselves for goal-accomplishment. The experimental group that learned these self-regulatory skills had significantly higher attendance than a control group, especially among employees who had a high degree of self-efficacy (belief in themselves).[10]

Social cognitive theory claims that most human behavior is learned observationally through modeling and it recognizes the role of both cognitive processes and vicarious experiences. Consequently, social cognitive theory is especially useful in leadership and managerial training. Modeling theory indicates that both desirable as well as undesirable behaviors can be learned through modeling and the challenge to managers is to provide effective models. Behavioral modeling usually involves extensive participant involvement by providing the participants with opportunities to observe the performance of new skills, to practice those skills, and to receive feedback on their performance. In cognitive modeling, it is helpful for the model to verbalize the cognitive thought processes so that the participants know what the model was thinking at each step in the decision process.[11]

ADULT LEARNING THEORY

For several years psychologists believed that the way adults learned was uniquely different from the way children learned, and they encouraged corporate trainers to revise the methods and content of their training. The adult learning process was called **andragogy**, to separate if from pedagogy. *Ped* is a Latin root meaning child, and pedagogy refers to the art of teaching and the methods of instruction that are used. *Andra* derives from a Greek word meaning man, and andragogy refers specifically to how adults learn— suggesting that it differs somehow from pedagogy. This new adult learning theory was especially popular with those who worked in training and development because it served to legitimate their profession and separate them from school teachers.[12]

The following principles of andragogy were proposed. They ostensibly recognize the maturity of the learner.

1. *Learning is experience-based*: The learning process should encourage participants to learn from their past experiences by introducing their experiences into the process and reexamining them in the light of new information. Learning is enhanced when learners can tie what they are learning into previous life events and apply new information to problems they have seen before. The "answers" they are learning in class are more meaningful if they have "asked the questions." If they haven't asked the questions they may not be prepared for the answers.

2. *Learning is problem-centered*: The learning should be problem-centered rather than content-centered. Adults are motivated to learn when the training is immediately relevant to help them solve a current problem. Learning something just because someone says it is important is not as motivating.

3. *Learning is enhanced by active participation*: Learning should permit and encourage active participation of the learner. The learning activities should be experiential rather than just informational. Therefore, the trainers should arrange the physical surroundings to facilitate small-group interaction and promote the sharing of ideas.

4. *Learning is collaborative*: The climate of learning should be collaborative rather than authority-oriented. The psychological climate should cultivate mutual respect and trust between trainers and trainees. The atmosphere should be one of openness, supportiveness, and collaboration.

5. *Learning requires involvement*: The planning, design, and evaluation of learning should be a mutual activity involving both the learner and the instructor. Since people feel more committed to decisions when they participate in making them, learners should play an active role in and be responsible for designing the training.[13]

In spite of the popularity of the andragogy theory, its proponents have been forced to recognize that the learning process is not uniquely different for adults and children. Adults want the information they are learning to be relevant to their current needs, but so also do children, even if their primary need is to pass an exam. Relevance is equally motivating for both adults and children. Likewise, an atmosphere of collaboration, trust, and mutual respect is equally important, regardless of age. Whether the learner should be involved in the design of training does not depend on the learner's age, but on whether the learner is capable of making these decisions. Children are sometimes as capable as adults of deciding what they need to learn and how the learning should be presented. At other times, neither children nor adults may be able to participate meaningfully in the design of their training because they have insufficient knowledge, time, or interest.

Thus andragogy cannot be considered a unique style of adult learning. The only principle of andragogy that seems to have survived as a universal characteristic of adult learners is the quantity and quality of their experience. Although all adults do not share identical experiences, it is safe to assume that with age come unique experiences that prepare older learners to acquire insights that are not available to younger learners.[14]

As the concept of andragogy has been refined, it no longer refers to a theory of adult learning separate from the learning of youth, but to a model of human learning for learners of all ages. As such, andragogy represents a type of experiential, participative, flexible learning that may be appropriate to learners of all ages, depending on the situation. Andragogy may be appropriate for most learning situations, but not all. For example, asking learners to design the instructional process or to learn from each other is inappropriate when the topics are extremely technical, when the nature of the learning calls for one set way, or when the learners face a novel situation.

PRINCIPLES OF LEARNING

The design and presentation of training programs should be based on the principles of learning proposed by both operant conditioning and social cognitive theory. The theoretical differences between these theories should not hide their similarities. Both theories recommend a similar set of principles for learning. Rather than getting lost in a debate over how they differ and which one is right, it is more useful to examine how each can improve training. Both theories contribute immensely by identifying the conditions that facilitate learning. Extensive research from both theories suggests that the following principles of learning are important in designing training programs: stimulus, response, motivation, feedback, transfer, learning curves, and forgetting.

STIMULUS: MEANINGFUL ORGANIZATION OF MATERIALS

To facilitate learning, the stimulus should be easily perceived and meaningfully organized. For example, learning calculus is easiest when the text describing how to do it is written logically so that one idea builds on another. Learning to drive is simplified when the visual field of stop signs, intersections, and other objects can be perceived easily. Learning safety procedures is easiest when they are explained in a logical and systematic order.

Most training environments contain dozens of potential stimuli besides the training material, such as the tone of the trainer's voice, the color of the walls, the noise of traffic passing outside, the feel of the collar that is too tight, and the discomfort that results from sitting too long. Sometimes getting the trainees to respond to the proper stimulus is difficult. If the trainer lectures for over an hour, the trainees probably will not attend to much of what is said, especially if the material is boring or difficult to understand. Even when the training is interesting, the trainees may not respond to the proper stimulus. Training films, for example, are sometimes so entertaining that the key insights are overlooked. In general, training is improved if the stimulus is meaningfully organized so that the trainees can easily perceive it. Sometimes telling the trainees what they are supposed to observe is helpful.

RESPONSE: PRACTICE AND REPETITION

In operant conditioning, learning consists of developing stimulus-response associations. When the appropriate stimulus is presented, the trainee should make the correct response. To increase the likelihood that the trainee will make the correct response on future occasions, operant conditioning recommends that the response be rehearsed through extensive practice accompanied by intermittent reinforcement. According to operant conditioning, an important principle of learning is to provide the learner with the opportunity for practice and repetition. To gain the full benefit of training, learned behavior must be overlearned to ensure smooth performance and a minimum of forgetting at a later date.

Social cognitive theory claims that practice is not necessary for learning certain behaviors. According to the theory, practice may be necessary for developing novel skills, but it is not important for behavior that is learned symbolically through "central processing" of the response information. Learning how to produce an income statement, for example, does not require extensive practice of each component activity, since the trainees already know how to write the numbers from zero to nine and do not need to practice them. Learning how to produce an income statement involves central processing of symbols to handle such items as cash, accounts receivable, and debts. Many human behaviors are performed with little or no practice. Studies of imitative behavior have shown that after watching models perform a novel behavior, observers can later describe the behavior with considerable accuracy, and, given appropriate incentives, the observers are able to reproduce the behavior exactly on the first trial.[15]

Both operant conditioning and social cognitive theory agree that practice is important in developing new skills, such as athletic or musical abilities. But even for skills such as these, social cognitive theory has demonstrated that mentally rehearsing a response can facilitate learning. Proficiency in learning and retaining a new skill is improved when individuals visualize themselves performing the new behavior. In fact, evidence suggests that the highest levels of learning are achieved by first organizing and rehearsing the modeled behavior symbolically and then by enacting it overtly.[16]

An important issue in scheduling practice involves deciding whether to use *massed* as opposed to *distributed* practice. For example, if a company decides to allocate twelve hours to supervisory training, would the training be most effective if it were massed, with the supervisors spending twelve consecutive hours in a one-day program, or if it were distributed over a twelve-week period of one hour per week? In general, the evidence suggests that distributed practice is better than massed practice. One study showed that a group of 300 supervisors trained over a two-week period made fewer mistakes in training their subordinates than a similar group that was trained in three successive days.[17]

MOTIVATION: REINFORCEMENT AND ACTIVE PARTICIPATION

Training programs will fail if trainees are not receptive to the instruction or if they have no reason to learn. Human behavior is goal-oriented and adequate motivation is essential to the success of any learning situation. Many different kinds of reinforcement facilitate training, including both extrinsic rewards and intrinsic satisfaction.

Most learning situations are intrinsically reinforcing because of the satisfaction associated with acquiring new knowledge or skills. However, intrinsic satisfaction by itself is not enough to perpetuate new learning.[18] Even safety training to avoid death and disability is not sufficiently self-rewarding to change behavior without additional incentives.[19] Companies are required to provide other forms of rewards or punishment, such as financial incentives, recognition, intergroup competition, or the threat of being fired.

FEEDBACK: KNOWLEDGE OF RESULTS

Performance feedback is a necessary prerequisite for learning. In an early study by Thorndike on the importance of feedback, blindfolded students were asked to draw three-inch lines.[20] Students who received no feedback on the lengths of their lines did not improve in their ability to draw three-inch lines even after several thousand trials. Although less variability in the lengths of the lines existed after many trials, the students were no closer to the three-inch standard after thousands of trials than at the start of practice. However, significant improvements were noted in the lengths of the lines of the blindfolded students who were told whether their lines were too long or too short.[21]

Feedback improves performance not only by helping learners correct their mistakes but also by providing reinforcement for learning. Knowledge of results is a positive form of reinforcement by itself. Learning activities have more intrinsic interest when performance feedback is available. Nevertheless, performance feedback should do more than inform learners whether they were right or wrong. Merely informing the trainees that they were wrong is not as effective as telling them why they were wrong and how they can avoid making mistakes in the future. Merely informing individuals of their incorrect responses can be very frustrating for those who want to know why they were wrong.

In general, knowledge of results is an essential feature of learning, and the sooner this knowledge comes after the learner's response, the better. Studies in animal learning suggest that the ideal timing of the feedback is to have it occur almost immediately after the response has been made.[22] Some training programs are able to provide this kind of ideal feedback, but not all. Management development programs often fail to provide any form of feedback, mainly because the managers are not given opportunities to respond until they are back on the job.

▌ HRM in Action

The Effects of Goal Setting and Knowledge of Results on Safety Training

A study by Robert Reber and Jerry Wallin demonstrated the benefits of providing feedback in addition to goal setting to improve occupational safety. The study was conducted in a farm machinery manufacturing firm that had an accident-frequency rate three times the national average for similar organizations. The previous training was considered inadequate, and the first-line supervisors unanimously agreed on the need for an improved safety-training program, preferably one that did not utilize extrinsic rewards.

Before the training was presented, thirty-seven behaviorally specific safety items were developed to assist in the training and to assess the employees' safety practices. These items described specific safety-related actions that could be directly observed, such as "approved safety glasses or goggles shall be worn when working beneath equipment where the danger of falling particles exists." These thirty-seven items were used by observers to evaluate the safety performance of each department. Each employee was observed approximately three times per week for twenty seconds, and the department's safety performance score was the percentage of employees being observed working in a completely safe manner.

The study involved 105 full-time employees in eleven departments that were separated into three experimental groups. Each group went through a sequence of four experimental conditions: (1) baseline, (2) training only, (3) training and goal setting, and (4) training, goal setting, and knowledge of results. The lengths of the baseline periods were fourteen, sixteen, and eighteen weeks so that the training started at staggered times. By starting the groups at different times, the researchers utilized a superior research design that controlled for extraneous factors, such as history and maturation.

The training phase of the study was ten weeks in length and started with a one-hour training program showing slides of safe and unsafe behaviors and explaining the thirty-seven item observational rating form that would be used to evaluate this behavior.

The goal-setting phase lasted sixteen weeks and began with a thirty-minute meeting in which each department was given a specific, difficult but attainable goal based on its previous performance.

The feedback phase lasted at least twelve weeks and consisted of showing the employees a chart on which was recorded their average weekly safety performance.

The results of this experiment indicated that providing knowledge of results significantly increased the employees' safety behavior. The average safety performance score for all three groups increased from a baseline of 62 to 71 after the first training session, to 77 when goal setting was added, and to 95 when knowledge of results was added. During this study the actual number of injuries, as measured by the lost-time injury rate, dropped from 21.2 to 9.9.

The researchers hypothesized that knowledge of results contributes significantly to the effectiveness of training for three reasons: (1) it leads to an increase in effort, (2) it encourages employees to set new and higher goals, and (3) it serves as an intrinsic reinforcer to reinforce performance.

Source: Robert A. Reber and Jerry A. Wallin, "The Effects of Training, Goal Setting, and Knowledge of Results on Safe Behavior: A Component Analysis," *Academy of Management Journal* 27 (1984): 544–60.

TRANSFER OF TRAINING

Because training often occurs in a special environment, an important question to ask is whether the learning will transfer to the actual job situation. Transfer of training occurs when trainees can apply the knowledge and skills learned in a training course to their jobs. If the learning that occurs in one setting does not transfer to the actual job situation, then the training has failed. Human relations training programs have been criticized frequently for their lack of positive **transfer of training**.

Three transfer-of-training situations are possible: (1) positive transfer of training when the training activities enhance performance in the new situation, (2) negative transfer of training when the training activities inhibit performance in the new situation, and (3) no observable effect of training. The conditions that determine whether positive, negative, or no transfer of training will result depend on the similarity of the stimulus and the response within the training and actual job situations. As shown in Figure 8.3, four situations are possible:

1. When the stimulus environments and the learned responses are the same in both the training situation and the job situation, a strong positive transfer of training will result.
2. When the stimulus environments of both situations are similar but the response that is learned in training is different from the response that is required on the job, a negative transfer of training will result. The responses that the trainee has learned will be inappropriate for the new situation.
3. When the stimulus environments are different but the responses are the same, a slightly positive transfer of training will result. The learner will have mastered the response, but it will have to be associated with a new stimulus.
4. When both the stimulus environments and the responses are different, no transfer of training will result.

The transfer-of-training problem can be illustrated by the example of learning to drive a car. In some driver education classes, the trainee sits in a simulated automobile while watching a film. The trainee operates the steering wheel, brakes, and turn signals

FIGURE 8.3 Predicting the transfer of training.

	Learned responses	
	Similar	Different
Similar	Large positive transfer +	Large negative transfer —
Different	Small positive transfer +	No transfer ○

Stimulus environments

in response to the curves, stop signs, and other stimuli shown in the film. When the trainee is in a real automobile and observes a stop sign, there will be positive transfer of training in learning how to stop because the stimulus is the same as that experienced while in the simulated car and because the response of pushing on the brakes and coming to a stop is also the same. However, if the simulated car has an automatic transmission and the actual car has a standard transmission, then the trainee's ignorance of how to operate a clutch will create a negative transfer of training because the responses are different to the same stimuli—the trainee will make an incorrect response.

Numerous factors influence the transfer of training, including factors associated with the design of training and how it is presented, factors associated with the trainees and whether the new learning is important to them, and factors associated with the work and whether the environment is conducive to changed behavior. In a survey of trainers the three factors ranked as the most serious impediments to effective transfer were: a lack of on-the-job reinforcement, interference from the immediate environment, and a nonsupportive organizational climate.[23] Some trainers have found that the most effective strategy for minimizing the transfer problem is to require the participants to develop a thorough action plan as part of the training program. If they have visualized and described in writing how they plan to apply the training, they are more likely to implement it.[24]

LEARNING CURVES

The rate of learning can be analyzed by examining **learning curves**, graphs that show the number or percentage of correct responses during successive learning periods. In unusual situations, learning may occur in a straight linear fashion, whereby each successive trial results in equal improvements in learning. Generally, however, learning progresses most rapidly in either the beginning or later trials, depending on what is being learned.

Four learning curves are illustrated in Figure 8.4. Curve A demonstrates a **negatively accelerating learning curve** in which increments in performance are large in the early stages of practice but become smaller as practice continues. A negatively accelerating learning curve is probably the curve that occurs most frequently.[25] Many of the everyday things that people have learned to do, such as walking, talking, and learning to write, involve rapid learning at the beginning and successively smaller increments of learning later.

Curve B is a **positively accelerating learning curve**. Here, the learning proceeds slowly at first and then gradually improves. This curve typically occurs when the material to be learned is very difficult or complex, when a trainee lacks the necessary background or aptitude, or when motivation is low at first but increases as mastery improves. Learning to swim the length of a pool proceeds as a positively accelerating learning curve. Until beginners have spent many hours in the pool, they cannot swim even a few yards. But after they have become accustomed to the water and have mastered some of the basic swimming techniques, their ability to swim the full length of the pool increases rapidly.

Curve C illustrates an **S-shaped learning curve**. This curve combines a positively accelerating learning curve at the beginning with a negatively accelerating curve in later

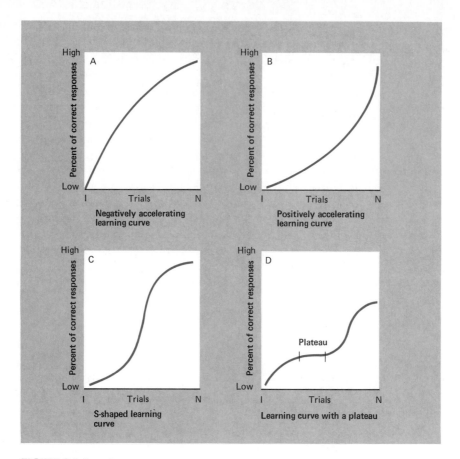

FIGURE 8.4 Learning curves.

trials. Evidence indicates that if performance were to be observed at the very beginning and very end of a training program, the S-shaped curve probably would describe most learning situations.[26] This idea stems from the belief that in the early stages of learning, improvement is always slow until the trainee is oriented to the learning process. Near the end of the learning process, when the trainee is trying to master the new skill, performance again progresses slowly. Performance improvements are most difficult to obtain at the very end when the trainee is perfecting the finishing touches of a highly developed skill.

Curve D illustrates a curve with a **plateau**. A plateau is a period where no learning seems to occur. The level of performance appears to remain constant, regardless of additional practice.

Because plateaus are common in many learning situations, three explanations for them have been proposed.[27] The first explanation, called the **hierarchy-of-habit** hypothesis, suggests that a plateau will be reached when a task requires a series of habits to be learned. The learner remains on a plateau until a new habit is acquired. An example of this is learning to type. Research in typing suggests that an individual learning to type goes through three stages of development.[28] The first stage is learning the keyboard. The second stage consists of letter-by-letter typing in which the individual thinks about each key and immediately strokes it. In the third stage, the learner types a series of short words, thinking of more than one letter at a time. The first plateau occurs at about ten to fifteen words per minute, and the learner stays on this plateau until the second stage is reached. The second plateau occurs around thirty to forty words per minute and lasts until the learner enters the third stage.

The second explanation for learning plateaus is that the learner experiences a decline in motivation. During the early part of a training program, including a college course, the learner is excited about the new topic and the opportunity to learn. After a while, however, the newness wears off and the rate of learning declines. When the time for an exam or some other incentive to learn approaches, the rate of learning again increases.

The third explanation for learning plateaus suggests that new learning is occurring but that it is not evident because incorrect learning is being eliminated at the same time. For example, basketball players sometimes appear to be making no progress because they are trying to unlearn incorrect ball-handling habits. Until such incorrect responses are extinguished, new learning and skill improvement do not occur.

Learning curves provide valuable information for designing a training program. It is useful for a trainer to be able to anticipate the rate of learning. If learning plateaus are a common occurrence, the trainer may want to examine the reason for a plateau. If the plateau is caused by a hierarchy of different habits that have to be mastered, the trainer may want to begin teaching a new habit even before the previous habit has been completely learned. If the plateau is caused by a lack of motivation, the trainer can provide incentives to provoke more interest in learning. If the plateau is caused by the elimination of incorrect responses, the trainer may want to identify the incorrect responses early so that the learner can avoid acquiring them.

FORGETTING

Being able to remember what has been learned is an important part of learning. Unfortunately, forgetting is a serious problem in training. Estimates of how much people remember from what they see, hear, read, and discuss one year later are very discouraging. Studies on how much information is retained by college students from the courses they complete show that students typically score about 20 percent on retakes of the final exams of courses they completed two years earlier.[29] And this low retention score probably overstates how much the students actually remembered, since they already may have known the material before they took the course or they relearned it in another course during the two-year period. If trainees forget what they are taught, does the training do any good? There are several theories that explain forgetting.[30] An understanding of these theories is useful in designing a training program that minimizes the amount of forgotten material.

PASSIVE DECAY THROUGH DISUSE

Forgetting is sometimes due to the fading or **passive decay** of memory traces in the brain. Such fading and decay could be the result of normal metabolic processes within the brain that occur with the passage of time. Material that has once been learned tends to fade and eventually may disappear altogether. Forgetting is a serious problem for many older people. However, some people who live long lives experience little difficulty with remembering.

Inadequately learned material can fade very quickly. Sometimes it is difficult to write down something immediately after hearing it. For example, important details of a phone message are occasionally forgotten as soon as the call has ended. Although passive decay appears to be a plausible explanation for forgetting, instances of vivid recall, such as when old people remember events in their youth, suggest that there may be other explanations for forgetting.

RETROACTIVE INHIBITION

Retroactive inhibition suggests that new learning interferes with the recall of old learning. An illustration of retroactive inhibition is provided by a story about Stanford University's first president, David S. Jordan.[31] Jordan, an authority on fish, had memorized the technical names of several thousand fish. When he was named president of the university, Jordan decided to learn the names of all the students. After learning the names of two or three thousand students, however, Jordan discovered, to his dismay, that he had begun to forget the names of fish, so he quit trying to learn the names of students. Although this story may not be entirely accurate, it does illustrate the process of retroactive inhibition in which new learning may interfere with the recall of old learning.

PROACTIVE INHIBITION

Proactive inhibition is a companion explanation to retroactive inhibition. It holds that old learning interferes with the retention of new learning. Both proactive and retroactive inhibition become particularly troublesome when the material being learned is similar to old learning. The greater the similarity, the more likely that interference will occur. Both processes can be illustrated by the example of an individual who is learning a second computer language. If the second computer language is similar to the language that has already been learned, it is easy for the learning of the first language to interfere with the learning of the second. Many students experience extreme frustration when learning a second, similar computer language because a simple mistake, like misplacing a comma, can prevent a computer program from running.

MOTIVATED FORGETTING

Occasionally, **motivated forgetting** occurs because the learner wants to forget the information. There are at least two reasons why learners might want to forget certain information. First, they may not want to remember information that is threatening to their self-esteem and damaging to their egos. This process is called repression. Another reason is because the information is no longer useful. Some flight attendants can take orders for drinks from many passengers and remember which passengers ordered which drinks. But once the attendants have served the drinks, they quickly forget the order information, since there is no further need to remember it. This tendency to remember unfinished tasks and to forget tasks that are finished was recognized many years ago and is called the *Zeigarnik effect*.[32]

LEVELS OF LEARNING

Although the principles of learning apply in general to all learning situations, the way in which they are used and the relative importance of each depends in part on the kind of learning that occurs. There are several different levels of learning. Four of the most important levels are motor response, rote learning, learning ideas, and value internalization.

MOTOR RESPONSE

Motor responses are physical acts involving various muscle groups. Some motor responses are simple, such as turning a knob, pushing a button, or pulling a lever. Other motor responses are complex, such as playing basketball, playing an organ, and operating heavy equipment. Motor-response learning frequently involves complex coordination, including finger dexterity, eye-hand coordination, and multilimb coordination.

Since motor responses depend largely on sensory control, the most important aspect in learning them is actual performance of the activity. For example, the best way to teach a child to ride a bicycle is by putting her on one, helping her develop a feel for pedaling and maintaining balance, and encouraging her to practice. Having the child watch other cyclists or letting her ride double with someone else can provide valuable imitative learning. But long lectures or discussions, even if they include diagrams and pictures, will do very little to help a child learn to ride a bicycle.

To help a learner develop appropriate motor responses, the trainer should:

1. Familiarize the trainee with the equipment, materials, and surroundings.
2. Demonstrate the activity.
3. Let the trainee begin practicing the activity.
4. Provide adequate guidance and feedback to make sure that incorrect responses are eliminated and correct responses are acquired. Verbal instructions may help to explain what the learner is doing wrong and what he or she needs to do differently, but physical demonstrations, showing exactly what needs to be done, are much more helpful.[33]

ROTE LEARNING

Rote learning refers to memorizing arbitrary associations between words, symbols, objects, or events. Examples of rote learning include memorizing a poem, learning the words to a song, and learning a new language.

Some people have an amazing ability to memorize large amounts of information and remember it. These individuals take advantage of memory devices that help people remember large amounts of new information. For example, the word HOMES is a useful mnemonic for remembering the Great Lakes. With the help of a memory device, some individuals can walk into a crowded room, be introduced to dozens of new people, and remember each individual's name. Most memory devices are based on some form of association whereby an individual learns new material by associating it with material that already has been learned. To help them remember the names of new acquaintances, many people envision the new person with an old acquaintance who has the same first name.

The following procedures help learners acquire rote learning:

1. Briefly familiarize the learners with the material to be learned.
2. Identify any patterns of association that may help the learners to remember the material, such as recurring themes or repeating patterns within the material to be learned.
3. Provide opportunities for the learners to practice repeating the new material. Practice should include both silent study and oral repetition. Distributed practice over a long period of time is superior to massed practice.
4. Provide accurate and immediate feedback so that the learners' errors can be corrected as soon as they are made.
5. Require repetitive practice so that overlearning occurs and trainees are given opportunities to demonstrate their learning.[34]

LEARNING IDEAS

The process involved in learning ideas is not open to observation and, therefore, is difficult to describe. The learner may be confronted with a complex stimulus environment and expected to make a response. Between the stimulus and the response, however, a complex, nonobservable process of thinking must occur. This thinking process has been referred to as an intermediary response, or a mediating response. The word *mediating* comes from the Latin word *medius*, which means "middle," referring to the processes between the stimulus and the response.

The process of learning ideas appears to depend on the development of symbols and associations within an individual's frame of reference. Much human learning appears to be a consequence of perceiving the total situation of stimuli and responses and of being able to organize them into meaningful patterns, mental images, and symbols.

The procedures recommended for learning ideas depend on whether the training follows operant conditioning theory or social cognitive theory. The procedures advocated by operant conditioning theory include the following:

1. Ideas must be divided into a sequential pattern of concepts and subconcepts.
2. Learners should be allowed to master one concept before proceeding to the next.
3. Learners should be required to practice each response and to demonstrate mastery of each concept.
4. Reinforcement should be provided to reward each step in the learning process.
5. Learners should be required to review the material frequently to avoid forgetting. Forgetting new ideas is less likely to occur if each idea is used as a building block for further learning.[35]

According to social cognitive theory, the process of learning ideas is grounded in symbolic learning. Here, learning is a process of discovery and trainees should actively participate in the learning process. The trainees should be allowed to explore situations so that they may eventually discover for themselves the operating principles or relationships involved. Sometimes this discovery process involves a sudden flash of insight and understanding. At other times it involves the gradual discovery of common elements, common principles, or sequential trends. The trainer can frequently assist the trainee not so much by instructing or presenting information as by asking questions and attempting to focus the trainee's thinking and discovery processes in a particular direction.

The early stages of most training involve rote learning while the trainees acquire the relevant facts and principles. Gradually, however, the students become involved in creating or actively reinterpreting knowledge and its applications. Skilled instructors can facilitate the process of idea learning by using a broad range of questions, beginning with simple factual inquiries and advancing to more complex interpretive questions.[36]

The learning of new ideas is both fun and frustrating. A sudden insight that solves a complex problem that an individual has been wrestling with for a long time can create an exhilarating feeling of joy and satisfaction. On the other hand, learning is frequently very frustrating and can cause a great deal of anguish as learners try to discover new relationships and solve new problems.

VALUE INTERNALIZATION

The process of acquiring personal values involves more than simply learning new information. For example, employees know that stealing merchandise or money is dishonest, but some do it anyway. If confronted with the evidence and asked why they did it, they offer excuses, but make it clear that they know stealing is dishonest and that they should not have done it. The problem is not that they have failed to learn or comprehend the right behavior.

How does cognitive information about proper standards of conduct become internalized as a personal moral value? Numerous studies have examined the **value internalization** process.[37] Moral behaviors are actions considered intrinsically desirable, valued, or good because of their contribution to society. Most of the research on moral development has focused on four moral behaviors: aggression, honesty, altruism, and the work ethic.

According to research on moral development, the most important techniques for developing value internalization are induction and modeling.[38] Induction refers to all forms of verbal explanation, such as reasoning, preaching, and teaching. Induction provides cognitive information describing appropriate behaviors and a justification for why such behaviors are important. It also includes various verbal reinforcements for appropriate behaviors, such as "thank you for reporting it," "you're an honest person," and "I appreciate your honesty." Abundant evidence indicates that induction is a useful, if not necessary, technique in moral development. Parents who use induction to explain the implications of their child's behavior on others generally have children who demonstrate consideration for others, resistance to temptation, and little aggression. Likewise, supervisors who provide logical explanations for why employees should behave honestly, why they should be helpful to others, and why they should be loyal to the company will help employees to acquire moral values of honesty, pride in work, and loyalty.

Modeling refers to the example that individuals observe in others' behavior. For instance, if a supervisor takes pride in his or her work and tries to hold down unnecessary costs, this behavior will set a good example for subordinates, who will be inclined to model their supervisor's behavior. Modeling serves to inform individuals about what they should do and indicates what is considered appropriate by others. The example of a model creates a general expectation for others to follow.

Through induction and modeling, individuals develop a general definition of moral behaviors that they internalize as personal standards of proper behavior. The value-internalization process usually takes a long time. Personal values are not created or changed significantly by a brief experience or by a simple training event. Values are acquired over time through a patient and persistent presentation of proper conduct using induction and modeling.

INTERNATIONAL HRM

Training programs worldwide are being influenced by the differences between the American and Japanese educational systems. The casual educational system in the United States and the intensively competitive system in Japan have produced dramatically different results, which has forced educators and trainers to reassess the value of rote learning, discipline, and conformity in learning. By most standards, Japan has the most efficient educational system in the world. Although the Japanese spend a smaller fraction of their national income on education than many other developed nations do, they have the highest literacy rate (99.7 percent) and consistently rank at or near the top in every international survey of achievement in mathematics and natural science.[39] Nevertheless, few scientists or scholars trained in Japan have produced significant original work, and many attribute this failure to the excessive use of rote learning in the schools and the heavy cultural demands for conformity.[40]

Education in Japan is compulsory for children age 6–15, but even noncompulsory education is common: about 95 percent of five-year olds and 70 percent of four-year olds attend kindergarten or nursery school. About 95 percent complete high school at either a public or private school and 40 percent finish college. Competition for admission to high school and college is extremely intense. Most students attend cram courses, called *juku*, after school and on weekends to prepare for high school and college entrance examinations. Since career opportunities are largely determined by the prestige of one's education, the pressure to excel academically begins in the early years of grade school.

Learning is much more intense for Japanese students than for U.S. students. Japanese children attend school 240 days a year compared with 180 days in the U.S., and many Japanese children spend Saturdays, Sundays, and vacations studying or being tutored. While high school students in the United States spend approximately six hours in class and one hour doing homework per day, Japanese students spend about eight hours in class and four hours doing homework. Much of this time is spent memorizing facts and information they might be asked on entrance exams.

Japanese high school graduates are almost as well-educated as many American college graduates. College entrance examinations in Japan in science and math test high school seniors at a level approximately equivalent to the third year of specialized courses in an American university. The average Japanese production worker is expected to understand complex charts, graphs, and statistics. All high school graduates have learned calculus.[41]

While high school students in the United States have been described as undisciplined and unruly teenagers who resist school, Japanese students are described as compliant youth who willingly conform to social expectations regarding the importance of education. These expectations are consistently reinforced throughout society, especially in the home by mothers who regard supervising their children's education as their primary responsibility. In the scientific community, the pressure to conform is manifested by an intolerance for mavericks and original thinkers who act individually. In Japanese science, as in Japanese society, taking risks and pursuing creative insights attracts personal attention, something that is censured in their group-oriented culture. The Japanese educational system is abundantly successful in teaching a plethora of facts, but educators question whether the rote learning and conformity found in the Japanese system are compatible with teaching students to think.[42]

SUMMARY

A. Learning refers to a relatively permanent change in behavior that occurs as a result of experience or practice. Both training and education contribute to the learning process. However, a distinction usually is made between training and education. Training refers to the process of acquiring specific skills and knowledge and normally results in a narrowing of the kinds of responses a trainee will make. Education, on the other hand, refers to providing students with general knowledge that can be applied in many different settings, and tends to broaden the range of responses that students will make.

B. Five of the major kinds of training programs include: (1) orienting and informing employees, (2) skill development, (3) safety training, (4) professional and technical education, and (5) supervisory and managerial training.

C. Training and development activities influence other organizational functions. Training and development activities should be based on a careful analysis of the overall organization using a systems approach to training. The major components of a systems approach to training are assessing the training needs, designing and presenting the training program, and evaluating the training.

D. The determination of training needs requires three types of analysis: organizational, operational, and personnel. An organizational analysis examines the kinds of problems an organization is experiencing and determines where they are located.

This analysis is performed by examining organizational-effectiveness indices, a personnel succession analysis, and an organizational-climate analysis. An operational analysis examines the specific behaviors required of the job incumbent to perform the job adequately. The personnel analysis examines how well the employees are performing their jobs and identifies which employees need training.

E. A training-needs analysis must be translated into specific behavioral objectives. Behavioral objectives identify the behaviors that the trainees should display after they have been trained. The criteria for good behavioral objectives are that: (1) the objectives should be described in behavioral terms, (2) they should specify a standard of performance, and (3) they should specify the constraints and time limitations for performing the behaviors.

F. The two major theories of learning are operant conditioning and social cognitive theory. According to operant conditioning, training primarily consists of developing stimulus-response associations through the proper presentation of reinforcement. Social cognitive theory suggests that learning occurs largely through vicarious experiences—imitating and observing others—and through symbolic learning using mental images, symbols, and ideas. Although operant conditioning and social cognitive theory are significantly different in the way they view cognitive thinking processes, they suggest a common set of principles for learning.

G. Training is improved if the stimulus environment is organized in a meaningful way so that trainees can easily perceive it. Sometimes training is facilitated if trainees are told what they should observe.

H. An opportunity should be provided for trainees to practice the response they learn. The development of motor skills and rote learning particularly require an opportunity for practice and repetition of the response. Generally, training time is most effective if practice periods are distributed over several consecutive training sessions rather than concentrated in one.

I. The training environment must provide adequate motivation for learning. Trainees should be allowed to participate actively in the training, and positive reinforcement should provide sufficient incentives to learn.

J. Performance feedback is a necessary prerequisite for learning to occur. To facilitate training, the trainees should receive immediate knowledge of the results of their performances.

K. The knowledge and skills that are learned in training must transfer to the actual job situation. To provide for a positive transfer of training, the stimulus environments of both the training and the actual job must be similar and the responses that are learned and practiced also must be similar.

L. Learning curves illustrate the number of correct responses during successive learning periods. The effectiveness of a training program can be evaluated by examining the learning curve. A learning curve may be positively accelerating, negatively accelerating, or S-shaped. A learning curve also may show a plateau in which no learning is apparent for a period of training.

M. These are three explanations for learning plateaus: (1) learning consists of a hierarchy of habits in which successive habits must be learned, (2) the learner experiences a decline in motivation, and (3) incorrect learning must be eliminated.

N. Forgetting what is learned is a serious problem in training programs. Four of the major explanations for why information is forgotten include: (1) passive decay through disuse; (2) retroactive inhibition, in which new learning interferes with old learning; (3) proactive inhibition, in which old learning interferes with new learning; and (4) motivated forgetting, whereby people intentionally forget information that either threatens their self-esteem or is considered useless.

O. Four of the most important kinds of learning are: (1) motor response, (2) rote learning, (3) learning ideas, and (4) value internalization. Motor-response learning refers to the development of specific physical skills, such as athletic and musical skills. Rote learning refers to remembering arbitrary associations between words, symbols, objects, or events. Learning ideas occurs through a complex process of thinking that uses mental images, symbols, and other cognitive constructs. Value internalization refers to the process of acquiring personal values in which beliefs and attitudes become internalized as important behaviors for the individual.

QUESTIONS

1. Should the growth of training and development activities in business organizations be viewed in part as a failure of the educational system? Why or why not?

2. How do training and development interact with other personnel functions?

3. What are the reasons why a company might decide to sponsor a training program? Which reasons are good and which are bad?

4. Since organizational effectiveness indices, such as labor costs, production efficiency, turnover, and absenteeism, can be influenced by so many different forces, how can they be used to indicate a training need?

5. What are the characteristics of good behavioral objectives? Do all behavioral objectives need to possess all three characteristics to be useful? Why or why not?

6. What are the major differences between operant conditioning and social cognitive theory in describing the learning process? How are these theories similar?

7. Operant conditioning and social cognitive theory are significantly different in their assessment of the need for practice and repetition. How can this difference be explained? What kinds of training require extensive practice and what kinds do not?

8. What are the conditions that explain whether a positive or negative transfer of training will result?

9. Identify several learning situations, and indicate whether you would expect them to produce a positively or negatively accelerating learning curve.

10. College students forget what they learn in class very rapidly. What should be done by both the students and the university to reduce the rapid rate of forgetting?

11. Trainers can help trainees learn new motor responses by showing them what to do and by providing performance feedback, but how helpful are trainers in aiding trainees to learn new ideas? What can a trainer do to facilitate learning new ideas that involve creative insight and problem-solving skills?

KEY TERMS

Andragogy: The adult learning process, which tends to be more experience-based, more problem-centered, more participative, and more collaborative than traditional grade school.

Behavioral objectives: The objectives of a training program, written in specific behavioral terms that describe the behavior the trainee is expected to learn, the standards of performance the trainee is expected to achieve, and the requirements and time limitations for how the behavior is to be performed.

Chaining: The process of combining several responses together to form a series of activities that are performed sequentially.

Education: The process of acquiring general knowledge and information that usually results in a broadening of the responses students are likely to make.

Hierarchy of habits: An explanation for learning plateaus that suggests that different habits must be acquired. Improvements in performance are not observed until new habits are learned.

Imitative learning: The process of learning new behaviors by observing others and by modeling their behavior (also called vicarious learning).

Learning curves: Graphs illustrating the number of correct responses or the percentage of correct responses during successive learning trials.

Method of successive approximations: A process of shaping behavior by selectively reinforcing closer and closer approximations of the correct behavior.

Modeling: A process for learning new behaviors in which the trainee imitates the behavior of a model.

Motivated forgetting: An explanation for forgetting information in which the individuals want to forget it either because it threatens their self-esteem or because it is no longer useful.

Motor responses: Physical actions or skills that an individual acquires through practice.

Negatively accelerating learning curve: A learning situation characterized by rapid learning in the beginning with successively smaller increments of learning in later trials.

Operant conditioning: A theory of learning that involves the development of stimulus-response associations acquired through selective reinforcement of the correct response.

Operational analysis: An examination of the behaviors that an employee must exhibit to be able to perform a task properly. An operational analysis is part of a training-needs analysis.

Organizational analysis: An examination of the kinds of problems the organization is experiencing and where they are located in the organization. An organizational analysis is part of a training-needs analysis, which examines organizational-effectiveness indices, personnel succession, and the organizational climate.

Passive decay: An explanation for forgetting in which information that is not used is gradually forgotten and lost from memory.

Personnel analysis: Part of the training-needs analysis that examines the abilities of individual employees to identify deficiencies in their performances.

Plateau: A horizontal part of a learning curve where no apparent performance improvements appear to be occurring.

Positively accelerating learning curve: A learning situation characterized by slow improvements in performance in the early stages followed by significant improvement in later trials.

Proactive inhibition: An explanation for forgetting in which old learning interferes with the acquisition of new information.

Reciprocal determinism: A basic philosophy of social cognitive theory that suggests that the environment influences individual behavior but that individuals also influence their environment and change it.

Retroactive inhibition: An explanation for forgetting in which new learning interferes with remembering old information.

Rote learning: A kind of learning that involves the association of words, symbols, objects, or events.

S-shaped learning curve: A learning situation characterized by slow learning at the beginning and end, with rapid learning occurring in the middle.

Shaping: A process of changing behavior that uses reinforcement to selectively reward successively closer approximations of the specific response that is desired.

Social cognitive theory: A major theory of learning based on observational and symbolic learning. Learning is influenced by what is reinforced, either extrinsically or through self-administered reinforcement, especially the anticipation of future rewards. The environment influences individual behavior, but individuals in turn influence their environment through a process called reciprocal determinism.

Symbolic learning: The process of learning that uses symbols such as words, mental images, and other cognitive associations.

Training: A process of learning characterized by the acquisition of specific information or skills. Training typically refers to the acquisition of specific skills or knowledge that reduce the variability of responding by trainees.

Transfer of training: The process of acquiring new knowledge or skills in a training environment and then transferring the same knowledge and skills to an actual job situation.

Value internalization: The process by which personal attitudes and beliefs are internalized into basic personal values.

Vicarious learning: The process of learning by observing the actions and behaviors of a model (also called imitative learning).

C O N C L U D I N G   C A S E

Defensive Drivers

After Jim Horton, the director of safety for Northern Public Utility, read the monthly accident report, he slammed it on his desk in anger and called the training office. George Geddes, the director of training, had to be called from a meeting to speak with Jim.

"George, our accident rate is 65 percent ahead of last year. That makes six straight months of record-setting accidents. Something needs to be done about it. If this rate continues, our people will soon have to walk or use their own vehicles."

Although he knew what Jim would say, George decided to ask for Jim's recommendation just to calm him down. "I know we've had a lot of accidents, but what do you suggest?"

Jim paused momentarily because he knew that he and George disagreed about the matter. "It's time we put together a driver education class and make all the service representatives attend it. I know you don't like that idea, but most of these accidents are caused by stupid mistakes and employee carelessness."

"What will you do with those who refuse to attend?" George asked. "Take away their company vehicles? You remember how poor the attendance was the last time we tried it on a voluntary basis."

Jim paused again and then concluded his conversation in a calm tone of voice. "I don't know what the answers are. That's why I called you. You're the training expert. Can't you design a defensive-driver training program that people will want to attend?

Our accident reports certainly tell us that we need such a program."

George replied by agreeing to prepare an outline for a new defensive-driving course for the company's eighty-five service representatives who spend a large part of each day driving company cars in both rural and metropolitan areas.

Questions:

1. What sort of training program should George propose that will be consistent with the principles of learning?
2. How can the training program develop defensive drivers rather than defensive employees?

NOTES

1. "Serving the New Corporation," Special bulletin published by the American Society for Training and Development (1986): 6–7.

2. Roger Roderick and Joseph Yaney, "Developing Younger Workers: A Look at Who Gets Trained," *Journal of Management* (Spring 1976): 19–26.

3. John C. Campbell, Marvin D. Dunnette, Edward E. Lawler, and Karl E. Weick, *Managerial Behavior, Performance, and Effectiveness* (New York: McGraw-Hill, 1970), Chapter 3.

4. See, for example, Todd Heider, "The Tailored Course: Saving Money and Time," *Training and Development Journal* 43 (February 1989): 42–45.

5. Craig E. Schneier, James P. Guthrie, and Judy D. Olian, "A Practical Approach to Conducting and Using the Training Needs Assessment," *Public Personnel Management* 17 (Summer 1988): 191–205.

6. Jennifer S. MacLeod, "Assessing Training Needs," *Employment Relations Today* 14 (Winter 1987/88) 341–44; James O. Mitchel, "Individualized Management Development Is Key to Field Managers' Success," *Market Facts* 7 (May 1988): 17–19; Barry Z. Posner, James M. Kouzes, and Roger T. Manley, "Increasing the Effectiveness of Management Development via the Managerial Problems Survey," *Journal of Management Development* 7, no. 7 (1988): 14–20.

7. B. F. Skinner, *The Behavior of Organisms* (New York: Appleton-Century-Crofts, 1938); B. F. Skinner, *Contingencies of Reinforcement* (New York: Appleton-Century-Crofts, 1969).

8. Albert Bandura, *Social Learning Theory* (Englewood Cliffs, N. J.: Prentice-Hall, 1977); Albert Bandura, *Principles of Behavior Modification* (New York: Holt, 1969); Albert Bandura, *Social Foundations of Thought and Action: A Social Cognitive Theory* (Englewood Cliffs, N. J.: Prentice-Hall, 1986).

9. Marilyn Jist, Benson Rosen, and Catherine Schwoerer, "The Influence of Training Method and Trainee Age on the Acquisition of Computer Skills," *Personnel Psychology* 41 (Summer 1988): 255–69.

10. Colette A. Frayne and Gary P. Latham, "Application of Social Learning Theory to Employee Self-Management of Attendance," *Journal of Applied Psychology* 72, no. 3 (1987): 387–92.

11. Phillip J. Decker, "Social Learning Theory and Leadership," *Journal of Management Development* 5, no. 3 (1986): 46–58.

12. Malcolm S. Knowles, *The Modern Practice of Adult Education* (New York: Association Press, 1970); Malcom S. Knowles, *The Adult Learner: A Neglected Species* (Houston: Gulf Publishing, 1973).

13. Ron Zemke and Susan Zemke, "30 Things We Know For Sure About Adult Learning," *Training* 25 (July 1988): 57–60.

14. Dale Feuer and Beverly Geber, "Uh-Oh . . . Second Thoughts About Adult Learning Theory," *Training* 25 (December 1988): 31–35.

15. Albert Bandura, ed., *Psychological Modeling: Conflicting Theories* (Chicago: Aldine-Atherton, 1971); J. P. Flanders, "A Review of Research on Imitative Behavior," *Psychological Bulletin* 69 (1968): 316–37.

16. R. W. Jeffery, "The Influence of Symbolic and Motor Rehearsal on Observational Learning," *Journal of Research in Personality* 10 (1976): 116–27.

17. W. R. Mahler and W. H. Monroe, "How Industry Determines the Need for and Effectiveness of Training," *Personnel Research Section Report* no. 929 (Department of the Army, 1952). Cited in Campbell et al., *Managerial Behavior*, p. 254.

18. Richard W. Malott, *Contingency Management in Education* (Kalamazoo, Mich.: Behaviordelia, 1972), Chapter 9.

19. "Adding Incentives to Safety Training Cuts Injuries, Boosts Productivity," *Training: The Magazine of Human Resources Development* 17, no. 7 (July 1980): A2–A3. See also A3–A15.

20. Edward L. Thorndike et al., *The Fundamentals of Learning* (New York: Teachers College, Columbia University, 1932).

21. M. H. Trowbridge and H. Cason, "An Experimental Study of Thorndike's Theory of Learning," *Journal of General Psychology* 7 (1932): 245–58.

22. George S. Reynolds, *A Primer of Operant Conditioning*, rev. ed. (Glenview, Ill.: Scott, Foresman, 1975), Chapters 2–4.

23. John W. Newstrom, "Leveraging Management Development Through the Management of Transfer," *Journal of Management Development* 5, no. 5 (1986): 33–45.

24. Timothy T. Baldwin and Kevin J. Ford, "Transfer of Training: A Review and Directions for Future Research," *Personnel Psychology* 41 (Spring 1988): 63–105; Marguerite Foxom, "Transfer of Training—A Practical Application," *Journal of European Industrial Training* 11, no. 3 (1987): 17–20.

25. Bernard M. Bass and James A. Vaughan, *Training in Industry: The Management of Learning* (Belmont, Calif.: Wadsworth, 1966): p. 43.

26. Ibid., p. 44.

27. Ibid., pp. 46–47.

28. Leonard J. West, *Acquisition of Typewriting Skills* (New York: Pitman, 1969), Chapter 20.

29. H. B. English, "The Psychology of Learning: A Study Guide." Columbus, Ohio (mimeographed), 1943. Cited in Ernest R. Hilgard, *Introduction to Psychology, 3rd ed.* (New York: Harcourt, 1962), p. 292.

30. Hilgard, *Introduction to Psychology*, pp. 288–310; See also Ian E. Glendon, Stephen P. McKenna, Karen Hunt, and Stephen S. Blaylock, "Variables Affecting Cardiopulmonary Resuscitation Skill Decay," *Journal of Occupational Psychology* 61, no. 3 (1988): 243–55.

31. Ibid., p. 298.

32. B. Zeigarnik, "*Das Behalten Erledigter und Unerledigter Handlungen*," *Psychol. Forsch.* 9 (1927): 1–85.

33. Bass and Vaughan, *Training in Industry*, p. 52.

34. Ibid., pp. 52–53.

35. Malott, *Contingency Management*.

36. Dennis P. Wolf, "The Art of Questioning," *Journal of State Government* 60 (March/April 1987): 81–85.

37. Larry C. Jensen, *What's Right? What's Wrong? A Psychological Analysis of Moral Behavior* (Public Affairs Press: Washington, D.C., 1975).

38. Martin L. Hoffman, "Moral Internationalization, Parental Power, and the Nature of the Parent-Child Interaction," *Developmental Psychology* 11, no. 2 (1975): 228–39; J. Philippe Rushton, "Generosity in Children: Immediate and Long-term Effects of Modeling, Preaching, and Moral Judgment," *Journal of Personality and Social Psychology* 31, no. 3 (1975): 459–66; J. Philippe Rushton, "Socialization and the Altruistic Behavior of Children," *Psychological Bulletin* 83, no. 5 (1976): 898–913.

39. Nigel Holloway and Bob Johnstone, "Japan: Education," *Far Eastern Economic Review* 144 (April 6, 1989): 64–72; "Swedish Schools: Working Class," *Economist* 309 (November 12, 1988): 15–18.

40. Michael E. Berger, "Japan's Energetic New Search for Creativity," *International Management* 82 (October 1987): 71–77; Merry I. White, "Learning and Working in Japan," *Business Horizons* 32 (March/April 1989): 41–47.

41. Ibid.

42. "Conformity vs. Creativity: Japan May Teach Its Kids More Facts but Unruly Americans Learn to Think," *Wall Street Journal* (November 14, 1988): R44.

Training and Development Programs

Learning Objectives

After studying this chapter, you should be able to:

1. Describe obsolescence and explain what an organization can do to reduce obsolescence among managerial and professional employees.
2. Explain the advantages and disadvantages of on-the-job training and development techniques versus off-the-job techniques.
3. List the major techniques for training both on the job and off the job.
4. Identify those training and development techniques that are used most frequently and those that should be used to achieve specific learning objectives.
5. Identify three areas of knowledge for managerial positions, and describe the relative importance of each area of knowledge to supervisors, middle managers, and top managers.
6. Describe the kinds of information that should be included in an orientation program for new employees.
7. List the four major criteria for evaluating a training and development program.
8. Identify four research designs for evaluating a training and development program, and describe the strengths and weaknesses of each design.

Chapter Outline

Need for Training
Illiteracy / Obsolescence / Responsibility for Personal Development

Training and Development Techniques
On-the-job Techniques / Off-the-job Techniques / Customer Education / Evaluation of Training Techniques

Orientation Training
Content of Orientation Training / Effective Orientation Sessions

Management Development Programs
Different Skills for Different Leaders / General versus Specific Training /
Commercial Management Development Programs

Evaluating Training Programs
Criteria of Evaluation / Research Designs

International HRM

Questionable Supervisor Training

This incident was described by the assistant director of transportation for a Midwestern state:

"For over a year, our state highway department sent groups of first-line supervisors to a two-day training program presented by our state university. The program covered the basic principles of management: planning, organizing, motivating, and controlling. It had been designed by members of the business school faculty.

"Each group consisted of about twenty supervisors, and we trained one group each month. At the end of each program we asked the supervisors to evaluate the program with a simple questionnaire asking how much they had learned from the program and whether they had enjoyed it. We had a three-year arrangement with the school, and over the three-year period, we expected all of our supervisors to go through the training program.

"No one seemed to question whether the training program was effective or not. We weren't getting any complaints from the supervisors, and most of the comments on the questionnaires were fairly positive. But

when one of the junior faculty said he thought the training was a waste of the taxpayer's money, we started to seriously question whether the training was doing any good. With the help of this junior faculty member, we evaluated the training. He suggested using a research design that involved a placebo training. The placebo training was presented by two members from the liberal arts faculty. We asked them to design a two-day training program on punctuation. We thought punctuation would be a reasonable placebo, since it involves some sort of learning but is not a critical activity in terms of how well the supervisors perform their jobs.

"The two liberal arts instructors who were asked to teach it were delighted to present a training program. We never told them that they were part of a training evaluation. They put together a two-day show that was very entertaining. It was a multi-media presentation that involved Mr. Comma and all the places that Mr. Comma liked to be and didn't like to be. It was a fast-paced show—something was always happening. While one instructor was explaining an idea, the other was flipping charts, writing on an easel, or operating a slide projector. At the end of this placebo training, we asked the participants to evaluate it, using much the same format as our previous evaluations.

"The results of this study were surprising. We expected the supervisors to say the placebo was more interesting than the management program since it was so entertaining. However, we did not expect the supervisors to say the placebo was more useful and valuable than the management program. One question specifically asked how much they expected to benefit from this program in their long-term development as a manager. The results indicated that punctuation was considered much more valuable than planning, organizing, motivating, and controlling. We had a hard time deciding what to think of this experiment. I'm sure that knowing where to place commas is not as important for our supervisors as knowing how to plan, organize, motivate, and control, but the results of our evaluation certainly didn't show that the supervisors felt this way."

Questions:
1. How do you explain the results of the experiment? What conclusions should be drawn?
2. Based upon the results of this experiment, what changes should the assistant director of transportation make in the supervisor training?

NEED FOR TRAINING

Two reasons largely explain the growing demand for training and development: illiteracy and obsolescence. A large number of employees are functionally illiterate, which means that they do not know how to read and write, and they are incapable of performing basic mathematical computations. Those who have been educated face the problem of obsolescence caused by forgetting and the expansion of new knowledge.

ILLITERACY

As noted in Chapter 2, the percentage of employees who are unable to read and write any language is increasing even though the percentage of students who finish grade school has increased. Finishing grade school and even high school is no guarantee that a student knows how to read and write or perform simple computations.

- 23 million adults cannot perform such tasks as reading a paycheck stub, completing a W-4 form, addressing an envelope, or reading an EEO announcement. Another 34 million have difficulty with these tasks.
- Among young adults ages 21 to 25, five percent cannot read at the fourth-grade level, 20 percent read below the eighth-grade level, and 40 percent read below the eleventh-grade level.
- Each year 700,000 youths who graduate from high school are functionally illiterate.
- Each year 1 million low-literate immigrants enter the United States.[1]

These results clearly illustrate the need for more and better basic education. Service and high-tech jobs requiring higher job skills are replacing lower-skilled manufacturing jobs. As the United States switches to a post-industrial economy, millions of workers will need to upgrade their job skills. Computer-integrated manufacturing, flexible manufacturing, and just-in-time delivery are transforming the demand for education and training. Craft occupations, such as tool-and-die maker and machinist, which were once considered highly skilled jobs, are now overshadowed by even higher-skilled jobs requiring a knowledge of electronics, computer technology, and statistical process control.

To evaluate current skill levels relative to future skill needs, the Department of Labor uses a six-point scale, as shown in Table 9.1. A level 1 job requires a reading vocabulary of only 2,500 words and the ability to write simple sentences, while a level 6 job requires advanced skills in writing technical journals, financial reports, and legal documents. Using the scale, the Labor Department estimated that the average skill level would need to increase from 2.6 in 1984 to 3.6 by the end of the century.[2]

The need for higher skill levels will place greater demands on organizations to provide basic education and specific job skills. The Bureau of Labor Statistics predicts that a significant proportion of new entrants to the work force will be high school dropouts (approximately 700,000 per year) and immigrants with inadequate language and education skills. In 1989, approximately 27 million workers were considered illiterate.[3]

OBSOLESCENCE

Obsolescence is another serious problem that is also getting worse. **Obsolescence** refers to a reduction in effectiveness because of a lack of knowledge or skill. The lack is sometimes due to forgetfulness, but more often it results from the creation of new knowledge and technologies that replace old ones. Obsolescence represents one of the most important reasons for the inauguration of training and development activities in organizations.

CAUSES OF OBSOLESCENCE

The rate of obsolescence grows with the expansion of new knowledge and new technology. The concept of half-life, taken from nuclear physics, provides a useful measure of the extent of obsolescence in different occupations. The term refers to the length of time

---

TABLE 9.1   Job skill levels

Level 1: Vocabulary of 2,500 words. Reading rate of 95–125 words per minute. Ability to write simple sentences.

Level 2: Vocabulary of 5,000–6,000 words. Reading rate of 190–215 words per minute. Ability to write compound sentences.

Level 3: Ability to read safety rules and equipment instructions. Able to write simple reports.

Level 4: Ability to read journals and manuals. Able to write business letters and reports.

Level 5: Ability to read scientific and technical journals and financial reports. Able to write journals and speeches.

Level 6: Same skills as level 5 but more advanced.

before a professional becomes roughly half as competent as he or she once was because of new developments. In engineering, the half-life of a 1940 graduate was estimated to be about twelve years. In 1965, the half-life of a well-trained college professor was estimated to be only five years. By 1990, the half-life of most professional and technical occupations was probably less than four years.[4]

Professional obsolescence is believed to be the major reason for the decline in performance in older engineers. A study of six engineering firms found that the average performance level of engineers increased for the first ten to fifteen years and then steadily decreased until retirement. Peak performance was achieved by the engineers who were 31 to 35 years old. A similar performance curve was found for managers and engineering supervisors. Performance levels increased for the first few years, then decreased. Peak performance levels were obtained by those who were 36 to 40 years old. The half-life of a supervisor's technical skills was thought to be considerably shorter than the half-life of his or her interpersonal and administrative skills.[5]

Obsolescence among professionals has become so serious that several states require professionals to return to school. In one state, lawyers must return to school for forty-five hours of legal course work every three years. Lawyers who fail to comply receive a restricted status that limits them to representing only a full-time employer or members of their family. Similar requirements for medical doctors also have been enacted. A number of medical boards require periodic recertification every six years. Several states require physicians to take fifty to sixty hours of continuing education annually to maintain their licenses. Other professions, including accounting and human resource management, also require their members to obtain **continuing education units (CEUs)** to maintain their professional certification.[6]

The quantity of knowledge is expanding in virtually every occupation. Furthermore, new knowledge is being created at an accelerated pace, especially in occupations that disseminate or use new information, such as engineering and teaching. The creation of new knowledge, however, does not necessarily mean that people will become obsolete. Even though the study of engineering firms showed that the average performance of older engineers declined, the researchers were quick to note that some older engineers were extremely competent and productive. Through study, work assignments, and training, these older engineers were able to maintain high rates of performance.[7]

Managerial obsolescence is not necessarily a function of age. The inevitable physiological changes that come with aging have little effect on executive performance. Mental abilities, as measured by intelligence tests, can actually improve over time, and particular improvement is often observed in verbal skills and conceptual exercises that involve the assembly of objects and designs. Creativity, which involves a synthesis of concepts, experience, and skills, is also little affected by aging. The effects of aging on vitality and energy levels, however, are more variable. Nevertheless, reduced stamina is seldom the major cause of obsolescence. There is no reason to assume that age is an automatic indicator of obsolescence; managerial incompetence is not a function of aging.[8]

PROGRAMS TO REDUCE OBSOLESCENCE

Organizations have tried several approaches to reduce the problems of obsolescence. The two basic strategies are (1) providing learning opportunities, and (2) creating a motivation within the learner to learn.

Numerous company actions have been proposed to provide opportunities for learning. Most of these suggestions are rather expensive, but because the costs of obsolescence are also high, the suggested actions usually are cost effective.

1. Continuing education appeals to many employees, with the most popular form being evening classes at a local college or university. Tuition and other expenses are normally paid by the company if the course is relevant to an employee's job and if the employee receives a passing grade.[9]
2. Training and development programs can be held at the company on company time or at some other site on weekends or evenings. These programs can be taught by competent members of the organization, by outside consultants, or by someone such as the service representative who sold the new equipment.[10]
3. Training materials can be purchased by the company and made available to employees. The materials might include reference books, manuals, professional periodicals, films, videotapes, and textbooks. These materials are often collected in the company library. However, the materials will more likely be studied if they are sent directly to the appropriate employees' offices.
4. Periodic seminars at which experts present information to a group of employees can be held.
5. Education sabbaticals can be arranged for managers and engineers, similar to those for college professors. Many executives feel that going to school full time for a semester is more profitable than going to evening school forever. Employee sabbaticals have been recommended as a way to reward employees for good performance and to motivate them to stay with the firm. Workers benefit from improved job skills and better mental health, while organizations benefit from greater creativity and loyalty.[11]
6. Job rotation and new project assignments can help employees gain new skills and knowledge. Although some lost time and frustration usually are associated with beginning a new assignment, the benefits of new learning frequently outweigh the lost time and effort.
7. Supervisors can encourage employees to maintain their competence by providing performance feedback, career counseling, opportunities for updating their skills, rewards for updating, and goal setting.

Companies that provide these opportunities create an organizational climate that encourages employees to update their skills. The benefits of providing these opportunities were observed in a survey of 447 engineers and 218 supervisors in ten diverse organizations. The organizations that had stronger updating climates had higher levels of involvement in continuing education and organizational commitment. They also had slightly higher levels of satisfaction and technical performance.[12]

RESPONSIBILITY FOR PERSONAL DEVELOPMENT

Company-sponsored training opportunities do not really focus on the root of the obsolescence problem—personal motivation. The motivation to learn and retain information must come from within an individual. If people are motivated to learn, they will do so, regardless of whether opportunities are provided by a company. If employees are involved in a training program because someone else wants them to be there and not because they want to be there, the training will not be of much value. In a study of six engineering firms, performance evaluations bore no relationship to the number of courses the engineers had taken.[13] One of the six firms spent much more time and money than the others to provide continuing education for its engineers, but in spite of this effort, the company's obsolescence problem was just as serious as the others. The engineers' motives for participating in the training explained why it was not having much effect. They had been pushed into the training by their supervisors because they were becoming obsolete. They apparently lacked the motivation to learn on their own, and the pressure of taking a formal course was not having much effect.

Organizations need to create healthy attitudes toward learning among managers. They should emphasize that the successful managers of tomorrow need to develop positive outlooks toward learning, overcome resistance to change, understand their own shortcomings as learners, and be more open to experiences and ready to learn from them. In essence, successful managers have to learn how to learn. They have to know how to skim material to obtain necessary information, how to vary their reading speed as a function of the material they are reading, and how to take advantage of opportunities to teach others in order to reinforce their own knowledge of particular material.

Another important strategy for helping to combat the problem of obsolescence is to foster in employees more favorable attitudes toward the importance of work.[14] To combat obsolescence and to help employees in their career development, a company should strive to strengthen the meaning of work for employees and to provide opportunities for them to be of service. Obsolescence is avoided more by promoting strong work values than by sponsoring company training programs.

TRAINING AND DEVELOPMENT TECHNIQUES

Companies use a variety of training and development techniques to increase the skills and competence of their employees. Some techniques, such as classroom instruction, are fairly standard and typical; others, such as taking a group of executives on a wilderness survival adventure, are unusual and novel.[15] Training and development techniques can be conveniently categorized as on-the-job or off-the-job techniques[16]

On-the-job techniques involve such activities as job-instruction training, apprenticeships, and internships where employees learn while actually performing the job. Off-the-job techniques involve learning activities that occur away from the actual job setting. These would include such activities as lectures, films, videotapes, and case studies that occur in such places as a university classroom or a special training room. On-the-job techniques are used more frequently than off-the-job techniques.[17] The greater use of on-the-job techniques probably reflects the fact that such techniques provide training oriented toward short-term production objectives. Off-the-job techniques tend to focus more on long-term development and education rather than on short-term training for production.

ON-THE-JOB TECHNIQUES

There are several advantages to on-the-job techniques that probably explain why they are used so frequently.

No special space or equipment is usually required for on-the-job training.

On-the-job training is practical since employees produce and earn while they learn.

On-the-job training provides an immediate transfer of training.

On-the-job training allows employees to practice what they are expected to do after training ends.

On-the-job training allows trainees to associate with their future coworkers and to observe and model the behavior of these coworkers.

JOB-INSTRUCTION TRAINING

Job-instruction training has been a popular and extensively used method of training new employees since it was first described by the War Manpower Board during World War II. Job-instruction training is the primary method by which most blue-collar and some white-collar employees are taught how to perform their work.

Before the actual learning occurs, job-instruction training requires a careful analysis of the job to be performed, an assessment of what the trainee knows about the job, and a training schedule. Job-instruction training begins with an introductory explanation of the purpose of the job and a step-by-step demonstration by the trainer of the job operations. After the trainer has demonstrated the job enough times for the trainee to comprehend the steps, the trainee is given the opportunity to try it alone.

During the demonstration, the trainer describes what is being done and why. The trainees also describe what they are doing while they are practicing. During the early practice sessions, the trainer maintains a close watch on the trainees to provide accurate and immediate feedback on their performances. As practice continues and the trainees reach satisfactory levels of performance, the close supervision is discontinued. However, periodic checks are made to ensure that the performance continues to be satisfactory.

APPRENTICESHIPS

Apprenticeship training refers to the process of having a new worker, called an apprentice, work alongside and under the direction of a skilled technician. In many of the skilled trades, such as plumbing, electronics, and carpentry, apprentice training is mandatory for admission into the trade. These programs are defined formally by the United States Department of Labor's Bureau of Apprenticeship and Training and involve a written agreement "providing for not less than 4,000 hours of reasonably continuous employment and supplemented by a recommended minimum of 144 hours per year of related classroom instruction."[18]

After an apprentice has worked under the direction of a skilled technician for a specified number of years, the apprentice automatically becomes a journeyman. The effectiveness of apprenticeship training largely depends upon the ability of the skilled technician to supervise the learning process. Individual differences in apprentices need to be recognized, and job assignments and instruction periods need to be carefully sequenced to maximize learning.

INTERNSHIPS AND ASSISTANTSHIPS

Internships and assistantships provide training similar to apprenticeship training; however, assistantships and internships typically refer to occupations that require a higher level of formal education than that required by the skilled trades. Many colleges and universities have developed agreements with local organizations to provide internship opportunities for students. These internships are part of what is called a **cooperative education** project. The students are employed by a business organization and work just the same as other full-time employees. However, they also work under the direction of a faculty member from the school or college where they are students. Students are frequently expected to write reports describing their experiences and what they have learned, and they typically receive academic credit toward graduation for such experiences.[19]

JOB ROTATIONS AND TRANSFERS

Job rotations and transfers are learning techniques that are usually provided only for managerial and technical occupations. Movement from one position to another provides managers with exposure to a number of different job functions and a broad grasp of the overall purpose of an organization. New management trainees may be rotated through different jobs, each lasting four to six months, to allow them to experience a broad range of functions that occur within an organization.

The disadvantage of job rotation is that a trainee always feels temporary and may not make a personal commitment to become involved in working and accomplishing much. A trainee may find job rotation particularly undesirable if it involves relocation of his or her family. Another disadvantage is that there is usually a certain amount of lost time in orienting a new trainee to a new situation.

In spite of these problems, the benefits of job rotation usually outweigh the difficulties. If a job rotation program is directed by a manager who can help the trainees to develop their goals and to focus on effective learning activities, the trainees can obtain valuable knowledge about the operations of many different parts of the organization and can practice the different management skills that are required.

JUNIOR BOARDS AND COMMITTEE ASSIGNMENTS

An alternative to transferring a trainee to a totally new job is placing the trainee on a committee that is responsible for making administrative decisions. The problems to be considered by the committee may be selected from a number of different functional areas, and the trainee may be required to gather a considerable amount of information before suggesting a solution. A **junior board** may be comprised totally of new trainees, or a trainee may be assigned as a member of a regular executive board to gain the opportunity of interacting with other executives and observing how they perform.

COACHING AND COUNSELING

Coaching and counseling activities are critical training activities in all on-the-job training techniques. Each of the techniques previously discussed requires systematic feedback on performance, encouragement by the trainer, and patient explanations of how to perform a job accurately.

For coaching and counseling techniques to function effectively, the proper relationship must be established between the trainer and the trainee. Coaching will not be effective if the trainer perceives the trainee as a rival. The trainee must be able to trust the feedback that is received from the trainer. The trainer also must recognize the trainee's dependency on him or her for information and must allow sufficient time for the trainee to develop the new behavior. Coaching and counseling require time, and the trainer cannot begrudge time spent in helping the trainee to develop. The trainer should remember that developing the trainee is part of the job of being a coach and that the reward for coaching is seeing improvement in the learner's performance.

An effective coach must (1) act as a good model with whom the trainee can identify, (2) set specific goals to help guide the trainee's behavior, (3) provide timely feedback on performance, and (4) provide the proper reinforcement and encouragement necessary for performance improvement.

OFF-THE-JOB TECHNIQUES

Many activities that occur off the job can help learners to perform better. Most off-the-job training programs are viewed as supplemental rather than as central to learning the job. Off-the-job training generally focuses more on long-term development and general education than on the skills and information needed to perform a specific job. The types of off-the-job training programs may vary from brief conferences and workshops held during the workday to formal education courses provided by a college or university.

The major disadvantage of off-the-job training programs is that they do not provide immediate transfer of training to real job situations. However, the advantages of off-the-job programs sometimes compensate for this transfer problem. Removing the learner from the actual job situation may facilitate the learning process. Expensive equipment is not tied up during the learning process, and errors and waste do not become troublesome problems because trainees are not holding up an actual production process. Because off-the-job programs focus more on learning and less on production, they provide trainees with an environment that is conducive to concentrating on new ideas and engaging in reflective thought.

Formal training away from the job also provides other benefits. A survey of 147 executives whose companies had used university executive programs indicated that 73 percent reported favorable evaluations of these programs. Three chief advantages were cited concerning university-sponsored programs:

1. They allow executives to get away from job pressures and to work in a climate in which party-line thinking is discouraged and self-analysis is stimulated.
2. They provide resource people and resource materials, such as faculty members, fellow executives, and books, that contribute suggestions and ideas for the executives to consider as they attempt to change, develop, and grow.
3. They challenge executives to increase their development and motivate them to improve.[20]

VESTIBULE TRAINING

Vestibule training is similar to on-the-job training except that it occurs in a separate training area equipped like the actual production area. The training that occurs in a vestibule is usually some form of job-instruction training. In vestibule training, however, the emphasis is on learning as opposed to the emphasis on production in job-instruction training. Vestibule training is typically used for teaching specific job skills.

Vestibule training provides several advantages over other forms of off-the-job training. A major advantage is that positive transfer of training results because the environments of the vestibule and the actual job setting are similar. Other advantages are that vestibule training provides ideal learning conditions, such as immediate reinforcement, accurate feedback on performance, and an opportunity for practice and repetition without excessive concern about making mistakes. However, a separate vestibule area that is used only for training can be expensive to maintain unless training sessions are held frequently.

LECTURE

An efficient means of transmitting large amounts of factual information to a relatively large number of people at the same time is the lecture. The lecture is the traditional method of teaching and is used in many training programs. A skilled lecturer can

HRM in Action

Retreading the Work Force

When Goodyear Tire and Rubber Company decided to rebuild its Kelly-Springfield bias-tire plant in Tyler, Texas, and make radial tires, it faced a massive retraining effort for 1,400 employees. The entire facility was gutted and rebuilt into a state-of-the-art computer-controlled factory. Almost every worker had access to and used a computer terminal in the office as well as in the factory.

Because of the change-over, many workers had to obtain training in basic skills of reading, writing, and math. Although the training in reading and math was voluntary, it was considered essential because learning to operate, maintain, and troubleshoot the high-tech equipment required it. The change-over also created a new social system that required a cultural change and new ways of managing and working together.

Each employee participated in at least 160 hours of training, and many employees had as much as six or seven months of training. This training was provided by several sources. The local community college and adult education association provided courses in math, reading, management, and other technical subjects, such as electronics. Consultants were used to teach employees about social skills and organizational culture. Vendors who provided the new equipment and computers were asked to assist with the training by teaching the employees how to operate and maintain the new equipment.

The workers responded very well to the retraining program because they recognized that their former technology and products were out of date. For them, the change to radial tires meant job security. For the company, the retraining and rebuilding program at the Tyler plant resulted in the on-time production of 25,000 tires per day and a work force with updated skills.

Source: Therese R. Welter, "New Wheels for the Old Workforce: Goodyear's Kelly-Springfield Plant," *Industry Week* (September 19, 1988): 56–57.

organize material and present it in a clear and understandable way. If the trainees are ready to receive it, a well-prepared lecture may succeed in transferring conceptual knowledge. However, a lecture does not allow active participation by the learners. Furthermore, since the lecture is a one-way communication process, it provides no practice, no feedback, no knowledge or results, and it may inhibit the transfer of learning.

INDEPENDENT SELF-STUDY

A considerable amount of training and development consists of independent learning by people trying to train themselves. The most frequent kinds of self-study activities are reading books and professional magazines, taking special courses through a local university, and attending professional meetings. The tremendous increase in new technology has increased the need for employees to train themselves using owners manuals and other handbooks. For individuals who are highly motivated, individual study and special training are excellent ways to increase job knowledge and skills. Independent study is especially important for employees who assume the responsibility of maintaining their own job skills. Although most employees do not have the motivation to undertake a special study program as an ongoing form of personal development, they can be motivated to do so if there are adequate opportunities for promotion and pay increases.[21]

VISUAL PRESENTATIONS

Visual training materials can appear in several forms, including television, films, videotapes, filmstrips, and slide-tape presentations. The films may portray actual people in real-life situations, or they may be animated cartoons. Both actual and animated films serve useful purposes. Real-life photography can make the training seem real and factual, but drawings can emphasize expressions, emotions, and ideas with few conflicting stimuli.

Television has become increasingly popular as a method of presenting business training. Some organizations have their own private networks that present training programs produced by the company. Another use of television is teleconferencing, which broadcasts programs that may be created live in broadcast studios located hundreds of miles apart.[22]

Films can be used for many purposes. Athletes often watch films of their performances to identify their mistakes. They also watch films of their opponents to identify weaknesses that they may use to their advantage. Videotaping actual behavior can be just as useful for management trainees. The trainees can observe how they responded in a particular situation and can diagnose their behavior.

Many training films have been developed to portray particular insights about management, supervision, and other technical skills. A major advantage of presenting information by film rather than by lecture is that films can be edited to minimize the amount of distracting information and to maximize learning efficiency for the trainee. Geographically dispersed companies have found videotapes a convenient way to transmit new ideas from headquarters or a training office.

One of the most promising uses of videotapes and films is to illustrate correct behavior patterns for imitative learning. Social cognitive theory has shown that observing the behavior of others is one of the most effective ways of developing new skills. Watching videotaped episodes of effective management behaviors is a powerful learning tool for management trainees. An excellent way to help supervisors learn new skills is to let them see how effective supervisors behave in situations similar to their own.

CONFERENCES AND DISCUSSIONS

Conferences and group discussions are used extensively for making decisions. However, they also can be used as a form of training. Conferences and discussions provide forums where individuals are able to learn from one another. A major use of group discussion is to change attitudes and behavior. Numerous studies have shown that individuals are much more inclined to change their attitudes if they participate in a group discussion and arrive at a group consensus regarding a topic than if they listen to a lecture.[23] An example of a group discussion that can be an effective means of training is one in which supervisors discuss the performance-evaluation procedure and develop common criteria for evaluating performance. One study showed that a group of supervisors who discussed their performance evaluations among themselves were more consistent and accurate in their ratings than supervisors who listened to a lecture or were simply given performance-evaluation guidelines by personnel. Group discussions have also been used successfully in empathy training to help nurses and other hospital workers develop greater sensitivity in caring for patients.[24]

TELECONFERENCING

With the advent of satellite broadcasting it is now possible for a trainer to be in one location while the learners are in many other locations watching the trainer on a television monitor. This type of training, called teleconferencing, may even include multiple trainers broadcasting from different locations as a panel of experts with the capacity to interact with their audience.

   Teleconferencing owes much of its growing popularity to its capacity to train many learners in different locations without the inconvenience or cost of bringing them together. The modes of teleconferencing, or teletraining, include computer, audio, video, or any combination of these three. Teleconferencing requires higher levels of skill for the trainers because they may be speaking only to a video camera and unable to observe how well their ideas are being received. Greater demands are also placed on the learners, who are encouraged to ask questions and provide feedback to the trainer. The comments of those who have participated in teleconferencing suggest that the motivation to learn is apparently not affected by teleconferencing, and the amount of practice and transfer of learning do not differ between teleconferencing and traditional learning.[25]

CASE STUDY

Case studies are used extensively in many business classes. They are designed to promote a trainee's discovery of underlying principles. Most cases do not have a single correct solution. Instead, a trainee is expected to analyze the problem and consider alternative solutions. Even though trainees may not agree on the best solution, a fair amount of agreement about the relevant issues should exist. Some cases are short and focus on a specific problem or issue. Other cases are long and unstructured, encouraging participants to consider a variety of diagnostic approaches and alternative solutions.

   The success of the case method as a training technique depends largely upon the skill of the discussion leader. Effective case discussions require skilled trainers who know when to focus the group's discussion on particular topics and when to allow free-floating ideas and exploration into alternative issues.

ROLE PLAYING

Role playing is a situation in which the participants assume specific characterizations and act out a particular situation or problem. Rather than simply talking about what the solution should be, the participants attempt to solve the situation as if they were the real individuals involved. Role playing usually creates a higher level of participation and enthusiasm among the participants than regular group discussion. Some participants enjoy role playing because it provides an opportunity to act out their uninhibited impulses. Other participants, however, feel that role playing is a bit immature.

One of the most effective uses of role playing is to facilitate attitude change. The best procedure for changing attitudes is to have participants play roles in which they are asked to express attitudes that are the opposite of their own personal feelings. A similar procedure is to ask participants to play the roles of people with whom they typically conflict. These situations are called counterattitudinal role playing and **role reversal**. In such situations the trainees are forced to verbalize a set of opinions that are contrary to their own private opinions. When individuals participate in such role-playing activities, their private opinions typically shift in the direction of the arguments they present.[26] This suggests that an effective training technique for reducing the conflict between a marketing manager and a production manager might be to have them reverse roles in a training situation and try to resolve their differences.

SIMULATION

Simulation refers to creating an artificial learning environment that approximates the actual job conditions as much as possible. In this regard, simulation is very similar to vestibule training. Simulation has been used extensively for learning technical and motor skills. Pilot training is facilitated by using a flight simulator that reproduces the cockpit of an airplane. One simulation for training Air Force pilots allows the trainees to fly missions against manned and computer-generated threats. Participating instructors, pilots, and controllers also can learn vicariously by viewing the progress of an ongoing simulation in a war room. In this theaterlike room, the scenes visible through the head-up display, radarscope, and radar-warning receiver of each engaged jet are presented on large monitors. The radio transmissions can also be heard.[27] Pilot trainees receive feedback on whether the responses they make are correct or incorrect. In the most sophisticated simulators, computers are used to analyze trainees' responses and provide feedback on their accuracy. The Air Force also has a very elaborate simulator that is a replication of an actual missile control room and is used to train missile crews.

Many different kinds of learning situations can be simulated with or without the use of a computer. The in-basket simulation is one of the simplest forms of simulation. In this exercise the trainee is asked to assume the role of a new manager or supervisor confronted with a set of instructions describing the new job and a series of memos outlining problems that need to be resolved. The trainee is given a limited amount of time, usually two hours, to read the memos and respond as if it were a real-life situation. The trainee makes decisions, replies to the memos, schedules meetings, and may even develop agendas for the meetings. Afterward, the trainee's decisions are evaluated, and feedback is given about alternative actions that could have been taken and about the advantages and disadvantages of the decisions that were made.

A more sophisticated form of simulation involves business games using a computer. Several computer simulations have been designed to approximate actual industrial settings. The trainees are asked to make business decisions as if they were operating a company.[28] In one particular simulation, the Business Management Laboratory, participants are asked to assume the leadership of a small manufacturing company competing with companies operated by other trainees.[29] The participants make decisions on production, pricing, hiring and training new sales representatives, and other production and financial concerns. The decisions are analyzed by the computer according to a program that approximates real-life conditions. The participants receive reports, such as an income statement and a sales report, that are similar to those actually received by managers. Each decision-making period within the simulation represents the decisions that a management team might make during a three-month period.

Computer simulations allow participants to examine the long-term effects of their business decisions in a relatively short period of time. If they make bad decisions, they can learn from their mistakes without having to suffer the actual consequences of real-life circumstances. Business simulations also motivate students to learn on their own. Students will voluntarily master even difficult concepts, such as break-even analysis and linear programming, if making an effective decision requires it.

PROGRAMMED INSTRUCTION

During the 1960s, **programmed instruction** was the newest fad in training and education. Programmed instruction is an application of the principles of operant conditioning, and some of its most enthusiastic proponents expected it to revolutionize the field of training and education. Although it did not replace other forms of learning, programmed instruction did become widely used as a method of training.

Several steps are involved in the development of programmed instruction material. First, the material must be divided into small learning segments, usually called frames. A series of frames are then combined into what is called a program. Each frame consists of certain information for the trainees to study. After studying a frame, the trainees are required to make a response evaluating their learning. The trainees are told immediately whether their responses are correct or incorrect. This feedback has the advantage of giving immediate reinforcement as well as knowledge of results.

The frames are organized according to a logical sequence in which earlier frames serve as building blocks for the development of more complex learning. Performance of the trainees is used as an indication of whether the learning material is properly described and appropriately sequenced. If most trainees have difficulty with a particular concept, then the material is rewritten to clarify it. The material is revised until most trainees can make the correct response on their first time through the material. Trainees work independently and proceed at their own pace.

Programmed instruction material can be presented to trainees in several ways. One method uses a teaching machine in which the material is presented one frame at a time. The trainees must make a response before they can advance the material. If their response is correct, they can proceed to the next frame. Otherwise they must go back and review previous frames. Another method uses a branching format. Here, a frame is presented on one page of a book, and at the bottom of that page, the trainees are given a question with alternative answers. Each answer instructs them to turn to another page where they learn whether their answer is correct or incorrect. If their answer is incorrect, the reason for its incorrectness is explained, and they are given further instructions and told where to proceed.

Programmed instructional material also has been presented on a computer in what is called **computer-assisted instruction** or computer-based training. Rather than reading the material from a book, the trainees read the material from a television screen. After they have read the material, they respond to a question, and the computer indicates whether their response is correct or incorrect. If the response is incorrect, the computer explains why and provides additional information to help trainees master the concept. If the response is correct, the computer proceeds to the next concept.[30]

INTERACTIVE VIDEODISC TRAINING

One of the newest high-tech forms of training uses an interactive laser-videodisc (IVD). Students sit in front of a video screen and interact with it in a self-paced learning session. The students listen to recorded instructions and watch visual images on the screen. Every few seconds the students are asked a question and they respond by touching one of the alternative responses shown on the screen or on a keyboard. Their answer determines the next voice they hear and the next image they will see, which could be a video, computer graphics, text, or a combination of all three.

A personal computer receives input from the touch-sensitive screen and directs a laser beam to specified frames on the disc. Each side of a videodisc carries thousands of still frames or several minutes of running video. The computer can superimpose graphic images on the video image coming from the videodisc machine. Thus an arrow can be used to identify an object on the screen just as a live instructor points to an illustration in a traditional classroom.

One of the learning benefits of an IVD is that each learner is required to respond to every question, something a traditional classroom does not typically provide. Another difference is the absence of embarrassment for wrong answers and the opportunity for learners to proceed at their own pace and even go back to review if they desire. Videodisc programs are infinitely patient, and repetition of a lesson can continue endlessly.

Hundreds of IVD courses have been developed, including programs for teaching basic literacy to nonreaders, instructing doctors how to diagnose ulcers, teaching executives how to manage, and training pilots how to fly. Producers of these programs claim that IVD training reduces the time required to learn by 30 percent or more in most cases and that retention is increased.[31]

Although most courses are expensive to develop and the equipment is costly, IVD can be less expensive than other forms of training if a large number of students need to be trained and if the training is not expected to change for several years.[32]

LABORATORY TRAINING

Laboratory training is also known as **sensitivity training** or T-group training. This type of training consists of an unstructured group discussion in which the participants talk about their personal feelings and reactions toward each other. The length of a laboratory training session may vary from as short as a couple of hours to as long as two or three weeks of all-day sessions. The training is designed to create greater self-awareness and increased sensitivity to the attitudes and emotions of others and to group processes. The leader of the group, called a facilitator, does not actively direct the group discussion but simply helps clarify the feelings and attitudes of group members. There is no agenda, and the group is free to discuss anything it chooses. The participants typically discuss their personal feelings and their reactions toward one another. Sensitivity training is designed to help trainees develop interpersonal-relations skills by enabling them to understand more about their own feelings and the attitudes and expectations of others.

PROGRAMMED GROUP EXERCISES

Programmed group exercises, sometimes called **experiential group exercises**, involve trainees working together in a discussion group to solve a specific problem. Although the problem may be artificial, the participation by each trainee within the group is not artificial. Participants interact with each other as if they were in a real problem-solving situation. After the decision has been reached, participants discuss what occurred, analyze the group processes, and analyze the behavior of each person in the group. Valuable learning occurs not only during the actual exercise but also during the following discussion.

One of the best-known experiential exercises is the NASA exercise. In this exercise the participants assume that they have crash-landed on the lighted side of the moon. They are asked to rank fifteen items in order of importance in helping them travel 200 miles to reach the mother ship. Each participant ranks the fifteen items, then groups of five to seven participants try to reach a consensus ranking. The groups often experience conflict in attempting to reach a consensus. Many important group processes can be observed during this exercise, such as leadership, communication, persuasion, decision making, problem solving, and conflict resolution. The most important insight for the participants is not whether fifty feet of nylon rope is more or less important than a magnetic compass for survival on the moon but how they can interact with each other to obtain the maximum sharing of knowledge.

Assessment centers represent a particular form of programmed group exercise. As discussed in Chapter 6, an assessment center involves a group of participants who work together on various group exercises. Assessment-center activities are useful in identifying potential managers as well as in providing training. Assessment-center activities help employees to achieve greater self-awareness and to learn valuable principles of management and supervision. Some companies have found that the observers learn as much as the participants, if not more. As a side benefit of the training they receive, the observers learn which behaviors they should acquire to increase their own effectiveness.

CUSTOMER EDUCATION

The fastest-growing type of training in recent years is customer education: teaching customers and clients how to use the organization's products and services. A 1985 survey indicated that for organizations with fifty or more employees, about half offered this type of training and considered it a strategic necessity.[33] Some organizations have been training customers for decades, such as General Mills with helpful hints from Betty Crocker, the Singer Company's sewing seminars, and Eastman Kodak's focus-and-shoot tips. In recent years customer training has become more elaborate and vital. It now occurs in a variety of forms, including owner's manuals, assembly instructions, job aids, troubleshooting guides, toll-free telephone numbers, user seminars, and demonstrations by field representatives. Financial institutions offer seminars and courses to teach potential investors about investment opportunities and the consequences of changes in tax laws. As consumer products and services become more complex, with built-in computers, timers, safety devices, legal restrictions, and programmable functions, customer training will continue to increase in frequency and importance.

EVALUATION OF TRAINING TECHNIQUES

Since so many different techniques are available, a training specialist must carefully evaluate the advantages and disadvantages of each technique to determine which is appropriate for a given situation. The selection of a training technique should be determined primarily by the objective of the training. For example, a lecture is ideal for disseminating a large amount of information to learners who are already motivated to receive it. But the lecture is not as useful for changing attitudes or teaching new motor skills.

The major principles of learning are described in Chapter 8: motivation, feedback, meaningful stimulus, practice, and transfer of training. The extent to which the various training techniques use these principles is indicated in Table 9.2. An ideal training program should be consistent with each of these principles; however, all five principles may not be equally important, depending on the particular training activity. For example, all five principles may not be important in training a group of sales representatives about changes in the product mix for the coming year; a carefully organized lecture or video-tape presentation of information may be adequate, and therefore, the four principles of active participation, knowledge of results, practice, and transfer of training would not be required.[34]

The various training techniques are used in a variety of different training programs. A survey by *Training* magazine of the general types of training offered by companies indicates that some kinds of training are much more popular than others.[35] The three most popular types of training include management development, supervisory skills, and technical skills, as shown in Table 9.3. Although basic remedial education does not occur very often, it is still provided by about one in three companies.

ORIENTATION TRAINING

An orientation program can have a positive influence on job expectations and job satisfaction and can establish a sense of identity for new employees at every level in an organization. As noted in Chapter 6, orientation training can reduce turnover, alleviate anxiety, create positive work values, reduce start-up costs, and save the time of supervisors and coworkers. To be effective, an orientation training program must be carefully designed. However, most trainers tend to provide too much detailed information in their orientation programs.

TABLE 9.2   Extent to which training techniques utilize five principles of learning

Principles of Learning

	Motivation: Active Participation of Learner	Reinforcement: Feedback or Knowledge of Results	Stimulus: Meaningful Organization of Materials	Responses: Practice and Repetition	Stimulus-response: Conditions Most Favorable for Transfer
On-the-job techniques					
Job-instruction training	Yes	Sometimes	Yes	Yes	Yes
Apprentice training	Yes	Sometimes	Possibly	Sometimes	Yes
Interships and assistantships	Yes	Sometimes	Possibly	Sometimes	Yes
Job rotation	Yes	No	Possibly	Sometimes	Yes
Junior board	Yes	Sometimes	Sometimes	Sometimes	Yes
Coaching	Yes	Yes	Sometimes	Sometimes	Yes
Off-the-job techniques					
Vestibule	Yes	Sometimes	Yes	Yes	Sometimes
Lecture	No	No	Yes	No	No
Special study	Yes	No	Yes	Possibly	No
Films	No	No	Yes	No	No
Television	No	No	Yes	No	No
Conference or discussion	Yes	Sometimes	Sometimes	Sometimes	No
Teleconferencing	No	Sometimes	Sometimes	No	No
Case study	Yes	Sometimes	Sometimes	Sometimes	Sometimes
Role playing	Yes	Sometimes	No	Sometimes	Sometimes
Simulation	Yes	Sometimes	Sometimes	Sometimes	Sometimes
Programmed instruction	Yes	Yes	Yes	Yes	No
Interactive videodisc	Yes	Yes	Yes	Sometimes	Sometimes
Laboratory training	Yes	Yes	No	Yes	Sometimes
Programmed group exercises	Yes	Yes	Yes	Sometimes	Sometimes

TABLE 9.3 Frequency of general types of training

Types of Training	Percent of Companies That Offer This Type of Training
Management skills/development	84.2
Supervisory skills	79.9
Technical skills/knowledge	79.8
Communication skills	75.7
Basic computer skills	69.3
New methods/procedures	68.8
Customer relations/services	66.4
Clerical/secretarial skills	65.4
Personal growth	61.9
Executive development	61.6
Employee/labor relations	52.1
Wellness	47.7
Sales skills	46.8
Customer education	42.2
Remedial basic education	31.7

Source: Beverly Geber, "Who, How, and What," *Training,* Vol. 26 (October 1989): 50.

CONTENT OF ORIENTATION TRAINING

In designing an orientation program, trainers should decide what information is needed *right now* by new employees. Orientation training should start with basic survival knowledge and progress to more general, but less pressing, information. This is the kind of information that is most useful:

1. Working hours, including breaks and lunch hours.
2. Location of facilities, especially the new employee's office, rest rooms, and eating places.
3. Special words and phrases used by the work group, particularly abbreviations.
4. Paydays and how the person will be paid.
5. Health and safety considerations, such as safe operating procedures, fire escapes, exits, first-aid supplies, and location of the nursing station.
6. Information on whom to contact in case of problems or difficulties.
7. Information on parking, bus stops, and car pooling.
8. Information about the phone system, such as how to be reached from outside and how to call outside.[36]

An effective orientation program actually begins before the new employees are hired. During the recruiting process, recruiters should effectively sell the organization to applicants. However, they must not oversell it and create unrealistic expectations about the work. New employees need to receive accurate and realistic job previews so that they do not expect working conditions that are significantly different from what they find. Negative aspects of the job should be presented to them factually so that they do not come as a surprise.[37]

EFFECTIVE ORIENTATION SESSIONS

In designing an orientation program, the trainer should carefully consider the kinds of impressions and expectations that the program should create. Initial expectations have a profound influence on the behavior and values of new employees. Since new employees do not know what to anticipate, the comments made during an orientation program have the potential of creating profound expectations. These expectations have a way of becoming self-fulfilling prophecies. For example, employees who are told that they are expected to become outstanding performers often become just that. The self-fulfilling prophecy has been observed frequently among management trainees, and it helps to explain why some individuals are able to achieve success and make rapid advancement within an organization.[38] An analysis of this concept suggests that expectations of success are created in the minds of trainees by: (1) the kinds of information and ideas given to them, (2) the output expected from them, (3) the type of feedback they receive, and (4) the encouragement and reinforcement they are given. If an organization wants to create a commitment to excellence among its new employees, the employee orientation is the best time to do it.[39]

During the orientation program, an attempt should be made to reduce the anxiety of new employees. Since new employees are usually concerned about being able to perform adequately on the job, they ought to know that their chances of succeeding are very good and that other individuals just like them have succeeded in the past. Anxiety is also reduced by acquainting new employees with their supervisors and coworkers.

New employees are likely to face some hazing by coworkers. Hazing refers to the harassment of new employees by senior coworkers, such as laughing at their mistakes, making derogatory comments, asking them to perform impossible tasks, and telling them they don't have what it takes. During the orientation training, the new employees should be warned about the possibility of being harassed and should be encouraged to accept it in good humor.

An experienced coworker or supervisor in the immediate environment should be assigned to each new employee as a "sponsor" or "mentor." The purpose of the sponsor is to provide specific job-related instructions and other information regarding the informal work-group norms and procedures. The sponsor should provide encouragement and advice and be available to answer questions as they arise. A major role of the mentor is to help introduce the new employee to other members of the work group. These introductions are generally best if they do not occur all at once. New employees should be introduced to their coworkers gradually.

Organizations often want to present the entire orientation training the first day and get it over with. If an employee is expected to remember all of the information presented, however, one massive training experience is not very effective. Two procedures help new employees retain information: receiving written instructions and spreading the training over a period of time.

Written instructions are particularly necessary for extensive, detailed information. Although new employees need to understand detailed information pertaining to company policies, benefits, and work procedures, the organization should not expect them to remember all of this information after one lengthy presentation. A superior procedure is to provide general verbal information followed by specific, detailed written information. The written information should be provided in an employee handbook that employees can study at their leisure when specific questions arise.

Orientation training is most effective when it is spread over several days rather than presented in one or two long sessions. Employees generally prefer several short orientation sessions combined with on-the-job training rather than one long session.[40]

In summary, the guidelines for developing an effective training program include the following:

1. Begin with the most relevant information.
2. Provide sponsors or mentors to help new employees learn the ropes.
3. Gradually introduce new employees to members of the work group.
4. Space the orientation training over a period of time rather than concentrating it in one long session.
5. Provide both oral and written information. Oral instruction should provide general orientation information, while detailed, specific information should be written.

MANAGEMENT DEVELOPMENT PROGRAMS

Selecting the appropriate content for a management development program is more critical than deciding which training technique to use. In other words, deciding what to teach is more important than deciding how to teach it. Moreover, the decision to use a lecture, a group discussion, role playing, or some other technique should be determined largely by the content of the training program.

Management development programs teach a bewildering variety of topics. In former years, the basic principles of management were considered to be planning, organizing, motivating, and controlling. Management development programs typically tried to describe these management functions and to present general principles for all managers to learn. In recent years, theorists have questioned the universal relevance of these principles of management, and they no longer believe that there are general principles of management that apply to all managers. The new philosophy of management, called contingency management, claims that the proper behavior for a manager depends on the situation the manager is facing. Since managers face a variety of different situations, it is difficult to design a generic curriculum for all managers.

DIFFERENT SKILLS FOR DIFFERENT LEADERS

The knowledge and skills required to be a good manager are not the same for all managerial positions. Management positions can be conveniently categorized into three major categories: top managers, middle managers, and first-line supervisors. Good theoretical reasons exist for using these three categories. Katz and Kahn have demonstrated that the three levels are significantly different in terms of leadership processes, attitudes, and skills.[41] Top-level managers must have an organization-wide perspective as they adapt the organizational structure to meet the demands of the environment. Supervisors, at the other end, are required to have technical knowledge and an understanding of the rules and procedures for getting the work done. Between these two levels, middle managers try to look both ways and translate the broad goals of top managers into specific procedures for supervisors to follow.

Management skills can be categorized into three dimensions: (1) technical and professional skills, (2) interpersonal relations skills, and (3) conceptual and administrative skills.[42] Technical and professional skills refer to the skills needed to perform a particular job, such operating or repairing a machine, completing and processing a particular form, writing a computer program, preparing a budget, and other specific actions involved in accomplishing direct work. Interpersonal relations skills are those that relate to the ability to interact with others, such as evaluating performance, providing positive reinforcement and feedback, and building a cohesive team. Conceptual and administrative skills are those that involve analyzing the functioning of an organization, such as understanding the business environment, diagnosing problems within the organization, and deciding what actions are needed to correct organizational problems.

These three skills are not equally appropriate for all managerial positions. Technical and professional skills are much more important for supervisors and lower-level managers than for top administrators. On the other hand, conceptual and administrative skills are much more important for top managers than for supervisors. Figure 9.1 illustrates the relative importance of these three skills for each level of management.

GENERAL VERSUS SPECIFIC TRAINING

Which topics can be taught in a management development program, and how applicable are they to each level of management?

FIGURE 9.1 Training and development skills of managers: hierarchy of management skills.

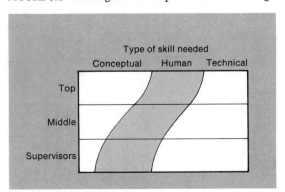

TECHNICAL AND PROFESSIONAL SKILLS

Technical and professional skills are generally specific to the job and to the organization. Safety training is an illustration of technical training. Although every organization needs some form of safety training, a specific training program describing safe operating procedures for one company may be quite different than that for another organization. Although some safety training is general, such as programs designed to raise the overall level of safety consciousness, most safety training needs to contain specific information relevant to specific jobs.

INTERPERSONAL RELATIONS

Interpersonal relations skills are generally relevant to all levels of management. A training program in interpersonal relations skills might cover such topics as communication, listening, handling grievances and complaints, and evaluating performance.

CONCEPTUAL AND ADMINISTRATIVE

Most conceptual and administrative skills are general in nature and relevant to all managers, especially top-level managers. For example, training in decision making would most likely explain the process by which any decision is made: identify the problem, identify alternative solutions, evaluate the alternatives, and select the best alternative. The decision-making process is essentially the same for all managers, even though top managers may spend more time making decisions. Likewise, training programs in managing time have universal relevance. All managers need to understand the processes of setting priorities, making "to-do" lists, scheduling meetings, and constructing agendas. Although the general principles regarding time management and problem solving may be applied to specific organizational problems, the principles have universal application in many different managerial settings.

COMMERCIAL MANAGEMENT DEVELOPMENT PROGRAMS

In recent years, management development programs have proliferated throughout the United States. This growth is based on simple economic considerations: training programs have the potential to produce sizeable revenues on the basis of small costs. Although large organizations sponsor many of their own management development programs, both large and small organizations increasingly use outside consultants and other training organizations.

TRAINING ORGANIZATIONS

The most popular form of management training is formal education; more management education and development occurs in colleges and universities than in other training settings. Almost every university and college has some form of management training, either to train new managers or to train current managers. The typical training for new managers is a masters of business administration (MBA) degree, and the design of most MBA programs worldwide is patterned after graduate business schools in the United States. However, the curriculum of the traditional MBA program has sparked growing criticism because of its excessive emphasis on quantitative decision-making models and

HRM in Action

Training Sponsored by Joint Labor-Management Committees in the Auto Industry

The first labor-management committees in the American auto industry started in the early 1970s. Until 1982, however, these programs were largely informal, plant-by-plant efforts in places where the climate was not too hostile. The need for greater cooperation was evidenced by problems attributed to antagonistic contract negotiations and growing international competition. Labor-management cooperation has long been hailed as a key to Japan's competitive edge.

In 1982 the United Auto Workers Union first negotiated a jointly administered labor-management program. In the 1984 negotiations the financing was substantially increased to 20 cents per worker-hour to fund national and local programs. This arrangement has provided for more than adequate funding of a variety of "jointness" activities.

The original focus of the labor-management committees was on ways to improve productivity. This focus changed, however, to more noncontroversial objectives that focused largely on the personal growth of the employees and only indirectly, if at all, on productivity.

The joint effort between General Motors and the UAW costs about $200 million per year, which funds a national training center near Detroit and eight regional centers around the country. These human resource centers offer a variety of programs in diverse topics, such as avoiding AIDS and buying real estate, plus basic literacy and education. The national training center is located on a twenty-two-acre "jointness" park equipped with designated rooms containing a communication network and TV monitors. GM and the UAW also issue a joint newsletter to keep the workers informed. In 1989 over 200 labor-management involvement groups were organized and meeting regularly.

The results of these joint efforts are mixed. The programs are costly and increasingly bureaucratic, but they have contributed to a better working relationship, and some think that quality improvements can be indirectly traced to them. Some argue that the improvements in basic education and job training alone are sufficient to justify the time and expense they require.

Source: Jacob M. Schlesinger, "Costly Friendship: Auto Firms and UAW Find that Cooperation Can Get Complicated." *Wall Street Journal*, August 25, 1989, p. 1.

its failure to prepare managers to think critically, analytically, and ethically. Many MBA programs, especially in Europe, are beginning to focus more on the development of interpersonal and diagnostic skills.[43]

Most universities also offer executive development courses for current managers as part of their extension programs. These courses range from broad executive orientation training for top executives to specific courses, such as just-in-time manufacturing or human resource planning, for other managers. Many companies rely heavily on public colleges and universities to provide current and relevant training for their managers. Other corporations, however, such as IBM, General Electric, Xerox, and McDonald's, have their own corporate colleges for training managers and executives. These campus-like training centers provide three major kinds of training: (1) generic management training, which usually focuses on interpersonal and conceptual skills; (2) specific skills applicable to a particular company, such as Dunkin Donuts' training for new franchise owners; and (3) developing a particular organizational culture. Some companies require all employees to complete a basic orientation program and then return after every promotion for more training that may include both a basic core of generic management skills plus specific functional training.[44]

The American Management Association (AMA), which was founded in 1923 to advance the science of management, is another leader in management development training. The AMA sponsors a vast array of both general and specific management development courses in dozens of metropolitan areas. Their course catalog contains almost as many listings as some colleges.

The Society for Human Resource Management (SHRM) is another professional association that conducts numerous seminars throughout the United States. The SHRM seminars, however, focus largely on personnel and industrial relations topics. Likewise, the American Society for Training and Development (ASTD) sponsors numerous seminars, especially programs designed to train company trainers.

Hundreds of independent trainers and consulting organizations are involved in providing management training. Many training companies were started by former personnel specialists who were at one time involved in developing and presenting training programs in their companies.

Faculty members of business schools also are involved in independently developing and presenting training programs. However, academic credentials and training experience are not essential prerequisites for conducting training programs. The list of those who offer management development seminars includes a broad array of people, such as professional athletes, coaches, former politicians, political aides, journalists, public relations specialists, and even ex-convicts.

Consulting organizations that specialize in providing management training and development are constantly coming and going. Some are as unstable as a group of undergraduate business students who design and sell a training program for a semester as part of a course requirement. However, other consulting organizations are very stable, representing a long-term commitment to a particular style of training and development.

COSTS AND BENEFITS

Are training programs cost-benefit effective? Most executives do not use the same tough-minded, cost-benefit criteria to evaluate training that they use in evaluating other business decisions. One rationalization for not evaluating the worth of training is that the costs and benefits are difficult to assess accurately. Executives also realize that the benefits of management development activities may be long-term benefits that cannot be observed immediately in profit-and-loss statements.

Even though the benefits may be hard to assess, a careful analysis should be made of the costs of management development activities. The costs are often much greater than realized. Most of the American Management Association conferences cost between $250 and $350 per day for members and more for nonmembers (1989 prices). For example, the AMA's course for new managers is a three-day program that cost $795. Other costs, such as transportation and living expenses, also are involved in attending these programs. Most of the management development seminars offered by ASPA, by universities, and by other private consultants cost at least that much or more. One private consultant charges companies $30,000 per day for his training. A survey of training budgets in 1989 found that 6 percent of budgeted training dollars was spent on seminars and conferences conducted by outside providers and another 4 percent paid for the fees of external consultants.[45]

A management development program that helps a manager develop new managerial skills or that stimulates creative insights into new ways of handling difficult problems can be worth many times the cost of its tuition. Therefore, determining whether management development programs are overpriced and whether they are cost-benefit effective is not a cut-and-dried process. Moreover, predicting whether a particular program will provide the valuable skills it promises and whether it will stimulate creative insight into new problems is a difficult, if not impossible, task.

The management training programs that probably have the greatest cost and least benefit are professional association meetings and annual conferences. The annual meetings of most professional associations are more like vacations than learning experiences. Attending a conference is essentially a paid vacation, since the cost of attendance, including travel, living expenses, and tuition, is paid by the employer. Critics of professional association meetings say that nothing is wrong with attending such a meeting as an extra paid vacation, but that it should be recognized as such.[46]

Since most management development programs are advertised by mail, advertising is a major variable in determining the success of a program. A well-advertised management development program can attract a large attendance even though the content of the program may be virtually worthless. Since the advertisements about a program can be very misleading, managers face a difficult task in trying to select carefully developed and useful programs to attend. The following suggestions identify additional sources of information that managers may want to examine before selecting a management development program.[47]

1. Talk to someone who has attended the program or to executives of other organizations that have sent managers to it. Managers who have already participated in a particular program usually are willing to describe the program objectively and to comment on its usefulness.
2. Investigate the trainers and instructors. The writings of most competent instructors who have developed an original technique or new ideas will be published in either professional journals or books. If a trainer has never written anything, the trainer could be asked to provide an in-depth course syllabus and copies of the training materials or outside readings that will be provided for program participants. Something in a written form should provide evidence of the quality of a good management development program.
3. Look for evaluation evidence, particularly research studies that evaluate the effectiveness of a program. Although evidence may not be available for all good programs, many of the better programs have been evaluated, and data are available to demonstrate the quality of these programs.[47]

EVALUATING TRAINING PROGRAMS

The three phases of training and development consist of assessing training needs, developing and presenting the training, and evaluating the training program. Considering the importance of evaluation, it is surprising to see how inadequately most training programs are evaluated. Many programs are not evaluated at all, and those that are evaluated are usually not assessed carefully.

Training programs are not evaluated carefully or frequently for several reasons. Evaluation takes time and effort. Usually the evaluation occurs after the training is over, and at that point, most managers are ready to pursue other projects. Nevertheless, evaluations are important because the evaluative feedback helps in the design of future programs and ensures that programs meet organizational needs.

Evaluating training programs is not especially difficult when the evaluation process has been built into the original training design and when provisions have been made for collecting the information. In evaluating training and development programs, two important issues should be addressed. The first issue concerns the criteria of evaluation: what are the important criteria by which training and development programs should be evaluated? Is the objective of training to achieve a change in behavior, a change in attitude, or a change in the organization? The second issue concerns the research design: when and from whom should data be collected to assess the effects of training?

CRITERIA OF EVALUATION

The criteria for evaluating a training program should be determined by the training objectives. If a training program is designed to disseminate new information, then the effectiveness of the training should be determined by how well the information was disseminated. Most training programs attempt to accomplish several objectives, such as to change behavior, to provide new information, and to make an organization more effective. Consequently, most evaluations should utilize multiple criteria. Four criteria have been proposed for evaluating training programs: (1) reactions, (2) learning, (3) behavior, and (4) results.[48]

REACTIONS

How well did the trainees like the program? Since the trainees are the consumers of the product, how well they liked the program is important information for evaluating the program. Did they feel that the information was worthwhile? Was it presented in a way that was meaningful and interesting? Did they believe the program was well-prepared and carefully organized?

These reactions can be obtained by having participants complete a simple questionnaire at the end of a training program. Although care is needed in designing the questionnaire to minimize response biases, the process of assessing participant reactions is quite easy. In fact, the ease of assessing participant reactions probably explains why this is the only information that is typically obtained regarding the effectiveness of most programs.

LEARNING

To what extent did the trainees learn and retain the information presented in the training program? Most training programs present knowledge that the participants are expected to learn. How well the participants learned and retained this information should be determined through the use of evaluations that are similar to the examinations used in schools and colleges to see how much students have learned. These tests can be based on traditional evaluation methods: true-false questions, multiple-choice questions, and essay exams.

Although many trainers are apprehensive about administering an exam, the participants usually respond more favorably than the trainers anticipate. In fact, when participants know in advance that they will be examined on the content of a training program, their attentiveness and retention usually increase.

BEHAVIOR

To what extent did the behavior of the trainees change as a result of the program? For example, if a time management seminar is expected to help trainees use their time more effectively by setting priorities and by developing "to-do" lists, did the participants actually change their behavior as a result of the training?

Changes in behavior can be assessed by two major methods. First, individuals can be asked to assess changes in their behavior by using a simple self-report questionnaire. Second, changes in behavior can be assessed by the observations of others. Supervisors, for example, can be assessed by their superiors or their subordinates. Several useful profiles have been developed to evaluate changes in a supervisor as perceived by subordinates.[49]

RESULTS

What final results were achieved from training—reduced costs, reduced turnover, improved productivity, or greater profitability? The primary reason for presenting most training programs is to improve organizational performance. The question, then, is whether the organization is actually performing more effectively or efficiently as a result of the training effort. After a training program on safety, is the frequency or severity of accidents declining? As a result of a new-employee orientation program, is the percentage of employees who leave within the first sixty days declining? As a result of a supervisory training program, are the departments of the trained supervisors obtaining higher levels of productivity, profitability, or morale?

RESEARCH DESIGNS

Numerous research designs may be used to evaluate training programs, and four are discussed in this section. The first two represent poor research designs, even though they frequently are used in evaluating training programs. The next two are excellent designs that should be used more frequently than they have been.[50]

THE POSTTEST-ONLY DESIGN

Many training programs are evaluated on the basis of a simple posttest-only design, also known as the case-study design, in which data are collected after the training program has been completed. This design is one of four designs illustrated in Figure 9.2. The symbols used in this figure are those used in research designs for behavioral science studies. *X* refers to the experimental treatment, or, as used here, to the training and development program. *O* represents an observation, or here, an evaluation of the training program. The evaluation could use any or all of the criteria discussed previously: reactions, learning, behavior, and results.

In a simple posttest-only design, the training program is presented and then evaluated. This is a poor research design for evaluating a training program because no standards of comparison are available for interpreting the observations. An evaluation may show that the participants are exhibiting the proper kinds of behavior, but they may have been displaying the appropriate behavior before the training program was ever presented. When nothing is known about behavior before training, a case study cannot show that a training program created a change in behavior.

Case-study designs are not entirely worthless. Although they are poor evaluation designs, they sometimes provide insightful information that helps in evaluating a program. The usefulness of a case study, however, depends on the skills of the observer. An astute observer may be able to evaluate what has occurred in a training program, assess the program's effectiveness, and prescribe changes that need to occur.

PRETEST-POSTTEST COMPARISONS

To provide a comparison for the posttest observations, some evaluators conduct a pretest evaluation. Although this design compensates for one of the problems of the case-study design, it is still an inadequate research design.

Improvements in performance or learning scores from the pretest to the posttest may or may not be attributed to the training program. For example, if a group of new trainees

FIGURE 9.2 Four research designs.

1. Posttest-only design (case study)
   X   O

2. Pretest-posttest comparison
   O   X   O

3. Pretest-posttest control group design
   R   O   X   O
   R   O   O

4. Solomon four-group design
   R   O   X   O
   R   O   O
   R   X   O
   R   O

Key
X = Experimental treatment or training program
O = Observation or measurement
R = Random assignment of participants to training condition

is exposed to one hour of training every day during their first week, improvements in their scores from the first of the week to the end of the week are typically attributed to the effects of training. Although the results may make the program appear successful, several competing explanations may also explain the change in the scores. Three of the most relevant competing explanations are referred to in experimental research as history, maturation, and the sensitizing effects of the pretest.

History refers to the historical events that transpire between the pretest and the posttest. While the training program is being presented, many other things are also happening that may influence the scores regardless of what occurs in training. **Maturation** refers to the development and growth that occurs within the trainees—processes that occur regardless of the training program. A group of new employees may show a significant improvement in their scores at the end of training compared to their scores at the onset of training because of the time they have spent on the job rather than the time they have spent in training.

Sensitizing effects of the pretest refers to the effects that pretesting might have on the trainees. Some attitudes and behaviors can be influenced simply by evaluating them. For example, studies in attitude change have found that asking people their opinions about racial prejudice influenced what they said on subsequent evaluations, even though nothing else happened between the pretest and the posttest.

PRETEST-POSTTEST CONTROL-GROUP DESIGN

This research design involves two groups—an experimental group and a control group. The R in Figure 9.2 represents randomization, meaning that the participants are randomly assigned to the two groups. Since the individuals are randomly assigned to groups, the pretest observations for both groups should be essentially the same. If the training program produces a significant effect, the posttest observations for the experimental group should be significantly greater than the pretests of either group and the posttest of the control group.

This research design is excellent for evaluating training programs and for determining whether the changes can be attributed to the training per se. The difficulty that this design typically presents for evaluating training programs is the problem of randomly assigning people to the two groups. This obstacle can be overcome, however, by randomly selecting certain individuals for training and by holding over the other individuals for a second training program. In many organizations, an entire staff cannot be trained at the same time, and therefore, having successive groups is sometimes a necessity.

THE SOLOMON FOUR-GROUP DESIGN

The **Solomon four-group design** is the most highly recommended research design for evaluating training programs. It requires four groups to which the participants have been randomly assigned. Only the first two groups are pretested. One of the pretested groups and one of the non-pretested groups participate in the training program. All four groups are observed after the training of the two groups has been completed.

This research design successfully eliminates alternative explanations for why the posttest scores of the experimental groups might be considerably higher than their pretest scores. If the scores are different, the improvement in performance can be attributed directly to the training program. Since this design appears complicated, many training specialists fail to seriously consider its usefulness. The difficulty, again, is in randomly assigning participants to the four groups. However, this problem can be conveniently overcome if the research design for evaluation is included in the initial design of the training program.

INTERNATIONAL HRM

Executives in the years ahead will need a much broader understanding of international business and global issues than was required in the past.[51] Before the 1980s, a typical executive received an undergraduate degree in finance or accounting and methodically advanced up the ranks of the organization without any international experience. It was not uncommon to see a company controller selected as a division head and then advance to a top-management job. A limited exposure to diverse cultures will not be adequate in the future.

The managers who will lead corporations in the twenty-first century will probably have a career record that includes several overseas assignments and even managing an international division. Just having an international perspective will not be sufficient; the executive will need practical experience in actually directing a significant segment of a foreign division. This on-the-job training will need to include both internal experiences (motivating and directing a culturally diverse work force) and external experiences (negotiating with prime ministers and ministers of trade and commerce).

Some organizations have already recognized that single-discipline experience provides inadequate training for positions in upper management and have instituted overseas assignments in their job-rotation training. Before he became the Chairman of Dow Chemical, for example, Paul Orrefice worked for Dow in Switzerland, Italy, Brazil, and Spain and was the president of its Latin American operations for a period of time. Other companies, such as Merck & Company and Coca Cola, have likewise internationalized their executive development to include overseas job rotations.[52]

Cross-cultural training will require considerable advance planning and career pathing. The selection and training process may require as much as twenty to twenty-five years of advanced planning. Having more managers work abroad creates additional training problems for organizations. Some managers and their families cannot adapt to the foreign culture and have to return home early. Premature returns result in enormous financial and emotional costs, and the expatriate failure rate for United States executives who are sent abroad is considerably greater than the failure rate of European or Asian executives. The high failure rate is largely attributable to inadequate selection and training. The following suggestions have been offered.

1. In selecting expatriates, companies should test both the candidates and their families to determine their cross-cultural skills and ability to adjust to life overseas.
2. Provide a cultural orientation for candidates and their families to help them understand the customs and practices of the new country.
3. Help candidates and their families learn the new language, if necessary, so they can communicate effectively and become acculturated.

4. Provide the expatriate managers with a long-term career orientation with adequate career pathing information to provide a sense of direction and purpose.
5. Provide a special support system for expatriates and their families to share feelings, experience, and insights.[53]

The global economy and increased international trade have also increased the demand for training at other levels in the organization. Other countries would do well to follow the lead of Japan. Japanese firms have learned that increased foreign trade requires an ongoing training effort, and all large enterprises have elaborate education and training programs. Some Japanese firms even have their own technical institutes that provide in-house training in such areas as quality circles, leadership, and technical job skills. Quality circle training is intended for everyone, not just those in QC teams, since Japanese managers believe quality is the duty of all employees. After workers become proficient in one skill, they continue to train in other areas. Cross-training is important in Japanese firms because knowing how to perform other jobs allows for transfers to accommodate fluctuating production requirements.[54]

SUMMARY

A. Obsolescence refers to a reduction in ability because of a lack of knowledge or skill. Obsolescence may be caused either by forgetfulness or as a result of the creation of new knowledge and technology. Obsolescence is a problem for all employees, but it is especially troublesome for professional and technical employees.

B. Training and development programs may utilize a number of both on-the-job and off-the-job training programs. On-the-job training generally provides better transfer of training and focuses more on immediate production. Off-the-job training is generally less structured and provides greater opportunities for general education.

C. The major techniques used in on-the-job training include job instruction, apprenticeships, internships and assistantships, job rotation and transfers, junior boards and committee assignments, and coaching and counseling.

D. Some of the major techniques used in off-the-job training include vestibule training, lectures, independent study, films and television, conference discussions, case studies, role playing, simulation, programmed instruction, sensitivity training, and experiential exercises.

E. An ideal training program should be consistent with these principles of learning: (1) the training should provide for active participation; (2) the learner should receive performance feedback; (3) the training materials should be meaningfully organized; (4) an opportunity for practice and repetition should be provided; and (5) conditions favorable for the positive transfer of training should exist.

F. The orientation training presented to new employees should contain information that is immediately relevant to the new work environment. Information that is highly specific and detailed should only be summarized and possibly included in an employee handbook. Orientation information should be presented over a period of time rather than concentrated in one lengthy presentation.

G. Management positions can be categorized into top managers, middle managers, and first-line supervisors. The basic managerial skills are: (1) technical and professional skills, (2) interpersonal relations skills, and (3) conceptual and administrative skills. These three types of skills are not equally essential for all managerial positions. Conceptual skills are more important for top managers, and technical and professional skills are more important to supervisors. Interpersonal relations skills are important to all managers.

H. The cost-benefit effectiveness of management development programs is difficult to assess. The benefits of training are hard to identify and sometimes occur over a long period of time. The costs of training are easier to measure, and a careful analysis shows that these costs usually are surprisingly high.

I. Two issues are involved in evaluating training programs: selecting the criteria and selecting an evaluation design. Four criteria have been proposed for evaluating training programs: reactions, learning, behavior, and results.

J. The most frequently used designs for evaluating training programs are the case study and the simple pretest-posttest comparison. However, serious methodological deficiencies make these two designs inadequate. Two designs that overcome these methodological problems and that ought to be used more frequently to evaluate training are the pretest-posttest control group design and the Solomon four-group design.

QUESTIONS

1. College students start to become obsolete within a few years after graduating because they forget what they have learned and because new information is created. What should students do to avoid the problems of obsolescence?

2. Why is job instruction training the most popular and extensively used method of training? Should it be used more or less frequently? Why?

3. Compensation is usually related to levels of education and training. Should four years of apprenticeship training be considered the equivalent of four years of college or technical training? Why or why not?

4. Do you agree or disagree that student interns in a cooperative education program should receive academic credit for their work experience? Explain your answer.

5. How important is the interpersonal relationship between the trainer and the trainee in helping the trainee to learn? Does a coach need to be well liked to be effective?

6. Do you think the lecture method is as ineffective as most studies indicate? Why or why not? If the lecture is so ineffective, why do you think it is used so frequently?

7. Some business courses rely almost exclusively on the case method. What are the advantages and disadvantages of using case studies? Do you think the case method is an adequate teaching tool, or should it be supplemented with other forms of training?

8. If you were a new employee, what information would you want to learn in an orientation program?

9. What problems would be created by trying to develop a general management course that described planning, organizing, motivating, and controlling and that all managers in the company would be expected to attend?

10. If you wanted to measure how much the trainees had learned from a training program, what kinds of exams could you construct? What effect do you think administering an exam would have on the participants?

11. Suppose a training program had a significant influence on the behavior of the trainees but did not influence the results of the organization, such as profitability, productivity, or costs. What went wrong? Does this mean that the training was ineffective?

KEY TERMS

Apprenticeship: A training technique in which the trainee, or apprentice, works with a skilled employee who teaches the apprentice how to perform the job.

Assessment centers: A series of problem-solving and decision-making activities in which groups of employees interact. Assessment centers are typically used to assess the management potential of employees; however, they also can be used for training purposes.

Computer-assisted instruction: A form of programmed instruction in which the trainee interacts with a computer to learn new information and answers questions asked by the computer.

Continuing education units (CEUs): To maintain their professional certification, many professionals are required to obtain credit for educational experiences.

Cooperative education: A learning experience that combines both work and education. Students work as employees in an organization under the direction of their supervisors and academic instructors.

Experiential group exercises: Activities that involve a group of individuals in making decisions and solving problems. The group members learn from participation in the group activity as well as from the group discussion about the activity.

History: The historical events occurring between the pretest and posttest of a research design that provide competing explanations for any effects that are observed.

Internship: A learning experience in which students are able to work for a period of time and apply the information they have learned.

Job-instruction training: The most extensively used technique of training, it consists largely of showing a trainee how to perform an activity and supervising the trainee's attempts to learn it.

Job rotation: A training technique that involves transferring trainees to different jobs to broaden their focus and to increase their knowledge.

Junior boards: A training technique that consists of assigning new trainees to an executive board responsible for making a decision.

Maturation: Internal changes within the trainees between the pretest and posttest evaluation that may provide alternative explanations for any effects that are observed.

Obsolescence: A reduction in ability or effectiveness caused by lack of knowledge or skill due either to forgetfulness or the creation of new knowledge and technology.

Programmed instruction: A training technique that arranges the training material in small sequential steps. The ideas are presented one at a time, giving the trainee an opportunity to respond to the material and to demonstrate mastery of it.

Role playing: A training technique in which participants are assigned to act out the roles of other people.

Role reversal: A form of role playing in which two or more participants exchange roles and act out a situation.

Sensitivity training: A training technique in which the trainees participate in an unstructured group discussion. The trainees share their feelings and emotions without the aid of a trainer or a scheduled agenda of topics to discuss.

Sensitizing effects of the pretest: Refers to the possible confounding influence that a pretest may have upon the posttest measurements.

Simulation: A training technique in which the trainee learns to respond in a training environment that is a reproduction of real-life conditions.

Solomon four-group design: A research design in which participants are randomly assigned to four training groups. Only two groups participate in training.

Vestibule training: A training technique in which trainees are placed in a special training room that is a replication of the actual job situation.

C O N C L U D I N G   C A S E

A Conference or a Vacation?

Rebecca Ashworth has been the training and development director of Ordway Engineering Company for the past four years. During that time she has tried to encourage the professional and technical employees to assume more responsibility for their own professional development. At her suggestion, the company approved a policy of paying for each employee to attend two professional conferences per year if prior approval is obtained.

Two months ago, Rebecca received a request from two members of the public relations staff to attend a conference being sponsored by the communications department of a university located 1,600 miles away. The cost of the conference per employee would be $525. After reviewing the program, Rebecca denied the request and suggested that the two employees look for another conference to attend. Now Rebecca has learned that the employees have gone over her head to the vice president of personnel to get the conference approved. The vice president wants to know why Rebecca refused to approve the request, since the employees claim that the conference will be an outstanding two-and-one-half-day event at which the latest communications theories and ideas will be presented by competent scholars.

Rebecca has a different evaluation of the conference. Both employees are alumni of the university, and the conference appears to be primarily an alumni reunion. The dates of the conference are February 3–5, an ideal time to take advantage of excellent skiing conditions at nearby slopes. The program consists of five three-hour sessions with topics that sound too esoteric to be applicable to corporate public relations. Most of the conference time looks as though it will be spent in long coffee-break periods. As far as Rebecca is concerned, the request amounts to a paid ski vacation for the two employees and a $1,050 subsidy to the university. In spite of her feelings, however, she must evaluate the program based on the quality of the program and what it can contribute to the employees and the company.

Questions:

1. What should her position be regarding a conference whose primary purpose consists mainly of reunion and vacation?
2. Where can she get better information about the program to evaluate it fairly?
3. Is there anything she can do to assure that the trip will be a good learning experience for the two employees rather than a paid vacation?

NOTES

1. Michael R. Fox and Catherine Baker, "Understanding the Illiteracy Problem." Issues Management Publication by the Society for Human Resource Management, Alexandria, Va., 1989, p. 3.

2. Aaron Bernstein, "Where the Jobs Are Is Where the Skills Aren't," *Business Week* (September 19, 1988): 104–8.

3. John S. McClenahen, "Training Americans for Work: Industry's Monumental Challenge," *Industry Week* (September 19, 1988): 52–59; Kirkland Ropp, "A Reform Movement for Education: Businesses Must Help Conquer the Illiteracy Crisis," *Personnel Administrator* 34 (August 1989): 39–41.

4. J. Lukaisiewiez, "The Dynamics of Science and Engineering Education," *Engineering Education* 61 (1971): 880–82.

5. Gene W. Dalton and Paul H. Thompson, "Accelerating Obsolescence of Older Engineers," *Harvard Business Review* (September–October 1971): 57–67; Zmira Laufer, "The Obsolescence of Administration and the Administration of Obsolescence," *International Journal of Manpower* 8, no. 1 (1987): 10–14.

6. J. B. Hickman, "Periodic Recertification," *Journal of the American Medical Association* 213 (1970): 1651–57; "Managing Your Career," *CMA Magazine* 62 (November 1988): 16–19.

7. Dalton and Thompson, "Accelerating Obsolescence."

8. Donald Norfolk, "When Senility Sets In . . . ," *Chief Executive* (December 1987): 58.

9. Eugene Raudsepp, "How Engineers Get Ahead and Avoid Obsolescence," *Machine Design* 61 (January 12, 1989): 107–11; John Folsom, "Educating an Industry," *Insurance Review* 49 (August 1988): 36, 37.

10. R. Lee Martin, "Career Obsolescence: Can It Happen to You?" *Manufacturing Engineering* 100 (February 1988): 46–52.

11. Edmund L. Toomey and Joan M. Connor, "Employee Sabbaticals: Who Benefits and Why," *Personnel* 65 (April 1988): 81–84.

12. Steve W. J. Kozlowski and Brian M. Hults, "An Exploration of Climates for Technical Updating and Performance," *Personnel Psychology* 40 (Autumn 1987): 539–63.

13. Dalton and Thompson, "Accelerating Obsolescence."

14. David J. Cherrington, *The Work Ethic: Working Values and Values That Work* (New York: AMACOM, 1980), Chapter 10; Paul Thorne, David West, and Ron Owen, "The Case for Salvaging the 'Throwaway' Executive," *International Management* 42 (May 1987): 49, 50.

15. David E. Sanger, "For Some Managers, Training Program Is Real Obstacle Course," *Wall Street Journal*, July 27, 1981.

16. Bernard M. Bass and James A. Vaughan, *Training in Industry: The Management of Learning* (Belmont, Calif.: Wadsworth, 1966), Chapter 7.

17. Wayne H. Smith and John W. Morrison, "High-Impact On-The-Job Training." *Industrial and Commercial Training* 18 (May/June 1986): 22–25; Stephen B. Wehrenberg, "Supervisors as Trainers: The Long-Term Gains of OJT," *Personnel Journal* 66 (April 1987): 48–51.

18. Bureau of National Affairs, "Planning the Training Program," *Personnel Management: BNA Policy and Practice Series*, no. 41 (Washington, D.C.: Government Printing Office, 1975): 205.

19. George T. Friedlob and Jerry E. Trapnell, "Faculty Micro-Internships: OJT that Is Priceless and Painless," *Internal Auditor* 45 (December 1988): 10–13; Sherry Southard, "Experiential Learning Prepares Students to Assume Professional Roles," *IEEE Transactions on Professional Communication* 31 (December 1988): 157–59.

20. W. Oberg, "Top Management Assesses University Executive Programs," *Business Topics* 2, no. 2 (1963): 7–27.

21. Ed Baranowski, "Planned Progression: How One Credit Union Prepares Its Own Employees for Management Advancement," *Credit Union Management* 11 (February 1988): 18–19.

22. David Green, "Business Television: A Dynamic New Training Channel," *Personnel* 65 (October 1988): 62–66.

23. Kurt Lewin, "Group Decisions and Social Change," in *Readings in Social Psychology, 2nd ed.*; G. E. Swanson, T. M. Newcomb, and E. L. Hartley, eds. (New York: Holt, 1952), 459–73.

24. Richard L. Prather, "Extending the Life of Performance Appraisal Systems," *Personnel Journal* 53, no. 10 (October 1974): 739–43; Julianne Morath, "Empathy Training: Development of Sensitivity and Caring in Hospitals," *Nursing Management* 20 (March 1989): 60–62.

25. Larry R. Smeltzer and Jeanette A. Davie, "Teleconferencing: Reach Out to Train Someone," *Personnel Administrator* 52 (June 1987): 211–19.

26. Alan C. Elms, *Role Playing, Reward, and Attitude Change* (New York: Van Nostrand, 1969).

27. Stanley W. Candebo, "USAF Controllers, F-15 Pilots Train for Combat Using Multi-Ship Simulation," *Aviation Week and Space Technology* 130 (March 27, 1989): 71–79.

28. Ernest R. Cadotte, "Filling the Gap in Business School Education," *Survey of Business* 24 (Fall 1988): 19–24.

29. Ronald Jensen and David J. Cherrington, *The Business Management Laboratory, 3rd ed.* (Dallas, Texas: Business Publications, 1984).

30. Nick Rushby, "Accommodating Individual Learning Styles," *Personnel Management* 20 (October 1988): 85; Joe Wehr, "Instructor-Led or Computer-Based: Which Will Work Best for You?" *Training and Development Journal* 42 (June 1988): 18–21.

31. Don Brenneman, "Computer-Based Training Results 1st Class," *Computing Canada* 15 (January 19, 1989): 18.

32. Sandra Helsel, "Interactive Videodisk and Special Education," *Optical Information Systems* 8 (July/August 1988): 186–90; David Weatherall, "Interactive Video," *Management Sciences* 32 (May 1988): 28–31.

33. Ron Zemke, "Customer Education: The Silent Revolution," *Training* 22 (January 1985): 27–34.

34. Bernard M. Bass and James H. Vaughan, *Training in Industry: The Management of Learning* (Monterey, Calif.: Brooks/Cole, 1966).

35. Beverly Geber, "Who, How, and What," *Training* 26 (October 1989): 49–63.

36. Gordon F. Shea, *The New Employee: Developing a Productive Human Resource* (Reading, Mass.: Addison-Wesley, 1981), Chapter 7.

37. John P. Wanous, "Effects of a Realistic Job Preview on Job Acceptance, Job Attitudes, and Job Survival," *Journal of Applied Psychology* 58, no. 3 (1973): 327–32.

38. J. Sterling Livingston, "Pygmalion in Management," *Harvard Business Review* (July–August 1969): 81–89.

39. Cherrington, *The Work Ethic*, Chapter 8.

40. Don Jones, "The Employee Handbook," *Personnel Journal* (February 1973): 136–41; Terry Newell, Ron Redfoot, and Lucy Sotar, "After the Layoffs: Orienting New Employees," *Training and Development Journal* 41 (September 1987): 34–36.

41. Daniel Katz and Robert Kahn, *The Social Psychology of Organizations, 2nd ed.* (New York: Wiley, 1978), Chapter 16.

42. Paul J. Guglielmino, "Developing the Top-Level Executive for the 1980s and Beyond," *Training and Development Journal* 33 (April 1979): 12–14.

43. Hugh Murray, "Management Education and the MBA: It's Time for a Rethink," *Managerial and Decision Economics* (Winter 1988): 71–78; Bill Walker, "Current Trends in Management Education," *Practicing Manager* 9 (Spring 1988): 47–48; Helen J. Muller, James L. Porter, and Robert R. Rehnder, "Have the Business Schools Let Down U.S. Corporations?" *Management Review* 77 (October 1988): 24–31.

44. Jack Gordon, "The Case for Corporate Colleges," *Training* 25 (March 1988): 25–31.

45. Jack Gordon, "Budgets, 1989," *Training* 26 (October 1989): 39–47.

46. Joel Hochberger, "Let's Stop Confusing Training Meetings with Vacations," *Training/HRD* 17 (April 1980): 116.

47. Malcolm Bull, "Are There Any Questions?" *Systems International* 16 (February 1988): 51.

48. Ralph F. Catalanello and Donald L. Kirkpatrick, "Evaluating Training Programs: The state of the Art," *Training and Development Journal* 22 (May 1968): 2–9.

49. William G. Dyer, Weldon Moffitt, and Philip B. Daniels, "As Others See You: Management Profiling for Team Effectiveness" (Distributed by Behavioral Science Associates, P.O. Box 411, Provo, Utah, 84601).

50. Donald T. Campbell and Julian C. Stanley, *Experimental and Quasi-experimental Designs for Research* (Chicago: Rand McNally, 1963).

51. Ronald W. Clement, "Management Development in the 1980s: A Field in Transition," *Journal of Management Development* 7 (1988): 45–55; Ray Watson, "New Visions for University-Sponsored Executive Education Programs," *Academy of Management Executive* 2 (November 1988): 321–23.

52. Amanda Bennett, "The Chief Executives in Year 2000 Will Be Experienced Abroad," *Wall Street Journal* (February 27, 1989): 1; Paul L. Brocklyn, "Developing the International Executive," *Personnel* 66 (March 1989): 44–47.

53. Mark E. Mendenhall, Edward Dunbar, and Gary R. Oddou, "Expatriate Selection, Training, and Career-Pathing: A Review and Critique," *Human Resource Management* 26 (Fall 1987): 331–45; Rosalie L. Tung, "Expatriate Assignments: Enhancing Success and Minimizing Failure," *Academy of Management Executive* 1 (May 1987): 117–29.

54. Eric Frank, "HRD in Japan," *Journal of European Industrial Training* 12, no. 5 (1988): 42–48; Arunodaya Sana, "Training as Major Factor in Japanese Economic Success," *Journal of European Industrial Training* 11, no. 7 (1987): 13–18.

C H A P T E R   1 0

Wage and Salary Administration

Learning Objectives

After studying this chapter, you should be able to:

1. Identify the objectives of a sound compensation plan.
2. Identify three labor markets, and describe the factors influencing pay in each market.
3. Explain the three decisions that must be made in determining how much an individual should be paid.
4. Describe the factors that influence the wage-level decision.
5. Explain how to conduct a wage survey, and describe the available surveys.
6. List four job-evaluation methods for determining the wage structure, and briefly explain each.
7. Describe the process for developing a wage curve, and explain how it is used and adjusted when necessary.
8. Identify the variables influencing individual pay.

Chapter Outline

Understanding the Wage Structure in Society
Objectives of Compensation / Ethical Considerations in Compensation / Three Labor Markets / Determinants of Pay / Three Wage Decisions

The Wage-level Decision
Establishing the Wage Level / Factors Influencing the Wage-level Decision / Wage Surveys

The Wage-structure Decision
Management Edict / Collective Bargaining / Job Evaluation

I N T R O D U C T O R Y   C A S E

Compensation Chaos of Earth's Herbs

The compensation system at Earth's Herbs has evolved over the past several years in a haphazard way and now the company faces some serious inequalities. Earth's Herbs is a small company that manufactures and distributes health foods and vitamins. It started as a family business and has expanded to fifty-five full-time employees and forty part-time employees. Only within the past few weeks has the company assigned someone to manage the human resource functions.

In the past, starting pay was decided when new employees were hired. Pay increases usually occurred when someone complained or threatened to leave. Consequently, pay was primarily based on how much was required to entice employees to stay—a practice that has created some serious inequalities.

The most serious compensation inequality is between the wages paid to the afternoon part-time workers and those paid to the evening part-time workers in the packaging department. Although both groups of employees perform the same work, the afternoon supervisor pays his workers a weekly salary and the evening supervisor pays her employees an hourly wage. The weekly salary amounts to more than twice the hourly wage. Another serious inequality is that the accountant, a recent college graduate who joined the company four months ago, receives $4,000 more per year than the financial vice president, who is four years older than the accountant and has been with the company for three years.

The vice president of operations does not think the company faces a serious problem, and he objects to making any drastic changes. He argues that people came to work here knowing what they would be paid and they should leave if they are dissatisfied. He thinks the company needs a policy

384

that prohibits employees from talking about their pay.

The vice president of finance, however, thinks the company needs to totally overhaul its compensation system and pay people according to what they do, rather than what they demand.

Questions:

1. How important is it to revise the compensation system, and should the system be modified slowly or totally overhauled?
2. What criteria should be used to design a compensation system?
3. What constitutes a "fair" compensation system? How should "fair" be decided?

UNDERSTANDING THE WAGE STRUCTURE IN SOCIETY

Total compensation consists of three major components: pay, incentives, and benefits. Employers try to offer an attractive package of base pay, incentives, and benefits to attract employees and retain them. Employees are interested in all three components and consider each carefully when evaluating a job offer or considering a change in jobs. Employees also consider nonfinancial rewards, such as the stability of employment, the physical environment, commuting distance, the social environment in which the work is performed, and the nature of the work itself. For example, electricians who work for a manufacturing company may be satisfied with pay rates far below those received by independent electrical contractors because they realize that working for a manufacturing company represents more stable employment than independent contracting.

Compensation administration is a major human resource function that has a significant impact on other human resource functions. Financial compensation can have a strong influence on job satisfaction, productivity, labor turnover, and several other processes within an organization. The relationship between compensation and other human resource functions is shown in Figure 10.1. Staffing, performance evaluation, training and development, and employee relations are all influenced by the compensation system, and they, in turn, influence compensation.

OBJECTIVES OF COMPENSATION

All employers have similar compensation objectives, regardless of whether they are profit, nonprofit, or government agencies, and regardless of size. The basic objectives are to attract qualified employees, to retain them, and to motivate them to perform their duties in the most effective manner. When pay decisions are made, several different objectives have to be considered simultaneously. For example, the decision to raise the pay of all maintenance mechanics might make the maintenance mechanics happy and facilitate hiring in that department, but this decision also could create several problems: it could destroy the conditions of equity with other craftsworkers; it could increase the organization's labor costs and destroy its competitive position; it could inhibit motivation by

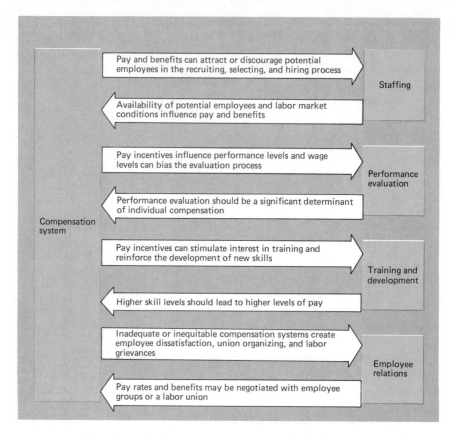

FIGURE 10.1 The relationship between compensation and other human resource functions.

destroying individual incentives; and it could be illegal if it was offered during a union election. Therefore, all pay decisions should achieve the following six objectives:

1. *Be legal.* The compensation system must be consistent with numerous federal, state, and local laws. (The major legislative constraints are discussed in Chapter 12.)
2. *Be adequate.* The compensation system must be large enough to attract qualified employees to join the organization and stay.
3. *Be motivating.* The compensation package should provide sufficient incentives to motivate employees to perform efficiently.
4. *Be equitable.* The employees should feel that their compensation is internally equitable relative to other employees in the organization and externally equitable relative to employees doing similar work in other organizations.
5. *Provide security.* Employees like to feel that their monthly income is secure and predictable. They need to feel that their pay is somewhat insulated from changes in employment, profitability, individual performance, and personal health.
6. *Be cost-benefit effective.* The organization must administer the compensation system efficiently and have the financial resources to support it on a continuing basis in the long run.

Each of these objectives is important in developing a sound compensation system. As shown in Figure 10.2, however, these objectives are not always compatible, and employers are frequently required to balance competing objectives. For example, providing an adequate wage to attract qualified employees may be inconsistent with the objective of making the wage cost-benefit effective because it requires excessively high wages. Furthermore, as wages become more secure, they become less motivating. Security is achieved by providing a predictable monthly income, regardless of performance, while motivation is achieved by paying for performance. Achieving an appropriate balance among these competing objectives is discussed at the end of Chapter 11.

ETHICAL CONSIDERATIONS IN COMPENSATION

In addition to practical considerations about what is legal and motivating, there are ethical considerations about what is just and fair. Some of these ethical issues, such as the size of executive salaries and the wage-slave issue (discussed in the next chapter), have been debated for many years. Other issues, such as the comparable-worth controversy (discussed later in this chapter) and mandatory health benefits (discussed in Chapter 12), are more recent.

Ethical issues concerning compensation are especially sensitive because money is such an important reason why people work. People expect to be treated fairly, and our concept of fairness is greatly influenced by such issues as why managers deserve more than laborers, why older workers should be paid more than younger workers, and whether people who need more should get it.

The idea of paying people according to their needs was prevalent prior to World War II. People who supported large families often received higher wages to help them meet their financial needs. This practice partially explains why male-dominated jobs have historically paid more than female-dominated jobs, and why many of these wage differentials still exist. In recent years, however, it has been generally viewed as wrong to allow considerations of need to influence pay—pay should be based on the requirements of the

FIGURE 10.2 Objectives of a compensation program.

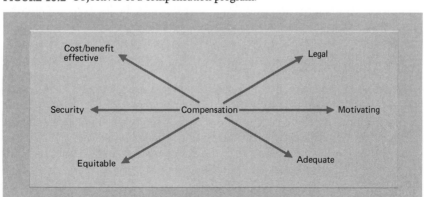

job and how well it is performed. Nevertheless, how much employees need to support themselves and their families continues to influence pay for both men and women. Since welfare payments are based on need, some managers ask if it is right to ignore need as a determinant of pay.

Compensation systems ought to be rational and established according to some kind of reasonable criteria. If employees are paid on a random basis, little purpose is served by studying compensation. Unless compensation programs are established on a systematic basis and adhere to some sort of logic and reason, there is very little to study.

Although the wage and salary system in the United States is largely determined by specific predictable factors, many people are more impressed by the system's apparent lack of order than by its predictability. A superficial examination of how much money different people make often gives the appearance of random chaos, where employees make demands and bargain for as much as they can get and employers pay whatever is necessary to keep employees. When people fail to examine a wage structure carefully, they often conclude that no systematic structure exists. For example, grade school teachers normally make less than half the income of university professors, even though their student contact hours are three or four times greater and they play a greater role in shaping social values. These differences in income cannot be satisfactorily explained by differences in educational preparation. School teachers are underpaid for a variety of social and political reasons. The annual salaries of some public school teachers are less than the fees some management consultants charge for a single day of training. Similarly, school bus drivers typically are paid much less than city bus drivers, and yet city bus drivers often have better hours and working conditions than school bus drivers. Long-haul truck drivers make more than either school bus drivers or city bus drivers. Apparently, hauling packages and consumer goods pays more than hauling people, for reasons that are unclear.

Although the wages and salaries that people receive appear to reflect unexplained variance, a fair degree of predictability does exist in the overall compensation structure of society. The amount of predictability and stability is sufficient to identify factors influencing pay and to allow organizations to establish pay rates that most employees consider fair. A rational wage structure is difficult to detect, however, when the entire labor market is considered simultaneously. Pay levels, for example, are significantly influenced by such factors as education and the supply and demand for labor. To identify meaningful relationships, the overall job market must be broken into smaller segments and analyzed separately.

THREE LABOR MARKETS

The labor force can be divided into **three labor markets**: (1) blue-collar and nonsupervisory white-collar workers, (2) professional employees, and (3) supervisors and executives.[1] This division provides a useful method for analyzing wage and salary levels because the three markets differ in terms of size, the normal method of computing pay, the range of pay, educational and training requirements, and factors that influence pay levels, especially the influence of key power groups such as labor unions, professional associations, and executive committees. The three labor markets and the determinants of pay for each are presented in Table 10.1. A fourth labor market, quite different from the other three, consists of professional athletes and entertainers.

BLUE-COLLAR AND NONSUPERVISORY WHITE-COLLAR WORKERS

The job market for blue-collar and nonsupervisory white-collar employees is usually a local market corresponding with the area where these workers would normally expect to look for work if they wanted to change jobs. Most blue-collar workers are paid on a weekly or biweekly basis in amounts determined by an hourly wage rate. The past several years, however, have witnessed a growing trend to pay monthly salaries to both blue-collar employees and nonsupervisory white-collar employees.

Only three or four classifications usually exist within each blue-collar or nonsupervisory white-collar job. For example, many union jobs have three classifications: appren-

TABLE 10.1 The determinants of pay in three labor markets

	Blue-collar and Nonsupervisory White-collar	Professional	Supervisors and Executives
1. Size of market	Local	National	Regional or national
2. Normal method of computing pay	Weekly or biweekly based on an hourly wage rate	Monthly based on an annual salary	Monthly salary plus bonuses and other incentives on a quarterly or yearly basis
3. Range of pay between classifications of an occupation	1:2 to 1:3	1:4 to 1:5	1:10 or more
4. Education and training required	Mostly on-the-job training ranging from less than a day to four or five years of apprentice training. Occasionally some technical or educational training beyond high school.	Usually six to ten years beyond high school	Formal education "helps." Most have a college degree. Some have a master's degree.
5. Factors that influence pay	Training and skill requirements; experience; degree of discomfort associated with the job; productivity; union-management negotiations	Educational training; academic degrees; years of service; professional recognition	Corporate revenues; level in the organizational hierarchy; responsibility for making decisions and supervising others

tice, journeyman, and craftsman. In the Bureau of Labor Statistics wage surveys, only two classifications are used for typists, order clerks, and data-entry operators; three classifications for file clerks; and five classifications for secretaries. The pay range for high- and low-paying jobs is usually a ratio between 1:2 and 1:3. In other words, the average wage for a high-paying job, such as tool-and-die maker, is usually only two or three times higher than the average wage for a low-paying job, such as janitor. Over time, the ratio tends to become reduced through a process called *wage compression*. As pay increases of specified amounts are added to every job in the company, the ratio between high- and low-paying jobs is reduced.

The amount of training required to learn a job is an important factor in determining the pay of blue-collar and nonsupervisory white-collar jobs. Training requirements, however, do not play as large a role in determining pay for these jobs as for professional jobs. Although some of the highly paid blue-collar jobs have lengthy training require- ments, most of the training occurs on the job during an apprenticeship or possibly in a technical school rather than in a college or university.

The rate of pay assigned to a particular blue-collar or nonsupervisory white-collar job is mainly influenced by skill requirements. Highly skilled jobs pay significantly more than jobs requiring less skill. However, pay levels also are influenced by working condi- tions, physical demands, job hazards, and other characteristics that may make jobs unpleasant or difficult to perform. Pay increases for nonsupervisory white-collar workers are closely related to pay increases for blue-collar employees, and the pay for both groups is influenced by collective bargaining. When a union raises the wage level of one group, the wages of the other groups usually are raised at the same time.

PROFESSIONAL EMPLOYEES

The labor market for professional employees tends to be nationwide and frequently crosses industry boundaries. A doctor, for example, might move to any part of the country to work in private practice, to teach in a medical school, or to work as a company doctor. Professionals usually are paid an annual salary, unless their income is derived from private practice.

Professional jobs usually have more classifications than blue-collar or nonsupervisory white-collar jobs. In its wage surveys, the BLS uses four classifications of auditors, five classifications of accountants, six classifications of attorneys, and eight classifications of chemists and engineers. Professional jobs have wider pay ratios than blue-collar jobs, in part because they have more classifications. The ratios for some professional jobs are as great as 1:4 or 1:5. New professionals starting in the lowest classification can expect to make only one-fourth to one-fifth as much as senior professionals.

Pay levels of professionals are primarily determined by educational training, aca- demic degrees, and years of service. Past performance and professional recognition also contribute significantly to the level of pay and to the possibility of advancing to a higher classification. Noteworthy is the fact that higher pay and higher classification may not mean a greater degree of supervisory responsibility in a professional job.

SUPERVISORS AND EXECUTIVES

The labor market for supervisors tends to be a regional market. When trying to change jobs, most supervisors limit their job search to the surrounding region. Middle managers and top executives, however, participate in a national job market, generally within the same industry. When executives change jobs, it is not unusual for them to move to a different geographical region, but they normally do not go from one industry to a totally different industry. Executive compensation usually includes base pay in the form of an annual salary, a bonus for performance, and several other forms of deferred compensation, such as stock options.

The number of classifications within supervisory and executive positions varies with the size of a company and its organizational structure. Although some large, complex organizations identify several classifications of managers, most discussions of managerial levels specify only three levels: first-line supervisors, middle managers, and top executives. The range of pay for supervisors and executives is extremely broad and often exceeds a ratio of 1:10. Some top-level executives receive 50 to 100 times as much as the average supervisor.

Educational training and academic degrees appear to have only a small influence on the pay of supervisors and executives. Academic preparation affects the starting salary and initial job assignments of new managers. College graduates with master's degrees in business administration or CPA certificates usually receive higher starting salaries and are placed in "fast-track" trainee positions. But after three or five years on the job, promotions and salary levels are largely determined by "track records" or past performance.

The compensation of executives is influenced by many factors, including both reasonable justifications and questionable excuses. One significant factor influencing the pay of chief executive officers is the level of revenues generated by their companies. As revenues increase the average pay of the top executives also increases. The same is true for human resource executives; their pay increases with the company's sales, as shown in Table 10.2.[2] The pay of middle managers and supervisors is primarily influenced by their level in the organizational hierarchy. As a manager's position on the organizational chart rises, so, too, does his or her average salary level. Executives' salaries also are influenced by years of experience.[3]

Most executives and supervisors endorse the idea of paying for performance. Therefore, the salaries and bonuses of managers should be related to the sales and profitability of their departments. The evidence indicates, however, that the relationship between sales and pay is only moderate and that the relationship between profitability and pay is about zero.[4] Apparently, executives and supervisors do not actually pay for performance as well as they think they should or claim to do. Since executives largely establish their own pay levels, there is some reason to speculate that their high salaries are related more to personal whims or the company's ability to pay than to their performances. This issue is examined further in Chapter 11.

PROFESSIONAL ATHLETES AND ENTERTAINERS

Professional athletes and entertainers do not conveniently fit into the preceding labor markets, and their pay is determined by a different set of variables. In 1988, the average annual salaries were $371,000 for professional baseball players, $340,000 for basketball players, $191,000 for football players, and $152,000 for hockey players.[5] Even more spectacular, however, are the news reports of all-stars who sign multi-year contracts for multi-millions per year. Some entertainers receive fabulous royalties on works of art, such

TABLE 10.2 Average salaries for top human resource executives based on company sales

Sales	Average Salary	Sales	Average Salary
Under $40 million	$71,100	$350–650 million	$93,100
$ 40–100 million	$75,700	$650–1.5 billion	$107,800
$100–200 million	$80,900	over $1.5 billion	$147,400
$200–350 million	$94,000		

Source: "1989 Human Resource Management Compensation Survey Results," ASPA, February 1989.

as films, records, and books; but they also receive fabulous fees for single appearances on stage or in concert.

The best way to understand the incomes these people receive is not by analyzing levels of skill, effort, or responsibility, but by making a simple supply-and-demand analysis. If two boxers can attract millions of viewers to watch them fight, they can earn millions of dollars for their performance. Likewise, the revenue generated by a rock concert is not determined by an objective assessment of the performers' skills but by the number of people they can attract and the price they are willing to pay.

An in-depth regression analysis examined the salaries of professional basketball players and the variables that influenced their salaries. Some merit, or individual performance, measures were related to their salaries, such as offensive-proficiency ratios, defensive-proficiency ratios, points per 48 minutes, and blocks per 48 minutes. However, other economic variables were also significant, especially player position, tier position, average team salary, draft position, and all-rookie team award.[6] It is obvious that talents and skill are very important for professional athletes and entertainers, but their salaries are primarily determined by how these skills are marketed to a consuming public.

DETERMINANTS OF PAY

Many factors besides the job market influence pay levels; these factors need to be considered as a whole. For example, blue-collar workers who labor in unpleasant working conditions generally receive wages that compensate them for their discomfort. But executives who have dingy offices generally get paid less than executives who have pleasant offices.

The major factors influencing pay are presented in Table 10.3. These factors are divided into four categories: external factors, organizational factors, job factors, and individual factors. Changes in labor supply and demand and in unemployment are the most important external factors influencing the amount of pay that employers must offer to attract and retain qualified employees. An external factor that is frequently overlooked is social expectations, or social customs. Although the Equal Pay Act forbids paying women less than men for equal work, certain jobs, such as nurse and secretary, have historically been viewed as "female" jobs that pay less than "male" jobs, even though these jobs are now held by both men and women.

Several organizational factors that also influence pay levels include industry standards, presence or absence of a union, and the size and profitability of the company. The organization's philosophy concerning pay is particularly important, since some organizations try to be wage leaders, establishing high pay levels, while others prefer to be wage followers, with below-average pay levels. An organizational variable that is often overlooked is the value of a job to the company. Higher pay is generally given for a job that makes an important contribution to the company. The contribution does not necessarily have to be a financial contribution. For example, a school wanting to have a first-class athletic program generally pays its coaches more than a school that is satisfied with a mediocre athletic program.

The number of job factors that influence pay levels is almost limitless. However, the most important ones are those associated with skill, responsibility, and effort. Skill factors include both mental and physical skills, including the education, training, and preparation necessary to acquire those skills. Jobs that involve a great deal of responsibility usually receive higher pay, regardless of whether the responsibility concerns physical assets, financial assets, human resources, or company goodwill. Pay levels are also higher for jobs that require more physical or mental effort. The influence of working conditions, however, is minor unless the conditions become extremely unpleasant or hazardous. The most important individual factors are productivity and seniority.

THREE WAGE DECISIONS

The development of a sound wage and salary system requires three basic decisions.[7] Each decision answers a critical question regarding an organization's compensation program.

The first decision, the **wage-level decision**, concerns the overall level of an organization's compensation. This decision answers the question: how much money do members of the organization receive relative to the money received by individuals performing similar work in other organizations?

The second decision, the **wage-structure decision**, concerns the pay awarded to different jobs within an organization. This decision answers the question: how much money is paid for one job relative to that paid for other jobs within the same company?

The third decision, the **individual wage decision**, concerns individual incentives and merit pay. This decision answers the question: how much money does one employee receive relative to the money received by other employees who perform similar work?

These three wage decisions illustrate the kinds of wage comparisons that employees make when they evaluate their wages. Accountants in Company A, for example, compare their wages with the wages of accountants in other organizations to see whether Company A has a higher or lower level of wages. The accountants also compare their wages with the pay of bookkeepers, computer programmers, and other members of Company A to learn whether the internal wage structure offers higher pay to jobs with more responsi-

TABLE 10.3   Determinants of pay

I. **External factors**
  A. Market factors
    1. Supply and demand for labor
    2. Educational and training institutions
    3. Transferability of skills between industries and geographical areas
    4. Changes in the composition of the work force
    5. Economic conditions and unemployment
  B. Unions—settlements in other organizations
  C. Geographical pay differences
  D. Government regulations and laws
  E. Social expectations—customs

II. **Organizational factors**
  A. Industry in which the organization is located
  B. Union or nonunion
  C. Profitability and ability to pay
  D. Size
  E. Capital or labor intensive
  F. Philosophies of the organization
    1. Wage leader versus wage follower
    2. Mix of pay and benefits
    3. Historical job relationships
    4. Compensation policies, practices, and procedures
    5. Part-time/full employment
  G. Value of the job—contribution to the company

III. **Job factors**
  A. Skill
    1. Mental requirements
    2. Complexity of duties
    3. Personal qualifications needed
    4. Ability to make decisions, judgments
    5. Managerial techniques
    6. Preparation for the job—education, training, and knowledge
    7. Social skills—capacity for getting along with others
    8. Ability to do detailed work
    9. Ability to do routine work
    10. Manual dexterity or motor skill
    11. Creative ability
    12. Initiative
    13. Resourcefulness
    14. Versatility/flexibility
    15. Previous experience
  B. Responsibility (for)
    1. Money, financial rewards, commitments
    2. Decision making
    3. Supervision—work of others
    4. Financial results
    5. Contacts with public, customers, and others
    6. Dependability and accuracy—quality of work
    7. Materials, equipment, property
    8. Determining company policy
    9. Confidential information
  C. Effort
    1. Physical requirements—fatigue
    2. Mental effort
    3. Attention to details
    4. Pressure of work
    5. Attention span required
  D. Working conditions
    1. Job conditions
    2. Physical hazards

IV. **Individual factors**
  A. Performance, productivity
  B. Experience
  C. Seniority, length of service
  D. Potential/promotability
  E. Personal preferences
    1. Desirability of the job itself
    2. Status, prerequisites, title
    3. Security of pay
    4. Hours of work
    5. Monotony
    6. Out-of-town travel

bility and greater difficulty. Finally, the accountants discuss their wages among themselves to determine whether each person's wage is the same or whether differences in wages are related to productivity, seniority, education, or something else.

THE WAGE-LEVEL DECISION
ESTABLISHING THE WAGE LEVEL

The wage-level decision primarily concerns the issue of pay adequacy: how much does one company pay relative to other companies with similar jobs? This decision is a policy decision made by top management. The organization can adopt a policy to pay the going market rate for each job, or it can choose to pay above or below the market rate. For example, a small manufacturing company with 200 employees adopted this wage policy: "The wages paid by our company will be at least as high as the wages paid in the surrounding area. Our goal is to have our wage rates fall in the third quartile."

Most organizations have a stated or implied wage-level policy, but they tend to communicate the policy verbally rather than in writing. The evidence indicates that a company with a policy to pay above-average wages is more likely to communicate its wage-level policy. The wage-level policies that some companies announce, however, are not necessarily the policies they follow. One study found that half the companies surveyed actually paid amounts that varied more than 5 percent from their stated policies. Since the largest variations resulted in both overpayment and underpayment, the conclusion of the study was that the errors resulted from ignorance of the going market rate rather than from a conscious effort to deceive the employees.[8]

A sound wage-level policy is expected to achieve three objectives: (1) to attract an adequate supply of labor; (2) to keep present employees reasonably satisfied with the level of their compensation; and (3) to avoid costly turnover. These objectives are essential for organizational effectiveness; however, wage-level changes seem to have only a small impact on them. Attracting and keeping an adequate supply of labor depends on many nonwage factors, particularly on unemployment levels in the economy. Extremely large increases in the pay level are probably required to attract a noticeably larger pool of job applicants, especially for blue-collar jobs. One study found that high wage levels did not seem to attract large numbers of blue-collar workers because they were generally unaware of the comparative wage levels in other organizations.[9] Another study found that equity comparisons had a major influence on pay satisfaction, but the important comparisons were internal rather than external. Social comparisons with what other companies paid their people were unrelated to pay satisfaction.[10]

Except for limited evidence showing that some employees will change jobs for higher pay, the consequences of wage-level changes are basically undetermined. It is probably safe to speculate that a 10 or 20 percent increase in the wage level would reduce turnover and create a temporary increase in satisfaction. But a wage increase probably would not increase productivity. A review of several case studies of organizations that paid significantly higher or lower wages than the market rate concluded that "some of the advantages that are assumed to result from keeping up with or paying above the market may not develop to the extent anticipated."[11]

FACTORS INFLUENCING THE WAGE-LEVEL DECISION

A company's wage level is most directly influenced by the policies and preferences of management. Top management can arbitrarily choose to pay wages and salaries that are above or below the market level. In some organizations the wage levels are extremely low to reduce labor costs and increase profits. In other organizations all employees are paid high salaries for humanitarian reasons. In the early years of one drug company, the president decided to pay high wages and have all employees participate in a profit-sharing plan. Although this decision has since been justified by economic outcomes, the original reason for the high wages was to make all the employees partners with management.

Wage levels also are influenced by other factors. According to the available evidence, the most significant factors influencing wage levels are organization size, unionization, and productivity (or ability to pay). Large organizations generally pay higher wages than do small organizations. In the United States, firms with 1,000 or more employees usually pay 10 to 30 percent more in direct wages per hour than smaller firms in the same industry, and larger firms spend about twice as much on benefits.[12] Similar wage differentials are usually found in European industries, while Japanese firms exhibit even greater differentials. Small Japanese firms with fewer than fifty employees pay only about 55 percent as much as large firms with over 1,000 employees. The reason larger organizations tend to pay more is not clear.

Some research suggests that larger firms pay more because workers who are better educated, more stable, and less prone to quit or be fired are more likely to work for larger companies where job tenure is rewarded. Opposing studies, however, have found that wage differences in large versus small firms are unrelated to the quality of employees, unionization, working conditions, or the need for workers who require less monitoring. It may be that large firms pay more simply because managers feel less accountable for monitoring wages.[13] Another explanation is that large organizations are able to pay higher wages because of their competitive advantage or improved ability to pay.

The wage levels of companies that bargain with unions generally tend to be higher than those of nonunion companies. In 1985, the Bureau of Labor Statistics (BLS) reported that the hourly pay of union workers was $2.44 higher than nonunion workers ($11.77 versus $9.33). This difference is even more pronounced when the costs of benefits are included. The difference in the total compensation packages, including both wages and benefits, was $5.09 higher for the unionized companies ($17.64 versus $12.55).[14]

Although BLS statistics concerning wage-level comparisons between union and nonunion workers can be misleading because of differences in the jobs and differences among companies, studies by economists using careful research techniques also show higher pay levels for union members. One particular study found that the wage levels of production workers in organizations with strong unions were 10 to 15 percent higher than those of nonunion production workers.[15] Strong unions apparently are able to raise an organization's wage level through aggressive bargaining. However, if an organization is financially weak, which is the condition of many school districts, aggressive bargaining might have little effect. While union bargaining has raised the wage levels of organizations that were low, it also has caused the wage leaders to drop back. Collective bargaining, at least, has reduced the variability in the wage levels of different organizations within a given industry.

As productivity and the ability to pay increase, it is reasonable to expect the wage level to increase, too. However, not much research has been done on this association because of the difficulty of developing a standardized formula for defining an organization's ability to pay and because of the confidentiality of such information. Nevertheless, the pay reductions by organizations in financial difficulty clearly suggest that wage levels are influenced by profitability. Several employee groups, most notably those in the steel, auto, and rubber industries, have accepted wage cuts to avoid plant closings.

WAGE SURVEYS

The major tool for making wage-level decisions is the **wage survey** (or pay survey). These surveys collect information about the compensation and benefits of other employees in similar industries or in the same geographical region. In a nonunion firm that has an average profit picture for its industry, the most compelling definition of an equitable wage is usually the going wage as determined by a wage survey. Both employees and managers are inclined to accept such a wage level as equitable.

TYPES OF SURVEYS

There are three primary kinds of wage surveys: (1) surveys conducted by government agencies, especially the BLS, (2) surveys conducted by professional organizations, and (3) surveys conducted by individual companies.

Wage surveys are conducted by numerous federal, state, and local government agencies. The most extensive government surveys are those conducted by the BLS. In addition to numerous unique reports and irregular publications, four series of continuing surveys are reported by the BLS: area wage surveys, Service Contract Act Surveys, industry wage surveys, and white-collar wage surveys.[16]

Area wage surveys report on the occupational earnings and benefits of selected blue- and white-collar jobs in 90 metropolitan labor-market areas, either annually or biennially. File clerks, stenographers, data-entry operators, secretaries, machinists, mechanics, laborers, and truck drivers are examples of the kinds of jobs surveyed. All industries within an area are studied except agriculture, mining, construction, and public administration. Information is published for occupations common to more than one type of industry. Every third year the BLS also publishes data on selected company practices, such as vacations and holidays, and employee benefits.

Service Contract Act surveys are reported for over 100 areas (in addition to the area wage surveys) at the request of the Department of Labor. These surveys are requested by the Employment Standards Administration under the Service Contract Act of 1965 to determine the prevailing wage rate. These surveys are very similar to area wage surveys except that less information is collected and published about employee benefits.

Industry wage surveys also are conducted by the BLS on twenty-five manufacturing industries, and fourteen nonmanufacturing industries. These surveys include earnings, benefits, and other human resource practices related to compensation. Industry surveys were started in 1950 and are updated periodically. Wage information is shown for the entire United States and for selected regions, states, or labor-market areas according to detailed occupation and industry characteristics. Examples of industries surveyed include banking, life insurance, communications, and bituminous coal.

White-collar surveys (on professional, administrative, technical, and clerical jobs) also are conducted annually by the BLS on a national basis. Some of the jobs included in these national surveys include accounting clerk, file clerk, secretary, typist, accountant, auditor, director of human resources, attorney, and engineer. Twenty-five occupations with over 100 work-level positions are included in these surveys. Table 10.4 illustrates a segment of a BLS survey.

Several professional organizations conduct wage surveys of their members. The American Management Association conducts surveys of managerial and professional occupations and publishes various reports on the salaries of top managers, middle managers, and supervisors. The Administrative Management Society surveys compensation for sixty clerical and data-processing positions in over 100 cities. The Society for Human Resource Management collects wage information from its members and publishes a report showing salary levels analyzed by position, geographic region, experience, and education. Wage surveys also are reported in various journals, including *Business Week, Compensation Review, Duns, Forbes, Fortune, Nation's Business,* and the *Monthly Labor Review.* For example, *Forbes* publishes a report regarding compensation awarded to the chief executive officers of the top companies. This report includes the salary and bonus of each CEO and other forms of remuneration that may be received by a CEO, such as stock options and deferred payments. The *Endicott Report* is a survey of starting salaries for college graduates, information which is generally available at college placement offices.

Wage surveys by government agencies and professional organizations are gaining greater acceptance. Wage and salary administrators are finding that these published surveys are very useful because they are reasonably current and inexpensive. However, the most frequently used surveys are still those conducted by a firm or a group of cooperating firms. For example, the human resource director of a small company might talk informally by phone or at a luncheon with other human resource directors in the area and share wage information regarding certain key jobs. In large organizations, a fulltime staff person or a task force may be responsible for designing and conducting wage surveys. In metropolitan areas, numerous business associations, such as an employers' association, an industrial relations council, or a chamber of commerce, may share wage information.

For these do-it-yourself wage surveys to be useful, four conditions must be met:

1. *Reciprocity.* Organizations conducting surveys must be willing to share their wage information in exchange for the information they collect from others.
2. *Anonymity.* The information should be reported in a way that does not identify the wages of individual organizations.
3. *Low cost.* The method used to collect and analyze the data must be efficient and inexpensive.
4. *Timely.* The information must be current, especially in times of high inflation.[17]

The major advantage of a do-it-yourself survey is that it can be designed to accommodate an organization's unique needs. If an organization is considering a pay increase for certain jobs, it can obtain timely information on these jobs by having the human resource department conduct a wage survey. Information from published surveys might

TABLE 10.4   Average salaries: United States*

Occupation and level	Number of employees	Monthly salaries		Middle range	
		Mean	Median	First quartile	Third quartile
Accountants					
I	10,638	$1,839	$1,833	$1,166	$2,000
II	29,945	2,169	2,141	1,969	2,335
III	28,520	2,784	2,749	2,499	3,015
IV	13,935	3,609	3,553	3,265	3,915
V	3,572	4,552	4,517	4,082	4,979
VI	686	5,688	5,482	5,306	5,998
Attorneys					
I	1,574	3,030	2,880	2,667	3,321
II	3,467	3,603	3,449	3,240	3,843
III	3,710	4,620	4,573	4,164	4,998
IV	2,958	6,212	6,164	5,489	6,824
V	1,195	7,634	7,496	6,747	8,288
VI	186	9,883	9,770	8,931	11,038
Personnel Specialists					
I	1,876	1,852	1,807	1,649	2,001
II	10,706	2,116	2,069	1,874	2,279
III	16,016	2,700	2,666	2,416	2,987
IV	8,635	3,518	3,458	3,090	3,915
V	1,694	4,485	4,415	4,116	4,855
Directors of Personnel					
I	867	3,436	3,415	3,182	3,749
II	1,792	4,409	4,457	3,929	4,911
III	795	5,951	5,833	5,416	6,248
IV	166	7,918	7,682	6,677	8,750

*Employment and average salaries in private service-producing industries for selected professional, administrative, technical, and clerical occupations, United States (except Alaska and Hawaii), March 1989.

[a] The middle range (interquartile) is the central part of the array excluding the upper and lower fourths of the employee distribution.

not be available for the specific jobs in question, or, if it is, it might be two or three years old.

The major advantages of published surveys are their low cost, large sample size, and degree of sophistication. Many published wage surveys can be obtained at no cost to a company because they appear in journals and published reports. The BLS area wage surveys also are very inexpensive and can be obtained from regional BLS offices or the Government Printing Office. Most published wage surveys are based on sample sizes that are much larger than an individual organization could hope to survey economically. The survey procedures used by professional organizations, especially the BLS, have become sophisticated in recent years, and thus the information collected by these organizations is reliable and useful. For example, the information for the BLS area wage surveys is collected by trained field interviewers who use elaborate job descriptions defining the positions being surveyed.

SURVEY METHODS

Three methods are normally used to conduct a wage survey: personal interviews, mailed questionnaires, and telephone inquiries. Personal interviews are the slowest and most costly method, but they are also the most accurate. Personal interviews by trained field interviewers are able to minimize some of the serious criticisms of wage surveys. These criticisms center on the difficulty of making valid comparisons between different job descriptions, earnings, and benefits. For example, many jobs have the same title, such as "secretary," but the responsibilities and demands of the jobs with that title vary significantly. Unless the level of each job is accurately classified, by someone such as a trained field interviewer, the wage data are meaningless. An employee's earnings can also be difficult to interpret because of such things as overtime, incentive pay, and bonuses. The hourly or weekly rates of pay for some positions are not related to their total earnings. Finally, benefits vary dramatically from organization to organization, and such things as paid holidays, free meals, and clothing allowances are part of the total compensation.

Trained field interviewers are better able to account for unique job differences than mailed questionnaires that rely on the personal interpretation of the individual completing the form. Mailed questionnaires are the cheapest and probably the most frequently used method of conducting individual wage surveys. For mailed questionnaires to be useful, however, the jobs, earnings, and benefits must be described carefully (which adds to the length and complexity of the questionnaires and makes the respondents less willing to complete it). Telephone inquiries are often used to clarify information from mailed questionnaires or simply to obtain a quick, informal survey of local wages. Detailed information on several jobs cannot be obtained very conveniently by phone.

THE WAGE-STRUCTURE DECISION

The wage-structure decision is the determination of how much each job should be paid relative to other jobs within the organization. Here the amount of money is based on the job demands and not on how well the job holder performs (although the wage structure must allow for individual variances based on performance, experience, and seniority). All jobs in an organization are not worth the same rate of pay. In comparison to other jobs, some jobs require greater skill and mental ability, some require greater physical effort, and some entail considerable responsibility. The major objective of the wage-structure decision is to provide equal pay for jobs of equal worth and an acceptable set of pay differentials for jobs of unequal worth.

The development of a wage structure involves a comparison of the jobs within an organization. Some organizations rely almost exclusively on wage surveys to make wage-structure decisions. However, wage surveys are not adequate, because organizations usually have unique jobs, plus jobs with unique tasks that cannot be analyzed using a wage survey.

Wage-structure decisions are typically made in one of these three ways: a unilateral determination by top management, collective bargaining between management and the union, and job evaluation.

MANAGEMENT EDICT

In small- and medium-sized organizations, the wage structure may be determined by management edict. The president of the company, sometimes with recommendations from officers in accounting or personnel, makes a unilateral decision concerning the wages paid for various jobs. In a small manufacturing company, for example, the president identified three levels of management and four levels of production. As a first approximation of how much each job should be paid, the president decided on the pay of the top management level (vice president of operations), and then set each successive pay level at 15 percent less than the level preceding it. This simple structure served as the basis for deciding how much each job should be paid, although individuals with greater experience and better performance received higher pay.

Wage structures determined by a unilateral management decision contain relatively wide pay differentials between high- and low-paying jobs. Most managers believe that employees should be paid for performance, and they also believe that outstanding performers deserve to be promoted. Consequently, the differences between high- and low-paying jobs are quite large.

Wage structures created by management edict are as good or as bad as the decisions that created them. If the decision maker knows the going market rates and understands the job requirements, the resultant wage structure might be acceptable. However, if some jobs are overpaid or underpaid, employees may become dissatisfied—even those who are paid fairly. If numerous complaints are expressed, the wage structure usually is changed. Unfortunately, the structure often becomes a patchwork of changes that cannot be defended, and then it contributes to continuing dissatisfaction. This festering situation probably explains why some consultants recommend that pay should have a low profile in an organization so that employees' attention is not drawn to wages.

COLLECTIVE BARGAINING

In most unionized organizations the wage structure is established through bilateral bargaining between management and the union. New contracts tend to preserve the wage differentials among the various jobs that existed before the union was elected. Over time, however, the wage structure tends to become so compressed that the differentials between high- and low-paying jobs grow small. This compression in the wage structure occurs because a large percentage of union membership holds lower-level jobs. As union leaders try to negotiate a contract that will be acceptable to the membership, they usually find it advantageous to ask for increases in the wages of jobs with the largest membership. Thus, the high wages of craftsworkers are sacrificed for large increases for low-level production jobs. When Walter Reuther, head of the United Auto Workers Union, announced a new wage settlement, he was pelted with tomatoes by dissatisfied craftsworkers who felt they had been sold out in favor of less-skilled coworkers.

Unions usually experience a great amount of dissatisfaction when the wage structure is established by collective bargaining. Management is primarily concerned about the total labor cost, whereas the allocation of money to the various jobs is the union's decision. However, a union usually is not well prepared to make wage-structure decisions. A union finds difficulty satisfying everyone, since an increase in pay for one group usually means a decrease in pay for another group. Union leaders have found that their members are seldom satisfied with what they get or with the explanations for their wages. Consequently, in union companies, both management and the union may realize advantages by using some form of job-evaluation technique to establish a wage structure.

JOB EVALUATION

The systematic approach to determining the relative worth or value of each job in an organization is referred to as **job evaluation**. The basic purpose of job evaluation is to eliminate pay inequities that exist because of unreasonable pay structures. The relative worth of each job is established by identifying factors that define "worth" and by comparing the requirements of each job with these factors.

Numerous surveys of business organizations have indicated that some form of job evaluation is used in most companies. One survey of 105 companies indicated that 70 percent of them used a formal job-evaluation program to determine internal job worth.[18]

To be successful, a job-evaluation program must be carefully designed and implemented. An effective program requires the cooperation of management and employees; both groups need to appreciate the value of the job-evaluation program and be willing to invest the time and money necessary to make it operate.[19] The job-evaluation committee typically consists of five individuals: two members of management, two employees or members of the union, and another person jointly selected by management and the employees. An industrial engineer or a job analyst often serves as an ex officio member of the committee and is responsible for clarifying the information on the job descriptions. Sometimes managers are reluctant to allow employees to participate in developing a wage structure, but the evidence indicates that managers' fears are largely unfounded. In fact, when one company discovered that the wage structure developed by a management committee was similar to one already developed by an employee committee, the company allowed the employee committee to determine the wage structure on its own. The composition of the committee does not seem to matter as long as the committee members are interested in the program and willing to perform the task thoughtfully. Trained job evaluators do not seem to be any more reliable than other employees who have been trained. Furthermore, research on the reliability of evaluator ratings indicates that a committee of three to five individuals is adequate.[20]

One study looked for evidence of sex bias in job-evaluation procedures and found that the ratings of different jobs were not biased by either the sex of the evaluator or the dominant sex of the job incumbents. These results suggest that job-evaluation methods can help to eliminate sex-biased compensation systems.[21]

The job-evaluation committee should have access to written job descriptions, and the committee members ought to be thoroughly familiar with the jobs being evaluated. The written job descriptions should describe each job accurately, and employees should examine their own job descriptions to ensure that they are correct and complete.

Many different job-evaluation systems have been developed and used in various organizations. Most of these systems consist of one of these methods or a combination of them:

1. Job ranking
2. Classification
3. Point
4. Factor comparison

Various computer-aided job-evaluation programs have been developed to improve the objectivity, consistency, and speed of the evaluation process. Some programs use data obtained directly from the job analysis and entered into the computer to identify a wage range for each job. For example, some companies use the Position Analysis Questionnaire (described in Chapter 4) to analyze jobs, and this information is entered into a computerized job-evaluation program that tells how much each job should pay relative to other jobs in the company.[22]

JOB-EVALUATION METHODS

Two job-evaluation methods, ranking and classification, are considered nonquantitative because they do not produce a precise numerical score for each of the jobs being evaluated. Instead, these methods produce a position for each job in a job-worth hierarchy. Ranking and classification methods also are called "whole-job" evaluation methods because they determine the relative worth of jobs on the basis of an overall, or global, assessment of the content of the jobs. The factor comparison and point methods, on the other hand, are quantitative. These methods evaluate the content of jobs on a factor-by-factor basis and produce a precise numerical score for each of the jobs evaluated.

One study suggested that the choice of which job-evaluation method to use does not matter much because they all produce similar results. It therefore advocated using the job-ranking method because it is the simplest. The methodology of this study was criticized, however, particularly when the profound effects of small wage differences on morale were noted. Consequently, the point method appears to be better than job ranking, especially for large or complex organizations.[23]

JOB-RANKING METHOD

The simplest method of developing a wage structure is to have the job-evaluation committee rank the jobs from highest to lowest in value. Although the committee could perform three or four rankings on three or four different factors, the jobs usually are ranked only once according to their overall worth. The advantages of the **job-ranking method** are that it is the simplest of all the evaluation methods and it requires little time or paperwork. The disadvantages are: (1) that the differentials between the ranks are assumed to be equal when they usually are not (e.g., there is usually very little difference in worth between jobs in the middle of the ranking, but big differences generally exist between jobs at the top and bottom ends of the ranking); (2) that evaluating each job as a whole is not conducive to a careful analysis and cannot provide an accurate measurement of worth; and (3) that the ranking method is difficult to use in organizations with large numbers of jobs.[24]

A useful technique to help evaluators rank a large list of jobs is to arrange them into clusters of related jobs, called job series, and rank each series separately. If an overall ranking is needed, it can be obtained easily by merging the job series that are already ranked.

CLASSIFICATION METHOD

The **classification method** (or predetermined-grading method) consists of establishing a predetermined number of grades or job classes. This method was originally developed by the federal government as a result of the 1923 Federal Classification Act, which established a system for fair compensation of federal white-collar employees. The classification process specifies a number of grades beforehand, and broad descriptions then are written of the types of jobs to be placed in each of the grades. Next, each job is evaluated by comparing its description with the descriptions for the grades, and it is then placed into the appropriate grade. The job grades range from high to low, and each grade has a verbal description with examples of the kinds of jobs that fit into it. A good classification system is difficult to develop and requires extensive knowledge about the dimensions of different jobs and the relative worth of the dimensions.[25]

The GS system used by the federal government is probably the best known classification system. This system contains eighteen grades (GS-1 to GS-18), with GS-1 being the lowest grade. The typical duties and responsibilities of a GS-1 are very simple and routine, as described in Table 10.5. Higher GS grades are associated with progressively more difficult jobs through GS-18, where high-level executive tasks are required. Many state and local governments also use a classification system.

One advantage of a classification system is that it standardizes the wages for similar jobs and maintains pay differentials between jobs within an extremely large organization. For example, a new chemical engineer starting work with the federal government should receive about the same pay regardless of the geographical region in which he or she works and regardless of which government agency is the employer. The disadvantage of using a classification system is that its stability makes it unresponsive to such factors as regional wage differences and labor-market variances. Managers have been known to manipulate job descriptions and job assignments to have a job placed in a higher or lower classification than "the rules" would indicate.

TABLE 10.5   Job class descriptions in the Civil Service System for General Schedule (GS) positions

Grade GS-1 includes those classes of positions the duties of which are to perform, under immediate supervision with little or no latitude for the exercise of independent judgment—

(A) the simplest routine work in office, business, or fiscal operations; or
(B) elementary work of a subordinate technical character in a professional, scientific, or technical field.

Grade GS-5 includes those classes of positions the duties of which are—

(A) to perform under general supervision difficult and responsible work in office, business, or fiscal administration or comparable subordinate technical work in a professional, scientific, or technical field requiring in either case—
    (1) considerable training and supervisory or career experience
    (2) broad working knowledge of a special subject matter or of office, laboratory, engineering, scientific or other procedures and practices and
    (3) the exercise of independent judgment in a limited field.
(B) to perform under immediate supervision and with little opportunity for the exercise of independent judgment simple and elementary work requiring professional, scientific, or technical training, or
(C) to perform other work of equal importance, difficulty, and responsibility, and requiring comparable qualifications.

Grade GS-9 includes those classes of positions the duties of which are—

(A) to perform, under general supervision, very difficult and responsible work along special technical, supervisory, or administrative lines in office, business, or fiscal administration, requiring—
    (1) somewhat extended specialized training and considerable specialized, supervisory, or administrative experience which has demonstrated capacity for sound independent work;
    (2) thorough and fundamental knowledge of a special and complex subject matter, or of the profession, art or science involved and
    (3) considerable latitude for the exercise of independent judgment;
(B) with considerable latitude for the exercise of independent judgment, to perform moderately difficult and responsible work requiring—
    (1) professional, scientific, or technical training equivalent to that represented by graduation from a college or university of recognized standing; and
    (2) considerable additional professional, scientific, or technical training or experience which has demonstrated capacity for sound independent work; or
(C) to perform other work of equal importance, difficulty, and responsibility, and requiring comparable qualifications.

POINT METHOD

The **point method** is the most frequently used job-evaluation method, because it is not very difficult to administer after it has been established and the decisions are defensible. The point method consists of analyzing the content of jobs from the written job descriptions and then allocating points for specific factors. The number of points assigned to each job determines a range of pay for that job as illustrated in Figure 10.3. The procedure for developing the point method consists of the following steps:

1. *Identify key jobs.* A list of twelve to twenty key jobs needs to be identified. By definition, **key jobs** (sometimes called benchmark jobs) are jobs that are equitably paid. They are not necessarily the most important jobs in the organization, but they should be jobs that are stable and well-defined. There should be a consensus of opinion that these jobs are equitably paid, because the wage structure for the entire organization will be based on them. Wage surveys help to identify key jobs.

2. *Identify job factors used to determine pay levels.* These factors are called **compensable factors** because they are the important factors for which compensation is given; they represent the critical dimensions that would justify paying one job more than another if all else were held constant. Some of the most frequently used factors include responsibility, physical demands, hazards, skill, working conditions, supervisory responsibilities, and mental requirements. Many point systems have ten or more compensable factors. However, research has consistently shown that three or four factors are highly correlated

FIGURE 10.3 Illustration on a wage curve using the point method of job evaluation.

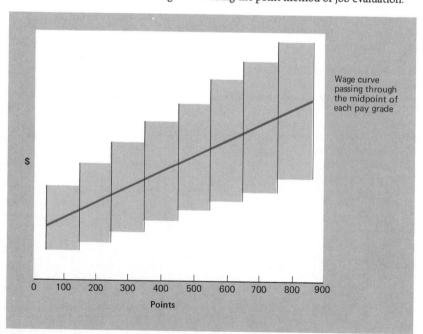

(greater than .90) with the overall results of an evaluation in which more factors are used. Studies have suggested that experience, responsibility, and skill requirements (or education/training) tend to be the most significant factors determining pay regardless of whether they are combined into one factor or separated into two or more factors.[26]

Even though the responsibility-education-experience factor seems to have by far the greatest impact on the wage structure in the United States as well as in other societies, other factors also should be considered. Such factors as working conditions, hazards, and physical demands may not have much impact on the wage structure, but they do influence some jobs. Moreover, employees believe that a multifactor system is necessary to consider all the relevant aspects of a job. Six to eight factors should usually be sufficient.

3. *Weight factors according to contribution to overall worth of the job.* The weights assigned to the factors will reflect the values of management and society. The most heavily weighted factors tend to be responsibility, knowledge, education, experience, complexity of duties, and supervisory responsibility. Sometimes unskilled workers are critical of the heavy weighting of education and skill, claiming that the only reason these factors are highly weighted is because the managers whose jobs require such factors are the ones who determine the weights. Although this criticism is often true, the heavy weighting of education and skill also can be defended on these grounds: (1) If education and skill are not heavily weighted, the final wage structure will be distorted and inequitable. (2) Jobs requiring high levels of skill and education usually go unfilled in the labor market and therefore need to pay well to attract qualified employees. (3) Financial incentives are considered equitable and necessary to reward individuals who have obtained additional skill and education. In Table 10.6, skill is weighted four times as heavily as working conditions.

4. *Divide each job factor into degrees that range from high to low and assign points to each degree.* An example of the degree assignments for the physical-demands factor is shown in Table 10.7. The degrees need to be described clearly so that evaluators can reliably determine the degrees for each factor from the job descriptions. The number of points assigned to each degree should correspond with the weighting of the factor. For example, if the factor of skill is weighted 40 percent, the factor of working conditions is weighted 10 percent, and both factors have five degrees, degree 2 for skill should have four times as many points as degree 2 for working conditions.

5. *Reach a consensus about degree assignments.* Before the committee as a whole discusses the evaluations and assigns the degrees and points to the jobs for each factor, each member should evaluate the jobs individually. The committee's decisions should then be reached by consensus rather than by voting or averaging. Reaching a consensus is important, even if the committee has to get more information about a job by interviewing the job holder or by observing the work performed. When evaluating jobs, the committee should follow these guidelines: (a) base the evaluation strictly on the requirements of the job, (b) consider only postorientation entry-level requirements, (c) focus primarily on what the worker does during the large majority of the time, (d) assess value relative to the total organization rather than the projected market value, and (e) avoid being influenced by the individual's performance level, education (since it may be more than is required by the job), or organizational level (since responsibility is usually a separate factor).

6. *Develop a wage curve using key jobs.* The total points for each job are calculated by summing the points assigned for each factor. The average pay for each key job can be obtained from payroll records; however, it is usually compared with wage survey data when possible to confirm its equity. Once the total points and the average pay of the key jobs have been determined, the data can be plotted on a graph. The **wage curve** is generally a straight line (linear curve), since the higher-level degrees are heavily weighted. The points usually are placed along the horizontal axis (the *x*-axis) and pay is placed along the vertical axis (the *y*-axis). Two methods of deriving a wage curve are: (a) the freehand method of drawing a line that comes as close as possible to the key jobs; and (b) the least-squares regression line that is derived by finding the slope and *y*-intercept from two statistical equations. The regression line is clearly the most accurate method, although pay administrators are sometimes frightened by statistical equations. (Fifteen key jobs plotted on a graph with a wage curve obtained from a regression line is shown in Figure 10.4).[27]

After the wage curve has been drawn, the total points are usually divided into labor grades, or job classes, and a range of pay is assigned to each grade. A wage curve divided into eight labor grades is shown in Figure 10.5. All jobs in the same grade have the same pay range. The purpose of using labor grades rather than the wage curve is for ease of administration. It is easier to administer fifteen or twenty labor grades than hundreds of separate points along the wage curve.

Once the wage structure has been established using the key jobs, the appropriate level of pay can be determined for other jobs. The committee decides how many points

TABLE 10.6   Point assignments for four compensable factors

Compensable Factor	Weighted Percentage	Degrees/Points				
		1	2	3	4	5
Skill	(40%)	20	32	48	72	100
Responsibility	(30%)	15	24	36	54	75
Effort	(20%)	10	16	24	36	50
Working conditions	(10%)	5	8	12	18	25

Example: Regrind Operator	Compensable Factor	Degree	Points
	Skill	3	28
	Responsibility	2	24
	Effort	4	36
	Working conditions	4	18
	Total points		126

TABLE 10.7 Physical-demands factor

This factor refers to the physical energy usually expended in standing, lifting, carrying, pulling, and pushing. Consider the amount in terms of the weight that is involved and the percentage of time the worker is normally required to perform these activities. The terms *occasional* and *frequent* are defined as follows:

Occasional: Observable during the normal workday routine but required less than 30 percent of the time.

Frequent: Required over 30 percent of the time.

Degree	Definition	Examples
1	*Very light work.* Occasional lifting, up to ten pounds. May frequently lift and/or carry materials of negligible weights such as dockets, ledgers, small tools, and the like.	Audit clerk, clerk-typist, condensor winder, draftsperson, payroll clerk, roller bearing inspector, sorter, timekeeper
2	*Light work:* Occasional lifting, up to twenty pounds. May frequently lift and/or carry objects weighing up to ten pounds. Jobs should also be rated in this category when they require continuous walking or standing even though the weight lifted is negligible, or when they require sitting most of the time but call for pushing or pulling arm and/or leg controls.	Barber, bevel saw operator, delivery clerk, die maker, drill sharpener, meter tester, loader boss, shaper operator, surveyor, production checker
3	*Medium work.* Occasional lifting, up to fifty pounds. May frequently lift and/or carry objects weighing up to twenty pounds. May be called upon to push or pull equivalent to lifting requirements.	Bricklayer, draw bench operator, machinist, tool and die maker, chipper, electrical repairperson
4	*Heavy work.* Occasional lifting, up to eighty pounds. May frequently lift and/or carry objects weighing up to forty pounds. May be called upon to push or pull equivalent to lifting requirements.	Blacksmith, boiler mechanic, heat treater, pipebender, steamfitter, rigger, drop-hammer operator
5	*Very heavy work.* Occasional lifting, more than eighty pounds. May frequently lift and/or carry objects weighing over forty pounds. May be called upon to push or pull equivalent to lifting requirements.	Feed loader, foundry laborer, hod carrier, longshoreman, miner, cross tie feeder, bending roll operator

other jobs should receive and refers to the wage curve to know how much these jobs should be paid. Unique jobs can be evaluated objectively, and logical explanations can be provided to justify their rates of pay.

FACTOR-COMPARISON METHOD

This method is conceptually similar to the point method but slightly more complex, and because of its added complexity, it is not as popular as the point method. Surveys indicate that it is used in only 10 to 20 percent of the organizations that use job-evaluation methods.[28]

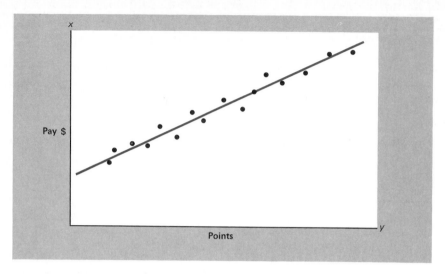

FIGURE 10.4 Illustration of a wage curve based on fifteen key jobs.

The **factor-comparison** method consists of the following steps:

1. *Identify key (benchmark) jobs.* As with the point method, these are equitably paid jobs. The difference is that only five to eight key jobs are normally used in the factor-comparison method in contrast to the twelve to twenty key jobs used in the point method.
2. *Identify job factors.* These factors should represent the important dimensions of worth, just as in the point method. Usually these five factors are included: mental requirements, physical requirements, skill, responsibility, and working conditions.
3. *Rank jobs.* The key jobs should be ranked with respect to each of the factors independently.
4. *Assign monetary amounts to each job on each factor.* The amount of money assigned to each job on a given factor should be consistent with how the jobs were ranked on that factor. When the dollar amounts assigned to a job are added for all five factors, their sum should equal the current rate of pay. This step is somewhat subjective, and the success of the method depends on how carefully the dollar amounts are assigned to each job on each factor.
5. *Compare unique jobs with key jobs.* This should be done, factor by factor, to determine how much each unique job should be paid.

The factor-comparison method is illustrated in Table 10.8. In this table, four student library jobs are considered equitably paid and serve as key jobs. Unique jobs, such as operating a copy machine, are compared against these key jobs to determine an equitable rate of pay. For example, the copy-center job is similar to a job at the circulation desk on three factors, but slightly lower on mental demands and higher on working conditions.

TABLE 10.8 The factor-comparison method using student jobs in a university library

Cents	Mental Demands	Physical Demands	Skill	Responsibility	Working Conditions
2.40	Reference (2.40)	Janitor (2.40) Sorter (2.10)	Reference (2.40)	Reference (2.40) *Circulation (2.10)	
1.80	Circulation (1.80) *				Janitor (1.50)
1.20	Sorter (1.20)	Reference (.90)	Sorter (1.20) *Circulation (.90)		
.60	Janitor (.30)	*Circulation (.60)	Janitor (.60)	Sorter (.60) Janitor (.30)	*Sorter (.60) Circulation (.30)
.00					Reference (.00)

Reference librarian = $2.40 + .90 + 2.40 + 2.40 + .00 = $8.10/hr.
Circulation desk   = $1.80 + .60 + .90 + 2.10 + .30 = 5.70/hr.
Sorters & Shelvers = $1.20 + 2.10 + 1.20 + .60 + .60 = 5.70/hr.
Janitor   = $ .30 + 2.40 + .60 + .30 + 1.50 = 5.10/hr.
*Copy center   = $1.50 + .60 + .90 + 2.10 + .60 = 5.70/hr.

PRICING THE JOB

After the jobs have been arranged in a hierarchy of job worth, specific amounts of pay need to be associated with them. The process of placing a dollar value on the worth of a job is referred to as **job pricing**. In pricing a job, most organizations assign a pay range rather than a specific fixed amount to allow for individual differences in performance. Similar jobs are grouped together into pay grades. Job pricing involves making decisions about **pay ranges** and **pay grades** in addition to developing a plan for adjusting the wage structure as necessary because of inflation. Developing the pay ranges is part of the individual wage decision discussed later.

PAY GRADES

Pay grades using the wage curve are illustrated in Figure 10.5. An organization could have fewer pay grades by expanding the width of each grade. How many pay grades to

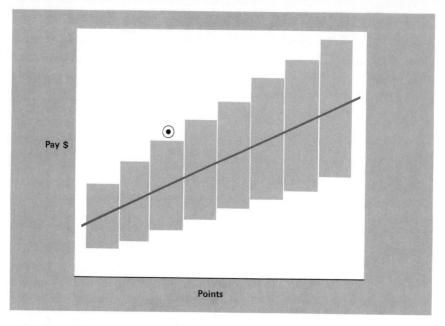

Pay $

Points

FIGURE 10.5 Illustration of pay grades constructed along the wage curve.

have could be decided arbitrarily by assigning a fixed width to each labor grade; however, a better procedure would be to plot each of the jobs on a chart to determine if natural clusters of jobs exist.

After all of the jobs have been evaluated, they can be plotted on a scatter diagram, as shown in Figure 10.4. Hopefully, the dot representing a job will fall within the pay range for its particular pay grade. Jobs that fall outside the pay ranges present special problems. These jobs are referred to as **red-circle job** rates because they are either overpaid or underpaid.[29] (Sometimes underpaid jobs are called blue-circle rates.)

Underpaid jobs are easy to correct; their pay levels can be raised immediately. Overpaid jobs are difficult to correct. An illustration of an overpaid job is shown in Figure 10.5. The job is represented by a dot with a circle around it, indicating that it is a red-circle rate. The employees performing this job have been earning more than the maximum amount that this job should pay. One obvious solution to the problem is to reduce the wages for this job. However, pay cuts usually produce bad feelings unless employees understand the job-evaluation procedure and agree that their jobs are over-paid. Large pay cuts force employees to suddenly change their standard of living, some-thing that is not easy to do.

A second approach to handling overpaid jobs is to notify the employees that their jobs are overpaid and that their pay will be systematically reduced by small increments over a period of time. If the employees understand the job-evaluation procedure and are given enough time to change their standard of living, this method will not produce as much dissatisfaction as an immediate pay cut.

A third approach is to hold the rates constant until inflation and other cost-of-living increases have increased the rest of the wage curve. These jobs are excluded from normal cost-of-living increases when pay rates are adjusted. Overpaid jobs can be brought back into line fairly quickly when there is a high rate of inflation.

A fourth approach is to redesign the job, usually by adding more responsibility; if the job is redesigned, it may no longer be overpaid. Finally, a fifth approach is to promote overpaid workers to higher-level positions. This is an ideal solution if the employees have the proper qualifications for promotion.

ADJUSTING THE WAGE CURVE

After a wage curve has been developed, it is generally easy to administer. As new jobs are created, the job-evaluation committee evaluates them and assigns an equitable pay range for them. However, some administrative problems may arise when the wage structure has to be adjusted due to inflation or internal changes within the organization, such as job redesign.

Two methods typically are used to adjust the wage curve. The first method is to provide an across-the-board increase of so many cents per hour for every job. An across-the-board increase amounts to a **fixed-rate-increase** and is illustrated in Figure 10.6 by line B. This curve shows a fixed increase of fifty cents per hour for every job. Many organizations have fixed-rate increases tied to the **consumer price index (CPI)**, which indicates the rate of inflation in the economy. Labor agreements that contain a **cost-of-living adjustment (COLA)** typically provide a fixed-rate increase with changes in the

FIGURE 10.6 Illustration of wage compression: fixed-rate increase versus percentage increase.

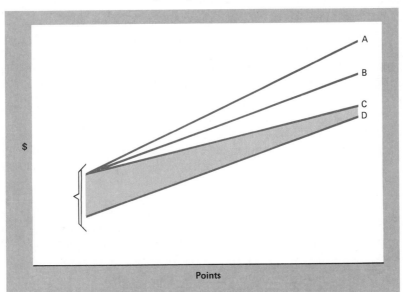

CPI. One major labor agreement, for example, provides for a one-cent-per-hour increase in every job for every .4 increase in the consumer price index.

The second method of adjusting the wage curve is to use a **percentage increase** whereby the rate for each job is increased by a specified percent. Line A in Figure 10.6 illustrates a percentage increase in the wage curve. Higher-paid jobs receive a larger cents-per-hour increase than lower-paid jobs. Ten percent of five dollars is only a fifty-cent-per-hour increase, whereas 10 percent of ten dollars amounts to a one-dollar-per-hour increase.

Occasionally, organizations raise the bottom end of the wage curve faster than the top end because of special situations. Such a situation is described by line C in Figure 10.6. Here the pay increases become successively smaller with higher-level jobs. The two situations that are most likely to result in a **decreasing-rate increase** typically are increases in minimum-wage legislation and collective-bargaining pressures that grant larger increases to lower-level jobs.

Over an extended period of time, both decreasing-rate and fixed-rate increases result in **wage compression**. The problem caused by wage compression is that eventually organizations are unable to promote employees to high-level positions because the financial incentives for accepting more responsibility and skill are too small to attract employees. Some organizations have faced serious staffing problems because of their inability to promote lower-level employees into higher-level jobs that do not provide adequate incentives. A small amount of wage compression occurs even with percentage increases because of the tax structure in society: people who have higher incomes are subject to higher income tax rates. To maintain adequate financial incentives to reward upper-level jobs, some organizations have found it necessary to use increasing-percentage increases as they adjust their wage curves.

COMPARABLE-WORTH CONTROVERSY

An important legal controversy in recent years, known as the **comparable-worth controversy**, centers on the issue of whether organizations should be required to evaluate the worth of every job according to a common set of criteria and to pay all jobs of comparable worth at the same rate. A major cause of the controversy is the fact that numerous jobs traditionally dominated by women (such as nurse, telephone operator, schoolteacher, and secretary), pay considerably less than jobs traditionally dominated by men (such as doctor, bus driver, professor, and messenger).

Two federal laws, the Equal Pay Act and the Civil Rights Act, prohibit discrimination on the basis of sex in paying employees. The Equal Pay Act prohibits employers from paying members of one sex less than members of the opposite sex for performing equal work. Jobs are considered equal if they require equal skill, effort, and responsibility and if they are performed under similar working conditions. Four exceptions are provided by the act: unequal payments can be based on (1) a seniority system, (2) a merit system, (3) a system that measures earnings by quantity or quality of production, or (4) any other factor other than sex. The Civil Rights Act is broader than the Equal Pay Act in prohibiting many kinds of discrimination, but it does provide similar coverage with respect to wage discrimination on the basis of sex. An employer is prohibited from discriminating against any individual with respect to compensation, terms, or conditions of employment because of the individual's sex. As a result of these laws, employers are required to pay both male and female employees performing the same job the same rate of pay. Therefore, all nurses who perform equal work have to receive the same pay, regardless of whether they are male or female. Similarly, all coal miners performing equal work have to receive the same rate of pay, regardless of sex. However, the comparable-worth controversy asks whether employers should be required to assess the overall worth of nurses and coal miners according to a common set of criteria and pay them equally if their worth is comparable.

The most highly recommended procedure for eliminating sex-based wage systems is through a job-evaluation program. The point method, especially, has been shown to be largely free from sex bias on the part of both the raters and the job incumbents.[30] Job-evaluation programs are designed to provide equal pay for jobs of comparable worth, and there is a popular myth that the gap between men's and women's pay would be eliminated if all companies used a job-evaluation system. Although the gap would narrow, a gap between the average pay of men and women would still exist because, on average, women typically choose careers that require less skill, effort, and responsibility than men. Consequently, a job-evaluation program would eliminate the gap only if equal percentages of men and women chose high-skilled jobs.[31] Data compiled by the Bureau of Labor Statistics indicate that the average pay of women compared to men increased from 60 to 70 percent from 1977 to 1987. The progress made by women in narrowing the wage gap was primarily due to the growing numbers of women entering professional jobs.[32]

Most courts have been reluctant to recognize the comparable-worth theory because of the legal and practical problems involved. The legislative histories of the Equal Pay Act and Title VII of the Civil Rights Act indicate that neither act prohibits an employer from paying unequal compensation for jobs that are not substantially equal. The courts also have made it clear that they do not want to engage in a wholesale reevaluation of an employer's pay structure to enforce their own concepts of economic worth. Legal interpretations suggest that Congress did not intend to substitute the judgment of the secretary of labor, the EEOC, or the courts for that of employers in compensation determinations. Instead, compensation for unequal jobs is to be determined by complex forces within a company and the labor market.[33]

Some courts have recognized the theory of comparable worth, and although they have given no guidance in regard to what standards to apply in establishing a case under the theory, they have prohibited compensation systems that are based on intentional discrimination. For example, in the case of *IUE* v. *Westinghouse Electric Corporation*, the Third Circuit Court agreed that Westinghouse had willfully set lower wage rates for those job classifications that were predominantly female than for those that were predominantly male. The court found that Westinghouse intentionally discriminated against women by assigning them to lower-paying jobs and by not transferring them out of such classifications. However, the court did not require Westinghouse to conduct an exhaustive evaluation of all jobs or to provide equal pay for jobs of comparable worth.[34]

In another landmark case, *County of Washington* v. *Gunther*, the U.S. Supreme Court ruled that four female jail matrons were victims of sex-based wage discrimination because their wages were only 70 percent as much as male guards in spite of the fact that the County of Washington had evaluated the jobs and determined that the matrons should be paid 95 percent as much as the male guards.[35] Here, a case of illegal sex discrimination was established even though the jobs were not equal. However, the Supreme Court was very clear in declaring that it was not basing its decision on the concept of "comparable worth." The decision was based on the fact that the County of Washington had evaluated the worth of the jobs and persisted in paying female matrons less than the county's own evaluation had determined. The Supreme Court, like other district and circuit appeal courts, refused to make its own subjective assessment of the worth of different jobs.

An employer's responsibility to rectify sex-based wage discrimination was challenged in the case of *American Federation of State, County, and Municipal Employees* v. *State of Washington*.[36] At the request of the Governor of Washington, a job-classification system was developed, in 1974, based on knowledge and skills, mental demands, accountability, and working conditions. However, the state failed to implement the system even though a study of government salaries indicated that women in predominantly female jobs were paid approximately 20 percent less than other jobs of similar worth. In 1984, the district court ordered the state of Washington to correct this disparity at a cost of $300 to $500 million; however, the Ninth Circuit Court of Appeals dismissed the case.

Although comparable worth is a dead issue at the federal level, several state legislatures have required job-evaluation studies for state employees and, in some states, for private employees also. These state laws, along with the growing application of job-evaluation programs, are reducing sex-based wage discrimination.

TWO-TIER WAGE SYSTEMS

Because of economic pressures during the 1980s, some companies negotiated two-tier wage settlements with their unions. Many leading firms, such as Boeing, Lockheed, McDonnell Douglas, American Airlines, and Safeway Stores, were among the list of companies that adopted multiple-level pay systems. The wage agreements generally provided that certain newly hired employees would receive substantially lower wages than current employees. Some of these two-tier systems were intended to continue indefinitely, while others were designed so that new employees would eventually reach parity with older workers, usually within 90 days.[37]

The purpose of a two-tier system is to make companies more competitive by reducing labor costs, and most companies that used the system realized these short-term benefits. The long-term effects were less favorable, however, and some two-tier systems have been eliminated. The basic problem with a two-tier system is that it creates feelings of inequity, causing people in both tiers to feel like second-class employees. Newly hired employees feel like second-class citizens because they are paid less than others for performing the same jobs. Employees in the higher tier also feel like second-class citizens because they cost more for their departments. Managers who are pressed to cut costs want to substitute new employees for long-term ones at the lower rate. Because they come with a higher price tag, longer-term employees are viewed as second-class citizens. Multiple-salary systems lead to isolation of the highly paid employees and the segmentation of activities in the company. Furthermore, they interfere with transfers, promotions, and other valuable training and development functions. Because of these problems, especially the

▌ **HRM in Action**

A Restoration of Wages and Benefits

During the 1980s, while the steel industry in the United States was downsizing, LTV Steel Corporation asked the employees at its Cleveland mill to accept reduced wages and benefits. When they made these concessions, many employees wondered if their wages would ever be restored. The answer was yes.

In April 1990, LTV Steel, Cleveland, approved a new labor agreement that restored their previous wages and benefits and provided other financial rewards, even though LTV's parent, Dallas-based LTV Corp., was still operating under Chapter 11 of the Bankruptcy Code. The new agreement, which covers 13,500 active employees, contains the following provisions:

1. A restoration of previous base wage concessions amounting to $1.61 an hour.
2. Additional pay increases of $1.50 an hour ($1.00 an hour increase on January 1, 1991, and 50 cents an hour increase a year later).
3. A restoration of shift differentials and Sunday premiums.
4. An immediate $1,000 payment: a $500 signing bonus and a $500 advance on the 1990 profit sharing.

Source: "Steel Unit's Hourly Workers Approve a Labor Contract," *Wall Street Journal*, April 3, 1990.

problem of inequity, many companies have initiated steps to abolish their two-tier pay systems.[38]

INDIVIDUAL WAGE DECISION

The third major wage decision in designing a compensation system is the individual wage decision. This decision concerns the relative pay of individuals who perform similar jobs in the same company. If workers perform similar jobs and their performance and experience are equal, it is reasonable to pay them all the same. But if some individuals are more productive or have more experience and training, then these workers should receive more money.

VARIABLES INFLUENCING INDIVIDUAL PAY

The individual wage decision influences feelings of job satisfaction and pay equity. Intense feelings of inequity can be created by unfavorable comparisons between coworkers regarding their pay. Higher-producing employees think they should receive higher pay than coworkers who produce less. Individuals who work together usually know how much each is paid, and they compare their performances. Some of the other variables influencing individual pay are listed in Table 10.3. These variables include experience, seniority, potential, and personal preferences.

PERFORMANCE

Performance differences are clearly the most reasonable and well-accepted justification for paying differential amounts. Most individuals accept the principle that workers who produce more should receive higher pay. This pay-for-performance principle is particularly strong among individuals who accept the work ethic. Studies have shown that individuals who score high on the Protestant work ethic scale tend to think high performers ought to be highly rewarded to establish a condition of equity. On the other hand, individuals with low Protestant work ethic scores tend to believe that the rewards should be distributed equally to both high and low performers.[39] Outstanding employees generally feel very demoralized when they are paid the same as less productive workers.

The attitudes of union leaders do not always endorse the pay-for-performance principle. Unions typically resist pay systems that base pay on performance. Union opposition to the pay-for-performance principle is dramatically illustrated by a Supreme Court case that involved three highly productive workers who were paid a piece-rate incentive. The Supreme Court upheld the union's right to fine members who exceeded the piece-work norm (*Scofield et al.* v. *National Labor Relations Board et al*).[40] Rather than pay for performance, most unions advocate paying for length of service or seniority.

EXPERIENCE

A common justification for giving some employees more money is that they have more experience. Years of experience are often related to productivity, and paying for experience is sometimes just another way of paying for performance. As workers accumulate more years of service, they become more productive. One study of 300 clerical workers found a rather high correlation (.60) between the efficiency ratings that the workers were given by managers and the workers' length of service. These results indicate that either length of service is related to performance, or that efficiency ratings are influenced by length of service, or both.[41]

A similar argument is usually made in justifying pay differentials for education. Individuals with more education are assumed to be more productive. For example, a school system usually has a wage schedule showing how much additional money should be paid to a teacher with a bachelor's, master's, or doctorate degree, or even with an additional thirty hours of graduate training. Some companies encourage their managers to return to school for additional training by offering educational incentives. The large enrollments in night MBA programs, extension courses, and educational centers on military bases indicate that these educational incentives are generally effective. Frequently, companies not only pay the costs of education but also pay higher salaries to employees who complete courses.

SENIORITY

Pay differentials based on seniority or length of service are found in many compensation systems. It is not uncommon for a wage decision to reflect the belief that long-term employees should be rewarded for faithful service even though their present performance might not justify pay increases. Several organizations, such as school systems and government agencies, have salary schedules that contain step increases within each labor grade. These step increases are based on years of service or seniority. Pay differentials based on seniority often are defended as legitimate even when no relationship exists between seniority and performance.

POTENTIAL

Occasionally, organizations pay higher than average wages to individuals who demonstrate outstanding potential. Many new employees are paid higher than normal starting salaries if they have the potential for becoming supervisors or high-level managers. Since recent college graduates have not had opportunities to demonstrate potential, the decision to pay them more is generally based on grades in college, leadership experiences, professional association memberships, and other academic activities. After new employees have been with an organization for a while, however, they are evaluated on what they have actually accomplished rather than on their potential for future performance.

POLITICS AND LUCK

Individual pay can be affected by politics and luck. The recommendations of influential people can create intense pressures on organizations to promote individuals and to provide pay increases. Pay levels also are influenced by being in the right place at the right time. Although being qualified and prepared are important prerequisites for being able to take advantage of opportunities, the fact that the opportunity is presented sometimes results from luck or chance. Political influence and luck should not be considered bona fide determinants of financial compensation, but overlooking them would amount to ignoring reality.

PAY RANGES

When a wage structure is developed, a range of pay rather than a specific wage is usually assigned to each pay grade to reward individual performance. Most pay grades have pay ranges that are 10 to 15 percent above and below the midpoint of each grade. The pay grades shown in Figure 10.5 have a pay range of 30 percent (15 percent above and below the wage line) to allow for individual incentives. One electronics company changed from a 20 percent range to a 37 percent range to provide greater individual incentives. New employees were started at the bottom of their pay ranges and advanced as their performance improved.

The height of a pay range has a great influence on the amount of individual incentive available for each job. A narrow pay range, such as 10 percent above or below the wage curve, provides for a small individual incentive. On the other hand, a wide pay range, such as 20 percent above and below the wage curve, provides for a large individual incentive. Figure 10.7 illustrates two different pay ranges. The solid lines indicate a small pay range (± 10 percent), and the dotted lines represent a large pay range (± 20 percent).

New employees usually are paid the minimum of a pay range. Advancement within the pay range typically is based on performance and years of service. A reasonable pay policy is to allow employees to advance from the bottom of a pay range to the midpoint based upon their years of service; advancement to the top of the pay range is only permitted for those employees who are outstanding performers. This policy allows long-term employees who are average performers to be paid more than new employees and still have some incentive to become outstanding employees.

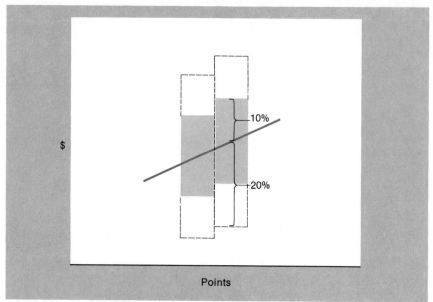

FIGURE 10.7 Illustration of two pay ranges.

In some compensation systems individual pay levels are based on step increases. The step increases for one labor grade are shown in Table 10.9. These step increases are based on performance and length of service. The table shows a labor grade that contains six step increases and three performance levels. The starting salary for this labor grade is $4.80, and the maximum salary is $7.50. To reach the maximum, an employee must have a high performance level and must advance through all six steps of the labor grade. The step increases can be automatic—advancing one step each year—or variable. Variable periods of time for the step increases provide an additional means for supervisors to control pay increases. Supervisors not only evaluate performance but also decide when it is appropriate to advance each employee to a higher step within the labor grade.

TABLE 10.9   Step increases based on performance and length of service

Performance Level	Minimum	Steps					Maximum
		1	2	3	4	5	
High	4.80	5.28	5.76	6.24	6.72	7.20	7.50
Medium	4.80	5.16	5.52	5.88	6.24	6.60	6.86
Low	4.80	5.04	5.28	5.52	5.76	6.00	6.24

TABLE 10.10 Merit-increase guidelines: fixed increase or discretionary increase

Performance Rating	*Expected Number of Employees	Fixed Increase Amount	or	Discretionary Increase Range
Outstanding: Truly exceptional performance	1 in 10	15%		14–18%
Excellent: Constantly exceeds standards	2 in 10	11%		10–13%
Good: Occasionally exceeds standards	4 in 10	8%		7–9%
Average: Occasionally meets standards	2 in 10	5%		5–6%
Fair: Marginal performance	1 in 10	3%		0–4%

*Note to supervisors: This column shows the number of employees in a typical department who would normally be rated in each category.

Advancement within a labor grade also may be based strictly on performance. To help supervisors make decisions regarding pay increases, the human resource department frequently provides merit-increase guidelines. Examples of two merit-increase guidelines are presented in Table 10.10. One guideline assumes a fixed increase amount, whereas the other provides a range for the supervisor to make a discretionary increase. The guidelines provide for the pay increases to be based on performance, and supervisors are told approximately how many employees should be rated in each performance category. One potential danger in relying on such a guideline is that outstanding employees may reach the top of their labor grade too soon. When employees reach the top of their grade, they are said to be "**topped out**." Once employees are topped out, they can receive pay increases only by being promoted to higher-level jobs or through cost-of-living increases that raise the entire wage curve.

Merit increases represent one of the many important ways by which individual performance can be recognized. Chapter 11 discusses the guidelines for using merit pay and identifies other methods of rewarding individual performance.

INTERNATIONAL HRM

Compensation managers throughout the world are required to answer the same three wage decisions—the wage-level decision, the wage-structure decision, and the individual wage decision—and similar criteria are used for making these decisions in most countries. Wage levels differ dramatically from country to country, but in almost every country, wage surveys are consulted in making wage-level decisions. The surveys that are the most useful are generally those that summarize data from other firms in the same country. But since benefits may differ greatly from company to company, many compensation analysts try to examine total remuneration, which includes all wages, bonuses, and benefits.

Job-evaluation systems are used extensively throughout the world to create a wage structure with a hierarchy of labor grades. For the most part, every culture uses similar factors to assign jobs to labor grades: skill, effort, and responsibility. Even in communist countries, jobs are classified according to their levels of complexity and skill requirements and paid accordingly. Cuba, for example, uses a classification system containing eight grades for its laborers, and the highest wage is 5.29 times the minimum wage. Managerial jobs are differentiated according to how much responsibility the manager assumes.[42]

The individual wage decision is almost universally determined by performance and seniority; however, the relative importance of seniority is much greater in Asian countries, especially Japan, than in the United States and Europe. After World War II an American-style job-classification system was installed in Japan to replace a system that relied almost exclusively on the status and seniority of the employees. While this system was not accepted initially, companies gradually began using ability and skills instead of seniority alone as a basis for job-grade assignments. In recent years the relative significance of seniority in the Japanese culture has declined considerably in favor of pay based on performance and job requirements. Nevertheless, seniority continues to influence pay more in Japan than in other cultures.[43]

Another significant difference between Asian and Western cultures is the concept of equal pay for equal work. Japan and other Asian countries have significant pay differentials that discriminate against women, part-time employees, and those who are employed in small companies. Reducing these differentials is not a priority and, indeed, the differentials are part of the new multi-track career-planning program for Japanese workers. On the other hand, some European countries have passed protective legislation similar to the Equal Pay Act in the United States. For example, England has an Equal Pay Law that gives women the right to request equal pay if their work is equal to a man's job in terms of effort, skill, and decision making. At least two Canadian provinces, Manitoba and Ontario, have also passed similar legislation.

Compensation practices are also somewhat unique in countries plagued by runaway inflation. During the 1980s, the cost-of-living index in Brazil more than doubled every year creating serious wage inequities. To keep up with inflation, employers indexed their wages and adjusted them monthly. Nevertheless, some wages had to be adjusted in the middle of the month because of turnover and other changes.

SUMMARY

A. Compensation decisions greatly influence other human resource functions, especially staffing, performance evaluation, training and development, and employee relations.

B. The design of a compensation system should attempt to satisfy six competing objectives. The pay system must be legal, adequate, motivating, equitable, cost-benefit effective, and provide adequate security for the employees.

C. Dividing the overall labor force into three job markets facilitates an understanding of the determinants of pay and helps to justify the wage structure that appears in society. The three job markets include: (1) blue-collar and nonsupervisory white-collar employees, (2) professional and technical employees, and (3) supervisors and executives.

D. Pay levels are influenced by many variables. Some of the major variables influencing pay include external factors, organizational factors, job factors, and individual factors.

E. The development of a sound wage and salary system requires three basic decisions. These three decisions are: (1) the wage-level decision, (2) the wage-structure decision, and (3) the individual wage decision.

F. The wage-level decision concerns the issue of how much money the members of one organization receive relative to individuals performing similar work in other organizations. A company's wage level is determined by the policies of top management. Companies that are large, unionized, and highly productive tend to have high pay levels.

G. The wage survey is the primary tool for making wage-level decisions. Three types of surveys are: (1) surveys conducted by government agencies, especially the BLS; (2) surveys conducted by professional organizations; and (3) surveys conducted by individual companies.

H. The wage-structure decision involves determining how much each job in the organization should be paid relative to other jobs within the organization. The wage structure can be determined by a unilateral decision of top management, through collective bargaining between management and a union, or through a job-evaluation method. The four job-evaluation methods include job ranking, classification, the point method, and factor comparison.

I. The job-ranking and classification methods are nonquantitative methods that produce a hierarchy of job worth. The point methods and factor-comparison methods, however, are quantitative methods that evaluate the content of jobs on a factor-by-factor basis. These quantitative methods produce a precise numerical score for each of the jobs evaluated.

J. The most frequently used job-evaluation method is the point method. This method consists of these steps: (1) identifying key jobs; (2) identifying the job factors that are used to determine pay levels; (3) weighting the factors according to their contribution to the company; (4) dividing each job factor into degrees; (5) reaching a group consensus about the degree assignments, and (6) using the total points and average pay of the key jobs to develop a wage curve.

K. Job pricing is the process of placing a dollar value on the worth of a job. Job pricing involves grouping similar jobs together into pay grades and assigning a pay range for each grade.

L. Two methods commonly are used to adjust the wage curve for inflation: an across-the-board increase, which is called a fixed-rate increase, and a percentage increase, which raises the rate of pay for each job by a specified percentage.

M. The comparable-worth controversy concerns the issue of whether organizations should be required to develop a common set of criteria and pay all jobs of comparable worth the same rates of pay. The Equal Pay Act and the Civil Rights Act require employers to pay men and women the same rate if their jobs are equal. However, these acts do not require companies to conduct an exhaustive evaluation of all jobs or to provide equal pay for jobs of comparable worth.

N. The individual wage decision concerns the relative pay of individuals performing similar jobs in the same company. Individuals typically receive higher pay levels if: (1) their performance is higher, (2) they have more experience, (3) they have greater education, (4) they have greater seniority, and (5) they have greater perceived potential.

QUESTIONS

1. What would be the influence of an increase or decrease in unemployment levels on a company's compensation system?

2. What are the objectives of a compensation system? What happens if all of these objectives are not considered simultaneously?

3. What would you say to a blue-collar worker to explain why the range of pay for supervisors and executives is so much greater than for blue-collar workers?

4. Economic forces of supply and demand seem to play a large role in determining the compensation of professional entertainers and athletes. How much influence do economic forces exert on the pay of other jobs?

5. What are the causes and consequences of wage compression?

6. What are the major factors influencing pay? As a general rule, what sort of advice would you give to someone whose goal is to earn a great deal of money?

7. What would be the consequences of a wage-level decision that pays wages that are significantly higher than the market rate?

8. Should employees participate in selecting the companies to be included in a wage survey? What advantages and problems might be created by such participation?

9. What are the major factors that need to be measured in a wage survey to ensure that the results will be meaningful?

10. What are the major limitations of information gained from wage surveys?

11. Explain the relative advantages and disadvan-

tages of the four job-evaluation methods of determining the wage structure: the job-ranking method, the classification method, the point method, and the factor-comparison method.

12. In the development of a wage curve, why is it so important for the key jobs to be equitably paid jobs?

13. In developing a wage curve using the point method, the average wage of the key jobs should be close to the wage line. What kinds of problems could account for a scatter diagram that shows the key jobs a significant distance away from the wage line?

14. In the development of a wage curve, why are responsibility, education, and experience weighted so much more heavily than working conditions, job hazards, and physical demands?

15. What are red-circle rates? What alternative methods does a company have for handling red-circle rates?

16. Describe the comparable-worth controversy. What has been the position of the courts in dealing with this issue?

KEY TERMS

Classification method: A procedure used to develop a wage structure in which the job descriptions for each job are compared with a classification scheme that ranks the jobs in a hierarchy of job worth.

(Cost-of-living adjustment) COLA: A procedure that provides for automatic increases in the level of pay based on the rate of inflation—usually indexed to the consumer price index.

Comparable-worth controversy: A controversy that centers on the issue of whether organizations should be required to establish a common set of criteria for evaluating the worth of jobs and to provide equal pay for jobs of comparable worth.

Compensable factors: The factors associated with the different jobs that justify paying one job more than another. Responsibility, education, and skill are usually considered the most important compensable factors.

(Consumer Price Index) CPI: A well-accepted measure of the rate of inflation.

Decreasing-rate increase: A procedure for adjusting the wage curve in which higher-level jobs are increased by successively smaller amounts.

Factor comparison: A method for developing a wage structure in which benchmark jobs are compared with other jobs, factor by factor, to determine how much money should be paid for each factor.

Fixed-rate increase: A procedure for adjusting the wage curve in which a fixed sum of money is added to every job in the hierarchy.

Individual wage decision: One of the major decisions that must be considered in the development of a compensation system. This decision considers the issue of whether individuals performing the same job should all receive the same rate of pay or whether individuals who have more seniority, experience, or higher productivity should receive higher pay.

Job evaluation: A procedure for developing a wage structure that is based on an evaluation of the job. The four job-evaluation methods are the job-ranking method, the classification method, the point method, and the factor-comparison method.

Job pricing: The process of deciding how much each job should be paid by determining which labor grade the job falls within and the pay range for that labor grade.

Job-ranking method: A procedure for developing a wage structure that involves ranking the various jobs in a hierarchy of job worth and then assigning monetary values to them.

Key jobs: Jobs that are considered equitably paid and are used in the point method to develop a wage structure. The pay levels for other jobs are determined from the wage curve that was developed using the key jobs.

Pay grade: A cluster of jobs along the hierarchy of job worth that are all paid the same rate of pay.

Pay range: The range of pay associated with each pay grade, which indicates how much individual incentive is associated with the job.

Percentage increase: A procedure used for adjusting the pay levels in which the pay for every job is increased by a fixed percentage amount.

Point method: The most popular job-evaluation method for developing a wage curve. The compensable factors of key jobs are used to develop the wage curve. Points are assigned to each factor, and the total points are associated with a specific pay level.

Red-circle jobs: Jobs that are either overpaid or underpaid relative to the amount the wage curve indicates ought to be paid for them.

Three labor markets: To gain an understanding of the diversity in wage rates in society, the overall labor force needs to be separated into three labor markets: blue-collar and nonsupervisory white-collar employees, professional and technical employees, and supervisors and managers.

Topped out: When employees receive pay increases to the point that their salaries are at the top of their pay ranges, they are said to be topped out. They are no longer eligible for pay increases based on performance and receive higher salaries only as the entire wage curve is increased.

Wage compression: A reduction in the relative wage differentials between high- and low-paying jobs. Upper-level jobs do not provide sufficient incentives to justify the higher levels of responsibility and skill required to perform them.

Wage curve: The line on a wage structure graph that shows higher levels of pay associated with higher-level jobs. Most wage curves using the point method are straight lines (linear curve) which are constructed by drawing a freehand line or through regression equations.

Wage-level decision: One of the major decisions involved in designing a compensation system; compares the wages paid in one organization with the pay in other organizations for employees performing similar work.

Wage-structure decision: A major decision in the design of a compensation system that examines how much money is paid for different jobs within the same organization.

Wage survey: A survey of the wages, salaries, and benefits offered by different organizations. The wage survey is the major tool used in making the wage-level decision. Many organizations conduct their own wage surveys, but the most sophisticated wage surveys are conducted by the BLS.

C O N C L U D I N G   C A S E

Education versus Supervision

"I'm his supervisor, I'm two years older, and I work just as hard as he does. There's no way he should get more money than me!" Warren T. believes his complaint is simple, direct, and obvious, and he cannot under-

stand why his annual pay is still $4,000 less than Stacey's. Both men work for Eastern Energy Controls, a small company with only sixteen employees that was founded four years ago. The company specializes in the design and installation of electronic panels that regulate the light and heat in large buildings.

Stacey joined the company two years ago after graduating from college with a degree in electrical engineering. Warren has been with the company almost since it was started. The company is too small to have titles and everyone generally works together doing similar work. However, Warren supervises an installation crew of four to six people, counting himself and Stacey. Stacey helps with the installation and handles most of the technical problems.

The company has made some significant technological improvements in the design of its control panels and expects to make many additional advancements. Many creative ideas have been suggested by members of the installation crew, especially by Stacey because of his technical training. Thomas S., the president of the company, claims that Stacey's salary is fair and has to be as high

as it is to keep him with the company. Warren thinks too much significance is attached to Stacey's education. Although Warren did not go beyond high school, he claims that he has learned how to do everything that Stacey does in installing an energy-control panel and that as a supervisor he should make more money, not less.

Before Stacey joined the company, Warren was quite happy with his salary. But now he feels underpaid, and his attitude is affecting his relationship with Stacey and other crew members. Stacey receives $33,000, Warren receives $29,000, and the next highest paid crew member receives $27,500.

Questions:

1. Does Warren have a legitimate complaint?
2. What is the worth of a college degree in annual salary?
3. Should Warren and Stacey be paid the same, or should one receive more? Explain your answer.

NOTES

1. See Leonard R. Burgess, *Wage and Salary Administration in a Dynamic Economy* (New York: Harcourt, 1968).

2. ASPA/Hansen Annual Survey, "Human Resource Management Compensation Survey," (June 1989).

3. Amanda Bennett, "A Great Leap Forward for Executive Pay," *Wall Street Journal*, April 24, 1989, p. B1; Amanda Bennett, "Salary Rules Aim at New Middle Manager," *Wall Street Journal*, April 10, 1987, p. 29.

4. A study by Graef S. Crystal of Towers, Perrin, Forster, and Crosby Consulting Firm, summarized in the *Wall Street Journal*, February 29, 1978.

5. Data supplied by *Sports Illustrated*.

6. Michael Wallace, "Labor Market Structure and Salary Determination Among Professional Basketball Players," *Work and Occupations* 15 (August 1988): 294–312.

7. Jill S. Kanin-Lovers, "Factors in Competitively Pricing Jobs," *Journal of Compensation and Benefits* 3 (March/April 1988): 302–4.

8. See Allan N. Nash and Stephen J. Carroll, Jr., *The Management of Compensation* (Monterey, Calif.: Brooks/Cole, 1975), p. 62.

9. Ibid., p. 66.

10. Leonard Berkowitz, Colin Fraser, Peter F. Treasure, and Susan Cochran, "Pay, Equity, Job Gratifications, and Comparisons in Pay Satisfaction," *Journal of Applied Psychology* 72 (November 1987): 544–51.

11. Nash and Carroll, *Compensation*, p. 67.

12. R. A. Lester, "Pay Differentials by Size of Establishment," *Industrial Relations* 7 (1967): 56–67.

13. Hong, W. Tan, "Wage Determination in Japanese Manufacturing: A Review of Recent Literature," *The Economic Record* 58 (March 1982): 46–60; Robert Evans, Jr., "Pay Differentials: The Case of Japan," *Monthly Labor Review* 107 (October 1984): 24–29; Labor Letter, "Big Firms Pay More," *Wall Street Journal*, February 21, 1989, p. 1.

14. Bureau of Labor Statistics, Department of Labor; Phone call with AFL-CIO Information Center.

15. Bureau of Labor Statistics, "Wage Rate Increases in Manufacturing," in *Chartbook on Prices, Wages, and Productivity* (Washington, D.C.: Government Printing Office, June 1979), from Table 14.

16. "Wage and Benefit Studies," Department of Labor, Bureau of Labor Statistics, August 1989.

17. Cited in Nash and Carroll, *Compensation*, p. 89.

18. David B. Balkin and Louis R. Gomez-Mejia, "Compensation Practices in High-Technology Industries," *Personnel Administrator* 30 (June 1985): 111–23.

19. Stephen Spencer, "How to Make Your Job Evaluation System More Efficient and Reliable," *Benefits and Compensation International* 16 (April 1987): 8–14.

20. Scott L. Fraser, Steven F. Cronshaw, and Ralph A. Alexander, "Generalizeability Analysis of a Point Method Job Evaluation Instrument: A Field Study," *Journal of Applied Psychology* 69 (November 1984): 643–47; Howard W. Risher, "Job Evaluation: Validity and Reliability," *Compensation and Benefits Review* 21 (January/February 1989): 22–36.

21. Dennis Doverspike and Gerald V. Barrett, "An Internal Bias Analysis of a Job Evaluation Instrument," *Journal of Applied Psychology* 69 (November 1984): 648–62; Donald P. Schwab and Robert Grams, "Sex-Related Errors in Job Evaluation: A 'Real-World' Test," *Journal of Applied Psychology* 70 (August 1985): 533–39.

22. Jill Kanin-Lovers, "Selecting a Computer-Aided Job Evaluation System," *Journal of Compensation and Benefits* 3 (September/October 1987): 104–7; Robert M. Madigan and Frederick S. Hills, "Job Evaluation and Pay Equity," *Public Personnel Management* 17 (Fall 1988): 323–30.

23. Lance A. Berger, "Using the Computer to Support Job Evaluation Decision Making," *Journal of Compensation and Benefits* 2 (July/August 1986): 15–19; Jill Kanin-Lovers, "Selecting the Best Job Evaluation Method for Your Organization," *Journal of Compensation and Benefits* 1 (March/April 1986): 292–95.

24. Terrence Walker, "The Use of Job Evaluation Plans in Salary Administration," *Personnel* 84 (March 1987): 28–31.

25. Nancy O'Rourke and Doyle Hoyt, "Achieving Equity in Classification and Compensation of Secretarial Positions," *Journal of Compensation and Benefits* 2 (September/October 1986): 80–85.

26. See Nash and Carroll, *Compensation*, p. 124.

27. Roger J. Plachy, "Compensation Management: Cases and Applications—The Point Factor Job Evaluation System; A step-by-step guide, part I," *Compensation and Benefits Review* 19 (July/August 1987): 12–27.

28. See Nash and Carroll, *Compensation*, p. 132.

29. Paul R. Reed and Mark J. Kroll, "Red-Circle Employees: A Wage Scale Dilemma," *Personnel Journal* 66 (February 1987): 92–95.

30. Gerald V. Barrett and Dennis Doverspike, "Another Defense of Point Factor Job Evaluation," *Personnel* 66 (March 1989): 33–36.

31. Peter B. Olney, Jr., "Meeting the Challenge of Comparable Work, Part I," *Compensation and Benefits Review* 19 (March/April 1987): 34–44; John F. Sullivan, "Comparable Work and the Statistical Audit of Paid Programs for Illegal Systemic Discrimination," *Personnel Administrator* 30 (March 1985): 102–11; Phillip C. Wright, "Equal Pay for Work of Equal Value and How to Achieve It: A Practical Approach," *Equal Opportunities International* 6, no. 2 (1987): 23–38.

32. "Pay Equity Reached," *Career Guidance Center Update* (March 1989): 4.

33. This controversy is reviewed in *Elements of Sound Base Pay Administration*, published by the American Society for Personnel Administration and the American Compensation Association, 1981, Appendix B. See also, Lawrence Z. Lorber, J. Robert Kirk, Stephen L. Samuels, and David J. Spellman III, *Sex and Salary* (ASPA Foundation, 1985).

34. *IUE v. Westinghouse Electric Corp.*, 23 EPD para. 106A (1980).

35. *Gunther v. County of Washington*, 623 F.2d 1303 (9th Cir. 1979). 452 U.S. 166 (1979).

36. *AFSCME v. State of Washington*, 578, F. Suppl. 846 (W.D. Washington, 1984).

37. Carl C. Hoffmann, "Are Multiple-Pay Systems Worth the Risk?" *Management Review* (July 1987): 39–44; Ken Jennings and Earle Traynham, "The Wages of Two-Tier Pay Plans," *Personnel Journal* 67 (March 1988): 56–63.

38. Mollie H. Bowers and Roger D. Roderick, "Two-Tier Pay Systems: The Good, The Bad, and the Debatable," *Personnel Administrator* 32 (June 1987): 101–12.

39. Jerald Greenberg, "Equity, Equality, and the Protestant Ethic: Allocating Rewards Following Fair and Unfair Competition," *Journal of Experimental Society Psychology* 14 (1978): 217–26.

40. *Russell Scofield et al. v. National Labor Relations Board et al.*, 394 US 423 (1969).

41. M. A. Bills, "A Method for Classifying and Rating the Efficiency of Clerical Workers," *Journal of Personnel Research* 1 (1923): 384–93.

42. Alexis Codina Jimenez, "Worker Incentives in Cuba," *World Development* 15, no. 1 (1987): 127–38.

43. Hong, W. Tan, "Wage Determination in Japanese Manufacturing: A Review of Recent Literature," *The Economic Record* 58 (March 1982): 46–60.

C H A P T E R · 11

Financial Incentives

Motivating with Money

E&S Electronics Company manufactures electronic components. To survive in a very competitive industry, the company must maintain a high level of productivity. Because of high fixed costs for expensive equipment, the company must efficiently produce quality products according to tight production schedules.

Management wants to ascertain whether the compensation system is being used to its fullest extent to stimulate maximum productivity. The vice president of operations would like to institute something like a piece-rate incentive system to reward individual performance. The employee relations director would rather have a monthly bonus program. The vice president of finance attended a business luncheon at which the speaker maintained that employees are motivated by job enrichment, achievement, and recognition rather than by money. Therefore, the finance vice president thinks that an incentive system will cause problems and that the company should give all employees a generous monthly salary. Other members of the executive team have mixed feelings about the situation. Would pay incentives actually increase productivity, and what would be their side effects?

The company has never had any type of incentive program. Employees are paid an hourly wage, and pay generally is kept secret.

Questions:
1. Should employees be paid a salary, or be told about the pay of their coworkers?
2. Should an incentive system be installed? If so, should the company use individual incentives, group incentives, or a profit-sharing plan? Should incentives be available to everyone or only to managers?

MONEY AND MOTIVATION

A long-standing controversy in compensation is whether pay should be used to increase performance. One of the most important reasons people work is to earn money. Even those who are intrinsically motivated to work because of the satisfactions they derive from their jobs must earn enough money. If their jobs do not provide adequate income, people are forced to seek other employment no matter how satisfying they find their jobs. But will people work harder or faster if they are offered more money?

Money is a significant factor in almost every theory of motivation. However, the effects of money are not similar in every theory. The theories of motivation predict varied, and in some cases contradictory, effects of money. Six of the major theories of motivation that consider the effects of money are McClelland's achievement need, Herzberg's hygiene/motivator theory, Maslow's need hierarchy, equity theory, reinforcement theory, and expectancy theory.

McCLELLAND'S ACHIEVEMENT NEED

David McClelland studied three needs: power, affiliation, and achievement. His most extensive research examined the need for achievement and how this need was fundamental to the development of successful managers and entrepreneurs.[1] McClelland found that successful managers and entrepreneurs had high needs for achievement. **McClelland's achievement need** studies described high-need achievers by three characteristics: they liked moderate levels of risk in their undertakings; they wanted personal responsibility for the success or failure of their ventures; and they wanted immediate and accurate feedback on their performance.

McClelland found that money did not have a very strong motivating effect on the performance of high-need achievers. In a laboratory study, for example, high-need achievers performed very well with or without financial incentives. Low-need achievers did not perform well without financial incentives, but when they were offered money for their work, they performed noticeably better. This study does not indicate that money is not important to high-need achievers or that it does not influence their performance. Although money may have a minimal effect on the performance of high-need achievers, it is still important as a form of feedback and recognition. When high-need achievers succeed, they look to monetary rewards as evidence of their success.

HERZBERG'S HYGIENE/MOTIVATOR THEORY

Frederick Herzberg proposed a two-factor theory of job satisfaction and motivation.[2] According to **Herzberg's hygiene/motivator theory**, one factor consists of variables relating to the content of the job, such as responsibility, autonomy, the work itself, and recognition. These job-content variables, which are called motivators, contribute to satisfaction and productivity when they are present. The second factor consists of variables relating to the organizational context in which the work is done, such as company policies, pay, coworkers, and supervision. These are called hygiene variables, and they contribute to dissatisfaction when they are absent or not managed well.

According to Herzberg, the motivators create satisfaction when they are present but do not create dissatisfaction when they are absent. The hygienes create dissatisfaction if they are absent or poorly managed, but no matter how much they are improved, they should not be expected to create satisfaction or motivation. Because pay is a hygiene factor, Herzberg advocates setting an equitable wage and then forgetting about it, since financial incentives and frequent pay adjustments only serve to keep a worker's mind focused on money and therefore create constant dissatisfaction. Herzberg recommends that managers avoid pay discussions and not use pay to motivate employees.

MASLOW'S NEED HIERARCHY

Abraham Maslow developed a theory of motivation based on a hierarchy of needs consisting of physiological, safety, social, esteem, and self-actualization needs.[3] According to **Maslow's need hierarchy**, higher-level needs do not become important to individuals and will not influence their behavior until lower-level needs are largely satisfied. Therefore, self-actualization needs, which are the highest needs in Maslow's hierarchy, will not be important until lower level-needs are essentially met.

The needs most directly related to money are physiological and security needs. Money contributes significantly to securing a comfortable and safe environment that satisfies an individual's safety and physiological needs. However, money is generally viewed as relatively unimportant for satisfying higher-level needs, and most American workers are mainly concerned about higher-level needs. Therefore, according to Maslow, money is not an effective motivator.

Frequently overlooked, however, is the role money plays in allowing people to pursue activities leading to self-actualization. Many people are prevented from pursuing self-actualizing activities because they do not have the necessary financial resources. Therefore, the money is not as unimportant in Maslow's theory as it at first appears.

EQUITY THEORY

Equity theory is useful in predicting whether employees will believe their pay is fair or unfair.[4] According to equity theory, an individual judges his or her own employment exchange and then compares it with the exchanges that others obtain. In other words, equity is based on a comparison between an individual's inputs and rewards and the inputs and rewards of others. While examining the employment exchange, individuals look at the inputs they bring to the exchange, such as education, skill, and effort, and compare these inputs with the rewards they receive, such as money, status, and recognition. If an individual's reward-input ratio is equivalent to the reward-input ratios of others, then he or she believes the condition is equitable.

Studies on equity theory have shown that individuals attempt to maintain conditions of equity. In laboratory studies, for example, subjects were led to believe that they had inferior skills and experience relative to others who were paid the same hourly wage. To correct the inequity, the subjects exerted greater effort to justify getting the same amount of money. Since the rewards were equal, the inputs also needed to be equal; the only way to compensate for inferior skills was to exert greater effort. When a condition of inequity is caused by not paying enough, underpaid subjects report strong dissatisfaction and reduce their level of effort until their rewards-inputs ratio is equal to the rewards-inputs ratios of others.

Equity theory can be diagrammed in this way:

$$\frac{\text{Individual's rewards}}{\text{Inputs}} = \frac{\text{Others' rewards}}{\text{Inputs}}$$

This diagram is extremely useful in analyzing the three wage decisions described in the previous chapter: the wage-level decision, the wage-structure decision, and the individual wage decision. Pay and other organizational rewards must be balanced with effort, skill, experience, and other inputs for a state of equity to exist.

REINFORCEMENT THEORY

According to **reinforcement theory** (also called **operant conditioning**), money is a generalized secondary reinforcer.[5] Primary reinforcers include rewards that are innately reinforcing because of their physiological nature, such as food, water, sex, rest, and removal of pain. Secondary reinforcers are those that are learned, such as social approval, status, and friendship. Money is called a generalized secondary reinforcer because it is a secondary reinforcer that has become generalized to a wide range of conditions. Money is a positive reinforcing stimulus for almost everyone in almost every situation, even if a person has no immediate opportunity to use it.

According to reinforcement theory, behavior is influenced by its consequences. When an individual is offered money to perform a task, reinforcement theory predicts that the individual will perform the task as long as the money is considered an adequate reward. If employees are to be rewarded for producing high-quantity and high-quality work and for not being absent, reinforcement theory predicts that the employees will achieve high-quantity and high-quality performance and not be absent. In general, reinforcement theory predicts that performance will improve as financial rewards become larger, when such rewards are directly tied to performance, and when they are given shortly after the task is completed.

The timing of the reinforcement is also important. Continuous reinforcement schedules, where employees are paid for each correct response, are sometimes preferred because the reinforcement is stable and predictable. However, partial reinforcement schedules that provide comparable amounts of money on a variable ratio schedule produce higher levels of performance than continuous schedules. An example of a variable ratio reinforcement schedule is the random payoffs that come from gambling, such as slot machines. Unfortunately, it is difficult to install these kinds of reinforcement schedules in industrial jobs even though studies endorse their value. In one study, college students worked under a continuous reward schedule or a variable reward schedule. The results of the study indicated that the students paid on a variable reward schedule performed better and continued working for a longer time after the rewards ceased than the students paid on a continuous reward schedule.[6]

EXPECTANCY THEORY

Expectancy theory suggests that money can be a powerful motivator if the proper relationships between effort, performance, and rewards are perceived. According to expectancy theory, three conditions are needed.[7] First, an individual must consider pay to be a valuable reward. For most individuals this condition already exists, especially for young employees who are heavily in debt. Second, the individual must believe that a strong correlation exists between performance and reward; that is, high levels of performance should be highly rewarded. Third, the individual must believe that a high probability exists that effort will result in successful performance. When an individual believes that he or she can perform well by expending more effort and knows that the performance will be reinforced by substantial monetary rewards, expectancy theory predicts a strong relationship between money and motivation.

$$\text{Effort} \longrightarrow \text{Performance} \longrightarrow \text{Rewards}$$

Expectancy theory is probably the most useful theory for predicting the effects of incentive pay on performance, and extensive research has generally supported the predictions of expectancy theory. When the three conditions are present, incentive pay usually produces a significant increase in performance. In summary, both reinforcement theory and expectancy theory suggest that money can be a powerful motivator when pay is based on performance. Extensive research has confirmed that performance-based pay systems significantly increase job performance.

INCENTIVE COMPENSATION

Incentive compensation plays a vital role in increasing organizational effectiveness, and it has attracted as much attention as other vital factors, such as new technology, organizational culture, and the work ethic. Intense foreign competition and stagnant productivity growth have forced American executives to explore ways of rejuvenating productivity. One of most popular recommendations is to offer financial incentives that are directly tied to productivity. These incentive programs, loosely referred to as **pay-for-performance**, have significantly increased productivity in companies where they have been installed, and surveys generally find that they also have a positive impact on employee morale.[8] There are numerous methods of rewarding individual efforts. Most pay-for-performance plans are either individual, group, or company-wide incentive plans or some combination of all three.

MERIT PAY

The most popular pay-for-performance method is the **merit-pay** increase. This method consists of periodically evaluating the performance of all employees and giving commensurate pay increases. High performers receive larger merit increases than low performers. The merit-pay increase is awarded in addition to cost-of-living increases or pay increases for additional education or years of service.

Some companies are concerned about the long-term consequences of increasing the base pay of their employees with every merit-pay increase and have adopted *lump-sum* merit increases. These lump-sum payments, awarded at the end of a quarter or the year, are treated as one-time rewards in recognition of outstanding performance and do not change the employee's base pay.[9]

Merit-pay increases are relevant to all jobs paid a fixed wage or salary. The most important requirement for awarding merit-pay increases is that the performance of each employee be carefully evaluated. But even when performance can only be evaluated subjectively, most employees still believe that pay increases should be related to performance.

Although merit pay is generally intended to reward employees for their productivity, other aspects of their performance may also be recognized, such as attendance, positive work attitudes, or initiative. Some companies also offer special incentives to compensate employees for their education and skills. These **skill-based pay** systems are designed to encourage employees to learn new skills and to develop additional talents. Team members who are cross-trained and capable of performing several jobs are especially valuable members of autonomous work groups. Skill-based pay systems usually provide an incremental addition to base pay for each significant skill an employee acquires.[10]

The procedures for giving merit-pay increases are presented at the end of Chapter 10. Organizations that use the point method to develop a wage curve usually have pay ranges associated with each labor grade. These pay ranges allow for individual incentives based on performance and seniority. A good compensation policy allows average employees to rise from the bottom of a pay range to no higher than the midpoint, based on seniority. Only outstanding performers should be able to rise to the top of the pay range, as illustrated in Figure 11.1.

Supervisors are generally responsible for evaluating performance and recommending merit-pay increases with the assistance of guidelines prepared by the human resource department. A merit-increase guideline showing both a fixed-percentage increase and a discretionary-range increase is presented in Table 10.10.

The following conditions must be met before an effective merit-pay program can be established:

1. Individual differences in job performance must be large enough to be worth the time and effort it will take for management to measure such differences and relate them to pay.
2. The pay range should be sufficiently wide (15 to 25 percent above and below the midpoint of the pay range) to allow for adequate differentiation of pay based on performance.
3. Differences in individual job performance should be measurable.

FIGURE 11.1 Merit-pay increases within a pay range.

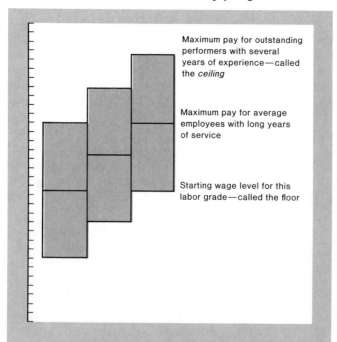

4. Supervisors and managers must have the competence to evaluate employee performance and provide meaningful feedback.
5. Management must be committed and employees must be receptive to making distinctions among employees based on performance.[11]

If supervisors are unable or unwilling to accurately assess employee performance, a merit-pay plan will fail. Careless evaluations by supervisors have been blamed for the failure of merit-pay systems among public employees. In 1984 Congress mandated that federal employees should be evaluated and receive merit-pay increases based on their performance. An evaluation in 1988 concluded that the merit-pay plan was a failure because supervisors rated almost all of their subordinates above average so they would qualify for a merit-pay increase. Only 1 percent of all employees was rated below average.[12]

PIECE-RATE INCENTIVES

Under a **piece-rate** incentive system workers are paid a fixed amount for each item produced. Piece rates have existed for many years, and several theorists have advocated paying workers on a piece-rate basis. The most ardent advocate of this incentive system was Frederick W. Taylor, the founder of scientific management. In his 1911 book, *Principles of Scientific Management*, Taylor argued that the best way to motivate workers to higher production was to offer them additional money for producing more. Taylor showed how higher productivity meant more income for the worker and greater profits for the company.[13] As a rule of thumb, the advocates of scientific management claimed that piece rates established by time-and-motion studies increased productivity at least 25 percent over "day work."

Over the years, Taylor's principles of scientific management have been severely misrepresented and unjustly criticized. The misrepresentation and criticism are unfortunate because research studies have consistently demonstrated that individual incentives have a greater influence on performance than any other variable.

Straight piecework is the oldest and most common incentive-wage plan, and it is used in over half of all incentive-wage plans. Originally, straight piecework plans paid a fixed rate per piece regardless of how little a worker produced. Today, most straight piecework plans have a guaranteed base rate that is at least as high as the minimum-wage rate.

Taylor advocated a **differential piece-rate plan**. This plan pays a low rate to workers who produce less than the standard amount and a high rate to workers who produce the standard amount or more. The plan significantly rewards productive workers since they are paid not only for producing more pieces but also are paid a higher rate for each piece (normally 20 percent higher than the lower rate). Taylor intended this system to encourage slower workers to quit and find more suitable employment. A comparison of straight piece rates and Taylor's differential piece-rate plan is shown in Figure 11.2.

Commission sales are a form of incentive piece rates. Commissions usually are associated with merchandising, such as the selling of cars, life insurance, and clothing. Some salespersons are paid on a straight commission basis; that is, they receive a fixed percentage of the sale price of each product sold. Most salespeople, however, are paid a combination of commission and base salary. Sometimes the base salary is a fixed amount,

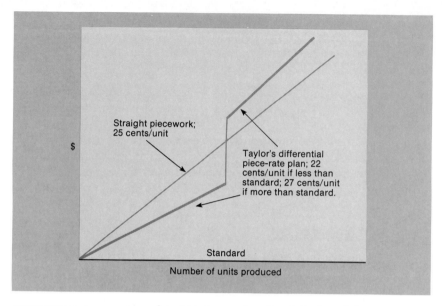

FIGURE 11.2 A comparison of straight piecework and F. W. Taylor's differential piece-rate plan.

either hourly or monthly, that salespeople receive in addition to their commissions. However, the base salary is usually a "draw" against commissions that assures a minimum income when sales are below the breakeven level.

The **standard hour plan** is another form of incentive piece rates. This plan, which is sometimes called a 100 percent premium plan, usually requires the establishment of performance standards through time-and-motion studies. If workers perform the standard amount each hour, they receive the hourly wage, but if they produce above standard, they receive proportionately more money. Standard performance is usually set at sixty units of work per hour, with a unit of work being that which a worker should be able to do in one minute. For example, if a worker consistently produces ninety units of work per hour, the worker receives one-and-one-half hour's pay for each hour worked.

An incentive plan similar to the standard hour plan is the *Halsey premium plan*, developed in the 1880s by an engineer, Fredrick A. Halsey. With this plan, the workers received a guaranteed hourly wage plus a percentage (33 percent was recommended) of the wage for any time saved. The actual production standards were determined by past performance, rather than by time-and-motion studies. For example, if a worker is paid $6.00 per hour and the task usually requires eight hours, the worker receives an additional $2.00 per hour for each hour saved under eight hours. A worker who completed an eight-hour task in seven hours would receive a $2.00 premium.

GROUP INCENTIVES

Piecework plans can be paid on either an individual or a group basis. Straight piece rates can be based on group production figures, with all members of the group sharing in the incentive pay earned by the group. Standard hour plans also can be applied to group productivity through the establishment of a group performance standard. If a group produces eighty units of work each hour when the standard is sixty units per hour, all members of the group will receive $1\frac{1}{3}$ times the hourly rate.

Group incentive plans have some important advantages over individual incentive plans. Group incentives create greater cooperation among coworkers than individual incentives. This climate of cooperation usually reduces the need for direct supervision and control since workers are supervised more by their coworkers than by their supervisor. In such a climate, slow workers are pressured by their coworkers to increase their productivity. Moreover, the flow of work and flexibility in job assignments are greatly facilitated by group incentives. When the normal work routine is disrupted by unique problems, such as illness or broken machines, individuals paid on a group incentive plan are more likely to adapt to the problem and solve it themselves.

Group incentives also have certain disadvantages. When the jobs of members of a group are independent, the members only feel responsible for their own jobs and think they should be paid only for their own work. In such a situation, group incentives provide limited motivation to produce more. Extra efforts by one worker will only result in a small increase in that worker's weekly pay. As the group gets larger, this problem becomes more severe. Thus, group incentives are most useful when jobs are interdependent, when the output of a group can be counted, and when a group is small.

Group incentives occasionally are paid to indirect labor departments. These incentives are called secondary, or indirect, labor incentives. They are relevant for those departments that do not produce a direct product but instead support other departments, such as safety and maintenance departments. For example, rewarding a maintenance department that breaks machines just to create work for themselves would be senseless. Instead, the department should be rewarded for fixing the machines so they will not break. Usually the incentives paid to indirect labor departments are determined by the performances of the direct departments that they assist. When the direct departments produce more than the standard, the indirect departments receive incentives.

NONFINANCIAL INCENTIVES

Companies also offer a variety of nonfinancial incentives to motivate and reward their employees. These programs, which include various award programs and suggestion systems, often have a greater impact on motivation and company loyalty than financial incentives.

AWARD PROGRAMS

Recognition awards can be highly motivating if they are part of an overall recognition program that includes a history of meaningful presentations. For example, a twenty-five-year service pin can be an extremely motivating reward, not because of its financial worth but because of the symbolic meaning associated with the way it is presented in an annual awards banquet where recipients are individually recognized. Employees who observe this ritual year after year come to appreciate the ceremony and see the pin as a highly valued reward.

To assess the popularity of recognition programs, the *Personnel Journal* asked its subscribers to describe (1) the kinds of programs they sponsor, and (2) the kinds of rewards they offer.[14] Length-of-service programs were the most popular; 90 percent said they recognized employees for the number of years spent with the organization, and two-thirds recognized employees at retirement. Attendance programs that recognize employees for not being tardy or absent were reported by one-fourth of the respondents. A quarter of the respondents also said they have safety programs to reduce accidents, and about the same percentage have some form of productivity-improvement program to save money or streamline procedures. Six percent have a suggestion program to reward employees for creative ideas. To recognize employees who make that extra service step, 13 percent of the companies have a customer-service program. Approximately one-third of the companies have a sales-incentive program that provides recognition beyond the regular sales commissions.

The most popular type of recognition award was a certificate or plaque sometimes accompanied by a gift certificate or cash award. Two-thirds of the companies reported using plaques and certificates in their award programs. Other rewards included accessory jewelry, watches, travel, rings, trophies, and ribbons. Travel and paid vacations have become increasingly popular in recent years, especially for sales incentives. Similar results were obtained in a survey of 171 companies by the Bureau of National Affairs.[15]

SUGGESTION SYSTEMS

Most organizations have formal suggestion systems that encourage employees to submit ideas for improving efficiency or profitability. Some organizations even provide attractive monetary rewards for good ideas. The reward usually is based on the estimated cost savings of the idea, although an upper limit usually restricts how much a person may receive for an acceptable suggestion. For example, one company pays $25 for every idea that is used and 10 percent of the estimated cost savings during the first year up to $1,000.

Maytag Company rewards its employees for submitting suggestions, and they have responded with great creativity. In 1987 the nonsupervisory employees submitted 6,346 suggestions, an average of three per worker, and more than 2,700 of these ideas were actually implemented. A total of $200,322 in awards was paid to employees for their suggestions, with the largest award being $7,500.[16]

Suggestions normally must be submitted in writing. A committee then evaluates them and prepares a written evaluation of each suggestion to show that it has been seriously considered. Some employees are highly motivated by suggestion plans and submit numerous creative ideas. For example, Raymond Roberts, a General Motors factory worker, has been awarded over $100,000 for various suggestions. The National Association for Suggestions Systems has reported a savings of $407 million from its 244 member companies. These companies reported that they received a return of $4.46 on each dollar that they invested in suggestion systems.[17]

EFFECTIVENESS OF INCENTIVE COMPENSATION

The effectiveness of incentive compensation has been studied for many years. For example, Frederick W. Taylor defended his recommendation of piece-rate incentives on the basis of his research, which showed that workers paid on a piece-rate basis produced more work and earned more money. Using the results of his research as proof, Taylor argued that scientific management was in the best interests of the workers, and he claimed that workers who tried it liked it. He also contended that piece-rate incentives were in the best interests of a company because they created lower labor costs per unit of production. (Even if variable costs remained constant, the fixed costs were spread over more units of production.)

PRODUCTIVITY INCREASES

In 1930 a survey of 1,214 compensation systems indicated that 37 percent of the workers were paid on a straight piece-rate basis.[18] The median increase in productivity for these piecework plans was estimated at 30 percent. Other surveys of piecework plans also have found significant productivity increases of varying percentages. In 1944 a survey of 302 incentive plans in New England showed an average increase in production of 29 percent.[19] A year later, two surveys of incentive systems showed average production increases of 39 to 41 percent.[20] In 1959 a survey of 2,500 incentive systems indicated that the average productivity of workers paid on a piece-rate incentive basis was 63 percent higher than that of hourly paid workers.[21] In addition to these surveys, the reports of numerous individual companies have indicated the achievement of significant productivity gains following the installation of piecework incentive plans.

Thus, the evidence shows that piecework incentive systems generally have a stronger influence on increasing productivity than any other single factor.[22] Increased productivity has been attributed to three factors associated with piece-rate plans: (1) financial incentives, (2) changes in the design of the work, and (3) higher performance goals. When a piecework plan is installed, a careful analysis of the job is conducted to ensure that it is being performed efficiently. This job analysis helps to identify more efficient methods of performing the task, if they are needed. Moreover, when the job is being timed to establish pay rates, a goal-setting process occurs, and this is followed by performance feedback. Some researchers have questioned whether the processes of goal setting, measurement, and job redesign might not be more responsible than pay incentives for increasing productivity. Studies generally show that each factor alone has a positive influence on productivity but that the impact is far greater when all three factors are present. Thus, individual and group incentive systems contribute to productivity increases due to: (1) improved methods and better organization of work, (2) higher performance goals with specific performance feedback, and (3) monetary incentives that induce greater effort.[23]

When pay incentives are eliminated, productivity typically falls, even when no changes have been made in job design or in performance goals. For example, a Midwestern papermill dropped an incentive-pay plan that provided semiannual bonuses to hourly workers. The bonuses were based on monthly evaluations of individual performance that were conducted by supervisors. The union objected to the subjective nature of the supervisors' evaluations and succeeded in pressuring the company to discontinue the incentive-pay plan. Following the plan's termination, productivity dropped 20 percent, and the turnover rate of top performers doubled. Poor performers liked their jobs better without the incentive-pay plan, but the satisfaction of top performers plummeted. Supervisors attempted to boost sagging productivity by using reprimands and threats of layoff, but these only served to create greater dissatisfaction.[24] Finally, the company decided to reinstate the incentive system.

The popularity of piece-rate incentives has declined, to some extent, not because they have lost motivating potential, but because of new technology. Piece-rate incentives are ideal when employees work independently and their productivity can be easily measured. However, new technology often forces employees to work together, and their work is machine-paced. Furthermore, some jobs change so quickly that it is not practical to establish a piece-rate standard for them. Consequently, some industries that have utilized piece rates for many years, such as the machine-tool and canning industries, are having to develop different pay systems. Piecework systems are being replaced with team-related and company-wide bonuses.[25]

RESTRICTION OF OUTPUT

Although many studies have shown that incentive-pay systems significantly increase productivity, numerous examples of incentive-pay systems that restrict output to arbitrarily low levels also have been reported. This **restriction of output** problem is at least as old as scientific management. Taylor referred to the problem as **soldiering**, and described several examples of work groups that had established arbitrarily low levels of productivity and pressured their members not to exceed these group norms.[26] Evidence of group norms restricting productivity is sometimes quite obvious when new employees join a work group. The influence of group norms on the productivity of a new employee is illustrated in Figure 11.3. Within two-and-one-half weeks, the new employee's productivity increased from thirty-two units of work per hour to seventy-four units of work per hour. Then suddenly the employee's productivity fell to fifty-six, the same as every other member of the work group.

Group norms restricting productivity are very troublesome to managers, and they are particularly perplexing because they seem to be irrational. Why should a group of workers collectively decide to hold down their level of production when they are paid only for what they produce? The problem centers around timing the job and establishing performance standards. Workers know that performance standards are somewhat arbi-

FIGURE 11.3 Illustration of group norms restricting productivity: individual productivity of a new employee.

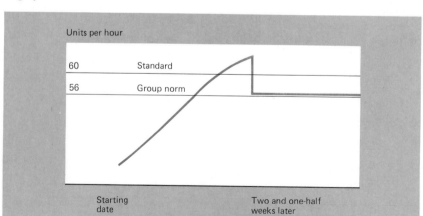

trary. They believe that if they consistently produce more than the standard, the industrial engineer will return and retime the job. Then they will be expected to produce more work for the same amount of pay.

Management has been guilty of retiming jobs often enough in some organizations to justify the workers' fears. Several interesting studies have closely examined the games that are played by workers and industrial engineers in setting performance standards. Since industrial engineers know that workers intentionally work slowly, they arbitrarily tighten the standards above the measured times. But the workers realize that the industrial engineers suspect them of working slowly so they add unnecessary and inefficient movements to look busy (which the industrial engineers expect and try to disregard).

One of Taylor's solutions to the rate-restriction problem was to have workers work alone. Group norms cannot restrict output if a worker is not in a work group. Another solution relies on better selection—only hire workers who will accept the performance standards and work as fast as possible. In recent years various organizational development techniques, such as group discussion and team-building sessions, have been proposed to change group norms.

COMPANY-WIDE INCENTIVE SYSTEMS

In addition to paying people according to their individual or group performance, pay can be based on the performance of the entire organization. The most common company-wide incentive systems include profit-sharing plans, gainsharing plans, and stock ownership plans.

PROFIT SHARING

In **profit-sharing** plans, employees receive a share of the company's profits in addition to their regular pay. The major types of profit-sharing plans are cash plans, deferred plans, or some combination of cash and deferred plans. Under a cash plan, payments are made to employees at the end of each period (usually quarterly or annually). Small companies generally prefer cash plans. Under a deferred plan, an employee's share is held until a later period, usually retirement, although workers who become unemployed or disabled may receive payments earlier than retirement under some deferred plans. Deferred plans not only motivate good performance but also contribute to the financial security of their participants. The money in deferred plans is normally invested, and as a result, some plans provide sizable sums of money to their participants.

Deferred plans are the most popular ones for large companies because of their significant tax advantages. A company's contribution to such a plan is a tax-deductible expense for the year in which the money is put into the plan, and the employee's share is not taxed until it is received, which usually is when the money has grown through investments and the employees may be in a lower income-tax bracket. (Predicting how extensively inflation will reduce this advantage is difficult, however). All deferred profit-sharing plans must be approved by the Internal Revenue Service.

Profit-sharing plans are increasing in popularity, particularly among small companies. The history of profit-sharing plans has been colorful. One of the earliest movements toward profit sharing occurred in France. In 1842 a Paris house painter and decorator, E. J. Leclaire, paid his workers a share of his profits, just as he had promised them at the beginning of the year. Leclaire's employees obviously liked the plan, but his competitors thought it was unfair and criticized Leclaire's generosity. The oldest profit-sharing plan still operating in the United States is Proctor and Gamble's, which was started in 1887. The oldest profit-sharing plan in England started just two years later at the South Metropolitan Gas Company.[27]

Many profit-sharing plans were started (or planned) between 1870 and 1900. Most of these plans were created for philosophical reasons: to create an ideal utopian society and to create equality among all members of society. Profit sharing was seen by nineteenth-century moralists as the answer to the challenges of communism and social inequality.[28]

From 1910 to 1930, profit-sharing plans were installed or advocated as a means of reducing the labor strife prevalent in America. After 1939, the dominant motive for instituting a profit-sharing plan was to increase profits. Although the attainment of a harmonious relationship between management and labor was cited as an advantage of profit sharing, the principal reasons for sharing profits were to promote employee efficiency and company profit. Comparisons between companies that do and do not have profit-sharing plans indicate that improved efficiency, reduced costs, and lower turnover are evident in profit-sharing companies. One survey compared the financial performance of department stores with and without profit sharing for the period 1952 to 1969. The survey found that the stores with profit-sharing plans had a 35 percent higher growth rate of sales, a 35 percent greater growth in net worth, and an 88 percent higher earnings per share than the stores without profit-sharing plans.[29]

Over 100,000 companies have installed profit-sharing plans tailored to their own specific conditions. Consequently, many different kinds of profit-sharing plans exist. Some plans have a *constant proportion* of profits that are contributed by the company, usually 20 to 25 percent. Other plans have a *discretionary* arrangement whereby the company's contribution is decided each year by its board of directors. Other plans have *ascending-* or *descending-scale formulas*, where the percentage of profits designated for a profit-sharing plan increases or decreases as a company's profits increase or decrease.

The **allocation formula** refers to the basis that is used to divide the money in a profit-sharing fund among the individual participants. Allocation formulas usually are based on level of responsibility, merit, base pay, and/or years of service. In one company, for example, allocation is based on units: 1 unit is given for each $200 of annual compensation up to 200 units, plus 2 units for each year of continuous service. Many companies allocate profit-sharing money according to base pay only because they assume that base pay is related to level of responsibility, merit, and years of service.

Profit-sharing plans have been successful in reducing conflict between managers and production workers. Many companies claim that their plans have succeeded in creating a sense of partnership between employees and management and in increasing employee interest in the company. In turn, many profit-sharing plans have contributed to the financial security of employees.

Profit-sharing plans also have certain limitations. Because each worker's share of the profit is not directly tied to individual productivity, a profit-sharing plan does not effectively motivate some employees. Immediate rewards that are directly tied to specific

| **HRM in Action**

Generous Incentives Create Loyalty, Satisfaction, and Profitability

Anderson Corporation, of Bayport, Minnesota, first began mass-producing window frames in 1905, and it has been one of the most effective and profitable companies in the lumber-yard business ever since. Much of its success is attributed to a profit-sharing plan started in 1914, a performance bonus plan started in 1924, and an employee stock ownership plan (ESOP) started in 1975.

The profit-sharing plan distributes 94 percent of the profit to employees according to their overall pay, which includes base pay and performance bonuses. This profit-sharing plan was designed by the company founder, Hans Jacob Anderson, who believed 6 percent was a reasonable return for those who created and managed the company. The rest of the profits, he believed, should be given to the workers to reward their efforts and help them save for retirement. In recent years, the profit-sharing awards for employees have amounted to as much as 84 percent of their annual pay, which in 1987 averaged $27,000 per employee.

Since 1924, all hourly wage employees have been eligible for bonus pay based on their individual or group productivity. The productivity bonus can raise an employee's pay to a maximum of 140 percent of the employee's base-pay rate. Knowing that their profit share is calculated on their total pay with bonuses included provides an added incentive for employees to perform well. Many employees earn the maximum 140 percent almost every day.

The ESOP, which began in 1975, has transferred 30 percent of the company into the hands of the employees. This ownership has contributed to the close feeling of "family" that has always existed at Anderson Corporation. Because the employees are loyal and dedicated, the company has never had to contend with a union or a strike. Employees say they love their work, and turnover is essentially zero. Although the leadership style is described as benevolent paternalism, the employees are very happy and the company is very productive.

Source: Carl M. Cannon, "Golden Shackles: Anderson Windowalls Knows How to Keep Unions and Government Bureaucrats out of its Town and its Factory—Money," *Business Month* 132 (September 1988): 56–63.

individual behaviors are more effective than profit-sharing plans for motivating employees who have short attention spans and cannot delay gratification. Furthermore, an effective profit-sharing program must have profits to share. Occasionally, profits are eliminated by economic forces that neither managers nor production workers can control. Profit-sharing plans do not provide much motivation during an economic recession. However, some employers argue that employees should carry part of the burden in years when losses are incurred since they share in the profits during good years. Another reason that a profit-sharing plan may not be very motivating is related to an organization's size. As an organization grows, workers may feel that their influence on the overall profit level is insignificant. Deferred plans are especially poor for providing employees with immediate incentives to work hard. Even small companies that produce large profit-sharing funds can fail to motivate young workers who do not expect to receive any of the benefits for another forty years.

GAINSHARING

Gainsharing is a company-wide incentive program similar to profit sharing, but the bonuses are based on improved productivity instead of on a percentage of the profit. Gainsharing plans normally reward employees on a monthly or quarterly basis, depending on how productivity is measured, whereas profit sharing is usually paid annually. The most popular gainsharing plans are Scanlon Plans, Rucker Plans, and improshare.

SCANLON PLAN

A **Scanlon Plan** is a combination of a gain-sharing plan and an employee-suggestion system. While a Scanlon Plan usually increases efficiency and productivity, it also is advocated as a means of reducing union-management conflict. A Scanlon Plan has come to represent a philosophy of industrial relations whereby management and employees work cooperatively to increase the efficiency of the company and to share in the rewards. Although Scanlon Plans were originally installed in unionized companies, the presence of a union is *not* necessary.

The Scanlon Plan was developed by Joseph Scanlon in 1937 to help reduce costs in a steel mill. Scanlon, who had been trained as a cost accountant, was acting as a union representative at the time. He formulated a plan based on the idea that the company should pay a fixed labor cost per ton of steel. If the employees produced more steel with fewer hours of labor, they then would share in the labor cost savings.[30] The results of installing the plan in the steel mill were very favorable, and as a result, Scanlon became employed by the national headquarters of the steel workers' union and helped to install other plans. Later, he joined the Massachusetts Institute of Technology, where he promoted his plan through writing and research.

A Scanlon Plan is installed by establishing a standard ratio of labor costs as a percentage of revenue; that is, the labor costs are divided by total sales or by the dollar value of the units produced. This standard is based on historical data for a company, such as the company's average ratio for the past five years. Once union and management have agreed on a normal cost of labor, the standard is not altered unless significant changes affect the production process or the products. After the ratio is established, all employees share in any labor-cost savings or productivity increases. For example, when the standard labor cost ratio is 45 percent and $200,000 of sales are produced, then $90,000 is the expected labor cost. But when actual labor costs are only $75,000, then the $15,000 savings goes into a bonus fund. Most of this fund, usually 60 to 75 percent, is paid directly to the employees, part is held in a reserve for possible deficits (usually 25 percent), and some may be paid to the company.

The purposes of the incentive are to increase cooperation and to stimulate creative suggestions for reducing labor costs. The suggestion system is a central factor in the Scanlon Plan. Normally a system of departmental committees is established in addition to a central committee that screens suggestions and evaluates them. Individuals generally are not paid directly for submitting suggestions but share with everyone else in any cost savings produced by the suggestions. The departmental committees meet periodically to eliminate problem situations that are reducing efficiency. These meetings are useful not only for improving efficiency but also for providing communication links between union and management.

Several studies have evaluated the effectiveness of Scanlon Plans. While the results have not been universally positive, most have indicated productivity increases of 20 to 25 percent after a plan has been established for one or two years. Case studies of firms using the Scanlon Plan indicate that it generally produces improvements in efficiency and in labor-management relations, favorable employee attitudes toward efficiency, and less resistance to change. Like other profit-sharing plans, however, Scanlon Plans probably work best in smaller companies.[31]

RUCKER PLANS

Allen Rucker developed an incentive plan during the 1970s called a **Rucker Share-of-Production Plan** that is similar to a Scanlon Plan but based on a more sophisticated accounting analysis of "value added." Here the ratio is calculated by dividing the labor costs by the "value added" rather than by total revenues as recommended by Scanlon. Under a Rucker Plan, a historical relationship is established between total employee earnings (i.e., total labor costs) and the value added by the employees through the production process. The value added by the firm is simply the sales value of output less the cost of materials used. A standard productivity ratio is calculated, which expresses the production value required for each dollar of compensation. As productivity increases, compensation increases and is shared between labor and management. The ratios are revamped if major changes in products or production processes occur.

IMPROSHARE

Improshare plans are similar to Scanlon and Rucker plans, but are tied directly to measures of productivity rather than to the dollar value of the product. The basic idea is that a firm sets a base level of performance, tracks improvements in performance, and then pays bonuses proportionate to the amount of time saved either to all workers or just to those in the group being measured. Improvements in productivity are shared with the employees, which explains why they are called improshare plans (*im*proved *pro*ductivity through *shar*ing). One advantage of improshare plans over Scanlon and Rucker plans is that improshare plans can be used in a broader variety of situations where a physical product is not produced. For example, the employees of a hotel could have bonuses tied to the occupancy rate, and employees in a training institute could receive bonuses tied to the number of people trained.

Gainsharing plans became very popular during the 1980s because they contributed significantly to productivity improvements, which were estimated to be as high as 35 percent in some companies.[32] Like profit-sharing plans, gainsharing creates greater motivation in small companies and requires careful record keeping and a cooperative attitude within the company.

STOCK OWNERSHIP PLANS

Another form of company-wide incentive is an employee stock ownership plan (ESOP). An ESOP is formed by creating a trust, into which a company makes tax-deductible contributions of cash or stock. The proceeds are used to buy shares of the company's stock which are allocated to individual employee accounts.

Employees who have an ownership interest in a firm are expected to be more concerned about the efficiency and profitability of the firm than employees who do not share in the ownership. Some organizations are wholly owned by their employees through an employee stock ownership trust (ESOT). One of the largest ESOPs is Wierton Steel Corporation (Wierton, West Virginia), which is wholly owned by its 7,000 employees.[33]

The popularity of ESOPs stems partly from a philosophy of sharing the wealth. ESOPs were first recommended in 1958 by economist Louis O. Kelso as a means of turning workers into capitalists through stock ownership. Favorable tax treatment and other economic advantages, however, have probably contributed much more to their growth. From 1974 to 1984, sixteen federal laws encouraging ESOPs were passed. Some of these laws temporarily allowed companies to reduce their taxes by whatever amounts they contributed to an ESOP as an inducement to start an ESOP. As a result, over 9,000 ESOPs have been created, and they enroll over 10 million workers.

Today, ESOPs are frequently used as financing tools for a variety of other economic transactions, including financing a leveraged buyout, preventing a hostile takeover, keeping a failing company from closing, providing an employee pension benefit, and creating a market for disposing of company stock by selling it back to the ESOP.[34]

The advantages of ESOPs can be illustrated by examining how they are created and managed. To create an ESOP, a bank lends money to the ESOP, which passes the loan to the company in return for an equivalent amount of company stock. The stock in the trust serves as collateral for the loan. The stock, which can be either newly issued shares of stock or stock purchased from shareholders, is held in a trust (ESOT) for the employees. Each year, the company places up to 25 percent of its payroll in the ESOP to pay off the ESOP loan and deducts the entire amount, both principal and interest, from its taxable income. The ESOP uses the company contribution to pay off the bank loan. As the loan is paid, the stock in the ESOP is allocated to each employee. When employees retire or quit, they withdraw their stock or sell it, often back to the ESOP. After they are hired, new employees join the plan and begin accumulating stock.[35]

One of the important tax advantages of ESOPs is that lending institutions, such as banks, pay taxes on only half of the interest income they receive from loans to ESOPs. Another tax benefit is that dividends paid in cash to ESOP participants are deductible as a pretax expense to the sponsoring company.[36]

The logic of stock ownership suggests that employees who are stockholders in their companies will work hard to increase the value of their stock. In fact, however, stock prices and dividends are even further removed from individual efforts than are profit-sharing plans. Nevertheless, ESOPs do seem to motivate employees, partly because of the monetary value of the stock and partly because of the threat of job loss. The economic advantages of ESOPs have been shown in two studies by the National Center for Employee Ownership. In one study of 360 high-technology firms, those firms that shared ownership with most or all employees grew two to four times faster than firms whose employees did not own stock. In another study of 52 employee-owned companies from various industries, the best performers were found to be those that made the largest stock payments to workers' ESOP accounts.[37]

The popularity of ESOPs will probably increase as a result of favorable federal legislation. The primary benefit of an ESOP is that it helps employees prepare for the future by developing a personal investment program. The disadvantages are that the employees' pensions are tied too closely with the success of one company and the employees are not allowed to vote as shareholders of the stock until they receive it at retirement.

EXECUTIVE INCENTIVES

The compensation of executives is much larger than that of other employees and tends to be determined by a different set of factors. It includes both monetary and nonmonetary rewards. Some nonmonetary rewards, such as a company car, reserved parking, and first-class air tickets, are available only to executives. An increasing number of chief executive officers (CEOs) receive over 1 million dollars a year in total compensation. This amount includes their base pay—which is often less than half the total—bonuses, stock options, director's fees, and several forms of deferred compensation. The median pay (salary plus bonus) of the top CEOs for 1978, 1980, and 1984 is shown in Table 11.1.

SALARIES

The compensation of executives is influenced by many factors, such as revenue, responsibility, and the fact that executives have a large role in setting their own salaries. Some factors, such as reviving a declining company, seem to be reasonable justifications for paying large salaries, while others may be questionable or even unethical excuses for exorbitant incomes. Sales are clearly the best predictor of a CEO's salary. Apparently, individuals who determine the pay for CEOs believe that the larger a company's revenues, the heavier the load on the chief executive, and therefore the greater the CEO's pay and bonus should be. As Table 11.1 shows, the median remuneration of CEOs in 1984 was $902,000 in companies with over $5 billion in revenue, almost triple the income of $337,000 for CEOs in companies with under $500 million revenue.[38]

TABLE 11.1   Salary and bonuses of chief executive officers

	1978 (802 Companies)	1980 (818 Companies)	1984 (785 Companies)
Median compensation	$ 306,000	$ 351,945	$ 560,000
Highest-paid CEO	3,423,220	7,865,831	22,900,000
According to company revenue:			
Under $500 million	169,000	not reported	337,000
$500 million to $1 billion	253,000	300,000	425,000
$1 billion to $5 billion	353,000	402,000	590,000
Over $5 billion	492,000	589,000	902,000

Source: "How Much Does Your Boss Make?" *Forbes* (June 11, 1979): 117–48; "How Much Does the Boss Make?" *Forbes* (June 8, 1981): 114–44; "Who Made What at the Top in U.S. Business," *Forbes* (June 3, 1985): 114–53.

The evidence suggests that CEO salaries are closely related to sales but not to profitability. One study of executive salaries in middle-sized manufacturing and distribution companies found that such salaries were almost directly related to sales. The only information needed to predict the salary of chief executives was a formula based strictly on sales. This study also found that the compensation of lower-level managers was a fairly predictable ratio of the CEO's salary and that the compensation of these managers was unrelated to company profits (in dollars) or profitability (ratio of profits to sales). Other studies also have shown that corporate performance is not related to either salaries or salaries plus bonuses, even though most executives claim that their pay is based on their performance.[39]

HRM in Action

Executive Perks

In addition to receiving exorbitant salaries, top executives also enjoy many other privileges that come with the job. Someone who was trying to comment on the cultural interests of the wealthy once said, "People who are wealthy are different than you and I." The listener simply responded, "Yes, they have more money." In the case of corporate executives, however, they also have more perks.

Here is a list of the most popular executive perks and an estimate of how many companies offer them:

Physical exam	91%	Chauffeur service	40%
Company car	68%	Airline VIP-club membership	34%
Financial counseling	64%	Reserved parking	32%
Company plane	63%	Executive dining room	30%
Income-tax preparation	63%	Home security system	25%
First-class air travel	62%	Cellular phone	22%
Country club membership	55%	Health club membership	19%
Luncheon club membership	55%	Financial seminars	11%
Estate planning	52%	Home use of WATS line	11%
Personal liability insurance	50%	Interest-free (or low-interest) loans	9%
Spouse travel	47%	Legal counseling	6%

Source: Survey conducted by Hewitt Associates, 1990.

Below the level of chief executive, most studies have found relatively consistent percentages representing the pay of the second- and third-highest executives. The second-highest executive is usually paid about 71 percent of the CEO's salary, except in retail trade where the second executive receives 84 percent. The third-highest executive normally receives 55 to 60 percent of the CEO's salary, and the next level down the pyramid receives 68 percent of that. These percentages reveal wide variations between the levels. Some question whether the responsibilities and demands of the CEO position justify such wide variations. The typical justification for such large pay differentials is based on the concept of a **just noticeable difference (JND)**, taken from the psychological literature on sensation and perception. A JND is the amount (weight, size, color) that is required to make a meaningful difference. At higher income levels a much larger dollar amount is required to make a noticeable difference between two income levels. But $50,000 to $100,000 or more seems to represent an exorbitant pay differential.

The pay of middle managers and supervisors is primarily influenced by their levels in the organizational hierarchy. A statistical analysis of the salaries of 150 managers found that a move from a first-level to a second-level managerial position resulted in a 12 percent pay increase. An additional 7 percent increase was obtained if such a move required the manager to report to a higher level in the structure. Education and age also were found to be related to pay. A master's degree in business administration was worth an additional 8 percent, and 50-year-old managers received 12 percent more than 40-year-old managers. Although a manager's pay is assumed to be closely related to sales and profits, this assumption was not sustained by the results of the analysis. A 15 percent increase in sales only produced a 4 percent increase in pay, and a 15 percent increase in profits produced a 1 percent *decrease* in base pay and only a 4 percent increase in salary plus bonus. Apparently all managers receive pay increases, but high performers receive larger bonuses than low performers who, instead, tend to get larger increases in base salary.[40]

BONUS PLANS

The most common incentive plans for upper- and middle-level managers involve bonuses. The basic philosophy behind **bonuses** is to reward managers for good performance. Bonuses are expected to stimulate managers to higher levels of effort and dedication. When bonuses are tied to the overall performance of a company, they are expected to create cooperation between managers and to increase flexibility and creativity.

The size of executive bonuses is typically larger for upper-level managers than for middle-level managers, even when expressed as a percentage of salary. At upper levels of a company, the bonus might be 50 to 80 percent of salary. At lower levels, supervisors and managers typically receive bonuses that are only 15 to 40 percent of their salaries, if they receive bonuses at all. The average bonuses of top corporate officers in 1985, expressed as a percentage of salary, are shown in Figure 11.4. Top corporate officers receive larger bonuses than lower-level managers, both in dollar amounts and as a percentage of salary.

Participation in bonus plans is typically determined by salary level, salary grade, or organizational level. An example of participation being determined by salary level is when executives earning between $30,000 and $50,000 receive a $5,000 bonus, those earning between $50,000 and $80,000 receive a $20,000 bonus, and those earning higher salaries receive a $50,000 bonus. In this situation, a manager whose base salary is $29,000 would not be eligible for a bonus, regardless of his or her performance. When eligibility is governed by salary grade, all employees in and above a given salary grade are automatically put on the bonus plan. When organizational level is used to determine eligibility, only the executives in certain levels of the organizational structure are allowed to participate.

A difficulty with all three of these methods is that the bonuses are determined by arbitrary formulas rather than by performance levels. Again, the basic idea behind bonuses is to reward outstanding performance and to provide an incentive for diligence

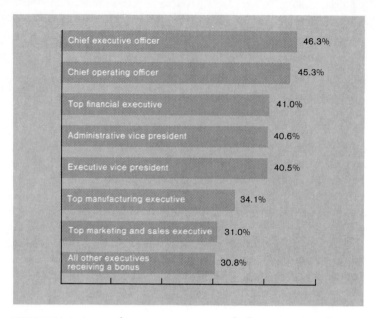

FIGURE 11.4 Average bonus as a percentage of salary. From Amanda Bennett, "Executives Face Change in Awarding of Pay, Stock Options," in *The Wall Street Journal*, February 28, 1986. Reprinted by permission of *The Wall Street Journal.* © Dow Jones & Company, Inc., 1986. All rights reserved.

in the future. When bonuses are based on salary level, salary grade, or organizational level rather than on individual performance, the bonuses lose their incentive and reward properties.

In recent years, greater efforts have been made to tie executive bonuses to company performance. After years of regularly receiving hefty increases in salary and bonus, regardless of their company's success or failure, more top executives are finding that their pay is now being linked directly to corporate performance. This pay-for-performance trend has also been observed at the division-manager and department-supervisor level, as their bonuses are becoming tied to the performance of their divisions and departments. To prevent managers from sacrificing long-term growth for short-term success, some executive bonuses are based on the company's performance over three to five years. These plans are growing in popularity because they create a better balance in motivated effort by rewarding both long-term growth and short-term profitability.[41]

Although bonuses are intended to improve the performance of individual managers and the organization as a whole, the research evidence does not entirely support their effectiveness. Several case studies have reported positive benefits from carefully designed and administered bonus plans in individual companies. One study compared the economic performance over a ten-year period of 100 bonus-paying companies with 100 companies that did not pay bonuses. The companies were matched according to size and industry. The results indicated that the paying of bonuses was associated with higher economic performance. A review of several case studies also concluded that a properly designed and administered executive incentive bonus plan tends to increase corporate net income and to benefit stockholders.[42]

In many companies, however, the bonus plans are not carefully designed and administered. In these companies, bonuses are not tied to operating goals or to company profits. A survey of 571 major companies over a two-year period found that bonus-paying companies were not necessarily more profitable than companies that did not pay bonuses. In this survey, bonus-paying companies and companies that did not pay bonuses were compared within sixteen industries. The bonus-paying companies, as compared to those not paying bonuses, had a higher return on investment in nine industries, a lower return on investment in six industries, and no difference in the remaining industry.[43]

Therefore, even though little research evidence supports the effectiveness of executive bonuses, they are widely used despite their high costs. Some have concluded that executive bonuses are an example of management's ability to pay itself what it wants, regardless of performance, and to pass the cost on to the consumers. Many executives prefer to have their bonuses paid at a later date for tax reasons. This policy of deferment contributes further to the ineffectiveness of the bonus as a source of motivation.

STOCK OPTIONS

In its simplest form, a **stock option** is the right to buy a company's stock at a certain price over a certain period of time, usually ten years. Stock options are viewed as an inexpensive benefit because they don't cost a business any cash or cause any charge to earnings. However, because they may dilute a company's stock if enough options are exercised, the Financial Accounting Standards Board believes the potential future impact of stock options should be included on a company's reports.[44]

Although numerous kinds of stock option plans exist, the basic premise of most is that employees are given the option of buying a specified number of shares at a fixed price. The option can be exercised over a period of time, which allows employees to wait and see if the value of the stock appreciates before buying it. During periods of rising stock prices, income from stock options can be sizable. For high-salaried executives, income from stock options can easily double their income from bonus plans and exceed their base salaries. In 1987, for example, Charles Lazrus of Toys "R" Us received $56.4 million in stock gains in addition to his $3.6 million in salary and bonus. The 1988 leader was Michael D. Eisner of Walt Disney, who received $32.5 million in stock gains in addition to his $7.5 million in salary and bonus.[45]

A survey of forty industrial companies found that the average stock option grants for the top executives were about 1.5 to 1.6 times their annual salaries, and some executives were given options for more than ten times their annual salary and bonus. Clearly, stock options are a significant part of an executive's compensation package.[46]

Like monetary bonuses, stock options were originally intended to be incentives for managers to perform well. The assumption was that managers would work hard and develop an interest in the economic success of the company if they shared in the ownership of the company.

Stock options usually are available only to high-level executives, particularly those who have a significant influence on company profits. As noted earlier, however, stock options have only a small incentive value, and therefore, the granting of stock should be viewed as a method of transferring money to executives at a lower tax rate.

In the past, stock option plans were extremely popular because of favorable tax laws. In the 1950s, for example, executives usually had ten years to exercise their stock options, and the option prices were sometimes as low as 85 percent of the stock's market value. If executives decided to exercise their options, they could buy the stock at its offered price, hold it for six months, sell it at its appreciated value, and only pay a 25 percent capital-gains tax. This plan was especially attractive since at the time the income-tax rate was as high as 91 percent at the highest level.

Between 1976 and 1981 the tax laws were changed, and all income from stock option plans was taxed as ordinary income. With the tax incentives eliminated, there was a drastic reduction in the number of stock options that were either granted or exercised. However, the 1981 Economic Recovery Tax Act provided for an incentive stock option (ISO) that allowed executives to defer paying tax on the appreciated value of their stock until they sold it, and then it was taxed at the capital-gains tax rate (20 percent) rather than as ordinary income (usually over 40 percent). Stock options once again became very popular and companies developed a variety of long-term incentive plans tied to the value of the company's stock. A glossary of these plans is shown in Table 11.2. In 1986 the capital-gains tax was eliminated, and once again stock options began to wane. The

---

TABLE 11.2 Long-term incentive plans tied to stock values

1. **Incentive Stock Option (ISO):** A qualified plan (meaning it conforms to the Internal Revenue Code) that allows companies to offer stock options to their employees at a price equal to the value of the stock. Employees have ten years to exercise their options; that is, to purchase the stock at the original offered price. Although the value of the stock at the time the employees purchase it may be greater than what they have to pay for it, the employees are not taxed until the stock has been sold.

2. **Nonqualified Stock Option (NQSO):** Similar to an ISO but without conformance to the Internal Revenue Code. The appreciated value of the stock is taxed as income when the option is exercised and the company obtains a corresponding tax deduction.

3. **Stock Appreciation Rights (SAR):** The company grants an executive the right to receive an amount of money equal to the appreciation in the underlying stock over time.

4. **Phantom Stock Plans:** Executive receives units analogous to company shares of stock and, at some future time, receives the value of the stock appreciation plus dividends.

5. **Restricted Stock Awards:** An executive receives outright as a bonus a grant of shares free (or with a discount), but is restricted from transferring the stock until certain conditions are met. The stock is forfeited if the conditions are not met.

6. **Performance Unit Plan:** A bonus plan where an executive earns specially valued units at no cost, based on achieving predetermined performance targets.

7. **Performance Share Plan:** A bonus plan where an executive receives shares of stock, based on achieving predetermined performance targets.

8. **Formula Value Stock Plan:** In companies where the stock is not publicly traded, an executive earns rights to stock that is valued according to a formula, such as book value.

popularity of stock options in future years will be greatly influenced by changes in the tax laws and whether the capital-gains tax is restored.

An employee stock ownership plan is advocated as an effective means of creating a sense of ownership or proprietorship in a company. However, an inherent conflict exists between the income purposes and the ownership purposes of stock options. To obtain money from a stock option plan, an employee must buy the stock and then resell it. Therefore, the feeling of ownership supposedly derived from holding the stock is not very great if the employee's intent is to immediately resell it.

Although stock options were originally intended to be incentives for performing well, they are now considered a membership reward rather than a performance reward. Employees participate in stock option plans because they are members of the organization rather than because they have performed well. The market value of the stock can be materially influenced only by a few top executives, and even these executives believe that the relationship between their performance and the stock price is very weak at best. Therefore, the incentive value of stock options is nil. Stock options are membership rewards, primarily for members of top management. As a method of reinforcing outstanding performance, however, stock option plans are seriously deficient.

DIRECTOR'S FEES

Many executives receive additional compensation for serving on a board of directors for their own corporation or for an outside corporation. Most outside directors receive an annual retainer fee, plus a separate fee for each board meeting or committee meeting they attend. A survey of the pay practices for outside directors in the top *Fortune* 100 industrials in 1985 indicated that the average annual retainer was $19,300, and the average fee was $790 for attending a board meeting and $730 for attending a committee meeting.[47]

Other benefits in addition to pay also are provided to some outside directors. Liability insurance coverage customarily protects board members from legal suits that may be brought against the board. Some board members' benefits include life insurance, travel insurance, and even group health and dental insurance. Stock purchase plans also are available for some board members.

NONFINANCIAL REWARDS

In addition to their many lucrative financial rewards, executives also receive numerous nonfinancial rewards. These nonfinancial rewards, known as perquisites (perks), should not be overlooked, even though they vary greatly from company to company. The number of perks available to executives normally depends on their level in the organizational hierarchy: top-level executives generally receive more perks than middle-level executives.

Some of the most popular perks include a large and elaborately furnished office, a choice location for one's office, a company car for personal use, reserved parking, and first-class air tickets. Other perks, as shown in Table 11.3, are memberships in private clubs, health spas, or athletic clubs; use of a company recreation center, such as a cabin; use of recreational equipment, such as a fishing boat; use of a special cafeteria; expense accounts; and free, long-distance telephone calls.

TABLE 11.3   Popular executive perquisites

1. Professional, trade, or business association membership
2. Reserved parking
3. Periodic medical examinations
4. Civic organization membership
5. Company car
6. Expense account for business entertainment
7. Social or country club membership
8. Executive luncheon club membership
9. Separate restroom and/or shower facilities
10. Executive dining room
11. Health or athletic club membership
12. Entertainment allowance
13. Financial counseling
14. Legal counseling
15. Career counseling
16. Use of company aircraft for personal trips
17. Chauffeured limousine
18. Psychological counseling
19. Company-owned country or social club
20. Company-owned vacation retreat
21. Official residence
22. Servants or servants allowance
23. Extended leaves of absence

Source: ASPA-BNA Survey No. 28, "The Status of Today's Executive," July 17, 1975.

Workers who have to pay for their own cars, food, and phone calls from a much smaller base salary than that of executives are understandably critical of executive perks. The most significant criticism of executive perks, however, concerns the ineffective way they are distributed—as membership rewards rather than as performance rewards. When all executives at the same level receive the same executive perks regardless of performance, companies overlook a potentially powerful motivating tool. For example, parking positions could be changed each month among division heads to reflect division sales. Use of the company cabin could be reserved for only those managers who are in the top half of the company. The awarding of perks according to performance could have a stronger motivating effect on executives than large financial bonuses.

THE ETHICS OF EXECUTIVE PAY

When most people learn about the enormous pay of chief executives, their initial reaction is, "How can anyone justify paying them such exorbitant salaries?" Indeed, the typical pay of chief executives is very high and very controversial. In some organizations the total compensation of the CEO is more than 1,000 times greater than the pay of the people at the bottom. Furthermore, the disparity is growing. During the 1980s, the average pay of top corporate executives more than tripled, while the pay of hourly production workers increased about 60 percent.[48]

Whether this discrepancy is fair depends greatly on one's personal values. Some people believe executives deserve large salaries and think the huge bonuses they receive provide a necessary incentive motivating them to create jobs and wealth. Other people think executive pay is absolutely exorbitant and simply immoral.

By international standards, American executives are overpaid. The average chief executive's salary in the United States is about 40 percent more than the average in Japan, over twice as much as the average in England, and almost four times as much as the average in Australia. Compared to the average entry-level college graduate, the American chief executive earns fourteen times as much, while the corresponding multiples in Japan, England, and Australia are ten, eleven, and four times as much.[49]

As a practical consideration, there is some indication that large pay differentials create an unhealthy climate within the firm. Years ago, J. P. Morgan discovered that poorly performing clients of J. P. Morgan & Company all had one characteristic in common: each company's top executive was paid more than 130 percent of the people in the next echelon, who, in turn, were paid more than 130 percent of the compensation of those below them. Morgan concluded that large pay differentials disrupted the teamwork and trust necessary for an effective executive team. Peter Drucker agrees with J. P. Morgan's conclusion and recommends that the ratio between the pay of the CEO and the average hourly worker never exceed twenty to one.[50]

Large CEO salaries are often excused by noting that they are only a fraction of what professional athletes and entertainers receive; however, the morality of athletes' and entertainers' earnings is just as questionable as executive pay. Rightly or wrongly, CEO pay tends to be enormous, especially when organizations get larger, when the company has shareholders, and when the company wants to keep its top executives.[51]

PAY ISSUES

In the design of a compensation system, three issues need to be addressed. The first issue is what percentage of an employee's pay should be base pay and what percentage should be incentive pay. This issue concerns the proper balance between two objectives of compensation: security and motivation. The second issue is whether employees should be paid an hourly wage or a salary. Some companies think that paying an annual salary rather than hourly wage amounts to more than just a difference in how the payroll is calculated. The third issue is whether a company's policy regarding pay levels should be open or secret. What is the appropriate balance between the right of personal privacy and the right to know what others earn? Although an open pay policy is not a serious threat to basic freedoms, many companies are concerned about whether it is a violation of their employees' rights to let employees know how much their coworkers earn.

BASE PAY VERSUS INCENTIVE PAY

Financial incentive systems do not always function smoothly. Some of the disadvantages include the following:

1. Incentive pay requires better record keeping and complicates the processing of weekly payrolls.
2. Incentive pay requires that performance be carefully evaluated and recorded; this becomes increasingly difficult as performance evaluations become more subjective.
3. Incentive pay requires greater managerial control in creating and monitoring incentive pay rates.
4. Employees may experience excessive anxiety and concern when incentives represent a large percentage of their total compensation, especially if they have only limited control over their performance.
5. Some employees complain that their bonuses are inadequate, regardless of the amounts.
6. Incentive pay systems require greater explanation and justification and are more frequently challenged, especially by poor performers.

Because of the problems financial incentives create, some compensation specialists are opposed to using them to motivate employees. Some companies refuse to tie pay to performance and prefer to pay straight base pay, either hourly wages or an annual salary. The disadvantage of base pay is that it does not motivate employees. When employees receive the same income regardless of their productivity, they have no incentive to work harder.

As discussed in Chapter 10, three of the six compensation objectives are *security*, *equity*, and *motivation*. Although straight wages and salaries provide a feeling of security, they are not very motivating and not generally equitable. To provide a sense of equity and an element of motivation, a compensation system must have some form of financial incentive in which pay is based at least partially on performance.

Union wage scales and commission sales illustrate two extremes of this issue. A fixed-pay system established by a union contract provides a feeling of security because raises are based on the cost of living, promotions are based on seniority, and layoffs are cushioned with layoff benefits. However, fixed-pay schedules are not equitable when large performance differences exist, nor are such schedules motivating. On the other hand, a sales commission that is based strictly on a percentage of sales volume provides little or no security, even though it may be equitable and very motivating.

To satisfy the objectives of a sound compensation system, a compensation manager must fine-tune the compensation system just as a mechanic fine-tunes an engine. The engine needs to be adjusted for the load it must pull, the quality of fuel it will use, and even the altitude at which it will operate. Similarly, a compensation system needs to be fine-tuned to meet its security, motivation, and equity objectives by balancing the base-pay and incentive-pay components. If the base-pay component is too large, inadequate motivation will result. If the incentive component is too large, several potential problems could develop, including increased turnover because of inadequate security, dissatisfaction caused by inaccurate performance evaluations, and dysfunctional competition between coworkers.

In **fine-tuning compensation**, the following variables must be considered:

1. The ability to *measure individual performance* accurately, objectively, and conveniently. As a larger portion of the total compensation becomes determined by individual incentives, the measurement of individual performance must become more precise. Occupations that are difficult to measure precisely, such as engineer, lawyer, and college professor, should not have as large an individual-incentive component determining their compensation as occupations that are easier to measure, such as sewing-machine operator.
2. The extent to which workers can *control the rate of production*. Individual incentives are not very useful if workers have little control over the quantity or quality of their performance. Assembly-line workers and security guards, for example, have very little control over the quantity of work they produce.
3. The degree of *interdependence and cooperation required* within the work group. When individuals work together as a cooperating group to produce a group product, their pay should be based on the level of group performance rather than on individual performance.
4. The *size of the work group* and organization. As work groups and organizations become larger, the measurable influence of a single worker shrinks. In large work groups and large organizations, group incentives and profit-sharing plans lose some of their motivating influence.
5. The organization's *ability to produce a profit* and obtain accurate and timely measures of performance. A profit-sharing plan requires not only profits to share (which largely excludes most nonprofit organizations) but also an acceptable procedure for measuring the profits and a formula for dividing them.

The fine-tuning process consists of adjustments to base pay, individual incentives, group incentives, and profit sharing to provide a feeling of security, equity, and motivation. Security is provided by base pay, while equity and motivation are provided through incentive plans. Some organizations pay small base salaries and give large bonuses to their executives, while others pay large base salaries and give small bonuses. General Motors and Ford, for example, pay their managers a small base pay but large bonuses, while General Electric does just the opposite. This means that an industrial relations manager at General Electric probably receives a higher base salary but a much smaller bonus than his or her counterpart at GM or Ford. The same sort of trade-off needs to be considered for all jobs within a company. The appropriate combination of base pay and incentive pay needs to be selected to maximize the pay objectives.[52]

The fine-tuning process can be illustrated by considering three jobs. The compensation for each of these jobs is shown in Figure 11.5. All three jobs offer both incentive pay and base pay, but the proportions are different. Job A is a clerical job in a credit union with 260 employees. The base pay is determined by a job-classification schedule. New employees start at the bottom of their classification. Pay increases, which can be granted twice a year, are based on performance evaluations by a supervisor. The super-

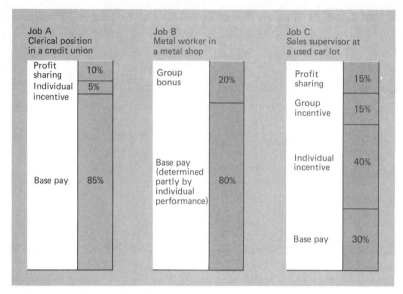

FIGURE 11.5 Fine-tuning of base pay and incentive pay for three jobs.

visor also can recommend a fifty-dollar monthly bonus for outstanding performance. The credit union has a form of profit sharing in which 20 percent of the undivided earnings at the end of each quarter are given to the employees according to their relative base-pay rates. The compensation plan is designated so that the average employee receives approximately 85 percent of total compensation in base pay, 5 percent from individual incentives, and 10 percent from profit sharing.

Job B is a job in a metal shop that consists of sixteen employees who make table and chair frames. Because most workers rotate from job to job throughout the day, maintaining accurate records of individual productivity is impossible. However, daily production records are kept for the group. The base pay of the metal workers is determined by their placement in one of five skill categories: learner, apprentice, intermediate, craftsworker, and skilled craftsworker. The company pays a monthly group bonus that is allocated according to skill category. Approximately 80 percent of each worker's income is derived from base pay and 20 percent from the group bonus. Individual performance is rewarded only in the sense that it determines the base-pay category to which each worker is assigned.

Job C is a supervisor at a used-car lot who monitors the performance of six other salespeople. The sales supervisor is paid a base salary that has been negotiated with the owner of the lot, a commission on the cars that she sells, a commission on the sales of her subordinates, and 1 percent of the monthly profit of the dealership. As percentages of the total compensation, these amounts are intended to represent 30 percent in base salary, 40 percent from personal commission sales, 15 percent from group commission sales, and 15 percent from profit sharing.

In summary, compensation systems can be designed in numerous ways. Different pay plans have significant effects on satisfaction, productivity, turnover, and absenteeism.

A good pay system that satisfies all six compensation objectives requires careful design-ing and patient adjusting. A new compensation system should contain some flexibility in its design, since its effectiveness is influenced by so many variables. As problems occur, the compensation manager can then make adjustments in the system to keep it finely tuned.

WAGES VERSUS SALARIES

The wage-versus-salary issue is a modern version of a long-standing philosophical debate. The basis on which a worker should be paid was one of the issues discussed in the slavery debates prior to the Civil War. Northern factory workers who received an hourly wage were called wage slaves. Many nineteenth-century philosophers saw little difference be-tween the plantation slaves in the South and the wage slaves in the North. "To put a man upon wages, is to put him in the position of a dependent," wrote Samuel Elliot in the *Journal of Social Science*, in 1871. The longer he holds the position, the more his capacities for independent judgment atrophy, and "the less of a man, in fine, he becomes." Factory wage earners were considered helpless conscripts in an economic battle, subject to the whims of their commanding chiefs. No lasting democracy, it was argued, could be built from conscripts and servants.[53]

A more recent issue concerns whether production workers should receive monthly salaries rather than hourly wages. Most supervisors and many nonsupervisory white-collar employees have been paid a monthly salary for years. Why not pay production workers on the same basis? Most employers think production workers will abuse the situ-ation. They fear that production workers who are paid monthly salaries regardless of their attendance will have high rates of absenteeism and tardiness.

In spite of these fears, several companies have begun paying monthly salaries in-stead of hourly wages to their production employees. Time clocks were retained for a time in some companies, but by now most have been eliminated. Among the companies that have changed to the salary method are Avon Products, Gillette, Black and Decker, Eaton Corporation, Kinetic Dispersion, and Polaroid.[54] The major advantage claimed for paying salaries is an improvement in employer-employee relations as a result of the elimination of distinctions based on pay methods. Most studies do not show that a salary system improves productivity. Moreover, some studies have found that absenteeism does initially increase after a salary program has been initiated, although peer pressure and subtle management controls usually bring it back to acceptable levels.

Paying salaries to everyone seems to improve employer-employee relations and to re-duce class consciousness. But the big question concerns how paying salaries will affect long-run profitability and job security. Organizations that do not have a stable work flow might not be able to afford fixed salaries for everyone. Regardless of its long-term con-sequences, this issue is not a very serious concern to the employees in many organiza-tions because of the generous income-continuation and personal-leave policies in their company benefit packages.

PAY SECRECY VERSUS OPENNESS

The final issue concerns whether information about the amount of money that individu-als earn should be public or secret. Some pay systems are entirely open to the public;

anyone who asks is told. In fact, some public agencies and school systems have even gone so far as to publish complete lists of their employees and the salary each receives in local newspapers. Most employees do not appreciate this degree of openness.

At the other extreme is a **pay-secrecy** system in which an individual's pay is known only by that person, his or her immediate supervisor, and the employees in payroll. In some secret pay systems, the employee's employment contract clearly specifies that individual salaries are not to be revealed or discussed.

Between these two extremes are varying degrees of openness and secrecy. Most private companies have pay systems that are moderately secret. A survey of human resource officers found that only 18 percent believed pay should be open to observation. Most enterprises do not provide anything more than general pay data and certainly no information about individual salaries.[55]

At issue here is whether pay should be open or secret and what criteria should be used to decide. If the criteria for deciding are based on individual privacy and personal freedom, then a secret pay system would be favored. If the criterion is job satisfaction, then the policy may have to vary from one company to another. Executives generally assume that most employees prefer a secret pay system, but the research evidence on this point is mixed. Although some studies have found that open pay systems increase job satisfaction, others have found that such systems decrease satisfaction.[56]

If productivity is the criterion for choosing a pay system, then an open system is generally superior. Again, however, the research evidence is mixed. Apparently, the benefit of an open pay system depends on: (1) how accurately employees estimate the pay of their coworkers in the absence of confirming information, (2) how accurately performance can be measured, (3) whether the financial incentives for rewarding outstanding performance are large enough to be considered significant, and (4) the employees' need for additional income. To increase performance, an open pay system depends on sizable financial incentives and accurate performance measures.[57]

Compensation managers thus have many decisions to make as they perform their work. Numerous forms of individual, group, and company-wide incentives can be used in the design of a compensation system. Furthermore, compensation managers can choose between an hourly wage or a monthly salary, and they also have the choice of making pay information secret or open to the public. Although this array of options makes compensation administration rather complex, it also provides an excellent opportunity to design an effective compensation system that provides security, motivation, and equity.

INTERNATIONAL HRM

Financial incentives appear to raise productivity in every culture. Canada and Western Europe have increased their application of pay-for-performance programs, and they have instituted many of the individual and company-wide incentive programs found in the United States. Even communist countries have acknowledged the importance of "material incentives" and have implemented a variety of individual, group, and company-wide incentives to improve their economies.

The effects of wage incentives on individual motivation and national productivity are clearly shown by the social experiments in Cuba following the 1958 revolution. In 1961 the Cuban government imposed on the entire economy a uniform wage scale based on the principle of equal pay for equal work, regardless of company and industry. This scale had eight labor grades, with a ratio of 3.08 to 1 between the highest- and lowest-paid grades. Premiums were paid for outstanding quantity and quality of work and for adverse working conditions.

The results of the first compensation plan were very impressive in terms of national productivity growth. However, the Cuban leaders, at the suggestion of the Che Guevara, decided that it was time to install a "true communist consciousness." Their plan involved eliminating work schedules and replacing them with "consciousness schedules." Wages were frozen and financial incentives were eliminated entirely. Workers received 100 percent of their normal wages when they missed work for justifiable reasons and when they retired. All jobs paid the same rate of pay and the payment of overtime work was discontinued.

This plan started in 1967, and by 1970 it was labeled a disaster. Absenteeism reached 20 percent, individual efficiency levels were less than 60 percent of what they had been, and per capita consumption was down to 91 percent of its 1961 level.

In the 1971 party congress, a new compensation plan was announced, which: (1) reinstated the payment of wages according to quantity and quality produced, (2) canceled the pay to absent workers, and (3) provided premiums for difficult work.

The application of material incentives was further strengthened by the General Reform of Wages in 1980, which encouraged the formation of autonomous work teams, called brigades. These groups were paid according to their group productivity, and the wages were distributed among members according to their participation in the collective tasks.[58]

Cuba's average annual increase in labor productivity of 5.2 percent in the 1980s was attributed largely to changes in the compensation system. Subsequently, other communist countries, including Russia and China, adopted the concept of brigades, where workers are paid as a group based on the group's productivity. At the heart of the economic reforms in Russia is a new incentive system that provides incentives for managers to innovate and for workers to improve productivity. Russian enterprises also enjoy new rights to hire and fire workers and to determine wage levels.[59]

Visitors to China report that some factories there have incentive systems similar to American firms, with piece rates, group incentives, and profit sharing at the end of the year. These year-end bonuses are typical of most Asian countries, where incentives are paid in the form of an additional one or two month's salary, depending on the profitability of the company and the performance of the work group. In Asian countries, individual incentives are rare, especially in Japan, where the culture emphasizes collective accomplishments rather than individual accomplishments.[60]

SUMMARY

A. The major theories of motivation predict different and, in some cases, contradictory effects of money. According to Maslow's need hierarchy and McClelland's need for achievement, money has the potential of being a useful motivator but other needs are far more important in influencing behavior. According to Herzberg's motivator/hygiene theory, money is a hygiene factor that can create dissatisfaction if it is not adequate but cannot be used effectively to motivate behavior. Equity theory claims that money is one of the valuable outputs of an employment exchange and that employee satisfaction and productivity are influenced by the reward-input ratios of individuals relative to the reward-input ratios of other employees. According to operant conditioning and expectancy theory, financial incentives have the potential to increase productivity significantly if the appropriate reward contingencies are established.

B. Merit-pay increases represent a common form of individual incentive used to reward outstanding performance. Merit-pay increases are particularly relevant for jobs that are paid a fixed wage or salary and can only be subjectively evaluated.

C. Piece-rate incentives are effective when individual productivity can be accurately assessed and when employees have control over their rate of production. The major types of piece-rate incentives include straight piecework, differential piece rates, commission sales, and standard hour plans.

D. Piece-rate plans can be used to reward either individual or group productivity. Group incentive plans are used to reward group productivity and are generally effective when the work requires the cooperation of the entire work group. However, group incentives are not very useful for extremely large groups or when the output of the group cannot be measured accurately.

E. Suggestion systems represent a form of individual incentive in which individuals are rewarded for submitting creative suggestions. The ideas produced in a suggestion system generally create significant cost savings.

F. Studies evaluating the effectiveness of piece-rate incentive plans indicate that the development of such a plan typically increases productivity by as much as 40 to 60 percent. Piece-rate plans appear to create greater effort, improved work methods, better organization of work, and higher performance goals—all of which increase productivity.

G. In some situations piece-rate incentives have failed to motivate employees to higher levels of performance. Group norms of rate restriction sometimes limit the output of the group to arbitrarily low levels. Group norms restricting productivity are generally caused by a lack of trust in management and a fear that the jobs will be retimed.

H. Profit-sharing plans allow employees to share in the company's profits and thereby motivate employees to greater productivity. Cash plans provide bonus payments to employees at the end of each period, and deferred plans provide a sum of money for each individual in the form of a savings or pension.

I. Gainsharing plans reward employees with more money if they are more productive. Three gainsharing plans are Scanlon Plans, Rucker Plans, and improshare plans. A Scanlon Plan is a combination of profit-sharing and employee-suggestion plans. If revenue is increased through higher productivity and creative suggestions from employees, a greater share of the revenue is given to employees. Rucker Plans are similar to Scanlon Plans but they base pay on value added rather than revenue. Improshare ties pay to actual productivity rates.

J. An employee stock ownership plan (ESOP) is another form of a company-wide incentive plan that is designed to give employees a feeling of ownership in the company. However, ESOPs do not appear to have much influence on motivation or productivity because their economic value is not closely tied to individual efforts.

K. Executive compensation typically consists of salaries, bonuses, stock options, directors' fees, and nonfinancial rewards. Although executives typically claim that their compensation is tied to their performance, the relationship is not very direct. Executive salaries are largely influenced by the size of the organization and how high the executive is in the organizational hierarchy. Bonuses also are largely determined by an individual's level in the organization and the organization's ability to pay. Stock options are intended to motivate executives to work harder and to help the organization succeed. Their popularity depends largely on the tax advantages associated with them.

L. The establishment of a compensation system that contains both adequate security and adequate motivation requires a careful balancing between base pay and incentive pay. Adjusting the compensation package to achieve a proper balance of base pay, individual incentives, group incentives, and company-wide incentives is referred to as fine-tuning the compensation package. The fine-tuning process involves an analysis of the size and interdependence of the work group, the degree of control that workers have over their rate of production, and the ability to measure individual performance.

M. Some compensation specialists recommend eliminating hourly wage systems and replacing them with a monthly or annual salary as a means of reducing class consciousness and creating a greater spirit of unity and trust between management and employees. However, organizations that experience instability in their work flow may have difficulty paying salaries.

N. A pay-secrecy policy that asks employees not to discuss their salaries is recommended when organizations cannot make accurate performance measures or offer large incentives for individual performance. However, an open pay policy is recommended when individual performance can be accurately measured, when an organization is able to provide large financial incentives to reward effort, and when individuals are able to control the results of their performance.

QUESTIONS

1. What are the effects of financial incentives, according to the major theories of motivation? What influence do financial incentives have on job satisfaction and productivity?

2. What conditions are necessary for the following individual incentive plans to operate effectively: piecework, merit-pay increase, commission sales, and the standard hour plan?

3. What conditions make a group incentive system superior to an individual incentive system?

4. What conditions make a suggestion system effective?

5. What is "restriction of output," and why does it occur? What can be done to avoid it?

6. What are the advantages and disadvantages of "cash" profit-sharing plans and "deferred" profit-sharing plans? Should allocation formulas be simple so that everyone can easily understand them or complex so that employees will not question them?

7. Is it morally right for a chief executive officer to receive ten to twenty times as much compensation as a production worker? Should restrictions be placed on executive perks? Should perks be taxed?

8. In fine-tuning an incentive system, what problems would occur if excessive weight were placed on individual incentives? On group incentives? On profit sharing? On base salary?

9. What are the arguments for and against paying all workers a monthly salary rather than an hourly wage?

10. What are the advantages and disadvantages of a pay-secrecy policy? When would a company want to have an open pay system, and when would it want to have a secret pay system?

KEY TERMS

Allocation formula: The formula used in profit-sharing plans that determines how the profit is allocated to individuals; it is normally based on seniority and performance.

Bonus: The incentive pay that individuals generally receive for outstanding performance; it is not a part of their base pay.

Commission sales: A form of incentive pay offered to sales representatives whereby they receive a commission based on a fixed percentage of the merchandise they sell.

Differential piece-rate plan: A piece-rate incentive plan that provides a low piece rate for individuals who produce less than the standard and a high piece rate for individuals who meet or exceed the standard.

Equity theory: A theory of motivation that compares the ratio of rewards to inputs for one individual with the rewards-inputs ratio of other individuals.

Expectancy theory: A theory of motivation that explains how behavior is influenced by the expectation that effort is related to performance and that performance is related to valued rewards.

Fine-tuning compensation: Adjusting a compensation package to achieve a balance between security and motivation. Security is provided by a stable base pay, and motivation is provided by incentives that associate pay with performance.

Gainsharing: A pay-for-performance plan, such as a Scanlon Plan, a Rucker Plan, or an improshare plan. Most gainsharing plans encompass employee participation in their design.

Herzberg's hygiene/motivator theory: A theory of motivation that identifies two categories of needs: motivators and hygiene factors. Motivators are associated with the content of the job and contribute to individual motivation. Hygiene factors are associated with the environment in which the work is performed. Poor hygiene factors can cause dissatisfaction but do not create motivation. Pay is considered a hygiene factor.

Improshare: A pay-for-performance plan whose name comes from *im*proved *pro*ductivity through *shar*ing.

JND (Just noticeable difference): The amount of money required to make a significant difference in the perception of an incentive. For an individual at a low pay level, a small amount of money would constitute a just noticeable difference, but for a highly paid executive, only a large sum of money would be perceived as a significant incentive.

McClelland's achievement need: A theory of motivation built around the need for achievement and its influence on behavior.

Maslow's need hierarchy: A theory of motivation based on a hierarchy of five needs: physiological, safety, social, esteem, and self-actualization.

Merit pay: Increases in an employee's basic wage level based on performance levels.

Pay for performance: A pay system that ties pay to performance levels.

Pay secrecy: A policy that restricts employees from discussing their pay and limits the amount of information about pay that can be made public.

Piece rate: The amount of money that an employee receives for performing a particular unit of work.

Profit sharing: A program that allows employees to share in the profits of a company based on the profitability of the company and an allocation formula determining each employee's share.

Reinforcement theory (operant conditioning): A theory of motivation that says behavior is determined by the types of rewards or punishments associated with the behavior.

Restriction of output (soldiering): The practice of producing less than is possible. This restriction occurs when peer-group norms establish an arbitrarily low standard of performance.

Rucker Share-of-Production Plan: A company-wide incentive plan in which compensation is based on a ratio of income to the value added by the employees in the production process.

Scanlon Plan: A company-wide incentive plan that combines profit sharing with a suggestion system.

Skill Based Pay: A pay system is which an employee's pay is partially determined by the employee's skills as a means of motivating employees to acquire greater skills.

Standard hour plan: An individual or group incentive plan that pays a fixed rate per hour where the hour is measured by an hour's worth of work rather than by a standard sixty minutes.

Stock option: A part of the executive compensation program that allows employees to buy shares of the company's stock, usually at a reduced price.

Straight piecework: An individual incentive plan that provides a fixed rate of incentive pay for each item produced.

C O N C L U D I N G   C A S E

Profit-sharing Problems

The Valley Manufacturing Company is a very successful manufacturer of industrial equipment. The company, which was founded in 1975, has grown at a steady rate through effective production and marketing activities.

In 1987 the company had a very profitable year, and as a result, Christmas bonuses were given to all of the supervisors and executives. Naturally, the members of management were delighted to accept the bonuses, and many of them expressed the feeling that all of the employees should share in the profits.

At the beginning of 1988, a profit-sharing plan was designed, and the employees were told that 50 percent of the company's profits would be shared with them after the company's operating profit exceeded 18 percent of owner's equity. Since most of the employees did not understand what would have to occur to achieve 18 percent of owner's equity, they largely disregarded the announcement of the profit-sharing plan. The company had a very good year in 1988, and at the end of the year, each employee received a special profit-sharing bonus check equal to approximately 12.5 percent of his or her annual salary. Since the employees had not expected this money, they were surprised and elated.

During the next year, the employees were excited about the profit-sharing plan. Supervisors would frequently remind employees to work hard and to take pride in their work because their efforts would influence their share of the profit. The employees also would encourage each other, and they would discuss the profit-sharing plan during lunch hours and breaks. During 1989 the company again had a very good year, and the profit-sharing bonus amounted to 14.5 percent of each employee's annual salary.

During 1990 the company appeared to be on its way to another profitable year. Relationships between the supervisors

and the employees were generally positive and pleasant. Production problems were quickly solved. Absenteeism, tardiness, and turnover had been significantly reduced, and everything seemed to be running smoothly. The wage levels were higher than similar jobs in the surrounding area, and the employees seemed to feel satisfied with their compensation.

Although the company was running smoothly internally, the local economy was not doing well in 1990. The construction industry in particular was struggling, and as a result, the company lost some of its major contracts. Consequently, the company's profit did not exceed 18 percent of owner's equity in 1990, leaving no profit to be shared with the employees.

The announcement that there would be no profit-sharing bonuses produced angry responses from the employees. They accused management of taking advantage of them, and they expressed a lack of trust and confidence in top management. Relationships between supervisors and production workers deteriorated rapidly, and the human resource department was flooded with complaints regarding job assignments and working conditions. Absenteeism, tardiness, and turnover increased, and several of the best employees left the company to work elsewhere. Although they could not prove it, several supervisors believed that broken equipment was a result of sabotage and intentional destructiveness rather than normal wear.

The top management of the company believes that they would be better off if they had never had the profit-sharing plan. Although the plan seemed to work well during 1988 and 1989, the consequence of having no profit to share in 1990 appears to have been extremely destructive.

Questions:

1. What went wrong with the company's profit-sharing plan?

2. Was the company wrong in instituting a profit-sharing plan in the first place? Why or why not?

3. How should the profit-sharing plan have been changed to avoid the kinds of problems that arose?

NOTES

1. David C. McClelland, *The Achieving Society* (New York: The Free Press, 1961); David C. McClelland, "Achievement Motivation Can Be Developed," *Harvard Business Review* (November–December 1965): 6–24.

2. Frederick Herzberg, *Work and the Nature of Man* (Cleveland, Ohio: World Publishing, 1966).

3. Abraham Maslow, "A Theory of Human Motivation," *Psychological Review* 50 (1943): 370–96; Abraham Maslow, *Motivation and Personality* (New York: Harper, 1954).

4. Karl E. Weick, "The Concept of Equity in the Perception of Pay," *Administrative Science Quarterly* 2 (1966): 414–39; I. R. Andrews, "Wage Inequity and Job Performance: An Experimental Study," *Journal of Applied Psychology* 51 (1967): 39–45.

5. Robert L. Opshal and Marvin D. Dunnette, "The Role of Financial Compensation in Industrial Motivation," *Psychological Bulletin* 66 (1966): 94–118. For an excellent introduction to operant conditioning, see George Reynolds, *A Primer of Operant Conditioning*, rev. ed. (Glenview, Ill.: Scott, Foresman, 1975).

6. G. A. Yukl and G. P. Latham, "Consequences of Reinforcement Schedules and Incentive Magnitudes for Employee Performance: Problems Encountered in an Industrial Setting," *Journal of Applied Psychology* 60 (1975): 294–98; G. A. Yukl, K. N. Wexley, and J. D. Seymore, "Effectiveness of Pay Incentives Under Variable-Ratio and Continuous Reinforcement Schedules," *Journal of Applied Psychology* 56 (1972): 19–23. See also Kae H. Chung, *Motivational Theories and Practices* (Columbus, Ohio: Grid, 1977), 60–73.

7. Donald Schwab, "The Motivational Impact of a Compensation System on Employee Performance," *Organizational Behavior and Human Performance* 9 (1973): 215–25; Edward E. Lawler, "Reward Systems," in *Improving Life at Work*, eds. Richard Hackman and Lloyd Suttle (Santa Monica, Calif.: Goodyear, 1977).

8. Robert L. Heneman, David B. Greenberger, and Stephan Strasser, "The Relationship Between Pay-for-Perfor-

mance Perceptions and Pay Satisfaction," *Personnel Psychology* 41 (Winter 1988): 745–59.

9. Jill Kanin-Lovers and J. D. Graham, "Variable Merit Pay Program Links Pay to Performance," *Journal of Compensation and Benefits* 4 (July/August 1988): 34–36.

10. James L. Whitney, "Pay Concepts for the 1990s, Part II," *Compensation and Benefits Review* 20 (May/June 1988): 45–50.

11. Thomas Rollins, "Pay for Performance: Is it Worth the Trouble?" *Personnel Administrator* 33 (May 1988): 42–46.

12. Jay R. Schuster and Patricia K. Zingbeim, "Merit Pay: Is it Hopeless in the Public Sector?" *Personnel Administrator* 32 (October 1987): 83–84; John F. Sullivan, "The Future of Merit Pay Programs," *Compensation and Benefits Review* 20 (May/June 1988); 22–30.

13. Frederick W. Taylor, *Principles of Scientific Management* (New York: Norton, 1911).

14. M. Magnus, "Surveying the Diversity of Rewards," *Personnel Journal* 65 (December 1986): 69–74.

15. "Employee Award Programs," Personnel Policies Forum, The Bureau of National Affairs, survey no. 145 (September 1987).

16. "When Do They Work," Labor Letter, *Wall Street Journal* (March 15, 1988): 1.

17. John Hein, "Employee Suggestion Systems Pay," *Personnel Journal* (March 1973): 218–21; Abraham Pizam, "Some Correlates of Innovation Within Industrial Suggestion Systems," *Personnel Psychology* 27 (1974): 63–76.

18. National Industrial Conference Board, *System of Wage Payment* (1930).

19. Reported in S. H. Slichter, J. J. Healey, and E. R. Livernash, *The Impact of Collective Bargaining on Management* (Washington, D.C.: The Brookings Institution, 1960): 494.

20. M. S. Viteles, *Motivation and Morale in Industry* (New York: Norton, 1953). See also, Allan N. Nash and Stephen

J. Carroll, Jr., *The Management of Compensation* (Monterey, Calif.: Brooks/Cole, 1975): 199.

21. R. T. Dale, "Wage Incentives and Productivity," *Personnel* 34 (1959): 4–5.

22. Mitchell Fein, "Restoring the Incentive to Wage Incentive Plans," *The Conference Board Record* 9, no. 11 (November 1972).

23. James S. Devlin, "Wage Incentives: The Aetna Plan," presented at the LOMA Work Measurement Seminar (April 1975); Peter Lorenzi, "Underestimated Effects of Goals and Rewards: A Systematic Replication," *Journal of Organizational Behavior Management* 9, no. 2 (1988): 59–71.

24. "Ending Incentive Pay Hurts a Plant's Productivity and Bosses' Morale," *Wall Street Journal* (November 24, 1981); personal communication with Professor Charles Greene of Indiana University.

25. Martin Brown and Peter Philips, "The Decline of Piece Rates in California Canneries, 1890–1960," *Industrial Relations* 25 (Winter 1986): 81–91; Michael A. Verespej, "Bye-Bye Piecework: Have Employees Design the New Plan," *Industry Week* 236 (June 20, 1988): 21–22.

26. Taylor, *Scientific Management*.

27. Esmond Lindop, "The Turbulent Birth of British Profit-Sharing," *Personnel Management* 21 (January 1989): 44–47.

28. See Daniel T. Rodgers, *The Work Ethic in Industrial America 1850–1920* (Chicago: University of Chicago Press, 1978), Chapter 2.

29. "As You Were Saying—Share Profits—Don't Freeze Them," *Personnel Journal* 54 (1972): 51. See also, Bert L. Metzger, *Profit Sharing in Perspective* (Evanston, Ill.: Profit Sharing Research Foundation, 1964).

30. Brian E. Moore and T. L. Ross, *The Scanlon Way to Improved Productivity* (New York: Wiley, 1978).

31. Metzger, *Profit Sharing*.

32. Thomas Owens, "Gainsharing," *Small Business Reports* 13 (December 1988): 19–28; Theresa M. Welbourne and Luis R. Gomez-Mejia, "Gainsharing Revisited," *Compensation and Benefits Review* 20 (July/August 1988): 19–28.

33. George J. McManus, "Weirton: Coming to Terms with Worker Ownership," *Iron Age* 4 (December 1988): 37–39; Michael Schroeder, "Has Weirton's ESOP Worked too Well?" *Business Week* (January 23, 1989): 66–67.

34. Barry B. Burr, "ESOPs Gaining More Forceful Roles," *Pensions and Investment Age* 17 (January 23, 1989): 1, 91; David H. Peirez, "ESOPs' Popularity on the Rise," *Pension World* 24 (October 1988): 59–61.

35. Mark Wachs, "ESOPs Bring Small Business Owners Tax Breaks," *Management Review* 77 (November 1988): 38–40.

36. Alan J. Schneider, "ESOPs: Now the Top Financing Card in the Treasurer's Hand," *Corporate Cashflow* 9 (October 1988): 56–59.

37. "ESOPs: Revolution or Ripoff?" *Business Week* (April 15, 1985): 94–108; "Gripes of Rath: Workers Who Bought Iowa Slaughterhouse Regret That They Did," *Wall Street Journal* (December 2, 1981); See also "Next: A Good, New Stock-Ownership Plan," *Business Week* (January 18, 1981): 120.

38. "Who Made What at the Top in U.S. Business," *Forbes* (June 3, 1985): 114–53.

39. Eugene F. Finkin, "How to Figure Out Executive Compensation," *Personnel Journal* 57, no. 7 (July 1978): 381–75; James T. Brinks, "Executive Compensation: Crossroads of the 80s," *The Personnel Administrator* 26, no. 12 (December 1981): 23–29.

40. A study by Graef S. Crystal of Towers, Perrin, Forster, & Crosby Consulting Firm, summarized in the *Wall Street Journal* (February 29, 1978).

41. Amanda Bennett, "More Managers Find Salary, Bonus Are Tied to Performance," *Wall Street Journal* (February 28, 1978).

42. Arch Patton, "Old Fashioned Initiative for Modern Enterprises," *Harvard Business Review* 32 (1954); 67–73; R. Smyth, *Financial Incentives for Management* (New York: McGraw-Hill, 1960).

43. J. Perham, "What's Wrong With Bonuses?" *Dun's Review and Modern Industry* 98 (1971): 41–44.

44. Amanda Bennett, "Executives Face Change in Awarding of Pay, Stock Options: Board Proposal Could Reduce Use of Benefit," *Wall Street Journal* (February 28, 1986).

45. Susan Chin, "The Power and the Pay," *Forbes* (May 29, 1989): 159–61.

46. Amanda Bennett, "A Great Leap Forward for Executive Pay," *Wall Street Journal* (April 24, 1989): B1.

47. Hewitt Associates, "Compensation and Benefits for Outside Directors in the *Fortune* 100 Industrials," survey (Lincolnshire, Ill., September 6, 1985).

48. Warner Woodworth, "The Scandalous Pay of the Corporate Elite," *Business and Society Review* 61 (Spring 1987): 22–27; "Corporate Leaders' Salary Ripoffs Disclose Double Standard Approach to Gain Union Concessions," *Operating Engineer* (November 1983): 20–23; Alan Farnham, "The Trust Gap," *Fortune* (December 4, 1989): 56–75.

49. Amanda Bennett, "Top Dollar: Corporate Chiefs' Compensation Far Outpaces Inflation and the Gains of Staffs," *Wall Street Journal* (March 28, 1988): 1, 12.

50. Alan Farnham, "The Trust Gap."

51. Amanda Bennett, "Top Dollar: Corporate Chiefs' Compensation Far Outpaces Inflation and the Gains of Staffs."

52. For illustrations of incentive adjustments, see Thomas H. Goodrich, "Just-in-Time With an Emphasis on Group Technology," *Manufacturing Systems* 6 (July 1988): 78–79; Edward P. Lazear, "Salaries and Piece Rates," *Journal of Business* 59 (July 1986): 405–31; Michael A. Verespej, "Strategic Manufacturing: Blue Collar Incentives (Part 18)," *Industry Week* 237 (July 4, 1988): 41–46.

53. Samuel Elliott, "Relief of Labor," *Journal of Social Change* 4, (1871): 139; E. L. Godkin, "The Labor Crisis," *Nation* 4 (1867): 335.

54. Robert Hulme and Richard Bevan, "The Blue-Collar Worker Goes on Salary," *Harvard Business Review* (March-April 1975); David Peach, "Salaries for Production Workers: What Happens?" *The Business Quarterly* (Spring 1974): 67–69.

55. Bureau of National Affairs, *Personnel Policies Forum*, Survey No. 97 (1972).

56. Edward Lawler, "Managers' Perceptions of Their Subordinates' Pay and of Their Superiors' Pay," *Personnel Psychology* 18 (1965): 413–22; Edward Lawler, "The Mythology of Management Compensation," *California Management Review* (Fall 1966): 11–22; George Milkovich and Phillip Anderson, "Management Compensation and Secrecy Policies," *Personnel Psychology* (Summer 1972): 293–302; Paul Thompson and John Pronsky, "Secrecy Disclosure in Management and Compensation," *Business Horizons* (June 1975): 67–74.

57. Thompson and Pronsky, "Secrecy Disclosure."

58. Alexis Codina Jimenez, "Worker Incentives in Cuba," *World Development* 15, no. 1 (1987): 127–37.

59. Robin Pringle, "Mr. Gorbachev's Economic Reforms," *Banker* 137 (February 1987): 15–17.

60. Robert E. Markland and Joseph C. Ullman, "Climbing the Great Wall," *Business and Economic Review* 33, no. 2, (January/February/March 1987): 30–34.

Employee Benefits and Pay Regulations

Learning Objectives

After studying this chapter, you should be able to:

1. Define employee benefits and explain why they have become such a significant part of employee compensation.
2. Identify and describe the major kinds of employee benefits that employers typically provide.
3. Explain four ways of calculating the costs of employee benefits.
4. List the three benefits that every employer is required to contribute toward and explain their provisions.
5. Describe the various kinds of pension and retirement programs and the laws regulating them.
6. Identify the major federal laws that regulate compensation and explain the central requirements of each.

Chapter Outline

Optional Benefits
Growth of Benefits / Costing the Benefits Plan / The Justification of Benefits / Health and Accident Insurance / Life Insurance and Income Continuation / Pay for Time Not Worked / Employee Services / Flexible Benefits

Required Benefits
Workers' Compensation / Unemployment Compensation / Social Security

Pay Regulations
Retirement Income / Company Pension Plans / Minimum-wage Standards / Fair and Equitable Wage Laws / Pay Deductions / Benefits Continuation

International HRM

Designing a Benefits Package

Six weeks ago the employees of the Silver Stone Company voted to organize a union. Since then, representatives of the union have been meeting with management representatives to negotiate a collective-bargaining agreement. The issues regarding work scheduling, discipline procedures, grievance handling, and promotions have been resolved. The issues still pending concern pay and benefits.

Before the election, Silver Stone provided very few employee benefits. No pension, no health insurance, no accident insurance, no life insurance, no dental insurance, and no paid vacations or sick leave were provided. A neighboring company in the electronics industry offers all of these benefits to its employees, and during the election campaign, the union organizers promised that the union would negotiate a similar benefit package for Silver Stone's employees. Many employees voted in favor of the union, thinking that they would no longer have to pay their own medical or dental expenses and that the company would provide a good pension.

During the past few days of negotiation, the union representatives have come to realize that they cannot continue to press for all of their benefits demands and still expect a significant increase in wages. A serious controversy has developed among the members of the union's bargaining team over which

benefits they should continue to demand. One member thinks they should drop dental coverage because of its expense and uneven usage. Another member thinks they should drop the pension plan because many employees have their own individual retirement accounts in addition to social security. The third member claims that the agreement will never be ratified by the membership unless both dental insurance and the pension plan are included. He thinks they should pursue their benefits demands even if they have to make significant wage concessions.

The union representatives need to reassess their position and decide what they really want. Since it is impossible for them to have everything they want, they must decide what they want most. Before they return to the bargaining table, they need to answer several questions.

Questions:
1. How can the union estimate how much each benefit will cost?
2. How should the union representatives decide which benefits are the most important to the union members? Should the decision be based on which benefits are the most popular?
3. What are the advantages of employer-provided benefits versus letting employees buy their own insurance and retirement coverage?

Employers are required by law to provide three benefits: social security, workers' compensation, and unemployment compensation. All other employee benefits are optional in the sense that the employer can choose not to offer them. Pension plans are optional, but if an employer decides to offer one, it must conform to the applicable state and federal regulations, especially the Employee Retirement Income Security Act (ERISA).

Workers today are seeking more, and different, benefits from their employers. Their desire for traditional benefits, including medical, dental, and life insurance, remains strong. But increasingly they also want new benefits, such as child-care assistance, flexible work hours, and parental leave. Future legislation may require employers to provide additional employee benefits. During the 1980s, congressional attention focused on taxing employee benefits as a means of increasing tax revenues. Legislation can have an enormous influence on the growth or decline of employee benefits.

OPTIONAL BENEFITS

In addition to their regular wages or salaries and the three benefits required by law, employees receive numerous supplemental rewards as part of the employment exchange. These **optional benefits** have different labels, including fringe benefits, employee services, supplementary compensation, indirect compensation, nonwage remuneration, and supplemental pay. In this chapter all of these supplemental rewards are referred to as employee benefits.

GROWTH OF BENEFITS

Before 1940 employee benefits were very limited. Only a handful of companies provided pension programs in which all employees were allowed to participate. Recreational facilities and social activities were sponsored by only a few companies. Company-sponsored dental, medical, and life insurance plans were virtually nonexistent. Most employees were paid only a wage and were expected to provide for their own medical care and retirement.

HISTORY OF BENEFITS

The rapid growth in employee benefits occurred in the 1940s during World War II. Because of war-time inflation, wage increases were strictly regulated by federal wage controls. Since no restrictions had been placed on benefits, however, employers who wanted to improve their compensation plans offered various employee benefits and services that did not violate the wage guidelines. At first, these new benefits were especially popular for managers and executives, but after the war, unions began to demand nonwage compensation increases for their members too. The right of unions to bargain for nonwage benefits was confirmed by court cases: *Inland Steel* v. *National Labor Relations Board* (1948) over pensions and *W. W. Cross* v. *National Labor Relations Board* over insurance.

Before 1970 benefits were usually called "fringe benefits," suggesting that they represented a small addition to the regular pay to make the compensation package more attractive. In recent years the word "fringe" has been dropped because benefits no longer represent a small addition to compensation. As a percentage of the total payroll costs, benefits have increased significantly. In 1929 the average benefits cost to the employer was only 3 percent of total wages and salaries. By 1949 the cost had increased to 16 percent, and by 1989 it was almost 40 percent.[1]

COSTING THE BENEFITS PLAN

Since employee benefits represent a major cost item for most companies, efforts to analyze and control benefit costs have become increasingly important. Four methods have been developed for analyzing the costs of employee benefit plans. The **annual-cost method** simply reports the total annual cost figure for each benefit. Although some benefits may seem difficult to measure, careful cost-accounting methods can be used to measure the cost of each benefit as well as the total cost for the entire benefit package.

The **cost per employee per year** is computed by dividing the total cost of each benefit by the number of employees receiving the benefit. Such an analysis might show that some very expensive benefits, such as legal counseling and alcohol and drug rehabilitation, are used by only a few employees. In addition to determining the cost per employee of each benefit, the company also may wish to aggregate the costs for all benefits. This figure, showing the total cost per employee, is especially meaningful when communicating with employees.

The **percent of payroll** shows the costs of benefits relative to the amounts spent for wages and salaries. This figure is particularly useful in making comparisons of the benefits costs of different companies. It is calculated by dividing the total annual cost of benefits by the total payroll cost. This produces a simple percentage figure that normally ranges between 20 and 60 percent for most companies. However, a company could feasibly spend more on benefits than on payroll, and as a result, the percent-of-payroll figure could exceed 100 percent. As noted earlier, the percent of payroll has increased dramatically, rising from 3 percent in 1929, to 16 percent in 1949, and to about 40 percent in 1989.

The **cents-per-hour** figure shows the costs of benefits per employee per hour. This figure is frequently used in expressing the costs of benefits, especially in union companies. It is also cited frequently in contract negotiations between unions and employers. Improvements in benefit plans are translated into cents-per-hour figures that become very important in the bargaining process.

The costs of employee benefits for various industry groups in 1988 are shown in Table 12.1 from data compiled annually by the United States Chamber of Commerce. The 1988 survey revealed that payments for employee benefits varied widely among the 932 reporting companies. At one extreme were twelve companies paying less than 18 percent of payroll for benefits, while nine firms paid 60 percent or more. Expressed as cents per payroll hour, the range was even more extreme. Ten percent of the firms paid less than $2.50 an hour, while the top 10 percent paid over $7.50 an hour. On an annual basis, the bottom 10 percent spent less than $5,200 per year per employee, while the top 10 percent paid over $14,684 per year per employee.[2]

THE JUSTIFICATION FOR BENEFITS

Why should companies provide employee benefits? Do employees have a right to receive benefits, and do employers have an obligation to provide them? These questions are especially relevant in view of the rising costs of health care and new laws requiring employers to assume a larger role in providing health and accident insurance.

TABLE 12.1 Major types of employee benefits, by selected industry groups

Industry group	Employee benefits as percent of payroll										
	Total, all employee benefits	Legally required payments (employer's share only)	Retirement and savings plan payments (employer's share only)	Life insurance and death benefits (employer's share only)	Medical and medically related benefits payments (employer's share only)	Paid rest periods	Payments for time not worked	Miscellaneous benefits	Total employee benefits as cents per payroll hour	Total employee benefits as dollars per year per employee	Number of companies
Total, all industries	37.0	8.9	5.0	0.6	8.7	2.3	10.6	0.9	519.8	10,750	932
Total, all manufacturing	36.4	8.8	4.5	0.6	9.7	1.7	10.2	0.9	557.8	11,758	273
Manufacture of:											
Textile products and apparel	33.3	9.5	3.6	0.3	7.5	4.9	7.2	0.2	316.4	6,605	15
Printing and publishing	30.4	9.2	4.8	0.5	5.0	1.2	8.9	0.7	439.9	8,282	19
Petroleum industry	46.1	8.9	9.8	1.2	10.2	2.6	12.8	0.4	881.3	18,381	13
Primary metal industries	42.8	13.2	2.1	0.4	17.2	0.8	7.6	1.4	645.1	13,635	8
Total, all nonmanufacturing	37.4	8.9	5.4	0.5	8.0	2.8	10.8	1.0	495.7	10,132	659
Public utilities (electric, gas, water, telephone, etc.)	42.3	8.0	6.8	1.0	10.5	2.7	12.4	0.8	721.4	15,195	113
Department stores	34.5	11.2	2.0	0.1	5.9	4.5	9.0	1.8	297.8	5,923	5
Insurance companies	34.4	8.0	5.2	0.5	7.2	1.8	10.3	1.5	505.6	10,018	114

Source: Reprinted with the permission of the Chamber of Commerce of the United States of America from *Employee Benefits 1988*. © 1989 Chamber of Commerce of the United States of America.

THE ETHICS OF REQUIRED BENEFITS

On one hand, it can be argued that no one has an inalienable right to receive benefits, and therefore employers do not have a moral responsibility to provide retirement pensions, paid vacations, or a safety net of insurance coverage for accidents and illnesses. Individuals are responsible for their own welfare. It can even be argued that employer-provided benefits are dysfunctional because employees become dependent on them and overlook their personal responsibility to provide for themselves.

On the other hand, even if employers do not have a moral responsibility to provide benefits, they do so for a combination of practical and humanitarian reasons. Some employers have developed attractive plans to help in recruiting and keeping employees. Other employers have established benefit plans to keep unions out or because unions are already present and have demanded benefit plans. Unions have tried to convince employers that benefit improvements are part of their social responsibility. Most employers also believe that a good benefit plan contributes to productivity and job satisfaction. The evidence, however, indicates that this belief is incorrect—benefits do not increase either satisfaction or productivity.[3]

The most important reason a majority of employers provide benefits is humanitarian. Most employees would not provide their own medical and accident insurance if the costs of these benefits were deducted from their paychecks. Consequently, many employers provide benefits because they believe the welfare of their employees is enhanced by the benefits. Benefit programs are based primarily on three philosophies:

1. Sharing the risks of accidents and illness
2. Forced savings for retirement or bad times
3. Sharing the costs of special services

In essence, benefit programs provide a dignified way for employees to receive a relatively secure and constant level of income, regardless of illness, accident, or time away from work. Benefit programs require employees to adopt an attitude of sharing and giving. Although wanting to get back as much as you put in is a natural attitude, many people must receive less than their fair share to fund those who have encountered serious misfortune. Benefit programs also force people to provide for themselves by requiring them to save for retirement. History has demonstrated that most people fail to provide adequately for their retirement years; therefore, society requires people to plan ahead. Rather than viewing this requirement as an unreasonable encroachment on individual liberties, it is typically viewed as a reasonable inducement to save for the future.

THE ETHICS OF UNEQUAL BENEFITS

Should all employees have equal access to employee benefits? In Mexico, the dominant pattern is that only salaried employees receive benefits. Blue-collar employees generally do not receive them and have to rely instead on an overloaded national health care system for their medical needs. In Argentina, likewise, private retirement pensions are provided by multinational companies, but only for senior management; other workers must rely on a social security plan that is struggling financially. In Germany, on the other hand, there has been an ongoing movement toward greater equality in both benefits and pay. In the German chemical industry, for example, similar benefits are available to all employees, and the distinctions between blue-collar and white-collar pay have mostly been eliminated.[4]

One ethical issue regarding unequal benefits concerns taxation and whether one group should receive more tax-free benefits than others. The allocation of benefits is usually unfair and discriminates in favor of those who are highly compensated. One of the central motives behind the historical development of benefits was the desire to give tax-free services to corporate officers. Employer-provided insurance, club memberships, and other benefits reduce the company's pretax income and protect executives from having to pay for them with their after-tax dollars. But this really isn't fair. In the United States, a federal law was passed in 1986 requiring employers to test whether their benefits favored highly compensated employees. Because the tests were so cumbersome, however, the law was repealed in 1989. Nevertheless, the issue of unequal benefits will not go away. It seems only fair that if highly compensated employees receive more or better benefits than others, the economic value of these extra benefits should be treated as taxable income.

The justifications for allowing benefits to skirt taxation are first, that benefits are a membership reward that everyone is supposed to share equally, and second, that individuals would not take the initiative to provide their own protection if the employer didn't do it. Allowing benefits to be distributed unequally is inconsistent with the first justification.

One radical proposal to correct these inequities is to treat all benefits that have a measurable economic value as taxable income. Individuals could then purchase whatever benefits or pensions they wanted and double coverage for two working spouses would be avoided. If individuals purchased their own health care, they would probably use medical services more restrictively, thereby slowing the advancing health care costs.

Judging by recent legislative changes to benefits coverage, it is apparent that Congress intends for employers to increase rather than decrease benefit coverage. Employers are required to continue benefits coverage for terminated workers and for the family members of deceased employees. Additional parental leave and dependent-care coverage are likely in the future.

VALUE OF EMPLOYEE BENEFITS

A careful cost-benefit analysis of employee benefits presents a very dismal picture. The costs of benefits have increased dramatically and now exceed 40 percent of the total payroll costs for many companies. Yet, employees place a minimal value on most benefits: they take benefits for granted, they assume that benefits will continue to increase, and they do not consider benefits as incentives to improve their work performance. Most employees do not understand either the breadth of their benefit plans or the costs of providing them. Most organizations have not performed an in-depth cost analysis of their benefit programs, nor have they carefully communicated this information to their employees.[5]

Many employers have been disappointed to discover that increased expenditures for employee benefits buy nothing for them. Studies suggest that no relationship exists between productivity and company benefits. Although good benefit plans seem to make recruiting easier, they do not increase productivity and their effects on satisfaction are not impressive. In some instances, benefits improvements have even decreased the satisfaction of employees who were unable to use the new benefits. One of the best studies on the growth of benefit plans found that organizational size was the best predictor of benefit improvements: large, bureaucratic companies tend to offer the most benefits. This study concluded that the tendency to improve employee benefits and services was just another manifestation of bureaucratization.[6]

Most employees have only a very limited knowledge of the benefits provided by their company. This tremendous lack of knowledge is illustrated by the results of a benefits survey of 3,300 employees in a large corporation. The employees were asked to answer a set of eighteen true-false and multiple-choice questions regarding important aspects of their benefits program. The average number of correct answers was only 7.5, not a very good score since they should have scored 6.0 by random guessing.[7]

In short, surveys on the effectiveness of employee benefit plans suggest that employees generally are not very knowledgeable about the benefits offered by their employers. Benefits do not increase job satisfaction, nor do they encourage employees to produce more. Whether benefits help in recruiting and retaining new employees is unclear. But what is clear is the enormous cost of benefits. The cost of benefits has increased even faster than the increase in wages and salaries. Employers apparently need to think more carefully about which benefits and services they should offer.

Although benefits packages vary dramatically from company to company, the various kinds of optional benefits can be classified into five major groups: (1) health and accident insurance, (2) life insurance and income continuation; (3) pay for the time not worked, (4) employee services, and (5) pensions. Because pensions are so extensively regulated, they are discussed later in this chapter under compensation regulations.

HEALTH AND ACCIDENT INSURANCE

The major forms of health and accident insurance are listed in Table 12.2.

1. Major medical and hospitalization coverage is provided by about 90 percent of most benefits plans. Major medical insurance usually covers surgeries and related expenses, such as anesthesia and in-hospital services. Childbirth was formerly covered by separate maternity benefit provisions. But childbirth, either by normal delivery or Caesarean

---

TABLE 12.2   Health and accident insurance

1. Major medical/hospitalization	5. Vision care and eyeglasses
2. Dental and orthodontic care	6. Health maintenance—
3. Chiropractic care	diagnostic visits/physical exams
4. Psychiatric care	

section, including ectopic pregnancy, is now treated as part of major medical coverage as a result of the 1978 pregnancy disability amendment to the 1964 Civil Rights Act. Expenses related to pregnancy, childbirth, and related medical conditions (but not abortions when the life of the mother is not endangered) have to be treated like other medical expenses in the benefit program. Hospitalization coverage usually includes the costs of a hospital room for an operation or an accident (sometimes limited to a semiprivate room), and many include treatment for mental illness or for alcohol or drug addiction. Some benefit plans also cover outpatient care and home care, such as visiting nurses or physical therapists. Since the care of employees with acquired immune deficiency syndrome (AIDS) is covered the same as other illness, the AIDS epidemic has significantly increased the costs of medical and hospitalization coverage. Efforts to contain these rising costs have included greater use of home care, nonphysician providers, and employee assistance programs.[8]

2. Dental and orthodontic coverage have been added to the majority of benefit plans. Most plans pay all expenses for the extraction or replacement of natural teeth when necessitated by an accident. Reimbursement is also provided for a percentage (usually 50 or 80 percent) of most other dental services, such as exams, crowns, X-rays, fluoride treatment, and cleaning.

3. For many years, chiropractic care was not covered by most benefit plans. In recent years, however, several plans have included separate provisions for chiropractic adjustments and orthopedic care. Other plans now treat chiropractic visits as regular doctor visits.

4. Psychiatric care is provided by a small percentage of benefit plans. Most psychiatric care benefits cover only part of the costs for psychiatric therapy for a limited number of visits, such as five sessions per calendar year. If the psychiatric care necessitates placing the employee in a hospital or mental institution, the costs are occasionally treated as part of the hospitalization coverage.

5. Vision care has been added to some benefit plans. Vision care normally provides employees with one eye examination and one pair of prescription glasses per year. Accidents causing damage to the eyes are usually covered under the major medical and hospitalization provisions of most benefit plans.

6. Diagnostic visits and physical exams are being covered by an increasing number of benefit plans. Avoiding poor health is less costly to both employers and employees than paying for accidents and illnesses. Many benefit plans now include special provisions for health maintenance. Health maintenance plans generally provide regular health and accident insurance coverage, and more importantly, they also provide preventive medical, dental, and eye care benefits for employees and their covered dependents. This form of health care was encouraged by the **Health Maintenance Organizations (HMO)** Act of 1973, which stimulated the development of *health maintenance organizations* (HMOs) for both public and private employees. The act requires that employers who are covered by the Fair Labor Standards Act and who have twenty-five or more employees offer employees the option of membership in a qualified health maintenance organization if they have a health benefit plan and if an HMO is located within fifty miles. An HMO is usually a clinic of participating physicians that provides medical care emphasizing preventive medicine. The cost to the employer is billed on a periodic basis without regard to the dates on which health services have been provided to employees; the cost is fixed, regardless of the frequency, extent, or kind of health service that has been furnished; and the cost is fixed under a community rating system. Essentially, employees can obtain basic health services as frequently as they need them at a fixed monthly cost.

Since the costs of medical services have increased dramatically in the past few years, insurance companies have been forced to raise the costs of health insurance premiums to cover benefit plans. The rising medical costs have been attributed to a lack of cost-consciousness on the part of hospitals and doctors, as well as employees. Hospitals and doctors have been criticized for charging exorbitant prices because they know that the bills will be paid by insurance companies. Employees sometimes request unnecessary medical services, and they are not particularly concerned about rising medical costs when they are fully covered by insurance.

Some companies have been forced to make changes in their medical benefits to reduce costs. The four most significant approaches to cost reduction include: (1) increasing the deductible amount or requiring an employee to pay the total cost of the first expense (e.g., $100 per year); (2) requiring employees to pay an increasing share of the insurance premiums; (3) changing the coinsurance percentage so that employees pay a larger part of the costs, such as increasing the percentage of chiropractic costs paid by the employee from 20 to 50 percent; and (4) holding the total coverage constant and adding new benefits only if others are deleted.

LIFE INSURANCE AND INCOME CONTINUATION

Benefit plans can create a valuable feeling of security by providing life insurance and various forms of income continuation. Accidents and illnesses that result in death are the most serious personal losses, but a permanent disability can also create a serious loss in the form of financial strain. If disabled employees cannot support themselves and their families and if they require extensive medical assistance, their financial burdens could become very great indeed. Life insurance and income-continuation plans help to alleviate such difficulties by sharing both the risks and the costs of accidents and illnesses. The major forms of insurance and income continuation are listed in Table 12.3.

1. *Group term life insurance* provides financial assistance to an employee's family if the employee dies. The costs of life insurance are normally lower under a group plan than under an individual plan. The amount of life insurance on each employee is usually some multiple of the employee's annual salary, such as one or two times the annual base salary. Most companies pay all of an employee's base premium, and employees are sometimes allowed to purchase additional coverage for themselves or other family members. Some group insurance plans have special features that: (1) cover all employees, regardless of health or physical condition; (2) allow an individual to convert from a group plan to an individual policy when leaving the company; or (3) continue coverage after retirement.

2. *Accidental death and dismemberment* is a special form of insurance coverage for accidents. If an accident results in death, the family or beneficiary receives a lump-sum payment.

TABLE 12.3   Life insurance and income continuation

1. Group term life insurance	5. Sick leave
2. Accidental death and dismemberment	6. Accident and sickness insurance
3. Long-term disability (LTD)	7. Supplemental unemployment
4. Severance pay	benefits (SUB)

If an accident results in the loss of limbs or sight, the injured person receives various benefits that are related to the seriousness of the loss, such as half the principal sum for loss of one foot, one hand, or sight in one eye and the full principal sum for loss of both hands or both feet or sight in both eyes.

3. Long-term disability (LTD) insurance is a method of providing disabled employees with long-term security. If an employee is unable to work because of an incapacitating accident or illness, LTD provides a continuing source of income until the employee returns to work or reaches retirement age. Most LTD payments do not begin until a fixed period of time (such as six months) has elapsed following certification by a doctor that the disability is one of long duration. During the waiting period, employees could receive workers' compensation benefits or accumulated sick-leave pay. LTD payments are usually about 60 percent of an employee's normal income, a sum that is reasonable since it is not taxed as ordinary income. LTD payments need to be large enough to provide adequate financial assistance but small enough to encourage disabled workers to return to work even if they need to develop new skills and find other employment.

4. *Severance pay* is designed to provide financial security when employees are terminated and have to look for new jobs. Severance pay typically amounts to one week's pay for each year of service. About one-fourth of union contracts require some form of severance pay.

5. *Sick leave* provides employees with the continuation of their regular pay when they are unable to work because of illness. Many organizations allow a specific number of sick days leave each year that may or may not be accumulated. The abuse of sick-leave benefits is a general problem in many organizations. For example, some employees call in sick when they want to go skiing or boating or when they wake up late and would rather miss the entire day than be tardy. Most organizations do not require evidence of illness unless strong evidence exists that sick-leave policies are being abused. As an incentive to discourage employees from abusing sick leave, some organizations allow employees to accumulate sick leave from year to year. Accumulated sick leave can then be used for extended periods of illness or recovery from an accident or applied toward early retirement. Another popular approach to the problem of sick-leave abuse is to give each employee a specified number of days off for *personal time* in addition to those allowed for sick leave.

These personal days can be added to an employee's annual vacation, or they can be accumulated for early retirement or recovery from a serious illness or accident.

6. *Accident and sickness insurance* provides income to employees who are unable to work because of accidents or illness. When this coverage is included in the benefit package, its terms are similar to those of medical and hospital insurance. The income is paid to an employee by the insurance company rather than by the employer. The benefits provided by these plans usually range from 50 to 75 percent of an employee's base pay and cover only the first six months of an illness after a one- or two-week waiting period.

7. Supplemental unemployment benefits (SUBS) are designed to increase the financial security of union members during periods of unemployment. Since regular unemployment compensation provides less than a full income for only a limited time period, some unions have attempted to protect the incomes of members who are unemployed through special SUB funds that have been established in contract negotiations with companies. About 6 million union members are covered by SUB clauses in their union contracts. SUBs are limited chiefly to unions in the auto, steel, and rubber industries, although scattered local unions in other industries also have negotiated SUB contracts. A company contributes a fixed amount, such as fifty cents per hour worked, into the SUB fund from which laid-off employees are paid. Under a United Rubber Workers plan, unemployed union members can receive about 80 percent of their former pay through state unemployment compensation and union SUB funds. The United Auto Workers plan provides laid-off auto workers with 95 percent of their take-home pay through SUB and unemployment compensation. During periods of recession, union members may be reminded that their SUB contract clauses do not guarantee financial security. For example, some of the SUB funds were exhausted during recent recessions.[9]

Additional disability and death benefits are provided through Social Security (and Medicare). Social security benefits are regulated by federal laws and are discussed later in this chapter under mandated benefits.

PAY FOR TIME NOT WORKED

Paid vacations and paid holidays create the impression that employees are being paid for not working and that the company is generously providing wonderful benefits. Consequently, vacations, holidays, personal excused absences, and other opportunities for not working are regarded as part of the benefit package. Some of the major forms of compensation for time off are listed in Table 12.4.

1. All employers consider it reasonable not to expect employees to work on holidays, but the question is, which holidays? In Charles Dickens's *A Christmas Carol*, an employee asks Ebenezer Scrooge for Christmas day off with pay. As Scrooge begrudgingly pays the employee, he remarks that Christmas is a poor excuse for picking a man's pocket once a year. Scrooge's philosophy about Christmas is not widely shared in the United States, where Christmas is the most generally acknowledged holiday.

The number of paid holidays in most companies has increased since 1970, when the norm was five to seven holidays per year. By 1989, most BLS area wage surveys indicated that about 80 percent of all industries had from seven to ten paid holidays.

TABLE 12.4 Major forms of compensation for time off	
1. Holidays	4. Union activities
2. Vacations	5. Reporting time
3. Personal time off	6. Sabbaticals

2. Paid vacations consist of continuing the employees' regular wages during vacation periods. Paid vacations are a relatively recent addition to many benefit plans. Before World War II, employees generally were not paid during their vacations; in fact, most employees were not even granted vacations. Today, however, paid vacations are a desirable employee benefit and are offered by 98 percent of all companies. Some employees would like to see the paid-vacation benefit further improved by the addition of a vacation bonus to cover recreational expenses.

Vacations generally benefit both the employees and the employer. Time away from the job provides opportunities for employees to rest and refresh themselves so that they will be more effective when they return. Some organizations insist that their employees take vacations and encourage them to go somewhere new and to spend the time doing something different. Other organizations tend to discourage vacations by providing a vacation-banking plan that enables employees to exchange their unused vacation time for additional salary or to accumulate the time and collect it upon termination or retirement.

The length of a vacation period is generally tied to an employee's length of service. A typical company vacation schedule is:

One week after six months to one year of service

Two weeks after one to four years of service

Three weeks after five to ten years of service

Four weeks after fifteen to twenty years of service

Paid vacations are the most expensive employee benefit. The costs do not seem so great, however, if the pay that employees receive during their vacations is regarded as money they have earned and held in a vacation reserve. This idea of a vacation trust is a useful concept that should be communicated to employees to counter the "something for nothing" notion that a paid vacation seems to create. Employees must perform well enough when they work to provide the resources to pay for their vacation time.

3. Personal time off with pay is provided for a variety of reasons, and most employees can be excused from work for good reasons, even if such reasons are not specified in the benefit plan. Employees who are summoned for jury duty are expected to be excused from work, although certain occupations are considered reasonable exemptions from jury duty. Most companies continue their employee's regular pay while they serve on a jury but reduce their pay by the amount they receive from the court. Marriage leaves of one to ten days are provided for employees who plan to continue employment after marriage. Military leaves are granted to employees serving in the armed forces. For short leaves, an employee's pay is usually continued (possibly reduced by the amount of military pay), but for long leaves, an employee is only assured of reemployment after discharge. Employees also may be excused from work with pay for various civic responsibilities. And on election days, employees are excused from work long enough to vote.

For family emergencies, such as illness, accident, or death, employees usually are given one to five days off with pay to assist in caring for family members or to attend a funeral. Parental leave of two to six months to care for a newborn or adopted child is provided for about three-fourths of the mothers and about one-sixth of the fathers. The role of men in child care is increasing, but not very rapidly. For example, Southern New England Telephone reports that in three years only seven men and 592 women have taken advantage of its unpaid leave policy.[10] Maternity and paternity leaves have been legislated in Sweden since 1974 and represent an interesting contrast to American practices. Employers in Sweden are required to hold open the jobs of new parents until they return to work. When a Swedish mother is employed outside the home, the husband and wife may decide which of them will stay home to care for the new child. Both parents are allowed 210 days of leave, and the spouse who remains at home is paid a salary that amounts to about 90 percent of his or her regular base salary paid by a state insurance program. This program is part of a major effort to actively involve fathers in the rearing of their children.[11]

4. Union activities often require union officers to be excused from work. The nature of the activities and the time allowed for them is specified in most labor contracts. For example, most unionized companies permit time off with pay to employees who are involved in a grievance procedure.

5. Reporting time guarantees that employees who report for work will receive a minimum amount of pay even if they do not work. In construction and manufacturing, for example, employees normally get paid for so many hours of work just for reporting to work even if there is nothing to do. If employees report for work and no work is available, they typically get paid for four hours of work. If the work is begun and is then stopped through no fault of the employees, each worker frequently receives a full day's pay.

6. Sabbatical leaves have been popular for college professors for many years. A few businesses have started to permit certain professionals and executives to have up to one year of sabbatical leave when they perform work that has value to society or that enhances their professional competence. For example, some executives are asked by their companies to become involved in urban development projects and other full-time civic activities.

EMPLOYEE SERVICES

Employee services include a broad range of benefits that are provided for a variety of reasons. Stock purchase plans, credit unions, and matched payroll-deduction savings

HRM in Action

Vested Vacations and Holidays

An employee handbook states that regular, full-time employees receive two optional days off (holidays) of their own choosing during each calendar year. Request for optional holidays must be made in advance and unused days cannot be carried over from one year to the next.

If an employee terminates without using his or her optional holidays, must the company pay the employee for those unused holidays? According to a published reply by the California State Labor Commissioner, the answer is yes. The response was based largely on the case of *Suastez* v. *Plastic Dress-Up Co.* (31 Cal 3d 774 1982), which determined that employees have a vested right to a prorated share of their paid vacations.

For example, if an employee who receives two weeks of paid vacation each year terminates after six months, this employee deserves one week of paid vacation and must be compensated for it. Based on these same principles of nonforfeiture, vesting, and proration, a company that offers two optional holidays must compensate employees who terminate early without using them for the portion they deserve.

This interpretation assumes that employee benefits are funded from the general assets of the company and employees have an absolute right to take these days for whatever purpose they wish so long as advance approval is obtained from the employer. However, paid sick leave and scheduled holidays would not be subject to proration, since these paid days off can be used only for their specific purpose.

Source: Letter by Lloyd W. Aubry, Jr., California State Labor Commissioner. Printed in *Personnel News*, May 1990, p. 7.

plans may be provided to encourage employees to save money and to develop their own financial estates. Legal services and emergency loans may be provided to help some employees keep their jobs or to stay out of jail. Charter flights, group tours, and other social and recreational facilities may be provided to create good morale and to satisfy the social needs of employees. Counseling services and alcohol and drug rehabilitation programs may be provided for humanitarian reasons to assist employees who need help.

Since about 1970, many organizations have established **employee assistance programs** that provide professional help for employees with personal problems. The most typical problems include alcoholism and drug use, financial indebtedness, emotional stress, and marriage and family problems. Alcoholism is the most frequent and most serious problem that is dealt with in employee assistance programs. Some programs have been described as worthless because of incompetent administration, inadequate professional help, and insufficient confidentiality. However, other programs (described in Chapter 15) have been highly praised for their success.[12]

Tax considerations are an important motive for providing employee services, since the monetary value of such services is not taxable to the employee and the company pays the same tax rate whether it spends the money on salaries or services. If, for example, an employee were allowed to use a company car as if it were his or her own, the value of this benefit would be much more than just the purchase price of the car. The total value would also include all car expenses, such as servicing, mechanical repairs, insurance, and property tax, plus the income tax the employee would have to pay if the value were added to his or her salary. Since 1985 the nonbusiness use of company cars has been taxed. The resulting cumbersome record-keeping and reporting requirements demanded by the Internal Revenue Service were designed to separate company-car business use from personal use in order to tax the personal-use portion. This example illustrates how the tax-free status of benefits significantly increases their monetary value to the employee. However, the monetary value of employee services may be reduced by future changes in the tax laws because the present system is more favorable to highly paid executives than to lower-level employees. The major employee services are listed in Table 12.5.

RETIREMENT COUNSELING

Within the past forty to fifty years, retirement has become a separate phase of life for which individuals plan and prepare. Longer life expectancies have contributed to the

---

TABLE 12.5   Employee services

1. Stock purchase plans
2. Credit unions
3. Matched payroll-deduction savings plans
4. Emergency loans
5. Matching gifts to charitable organizations or schools
6. Tuition for the employee and/or family members
7. Clothing and uniforms
8. Service awards
9. Christmas bonuses
10. Food services and cafeteria
11. Transportation and parking
12. Company car
13. Auto insurance
14. Liability coverage
15. Child care and day-care center
16. Child adoption
17. Moving and transfer allowances
18. Personal counseling
19. Legal assistance
20. Alcohol and drug rehabilitation
21. Gymnasium and physical training center
22. Recreation center
23. Group tours and charter flights
24. Discount privileges on purchases from the company

importance of retirement preparations. In 1920 the average life expectancy was only 47.3 years, largely because of the high infant-mortality rate. The average life expectancy in 1988 was 74.7 years. Although the longer life expectancy means that individuals could extend their working years, the trend is toward early retirement.

Prior to passage of the Social Security Act in 1935, a generally accepted age for retirement did not exist. Older individuals continued to work if their health permitted. After the passage of the Social Security Act, however, 65 became the generally accepted age for retirement, and many organizations established 65 as the mandatory retirement age. From 1900 to 1987, the percentage of the population over age 65 increased from 4 to 12 percent, while the percentage of men over age 65 who continued to work decreased from 67 to 17 percent.

In 1986 the mandatory retirement age was eliminated, primarily to encourage later retirement and to reduce the financial strain on Social Security funds. Nevertheless, the trend toward early retirement continues. Most individuals who have decided to retire are apparently not willing to reconsider their decision.

To help employees prepare for retirement, many organizations sponsor informal discussion groups in which workers can discuss their future plans. A survey of 267 companies found that 36 percent of them have formal preretirement counseling programs. About two-thirds of these programs include the spouses of employees in the counseling sessions. The majority of the counseling sessions examine Social Security, company pension plans, and other types of benefits or services provided by the employer after retirement. Some of the important topics that are covered include financial planning, wills and inheritance provisions, earning money after retirement, recreation and hobbies, health problems of older persons, and organizations for retirees. Some employers provide tuition aid, educational assistance, and publications describing activities for retired persons to encourage employees to prepare both financially and psychologically for the change. To help employees ease into a new style of life gradually, 15 percent of the companies surveyed even have "tapering off" programs that allow employees to reduce their work hours as they approach retirement.[13]

TRANSFER ASSISTANCE

When employees are transferred to new locations, they often receive **transfer assistance** in the form of allowances and other personal assistance. Most organizations have a policy of reimbursing reasonable moving expenses. Studies show that most major corporations pay over 90 percent of all direct out-of-pocket moving expenses, and in recent years, some companies have started to do even more to make transfers acceptable. Since both husband and wife may be employed, transferring one creates problems for both. Therefore, some companies now attempt to arrange a new position for the spouse of a transferred employee, even if the new position is with another organization. If the cost of living is higher in the new location, some companies offer a cost-of-living allowance that is usually a percentage add-on to the transferee's base salary. Moving to New York City or Honolulu, for example, might result in a 10 to 25 percent pay adjustment. To facilitate the change in residence, some companies agree to buy the employee's old home (which they resell) at a fair market value and to arrange a low-interest loan to buy a new home. If an income-tax liability results from the transfer allowances, the transferee also might receive an additional allowance to offset the liability. All of these benefits are in addition to the salary increase that typically is awarded with a promotion to a new position or given as an incentive to move.[14]

EXPATRIATE ALLOWANCES

It is expensive to station an executive overseas. When managers of multinational companies are assigned to work abroad, they normally draw additional compensation in the form of special **expatriate allowances**. These allowances are often as much as three or four times the executive's base salary, and they become complicated because of tax considerations. A typical compensation package includes base salary, premiums for foreign service and hardship, and allowances for cost of living, housing, storage, and taxes. Most companies pay on average an extra $10,000 a year for accepting the foreign post, plus another $8,000 if the assignment is considered hazardous or a hardship. Because living quarters overseas are often more expensive, most companies pay housing differentials that can range up to $100,000 for a family of four in Tokyo. Other differentials may include over $20,000 for goods and services, $5,000 or more for a car, $10,000 or more for travel to bring executives and their families back home each year, and several thousand dollars to pay the expatriates' increased tax liability.[15] These amounts illustrate how costly overseas assignments are for multinational organizations. The foreign-service premium and the area, or hardship, allowance are amounts that the employee is paid to accept the foreign assignment. All other allowances are intended to equalize the financial costs so that the costs of living abroad are comparable to the costs of remaining at home. The tax allowance is so costly because it involves a tax on a tax; that is, it is the amount paid to the expatriate to cover the high tax burden due to his or her overseas assignment, an amount which is itself taxable.

DEPENDENT CARE

An increasing number of employers try to help their employees shoulder the pressing responsibilities of caring for their families. These responsibilities include both elder care and child care, often referred to collectively as dependent care. The significant increase in female employment in recent years means that a large number of those who formerly provided dependent care in the home have now entered the work force, making child care and elder care very important benefits to these families. Many employers have discovered that dependent care is more than a humanitarian issue, it is also an economic issue since caring for a dependent tends to reduce attendance, increase stress, and decrease productivity.[16]

A much larger percentage of the work force has a responsibility to care for an aging family member than is generally recognized. It is estimated that between 23 and 30 percent of workers have some type of elder-care responsibility, and two-fifths of these people have been providing elder care for more than five years.[17] Caring for an aging parent can be very stressful, both physically and emotionally. For example, a large number of people who care for older people suffering from Alzheimer's disease experience upper respiratory illnesses. It is believed that the stress of caring for an Alzheimer's patient weakens the care-giver's immune system.

Employers have experimented with a variety of child-care programs, and most of their efforts have been judged successful. Probably the greatest deterrent to more extensive child-care programs is a philosophical belief that child-rearing is a responsibility better performed by parents than by companies or day-care centers. Although research in moral development abundantly demonstrates the vital role parents play in teaching moral values, some parents choose to work and others are required to work by economic necessity. Finding a dependable and affordable source of child care is a high priority for many working parents. The following are the five most popular forms of child-care benefits:

1. *On-site child-care facility.* The companies that have an on-site child-care facility number in the hundreds. They tend to be large companies, and many of them are hospitals. Sometimes neighboring companies form a consortium to provide an on-site facility. The major advantage of an on-site facility is that parents can visit their children during their breaks and lunch periods. The major disadvantages are legal liability for accidents and the cost of creating and maintaining the facility. Apple Computer and Campbell Soup Company created on-site child-care centers, which cost about $5,200 per year per child.[18] Another disadvantage shared by on-site child-care facilities is the spread of illness, which causes parents to have to stay home with sick children. One study found that parents who were able to arrange care for their children in their homes only lost .19 day per month because of sick children, while those whose children were in a day-care center missed an average of .52 day per month. In spite of the costs of on-site facilities, some companies believe they are cost effective due to improved attendance, productivity, and retention.[19]

2. *Child-care allowances and flexible spending accounts.* Since on-site day-care centers are not very feasible for small and medium-sized companies, some of these companies try to help employees by subsidizing their expenses in off-site centers or in their homes. A flexible spending account allows employees to pay their own child-care expenses with pretax dollars, which costs the employer nothing.

3. *Day-care information.* Some employers have provided excellent help for their employees by simply providing a resource and referral system. This information often includes names of day-care centers, rest homes, clinics, and babysitters.

4. *Flexible scheduling.* Being able to adjust work hours is occasionally very important to employees who are caring for others and cannot always control their schedule. Some of the most helpful schedule changes include flextime, permanent part-time jobs, and job sharing.

5. *Parental leave.* Some companies and the state of Washington have created a parental-leave policy that allows mothers and fathers of newborn or adopted children to take an unpaid leave for a period of time. Most European countries have had legislated parental-leave policies for several years, and this issue has been debated by the United States Congress. So far Congress has chosen to let companies create and regulate their own leave policies. About three-fourths of all companies have a formal maternity-leave policy, and some also provide paternity leave. For example, Colgate-Palmolive allows twelve weeks of unpaid leave for all salaried men and women for birth, adoption, family illness, or elder care. Eastman Kodak offers seventeen weeks of unpaid leave, and Aetna Life and Casualty offers up to six months of leave. After the first year of its new family-leave plan, Aetna found that the number of women who quit working after childbirth dropped from 23 to 12 percent.[20]

FLEXIBLE BENEFITS

One of the latest developments in employee benefits is not a new benefit but a change in the way benefits are offered. Benefit plans that include optional coverage, supplements to a standard program, or a choice in the kind of benefits desired are called **flexible benefits**. These plans also may be called **cafeteria benefits** or smorgasbord benefit plans, suggesting that the employees are permitted to choose their own benefit plans.[21]

A flexible benefit plan typically is a standard plan with a stated dollar value that employees are able to alter to fit their individual needs. Each employee selects his or her own benefit plan. Sometimes the individualized plans are required to have the same economic value as the standard plan. Other times, employees are allowed to select additional coverage if they pay the extra cost.

To illustrate, one flexible benefit plan offers employees a choice of three major medical plans: the standard plan, an improved plan with greater coverage and a small deductible, and a low-cost plan with a large deductible that requires employees to pay the first $500 of medical expenses each year. The company pays the cost of the standard plan, which is available to all employees unless they choose something different. If employees choose the improved plan, they must pay $2.54 a week for it. If they select the low-cost coverage, they receive a $3.35 credit that can be used to purchase increased life insurance, accidental death and dismemberment insurance, or dependent life insurance.

Flexible benefits plans are a tax-efficient form of compensation because of Section 125 of the Internal Revenue Code, which allows employees to choose between nontaxable benefits, taxable benefits, or cash. Although they have to pay income tax on the cash and taxable benefits they select, employees do not pay tax on the nontaxable benefits they select. Some examples of nontaxable benefits are group term life insurance (up to $50,000), medical insurance, dependent care for children, and group legal assistance.

Although there are several basic approaches to structuring a flexible benefits plan, the most highly recommended type for controlling costs involves a *flexible spending account*. A flexible spending account plan enables participants to pay health and dependent-care expenses with pretax dollars rather than after-tax dollars. This plan, sanctioned under Section 125 of the Internal Revenue Code, allows employees to designate how much of their income should be placed into their flexible spending account, and this money can be used to pay for any medical expenses, such as dental care, vision care, coinsurance, deductibles, and prescription drugs. The plan requires advanced annual withholding and money not used during the year is forfeited.[22]

Employer interest in flexible benefits has increased because such a plan enables a company to offer additional types of benefits without a corresponding increase in costs. Indeed, the costs of a flexible benefit plan seem to increase more slowly than those of a regular benefit plan because cost levels are reestablished and controlled more closely. Employees generally prefer a flexible benefit plan because it allows them to meet their own unique needs. Companies that have adopted flexible benefit plans generally find that about 80 percent of the employees make some change in their benefit plans. The tendency is to choose additional coverage.[23]

There are some major disadvantages to flexible benefits. (1) Designing and administering numerous individual plans can be extremely cumbersome; however, computerized systems can eliminate much of the administrative difficulty. (2) Implementing a

HRM in Action

Benefits Cost Containment Without Union Resistance

The Von's Companies, Inc., a 34,000-employee grocery company headquartered near Los Angeles, implemented a flexible benefits program designed to better meet employee needs and reduce benefit costs. The flexible program, first piloted in 1986 to 1,200 salaried and nonunion hourly employees, offered a variety of options in health insurance, life insurance, and vacation days through a flexible spending account.

As part of Von's total compensation philosophy, the flexible benefit program is tied to the company's annual profit-sharing allocation. Under this program, employees receive their share of the profits each year in the form of "flex dollars." These flex dollars can be deposited in the profit-sharing plan (and matched on a dollar-for-dollar basis by the company), taken in cash, or used to purchase benefits. The profit-sharing allocation has amounted to about 4 percent of each employee's annual pay. The benefit options that employees may select have real price tags that are tied to the actual costs of each benefit. Consequently, employees know how much both they and the company spend on benefits, and they have a better appreciation of the need to control these costs.

Before the flexible plan was introduced, the company had long maintained an expensive, noncontributing medical coverage plan, largely as a result of union pressure. To avoid creating opposition and resentment, the company decided to retain the expensive medical plan as an option, but it also introduced three other comprehensive plans with varying deductibles. After three years, employees had gradually abandoned the expensive plan in preference for other plans requiring employee contributions.

The flexible benefits program has provided Von's with a framework for incorporating employee cost sharing, and this cost sharing has resulted in reduced health-care expenditures.

Source: "On Flexible Compensation," by Hewitt Associates, October 1989.

flexible benefits plan requires extensive communication to educate employees about their benefit options and to help them make wise decisions. (3) The cost-savings and shared-risk components of flexible benefits are largely lost through *adverse selection*, in which bad-risk employees choose a benefit and good-risk employees do not (for example, orthodontia coverage is predominantly selected by employees with children between ages five and fifteen who need braces).

A few studies have examined the benefits preferences of employees and have found that the kinds of benefits employees want are significantly influenced by their age, marital status, and number of dependents. The results of one study are shown in Table 12.6. This study used a paired-comparison technique in which employees were asked to evaluate eight benefits by comparing two at a time. Each benefit was matched with every other benefit, and the numbers in the table indicate how often each benefit was preferred over the others. The eight benefits were: (1) a shorter workday of seven hours and thirty-five minutes; (2) a four-day workweek of nine hours and thirty minutes each day; (3) ten Fridays off each year with full pay; (4) early retirement; (5) two additional weeks of paid vacation per year; (6) a 5 percent pay increase; (7) a pension increase of seventy-five

TABLE 12.6   Preference ratings and *F*-ratios of eight benefits (*n* = 149 employees in a public utility company)

Option	Age in Years				Marital Status			Dependents			
	18–35 (*n* = 52)	36–49 (*n* = 58)	50–65 (*n* = 39)	F	Single (*n* = 62)	Married (*n* = 97)	F	0 (*n* = 33)	1–3 (*n* = 60)	4 or more (*n* = 66)	F
Extra vacation	5.00	4.67	5.21	1.12	4.86	4.88	.04	4.72	4.93	4.97	.19
Pay increase	4.70	4.71	4.09	1.50	4.68	4.34	1.17	4.79	4.40	4.44	.55
Pension increase	3.00	4.08	5.59	19.82†	3.56	4.23	3.93*	4.67	4.42	3.32	6.16†
Dental plan	4.35	3.69	1.71	12.09†	2.78	3.91	6.52†	1.79	3.03	4.93	21.42†
Early retirement	2.81	3.48	3.65	1.91	3.20	3.32	.10	3.64	3.30	3.07	.74
10 Fridays off	3.19	2.67	3.48	2.63	3.20	3.04	.30	3.48	2.97	3.05	1.12
Four-day week	3.63	2.67	2.26	3.48*	3.06	2.73	.61	2.67	2.60	3.30	1.40
Shorter workday	1.23	1.42	1.47	.26	1.54	1.19	1.80	1.94	1.28	.96	4.70†

*p < .05   †p > .01

The numbers refer to how often each benefit was preferred when compared with the other seven benefits in a paired-comparison technique.

Source: From Chapman, J. Brad, and Robert Otteman, "Employee Preference for Various Compensation and Fringe Benefit Options." Reprinted with permission from the November 1975 issue of *Personnel Administrator.* Copyright © 1975 by The American Society for Personnel Administration, Berea, Ohio.

dollars per month; and (8) family dental insurance. The overall results indicated that extra vacation and a pay increase were the most preferred items and that a shorter workday was the least preferred benefit. However, there were significant demographic variations in preferences. Younger employees were more in favor of the family dental plan and the four-day workweek, while older workers preferred a pension increase. Married workers had stronger preferences for a pension increase and the family dental plan than single workers. The desire for the family dental plan also was significantly related to the number of dependents. Employees with four or more dependents had a much stronger preference for dental coverage than employees with no dependents.[24]

REQUIRED BENEFITS

Employers are not required to provide medical insurance, life insurance, and other employee services, but they must participate in providing three mandated benefits. The **mandatory benefits** are workers' compensation, unemployment compensation, and

Social Security. Also, although employers are not required to provide pensions for their employees, they must abide by extensive laws governing pension plans if they choose to provide such plans. Because the existing laws are frequently amended and new laws are created, students and managers who want to know the current laws should consult the publications of an agency such as the Commerce Clearing House, available in most libraries.

WORKERS' COMPENSATION

Before the level of social consciousness regarding sex discrimination was raised in the 1970s, **workers' compensation** was known as workmen's compensation. Many legal publications continue to use the label workmen's compensation, and students desiring to study the background of workers' compensation will need to use the earlier label for their research.

The conditions that created the need for workers' compensation laws are illustrated by this account:

> On October 17, 1906, Adam Rogalas, a Russian laborer paid $1.60 a day by the Iron City Grain Elevator Company of Pittsburgh, was sent with two other men to do some work in an adjoining building that was used by the company for storage. The supports of the floor above the workers gave way, and the floor fell onto the workers. One of the workmen escaped, another was injured, and Rogalas was killed. At the inquest into Rogalas's death, a building inspector testified that the floor supports were obviously inadequate. Rogalas had a wife and four children, ages ten, six, five, and two, but he had no savings. According to Mrs. Rogalas, the claim agent of the company had offered to settle with her for $400, which she had refused. Instead, she put her case into the hands of a lawyer, and a suit for $20,000 was entered. Meanwhile, to make ends meet, Mrs. Rogalas took in washing, accepted six-dollars worth of groceries monthly from the city poor relief, and begged at the door of her Catholic church on Sundays. Mrs. Rogalas's sister, who had a family of six, did what little she could to help, and the widow's lawyer occasionally advanced her ten dollars. Mrs. Rogalas, who had another child six months after the accident, was seen, in severe winter weather, wearing shoes so old that her feet were exposed. It was the end of the year before Mrs. Rogalas's suit came to trial. The court instructed the jury to return a verdict for the defendant and the widow lost her case.[25]

This episode, which was published in 1910 along with hundreds of similar stories, illustrates the difficulty that survivors faced in seeking compensation for industrial accidents. Such stories greatly influenced public sentiment and led to the passage of state workers' compensation laws, starting in 1910. Although public sentiment generally supported the idea that injured workers deserved some sort of compensation, making employers liable to exorbitant civil suits also seemed unfair.

COMMON LAW DEFENSES

Prior to 1910 the liability for an industrial accident was decided according to the English common law system. During the nineteenth century, legal protection was definitely on the side of the employer. Three common-law defenses were available to employers to protect them from liability suits by injured employees:

1. The *assumption-of-risk* doctrine held that employees, upon entering into employment, agreed to assume the ordinary risks incident to the job. Hence, the employer was not liable.
2. The *fellow-servant* rule held that the employer was not liable if coworkers of the injured employee had been negligent.
3. The *contributory negligence* doctrine held that the employer was not liable if an injured worker's own negligence in any way contributed to the cause of the accident.

These three common-law defenses made it almost impossible for injured workers to sue an employer. Injured workers had to prove that neither they nor their coworkers had contributed in any way to the accident and that it had been caused entirely by negligence on the part of the employer. This standard of proof was almost impossible to meet because coworkers and professional witnesses were reluctant to testify against an employer. But even if the court decided in a worker's favor, the victory did not amount to much. Most of the money that was awarded had to be used to pay legal expenses and court fees, and if the injured worker received anything, it was usually only a small amount received years after the injury in question.

LIABILITY WITHOUT FAULT

The situation changed in 1910, when the New York state legislature passed the Workmen's Compensation Act. Even though the New York law was declared unconstitutional, ten more state legislatures adopted similar compensation acts in the following year. These laws were passed in response to the reports of several state commissions that had investigated employer's liability acts. By 1921 workers' compensation laws had been enacted by forty-two states, by three territories, and by the federal government for its civil employees.[26] Since 1948 all states have had some form of workers' compensation.

New York's law was compulsory. When it was declared unconstitutional, some state legislatures decided to make their laws elective. New Jersey, for example, adopted an elective law that permits employees and employers to choose whether they will come under the statute. If they do not elect coverage under the statute, both parties must sign a written contract of hiring indicating that the workers' compensation law does not apply to them and that the employer is not allowed to use the three common-law defenses if an injured worker brings suit. About half of the states have similar elective laws.

The basic concept underlying workers' compensation laws is *liability without fault*, meaning that an injured employee is entitled to a moderate and reasonable amount of compensation, regardless of who causes the accident. A second underlying concept is that such compensation is part of the expense of production and therefore is chargeable to the employer. Worker's compensation laws provide immediate financial aid for injured workers and remove the need for lawsuits and the common-law defenses.

COVERAGE

Because each state has its own workers' compensation law, the provisions are not all the same.[27] To be covered by a workers' compensation law and be eligible for benefits, employees must work for a covered employer in a covered job. Some state laws only cover jobs in industries involving hazardous occupations. Other laws exempt employees in agriculture and domestic service. Most states exempt small businesses, such as those with fewer than five employees; however, they provide elective coverage for sole proprietors, partners, and corporate officers.

INJURIES COVERED

The various state laws are not very explicit in describing what kinds of injuries are covered and how they must occur if workers are to receive benefits. Most laws simply say that they cover injuries "arising out of *and* in the course of" the employment. Most of the state laws also explicitly cover occupational diseases arising out of employment. Mental injuries resulting from stress are covered by some state's laws; but excessive litigation and exorbitant costs are forcing some states, especially California, to reevaluate their coverage of mental health problems.[28]

WAITING PERIOD

After an injury occurs, almost all of the state laws require a certain waiting period, usually one or two weeks, before compensation becomes available. Sometimes, when the injury is severe or disables the employee for a long time, compensation may later be paid for part or all of the waiting time. The purpose of the waiting period is to reduce the costs. The laws assume that employees should bear some of the cost of their injuries and that a short waiting period is not too great a loss. The laws also seem to assume that a longer waiting period reduces the likelihood that an injured employee will exaggerate a trivial injury.

BENEFITS

Under workers' compensation laws, three types of benefits are provided by most states: death benefits, medical expenses, and wage-replacement payments. The death benefits are a one-time lump sum paid to the survivor. Hospital and medical payments are usually paid immediately after the injury without a specified waiting period. Some states place limits on the amounts that will be paid for each injury and the length of time a disability is covered. Other states have no limitations on time and amount.

Wage-replacement payments, after the waiting period, are usually between 50 and 70 percent of a worker's average weekly wages. In some states, however, the rate varies according to marital status, number of children, or other conditions. To reduce their worker's compensation costs, many companies try to involve injured workers in therapy and rehabilitation programs, thereby helping them return to their former jobs or re-stricted-duty jobs as quickly as possible.[29]

FUNDING

Workers' compensation benefits are basically funded under an insurance program through one of four methods. First, the benefits might be provided by a private insurance company. Second, a company might be self-insured if it is large enough and can demonstrate that it has sufficient capability to handle such funding. Third, a state might have its own exclusive fund and act as a monopolistic insurer of accidents. Fourth, a state fund

▌ **HRM in Action**

Early Return to Work Programs

The ultimate method for reducing worker's compensation costs is to prevent accidents from happening. But after they have occurred, the key to containing costs is to get injured workers back on the job as quickly as possible.

Companies that have developed early return to work programs report that they have significantly reduced their insurance costs and increased worker morale. With an early return to work program, injured employees are required to report to work as soon as it is physically possible for them to do so, even if they can only sit on a chair or lie on a couch. If they cannot perform their regular jobs, they are reassigned to other jobs consistent with their limitations. They receive their normal pay even if they can only sort papers or answer phones.

The benefits of an early return to work program were demonstrated by two matched hospitals. Hospital A implemented an early-return policy in 1980 and during the next three years its average lost work days per accident was only 13.5 compared with 18.5 for Hospital B. Hospital A also obtained a 39 percent reduction in its insurance premium rate because of an improved experience rating.

In 1987, Consolidated Freightways started a program it called a "Transitional Return to Work Program" (TRWP). The program was credited with reducing the number of lost time injuries rate from 66 in 1986, to 41 in 1987, and to 29 in 1988.

A matched comparison of two mining companies also provides an impressive contrast. Barrick Mercur Mining, which has an active early return program, has an experience rating that is only 42 percent as much the experience rating of C. W. Mining, which has no program. Barrick Mercur's loss ratio of lost days per accident is only .25, compared with 9.07 for C. W. Mining.

The improvement in worker morale may be even more significant than the financial benefits from reduced insurance costs. By returning to work injured employees tend to view themselves as productive and self-sustaining rather than as invalids or handicapped.

Data supplied by Elliot Morris, Legal Council for the Utah State Worker's Compensation Insurance Fund, 1990.

might be a competitive fund that competes with private insurers to insure companies. In each method, the insurance premiums are paid by the employers. The costs to a company are determined by its **experience rating**, which is based on the number of payments made under workers' compensation to the employees of that company. For example, companies that have poor safety records are required to pay high workers' compensation premiums. This approach is intended to encourage employers to improve their safety records.

The initial cost of workers' compensation depends largely on a company's industry classification and the state in which it is located. In states with the lowest costs, the cost of workers' compensation is about 2 to 5 percent of payroll for reasonably safe industries, such as 3.9 percent for carpentry, 1.4 percent for electronics, and 3.4 percent for cement products. In high-accident industries the costs can be considerably greater, such as 22 percent for explosives manufacturing and 36 percent for building demolition. In states with the highest costs, employers in unsafe industries may be required to pay as much for workers' compensation as they do for wages.

UNEMPLOYMENT COMPENSATION

Unemployment compensation was established as part of the Social Security Act of 1935. During the Great Depression, the unemployment rate was extraordinarily high (almost 25 percent), and public sentiment was sympathetic to people who were out of work through no fault of their own. A national unemployment compensation program was created by two titles of the Social Security Act. One of these titles, the one regulating the tax on employers, was later incorporated into the Internal Revenue Code as the Federal Unemployment Tax Act (FUTA). The purpose of this act is to provide short-term subsistence to laid-off workers while they are looking for other employment. FUTA applies to employers who employ one or more employees for twenty weeks or who pay wages of $1,500 or more in any quarter of a calendar year.

Unemployment compensation programs are administered jointly by the federal and state governments, but the bulk of the responsibility falls on the state. Initially, the federal tax levied on employers was only 1 percent of the first $3,000 they paid to each employee. These rates increased over the next fifty years, so that by 1985 the tax rate was 6.2 percent on the first $7,000 of annual wages paid to each employee. However, the Social Security Act encouraged states to create and administer their own unemployment programs by allowing a tax credit to employers. In 1985 the tax credit was 5.4 percent to employers who paid state taxes under an approved state plan. Since all states have approved plans, the federal tax rate for all employers is only .8 percent (6.2 minus 5.4).

The federal tax is used to pay all of the administrative costs, both state and federal, associated with unemployment compensation programs. Money to administer the programs is sent back to the states through the congressional budgeting process, in accordance with standards established by the federal government. However, each state has its own procedures for administering the program, and some states are much more efficient than others. To have an approved plan, the state unemployment compensation programs must meet federal requirements for financing and coverage.

States are free to assess different tax rates to employers, depending on their unemployment rates. As a result, actual tax rates vary greatly among the states and among individual employers within each state. In 1988 the estimated average tax rate was 2.4 percent of taxable wages, ranging from a high of 5.4 percent in Michigan, with a taxable base of $8,500, to a low of .7 percent in Florida, with a base of $7,000. As a percentage of total wages, the national average tax rate was 1.0 percent.[30]

There are no federal standards for benefit amounts, qualifying requirements, or duration of regular benefits. Consequently, the states have developed diverse and complex formulas for determining benefits. Payment is typically about 50 percent of a worker's former weekly wage. The Social Security Act initially provided twenty-six weeks of coverage, but during periods of high unemployment, this has been extended by Congress and/or state legislatures to as much as sixty-five weeks.

To be eligible for unemployment compensation, individuals must have been employed a minimum length of time in jobs covered by the Social Security Act, must be currently unemployed, and must be willing to accept suitable employment if it is offered to them. Employees can be disqualified for unemployment compensation if they quit or were fired. Individuals are usually expected to demonstrate that they are willing to accept work by periodically reporting to the local employment service to seek suitable job opportunities. However, the term "suitable employment" is subjectively defined, and some individuals do not accept employment until their benefits are about to end or unless a new job pays very well.

Except for four states that require employees to contribute to the funds, the costs of supporting an unemployment compensation program are born by employers. However, costs are not uniform for all employers. The costs to each company are based on the average number of employees from that company who are drawing the funds—called the experience rating. A separate account of unemployment compensation claims is maintained for each employer, and if a surplus is accumulated in an employer's account, the tax rate is reduced. Since new employers do not have an experience rating, they are assigned the average of their industry for the first year. As unemployment in a geographical region increases, both the unemployment compensation claims of employees and the costs to employers increase. To minimize their unemployment compensation tax payments, employers strive to smooth their employment demands and avoid layoffs.

SOCIAL SECURITY

During the Depression, one-fourth of the work force was unemployed, and many older workers had little or no savings. For most Americans, government handouts were not socially acceptable, no matter how badly they were needed. Programs such as the Townsend Plan, which proposed to retire all workers at a specified age and to have them receive government doles, were defeated in Congress. Finally, in 1935, the **Social Security** Act was passed as the Old Age Survivor's Insurance (OASI) Act. This act was more acceptable than previous plans because, rather than providing government doles, it forced employees to save for their retirement years during their working years. The original tax rate of this savings plan was 1 percent of the first $3,000 earned, which meant that the most an employee had to pay was $30 per year. Employers were required to pay matching contributions to the fund.

At first, Social Security only covered a worker upon retirement, but in 1939 the law was amended to pay survivors when the worker died as well as certain dependents when the worker retired. Social Security only covered workers in private industry, until 1950, when it was extended to include most self-employed persons, most state and local employees, members of the armed forces, and members of the clergy. Today, almost all jobs in the United States are covered by Social Security, except state and local government employees who have their own pension plans that were created before 1983.

Disability insurance benefits were added to the Social Security Act in 1959, making it the Old Age Survivors and Disability Insurance Act (OASDI). The disability insurance provided protection against loss of earnings due to total disability. The Social Security program was expanded again in 1965, with the addition of Medicare, which provided hospital and medical insurance protection for individuals aged 65 and older. Since 1973 Medicare benefits also have been available to individuals under age 65 if they are disabled or have kidney failure. In 1972 a significant amendment to the act provided for automatic increases in benefits as the consumer price index changed, and in 1977 an amendment allowed tax rates to be raised to pay for the added benefits. The 1983 amendment increased the self-employed tax rate to make it equal to the combined rates of the employer and employee.

SOCIAL SECURITY BENEFITS

Individuals who want to know if they are covered by Social Security or how much they could receive should contact their local Social Security office. Four basic types of insurance benefits are provided by the Social Security Act:

1. *Old-age or disability benefits.* Workers who retire or become severely disabled may be eligible to receive a monthly Social Security check. The normal retirement age is 65, although it is possible to retire at age 62 with a 20 percent reduction in benefits. Retirement age is scheduled to rise gradually from 65 to 67 after the turn of the century. To be considered disabled, a worker must have a severe physical or mental condition that prevents him or her from working and that is expected to last at least twelve months.

The monthly cash benefits paid to retired or disabled workers are determined by their work credits and by their average earnings. Work credits are based on "quarters of coverage," which is essentially a measure of how long an individual worked at a job that contributed to the Social Security funds. In 1990 workers received one quarter of coverage for every $520 of covered earnings (an amount tied to the CPI), but not more than four quarters of coverage in a year. The number of work credits needed for various benefits depends on an individual's age, but after forty quarters (ten years) of coverage, a worker is fully insured. The maximum monthly benefit for a worker retiring at age 65 in 1990 was $975.

2. *Benefits for dependents of retired, disabled, or deceased workers.* Monthly Social Security checks are paid to certain dependents of a worker who has retired, has become disabled, or has died. Again, the monthly cash benefit is determined by the number of work credits and the average earnings. If a worker retires or is disabled, monthly payments can be made to unmarried children under the age of 18 (or 22 if full-time students), a spouse who is age 62 or older, and a spouse under the age of 62 if she or he is caring for the worker's child. If the worker dies, monthly payments can be made to unmarried children under the age of 18 (or 22 if full-time students), a widow or widower who is age 60 or older, and dependent parents who are age 62 or older.

3. *Lump-sum death benefits.* When a worker dies, a lump-sum payment is made to the worker's survivors. This payment normally goes to the widow or widower. In 1990 the lump-sum payment was $255.

4. *Medicare.* Although **Medicare** is an amendment to the Social Security Act, it is often treated as a program separate from Social Security. The primary purpose of Medicare is to protect people age 65 and older from the high costs of health care. Medicare benefits also are provided for people under age 65 if they are disabled for twenty-four or more consecutive months or if they or their dependents need dialysis treatment or a kidney transplant because of permanent kidney failure. Medicare consists of two parts that are generally called Plan A and Plan B. Plan A is the hospital insurance part that helps to pay the cost of in-patient hospital care and other related costs. Plan B is the medical insurance part that helps to pay the costs of physician's services, out-patient hospital services, and certain other medical items and services not covered by hospital insurance. Everyone who is 65 or older and who is eligible for Social Security benefits automatically receives the Plan A hospital insurance protection. However, to receive the Plan B medical insurance, people age 65 and older must pay a monthly premium ($28.60 per month in 1990).

EVALUATION OF SOCIAL SECURITY

Like other government programs, Social Security has frequently been criticized for its high administrative costs, the heavy tax burden required to support it, and the inequities and fraud associated with the dispersal of benefits. In 1976, and again in 1982, concern over the financial soundness of Social Security grew because projections showed that the two major Social Security funds (the Old Age Survivor's Fund and the Disability Insurance Fund) would soon be bankrupt. Benefits had been greatly increased, especially with the addition of Medicare, and income levels were grossly inadequate.

Significant changes were made in 1977 to keep the Social Security system solvent. The matching tax rates paid by both employee and employer were raised as well as the self-employed tax rate. Furthermore, the income limits subject to the Social Security tax were increased. Although these changes significantly increased the revenues, it was obvious by 1982 that the changes had not been adequate and that further increases in the tax rates or a reduction in the benefits would be needed to keep the system solvent. The history of these changes is detailed in Table 12.7.

Unlike private pension plans and insurance companies, the Social Security system does not have a large reserve of funds to pay future liabilities. Instead, Social Security relies on current income to pay current liabilities and only has a small reserve to cushion

TABLE 12.7   Social Security tax rates for selected years*

	Employee/ Employer Tax	Self-employed Tax	Maximum Taxable Income	Maximum Tax
1937–1949	1.0 %	–	$ 3,000	$ 30.00
1955	2.0	3.0 %	4,200	84.00
1960	3.0	4.5	4,800	144.00
1965	3.625	5.4	4,800	174.00
1970	4.8	6.9	7,800	374.00
1975	5.85	7.9	14,100	824.85
1980	6.13	8.1	25,900	1,587.67
1985	7.05	14.10	39,600	2,791.80
1990	7.65	15.30	51,300	3,924.45

*The 1977 law provided for an automatic escalator that will raise the earnings base any time the annual cost of living rises 3 percent or more.
Source: Data provided by Social Security Administration.

the irregularities in income. In 1988 the total income of the Old Age Survivors and Disability Insurance Trust Funds amounted to $251.5 billion, whereas the expenditures totaled $219.2 billion. The income was obtained from about 120 million workers who had taxable earnings that year, and the disbursements were paid to 38.8 million individuals who received monthly cash benefits. Thus, the ratio of recipients to workers was about 1:3.1. The change that has occurred in this ratio is alarming: in 1950 the ratio was 1:14, and in 1960 it was 1:5. By the year 2005, the ratio is expected to be 1:2. To continue funding the present system, either the benefits need to be reduced or the Social Security costs as a percentage of income need to rise substantially. The problem will become especially acute if the birthrate continues to decline, leaving few young workers to support a growing population of people over age 65. Although Congress has attempted to encourage older workers to continue working, the trend toward early retirement continues, and it appears to be an economic issue rather than a health issue.[31] Many people decide to retire when their retirement income appears adequate and secure even though their health is good and they could continue working.

PAY REGULATIONS

Compensation systems are influenced by various state and federal laws. Managers need to understand these regulations to develop compensation systems properly because the regulations serve as constraints that must be followed. Legislation has been primarily directed at regulating five aspects of wage and salary administration: retirement income, minimum-wage standards, equity, pay deductions, and benefits continuation.

RETIREMENT INCOME

The three major forms of retirement income are Social Security, individual savings plan, and company pension plans. A **pension** is the income individuals receive during retirement as a deferred payment for past services rendered.

INDIVIDUAL SAVINGS PLANS

Employees normally have between forty and fifty productive years to accumulate a personal estate. During these working years, individuals ought to prepare for later years of life, when their health might not allow them to continue in the same line of work or when they may want to retire from work and pursue other activities. Even though individuals know they will eventually retire many reach retirement age without adequate financial security.

As noted earlier, the Social Security system was created primarily because many people were reaching retirement age with inadequate personal savings. When the Social Security system was originally designed, it was intended to provide only a supplement to other forms of retirement income or pensions. Individuals were expected to provide for their own retirement, either through personal savings or a company pension plan.

To encourage individuals to provide their own pensions, Congress has provided attractive tax benefits for a variety of deferred-compensation plans. By placing part of their income in a deferred-compensation plan, employees avoid paying tax on either the amount they invest or the interest income the investment earns until they receive it later. Four of the most popular plans include the following:

1. 401(k) plans, sometimes called "salary-reduction plans," allow participants to place about $7,979 in 1990 (indexed to inflation) or 15 percent of their income, whichever is less, in a retirement account. This amount is not included in the employees' gross income, which shelters it from both Social Security tax and income tax. Early withdrawal is possible if a hardship is established. About half the time, employers make matching contributions to an employee's 401(k) plan to supplement what the employee saves. Deferred profit-sharing allocations are often placed in a 401(k) plan.[32]

2. Individual retirement accounts (IRAs) allow workers to set aside 100 percent of their earned income or $2,000 ($2,250 for a married couple if only one spouse is employed), whichever is less. This money is invested and the interest income is not taxed until it is withdrawn; however, there is a 10 percent tax penalty for withdrawals before age 59½. Furthermore, money invested in an IRA reduces the taxable income of employees who do not have an employer-provided pension plan or who make less than $25,000 (or $40,000 if a married couple).

3. Simplified employee pensions (SEPs) permit an employer to contribute to an employee's IRA an amount equal to $30,000 or 15 percent of the employee's income, whichever is less, provided this is done for each eligible employee.[33]

4. Keogh (H.R. 10) plans allow self-employed persons to place $30,000 or 25 percent of their income, whichever is less, in a tax-sheltered investment. As with an IRA, individuals can manage their own Keogh investments, and they are free to use a variety of investments, such as mutual funds, commodities, securities, or real-estate shares.[34]

COMPANY PENSION PLANS

About 89 percent of private industry employees and 98 percent of public employees in the United States participate in private pension plans.[35] There are basically two types of qualified benefit plans: a **defined contribution plan** and a **defined benefit plan**. A defined contribution pension plan requires a separate account for each participant. Retirement benefits are based on the amount contributed plus the interest income that accrues to each participant's account.

A defined benefit pension plan uses a formula that defines the benefits employees are to receive. Here, employers must make annual contributions, based on actuarial computations, that will provide sufficient funds to pay the vested retirement benefits. Separate accounts are not maintained for each participant. These plans are usually designed to pay a fixed monthly amount to retired employees based on a benefit formula. The formula usually involves an earnings base (the average earnings during the final working years) times the years of service, times a stipulated percentage (generally between 1 and 3 percent). This formula typically provides a monthly pension that is about 50 to 70 percent of a person's previous salary.[36]

In recent years, because of escalating administrative costs, firms have been slowly turning away from defined benefit plans in favor of defined contribution plans, especially 401(k) plans. Traditional defined benefit plans lock employers into paying benefits in good and bad years, while defined contribution plans allow contributions to be determined on an annual basis, and employees can withdraw part of the assets as a loan to themselves.[37]

EMPLOYEE RETIREMENT INCOME SECURITY ACT (ERISA)

Before 1974 private pension plans were highly criticized for several reasons. Many workers were greatly disappointed to learn upon retirement that they were not covered by a company pension plan because of complicated rules or insufficient funding. Some pensions required unusually long vesting periods (years of service), and employees were sometimes laid off early so that their employer could avoid paying them a pension. Some pension funds, including both employer-managed and union-managed funds, were very poorly managed due to incompetence, fraud, or labor racketeering. When companies went bankrupt, their pension funds usually collapsed along with them, creating disappointment and hardship for employees who had counted on a secure pension for retirement.

To reduce the injustices and mismanagement of private pension funds, Congress passed the Employee Retirement Income Security Act (ERISA) of 1974.[38] This legislation was designed to ensure that employees covered under private pension plans would receive the benefits promised. ERISA does not require employers to have a pension plan; indeed, many pension plans were terminated because of the difficulty of following the standards set by ERISA. However, if an employer chooses to have a pension plan, the employer must comply with the following:

1. *Eligibility requirements.* In general, all employees who have two years of service (1,000 hours of employment in twelve months is one year of service) must be eligible to participate in the pension plan.

2. *Vesting requirements.* **Vesting** refers to the employee's right to participate in the pension plan and to be assured of receiving money paid by the company into his or her pension fund. The plan may specify how many years of service are required before the employee is said to be fully vested. Employees who terminate before they are fully vested are entitled to only a certain percentage of the normal pension payments. The 1986 Tax Reform Act shortened the time limits for full vesting. The two minimum vesting schedules contained in this act are: (1) 100 percent vesting upon completion of five years of service, or (2) 20 percent vesting after three years of service and then 20 percent per year thereafter until 100 percent vesting after seven years of service.

3. *Portability practices.* **Portability** refers to the ability to transfer pension credits or funds from one fund to another when an employee changes employers. Portability is not required under ERISA; it is a voluntary option that employees like. If the employer agrees, vested employees leaving the company are allowed to transfer the assets in their pension, profit-sharing, or savings plans to an IRA without paying tax.

4. *Funding requirements.* To ensure that sufficient funds will be available to cover future pension payments, companies are required to set money aside in special funds. Unlike Social Security, which is a nonfunded, or pay-as-you-go, pension plan, private plans must be funded. Companies that had inadequately funded plans were required by ERISA to accelerate their rates of funding.

Pension plans can be either *contributory* or *noncontributory*. In a contributory plan, both the employees and the employer make contributions to the pension fund. In a noncontributory plan, the contributions are made solely by the employer. Most private pension plans are noncontributory (about 80 percent), while government pension plans are usually contributory.

The funding of pension plans can be either *insured* or *trusteed*. In the case of insured plans, the contributions are given to an insurance company to purchase an annuity for the employees' retirement years. In the case of trusteed plans, the contributions are placed in a fund managed by a trustee or a bank. The money in this fund is invested in stock, real estate, or securities to increase the value of the fund. However, the value of the fund also can decline, particularly during a recession.

5. *Fiduciary responsibilities.* **Fiduciary responsibilities** are those required of the individual who is responsible for administering a pension fund, such as a pension trustee, an officer of the company, or an attorney. ERISA established the "prudent-man" rule requiring fiduciaries to make rational decisions that would be consistent with the thinking of any prudent person. Fiduciaries are held responsible for negligent acts that violate the prudent-man rule. They are expressly prohibited from engaging in certain actions, such as making loans to a "party-in-interest" or investing more than 10 percent of the assets in the securities of the employer.

6. *Reporting and disclosure requirements.* ERISA contains extensive reporting and disclosure provisions that have created additional work and problems for pension-plan administrators. The reports required by ERISA are summarized in Table 12.8. All participants in a pension plan must receive a comprehensive booklet describing the major provisions of the plan *in language they can understand.* Anytime the plan is changed materially, the participants must be notified, and a participant may request a special report about the financial condition of the plan at any time. A summary report showing each employee's status in the plan must be distributed annually to each employee. The secretary of labor also must receive an annual report containing detailed information about the operation and financing of the plan.

Most students and young workers are not especially interested in pension plans because retirement seems so far away. However, a good retirement income is only derived from many years of careful planning and saving. Therefore, an individual needs to evaluate a company pension plan early in his or her working life and to supplement the plan and Social Security with a personal savings account. Careful planning also can result in tax benefits.

MINIMUM-WAGE STANDARDS

Before the Great Depression, it was not unusual for employers to reduce wage rates during adverse economic conditions. In fact, many of the nineteenth-century union-management battles began over reductions in wage levels. During the Depression, however, three major laws were passed to establish minimum-wage standards: the Davis-Bacon Act of 1931, the Walsh-Healey Act of 1936, and the Fair Labor Standards Act of 1938.

TABLE 12.8   Reports required by ERISA

1. Communications required for all employees
    a. Summary plan description
    b. Announcements of material modifications (within 120 days after the end of the year in which the changes were made)
    c. Summary annual report (including assets and liabilities, receipts and disbursements, and other information necessary for an accurate and readable summary)
2. Information available to employees for examination
    a. Plan document (clearly identified copies must exist at each geographic location at reasonable times for viewing)
    b. Annual report
3. Information to be furnished to employees on request
    a. Annual report (employee may be charged twenty cents per page)
    b. Plan document
    c. Vesting statement
4. Information to secretary of labor (may also go to SEC, IRS, and the Treasury Department)
    a. Summary plan description
    b. Plan modifications
    c. Financial statements, an actuarial report, and an insured plan report

DAVIS-BACON ACT

The Davis-Bacon Act of 1931, sometimes called the Prevailing Wage Law, was the first federal law that attempted to protect the amount of pay received by employees. The act covers work on the construction or repair of federal buildings for which the contract involves more than $2,000. It requires organizations holding federal contracts to pay laborers and mechanics the prevailing wages of the locality in which the work is performed. Overtime must be paid at one-and-one-half times the local rate. The purpose of this law is to ensure that the local areas where the public-works projects are awarded receive the intended employment benefits. It prevents contractors from importing cheap labor from other areas and from auctioning jobs to the lowest bidders.

In recent years some attempts to have been made to rescind the Davis-Bacon Act because of its contribution to inflation. Construction unions have argued that the prevailing wage rates are "prime" wage rates that have made federal construction projects very expensive.

WALSH-HEALEY ACT

The Walsh-Healey Act of 1936, officially called the Public Contracts Act, extended the Davis-Bacon Act to nonconstruction federal contractors. This act sets basic labor standards and minimum-wage rates for all work done under a federal contract exceeding

$10,000. The minimum-wage standards, however, are industry minimums established by the secretary of labor rather than local prevailing rates. The act requires that overtime be paid at the rate of one-and-one half times the base rate for work exceeding forty hours per week. This act also contains safety requirements that were intended to reduce accidents; however, the safety rules were superseded by the Occupational Safety and Health Act of 1970.

FAIR LABOR STANDARDS ACT

The Fair Labor Standards Act of 1938 is commonly referred to as the Wage and Hour Law or FLSA. It has been amended many times and is the most important law regulating compensation practices. This law is the result of Congress's decision to extend the provisions and controls of the Davis-Bacon Act and the Walsh-Healey Act to all organizations involved in interstate commerce. It sets minimum-wage standards, overtime pay standards, and child-labor restrictions. FLSA is administered by the Wage and Hour Division of the Department of Labor, which tries to correct injustices via conciliation, the assessment of fines, or legal decisions through the federal courts.

Minimum-wage rates have increased dramatically since FLSA was first passed in 1938. The original minimum was 25 cents an hour, which only covered laborers working in the production of interstate commerce. By 1991 the minimum wage had been raised to $4.25 an hour, and the coverage had been extended to almost all employees, including agricultural laborers and domestic workers. The legislative history of minimum-wage

TABLE 12.9   Minimum-wage increases since passage of the Fair Labor Standards Act in 1938

Year	Minimum Wage	Year	Minimum Wage
1938	.25	1974	2.00
1939	.30	1975	2.10
1945	.40	1976	2.30
1949	.75	1978	2.65
1955	1.00	1979	2.90
1961	1.15	1980	3.10
1962	1.25	1981	3.35
1966	1.40	1990	3.80
1968	1.60	1991	4.25

increases is presented in Table 12.9. Teenagers (16 to 19 years of age) on their first job can be paid a subminimum training wage equal to 85 percent of the minimum for their first three months.

Minimum-wage laws have been severely criticized by economists. The purposes of minimum-wage standards are to ensure a living wage for all laborers and to reduce poverty. In particular, the laws are intended to help low-income families, females, and minority workers. However, studies on minimum-wage laws indicate that their overall effects are undesirable. Minimum-wage laws tend to have the most destructive effect on the very people that they are intended to help. The evidence indicates that employers are not willing to pay minimum wage to marginal workers. Therefore, employers eliminate marginal jobs by replacing them with mechanization and new technology. Teenage employment has been especially hard hit by rising minimum wages; each rise in the minimum-wage rate has increased the teenage unemployment level. Finally, minimum-wage rates are highly inflationary. When the minimum-wage rate is increased, there are direct and indirect effects on the wage structure. The *direct* effect of a minimum-wage increase refers to the increase in wages for jobs at the bottom of the wage curve that have been below the minimum wage. The *indirect* effect of a minimum-wage increase refers to the changes in the remainder of the wage curve to maintain appropriate wage differentials for jobs that deserve higher pay. An analysis of the effects of minimum-wage increases in numerous industries indicates that the indirect effect is usually greater than the direct effect; that is, companies spend more money on increasing the pay of high-level jobs than they spend on raising the pay of low-level jobs to the new minimum. The direct and indirect effects of an increase in minimum wages are illustrated in Figure 12.1. In spite of most companies' attempts to raise high-level jobs and to maintain appropriate wage differentials, a minimum-wage increase typically results in a compression in wage rates.[39]

FIGURE 12.1 Illustration of the direct and indirect effect of a minimum wage increase

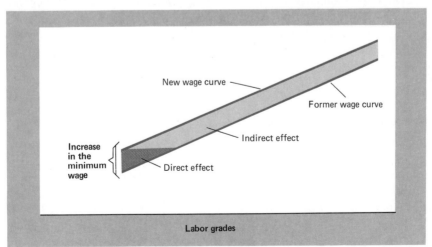

Overtime provisions require that covered employees receive one-and-one half times the base rate for all hours worked in excess of forty hours during a given week. If an employee receives a straight hourly wage, the calculation of overtime payments is simple. However, since the overtime provisions also apply to bonus payments, time off in return for overtime work, and work done on a piece-rate basis, the calculations can become complex. Consider the example of an employee who earns $5.00 per hour for a 48-hour week, receives a $24.00 weekly bonus, and gets eight hours of overtime pay *based on a rate that includes the bonus*. The employee really earns $5.50 per hour ($5.00 per hour base pay plus the $24.00 bonus divided by the forty-eight hours required to earn it, or $.50 per hour) and an overtime rate of $8.25. The employee's earnings for that week would be calculated in this way:

Regular time   40 × $5.50 = $220.00
Overtime   8 × $8.25 =   66.00
Weekly earnings   = $286.00

Child labor is restricted by FLSA. Minors between the ages of 16 and 18 are not allowed to work in hazardous occupations, such as mining, meat-cutting, and logging. Children under age 16 are restricted from all work in interstate commerce, unless they are working for their parents or an employer who has received a temporary permit from the Department of Labor. FLSA was the first federal law restricting child labor that was not declared unconstitutional. For almost a century, state laws had attempted unsuccessfully to regulate child labor.

FLSA exempts certain employees from both its overtime and its minimum-wage provisions. The **exempt employees** include executive, administrative, and professional personnel; outside salespersons; workers in service and retail establishments with mainly intrastate sales; and workers in seasonal industries. The exempt status for executives and administrators is determined by the percentage of time (50 percent or more) they spend in administrative activities that require them to exercise discretionary authority. Many organizations make clear distinctions between exempt and nonexempt personnel. Exempt personnel usually are nonunion administrators or professional employees who are paid salaries. Nonexempt personnel usually are paid hourly wages and may belong to a union. It is important to remember, however, that whether a job is exempt or not is determined by the requirements of the job and not by whether it is paid a salary or an hourly wage.

FAIR AND EQUITABLE WAGE LAWS

Wage inequities have been recognized for many years, and several laws have been passed to eliminate wage discrimination based on sex, race, and age. These laws do not, however, guarantee a job, a pay increase, or a stated income level. None of these acts prohibits wage differentials or promotions based on factors such as seniority, merit, or measures of performance. However, a company must be able to defend its compensation system by demonstrating that a merit-pay plan is actually based on valid performance measures.

HRM in Action

Computer Operations Manager Is an Exempt Employee

The Fair Labor Standards Act (FLSA) of 1938 is one of the most frequently litigated laws because of disputes about who should receive overtime pay. The law requires employers to compensate employees at a rate not less than one and one-half times their normal rate of pay for hours worked in excess of 40 hours a week. However, employees are exempt from the overtime requirements if they perform executive, administrative, professional, or outside sales jobs.

Although many think an exempt employee is anyone who receives a salary, the distinction between exempt and nonexempt is based on the requirements of the job. The definitions of executive, administrative, professional, and outside sales jobs are contained in a 28-page Department of Labor publication. Sometimes, however, it is very difficult to apply these definitions to a specific job.

A federal district court in Missouri concluded that a computer operations manager was an exempt employee. Interestingly, the court decided that the employee's job included *both* executive and administrative duties and it was the combined aspects that made it exempt.

An executive is defined as an employee (1) whose salary exceeds $250 per week; (2) whose primary duty consists of managing an enterprise or subdivision thereof; (3) who regularly directs the work of two or more other employees; (4) who has the authority to hire, fire, and evaluate other employees; (5) who regularly exercises discretionary powers; and (6) who performs executive duties at least 80 percent of the time.

An administrator is defined as an employee (1) whose salary exceeds $155 per week, (2) whose primary duties consist of performing office or nonmanual work directly related to management policies or general business operations, (3) who regularly exercises discretion and independent judgment, (4) who regularly assists a proprietor or who performs under only general supervision, and (5) who performs administrative duties at least 80 percent of the time.

The computer operations manager supervised the computer department and assisted in recruiting, interviewing, and hiring other computer operators, handled disciplinary problems, evaluated performance, and recommended pay increases and bonuses. The manager also exercised discretion and independent judgment in identifying vendors, ordering supplies, and scheduling work. The court decided that some of these duties were executive and others were administrative, and the combination made this an exempt job.

Source: McKeever v. J. E. Stowers & Company, 112 L.C. 35, 247 (W.D.Mo. 1989).

EQUAL PAY ACT

The Equal Pay Act was passed in 1963 as an amendment to the Fair Labor Standards Act. This act states:

> No employer shall discriminate between employees on the basis of sex by paying wages to employees less than the rate at which he pays wages to employees of the opposite sex for equal work on jobs which require equal skill, effort, and responsibility, and similar working conditions.

This law has been interpreted very broadly to prohibit the unequal payment of wages to men and women working in the same job category. Very few arguments for paying unequal wages have been accepted. For example, requiring a male worker to occasionally lift a loaded box of parts onto a conveyer belt has not been considered sufficiently unequal to entitle him to be paid more than his female coworkers.

In spite of the Equal Pay Act, the average income of females is considerably less than that of males. The Wage and Hour Division of the Department of Labor, which is the agency responsible for enforcing the Equal Pay Act, has exerted an enormous effort to eliminate the disparity in income by means of education, conciliation, and legal action. Several large settlements involving millions of dollars have been awarded to female employees as a result of class-action suits. In one of the largest settlements, AT&T was required to pay $23 million to female employees for past discrimination in wages.

The disparity existing between the average incomes of males and females must be interpreted carefully, since it does not result entirely from illegal sex discrimination. A major cause of the disparity stems from the employment patterns of female workers. Large numbers of women joined the work force in the 1970s and started in entry-level positions that legitimately pay less than higher-level positions. Many women also choose low-paying temporary jobs or part-time employment because they are actively raising families. Finally, many women work in traditionally low-paying, female occupations, such as secretary or receptionist. The comparable-worth controversy, discussed in Chapter 10, concerns the issue of whether traditional female occupations should continue to be paid less than traditional male occupations. To date, the courts have not required companies to develop a common set of criteria for evaluating the worth of different jobs. However, many companies have tried to eliminate some of the disparity that exists between traditionally female-dominated and male-dominated occupations.

CIVIL RIGHTS ACT

Title VII of the Civil Rights Act of 1964, as amended in 1972, prohibits the unequal payment of wages to employees because of race, sex, color, religion, or national origin. The Equal Employment Opportunity Commission enforces the Civil Rights Act, and the commission can bring class-action suits against employers who have discriminatory compensation systems.

AGE DISCRIMINATION IN EMPLOYMENT ACT

The Age Discrimination in Employment Act of 1967, as amended, protects employees and prospective employees over age 40 from unfair treatment due to age. Pay increases, bonuses, and employee benefits cannot be denied to older workers simply on the basis of age. The enforcement of this act is a responsibility of the EEOC.

PAY DEDUCTIONS

Three federal laws have been passed to protect employees' earnings. These laws regulate the deductions that can be made from a worker's paycheck.

COPELAND ACT

The Copeland Act of 1934 was passed during the Great Depression to prohibit the unfair treatment of employees who needed jobs so desperately that employers could take advantage of them. The Copeland Act authorizes the secretary of labor to make reasonable regulations concerning the deductions that a federal contractor can make from employees' wages. Contractors have to demonstrate that their payroll deductions are proper, and they have to file weekly statements showing the wages actually paid and the deductions made.

ANTI-KICKBACK LAW

The Anti-Kickback Law was passed in 1948 as an amendment to the Copeland Act, making it illegal for a federal contractor to threaten or otherwise induce employees to give part of their rightful compensation to the contractor.

FEDERAL WAGE GARNISHMENT LAW

The Federal Wage Garnishment Law of 1970 restricts the amount of an employee's disposable earnings that can be deducted to pay a **garnishment**. A garnishment is a civil judgment brought against an individual for failure to pay a debt which gives the creditor the right to have part of the debtor's wages paid directly to the creditor. The law limits the amount that can be garnished in one week to not more than 25 percent of an employee's disposable weekly earnings or the amount that is thirty times the FLSA minimum wage, whichever is less. There are certain exceptions to these limits, however. For example, larger sums can be garnished if an employee has an obligation to pay alimony or child support. The law also makes it illegal to discharge an employee because of wage garnishments.

BENEFITS CONTINUATION

When employees are laid off or quit, they typically lose their benefits coverage from their former employer. This loss of coverage can create a difficult economic hardship for some individuals who have heavy medical or hospital expenses. To protect people who leave an employer from losing their benefit coverage, Congress passed a law in 1986 (amended in 1989) that requires employers of twenty or more employees to extend health-insurance group benefits to terminated employees and employees with reduced hours for twenty-nine months.

Widows and divorced and legally separated spouses may elect this coverage for up to three years. This law allows employers to charge those who elect to continue their benefits 102 percent of the cost of this coverage to pay for the benefits plus a small fee to cover administrative expenses. This law does not require employers to have a benefit plan, it simply requires that employers allow terminated employees or the spouses of former employees the opportunity to continue participating in the same group benefit program as other employees.

INTERNATIONAL HRM

Employee benefits vary dramatically not only from country to country but within a single country. For example, Japanese workers rarely have more than three to five days of vacation per year. However, one large Japanese retail company, Mauri Co. Ltd., has introduced a vacation plan that allows its 9,000 employees to take a one-month leave of absence each year: twelve days every six months.[40]

Because benefits vary so widely, it is essential to include them when making cross-cultural comparisons of compensation. Benefits and perks are a much larger part of the total remuneration package in Europe than in the United States. Sweden, for example, has often been recognized for the generosity of its national health care and pension plans, and wages in Sweden have been comparatively high; however, Swedish workers pay 55 to 65 percent of their wages in taxes to fund these national programs, and in recent years the programs have become less generous because of large government deficits.[41]

In China, where the government owns most of the factories, the average wage of factory workers is only 3 to 5 percent that of an average United States worker, but this statistic is misleading because it ignores benefits. Chinese workers do not pay income or social security taxes, and health care and pensions are provided from public funds. Furthermore, most employees are provided housing and utilities by their employer at a cost of about one dollar per month (roughly 3 to 5 percent of their monthly income). Therefore, even though the wages of Chinese and American workers are significantly different, the differences are much narrower when benefits are considered. Pensions are new and accessible to only a few international workers because the care of older workers in China is viewed as a family responsibility.[42]

In the United States, favorable tax laws have encouraged employees to purchase shares of their company's stock. Firms outside the United States have been slow to distribute stock to employees; however, employee ownership is increasing worldwide. In England, for example, a new law is pushing corporations to provide more stock options for their employees. In India, stock ownership in private companies was not introduced until 1985, and then only a few Indian managers showed much interest in purchasing stock.

In European countries, retired workers are expected to have three sources of retirement income: company pensions, national social security, and personal savings. Company pensions are predominantly defined benefit plans based almost exclusively on years of service. To encourage more personal saving, some European companies have started defined contribution plans as a supplement to their defined benefit plans. National social security payments have usually been very generous, which has created severe funding difficulties for most countries. The funding problems have been exacerbated by workers who have been encouraged to take early retirement. By pushing employees to retire early, these countries have reduced their unemployment problems but older workers have sometimes been forced into premature poverty with inadequate social security and reduced company pensions.

SUMMARY

A. Employee benefits have increased significantly in recent years, both in respect to the number of benefits offered and the costs of providing these benefits. As a percentage of payroll, the costs of benefits have increased from 3 percent in 1929 to 16 percent in 1949 and to almost 40 percent in 1989.

B. Good benefit plans are very costly, but they buy almost nothing for the employer. Although some human resource managers believe good benefit plans facilitate recruiting and hiring new employees, good benefit plans do not increase either satisfaction or productivity. Furthermore, most employees know very little about the benefits offered by their company.

C. The major optional benefits offered by companies generally include: (1) health and accident insurance, (2) life insurance and income continuation, (3) pay for time not worked, (4) employee services, and (5) pensions.

D. Health and accident insurance typically pays for hospital and doctor expenses, including chiropractic and psychiatric visits. Many companies also offer dental plans.

E. Most employers are required to offer employees the option of participating in a health maintenance organization, which provides health care at a fixed monthly cost regardless of the frequency of usage. Health maintenance plans emphasize preventive health care.

F. Life insurance and income continuation benefits typically provide group term life insurance, long-term disability, accident and severance pay, and sick leave.

G. A very expensive employee benefit is pay for time not worked, such as paid holidays, vacations, personal time off, and sabbaticals.

H. Some employers offer a large variety of employee services such as stock purchase plans, credit unions, matched payroll-deduction savings, tuition reimbursement, Christmas bonuses, food services, company cars, personal counseling, and recreation opportunities.

I. Four methods of estimating the costs of employee benefits plans are: (1) the annual cost, (2) the cost per employee per year, (3) the percent of total payroll, and (4) the cents per hour.

J. All employers are required to provide three mandated benefits: (1) workers' compensation, (2) unemployment compensation, and (3) Social Security. The costs of workers' compensation are determined by the safety record of the industry to which a company belongs and the state in which the company is located. The costs of unemployment compensation are related to how often employees are laid off by a company. The Social Security tax rate is established by Congress. The tax rate has increased significantly in recent years and is expected to increase further in the future.

K. The United States Congress has established tax incentives to encourage individuals to establish individual retirement accounts. Income placed in an IRA, a Keogh, a 401(k), or an SEP is not taxed until it is withdrawn.

L. Company pension plans must conform to the requirements of the Employee Retirement Income Security Act (ERISA), which include: (1) eligibility, (2) vesting, (3) portability, (4) funding, (5) fiduciary responsibilities, and (6) reporting and disclosure requirements.

M. Three major laws establishing minimum-wage standards have been passed. The Davis-Bacon Act and the Walsh-Healey Act require government contractors to pay the prevailing wage rates. The Fair Labor Standards Act requires all employers involved in interstate commerce to pay a minimum wage rate. In 1938, when FLSA was passed, the minimum wage was only $.25 per hour; in 1991, the minimum wage was $4.25 per hour.

N. The Equal Pay Act of 1963 and the Civil Rights Act of 1964 require employers to pay men and women the same rate of pay if the jobs that they perform are equal.

O. The Copeland Act and the Federal Wage Garnishment Act protect the employee's pay and restrict the amount of money that can be deducted for such things as wage garnishments.

QUESTIONS

1. Why should an employer provide an employee benefit program? What does such a program do for the employer?

2. What is a Health Maintenance Organization (HMO)? What are the advantages of an HMO?

3. The costs of benefits as a percentage of payroll have increased dramatically in the past fifty years. Do you expect them to level off, decrease, or continue increasing? Why?

4. What can an employer do to better inform employees about their benefits? Should employees be better informed? Why or why not?

5. Should employees have insurance protection against all kinds of accidents and illness? Why or why not? Should such insurance be provided by the company, private insurance companies, or the government?

6. Since so many employees use sick leave to take a day off, do you agree or disagree that employees should simply be given so many days of personal time to use as they choose?

7. Since some employee services are used by only a small number of employees (such as alcohol and drug treatment, psychiatric care, and legal assistance), should employees who do not use such services receive other benefits or cash refunds? Why or why not?

8. What are the advantages and disadvantages of flexible benefits?

9. Who pays for unemployment insurance compensation? What motive would a company have to list a worker as fired rather than as laid off? How can such problems be corrected?

10. Is Social Security a viable program that can survive the next 100 years? How does it work, and how can it be improved?

11. What is meant by *vesting, portability, fiduciary, contributory*, and *noncontributory* as they are used to describe pensions?

12. Are minimum-wage laws inflationary? Should the minimum-wage rate continue to be raised? Should it be tied to the Consumer Price Index?

13. Who would be an exempt employee? A nonexempt employee?

14. Should an employer be expected to pay overtime to employees who work overtime on their own initiative, without authorization by their supervisors, and contrary to the officially stated company policy?

KEY TERMS

Annual-cost method: A method of computing the costs of benefits by calculating the total annual cost of each benefit.

Cents per hour: A method of calculating the costs of benefits by computing the cost of each benefit in terms of how much it costs per each employee hour.

Cost per employee per year: A method of calculating the costs of employee benefits by dividing the total annual cost by the number of employees.

Defined benefit plan: A pension plan that provides a retirement income to retirees based on a formula that usually combines the retiree's years of service and average annual income for the last five years.

Defined contribution plan: An individual pension fund created for each employee into which the company invests a specified amount of money each year until the individual retires.

Employee assistance program: A benefit program that provides counseling to employees with such problems as marital conflict, indebtedness, alcoholism, and drug abuse.

Exempt employees: Employees who are exempt from the overtime requirements of the Fair Labor Standards Act, such as outside salespeople and executives who have administrative or managerial responsibilities.

Expatriate allowances: The additional income and benefits provided for employees who are transferred to a foreign country.

Experience rating: A rating computed for each employer that is based on the number of accidents or the number of employees laid off. This rating is used to adjust the unemployment compensation and workers' compensation tax rates for each employer.

Fiduciary responsibilities: Responsibilities of the person who manages a pension fund.

Flexible benefits (cafeteria benefits): Employees choose the benefits they desire, subject to certain limitations and total cost constraints.

Garnishment: Money taken from an employee's paycheck as a result of a court judgment brought against that employee by a creditor.

HMO (Health maintenance organization): Provides health care services emphasizing preventive medicine at a fixed monthly rate.

IRA (Individual retirement account): A personal retirement investment program in which an employee can put a percentage of his or her income. The money in the account is not taxed until it is withdrawn.

LTD (Long-term disability): Insurance that provides disabled employees with long-term security.

Mandatory benefits: Benefits that each employer is required to provide: unemployment compensation, workers' compensation, and Social Security.

Medicare: A Social Security benefit that pays medical expenses of employees over age 65 and permanent disability payments for individuals under age 65.

Optional benefits: Benefits that employers choose to provide that are not required by law, such as health and accident insurance, pensions, and pay for time not worked.

Pension: The income that an employee receives after retirement.

Percent of payroll: A method of calculating the costs of employee benefits by expressing the cost as a percentage of the total payroll costs.

Portability: The ability to transfer pension monies from one pension fund to another when an employee changes employers.

Social Security: Program designed as a forced savings plan in which employees save money during their working years to provide a pension after they retire.

SUB (Supplemental unemployment benefits): Special funds provided by employers as a result of a labor agreement that provides supplementary benefits to employees who are laid off.

Transfer assistance: The special assistance provided to an employee who is transferred to a new location. Examples include a transfer bonus, moving allowance, assistance in buying and selling a home, and help in finding employment for the employee's spouse.

Unemployment compensation: Money provided by the unemployment compensation funds to temporarily assist employees who are laid off through no fault of their own.

Vesting: The employee's right to receive the money contributed to his or her pension fund by an employer even if the employee terminates employment with the employer.

Workers' compensation: The compensation provided for employees who are injured on the job regardless of who was responsible for the accident.

CONCLUDING CASE

Pay or Benefits

Carl and George work for a mining and smelting company, but their jobs have nothing to do with either the mining or smelting of ore. They take care of the grounds around the corporate offices. In their view, the company spends too much money on benefits, and they would like to receive more pay instead of benefits.

Some time ago, the company terminated its road-building crew, and all road building is now contracted to a company that specializes in this work. Carl and George think that they ought to form their own business and contract to do the ground work for the company. They believe that such a business would not only put them ahead financially but that it would also save money for the mining company because the company would no longer have to pay the cost of their benefits. The company recently announced that the cost of benefits was 68 percent of its payroll.

Carl and George reason that they could get at least 50 percent higher pay and still provide their own benefits if they became independent contractors. They think they could purchase their own medical coverage, start their own retirement accounts, and still have money left if they received 50 percent higher pay.

Questions:

1. Would Carl and George be ahead financially if they formed their own company and contracted to do the work for 50 percent more than they presently receive?
2. What would be the likely benefits implications?

NOTES

1. Chamber of Commerce of the United States, *Employee Benefits Historical Data: 1951–1979* (Washington, D.C., 1981).

2. Chamber of Commerce of the United States, *Employer Benefits: 1989 Edition* (Washington, D.C., 1989).

3. Robert Ashell and John Child, "Employee Services: People, Profits, or Parkinson?" *Personnel Management* (Fall 1972): 18–22.

4. Laurie W. Letts, "Voluntary Benefits in Mexico Include Health, Group Life, Pension Insurance," *Employee Benefit Plan Review* 39 (1984): 84–85; J. Douglas Buchanan, "Keeping an Eye on Pensions in Argentina," *Benefits and Compensation International* 18 (September 1988): 9–13; Peter A. Doetsch, "Private Pension Plans in West Germany," *Benefits and Compensation International* 17 (March 1988): 6–9.

5. H. W. Hennessey, Jr., "Using Employee Benefits to Gain a Competitive Advantage," *Benefits Quarterly* 5, no. 1 (1989): 51–57.

6. Robert Ashell and John Child, "Employee Services: People, Profits, or Parkinson?" *Personnel Management* (Fall 1972): 18–22.

7. A benefits survey conducted by the author in a large international construction company.

8. Willis B. Goldbeck, "AIDS and the Workplace: Business Fights the Epidemic," *Futurist* 22 (March/April 1988): 18–19.

9. Andrew J. Oswald, "Unemployment Insurance and Labor Contracts Under Asymmetric Information: Theory and Facts," *American Economic Review* 76 (June 1986): 365–77.

10. Labor Letter, *Wall Street Journal* (July 19, 1988): 1

11. Eric Morgenthaler, "Dads on Duty: Sweden Offers Fathers Paid Paternity Leaves; About 10% Take Them," *Wall Street Journal* (January 29, 1979).

12. Roger Ricklefs, "In-House Counsels: Firms Offer Employees a New Benefit: Help in Personal Problems," *Wall Street Journal* (August 13, 1979).

13. "Retirement Policies and Programs," ASPA-BNA Survey No. 39, 1989.

14. "Employers Devise Ways to Help Spouses in Worker Transfers," Labor Letter, *Wall Street Journal* (April 11, 1989): 1.

15. Nancy J. Carter, "Moving Managers Internationally: the Need for Flexibility," *Human Resource Planning* 12, no. 1 (1989): 43–7; Calvin Reynolds, "Cost Containment and Expatriate Tax Policies of U.S. Multinationals," *Benefits and Compensation International* 17 (October 1987): 28–31; "It's Expensive to Station an Executive Overseas," Labor Letter, *Wall Street Journal* (October 13, 1987): A1.

16. Raymond C. Collins and Renee Y. Magid, "Taking the Myths out of Childcare Planning," *Management Review* 78 (January 1989): 18–22.

17. "Eldercare Benefits Meet New Employee Needs," *Employee Benefits Plan Review* 42 (June 1988): 21, 24.

18. Toni A. Campbell and David E. Campbell, "Benefits: Seventy-One Percent of Employers Say They Could Be Part of the Child Care Solution," *Personnel Journal* 67 (April 1988): 84, 86; "On-Site Child Care Works at Apple and Campbell: Two Companies Help with Child Care Costs," *Employee Benefit Plan Review* 43 (September 1988): 239–42.

19. "Child Care is a Hard Dollars and Cents Issue for Employers," Labor Letter, *Wall Street Journal* (April 25, 1989): A1; Susan Jones Ainsworth, "Kids Get a Vote of Confidence from the CPI," *Chemical Week* 142 (June 15, 1988): 29–30; Margaret LeRoux, "California Bank Offers On-Site Day Care," *Business Insurance* 20 (September 15, 1986): 13; Wendy Wayne, "A Hospital's On-Site Child Care Center Proves to Make Business Sense," *Health Care Management Review* 11 (Summer 1986): 81–87.

20. "Parental Leave," *Wall Street Journal* (June 8, 1988): B1; "Family Leave and Elder Care Policies Show Mixed Results After a Year," Labor, *Wall Street Journal* (December 19, 1989): A1; "Surveying Employees to Assess Child Care Needs," *Employee Benefit Plan Review* 43 (September 1988): 24–28.

21. Commerce Clearing House Editorial Staff, *Flexible Benefits* (Chicago, Ill.: CCH, 1983).

22. David Langer, "How a Flexible Spending Account Plan Works," *Practical Accountant* 22 (March 1989): 77–78.

23. Polly T. Taplin, "Flexible Benefits after Two, Three, and Five Years," *Employee Benefit Plan Review* 42 (June 1988): 30–34.

24. J. Brad Chapman and Robert Ottemann, "Employee Preference for Various Compensation and Fringe Benefit Options, the 1975 Research Award Winner sponsored by ASPA Foundation, Box A, Berea, Oh. 33017. See also S. M. Nealey, "Determining Worker Preferences Among Employee Benefit Programs," *Journal of Applied Psychology* 48 (1964): 7–12; S. M. Nealey and J. G Goodale, "Worker Preferences Among Time-off Benefits and Pay," *Journal of Applied Psychology* 51 (1967): 356–61.

25. Crystal Eastman, *Work Accidents and the Law* (New York: Charities Publication Committee, 1910), pp. 3–4.

26. Walter F. Dodd, *Administration of Workmen's Compensation* (New York: The Commonwealth Fund, 1936).

27. LaVerne C. Tinsley, "State Workers' Compensation: Enactments in 1988," *Monthly Labor Review* 112 (January 1989): 66–71.

28. Linda D. McGill and William C. Nugent, "Compensation for Work-Related Stress: A New Employee Right?" *Employment Relations Today* 14 (Autumn 1987): 249–56; Sandy Moretz, "Can California Achieve Workers' Comp Reform?" *Occupational Hazards* 51 (February 1989): 77–79.

29. Jill Lambert, "Workers' Comp Crunch Stimulates Tougher Claims Management," *Corporate Cash Flow* 10 (February 1989): 24–27.

30. Social Security Bulletin, U.S. Department of Health and Social Services, Vol. 52 (July 1989): 26.

31. A. Haeworth Robertson, "The Outlook for Social Security," *Topics in Total Compensation* 3 (Winter 1988): 123–29; Don Dunn, "Early Retirement: It Pays to Plan

Early," *Business Week* (February 27, 1989): 134–35; Dorcas R. Hardy, "The Future of Social Security," *Social Security Bulletin* 50 (August 1987): 5–7.

32. Rory Judd Albert and Neal S. Schelberg, "IRS Issues 'Hardship' Regulations," *Pension World* 24 (November 1988): 63–64; Craig H. Westbrook, "Section 401 (k) Plans and the Tax Reform Act of 1986," *Journal of Pension Planning and Compliance* 14 (Summer 1988): 117–31.

33. Christy Milner Farrell, "Simplified Employee Pension Plans (SEPs): Past, Present, and Future," *Journal of Pension Planning and Compliance* 14 (Fall 1988): 233–70.

34. William H. Hoffman and Eugene Willis, *1986 Annual Edition, West's Federal Taxation: Individual Income Taxes* (St. Paul, Minn.: West, 1985), Chapter 19.

35. Lora Mills Lovejoy, "The Comparative Value of Pensions in the Public and Private Sectors," *Monthly Labor Review* 111 (December 1988): 18–26.

36. Bob G. Kilpatrick and Nancy L. Wilburn, "Benefit Limitations on Qualified Defined-Benefit Plans," *Journal of Pension Planning and Compliance* 14 (Winter 1988): 293–312.

37. Nancy Connors, "Pension Benefits: Which Nest Is Best for Your Eggs?" *CFO: The Magazine for Chief Financial Officers* 4 (July 1988): 51–52.

38. "What You Should Know About the Pension Law," U.S. Department of Labor (May 1988).

39. See J. M. Peterson and C. T. Steward, *Employment Effects of Minimum Wage Rates* (Washington, D.C.: American Enterprise Institute for Public Policy Research, 1969). See also Leonard R. Burgess, *Wage and Salary Administration in a Dynamic Economy* (New York: Harcourt, 1968), pp. 18–28.

40. "One-Month Vacation System Offered by Leading Retailer," *Productivity in Japan* 4 (Autumn 1989): 5.

41. Heather Bowker, "Total Compensation Planning in Europe: Challenge or a Mystery," *Topics in Total Compensation* 2, no. 4 (1988): 379–89.

42. James A. Nelson and John A. Reeder, "Labor Relations in China," *California Management Review* 27 (Summer 1985): 13–32; Robert E. Markland and Joseph C. Ullman, "Climbing the Great Wall," *Business and Economic Review* 33 (January–March 1987): 30–34.

Labor Relations

Union Structure and Leadership

Local Unions / National Unions / The AFL-CIO

Collective Bargaining

Bargaining Structures / Preparation for Negotiations / Contract Issues / The Labor Agreement / The Bargaining Process / Bargaining Strategies / Concession Bargaining

Bargaining Impasses

Strikes / Lockouts / Picketing / Boycotts / Mediation and Conciliation / Arbitration

Labor Relations in the Public Sector

International HRM

INTRODUCTORY CASE

The Cost of Concessions

The decade of the 1980s tested the flexibility of the United Food and Commercial Workers (UFCW) union and its willingness to cooperate with the meat packing industry. Signs that cholesterol-conscious consumers had permanently reduced the demand for red meat were apparent early in the decade. The meat packing companies faced intense competition for a dwindling market share, and by 1986 analysts predicted that only five or six of the sixteen major meat packing companies would survive the shakeout.[1]

In 1982 the international UFCW union leaders urged members to accept-wage and benefit concessions at high wage packing plants to keep companies, and even the industry, alive. Local leaders who followed this advice, however, faced a backlash that removed them from office. At Morrell's Sioux Falls packing plant, for example, a new slate of officers were installed to re-

place leaders who had agreed to a $2.40 per hour cut in wages in 1983. Under the new leadership, 2,500 workers struck for eleven weeks at the end of 1985 and won a one dollar an hour boost in pay.

In Austin, Minnesota, the George A. Hormel & Company asked union members to accept a reduced wage rate, from $10.69 to $8.25.[2] Hormel's total labor costs were about $17 per hour compared to $13 per hour or less for the industry. The leaders of Local 9 of the UFCW, however, refused to accept any wage reductions. They turned down a company offer of $10 an hour, which other Hormel plants had accepted, and led 1,500 workers on strike.

While the UFCW international was negotiating for increased wages, Local 9 hired a New York consultant to conduct a "corporate campaign" of harassment against banks, insurance companies, and other

517

institutions linked to Hormel. One target was the First Bank of Austin where the union and many members closed their accounts and picketed, and another target was a Minneapolis bank that acted as trustee for company stock held in pension and profit-sharing plans. These pressure tactics were ineffectual, however.

The strike was a bitter struggle that divided the town of Austin and created such animosity and hatred that the community still has not fully recovered. Five months after the workers walked off the job, and after the local union refused to accept a federal mediator's proposal for a settlement, the company reopened the plant with 700 nonunion workers. Harassment, vandalism, and threats of violence forced the governor to send National Guardsmen and armored trucks to restore order. The international union finally settled the strike after it replaced the leaders of Local 9 and placed it in trusteeship. Nearly 500 members of the union decided to return to work in spite of the ill feelings their decision created among those who stayed on strike.

Before the strike, Austin, a one-company town with a population of 22,600, of whom 1,800 worked for Hormel, was considered an ideal community. Since the strike, it has been torn apart with a continuing campaign of hatred and vandalism: obscene phone calls, broken windows, damaged vehicles, and vandalized homes. Strikers continue to boycott stores that support Hormel and restaurants are often segregated between strikers and nonstrikers. Four years after the strike, wages were restored and the company become profitable again, but the community was still divided.

Questions:

1. If you were advising Local 9 or Hormel, what recommendations would you have made along the way? Was the conflict inevitable?
2. How effective are strikes? Why do strikes have such a potential for violence? What alternative methods can be used to resolve conflicts?
3. How flexible should unions be in their negotiations with management? If they continue to push for greater cooperation, at what point do they lose their power as a bargaining unit?

UNILATERAL VERSUS BILATERAL DECISION MAKING

Approximately 15 percent of the nonagricultural work force in the United States belong to a union.[3] For them, the human resource functions are considerably different than for employees who work in a nonunion organization. In a nonunion organization, employers are free to make decisions regarding wages, hours of work, and working conditions without any input or approval from the employees. In this system, called **unilateral decision making**, employees must either accept management's terms, negotiate individually to change them, or leave. When employees have a union represent them, however, employers are required to negotiate with the union regarding wage levels, hours of work, working conditions, and other matters of employment security. In this system, called **bilateral decision making**, employers deal not with each employee individually but with a union that represents the workers.

The presence of a union significantly alters several human resource activities. Recruiting processes, selection procedures, wage levels, pay increases, benefits packages, complaint systems, and discipline procedures may be altered drastically by the requirements of a labor agreement.

Unions typically try to extend their influence into other areas of management, such as the scheduling of work, the establishment of work standards, job redesign, subcontracting, and the introduction of new equipment and methods. Employers usually resist union encroachment into these areas by claiming that these issues are exclusive **management prerogatives**. Whether an employer succeeds in maintaining exclusive control over these prerogatives depends on the relative strength of each side in collective bargaining and on the resolution of other conflicts, such as grievances, strikes, and slowdowns.

THE ETHICS OF UNIONS

Labor unions are one of the most highly charged, emotional topics in the field of human resource management. Most people have strong feelings about unions—either positive or negative. The central ethical issue regarding unions is whether employers should have unilateral control over wages, hours, and conditions of employment or whether they should be required to share this power with employees. Since 1935, public policy has required employers to share the power when a majority of employees favor it.

Some people criticize labor unions for generating restrictive work rules, demanding exorbitant wage rates, disrupting important public services, creating inflationary pressures, protecting incompetent workers, limiting the rights of nonunion workers, and instigating violent acts. Other people praise them for protecting employees from arbitrary management decisions, providing working conditions that are safe and pleasant, and increasing wages and benefits so that workers can have a decent standard of living. Union sympathizers claim that unions are necessary to protect employees from arbitrary management actions. They say that unions provide a *balance of power* in negotiations with large, powerful corporations. Union critics claim that unions abuse their power by disregarding productive efficiency and that they threaten rather than protect the rights of individual workers to have secure jobs.

Like political issues, these arguments could be debated endlessly. Deciding whether one side is right or wrong, however, is not as important as understanding both sides of the issue. Human resource specialists should be able to present both union and management views on an issue, regardless of their biases. Another reason to study labor unions is to be able to evaluate public policy and labor regulations. Collective bargaining was established by federal legislation. The field of labor relations and the activities of labor unions have been greatly influenced by federal laws that define the rights, duties, and obligations of both unions and employers in the areas of collective bargaining and employee relations. Because these laws have an enormous social and economic impact, citizens should be prepared to evaluate them and change them as needed.

WHY PEOPLE JOIN UNIONS

The reasons workers choose to join or not join a labor union vary from general ideological beliefs to simple pragmatic reasons. To some people, labor-management struggles represent class conflicts between the "haves" and the "have nots," or between capitalists and laborers. To the average worker, however, philosophical issues are probably much less important than practical considerations. Some workers join a union because the union has a union shop clause in the contract and workers must join to keep their jobs; if the workers were given a choice, some would undoubtedly choose not to join. Other workers join to satisfy their needs for affiliation; some labor unions provide social interaction in much the same way as fraternities and sororities on college campuses.

For most workers, the decision to join a union rests on two primary issues: economic advantages and the elimination of unfair conditions.[4] Most union members believe unions should be credited for having created many economic benefits, including higher wages, improved medical benefits, bigger pensions, longer vacations, more rest breaks, protection against inflation, and political pressure through lobbying. Union members also believe that unions protect them against unfair and discriminatory treatment by management. For example, if there is a union contract, then promotions, pay increases, and easy job assignments cannot be unfairly given to favored employees, and supervisors cannot act harshly and capriciously by firing a worker without a fair hearing. Workers join unions because of low wages and unfair personnel policies.

There are three major reasons why people decide *not* to join a union. First, employees may consider themselves professionals and believe they should join a professional association rather than a trade union. Teachers, nurses, and engineers, for example, could join a union, but many in these professions feel that unions are for production workers and that as professional employees they should rely on their professional associations for help. Second, an increasing number of people disagree with the goals and activities of labor unions. These people believe that unions should discontinue negotiating for a larger piece of a shrinking pie and begin to cooperate with management in trying to increase the size of the pie. Third, some employees identify with management. They work closely with management, especially in small companies, and they think unions are inefficient adversaries. Again, fair wages and sound human resource policies seem to be important determinants of the decision not to join a union.[5]

Union membership has gradually declined from a high of about 35 percent of the work force in 1953 to about 15 percent in 1990. Although union leaders predict a reversal in this trend over the next few decades, others predict that organized labor will cease to be a bargaining unit and simply become a fraternal association.[6] Both positions are probably overstated, but it is true that union membership has declined. Most of the economic and political forces causing the decline are expected to continue.

1. Contingent employees, such as part-time, temporary, and leased employees, seldom form unions, and the percentage of contingent employees is expected to increase.
2. A larger percentage of the labor force will work in small companies, and small companies are more frequently nonunion.
3. Most union members have held blue-collar jobs, and technological advancements are creating fewer blue-collar jobs and more white-collar and service jobs.
4. The protections that were formerly provided by labor agreements are being provided by federal legislation, making unions unnecessary.
5. Increased competition from both foreign and domestic firms requires flexibility and restructuring that often conflicts with inflexible labor agreements.
6. The image of unions has been tarnished by reports of fraud and ties to organized crime.[7]

EARLY LABOR MOVEMENT

This section briefly reviews the history of labor unions during the past few centuries. An understanding of this labor history is necessary to comprehend many current labor issues. The laws that exist today were passed in response to specific problems that existed in earlier years.

In 1935 the National Labor Relations Act (Wagner Act) established the legal right for labor unions to exist. Before that time, the existence of unions was uncertain and threatened. Labor leaders had lobbied for the passage of several state and federal laws only to see the laws used against unions after they had been passed. During the 1800s four major tactics were used against unions: the conspiracy doctrine, court injunctions, yellow-dog contracts, and antitrust statutes.

CONSPIRACY DOCTRINE

Before 1800 labor unions in America were patterned after the guilds of the Middle Ages. A guild consisted of workers in a particular skilled trade who had joined together to form an association. The association established standards of professional conduct and regulated the entry of new members into the trade by controlling the training process. New members often had to serve long apprenticeships before they could advance to the levels of journeyman or craftsman. These craft unions were generally small and did not engage in strikes or collective bargaining.

One of the first instances of collective union activity occurred in 1794 when the Philadelphia Cordwainers (shoemakers) refused to work in protest against reduced wages.[8] The shoemakers' unions were so powerful that the shoemakers' employers formed associations to neutralize the power of the unions. The most effective weapon used by the employers was the hiring of replacements who worked for wages below the scale demanded by the unionists. After the craftsmen had formed a highly organized union, however, the employers could not hire sufficient replacements.

In 1806 the employers' associations sought the help of the courts. This date marks the beginning of government intervention in labor relations.[9] In the *Philadelphia Cordwainers* case, the shoemaker employers charged that labor unions were illegal conspiracies in restraint of trade. A conspiracy, generally defined, is a combination of two or more people who join together to damage the rights of others. For conspiracy to be charged, the only evidence necessary is that the group has caused or *plans* to cause an injustice to other people or to society.

A significant feature of the legal definition of a conspiracy is that something one person is allowed to do when acting alone may be illegal when done by a group. This concept of group action was an important consideration in the outcome of the early conspiracy trials. The courts held that workers as individuals had the right to take actions to increase their wages or to quit if they were dissatisfied. But workers were found guilty of conspiracy when they acted as a group to demand high wages or withhold their labor by collectively striking. From 1806 to 1842, seventeen verdicts declared that labor unions were illegal conspiracies in restraint of trade.[10]

In 1836 mass demonstrations were held in New York and in Washington, D.C., protesting the use of the conspiracy doctrine. Two judges who had previously convicted unionists as criminal conspirators were burned in effigy during these demonstrations. Finally, in 1842, the conspiracy doctrine was redefined in the landmark case of *Commonwealth* v. *Hunt*. Chief Justice Shaw of the Massachusetts Supreme Court ruled that a union could be found guilty of conspiracy if either its objectives or its methods of achieving the objectives were illegal. But Shaw ruled that collective bargaining to raise wages was not illegal, nor was collectively striking, even if the effect of such actions was to reduce profits or to raise the price of the product.

INJUNCTIONS

When employers could no longer use the conspiracy doctrine to control union activities, they turned to the use of court injunctions. An **injunction** is a court order that directs a person or group to refrain from pursuing a course of action. In most cases an injunction is used to protect property rights, which include the rights to hire workers, to sell goods, and to run a business in a profitable manner. Injunctions are issued when it is believed that without them irreparable damage to property will occur, leaving the property owner without adequate remedy to obtain compensation for the loss. Irreparable damage to property can be inflicted not only by violent destruction of physical items but also by activities that interfere with the normal running of a business.

Injunctions are issued by judges acting alone in an "equity court." An equity court is different from a trial court that has a judge, jury, witnesses, and cross-examination. In an equity court, the judge alone decides whether sufficient evidence exists to issue a restraining order. If one judge refuses to issue an injunction, employers are free to look for another judge who will. A person who violates an injunction can be held "in contempt of court," and the judge who issued the injunction determines whether it has been violated. Severe penalties, including the payment of heavy fines and imprisonment, can be inflicted on violators of injunctions.

The blanket injunction used sweeping terms to enjoin unions and "all other persons whomsoever" from "interfering in any way whatsoever" with the normal conduct of business. Injunctions were used frequently to restrain union activities. Prior to 1931, state and federal courts issued 1,845 labor injunctions.[12] Most of them were issued after 1895, when the Supreme Court upheld the constitutionality of labor injunctions in the celebrated *Debs* case.[13] This case involved the nation's railroads and a serious threat to interstate commerce. The case grew out of a dispute between the American Railway Union and the Pullman Car Company. In 1894 the railway workers struck to protest reduced wages and the discriminatory firing of union leaders. When the union realized that it could not win its strike by direct action, it attempted to force the railroads to engage in a secondary boycott against the use of Pullman sleeping cars. When the railroads refused this request, the union induced a series of strikes against the railroads. Because the strikes disrupted interstate commerce, especially delivery of the U.S. mail, the government obtained an injunction ordering the union and its officers to cease striking against the railroads. Eugene F. Debs, president of the union, and other union leaders were imprisoned for violating the terms of the injunction. When this case reached the Supreme Court, the court endorsed the use of injunctions in labor disputes. This case was a serious blow to union leaders, who believed that unfair employers could conspire with capricious judges to issue an injunction against any form of union activity, legal or illegal.

YELLOW-DOG CONTRACTS

Court injunctions were especially effective when they were used to enforce **yellow-dog contracts**. A yellow-dog contract was a written statement that workers had to sign as part of their application for employment to confirm that they were not presently members of a union, that they accepted the company as a nonunion employer, and that they promised not to join a union or to encourage others to join a union. The yellow-dog contract was first used in the 1870s, and from then until 1932 it had a chilling effect on union activity. In 1908 and again in 1912 the Supreme Court ruled that federal and state statutes designed to outlaw the use of yellow-dog contracts were unconstitutional. Not only was a yellow-dog agreement legal but it could also be enforced with a court injunction.

ANTITRUST STATUTES

During the late 1800s the concept of free enterprise was threatened by large corporate trusts and combinations that attempted to monopolize the production and sale of selected products, especially oil, sugar, tobacco, whiskey, and shoemaking machinery. Congress responded to this threat by passing the *Sherman Antitrust Act* of 1890.[14] Although this law made no specific references to labor organizations, unionists found that it limited a variety of vital union activities. Unions were interpreted by the courts as illegal combinations in restraint of interstate commerce when they attempted to strike an employer or to boycott an employer's products.

The application of antitrust legislation to restrict union activities is illustrated by the famous *Danbury Hatters* case.[15] In 1902 the United Hatters attempted to organize the employees of Loewe & Company in Danbury, Connecticut. The company refused to recognize the union. An organizational strike designed to force union recognition was unsuccessful because the company found replacements for the striking workers and continued to operate successfully. Of the eighty-two firms in the felt hat industry, seventy were organized. Some of the nonunion firms had a significant competitive advantage because of their low labor costs and high productivity. Since the survival of the hatters' union depended on its ability to organize the remaining twelve firms, it decided to make a show of strength and therefore instituted a boycott against the purchase of Loewe's hats with the help of the American Federation of Labor. The boycott was successful; Loewe's reported an $85,000 loss in one year. Subsequently, the company sued the United Hatters and its members for damages under the Sherman law. The Supreme Court ruled that the union's boycott was a restraint of interstate commerce and awarded treble damages ($252,000) to be paid by the union and its individual members.

After the *Danbury Hatters* case, labor unions intensified their efforts to exert political pressure. The unions decided that they needed protective legislation since the existing laws were being interpreted adversely by judges who had been appointed for life. In 1914, when the Clayton Act was passed, the unions believed that they had finally succeeded in winning their freedom. This law stated that labor was not a commodity or an article of commerce and that the antitrust laws could not be construed to forbid the existence of labor unions.

To their dismay, unionists soon found that the Clayton Act was worthless. They already had the right to exist. What they needed was the right to use economic sanctions, especially strikes, against employers who refused to recognize them and bargain collectively. The Supreme Court had continued to interpret the laws with such sweeping pronouncements that any strike for any purpose was considered unlawful if it diminished the amount of goods in interstate trade.

By 1933 union membership was only about 2 million members. The survival of the unions was threatened because they were constrained from performing several essential activities. Strikes, pickets, and boycotts could be squelched immediately by a temporary injunction. Membership in a union could be restricted by a yellow-dog contract that was required as a condition of employment. Any union activity that served to reduce interstate commerce was considered illegal, and unions and their members could be fined up to three times the loss.

During this period, unions struggled to survive in a very hostile environment. Only a small percentage of the work force joined a union, and organized labor might have disappeared entirely if working conditions had been more tolerable. However, because enough workers felt abused and exploited due to low wages, poor working conditions, and unfair management, they continued to organize. They hoped to force employers to respond to their demands through united efforts at picketing, strikes, and boycotts.

Workers often felt frustrated in their attempts to create peaceful change and therefore resorted to violence. The violence usually created prejudice against the unions when cases reached the courts, and in condemning violence, the courts also ruled against the activities of labor unions. A good illustration of the courts' reactions to union violence is provided by the *Coronado* case. The Coronado Coal Mine was operated by members of the United Mine Workers. In 1914, however, the mining company decided to operate the mine on a nonunion basis. Since the company expected this decision to cause trouble, it hired armed guards, purchased rifles and ammunition, evicted union members from company houses, and built a cable fence around the mine. The anticipated violence followed. Several nonunion workers and guards were murdered, and many individuals on both sides were injured. The mine was damaged once by flooding and was ultimately destroyed by dynamite. The violence was succeeded by lengthy litigation that ultimately reached the Supreme Court on two separate occasions. In its second ruling, eleven years after the event, the Court ruled against the union and even disregarded the Clayton Act by convicting the union of antitrust violations of the Sherman Act.[16]

Widespread labor disputes marked by occasional violence finally induced society to consider this fundamental issue: Are property rights more important than individual rights? The early laws and court rulings governing labor relations definitely endorsed the supremacy of property rights. But legislators gradually began to think that individual rights were more important than property rights. Proponents of individual rights held that an individual should have the right to hold a job and to improve his or her life and that an organization should serve its members rather than members serving the organization.[17]

LABOR LAWS

From 1806 to 1932 the legal climate surrounding the collective bargaining process was very restrictive. Theoretically, unions were lawful organizations; workers could join a union, and they had the right to strike. But in practice, the courts controlled the rights of workers to join unions and denied unions the liberty of engaging in the activities that made collective bargaining effective. The evidence of a century of labor activity demonstrated that unions needed protective legislation to neutralize the power of employers.

The strong antiunion atmosphere of the early 1900s might have continued if the Great Depression had not provided a strong impetus for change. Nearly 25 percent of the work force was unemployed during the Depression, and workers had to struggle for economic survival. Many banks were forced to close, businesses went bankrupt, and many people lost their homes, farms, and personal possessions. Several laws designed to alter the economic structure were passed during the period. Two of these laws—the Norris-LaGuardia Act and the Wagner Act—concerned labor unions. These laws provided unions with the power that they had lacked for so long.

NORRIS-LAGUARDIA ACT

The Norris-LaGuardia Act, passed in 1932, encouraged the formation of labor unions by neutralizing the differential power between employees and employers.[18] It recognized the basic inequality that existed between the employer and the individual worker. To achieve a balance of power between the employer and the worker, Norris-LaGuardia limited the power of the courts to intervene in labor disputes. It established an area of industrial freedom in which court actions are constrained. The primary focus of the act was to limit the use of the court injunction. The major provisions of the Norris-LaGuardia Act are presented in Table 13.1.

Although Norris-LaGuardia restricted court interference in labor disputes, it did not restrict interference from other parties, especially employers. The act was intended to encourage collective bargaining, but workers still lacked the protection they needed to engage in collective bargaining activities. An extensive congressional investigation in 1936 by the LaFollette committee documented numerous antiunion activities.[19] Four of the most threatening activities to collective bargaining were industrial espionage, attacks on union leaders, strike-breaking tactics, and the formation of company unions.

INDUSTRIAL ESPIONAGE

The LaFollette committee found that employers frequently hired agents from their own organizations or from professional detective agencies to spy on union members. These spies not only identified union members but also tried to destroy the union from within by advocating violence and destruction, by discrediting union leaders, and by destroying the faith of other workers in the union.

ATTACKS ON UNION LEADERS

Many union leaders were killed or beaten by hit men hired by employers to discourage union activity. The LaFollette committee also disclosed the practice of rough shadowing,

TABLE 13.1   Major provisions of the Norris-LaGuardia Federal Anti-Injunction Act

- The courts are not allowed to decide the legality of a strike. The responsibility for deciding whether some strikes are contrary to the public interest is assigned to the legislative arm of government. Therefore, a court cannot issue an injunction against a strike just because the judge objects to its purpose.
- The courts are not allowed to restrict labor unions from giving aid, such as strike-relief funds, to members engaged in a labor dispute.
- The courts are not allowed to restrain the picketing activities of unions as long as such activities are free from violence and fraud.
- Unions are allowed to encourage nonstriking members to join in the conflict provided that the campaign for participation is free from violence and fraud.
- The courts are not allowed to restrict unions from assembling peacefully or from conducting meetings.
- The courts are not allowed to enforce yellow-dog contracts. Employers can still require workers to sign an agreement stating that they will not join a union, but such agreements cannot be legally enforced in court.

where union leaders were kept under open surveillance to intimidate and harass them and their families. Attacks were also made on the character and loyalty of union leaders to discredit them in the eyes of union members. Damaging false rumors that claimed that union leaders were "communists," "foreign elements," or "labor racketeers" were often circulated.

STRIKEBREAKING

Once a union had been formed, many employers tried to destroy it by making strikes ineffective. Some strikes were broken when employers refused to negotiate with the union and encouraged workers to return to work. In some widely publicized cases, employers hired professional strikebreakers and fortified their companies with munitions and barricades. Some of the professional strikebreakers were former criminals who incited violence among the strikers, causing the national guard or state police to be called in. The violence was intended to create antiunion sympathies in the eyes of the public.

COMPANY UNIONS

A less violent method of controlling union activities was for a company to organize and dominate a union. Such a company union was sometimes able to represent worker grievances, but it usually did not allow genuine collective bargaining over wages and other important issues. A company union ultimately represented the interests of the company, not the employees.

WAGNER ACT

The long record of violence and strife in labor relations convinced many that legislation was needed for the benefit of both unions and employers. A depressed economy with high unemployment also lent credence to the idea that union activities should receive government protection. Therefore, in 1935, Congress passed the National Labor Relations Act, popularly called the Wagner Act after its sponsor, Senator Robert Wagner of New York.[20] This law was designed to be an economic stabilizer for a depressed economy and to establish collective bargaining as the vehicle for industrial relations. In 1937 the Supreme Court upheld the constitutionality of the Wagner Act, and it quickly became the legal foundation of union growth.

The basic intent of the Wagner Act is summarized in Section 7 of the Act:

Sec. 7. Employees shall have the right to self-organization, to form, join, or assist labor organizations, to bargain collectively through representatives of their own choosing, and to engage in concerted activities, for the purpose of collective bargaining or other mutual aid or protection.

To guarantee these rights to employees, Congress identified five unfair labor practices and declared them unlawful. These practices, which are defined in Section 8 of the Wagner Act, are summarized in Table 13.2.

The Wagner Act established the National Labor Relations Board (NLRB) and gave it the authority to administer the act in a peaceful and democratic manner. When a sufficient number of employees request a representation election, the NLRB conducts the election and determines the bargaining agent. If charges of unfair labor practices

---

TABLE 13.2   Unfair labor practices as specified by the National Labor Relations Act

It is an unfair labor practice for an employer to "interfere with, restrain, or coerce employees in the exercise of their rights under Section 7." This means that employers cannot threaten employees with job loss for union activity. They cannot grant wage increases that are timed to discourage union membership. They cannot question employees about union activities or spy on union meetings or leaders, nor can employers try to openly induce employees to discontinue union activities by offering them better jobs or more money.

It is an unfair labor practice for an employer to dominate or interfere with the formation or administration of a labor union. This means that company unions that are formed or directed by a company are illegal. A company cannot even contribute financially to the union or pay delinquent membership dues for its employees.

It is an unfair labor practice for employers to allow union membership or activity to influence hiring, firing, promotion, or other employment decisions. An employer can still fire employees for disciplinary reasons such as disobedience, drinking on the job, or careless work, but an employer should be prepared to show that employment decisions are not intended to discourage union membership or activity.

It is an unfair labor practice to discharge or discriminate against an employee who has filed a charge with the NLRB or given testimony to the NLRB. This restriction is intended to protect the integrity of the board and to allow it to collect information without the threat of reprisals being made against its witnesses.

It is an unfair labor practice for an employer to refuse to bargain in good faith with representatives of the employees.

are made, the board is responsible for investigating and resolving them. From 1936 to 1947 the NLRB was extensively involved in employee relations disputes. It reinstated 76,268 workers who had been discharged because of union activities; it awarded $12,418,000 in back pay to workers who had been discharged; it disestablished 1,709 company-dominated unions; and it ordered employers to bargain in good faith on 5,070 occasions.[21]

TAFT-HARTLEY ACT

In 1947 the general feeling in Congress and society was that the Wagner Act had provided too much power for unions. Some union activities seemed to represent an abuse of power. In 1943, for example, the defiance by the United Mine Workers Union of a no-strike order issued by the National War Labor Board resulted in the federal government seizing and operating the coal mines. When wartime controls were removed at the end of World War II, many unions tried to exert their new power. In 1946, 4,985 strikes occurred, which resulted in an unprecedented 116 million workdays of lost production.[22] Events such as these, plus the public's misunderstanding of the provisions of the Wagner Act and the functions of the NLRB, created the feeling that union activities needed to be controlled.

The Wagner Act was amended in 1947 by the Labor Management Relations Act, popularly called the Taft-Hartley Act.[23] Under the provisions of this act, collective bargaining was retained as the basic direction of national labor policy, but greater restrictions were imposed, especially on unions.

The Taft-Hartley Act amendments concern four basic issues: (1) unfair labor practices by unions, (2) the rights of employees as individuals, (3) the rights of employers, and (4) national emergency strikes.

UNFAIR UNION PRACTICES

The Wagner Act identified specific actions of employers as unlawful. The Taft-Hartley Act, in turn, identified specific union activities as unlawful. Six unfair union practices are prohibited by the act. These restrictions, which are summarized in Table 13.3, prevent unions from restraining, coercing, or threatening an employer or employees who choose not to join a union. The restrictions also require unions to bargain in good faith, prohibit unions from using secondary boycotts and featherbedding, and prohibit unions from charging excessive membership dues or initiation fees.

Featherbedding refers to restrictive work rules that require more workers than are necessary to perform a job. The term comes from the beds on which firemen helpers slept after nonsteam locomotives made their jobs unnecessary. The Brotherhood of Locomotive Firemen and Enginemen insisted the job was necessary despite its obsolescence and succeeded in preserving it in their negotiations.

The Taft-Hartley Act prohibits unions from featherbedding, that is, forcing employers to pay for work or services not performed. Although this provision seems reasonable, it has had little effect. The NLRB has ruled that the provision does not prevent unions from seeking employment for their members "even in situations where the employer does not want, does not need, and is not willing to accept such services." This ruling of the NLRB was upheld by the Supreme Court in 1952, when the Court ruled that featherbedding was illegal only when it resulted in payment for services not performed or not to be

TABLE 13.3   Unfair labor practices by unions as specified by the Taft-Hartley Act

Unions are not allowed to restrain or coerce employees in the exercise of their collective bargaining rights. Therefore, unions cannot threaten antiunion employees with job loss should the union gain recognition. Picket-line violence and threats to employees who cross picket lines are illegal. Threats of reprisal against employees subpoenaed to testify against the union at NLRB hearings are illegal.

Unions are not allowed to force an employer to discriminate in any way against an employee in order to encourage or discourage union membership. Employers cannot be forced to fire or assign unpleasant jobs to employees who refuse to join a union, fail to attend union meetings, or oppose union policies. An exception to this provision is when a valid union-shop agreement has been negotiated which demands the discharge of employees who fail to pay initiation fees or periodic dues.

Unions are required to bargain in good faith with employers in regard to wages, hours, and conditions of employment. This requirement means that unions must make the same good faith efforts as employers to meet and make counterproposals in a sincere effort to reach agreement.

Unions are not allowed to conduct certain types of strikes or boycotts. For example, union activities cannot try to force an employer or self-employed person to join a cause or cease dealing with another employer. This means that secondary boycotts against another company, such as a supplier or purchaser, are illegal. It is also illegal for a union to strike to force an employer to assign particular work to a particular craft.

Unions are not allowed to charge excessive initiation fees or membership dues when all employees are required to join a union shop.

Unions are not allowed to force employers to pay for work or services that are not performed—a practice called featherbedding.

performed. The Court did indicate, however, that whether a job was or was not necessary should be decided in collective bargaining.[24]

RIGHTS OF EMPLOYEES

In addition to the protections specified in its unfair union practices section, the Taft-Hartley Act provides rights for individual employees. First, it prohibits the **closed shop**, an arrangement that requires all workers to be union members at the time they are hired. (However, an exception was later made by the Landrum-Griffin Act to allow a closed shop in the construction industry).

The act also affects the **union shop**, an arrangement that permits an employer to hire workers who are not union members with the stipulation that they will join the union once they are hired. The Taft-Hartley Act allows union shops but empowers the states to pass legislation prohibiting them. Such **right-to-work** legislation has been passed by twenty states, mostly in the South and West. Individual employees in these states may refuse union membership even if the majority chooses to have a union represent them. Advocates of right-to-work laws claim that they are necessary to guarantee basic individual freedoms. Opponents claim that it is unfair for nonunion members to enjoy the benefits of union membership without paying union dues or participating in union activities and that this legislation threatens union security. The evidence does not

HRM in Action

Are Work Groups Legal?

Work groups are popular in many industries, and some companies view them as an essential element in their struggle to remain competitive. The most popular work groups are quality circles, labor-management committees, design teams, and participation groups. In many organizations these work groups have contributed importantly to a variety of organizational improvements, such as better quality control, product design, work scheduling, and labor-management cooperation. Yet, it appears these work groups are illegal if the union objects to them.

A design team was established at DuPont's Chambers Works in Deepwater, New Jersey, in May 1987. The team consisted of twenty-three people—twelve supervisors and eleven operatives, of whom five were union members. The team held regular meetings to consider such issues as flextime, understocked candy machines, and an employee fitness center. After several meetings, however, the local union filed an unfair labor practice.

The Chemical Workers Association claimed that the work group infringed on its domain by discussing issues that were subject to collective bargaining. When an administrative law judge agreed, the union asked that seven other work groups at Chambers Works be disbanded.

The legal foundation for the union's objection is the National Labor Relations Act (1935), which prohibits employers from giving "financial or other support" to a labor organization. The work groups can be considered labor organizations since labor organizations are broadly defined in the law as "any organization of any kind, or any agency or employee representation committee or plan" that deals with wages, hours, or conditions of work.

Most unions (including the United Auto Workers, the United Steelworkers of America, and the Communication Workers of America) have endorsed work groups and included provisions for them in their labor agreements. Other unions (including the American Postal Workers Union) have resisted employee-involvement groups. And when the union objects, it appears they are illegal.

Source: Richard Koenig: "Quality Circles Are Vulnerable to Union Tests," *Wall Street Journal*, March 28, 1990, p. B1.

support either side. Right-to-work laws are difficult to enforce because of the strength of peer pressure, and as a result, union security has not been seriously undermined in states with these laws.[25]

The Taft-Hartley Act protects union members who choose to cross the picket lines. During a strike, unions try to prevent employees from returning to work by fining them and refusing to let them leave the union to avoid the fines. Recently, however, the U.S. Supreme Court has decided that a union constitution may not prohibit members from resigning their membership during a strike to return to work.[26]

The Taft-Hartley Act also provides for two other individual rights. Employees are allowed to present grievances directly to their employer without union intervention, and a dues check-off arrangement, in which membership dues are taken directly from an employee's wages by the employer and sent to the union, cannot be used unless the employee authorizes this arrangement each year.

RIGHTS OF EMPLOYERS

Under the Taft-Hartley Act, employers enjoy some of the same rights that the Wagner Act gave to unions. Employers are given the right to file unfair labor practices complaints against unions. Employers also can call for elections to decide questions of representation. The most important right, however, is employers' increased freedom of expression. Employers are free to express their views concerning union organizations, provided that there is "no threat of reprisal or force or promise of benefit." This provision allows employers to tell their employees why they think unions are worthless, dangerous to the economy, or corrupt, provided that the employers avoid threats, promises, coercion, and libelous slander.

NATIONAL EMERGENCY STRIKES

National emergency disputes normally involve critical services or industries such as railroads, oil, steel, coal, and ocean shipping. If the president of the United States believes that a strike would "imperil the national health and safety," the president may apply for a court injunction to restrain the strike for sixty days. If no settlement is reached during this time, the injunction can be extended an additional twenty days. After this eighty-day "cooling off" period, the employees may strike and the president must submit a full report to Congress with recommendations for its consideration. In the thirty times that the national emergency strike provisions have been used, the injunction has not proved to be a very effective tool in resolving labor disputes. However, the high-level investigators assigned by a president to deal with a national emergency dispute have often been effective mediators.

LANDRUM-GRIFFIN ACT

Government control of labor relations was increased in 1959 by the passage of another amendment to the National Labor Relations Act, the Labor-Management Reporting and Disclosure Act.[27] This law, commonly called the Landrum-Griffin Act, primarily regulates the internal conduct of labor unions. Between 1957 and 1959, a congressional committee, known as the McClelland Anti-Racketeering Committee, investigated improper actions of labor unions. The Committee's investigation revealed widespread misuse of union funds, acts of violence against union members, organizational picketing to extort money from employers, infiltration by criminals into union leadership positions, and a loss of power among the rank-and-file union members. The Landrum-Griffin Act was designed to control these alleged wrongdoings. The act focuses on five major areas: (1) a bill of rights for union members, (2) reports to the secretary of labor, (3) union trusteeships, (4) conduct of union elections, and (5) financial safeguards. The major provisions of this act are summarized in Table 13.4.

The Landrum-Griffin Act provides union members with some of the same basic rights within their union that American citizens enjoy under the Bill of Rights of the United States Constitution. The act requires unions to follow democratic procedures in electing officers and creating union policies. Many union leaders have objected to this requirement, arguing that business organizations and even government agencies do not have to function so democratically. Some union leaders think that democratic procedures

TABLE 13.4   Provisions of the Landrum-Griffin Act

The law grants equal rights and privileges to every union member with regard to nomination of candidates, voting in elections, attendance at union meetings, and voting in these meetings. Every member is given the right to meet and assemble freely with other members to express views, arguments, and opinions. Increases in dues and fees must be approved by the union membership majority. Members who have been wronged by the union and cannot obtain justice through normal union procedures are guaranteed the right to sue the union in a civil suit. Union members may not be fined, expelled, or otherwise disciplined, except for nonpayment of dues, unless certain procedural steps are taken to insure due process. The member must be (1) served with written specific charges, (2) given a reasonable time to prepare a defense, and (3) afforded a full and fair hearing.

Each labor organization is required to submit a copy of its constitution and bylaws plus annual financial reports. These reports are open to the public. Union members can challenge the accuracy of the reports in a court suit and if they are successful, the union is required to pay the court costs and attorney's fees. Employers are required to report any expenses or payments regarding efforts to influence union activities or the union attitudes of employees. Labor relations consultants also must report their receipts and disbursements and the nature of their arrangements with employers when they are paid to influence employees' union attitudes.

If an international union takes control of a local union, it is required to provide a rational justification for its action and detailed reports of its activities, especially its financial transactions.

National unions are required to hold elections at least once every five years; local unions, at least once every three years; and intermediate bodies, every four years. Voting must be by secret ballot and among members in good standing or by delegates chosen by secret ballot. Election results must be retained for at least one year. If a union member complains of voting irregularities, the secretary of labor can direct that a new election be held, call for a recount, or take some other corrective action. Unions may not impose unreasonable eligibility requirements on candidates for union office. Unreasonable requirements, such as 50 percent attendance at all union meetings during the preceding three years, are not legal. However, a person convicted of certain crimes is barred from union office during the first five years after his or her sentence expires. The law also provides that union officers can be removed from office for serious misconduct, although the removal procedures are rather cumbersome and time consuming.

Union officers are required to manage and invest union funds in strict accordance with the constitution and bylaws of the union. Embezzlement of union funds is a federal crime. All union personnel who receive or handle union funds must be bonded. Unions are not allowed to loan over two thousand dollars to their members, and unions and employers are prohibited from paying the fines of officers or members convicted of willful violation of the act.

are inefficient. They argue that many union positions should be appointive rather than elective and that certain decisions should be made by union leaders without requiring ratification of the membership.

To reduce the likelihood of fraud and improper actions, the Landrum-Griffin Act requires several parties to file reports with the secretary of labor. A union is required to submit copies of its constitution, bylaws, and financial records to the secretary. Employers and labor relations consultants are required to report to the secretary concerning any money spent or received to influence unions or attitudes about unions.

The constitutions of many international unions authorize the international officers to suspend the normal governing processes of local unions, to supervise their internal activity, and to assume control of their property and funds. This takeover of a local union by its international union is called a trusteeship or supervisorship. A trusteeship is an effective way for international unions to prevent corruption, mismanagement, and the violation of collective bargaining agreements by local unions. However, a trusteeship can be abused. In some instances, local treasuries have been plundered by an international union. To prevent such abuses, the Landrum-Griffin Act requires frequent reports on trusteeships, including detailed justification for actions taken. This provision of the act has contributed to an enormous reduction in the number of trusteeships.

To protect union funds, the act stipulates that union officers fulfill certain fiduciary responsibilities and bonding requirements. The fiduciary requirements demand that union officers wisely manage and invest union funds according to the union's constitution. Limits are placed on how much money a union member can be loaned in order to reduce the possibility of embezzlement through loan defaults. These provisions were designed to eliminate some of the improper acts that had been observed in a small number of unions.

ORGANIZING A UNION

THE NLRB

The National Labor Relations Board (NLRB) was established by Congress through the Wagner Act. The purpose of the NLRB is to protect the rights of employees, employers, unions, and the general public. To protect these rights, the NLRB performs two major functions: conducting representation elections and resolving unfair labor practices.

The NLRB has two divisions.[28] One division consists of a five-member board that hears and decides cases involving unfair labor practices and disputed elections. The board reviews a large number of cases each year, but it rules on only a small number that contain precedent-making issues or that provoke suspicion of a serious error. These cases are referred to the board by the other division of the NLRB.

The other division consists of a general counsel and a large staff. The general counsel is appointed by the president and approved by Congress. The staff consists of employees in thirty-one regional offices and three subregional offices. Each regional office has a director who supervises field examiners and labor attorneys. Most of the work of the NLRB is accomplished in these regional offices. The field examiners investigate unfair labor practices and conduct elections. The attorneys perform the same kinds of work as the field examiners, and also may appear in court proceedings.

REPRESENTATION ELECTIONS

If employees want to organize a union, they must follow the procedure established by the NLRB to provide for peaceful elections. The first step is to get at least 30 percent of the workers in a company to sign authorization cards calling for a union to represent them. After 30 percent of the workers have expressed an interest, they can petition the NLRB for a representation election.

The NLRB then investigates four issues: (1) whether the company falls within the jurisdiction of the NLRB, (2) who should represent which workers, (3) whether there is enough worker interest (at least 30 percent), and (4) whether another petition has been filed within the past year. A company must exceed a certain dollar volume of business, such as $1 million in sales, or the NLRB will not respond to the petition. If a company is too small to come under the jurisdiction of the NLRB, its case is left to the jurisdiction of state laws, which may or may not exist.

The NLRB must decide how to form appropriate bargaining units. In a hospital, for example, the NLRB normally forms separate unions for registered nurses, technical employees, business office and clerical employees, and general service and maintenance employees. New elections cannot be conducted if a valid election was held during the preceding twelve months.

Elections using secret ballots are conducted by the NLRB's regional offices. Representatives of both management and the union are entitled to observe the election procedures to determine that only legitimate employees are given ballots. Once the election has been conducted and any problems associated with it settled, the outcome is certified. If the union has won, the employer is obligated to enter into collective bargaining negotiations with certified representatives of the union.

The process for decertifying a labor union follows the same procedure. The NLRB must receive a petition from at least 30 percent of the workers calling for an election. After the usual investigation, an election is held. If fewer than 50 percent vote in favor of the union, the union is decertified. Between 1936 and 1947 unions won about 80 percent of the representation elections. During 1984 unions only won 46 percent of the 3,561 representation elections conducted by the NLRB. The win-loss record for unions is even lower in decertification elections. In 1984 unions only won 23 percent of 874 decertification elections.[29]

The NLRB has held that employers cannot initiate decertification activity if employees show no interest in decertification. Firms cannot recommend, circulate, or assist in preparing a petition for decertification. During the campaign stage, employers can provide only minimal assistance and cannot allow employees to work for decertification during working hours.[30]

UNFAIR LABOR PRACTICES

An **unfair labor practice** is any action by either the union or management that is prohibited by law or NLRB ruling. Every case originates in one of the regional offices as a charge or petition that has been filed by an individual or organization. The regional office investigates the charges by assigning a field examiner or an attorney to take written statements and affidavits from available witnesses. Regional offices try to dispose of the cases informally through withdrawal, settlement, or dismissal. If a case is not closed by one of these informal methods, a formal complaint is issued by the regional director to the general counsel. The general counsel may dismiss the case, leaving the complaining party with no recourse other than to sue the NLRB in the federal courts, or the general counsel may refer the case to the board for a ruling. During this period the case can be withdrawn by the charging parties; however, the general counsel may pursue the case on its own, irrespective of a settlement, to correct a serious inequity or to allow the case to serve as a precedent. Before a case goes before the full board, a formal hearing is held. An administrative law judge conducts the hearing according to the rules of evidence and procedures of the United States District Courts, and then issues a decision. Any party that disagrees with the judge's decision may appeal within twenty days to the five-member board of the NLRB.

The NLRB handles an enormous number of cases each year. In 1989 the number of elections and unfair labor practices cases totaled 44,190. Almost 80 percent of these cases involved unfair labor practices. Fortunately, almost 90 percent of the unfair labor charges are settled informally.[31] Many charges are dropped after a contract has been successfully negotiated. Other cases are dismissed by the NLRB because they are trivial or because the NLRB does not have enough time to handle them. The NLRB faces a constant challenge to improve its efficiency since the full procedure from charge to complaint to hearing by a law judge to board ruling normally requires a full year.

After the NLRB issues a decision, a dissatisfied party may appeal to the federal court of appeals, and then ask the Supreme Court to review the case. This process may take several years. In a typical year, about 50 percent of the NLRB's rulings are appealed, and approximately 85 percent of these rulings are upheld.

LEGAL AND ILLEGAL CAMPAIGN TACTICS

Many of the unfair labor practice charges submitted to the NLRB arise from improper campaign activities. The time just prior to an election is an intense period when employers and union representatives are campaigning for employee support. Both sides are quick to notice improper actions and to charge one another with unfair labor practices. Consequently, both sides need to know the laws limiting what they can do. Many activities that are normally legal become illegal prior to a representation election.

Before passage of the Taft-Hartley Act, an employer was not allowed to campaign actively against a union during a representation election. This severe restriction on the right of an employer to express an opinion was inconsistent with the constitutional guarantees of freedom of speech. The Taft-Hartley Act corrected this imbalance by allowing employers to express their views and to disseminate information as long as it "contains no threat of reprisal or force or promise of benefit."

Through its efforts to administer this law, the NLRB has established a lengthy list of guidelines for fair elections. The general intent of the board is to provide conditions that are as ideal as possible so that the uninhibited desires of the employees can be determined. Any evidence or suggestion of violence by either management or the union is certain to be condemned by the board. Many other actions also are illegal because they violate the employees' freedom of choice. When violations by either side are observed and when the guilty party receives a majority vote, the NLRB can order a new election.

The board has ruled that an election is invalid when an employer visits employees in their homes or assembles them in a manager's office for the purpose of urging them to reject the union. Employers cannot single out certain employees and talk with them individually or in small groups. Nor can an employer question employees about their union sentiments.

An employer must not threaten economic retaliation if the union wins the election. The employer cannot suggest that there will be a loss in wages or benefits if a union is elected, nor can an employer threaten to divert production to another nonunion facility, threaten to close the plant, or in any other way intimate that the employees might lose their jobs if they vote in favor of a union. However, the employer is not prevented from presenting factual information to employees about the economic effects of union representation.

During an election campaign, employers generally are not free to grant wage increases or benefits improvements unless they can demonstrate that these changes are completely unrelated to the campaign. Normally this means that all wage and benefit improvements have to be announced either before or after the election campaign. Nor can an employer announce a wage or benefit improvement that will begin after the election regardless of the outcome. Such an announcement appears to imply an incentive to defeat the union by showing that the union is not needed to obtain better wages.

Employers are allowed to assemble their employees on company time and to disseminate information without being required to provide equal time for the union. The meeting place, however, must be a customary meeting place and not a place having a "special impact of awe," such as the company president's office. Since the union is generally not given equal access to a captive audience of employees on company time, union representatives often meet with employees in their homes. Within seven days after an election has been scheduled, the company is required to provide the names and addresses of all employees eligible to vote to both the union and the NLRB.

Even though employers are not allowed to threaten employees, to promise rewards, or to use inflammatory rhetoric during an organizing campaign, they are free to aggressively describe the disadvantages of a unionized company. An employer can inform employees that if they become union members they will have to pay union dues. The employer can show employees the union's financial reports, and tell them that if they become union members most of their dues will be used to pay the salaries and expense accounts of union officials. The employer can explain that collective bargaining and grievances are costly because both sides need to call in highly paid experts to settle the disputes and that the company would prefer to see both sides keep their money. An employer also can show how costly union activities such as strikes, bargaining, and grievances are to the employees, the company, and society because of lost production and lost time during these periods. The employer can present information showing the indirect costs of unionization that the company wants to avoid: executive time spent in bargaining sessions, working time of employees spent on union business, payment of arbitrator's fees, and costs of hiring lawyers and labor relations experts. Money spent for such costs obviously cannot go to the company in the form of profits or to the employees in the form of higher wages.

An employer also is free to explain how a union can limit the employees' personal freedoms. Employees who join unions have to obey the orders of union officials, within the scope of their authority, which means that the employees will have two bosses instead of one. Once employees join a union, the union's constitution becomes a binding contract between them and the union, and they will be expected to obey all the union rules. An employer is free to explain that a union's constitution contains provisions for punishable union offenses, union trials, suspensions, expulsions, and fines. Finally, the employer can point out that a union represents a threat to job security since the union may call a strike regardless of a given employee's feelings and can fine employees who cross its picket line.

In summary, the NLRB has the responsibility of creating an election climate that provides employees with maximum freedom to accept or reject a union.[32] Employers and unions are allowed considerable latitude in presenting their positions to employees and in campaigning for their votes. However, neither side can use violence, threats, or coercion to influence employee votes. Employers also are restricted from promising benefits or from using inflammatory speeches to discourage unionization.

UNION STRUCTURE AND LEADERSHIP

Labor unions have three major levels of formal organizational structure: (1) the local union, (2) the national or international union, and (3) the federation of unions.

LOCAL UNIONS

Local unions generally represent a group of employees working in one area for a particular employer. These local unions have the most direct contact with union members, and the members rely on their local union for social interaction, economic support, and political power. The typical functions of a local union include negotiating an agreement with the company, administering the contract after it has been negotiated, settling disputes and grievances that arise from contract violations, organizing nonunion employees, and operating the local headquarters.

Local unions vary greatly in size and power—from as small as 10 members to as large as 40,000 members. There are approximately 70,000 local unions in the United States.[33] The officers of a local union are selected by a democratic process that includes nominations, campaigns, and elections. The typical officers are president, vice president, secretary/treasurer, business representative, union steward, and committee chairpersons. In small unions these officers normally perform their union responsibilities in addition to their regular work. In large unions, however, the officers may serve on a full-time basis, which often creates a strong desire for reelection to avoid going back "on the line." Two of the most important positions in a local union are the business representative and the union steward.

BUSINESS REPRESENTATIVE

The **business representative** performs a crucial role in contract negotiations, in grievance proceedings, and in managing the local union headquarters. This person usually works full-time for the local union. Business representatives usually take the lead in representing their unions at the bargaining table. They counsel members about both personal and job-related problems. Sometimes they help employers correct members who are creating disciplinary problems. They also are responsible for administering the daily affairs of the local organizations, such as maintaining the local headquarters, supervising the administrative staff, collecting dues, and recruiting new members.

UNION STEWARD

A **union steward** represents the interests of union members in their immediate relations with a company. The union steward generally performs his or her regular job and gets released time as needed for union activities. When union members have grievances about the treatment they have received or disputes about the labor agreement, they see the union steward as the first step in the grievance procedure. The union steward tries to resolve problems between supervisors and members on an informal basis without issuing formal complaints or relying on arbitration. The smooth operation of a labor agreement is greatly influenced by the skill of a union steward.

NATIONAL UNIONS

National and international unions are collections of local unions, usually in the same industry. Each of the 173 national unions has its own constitution, which establishes the rules and conditions for chartering the local unions. Most national unions have the power to approve or disapprove agreements negotiated at the local level, to decide whether a strike by a local union is legitimate, to supervise elections of local officers, to audit the records of local unions, to remove local officers for improper actions, and to place the local union in trusteeship for violating the national union's rules. Local unions also are required to pay dues to their national union.

In return for what they receive from local unions, national unions provide a variety of services for the local unions. During contract negotiations, local unions can request the national union to provide legal assistance and help at the bargaining table. The national union also may provide financial assistance during organizing drives and strikes. In multi-employer contract bargaining, the national union usually negotiates the contract for a group of local unions.

National unions also provide various indirect services such as education and research, public relations campaigns, lobbying activities to influence legislation, communications to members, and administration of benefits and pension plans.

The national unions are governed by national officers who are elected at periodic conventions by delegates representing the local unions. The delegates also vote on all proposed changes in the national constitution at these conventions.

THE AFL-CIO

The AFL-CIO is a large and powerful federation of labor. Ninety-six national unions plus numerous independent, local, and regional unions belong to this federation. The AFL-CIO represents approximately 75 percent of all unionized workers.[34]

The American Federation of Labor (AFL) was organized in 1886 after thousands of workers became dissatisfied with an earlier labor organization, the Knights of Labor. The Knights of Labor was an unwieldy combination of **craft unions**, industrial unions, and social reformers. The AFL was originally a federation of crafts unions, that is, unions composed of members in a specific craft or trade. **Industrial unions**, which include all workers in a plant or industry regardless of craft, were excluded from membership in the AFL. Samuel Gompers, the first president of the AFL, believed that trade unionism could best succeed when it was confined to craftsworkers who limited their bargaining to immediate issues of improving wages and working conditions.

Socialist movements associated with agrarian reform, the greenback movement, women's suffrage, and prohibition were not relevant issues for the AFL.

Samuel Gompers was a Dutch immigrant and cigarmaker who had taken an active role during his early years in organizing the Cigarmakers' Union. He later served as president of the AFL every year but one until his death in 1924. Under Gompers's leadership the AFL became a powerful labor federation because it advocated principles of free enterprise. Gompers was opposed to federal minimum-wage laws and against government unemployment insurance or other forms of social security. He believed that such welfare programs would weaken democracy by making citizens too dependent on the government. He felt that protection and security should come through trade unionism.

The AFL refused to grant charters to industrial unions for many years. But in 1935, John L. Lewis, an officer in the AFL, began to organize industrial unions within the AFL. When the AFL expelled these unions, Lewis left the AFL and formed a separate federation of unions called the Congress of Industrial Organizations (CIO). Lewis hired hundreds of communists and placed them in CIO jobs. The communist influence in some CIO unions was relatively strong for many years, until public opposition and World War II made communism unacceptable. For twenty years, the AFL and the CIO competed for union membership and lobbied Congress for legislation favorable to their own special interests. Finally, in 1955, an agreement was negotiated that brought the CIO back into the AFL. This new organization became known as the American Federation of Labor and Congress of Industrial Organizations (AFL-CIO).

The chief governing body of the AFL-CIO is its executive council and representatives from the national unions who meet in a national convention every two years. The executive council includes the president, the secretary/treasurer, and thirty-three vice presidents. This group meets three times a year and sets policy between conventions. The AFL-CIO also has a large staff that provides information, advice, research, and public relations for the national and local unions.

COLLECTIVE BARGAINING

The heart of labor relations is collective bargaining. Early labor struggles centered on the rights of workers to force employers to negotiate a collective agreement. Most labor agreements are negotiated uneventfully, with little public awareness, and at only a small cost to either party. Only a few agreements attract national attention and involve massive costs and economic disruptions.

Collective bargaining basically consists of management and union representatives coming together to reach an agreement that will be acceptable to their constituents. The process can be smooth and uncomplicated if both parties are willing to negotiate cooperatively to reach an agreement. However, the process can also be extremely complex and time consuming. The major issues surrounding collective bargaining are who will represent the workers, which issues will be negotiated into the contract, what strategies will be used in bargaining, how bargaining impasses will be resolved, and how the contract will be administered.

BARGAINING STRUCTURES

Traditionally, most labor agreements have been negotiated between a single union and a single employer. The growing size and complexity of both unions and corporations, however, has led to the use of alternative bargaining structures. There are four kinds of bargaining structures:

1. *Single union–single employer bargaining* is the typical bargaining structure and is preferred by most employers. Employers usually prefer to negotiate with a single union since this gives them the greatest freedom and the strongest power position to decide what is acceptable. Employers like to avoid having to negotiate a number of contracts with separate unions because of the threat that one group will disrupt the agreements negotiated with the other groups.

2. *Multi-employer bargaining* consists of a single union negotiating with more than one employer. If an agreement applies to all employers in an industry, it is called *industry-wide bargaining*. This structure allows all the employers to get the same wage rates. Multi-employer bargaining is used in construction, retailing, and service industries.

3. *Coordinated bargaining* sometimes called *coalition bargaining*, consists of several unions bargaining with a single employer. Coordinated bargaining increases the power of many small unions in dealing with a large employer. All of the unions that deal with a single employer have an economic interest in the negotiated settlements of the other unions. Therefore, unions such as the IUE, UAW, and UE will form a coalition to negotiate a coordinated agreement with General Electric.

4. *National/local bargaining* consists of an agreement that is negotiated at the national level on economic issues and at the local level on working conditions or other specific contract issues. The United Auto Workers and the car manufacturers use this form of bargaining.

PREPARATION FOR NEGOTIATIONS

Before coming together, each side needs to prepare carefully for the negotiations. Both sides should have factual information supporting their arguments. In addition to knowing about their own, specific situation, each side should have a broad understanding of changes in the cost of living, unemployment rates, profit outlook for business, technological changes, job-redesign experiments, changes in the wages and benefits at competing companies, and other economic conditions.

Union representatives must thoroughly understand the interests of their members. They must know what the members want and how far they are willing to go to get it. When union representatives negotiate an agreement with management, they must know whether the union membership will be willing to ratify the agreement.

Management representatives need to know how much each union demand will cost, and be able to predict how each concession to the union will influence the profitability and efficiency of the company.

Both sides should assess how well the previous agreement has served. Problems in administering the old agreement, inconsistencies in its application, and uncertainties in its interpretation that may apply to the new agreement need to be clarified. This information should be obtained from supervisors, executives, and union leaders who have to administer the agreement and live with it.

CONTRACT ISSUES

The Taft-Hartley Act requires that union and management negotiate on "wages, hours, and other terms and conditions of employment." Some terms and conditions of employment, however, are outlawed by the act. The NLRB and the courts have classified bargaining issues into mandatory, voluntary, and illegal items.[35]

1. Mandatory items include wages or salaries, hours of work, subcontracting, stock purchase plans, profit-sharing plans, pension and employee welfare plans, Christmas bonuses, work loads and production standards, and plant rules. Labor and management must bargain in good faith on these mandatory items, and they may bargain to an impasse without violating the unfair labor practice provisions. Unions may strike to obtain mandatory items, and employers may refuse to sign a contract unless their version of these is included in the contract.
2. Voluntary items are issues that may be discussed at the bargaining table but may not be bargained to an impasse. Employers cannot make voluntary items a condition for signing a labor contract, such as demanding that the union withdraw fines on members who crossed picket lines during a strike. Unions may not strike over voluntary items, such as demanding that a company contribute to an industry-wide promotion fund or a strike insurance plan. The Supreme Court has ruled that employers may legally demand that promotions, discipline, and production scheduling be matters of exclusive management control and not subject to arbitration. This decision appears to make these items voluntary.
3. Illegal items are issues that may not be negotiated at the bargaining table, such as yellow-dog contracts, closed shop agreements, compulsory check-off programs, and hot-cargo agreements, which forbid employers to handle nonunion goods.

THE LABOR AGREEMENT

A labor agreement can cover many issues or only a few, depending on the interests of both parties. The agreement does not have to be written in technical language, but it should not be ambiguous. The wording of an agreement should be carefully considered so that misinterpretation leading to costly grievances may be avoided. One survey of the readability of forty-nine collective bargaining agreements concluded that college-graduate-level reading skills were necessary to understand them and that the complexity contributed to unnecessary grievances, costly arbitration, and added friction between management and labor.[36]

Most labor agreements cover seven major bargaining issues: compensation and benefits, working conditions, job security, discipline procedures and individual rights, union security, management prerogatives, and contract duration.

COMPENSATION AND BENEFITS

The economic issues negotiated at the bargaining table are usually the most important issues in the agreement. The agreement might contain a basic wage structure plus an incentive pay system, a cost-of-living adjustment (COLA), shift differentials, and other provisions for determining pay. Medical insurance, life insurance, sick days, vacations, and other company benefits might also be included in the agreement.

WORKING CONDITIONS

Working conditions include work rules, performance standards, rest periods, work schedules, and safety and health procedures. The trend in recent years is to negotiate a shorter workweek with less rigorous work rules.

JOB SECURITY

Job security usually involves two forms of protection: financial security during a layoff and protection from unfair treatment on the job. To protect members who are laid off, the agreement might provide supplemental unemployment benefits, severance pay, and other forms of protection. The primary protection against unfair treatment is through seniority provisions. Union members almost universally accept seniority as the most legitimate basis for making fair decisions involving workers—favoritism should be shown to those who have the longest uninterrupted years of service. Most labor agreements specify that actions such as promotions, layoffs, transfers, and overtime opportunities will be based on seniority.

DISCIPLINE PROCEDURES AND INDIVIDUAL RIGHTS

The procedures for disciplining employees are normally described in the agreement. These procedures allow management to take necessary actions against problem employees and still guarantee the rights of due process to those who are disciplined.

UNION SECURITY

Most unions try to negotiate some form of union security into the agreement. They want to avoid the constant strain of having to entice new employees to join the union and the financial insecurity created by members who are delinquent in paying their dues. Union security can take several forms:

1. A closed shop requires that only union members be hired. The Taft-Hartley Act outlaws a closed shop, except for hiring halls in the construction industry, but they exist anyway in such industries as the longshore workers.
2. A union shop requires everyone who is hired to join the union within a prescribed period, usually thirty days. Temporary workers, part-time help, and student interns may be exempted from membership in what is sometimes called a *modified union shop*. Union shops are not legal in the twenty states that have right-to-work laws.
3. A *maintenance-of-membership shop* requires that employees who join voluntarily must continue paying their membership dues until the present contract expires.
4. An **agency shop** recognizes the union as the bargaining agent for both union and nonunion employees and requires everyone to pay union dues, regardless of whether they are members or nonmembers.
5. A *dues check-off* provision allows union dues to be paid directly to the union by the company's payroll office if a member signs an affidavit agreeing to such a payroll deduction. Union members can insist, however, on paying their own dues, which usually results in delinquent accounts.

MANAGEMENT PREROGATIVES

Most labor agreements contain a section describing management rights or prerogatives. Such a section typically identifies specific decision areas where management is free to make unilateral decisions, such as changing the work rules, tightening labor standards, altering the production processes, or assigning jobs according to competence as well as seniority.

The management-rights provision in most agreements is a general statement that gives the company's management all rights, powers, and privileges to direct the company except as specified elsewhere in the agreement. This general statement is consistent with the *reserved-rights theory* of collective bargaining, which claims that management's authority is supreme in all matters except those it has expressly conceded in the labor agreement. Over time, many unions have succeeded in reducing the number of issues that are strictly management prerogatives. As voluntary items in the negotiations, some unions have demanded and obtained the right to participate in such decisions as work scheduling, changing the work rules, and making job assignments.

CONTRACT DURATION

Most contracts cover a two- or three-year period. Unions usually prefer a short contract period so that they can negotiate frequent pay raises and other improvements. Companies usually prefer a long contract period to avoid the disruption and turmoil caused by negotiation of a new contact. Since inflation is so unpredictable, some unions have demanded an automatic cost-of-living adjustment (COLA) in their contracts in lieu of a short contract period.

THE BARGAINING PROCESS

The actual negotiations usually involve two teams of negotiators sitting on opposite sides of a bargaining table. At the local level, the union team often has about seven members, including local officers, the union steward, and sometimes regional or national representatives. The management team is usually smaller than the union team, consisting of three or four members from human resources and line management. Top management often avoids participating directly in the bargaining sessions to reduce the possibility of making rash and unwise compromises.

The bargaining process usually consists of four stages:

1. *Opening presentation of demands.* During the first formal bargaining meeting, both sides present their demands, unless they have been exchanged beforehand. The union typically goes first, and the management team asks questions to clarify the issues and to assess the importance of each demand. The first meeting is especially crucial in establishing the climate of negotiations—whether the bargaining will be a combative struggle or a cooperative, problem-solving effort. The rules and procedures that will be followed throughout the negotiations usually are decided at the first meeting.

2. *Analyzing the demands.* The demands submitted by each side usually include some that absolutely must be fulfilled before an agreement can be reached, others that are desirable but not necessary, and a few that are included just for trading purposes. The negotiators have to examine each other's lists and try to identify which are the real issues. Sometimes negotiating teams include frivolous demands and later find that they have become serious obstacles to reaching an agreement. Unrealistic demands tend to antagonize the other team and to cause unnecessary deadlocks.

The areas in which each side is willing to negotiate comprise the **bargaining zone**. Each side has a tolerance limit and will refuse to negotiate on issues that exceed its limit. A bargaining zone is illustrated in Figure 13.1. For example, anything less than a 12 percent pay increase might be below the union's tolerance limit, and anything greater than an 18 percent increase might be above management's tolerance limit. Therefore, as shown in the figure, the bargaining zone for pay increases is between 12 and 18 percent. Dental insurance may or may not be in the bargaining zone. A company might be willing to consider a dental plan if other benefits are reduced. Or it might consider dental insurance to be prohibitively expensive and refuse to accept it.

The order in which the demands are discussed can become a serious negotiating issue in itself. Unions prefer to strike over the most important issues, and they like to have these issues discussed at the end of a bargaining agenda. If agreement is not reached, it is easier to call a strike at the end of an agenda than midway through it.

3. *Compromise.* When the interests of both sides are not identical, a compromise must be achieved. In local negotiations, these compromises can be worked out at the bargaining table by both teams. Sometimes, however, subcommittees of representatives from both sides investigate the issue and try to develop acceptable alternatives. Compromises also can be obtained by each side making counterproposals until an agreement is reached.

4. *Informal settlement and ratification.* After both sides have obtained what they feel is their best compromise, they have to return to their reference groups for approval. Top management must examine the tentative agreement and decide whether it allows them to

FIGURE 13.1 Bargaining zone.

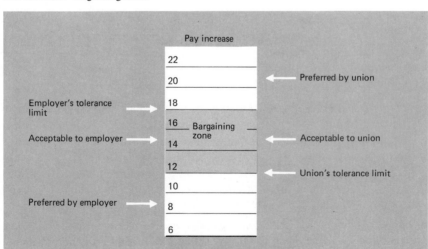

operate the company efficiently and profitably. Union representatives have to decide whether the membership will ratify the contract.

After top management has approved the agreement, it goes before the union membership for approval. If the majority of those who vote approve the agreement, then it is *ratified* and becomes a binding agreement between the company and union for the duration of the contract period. Written copies of the agreement are prepared and distributed to each member.

In years past, almost every agreement negotiated by union representatives was ratified by the union membership. In recent years, however, only about 90 percent of the tentative agreements are ratified. When the union membership refuses to ratify a contract, union representatives are faced with the difficult and unpleasant task of going back to the bargaining table and trying to win more concessions from management.

BARGAINING STRATEGIES

There are many strategies for bargaining and reaching an agreement. Two opposing strategies have been labeled distributive bargaining and integrative bargaining.[37] **Distributive bargaining** refers to a conflict situation in which each side struggles aggressively to receive the largest share of the rewards. A win-lose relationship exists and each side sees the confrontation as a situation in which the total rewards to be allocated are fixed and each is struggling to maximize its own share. Getting more is sometimes achieved by threats, deceit, and misinformation.

Integrative bargaining refers to a cooperative problem-solving form of negotiation. Both parties investigate problem areas and try to reach mutually acceptable solutions. A working relationship of trust, respect, and acknowledged legitimacy exists in this situation. Communication between the parties is open and frequent. The total rewards are not viewed as a fixed amount to be divided but as a variable amount that both sides can increase and share through cooperative teamwork.

The dominant negotiating strategy in American unions has been distributive bargaining. When employers and employees have an open and trusting relationship, the employees generally do not vote to have a union represent them. Where a union exists, distrust, conflict, and a "them-versus-us" mentality tend to exist. Consequently, most negotiations are a power struggle between the union and management.

CONCESSION BARGAINING

In 1980 Chrysler Corporation was teetering on the brink of bankruptcy in spite of receiving federally insured loans. Lee Iacocca told members of the United Auto Workers union that Chrysler would soon have no more twenty-two dollar an hour jobs, but that if they agreed to his proposed wage concessions they would still have many seventeen dollar an hour jobs. The union members accepted the wage reductions partly because the white-collar employees had accepted similar reductions (Iacocca's salary was just one dollar), and partly because it was obvious that the concessions were necessary to save the company and their jobs.[38]

The concessions won by Chrysler set a pattern for many collective bargaining agreements during the 1980s by companies that were struggling financially. Negotiations that resulted in wage reductions or work rule "give-backs" were called concession bargaining. The major economic factors that led to concession bargaining included increased international competition, deregulation of key industries, and technological innovations.

An examination of the reasons union leaders were willing to accept wage reductions indicated that the most important motive was their belief that the concessions were necessary. Union leaders recognized that they could not demand twenty dollars per hour and expect the employer to compete successfully when foreign workers perform the same job for less than five dollars per hour.[39]

Most of the give-backs were not free, however. In almost every case the union extracted some kind of promise that they would share in the economic success of the firm when times were better. Some agreements called for profit sharing, others called for wage increases as profits rose, and some required that union leaders be given positions on the board of directors. Most concessions were also contingent on improved job security, such as promises that jobs would not be eliminated without advanced notice, or that the union would be consulted before a plant-closing decision was made.[40]

BARGAINING IMPASSES

When both sides want to reach an agreement and are willing to compromise, the bargaining process usually results in a peaceful settlement. A good settlement may require lengthy negotiations, however, since the process of obtaining a good settlement often requires conferences, investigations, and counterproposals.

Occasionally, negotiations reach an impasse because neither side is willing to give. The Taft-Hartley Act requires that both parties engage in **good-faith bargaining**, or they will be guilty of an unfair labor practice. The conditions for good-faith bargaining, as defined by the courts and the NLRB, include the following:

1. A serious attempt must be made to adjust differences and to reach an acceptable common ground.
2. A counterproposal must be offered when another party's proposal is rejected. This must involve the "give and take" of an auction system.
3. A position on contract terms may not be constantly changed.
4. Evasive behavior during negotiations is not permitted.
5. There must be a willingness to incorporate oral agreements into a written contract.

Offering a counterproposal is an important indication of good-faith bargaining since it demonstrates a bona fide intent to reach an agreement and shows that bargaining is more than just a series of empty discussions. Although the law says that the parties must engage in good-faith bargaining, it does not say that they must reach an agreement. The good-faith concept encourages the parties to reach agreement, but it does not mean that a bargaining impasse cannot occur. The NLRB cannot order the parties to reach agreement, nor can it direct the parties to incorporate a particular provision into their labor agreement. When an impasse occurs, several things might happen, including strikes, lockouts, picketing, boycotts, mediation and conciliation, and arbitration.

STRIKES

A **strike** occurs when a group of employees refuses to work. If the entire work force of a company acts in concert and refuses to perform their work, they can exert strong economic pressure against the company. Before union leaders enter into negotiations with a company, they may call for a strike vote of the members. This vote does not mean that the union wants or expects to strike. It simply indicates that the union representatives are authorized to issue a strike order if the bargaining reaches an impasse.

A strike is one of the union's strongest negotiating weapons, but it must be used carefully. Before going on strike, union members should know why they are striking and what they hope to gain. Although strikes are usually called for economic reasons, they cannot ordinarily be justified economically. More income is usually lost during the strike than the workers can hope to recover through higher wages and benefits in a new contract. Strikes can be costly in other ways, too. If the strike does not succeed in achieving its purpose, union leaders may be voted out of office, the union may be defeated in a decertification election, and the union could lose its public support.

Occasionally, workers may engage in slightly different forms of refusing to work. Employees may report to work but not work or accomplish anything. This is called a *sit-down strike*. A *work slowdown* is similar: employees report to work, but they accomplish very little. A *wildcat strike* occurs when a group of workers walk off the job in violation of a valid labor agreement and usually against the direct orders of the labor union. Under many labor agreements, the employer has the right to discharge employees engaging in such strikes or to otherwise penalize them for these forms of work stoppage. Employees who participate in a wildcat strike lose their status as employees under the provisions of the Taft-Hartley Act. If the employees are discharged, the NLRB will not direct that they be reinstated.

A **sickout** occurs when several employees claim they are not working because of illness. Employers dislike paying sick leave to striking workers but they usually have to pay because it is extremely difficult to prove a *prima facie* case of employee conspiracy.[41]

Workers are free to withhold their services and withdraw from employment anytime they choose. Since 1842 they also have been free to stop work in concert without the threat of a conspiracy charge. Employers are free to hire temporary replacements and to continue operating during a strike.[42] However, if employees want to enjoy the protection of labor laws and the judicial system, they have to abide by certain restrictions when they strike. The basic protections that they enjoy are the right to vote and the possibility of reinstatement. For at least one year after a strike has been called, strikers have the privilege of voting in union elections along with the temporary replacements who have been hired. If strikers hope to be reinstated after an agreement is reached, they must avoid all forms of violence and coercive misconduct. If they are guilty of misbehavior, they are not entitled to reinstatement. When a new agreement is finally negotiated, strikers usually are reinstated in their jobs as a condition of the settlement. But reinstatement is not guaranteed to all strikers, especially if their jobs have been eliminated.

Strikes can be called only when an impasse has been reached over a mandatory item, such as wages, hours, and other conditions of employment. **Jurisdictional strikes** are illegal. A jurisdictional strike results from a dispute between two or more unions over which union should be allowed to perform a particular job. Jurisdictional disputes are

▌ **HRM in Action**

Union Demands versus Economic Realities

When unions refuse to accommodate economic realities, their own survival is threatened. Such was the case of the unions that opposed Phelps Dodge. During the 1980s, copper prices dropped to as low as sixty cents per pound and threatened the survival of the copper industry in America. While other copper producers, including giants like Kennecott and Anaconda, were forced to either leave the mining business or lose their independence, Phelps Dodge decided to take drastic steps to restore profitability. Because the unions refused to accept these changes, they were ultimately removed.

Since it cost Phelps Dodge over eighty cents to produce a pound of copper and projections indicated that the price of copper would remain about sixty-five cents per pound, management decided to sell some of its assets, close inefficient smelters, move the company headquarters from New York City to Phoenix, and reduce its labor costs.

The greatest resistance to their restructuring plan came from about a dozen labor unions representing their employees. Phelps Dodge cut its work force to 56 percent and demanded the elimination of the automatic cost-of-living adjustment, which had raised wages about 12 percent annually over the previous decade. The company also asked employees to contribute to the cost of their medical coverage and to accept a two-tier wage system paying new hires a lower wage. The pay of salaried employees was cut by as much as 10 percent, and executive perks, such as personal secretaries and first-class air flights, were dropped.

The union responded with a bitter strike that lasted two years and created such conflict and tension that the governor of Arizona felt compelled to mobilize the National Guard. The greatest tension occurred when several union members decided to cross the picket lines and return to work with the replacement miners. Finally, the workers voted to decertify all of the unions. The election, however, did not end the feuding. The unions continued to fight Phelps Dodge and its banks both in civil courts and before the NLRB alleging civil rights violations on the picket lines and unfair labor practices.

As a result of their restructuring, and aided by higher copper prices, the economic outlook for Phelps Dodge gradually improved. Mining efficiency significantly increased: with 52 percent fewer employees the company produced 55 percent more copper. Turnover declined from 18 percent per month to less than 1 percent per month. Lost-time accidents were reduced from 14.1 per million hours worked in 1981 to 3.7 per million hours worked in 1988. The miners share in the economic improvement of the company through a profit-sharing program that pays bonuses worth several weeks' pay.

All of these improvements reduce the likelihood that the union will be reinstated anytime soon as the bargaining agent for the workers. The unions pursued an aggressive and inflexible battle against the company that ultimately led to their defeat.

Source: Alecia Swasy, "Long Road Back: How Phelps Dodge Struggled to Survive and Prospered Again," *Wall Street Journal*, November 24, 1989, p. 1.

particularly prevalent in the construction industry. The procedure for resolving such disputes is to rely first on a private forum (such as the impartial Jurisdictional Disputes Board of the AFL-CIO) and then on the NLRB.[43] The federal courts and the Supreme Court will get involved only if there is some indication of inconsistency in the decisions. Finally, another type of strike that is strictly illegal is a *certification strike* (also called a recognitional strike), which is called by a group to protest the results of a certification election and to force the employer to recognize it rather than the union that won certification.

LOCKOUTS

A **lockout** occurs when an employer refuses to allow employees to work. In some ways a lockout is management's counterweapon against the union's strike. However, a lockout is not a legal economic weapon if its use is intended to discourage union membership. Like a strike, a lockout is permissible only after a deadlock has been reached on mandatory bargaining items.

Lockouts are used primarily for two defensive purposes. First, a lockout may be instigated to prevent unusual economic hardship created by slowdowns, destructiveness, or uncertainty about a work stoppage. Second, a lockout may occur when employers in a multibargaining unit see a union trying to use a whipsawing strategy against them. Whipsawing refers to successive strikes against members of a multi-employer bargaining unit, usually starting with the most profitable employer in an effort to use the gains obtained from one employer as leverage against the others. To avoid whipsawing, all employers close their doors until all settlements are reached.

During a lockout an employer can legally hire temporary replacements, provided that the purpose is not to "destroy the protected rights of the workers or the union." The logic here is that employers can hire temporary help to sustain their firm's economic health just as locked-out employees can engage in temporary work to support their families.[44] As long as the employer has a legitimate business objective, the union employees can be locked out of the company and replaced by temporary employees until an agreement is negotiated. In actuality, lockouts are rarely used.

During a labor dispute, striking employees may receive financial assistance from their own union and other sympathetic unions, but originally they were not supposed to receive public benefits. The statutes in all states initially disqualified employees from receiving unemployment compensation benefits if they were unemployed as a result of a labor dispute, regardless of which side was responsible for the work stoppage. In many states, however, the law has evolved to allow unemployment compensation benefits if the stoppage can be blamed on the employer.[45]

PICKETING

When a union calls a strike, it usually establishes picket lines to advertise the strike and discourage the employer from continuing operations. Picket lines typically consist of striking workers who stand at the entrance to the company and advertise their strike by carrying signs and distributing literature. During the first few days of a strike, picket lines are staffed around the clock with large numbers of enthusiastic strikers who try to persuade the public and other unions to cease dealing with the company. If the strike persists for several months, the enthusiasm of the pickets declines and only those assigned to duty are usually on the lines.

Picket lines do not always need a large mass of strikers to be effective. A small group of pickets can force operations to cease if they can gain the cooperation of other employees or other unions. If transportation workers refuse to cross picket lines to deliver supplies or pick up goods, a company can be forced to stop even though management personnel and temporary help are available to work.

Although picketing is a legal activity, it is subject to certain restrictions. The Taft-Hartley Act says that employees shall have the right to picket, but it also says that employees shall have the right to refrain from picketing or participating in a strike. Therefore, employees can refuse to picket. They also have the right to cross picket lines to go to and from work without restraint or coercion while a strike is in progress. Picketing that prevents employees from working during a strike is illegal. However, union members can be fined by the union for crossing the picket lines. The Supreme Court held that a union may fine union members who work during the strike and sue them in state courts to collect fines, provided that the fines are "reasonable."

Picketing is supposed to be a peaceful activity for the purpose of advertising a labor dispute. All forms of picketing that involve violence or the threat of violence are illegal. **Mass picketing**, in which a large group of people participate in the picketing, may be illegal if it blocks the path of people trying to enter or leave the company, disrupts traffic around the company, or creates a threatening and unruly atmosphere. However, the NLRB and the courts have avoided specifying the maximum number of legal pickets. The NLRB also has chosen not to prohibit name-calling by picketers. Strikebreakers usually are called a variety of foul names when they cross picket lines. The board has allowed virtually any form of name-calling as an expression of free speech as long as it does not contain threats of violence.

BOYCOTTS

When a group of customers collectively refuses to transact business with a company, this action is called a boycott. Boycotts are powerful economic weapons for demanding change in organizations. A union can call for its members to boycott an employer's goods or services and can fine members who violate the boycott. A union also can solicit public support for a boycott; distributing handbills to consumers in a shopping mall, for example, is protected by the freedom of speech.[46]

As long as the refusal to transact business is aimed directly at the employer, this action is called a primary boycott. But if the union exerts pressure on another organization or union to boycott the employer, this action is called a **secondary boycott**. Primary boycotts are generally legal. Secondary boycotts are outlawed by the Taft-Hartley Act.

The distinction between primary and secondary boycotts is not entirely clear. For example, it is legal to picket in front of a secondary store and ask consumers not to purchase items made by a struck company, but is not legal to ask consumers of a secondary store to boycott products of companies not on strike. Consumer picketing can only focus on the products of the struck company. Although primary boycotts are legal, they usually are not very effective unless they generate public support. This strategy can be a very dangerous and self-defeating act, however. Once the public turns against a company, it is difficult for the company to reestablish a clientele. Therefore, the negative effects of a boycott might continue long after an agreement has been negotiated and may threaten the job security of the union members.

Another boycott that is very powerful, but also illegal, is when unions threaten to withdraw their pension funds from lending institutions that support antiunion companies. Unions have obtained financial information and attempted to pressure money managers and stockholders into forcing recalcitrant employers to accept union demands. The substantial size of some pension funds makes this a serious threat. However, secondary boycotts are illegal, and pension plan fiduciaries are expected to act solely in the interests of plan participants.[47]

HRM in Action

Government's Role in Labor Disputes

In 1989 the Machinists Union requested help from the federal government to settle a dispute with Eastern Airlines. The Machinists Union wanted President George Bush to create a special emergency board to evaluate their dispute. Union leaders were confident that an impartial board would agree that Eastern's bankruptcy was largely a pretext to set aside their union agreement. President Bush refused to name an emergency board and justified his decision by saying that the government should not intervene in private labor disputes.

Only a short time later, however, the federal government announced that it was actively involved in resolving the long and bitter strike between the United Mine Workers and Pittston Coal Company. This strike crippled the company, threatened the survival of the union, and created widespread violence and vandalism. Secretary of Labor Elizabeth Dole named a "super mediator" who successfully engineered a settlement to the dispute. Later she appointed an eleven-member commission to formulate solutions to sky-rocketing health care expenses. Exorbitant benefits costs was the core issue in the Pittston strike and a central issue throughout the coal industry. The government's involvement was lauded as a valuable, and perhaps necessary, contribution to resolving this bitter dispute.

For government intervention to be successful, both sides must welcome third-party help and agree to work toward a solution. In the Machinist Union's strike, Eastern Airlines didn't want an emergency board. Eastern wanted to reduce its labor costs immediately through wage reductions and other cost-cutting measures, and it didn't want its plan stalled by an emergency board's investigation.

On the other hand, both the rail union and the railroads requested governmental help during the summer of 1990 to help them resolve an impasse in bargaining over health care costs. Either side could have requested an arbitrator to resolve the impasse, but both sides wanted an emergency board to study the issue and recommend a solution. In their request for assistance, both the unions and railroads suggested a September 15 target date for the emergency board to submit its recommendations. As an indication of their cooperative spirit, the twelve unions involved in the agreement said they would forgo a strike, and the railroads agreed to forgo making unilateral changes until at least thirty days after the emergency board made its recommendations.

Source: Albert R. Karr, "Railroads, Unions Request Assistance in Reaching Pact," *Wall Street Journal*, March 30, 1990, p. A8.

MEDIATION AND CONCILIATION

The collective bargaining process assumes that the two parties will successfully negotiate an acceptable agreement. When an impasse is reached, however, it is sometimes helpful to request the assistance of a neutral third party. This process, called **mediation** or **conciliation**, usually consists of having the third party listen to both sides, evaluate the conflicting issues, clarify differences, propose new compromises, and identify common grounds for further negotiations. The Federal Mediation and Conciliation Service (FMCS) publishes a list of people who are qualified to serve as mediators. The FMCS must be notified about unresolved disputes at least thirty days before a contract expires. Mediators usually enter a dispute when either the union or management or both have requested their assistance. In the airline and rail industries, the National Mediation Board has the authority to enter the dispute without an invitation from either party. Mediation and conciliation are especially prevalent in public-sector bargaining when strikes are prohibited. Unwanted assistance, however, does not seem to help much. Mediation efforts that are not requested by both sides have received widespread criticism.

ARBITRATION

The final step in overcoming a bargaining impasse is **binding arbitration**. Here, both parties agree to refer the dispute to a judge, called an arbitrator, and to accept the arbitrator's decision. Arbitration has been used to reach agreement between professional baseball players and managers; however, this process has been sharply criticized for producing exorbitant salaries. Arbitration is used more frequently for settling grievances than for settling contract disputes. Most employers and union leaders are not willing to let an arbitrator bind them to a contract. They prefer to continue bargaining on contract issues. The arbitration process is described in Chapter 14.

LABOR RELATIONS IN THE PUBLIC SECTOR

For many years, the *doctrine of sovereignty* was used by government bodies to deny the collective bargaining process to public employees. Sovereignty refers to the absolute and supreme power by which the state is governed. Union activities such as strikes or collective bargaining were clearly inconsistent with the sovereignty of the government. In fact, all government employees were deliberately excluded from the provisions of the Wagner Act and the Taft-Hartley Act. It was generally believed that the public would be deprived of essential services if a bargaining impasse resulted in a strike, and public law 330 (1955) made it a felony for a federal employee to strike.

Another argument used against collective bargaining in the public sector was that the employer—the public—could not be realistically represented at the bargaining table. Only elected officials with temporary, uncertain power could sit at the bargaining table.

During the 1960s, however, collective bargaining appeared in the public sector. One reason for its acceptance was the growth in the number of public employees. In 1930 only 6 percent of the civilian work force worked for the government; by 1990 that figure was over 15 percent.[48] This growth in numbers created the need for a well-defined system of labor relations and also gave government workers a power base. But the most important reason for the sudden appearance of public-sector collective bargaining was the issuance of executive orders by President John F. Kennedy and later presidents. Then, in 1978, Congress passed the Civil Service Reform Act to provide federal employees with many of the same collective bargaining protections as the National Labor Relations Act. In addition, forty-two states have passed some form of labor legislation to protect the collective bargaining rights of state and local employees.

The basic intent of labor regulations in the public sector is the same as in the private sector: employees should have the rights to organize, free of restraint and coercion, and to negotiate a labor agreement through peaceful collective bargaining. However, there are differences between the practices and procedures of the public and private sectors.

For federal employees, the Federal Labor Relations Council performs some of the same functions as the NLRB does for private employees. The council determines the makeup of bargaining units, orders and supervises elections, disqualifies elections for corrupt or undemocratic actions, and decides unfair labor practice charges. Experience shows that the council has adopted many of the NLRB guidelines.

For a group of federal employees to organize a union, a majority must vote, through secret-ballot elections, in favor of having a union represent them. Exclusive recognition of all employees in the unit is the only form of recognition available. In other words, the labor union must represent only federal employees, since unions that represent workers in the private sector do not qualify. Although the union must represent all employees in the bargaining unit (even if they do not hold membership in it), it cannot require union membership as a condition of employment. This provision is similar to right-to-work laws in the private sector.

In federal employee collective bargaining, the parties are expected to conduct good-faith bargaining on negotiable issues. The obligation to bargain in good faith and the issues that can be negotiated are similar to what is called for in the private sector. A major difference, however, is that federal unions are prohibited from striking against the federal government or any agency of it. A Federal Service Impasse Panel is responsible for settling impasses in bargaining. The panel often obtains assistance from the Federal Mediation and Conciliation Service.

The legality of a strike by public employees was challenged in 1981, when the air traffic controllers' union went on strike for higher wages. The strike occurred in spite of extensive mediation, concessions, and warnings that strikers would be fired. Finally, President Ronald Reagan announced that those who refused to return would be fired and replaced by new employees. This confrontation had a chilling effect on strikes by federal employees, since many who were fired were denied employment later when they attempted to return to work.

Many government employees believe their inability to strike creates a serious disadvantage for them. They feel their employer will not negotiate in good faith unless they have the right to strike. At the state and local level, strikes are permitted to some extent in fourteen states. Other states do not permit strikes but have moderate strike penalties that do not prevent them. In general, laws prohibiting public employee strikes have not been successful in eliminating strikes.[49] Numerous strikes have occurred at the state and local level, and they have become increasingly frequent in recent years. The problem stems partly from an inadequate system of resolving labor disputes. Some states have better labor policies than others. But a basic generalization is that whatever rights exist at the state and local level lag far behind those at the federal level and obviously behind those available to private-sector employees.

Two impasse-resolution procedures that have been used frequently are mediation and fact finding. However, a review of the effectiveness of these two procedures found they were largely ineffective in preventing or ending strikes.[50] Penalties for striking public employees appear to be moderately successful, but only when the penalties are moderate. The likelihood of a strike decreases as the severity of the penalties increases, but only to a point, after which severe penalties cause strike activity to increase.[51] The most effective resolution strategy appears to be interest arbitration. Between the Civil War and World War I, many state and local governments used compulsory binding arbitration by *ad hoc* boards. However, the U.S. Supreme Court prohibited compulsory arbitration but allowed voluntary interest arbitration. In 1970 the Postal Reorganization Act provided for interest arbitration among postal employees, and several states have enacted compulsory interest arbitration provisions. Experience suggests that interest arbitration, which requires the voluntary consent of both parties, tends to reduce strikes by public employees by giving them a viable substitute for resolving impasses.[52]

INTERNATIONAL HRM

Trade unions play a much more prominent role in some countries than others. While union membership has declined in the United States, in several other countries, especially Denmark and Sweden, a majority of the workers still belong to trade unions. Making comparisons of union density among countries is somewhat imprecise due to inconsistencies in how the measures are obtained (for example, retired workers are still union members in most Scandinavian countries) and whether professional and employee associations are included. Nevertheless, as Table 13.5 shows, the United States and France have much lower union-density rates than Norway and Sweden.

Labor relations in many countries of the world have been greatly influenced by labor laws in England and the United States. British law has served as a pattern for many developing countries, especially Australia, New Zealand, and other former colonies. The labor laws in Japan and the Philippines, however, have been influenced more by laws in the United States.

Although England, Australia, and New Zealand share a common legal philosophy in their labor relations, their applications are somewhat different. In England, employers and unions have the greatest freedom to determine the content and procedure of their collective bargaining. Labor disputes may result in prolonged strikes. In Australia and New Zealand, however, where 80 percent of all employees are covered by tribunal awards or collective agreements, collective bargaining is supplemented by compulsory arbitration. Third-party involvement in the form of mediation, conciliation, and arbitration is much more active when disputes arise.[53]

Labor relations in Japan are regulated by a combination of social norms and national law. Japan has historically maintained strong social norms regarding the proper treatment of workers to ensure the smooth operation of businesses. In 1947 the Labor

Nation	Percent in Unions		
Australia	46	Italy	41
Austria	61	Japan	29
Britain	52	Netherlands	28
Canada	38	Norway	65
Denmark	93	Sweden	83
France	17	United States	17
West Germany	38		

TABLE 13.5   Union density rates: Percent of wage and salary workers who are trade union members

Source: T. Viser, "Trade Unionism in Western Europe: Present Situation and Prospects," *Labour and Society* 13, No. 2 (1988), pp. 125–82; U.S. Department of Labor, BLS statistics, 1988 data.

Standards Act transformed some of these social norms to legal requirements protecting workers. The act requires employers to establish work rules that do not infringe upon any laws or collective agreements applicable to the workplace. The work rules cover: (1) personal matters, such as recruitment, transfer, dismissal, contract suspension, and termination; (2) dismissal; (3) working conditions, including working hours, overtime, breaks, rest days, and leave; (4) wages; (5) training; (6) welfare; (7) occupational safety and health; and (8) accident compensation.[54] The authority for these work rules is established in Japan under two main theories: a contractual obligation according to what the employer has stated, and a legal obligation according to the law.

In practice, almost all major Japanese firms are unionized, but Japanese unions are not as independent of management as U.S. unions. During the 1950s, while the cultural norms were being revised, Japan had many strikes. In recent years, strikes are rare and usually only token displays lasting an hour or so. Rather than striking, employees may wear black arm bands to evidence their displeasure. Most Japanese labor agreements are negotiated at the same time (the first of April), which produces a consistent pattern of wage increases.

SUMMARY

A. An employer's ability to make unilateral decisions is curtailed when a union is present. When a union has been chosen to represent employees, management and the union have a mandatory requirement to engage in bilateral decision making on wages, hours of work, and conditions of employment.

B. The most important reasons employees decide to join or not join a union depend on their perception of the fairness and equity of treatment they receive at work.

C. Prior to 1932, the legal environment was not favorable to collective bargaining. Unions had the right to exist but they did not have the economic power to force employers to negotiate a peaceful collective bargaining agreement. Union activities were limited by antitrust laws, yellow-dog contracts, court injunctions, and, for a time, conspiracy laws—all of which made union activities illegal and punishable with prison terms and fines.

D. Federal legislation was required to establish collective bargaining. Four major laws were passed to encourage labor unions and to regulate them. The Norris-LaGuardia Act eliminated the use of court injunctions against labor disputes. The Wagner Act established the rights of employees to organize a union without reprisals, and it created the National Labor Relations Board (NLRB) to oversee union elections and to prosecute unfair labor practices. The Taft-Hartley Act limited the actions of unions and created a balance of power between management and unions. The Landrum-Griffin Act regulated the internal affairs of unions by requiring them to function democratically and free of fraud.

E. The major responsibilities of the NLRB are to conduct representation elections and to investigate and determine unfair labor practices.

F. Labor organizations have three major levels of organizational structure: local unions that negotiate and administer most contracts; national or international unions that are collections of local unions, usually from the same industry; and the AFL-CIO, which is a federation of national unions.

G. Collective bargaining, which is the heart of labor relations, consists of management and union reaching an acceptable agreement about wages and benefits, working conditions, job security, discipline procedures, union security, and management prerogatives. The typical bargaining approach is a distributive approach, in which each side tries to maximize its own rewards at the expense of the other side, rather than an integrative approach, which seeks the best overall solution for both sides.

H. An impasse in the collective bargaining process may result in: (1) a strike, if employees refuse to work; (2) a lockout, if the employer refuses to let employees work; (3) picketing, if the employees advertise their dispute; (4) boycotts, if employees cease to transact business with the employer and encourage others to cease business also; or (5) mediation and conciliation, if outside parties intervene to settle the dispute.

I. Labor relations in the public sector are not as well-defined as in the private sector. Federal government employees are permitted to join only those labor unions that represent government employees, which are permitted to negotiate agreements similar to those of private unions. However, federal employees are not allowed to strike. Employees of state and local governments are subject to a mixed set of rules that vary from state to state.

QUESTIONS

1. Do you tend to be for or against unions? How do you justify your position? What arguments can you develop for the opposite point of view?

2. Would you join a labor union? What would you say to coworkers who disagreed with you and were trying to persuade you to follow them?

3. Do labor unions still depend on favorable legislation for their existence? Which laws do you think ought to be eliminated, revised, or added? Why?

4. Many unfair labor practices are filed with the NLRB because of trivial complaints during elections. Since the NLRB has such a heavy case load, what action would you recommend to reduce the number of frivolous complaints?

5. The "right-to-work" issue resulting from section 14-b of the Taft-Hartley Act has created an ongoing debate. What are the arguments for and against the "right-to-work" clause, and what is your personal position?

6. Are current procedures for representation elections more favorable to the employer or to the union organizers? What changes would you recommend in the interpretation of rules regarding what is fair or unfair during an organizing campaign?

7. If you were a union leader in a national union, would you be for or against affiliation with the AFL-CIO? Why?

8. Collective bargaining is almost always a distributive bargaining strategy. Is it possible for an integrative bargaining strategy to be used? What conditions would have to exist, and what would be the probable long-term effect?

9. What are the issues that must be considered by each side before a strike or a lockout is declared?

10. What are the advantages and disadvantages of compulsory binding arbitration?

11. Should public employees be allowed to strike? How should labor disputes in the public sector be resolved?

KEY TERMS

Agency shop: A union security provision requiring both union members and nonmembers to pay dues to the union.

Bargaining zone: The range of feasible alternatives on each bargaining issue that both management and union are willing to consider during negotiations.

Bilateral decision making: A decision-making process that uses two-party bargaining to reach agreement.

Binding arbitration: A means for overcoming a bargaining impasse by referring the labor dispute to an outside party with agreement beforehand that both sides will accept the arbitrator's decision.

Business representative: A full-time union employee who supervises the local union headquarters and helps to administer the union contract.

Closed shop: A union security provision that an employer hire only union members. Closed shops are illegal except in the construction industry.

Craft union: A union comprised of members who work in the same craft, such as carpenters or electricians.

Distributive bargaining: A bargaining strategy in which each party tries to maximize its own outcomes at the expense of the other party.

Featherbedding: The practice of requiring employers to hire extra workers who are not wanted or needed. Although featherbedding provisions in a labor agreement are illegal, the courts have said that the collective bargaining process—not the courts—should decide which jobs are necessary.

Good-faith bargaining: The requirement that both parties meet and make offers and counter-proposals in an effort to reach an agreement.

Industrial union: A union comprised of members who work for the same company or industry regardless of their particular crafts.

Injunction: A court order prohibiting a person or group from carrying out a given action, such as a strike or boycott, that would cause irreparable damage.

Integrative bargaining: A bargaining strategy in which both parties work together cooperatively to achieve the best outcome for both.

Jurisdictional strike: An illegal strike resulting from a dispute between two unions about which union has jurisdiction over certain jobs.

Lockout: The employer closes the doors of the company and refuses to allow the employees to continue working.

Management prerogatives: Areas of managerial responsibility for which employers claim the power to make unilateral decisions.

Mass picketing: A large number of individuals parading in front of a company to advertise their labor dispute.

Mediation (conciliation): Intervention by a third party into a labor dispute to reduce conflict and help both sides compromise to reach agreement.

Right to work: A provision granted by Section 14-b of the Taft-Hartley Act that allows states to forbid union shops, thus making union membership an optional rather than a mandatory requirement to hold a job.

Secondary boycott: An illegal action that creates economic pressure on a secondary business, such as a supplier or customer of the primary business, and is thereby designed to create pressure on the primary business.

Strike: A refusal to work by a group of employees.

Unfair labor practice: Any action by either the union or management that is prohibited by law or NLRB ruling.

Unilateral decision making: A decision-making process in which one party (management) can make decisions without the involvement of the other party (employees).

Union shop: A union security provision that all employees must belong to the union. If new employees are not members, they are required to join, usually within thirty days.

Union steward: An elected union officer who usually holds a regular job but is given time off to help administer the labor agreement and to represent the interests of union members when problems occur.

Yellow-dog contract: A statement employees were required to sign in which they agreed not to join a union.

CONCLUDING CASE

Crossing a Picket Line

At the end of April, most of the large hotels in the metropolitan area had not reached an agreement with the hotel and restaurant workers' union. Consequently, when their contract expired May 1, the workers went on strike and established picket lines at the entrances to the large hotels. The hotel managers were well prepared for the strike and continued to operate normally by using managers and a few temporary employees and by offering buffet meals where the customers could serve themselves.

Realizing that the strike was not succeeding, the union contacted other unions and asked them to honor their picket lines by refusing to make deliveries. The leaders of the Teamsters Union agreed to issue a notice of support for the hotel and restaurant workers' union but said that the decision about crossing the picket lines would be left to each individual truck driver.

Union leaders for the Blue Dot Cab Company drivers agreed to support the strike by refusing to deliver guests to the hotels. Notices were sent to the cab drivers informing them that their union was honoring the picket lines at the hotels and they could be fined twenty-five dollars if they crossed the picket lines. In spite of this announcement, however, many Blue Dot drivers failed to honor the picket lines. Some drivers delivered guests to the side entrances of the hotels to avoid crossing picket lines at the front entrances. Other drivers simply avoided crossing the lines by asking hotel guests to walk the last fifty feet to a hotel entrance. A few drivers drove right up to the hotel entrance, ignoring the pickets.

Within three days, the cab drivers' union was flooded with complaints from the hotel and restaurant union about violations by cab drivers. However, the cab drivers also began to complain about the decision of their local leaders. Their major complaints included the following:

1. If we refuse to transport the guests, one of the independent cabs will be glad to do it. Therefore, we are the ones who are being hurt financially, not the hotels. People will still get to the hotels one way or another.
2. If we went on strike, the hotel and restaurant union members would not go on strike for us, and even if they did, it would not help us.
3. The strike by the hotel and restaurant union does not concern us; we should only strike when we are dissatisfied with our own agreement.

4. Refusing to give someone a ride after they are already in your cab is embarrassing and unpleasant and creates bad feelings toward the cab company.

Questions:

1. Should the leaders of the cab drivers' union put teeth into their decision and immediately assess the fines against violators, or should they reverse their decision?
2. What are the potential consequences to both unions and their members of one union supporting another union's cause?

NOTES

1. Marj Charlier, "Meat Packing Industry Faces Shakeout: Union Resistance to More Concessions Widens," *Wall Street Journal*, February 5, 1986, p. 2.

2. Most of the information for this case came from Michael H. Brown, "Hormel's Bitter Legacy," *Business Month* 131 (May 1988): 56–62.

3. U.S. Department of Commerce, *Statistical Abstract of the United States*, 108th Edition (Washington, D.C.: Government Printing Office, 1988).

4. Jack Fiorito, "Political Instrumentality Perceptions and Desires for Union Representation," *Journal of Labor Research* 8 (Summer 1987): 271–89; Duane E. Leigh and Stephan M. Hills, "Public Sector-Private Sector Differences in Reasons Underlying Expressed Union Preferences," *Journal of Collective Negotiations in the Public Sector* 16, no. 1 (1987): 1–14.

5. P. B. Beaumont and J. Elliot, "Nurses: RCN or Union Membership?" *Employee Relations* 8, no. 4 (1986): 2–4; Christine Maitland and Charles Kerchner, "The Tone of Labor Relations in the Schools: Correlates of Teacher Perception," *Journal of Collective Negotiations in the Public Sector* 17, no. 4 (1988): 279–84.

6. Don Nichols, "The Management Revolution and Loss of Union Clout," *Management Review* (February 1988): 25–26; Peter F. Drucker, "Peter Drucker Asks: Will Unions Ever Be Useful Organs of Society?" *Industry Week* 238 (March 20, 1989): 16–22.

7. Rod Willis, "Can American Unions Transform Themselves?" *Management Review* (February 1988): 14–21.

8. Two excellent references on the early history of labor unions are: John R. Commons and Eugene A. Gilmore, *A Documentary History of American Industrial Society, III* (Cleveland: Arthur H. Clark, 1910); and Selig Perlman, *A History of Trade Unionism in the United States* (New York: Macmillan, 1929).

9. See Commons and Gilmore, *Documentary History*, p. 64; Benjamin J. Taylor and Fred Whitney, *Labor Relations Law*, 5th Edition (Englewood Cliffs, N.J.: Prentice-Hall, 1987), p. 17.

10. Taylor and Whitney, *Labor Relations Law*, p. 18.

11. *Commonwealth of Massachusetts* v. *Hunt*, Massachusetts, 4 Metcalf III(1842).

12. Taylor and Whitney, *Labor Relations Law*, p. 18.

13. *In re Debs*, Petitioner, 158 U.S. 564, (1895).

14. The Sherman Antitrust Act of July 2, 1890, 26 Stat. 209, as amended.

15. The first *Danbury Hatters* case is officially called *Loewe* v. *Lawlor*, 208 U.S. 274 (1908); the second case is *Lawlor* v. *Loewe*, 235 U.S. 522 (1915).

16. The first case was *United Mine Workers* v. *Coronado Coal Company*, 259 U.S. 344 (1922); the second case was *Coronado Coal Company* v. *United Mine Workers of America*, 268 U.S. 195 (1925).

17. Haggai Hurvitz, "American Labor Law and the Doctrine of Entrepreneurial Property Rights: Boycotts, Courts, and the Juridical Reorientation of 1886–1895," *Industrial Relations Law Review* 8, no. 3 (1986): 307–61.

18. The Norris-LaGuardia Act of March 23, 1932, 47 Stat. 70.

19. La Follette Committee, *Report on Industrial Espionage*, Report No. 46, Parts I to XXI, 75th Congress.

20. The Wagner Act of July 5, 1935, 49 Stat. 449.

21. Taylor and Whitney, *Labor Relations Law*, p. 188.

22. Ibid., p. 211.

23. Labor Management Relations Act of June 23, 1947, 61 Stat. 136, amended by Act of September 14, 1959, Stat. 519.

24. *American Newspaper Publishers Associations* v. *NLRB*, 345 U.S. 100 (1952).

25. Indiana passed a right-to-work law in 1957 and repealed it in 1965. Labor conditions before, during, and after the law did not appear to change much.

26. *Patternmaker's League of North America* v. *National Labor Relations Board* 105 S.Ct. 3064 (1985); Rebecca A. Campbell, "The Board Upholds Suspension from the Union for Strike Breaking Activity," *Employee Relations Law Journal* 13 (Spring 1988): 689–93.

27. The Landrum-Griffin Act of 1959, 73 Stat. 519.

28. *Forty-Ninth Annual Report of the National Labor Relations Board* (Washington, D.C.: U.S. Government Printing Office, 1984), p. 3–7.

29. Ibid., p. 18.

30. Ellen R. Peirce and Richard Blackburn, "The Union De-certification Process: Employer Do's and Don'ts," *Employee Relations Law Journal* 12 (Autumn 1986): 205–20.

31. Information provided by the National Labor Relations Board, information services. (Washington, D.C.) January 1990.

32. John J. Sicilian, "Is NLRB Really Pro-Management?" *Employment Relations Today* 13 (Winter 1986/1987): 333–40.

33. Information supplied by the AFL-CIO National Headquarters Information Service, January 1990.

34. Personal correspondence with AFL-CIO National Headquarters, January 1990.

35. Described in Taylor and Whitney, *Labor Relations Law*, p. 400.

36. Clyde Scott and James Suchan, "Public Sector Collective Bargaining Agreements: How Readable Are They?" *Public Personnel Management* 16 (Spring 1987): 15–22.

37. Richard E. Walton and Robert B. McKersie, "*A Behavioral Theory of Labor Negotiations* (New York: McGraw-Hill, 1965).

38. Patricia O'Toole, *Corporate Messiah* (New York: Signet, 1985), Chapter 10.

39. Suhail Abboushi, "Union Leaders' Willingness to Negotiate Concessions," *Journal of Labor Research* 8 (Winter 1987): 47–58.

40. Brian E. Becker, "Concession Bargaining: The Meaning of Union Gains," *Academy of Management Journal* 31 (June 1988): 377–87; Everett M. Kassalow, "Concession Bargaining: Towards New Roles for American Unions and Managers," *International Labor Review* 127 (1988): 573–92.

41. James A. Keim and David L. Quigg, "The Sickout: Using and Evaluating Statistical Evidence in a Prima Facie Case," *Employee Relations Law Journal* 13 (Winter 1987/1988): 445–64.

42. Thomas P. Murphy, "Lockouts and Replacements: The NLRB Gives Teeth to an Old Weapon," *Employee Relations Law Journal* 14 (Autumn 1988): 253–61.

43. James K. McCollum and Edward A. Schroeder, IV, "NLRB Decisions in Jurisdictional Disputes: The Success of the 10 (k) Process," *Employee Relations Law Journal* 13 (Spring 1988): 649–65.

44. David P. Brenskelle, "Employers Win the Right to Hire Temporary Workers After a Lockout," *Employee Relations Law Journal* 12 (Winter 1986/1987): 505–9.

45. Craig S. Weaver, "Should Workers Be Paid to Strike?" *Personnel Administrator* 33 (June 1988): 108–12.

46. *Debartolo Corporation* v. *Florida Gulf Coast Building and Construction Trades Council*, 108 S.Ct. 1392 (1988); Thomas P. Brown, IV, "The Supreme Court Affirms a Union's Right to Distribute Handbills to Consumers," *Employee Relations Law Journal* 14 (Summer 1988): 117–22.

47. Joel Chernoff, "Union Muscle Bolstered by Pension Plans," *Pensions and Investment Age* 13 (April 1, 1985): 1, 36–37; Peter A. Susser, "Changing Union Tactics: New Problems For Employers," *Employment Relations Today* 15 (Winter 1988/1989): 313–20.

48. Information provided by the Bureau of Labor Statistics, Washington, D.C. January 1990.

49. Jay S. Siegel, "When Strikers Become Privileged Law Breakers," *New England Business* 8 (June 16, 1986): 57–58.

50. Michael W. Hirlinger and Ronald D. Sylvia, "Public Sector Impasse Procedures Revisited," *Journal of Collective Negotiations in the Public Sector* 17 (1988): 267–77.

51. Dane M. Partridge, "A Reexamination of the Effectiveness of No-Strike Laws for Public School Teachers," *Journal of Collective Negotiations in the Public Sector* 17 (1988): 257–66.

52. Charles J. Coleman, "Federal Sector Labor Relations: A Reevaluation of the Policies," *Journal of Collective Negotiations in the Public Sector* 16 (1987): 37–52; Homer O.

La Rue, "An Historical Overview of Interest Arbitration in the United States," *Arbitration Journal* 42 (December 1987): 13–22; Arlyne K. Liebeskind, "Compulsory Interest Arbitration for Public Safety Services in New Jersey—The First Three Years," *Journal of Collective Negotiations in the Public Sector* 16, no. 4 (1987): 343–61.

53. Kevin Hince, "Wage Fixing in a Period of Change: The New Zealand Case," *International Labor Organization* 125 (1986): 463–72.

54. Toshiaki Ohta, "Works Rules in Japan," *International Labor Review* 127 (1988): 627–39.

55. Yves Delamotte, "Workers' Participation and Personnel Policies in France," *International Labor Review* 127 (1988): 221–41.

C H A P T E R   1 4

Grievance and Discipline Procedures

Learning Objectives

After studying this chapter, you should be able to:

1. Identify the two basic procedures for resolving labor relations problems and explain how they interact.
2. Define what a labor grievance is, and describe the conditions that generally cause grievances to be submitted.
3. List the typical characteristics of individuals who are prone to submit grievances.
4. Describe the typical grievance procedures in both union and nonunion companies.
5. Explain the arbitration procedure and the problems and benefits of using arbitration to resolve labor disputes.
6. Describe the positive and negative approaches to employee discipline and their consequences.
7. Identify the four major causes of disciplinary problems.
8. Describe the concept of administrative justice in employee relations.
9. Describe the steps of a progressive discipline system.
10. List the characteristics of an effective discipline system.

Chapter Outline

Grievance and Complaint Procedures

Protecting the Rights of Employers and Employees / Grievance Defined / Causes of Grievances / Reducing the Number of Grievances / Characteristics of Grievants / Grievance Procedures in Union Organizations / Complaint Procedures in Nonunion Organizations / What Makes a Complaint Procedure Effective? / Arbitration

Discipline Procedures

Approaches to Discipline / Diagnosing Disciplinary Problems / Administrative Justice / Disciplinary Process / Principles of Effective Discipline

Legal Protections

Age Discrimination / Sexual Harassment / Handicap Discrimination /
Religious Discrimination / Wrongful Discharge

International HRM

I N T R O D U C T O R Y   C A S E

An Offensive Working Environment

When she was in high school, Margo was proud of her physical appearance, and she realized that her attractiveness contributed to her popularity and helped her to win several beauty contests. At work, however, she finds that her appearance seems to create problems and is now interfering with her work. Struggling to be accepted as a person rather than a sex object is not new to Margo, but her present situation has become too much for her.

When she goes to the mail room or copy machine, Margo must pass through a room where seven male employees work. As she walks through the room, she is subjected to a series of suggestive and indecent comments, and occasionally some of the men reach out and pat her on the rear end. At first she simply tried to ignore the problem, but one day after being pinched as she walked through, she complained to her supervisor. He promised to talk to the supervisor of the other department and ask him to put an end to the problem. He did talk, but the problem didn't end. Margo continued to be verbally molested. On one occasion, one of the men told her that he wanted to have sex with her. Another added that the whole department wanted to have sex with her.

Since talking to her supervisor did not help, Margo finally refused to go through the room when the men where there. She would either come in early or stay after work to use the copy machine and deliver mail. This strategy helped somewhat, but it has now created a problem between Margo and her supervisor, who thinks that her refusal to walk through the room is ridiculous. He told Margo that she should consider the men's comments as compliments and should feel proud that they notice her. Margo, however, does not believe that she should have to accept this sort of treatment. The company handbook states that "the company assumes the responsibility of maintaining a work place free from fears of threats and intimidation." Margo does not believe she in any way encourages the men's behavior. She is careful of her own behavior and she wears modest clothing. In talking with some of the other female employees, Margo discovered that many of them experience the same humiliation when they must pass through the room.

Questions:

1. Should Margo try to find another job, stay with her job and ignore the problem, pursue her complaint through the employee complaint system, or contact the EEOC?

2. How should the company respond to this problem? Most of the sexual harassment comes from three of the male employees. Should the company take disciplinary action against these three employees? If so, what action would you recommend?

3. What action do you think the EEOC should take?

GRIEVANCE AND COMPLAINT PROCEDURES

Effective human resource management should create a pleasant and rewarding place to work. If employees are treated fairly, complaints will be minimized. Good policies should lead to highly motivated, effective workers. Unfortunately, problems are likely to occur regardless of how well the human resource policies and practices are designed.

PROTECTING THE RIGHTS OF EMPLOYERS AND EMPLOYEES

To maintain fair and effective employee relations, every organization needs both a grievance procedure and a discipline procedure, as illustrated in Figure 14.1. Both procedures are needed whether the employees are represented by a union, a professional association, or no organization at all.

Grievance procedures provide a systematic process for hearing and evaluating the complaints of employees and tend to be more highly developed in union companies than in nonunion companies because they are specified in the labor agreement. These procedures protect the rights of employees and eliminate the need for strikes or slowdowns every time a disagreement occurs about the labor contract. Disagreements are almost inevitable regardless of how well the agreement was written. Even well-written labor agreements leave some issues open to interpretation since the negotiators cannot anticipate all future conflicts.

Discipline procedures provide a systematic process for handling problem employees. Employee discipline is one of the most challenging responsibilities of managers and human resource specialists. The reasons for unacceptable behavior are complex and

FIGURE 14.1 Two procedures for maintaining effective employee relations.

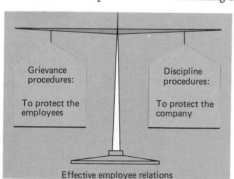

difficult to diagnose. The goal of a good discipline system is to help employees perform better, but if they fail to respond, a procedure is needed for firing them as a last resort. A good discipline system can make terminations "stick" without fear that the fired employees will be reinstated.

Every organization ought to have both a grievance procedure and a discipline procedure. Discipline procedures are needed to correct unacceptable behavior and to protect the company. Grievance procedures are needed to protect employees from inconsistent and unfair treatment. Both procedures are valuable in union and nonunion companies. Some managers, especially those in nonunion companies, think grievance or discipline procedures are unnecessary, and they rely on the skills of their supervisors to handle employee complaints and to correct problem behavior. However, many supervisors do not have adequate interpersonal skills to resolve employees' complaints. Furthermore, if a supervisor is the cause of the unfair treatment (such as sexual harassment), the employee cannot take the problem back to the supervisor and expect a fair hearing. In such a situation, a higher official is needed so that the employee can appeal the case.

A formal grievance procedure increases the amount of upward communication to top management and makes their decisions more sensitive to employee feelings. As grievances are expressed, top management becomes aware of the problems and frustrations of employees. Just knowing that there is a formal grievance system usually makes employees feel better. Even when employees cannot change a problem situation, they are reassured by the knowledge that others have listened and have tried to understand. Therefore, every organization, union or nonunion, ought to establish a procedure for responding to employee complaints.

GRIEVANCE DEFINED

A grievance is a work-related complaint or formal dispute that is brought to the attention of management. Union companies use a more limited definition in which grievances refer only to specific disputes concerning the labor agreement. This definition is restrictive and ignores many relevant criticisms that ought to be considered even though they are not covered by the agreement. At the other extreme, in nonunion companies grievances are sometimes defined very broadly to encompass any discontent or sense of injustice, even criticisms that are never expressed by employees. Such a definition has little validity because complaints have to be expressed before management can be expected to respond to them. Even so, managers need to be sensitive to unexpressed complaints that are evinced by sullenness, moodiness, criticism, insubordination, tardiness, and declining work performance.

Some examples of grievances include: (1) A senior employee submitted a grievance claiming that a younger employee with less seniority was promoted to fill a job vacancy in violation of the promotion and transfer provisions of the labor agreement. Management argued that the agreement had not been violated since the younger employee was more qualified for the job. The senior employee persuaded his union steward to talk with the operations manager about the issue. As a result of the discussion, the union steward told the senior employee that the labor agreement had not been violated and that the union would not submit this case for further grievance. The senior employee accepted the explanation and withdrew the grievance. (2) Two employees were discharged for fighting during an off-duty poker game. They submitted grievances claiming that their off-duty misconduct should not come under the jurisdiction of the employer. An arbitrator agreed with them. (3) Some employees who were required to work a 40-hour week plus a Saturday holiday claimed that they should receive triple-time wages (three times their normal wage rate) for the additional day. They based their contention on the terms of the labor agreement that provided time and one-half for overtime and an "additional" time and one-half for holidays. An arbitration board agreed with their interpretation of the labor agreement.[1]

CAUSES OF GRIEVANCES

Most of the behavioral science literature suggests that grievances are caused by seething discontent and unfair management practices. This is partially true. The number of grievances is usually much higher when morale is low and when employees feel frustrated and discontented. Changes in the number of grievances have sometimes been used to measure the effectiveness of management decisions and human resource policies.

Although the number of grievances tends to increase when job satisfaction declines, dissatisfaction with the job is not the only source of grievances. Grievances may arise because of:

Unclear contractual language that creates differing interpretations of the labor agreement.

A violation by management of the labor agreement.

A violation of the law, such as not following the overtime provisions of the Fair Labor Standards Act.

A violation of normal work procedures or other precedents.

Perceived unfair treatment of the employee by the supervisor.

Promoting a more qualified junior employee over an employee with more seniority.[2]

Even though grievances are related to dissatisfaction with the job, they are not related to any particular kind of job. Grievances do not appear to be more prevalent in one kind of work than in another. All jobs can produce grievances if the employees are not well-suited for the jobs, if the employees are treated unfairly, or if the employees are expected to do something they believe is wrong.

Certain styles of supervision can increase the grievance rate. The number of grievances frequently mounts when supervisors behave dictatorially, when they refuse to listen empathetically to employee complaints, when they confront employees with take-it-or-leave-it attitudes, when they are unfair or inconsistent in disciplinary actions, when they give inadequate and unclear instructions, and when they fail to keep employees informed. On the other hand, employees are much less likely to submit grievances if they feel that supervisors are genuine, are concerned about the employees' best interests, are trying to be fair, and are trying to follow the labor agreement. A study of leadership styles demonstrated that grievance rates are inversely related to measures of consideration. The results of the study indicated that supervisors with high consideration scores, which indicate that supervisors display trust, respect, and warmth toward group members, tend to have low grievance rates.[3] Most employees will tolerate a certain amount of injustice without complaining if they think their supervisor cares and is trying to be fair.

Being fair and empathetic, however, is not the same as being participative and democratic. A study of seventeen supervisors in a large industrial machine manufacturing company compared autocratic and democratic leadership styles. A short questionnaire measuring attitudes toward participation, authority, and sharing information was used to identify six autocratic supervisors and eleven democratic supervisors. The results indicated that democratic supervisors had a significantly higher rate of grievances than autocratic supervisors. The democratic supervisors were able to resolve a larger percentage of grievances at the first stage of the grievance process than the autocratic supervisors. However, at later stages of the process, the democratic supervisors had a higher percentage of their decisions overturned by upper management than the autocratic supervisors. In this company, at least, autocratic supervisors seemed to have the best understanding of the labor agreement, and they administered the agreement in the most authoritative fashion, which produced the fewest grievances.[4]

The grievance rate is also influenced by union leaders. One study of fifty-four union stewards concluded that their attitudes had a greater impact on the grievance rate than either the characteristics of the grievant or the grievant's supervisor.[5] Some union stewards are oriented toward submitting grievances and constantly look for opportunities to do so. Even when an offended employee decides not to file a grievance, some stewards will file the grievance in the name of the union anyway. Other union stewards are oriented toward resolving problems and try to do so without submitting a formal grievance. Some union representatives will solicit grievances because they want to retain their union position. They think that submitting a large number of grievances will make them look good and win the support of other union members. They may even solicit grievances just to divert the attention of members from weaknesses or leadership deficiencies within the union.

REDUCING THE NUMBER OF GRIEVANCES

To reduce the number of grievances, the conditions that cause grievances must be eliminated. Company policies need to be followed carefully. If there is a labor agreement, it must be carefully worded. During collective bargaining, both sides should attempt to resolve uncertainties and ambiguities and ascertain that the written agreement contains what they want it to say.[6] All supervisors should know what the agreement says and be adequately trained to follow it. They also need training in the basic principles of good supervision. If they can learn to be fair and understanding, there will be fewer grievances.

Although grievances are an indication of problems and complaints, the elimination of all grievances would be an unrealistic goal. Frequently, an organization is surprised to find that its grievance rate increases after the start of an organizational development and improvement project. As working conditions in the company improve and as employees are given greater freedom and participation, management assumes that the grievance rate will decline. Usually it does decline, but not until six months to a year after the change starts. The initial effect is usually an increase in grievances. As employees see a more open and responsive attitude among managers, they tend to submit more grievances than usual. The flurry of complaints originates from past injustices that employees formerly thought would be ignored. Consequently, changes in grievance rates have to be interpreted carefully. An increase in the rate of grievances does not always mean that conditions are deteriorating.

CHARACTERISTICS OF GRIEVANTS

Several studies have examined the characteristics of employees who submit grievances. Most of these studies have compared a sample of grievants with a matched sample of nongrievants with similar age, seniority, and job classifications. One study found that grievants are younger, predominantly male, less likely to be married, more likely to be American citizens, and more often rehires than nongrievants.[7] A second study found that grievants have more education, are more active in the union, and have higher rates of absenteeism and tardiness than nongrievants.[8]

A third study suggested that two different kinds of grievants exist. One type is the "problem employee" who is protesting a disciplinary action. Such an employee generally has a history of disciplinary grievances, terminations, suspensions, absences, arrests, sick leaves, and derogatory statements in his or her personnel file. This individual's grievance rate, poor work performance, and personal difficulties suggest the possibility of a serious personality disorder. The other type of grievant, the "chronic complainer," is the person who has not settled down in the job. This employee is younger and more highly educated, has missed more work by requested leaves or absences, and has more derogatory information in his or her personnel file than a nongrievant. But this grievant tends to receive more wage increases and promotions than the nongrievant, which suggests that this type of grievant is ambitious, outspoken, and generally resistant to the conventions of society. Some of the complaints submitted by this type of grievant may represent constructive complaints regarding inappropriate company practices or unfair personnel policies.[9]

These studies suggest that most, but not all, grievances are submitted by problem employees and chronic complainers. Some grievances are submitted by productive and creative employees who use the grievance system to create their own kind of change. The complaints of this latter group should not be summarily disregarded since they might contain insightful recommendations for improving the organization.

GRIEVANCE PROCEDURES IN UNION ORGANIZATIONS

The essence of the grievance procedure is to provide a means by which employees can express complaints without jeopardizing their jobs and by which they can obtain a fair hearing through progressively higher levels of management. Each year thousands of grievances are filed. Without a peaceful process for resolving them, the economic costs of lost output due to strikes or lockouts would be substantial, and industrial relations would be chaotic.

The general procedure for handling grievances has become standardized for unionized companies, although specific details vary from company to company. In large organizations the process generally contains more steps than in small organizations, as shown in Figure 14.2. The full grievance procedure consists of these five steps:

Step 1. The first step in most labor agreements calls for the complaint to be submitted to the supervisor. Some agreements require a complaint to be submitted in

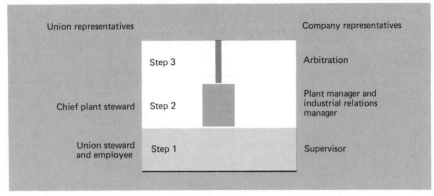

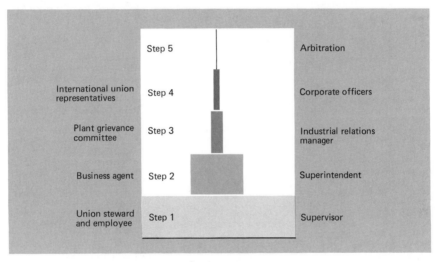

FIGURE 14.2 Grievance process for large and small companies.

writing on a prepared form. Other agreements allow an employee to express a complaint verbally. Employees usually can request the presence of the union steward to support them. The union steward may even take the lead in presenting a grievance. However, the first meeting may involve only an aggrieved employee and a supervisor in an informal exchange. A vast number of workers' complaints are settled satisfactorily by a simple discussion.

Step 2. If an employee is not satisfied with the actions of the supervisor, the grievance can be appealed to the step 2. At this point the grievance is almost always written. The employee is represented by the chief plant steward or business agent, and the employer is represented by the superintendent or industrial relations office. In smaller companies, this step is usually bypassed.

Step 3. If the union is not satisfied with the decision of the superintendent or industrial relations office, the grievance can be appealed to step 3. Here, the plant manager or director of industrial relations represents the employer, and the union is represented by the plant grievance committee. In smaller organizations, these groups, as the highest ranking officers for both management and union, represent the second step in the grievance procedure. Grievances that are not settled at this step may go directly to arbitration.

Step 4. Large corporations may have a fourth step in the grievance process where top corporate officers meet with representatives of the international union to resolve unsettled grievances. The number of grievances that reach this level represents a very small percentage of the total. Only those issues that have a broad and general interest to the union and corporation are usually considered at this level.

Step 5. The final step in the grievance process is binding arbitration by an outside third party acceptable to both management and the union. Both parties agree beforehand to abide by the arbitrator's decision.

Most grievance procedures specify time limits for each stage of grievance processing. An agreement may stipulate, for example, that a grievance must be filed within a certain number of days after an alleged violation takes place. The organization is required to respond within a certain number of days at each stage of the procedure. The union also has a time limit for appealing a decision to the next stage if it is not satisfied. Failing to respond within a specified time limit may result in forfeiture of the grievance by the union or in granting the grievance by the company. Extensions of time limits are usually granted upon request for legitimate reasons. Many agreements provide an interval of three to five working days between steps of the grievance procedure; others provide a somewhat longer interval. The purpose of such time limits is to force both the company and the union to address grievances immediately. If grievances are resolved promptly, friction and discontent are reduced.

To resolve a grievance, both management and union representatives must be willing to discuss the issue rationally and objectively. Both sides must desire to resolve the dispute and to seek a satisfactory solution. A grievance should not be treated as a form of competition in which each side keeps track of its win-loss record. Instead, each side should seek to resolve conflict and remove inequities.

Most grievances are resolved at the first step of the process by competent supervisors who are willing to listen and act fairly. To reduce the number of grievances that are appealed, supervisors are encouraged to follow these recommendations:

Treat all complaints seriously.

Investigate and handle each case as though it may eventually result in arbitration.

Talk with an employee as soon as possible about his or her grievance and give the employee a full hearing.

Correct the problem if the employee or the company is wrong.

Examine the labor agreement carefully, and obtain clarification from the human resource office if necessary.

Collect evidence and determine if there were any witnesses.

Remain calm.

Carefully examine all the evidence before making a decision.

Avoid lengthy delays. When all the information is in, make a decision and communicate it.[10]

Sometimes a supervisor is not in a position to resolve a grievance because it concerns a company policy. Such a dispute may have to be appealed to the second, third, or even fourth step of the grievance procedure before the appropriate people who can change or interpret the policy become involved.

A labor union is frequently placed in the awkward position of having to process a grievance that it does not support. The Taft-Hartley Act requires a union to represent all employees in the bargaining unit, even if they are not members of the union. However, a union may understandably feel reluctant to press the grievance of a nonmember because it may involve a costly and time-consuming process. Union leaders also may dislike having to process the grievances of some of their own union members because they do not agree with their complaints. Some employees are chronic complainers who create headaches for both management and unions with their endless strings of grievances.

Since a union has a duty to provide fair and equal representation in the handling of grievances, it can be sued by employees for arbitrary, discriminatory, or unfair conduct. The labor organization is required to accept a complaint for unbiased investigation before declining to process it. But the Supreme Court has ruled that a union does not have to process all grievances, regardless of merit.[11]

Union leaders may try to persuade a member to drop a frivolous complaint, or they may present the grievance to management in a half-hearted fashion. If an employee feels that he or she has not been represented fairly, the employee may sue the company and the union in federal courts or before the NLRB. This situation explains why labor agreements often contain so many legal technicalities—they are partially intended to protect union leaders from the members.

COMPLAINT PROCEDURES IN NONUNION ORGANIZATIONS

Unlike the well-defined grievance programs found in most union companies, those found in nonunion companies are informal, if they exist at all. However, a growing number of managers in nonunion companies favor the provision of increased human rights and freedoms for employees. In nonunion companies, grievance procedures are often referred to as **complaint systems**. A Conference Board survey of 652 companies with some union presence found that almost half of them had adopted a complaint system for their nonunion employees. Among the 96 nonunion companies surveyed, an even higher percentage—68 percent—indicated that they had such a system. The survey indicated that complaint systems were most prevalent among larger companies and in the manufacturing industry.[12]

When employees in nonunion companies have complaints, they are encouraged to speak up. Many executives claim that their organizations have adequate grievance protection because employees who have complaints are encouraged to say what they think with the assurance that they will be heard. The problem with speaking up, however, is not a fear of being ignored but a fear of being fired. Usually, the person who suffers the most severe consequences when an employee blows the whistle on corporate misconduct is the whistle blower. **Whistle blowers**—employees who observe an illegal or immoral action and make the information public—are usually fired or treated so badly that they resign.[13]

Surveys indicate broadening support for methods of assuring due process to employees who believe they have been wronged by management. The most popular procedures in nonunion companies include the grievance committee, ombudsman, grievance appeal procedure, open-door policy, and investigative officer.[14]

GRIEVANCE COMMITTEE

Some nonunion organizations have established a grievance procedure that allows individuals to submit their grievances to a grievance committee. The members of the committee may be appointed by top management or elected by the employees. Some colleges have capricious grading committees or student governance committees to which students who think they have been treated unfairly may appeal. Such committees hear the evidence and issue a judgment. In some companies, the grievance committee hears the evidence and makes a recommendation to the president, rather than making a binding decision on its own.[15]

OMBUDSMAN

The term **ombudsman** originally referred to a politically neutral and independent person who represented ordinary citizens in their disputes with government officials. The concept first originated in Sweden and Finland in 1809. In recent years, numerous organizations have appointed one of their employees to be an ombudsman. Such an individual is charged with investigating and settling employee complaints. Xerox Corporation has an ombudsman system. The ombudsman reports to the president, who is the only person with the authority to reverse the ombudsman's decision.[16] The use of an ombudsman appears to be gaining popularity in both business and nonbusiness organizations. Many colleges have adopted the system to handle student complaints. Several newspapers, radio, and television stations also have appointed ombudsmen to hear complaints of citizens and to render help either directly or by means of publicizing the problem.

GRIEVANCE APPEAL PROCEDURE

Some companies allow employees to submit grievances to successively higher levels in the organization, as illustrated by Table 14.1. In some cases, the aggrieved employee is represented by an attorney, a peer, or a member of the human resource department. The hearing is normally conducted by a neutral company executive who hears the evidence and makes a judgment.[17] This procedure is similar to the appeal process in a union agreement, but with two exceptions. First, it is usually an informal system, and an appeal can be stopped anytime at management's discretion with no guarantee that it will reach the top officers. Second, ultimate appeal is usually made to top management and does not go to arbitration. Allowing a grievance to go to binding arbitration would make this procedure more fair, but most employees do not have the skills necessary to prepare their own cases nor the resources to pay their portion of an arbitrator's fees, and most companies do not want to relinquish control to an outside party.

TABLE 14.1 Complaint procedure for a retail store

Problem-Solving Procedure

Objective: The purpose of this problem-solving procedure is to provide a formal process for solving problems and for protecting the rights of employees.

Step 1:   Supervisors are responsible for hearing and resolving work-related problems. The problem should be fully discussed with your immediate supervisor. However, in unusual cases or because of personal conditions between you and your supervisor, you may want to discuss the problem directly with the employee relations office.

Step 2:   If your supervisor does not resolve the problem to your satisfaction, it can be appealed to your functional manager. This manager will explore all the facts of the case and render a decision.

Step 3:   If you are still dissatisfied with the resolution of your problem, it can be discussed with the store manager. The employee relations manager will make the appointment for you. After the discussion, the store manager's decision at this level will be considered final.

The following time limits have been established:

Step 1 —   5 working days

Step 2 —   5 working days

Step 3 — 10 working days

OPEN-DOOR POLICY

The most popular procedure for responding to employee complaints is the open-door policy. Approximately two-thirds of nonunion organizations have explicit open-door policies.[18] Such a policy usually means that all employees, regardless of their positions, have the right to discuss a complaint with top corporate officers without being forced to go through a chain of command. After an investigation of a reasonable complaint has been completed by an executive, the aggrieved employee is informed about the outcome.

Although an open-door policy provides an avenue for employees to express their complaints, it does not always function effectively. The social distance between production workers and the company president is usually exaggerated when viewed from the bottom of the hierarchy, and it can destroy an employee's willingness to share a problem. The open-door policy needs to exist throughout the organization so that complaints can be taken to lower levels of management as well as to higher levels. Many complaints concern day-to-day issues that are far removed from top officers. An open-door policy that requires taking all complaints to the company president for resolution is ineffective and undesirable.

INVESTIGATIVE OFFICER METHOD

Approximately half of all organizations have a grievance procedure that provides for some form of investigation of employee complaints. The investigation is normally conducted by a human resource executive or by an assistant to either the president or a vice president; a report is then submitted to top management. This procedure is similar to the Inspector General system used in the military. A representative of the Inspector General's office visits each military unit once each year to hear and investigate complaints by soldiers. In business organizations, however, the investigations are usually conducted as needed rather than on an annual basis, and the investigations probe only the most severe complaints.

WHAT MAKES A COMPLAINT PROCEDURE EFFECTIVE?

To have an effective complaint procedure, employees must believe that:

1. their complaints can be presented without a lot of hassle, embarrassment, or paperwork;
2. their complaints will be evaluated by a fair and impartial third party; and
3. they will not be fired or mistreated for submitting their complaints and pressing them to a resolution.

This protection against being fired or mistreated is necessary for the success of both union and nonunion grievance procedures. Union employees usually have greater protection than nonunion employees because their labor agreement is written and it can be enforced by collective action. But any employee, union or nonunion, can become the object of persecution by managers who want to force the employee to resign. Actions spurred by the vindictive feelings of executives toward subordinates who have submitted grievances are sometimes cruel. An employee who has exposed the wrongdoings of corporate officers may become the object of a campaign of abuse and harassment including false accusations, embarrassing work assignments, and low performance evaluations. The fear of being fired or mistreated for submitting a grievance is a real fear, especially in a nonunion company. Fears of retaliation must be countered before a complaint procedure will function effectively.[19]

ARBITRATION

Arbitration is the process of having a labor dispute resolved by an impartial third party who examines information from both sides and renders a judgment. The parties agree beforehand to accept the decision of an impartial judge called an arbitrator. As discussed in Chapter 13, arbitration can be used to settle contract issues during collective bargaining. It is more frequently used, however, to resolve labor grievances involving the interpretation or application of the labor agreement and discharge and disciplinary actions.

For many years a nagging question challenged the arbitration process: Could labor disputes be legally settled by arbitration, or should they be settled in the courts as contract issues? The legality of grievance arbitration was questioned because it was viewed as a device to avoid court jurisdiction over contractual matters. Neither side wanted to submit an issue to arbitration if they knew it might later be overturned in the federal courts. During the 1960s, the situation changed as a result of several Supreme Court decisions that significantly strengthened the grievance process.

The present status of arbitration is reasonably secure. The Supreme Court and federal courts endorse the arbitration process, and the NLRB also has indicated its support of arbitration when certain conditions are met. The proceedings must be fair and regular, the parties must agree to accept an award as final and binding, the award must not be a clear contradiction of the purposes and policies of the board, and the award must deal with the statutory rights of the parties.[20]

In wrongful-discharge cases, the courts have been fairly consistent in holding that the grievance process outlined in a collective bargaining agreement preempts state laws and the resolution of the case in court. In *Friday* v. *Hughes Aircraft Company*, for example, a California Court of Appeal refused to allow a chemical storekeeper with twenty-eight years of service to sue his employer in court rather than use the grievance procedure.[21] He was terminated after several reprimands and suspension and tried to sue in court rather than file a grievance that could go as far as arbitration. The court required him to use the arbitration process.

In *United Paper* v. *Misco Inc.*, the U.S. Supreme Court unanimously held that, absent proof of fraud or dishonesty, a federal district court cannot overturn an arbitrator's decision. An arbitrator reinstated an employee who had been fired for alleged marijuana use while on the company premises. The company succeeded in having the decision overturned in federal district court by arguing that the arbitrator misinterpreted the contract and followed improper fact finding. The Supreme Court ruled, however, that

HRM in Action

Job Security Is Not Guaranteed

In 1988 General Motors announced that it would close its Fiero assembly plant in Pontiac, Michigan, because of slumping sales. The announcement came as a surprise to the 1,700 employees who would be laid off because they had assumed their jobs were guaranteed.

When the current labor agreement was signed almost three years earlier, union leaders told members that the agreement provided "unprecedented" job security. Union members believed their agreement prohibited General Motors from closing plants and laying off workers. GM explained that the plant was not closed, but "indefinitely idled," and that the layoffs did not violate the agreement.

The United Auto Workers union challenged the decision to shut the plant and the issue was submitted to arbitration. The arbitrator ruled in favor of the company. The ruling also affected 8,100 other employees in idled plants in Leeds, Missouri, Framingham, Massachusetts, and Lakewood, Georgia. If the company is not producing a product that consumers are buying, the assembly plants cannot remain open. Job security is determined more by economic success of the company than by the job-security provisions negotiated in a labor agreement.

Source: Gregory A. Patterson, "GM Wins Arbitration in UAW Dispute Over Firm's Closing of Michigan Plant," *Wall Street Journal*, March 30, 1990.

the arbitrator's decision should not be reversed by federal courts unless it violates an explicit law.[22]

The arbitration procedure is usually outlined in the labor agreement's provisions. These provisions generally describe the issues that may be arbitrated, the selection of an arbitrator, the arbitration procedure, and limitations on the authority of the arbitrator.

ISSUES FOR ARBITRATION

Although many grievances originate from discourteous or unfair treatment, most of the grievances that reach arbitration involve disputes about the specific application or interpretation of a labor agreement. Some of the issues referred to arbitration most frequently include the following:

Discharge and disciplinary actions

Seniority and its application

Leaves of absence

Promotions and transfers

Vacations and vacation pay

Holidays and holiday pay

Health and welfare benefits

Management rights

Union rights

Strikes and lockouts

Union security

Wages and hours[23]

CHOOSING AN ARBITRATOR

Once the parties decide to have a dispute settled by arbitration, the first step is to select an arbitrator or board of arbitration. Occasionally, a **tripartite board**, consisting of representatives from management and union plus an impartial chairperson, is appointed.[24] Some companies and unions have an arbitrator that they call on regularly. Others compile a list of people acceptable to both sides and rotate through the list. The names of experienced arbitrators can be obtained from lists compiled by the American Arbitration Association or by the Federal Mediation and Conciliation Services. The choice of an arbitrator may become a serious labor dispute in itself. Sometimes the previous award decisions of prospective arbitrators are carefully scrutinized to determine whether they have made more awards in favor of management or the union. However, since each case is different, this exercise is generally not very useful.

Although most arbitrators are lawyers or professors, there are no set requirements that a person must satisfy to serve as an arbitrator. Any person who has a reputation for fairness and impartiality might be asked to hear a dispute. An arbitrator is not bound by precedents. His or her job is to render the best judgment possible about the meaning of a particular labor agreement with respect to the specific case. The fact that one arbitrator decides a case in one way does not necessarily mean that another arbitrator will do likewise in a similar case. However, arbitrators usually review the rulings handed down by one another, and as a result, a set of general principles has slowly accumulated.

ARBITRATION PROCESS

After an arbitrator has been chosen, an arbitration hearing is held. A statement called the **submission agreement** is usually prepared; this statement formally outlines the issues for arbitration and grants final authority to the arbitrator to settle the issue.

The hearing may be as formal as a civil court hearing and involve written testimony, signed statements and affidavits, the swearing in of witnesses, cross examination, and a recorded transcript of the proceedings. Or, the hearing might be very informal, with just an opening statement by each side and then questioning by the arbitrator. To save time, most testimony by witnesses is obtained in advance and presented to the arbitrator. Normally, the hearing does not last more than one day.

Most arbitrators stipulate that the burden of proof is on the party that initiates the complaint. If the union alleges violation of the agreement, it must provide evidence of what happened and describe how the agreement was violated. If an employee was disciplined or discharged, the company must provide evidence showing that the action was legitimate.

After all of the evidence has been presented, the hearings are adjourned. The arbitrator reviews the evidence, examines the labor agreement, and usually looks at previous arbitration awards in similar cases before reaching a decision. Within thirty days, the arbitration award is usually announced to both parties along with a written review of the case. The written review is important because it contains a rationale for the decision and helps each side understand the decision.

Women have a higher probability of winning arbitration awards than men from male arbitrators. Female arbitrators, however, do not show the same preferential treatment for female grievants. Three investigations of over 2,500 discharge cases indicated that women are almost twice as likely as men to have their grievances sustained. In cases where they are sustained, women are much more likely than men to receive full reinstatement than partial reinstatement. In cases where suspension is imposed rather than discharge, women usually receive shorter suspensions than men. These results are generally consistent with the favorable treatment of women in the criminal justice system.[25]

PROBLEMS WITH ARBITRATION

Most representatives of management and labor are generally satisfied with the arbitral process, especially if the arbitrator is objective and actively controls the hearing.[26] Grievance arbitration contributes to the peaceful resolution of labor disputes. Nevertheless, it has its problems. Grievance arbitration is generally criticized for three reasons: it costs too much, it takes too long, and it has become too formal. The costs of arbitration generally increase each year because arbitrators increase their fees and because their expenses grow higher. The average time involved in processing a grievance through arbitration is so long that it is discouraging to most employees. The average time between the initial grievance filing and the final arbitration award is about 250 days.[27] The growing cost and increasing time delays are partially attributed to what critics call "creeping legalism." The trends in arbitration are toward greater use of lawyers, more formal grievance hearings, longer testimony to examine, and more technical language in the labor agreement. Creeping legalism, however, occurs for a reason. If one party uses a lawyer and the other does not, the party represented by the lawyer tends to win, according to a survey of over 1,200 arbitration cases involving discharge for just cause. If both sides have lawyers, the likelihood of winning is about the same as when neither side is represented by a lawyer.[28]

To overcome delays in arbitration, several companies have developed systems designed to expedite grievance cases as efficiently as possible. Employees in one steel company, for example, can obtain an arbitration hearing within ten days of filing an appeal. An arbitrator selected from a panel of arbitrators hears the case, which is presented by local plant and union representatives and involves no written transcripts or briefs. Since the award is made within forty-eight hours of the hearing, costs are greatly reduced by this method. Moreover, such a speedy hearing appears to promote better employee relations and seems to lose little in legalistic thoroughness.[29]

DISCIPLINE PROCEDURES

Discipline has many definitions. Most people equate discipline with punishment, such as spanking a child or discharging an employee. However, discipline is not synonymous with punishment. A discipline procedure may consist of several different consequences, including training, correction, evaluation, punishment, and ultimate termination. The overall objective of disciplinary action is to remedy a problem and to help employees achieve success in their work. It is to the advantage of both an organization and its employees that a smoothly functioning state of order be maintained. To maintain a state of order, an organization must have an accepted standard of appropriate conduct, a fair procedure for evaluating behavior, and a sequence of progressively severe penalties for rule violators.

APPROACHES TO DISCIPLINE

The violation of company rules can be handled in many different ways. At one extreme, a supervisor seeing a mistake may scream at the offender in front of other workers and issue snap decisions aimed at punishing the offender and at deterring others from wrongdoing. At the other extreme, a supervisor seeing a mistake may respond in a calm and considerate manner with the intent of improving future performance, not of punishing past performance.

Why are there such dramatic differences in the ways supervisors respond? First, supervisors have developed their own characteristic ways of responding to disciplinary problems. How they were disciplined by their parents when they were children and how they were treated by superiors earlier in their careers have an enormous influence on their styles of disciplining. Supervisors tend to model the disciplinary styles of other people who have been influential in their lives. Disciplinary styles also are influenced by the company's formal discipline procedures and dominant style of management. If the organization has a formal discipline system with a sequence of penalties, supervisors usually follow the sequence in a calm and rational manner. If the dominant style of management shows a concern for the personal growth and development of employees, supervisors are inclined to help employees solve problems and improve their performances.

NEGATIVE APPROACH

The negative approach to discipline, sometimes called punitive or autocratic discipline, is summarized in Table 14.2. The purpose of punitive discipline is to punish employees for mistakes. The punishment is usually severe to remind others of the consequences of wrongdoing. To produce the desired effect, the punishment is usually administered publicly, such as a verbal reprimand in the presence of other employees or firing on the spot. When the mistake is discussed, there may be an emotional outburst. The supervisor may become angry and make irrational decisions. Even though employees may be suspended or discharged only infrequently, they live in constant fear that it could happen at any time.

The basic problem with punitive discipline is that it motivates employees to achieve only the minimum acceptable performance. Employees who are motivated by fear are not oriented toward becoming outstanding performers. Instead, they are motivated to avoid failure and to produce only the minimum amount of work to avoid punishment. Another problem with punitive discipline is that severe punishment does not necessarily deter troublemakers. For example, people who break laws usually are thinking about their immediate wants rather than the long-term consequences of their actions. Likewise, employees who repeatedly make errors usually do not think about the consequences of their acts. Severe punishment and threats of being terminated are not usually very effective methods of discipline for such employees.

TABLE 14.2   Comparison between positive and negative approaches to discipline

	Negative Approach	Positive Approach
The motive for discipline	Retribution—punishment for errors	To correct behavior and eliminate further errors
The emotional tone of the meeting	Expression of anger, loss of temper, irrational punishment or threats	Calm explanation of the error and why it is unacceptable
Desired result of discipline	To severely punish or terminate the offender, to serve as an example and create fear in others, to serve as a deterrent to others	To rehabilitate problem employees and turn them into productive employees
Probable consequence	Employees will achieve only the minimum acceptable performance	Those who respond will become good employees; those who do not respond will be terminated

POSITIVE APPROACH

The positive approach to discipline, sometimes called constructive discipline, is summarized in Table 14.2. The purposes of constructive discipline are to eliminate future problems and to create effective employees. Employees' mistakes are used to help them learn how to change. The disciplinary discussion is a calm consideration of the problem—what caused it, why it needs to be corrected, and how it can be corrected. The discussion focuses on the problem and how it can be solved rather than on who is to blame and why.

A necessary prerequisite for the positive approach to discipline is a clear understanding of the rules and expectations. The rules do not need to be an exhaustive list of detailed regulations. In fact, an informal list of general guidelines requiring individual interpretation is sometimes most useful because it creates greater acceptance and commitment among employees than formal rules. Regardless of the structure of the rules, employees need to know what behavior is expected of them and what behavior is unacceptable. The performance standards must be fair and reasonable, and the rules must be administered fairly.

The positive approach to discipline does not mean that a supervisor should ignore errors or casually disregard problems. It does not mean lax discipline. When an employee arrives late for work, drinks on the job, willfully damages company property, or commits any other wrongs, supervisors need to act. According to the constructive approach to discipline, the supervisor's actions should be directed toward the rehabilitation of the employee and the elimination of the problem. The supervisor may need to be very firm, and repeated wrongdoing may have to result in suspension and discharge. But the intent is to help the employee correct problem behavior and become an outstanding performer.

The positive approach to discipline is closely tied to the development of personal responsibility. When employees are given specific performance expectations, when their performances are evaluated, and when problems are addressed in a constructive environment, the employees tend to develop a strong sense of personal responsibility. These conditions also contribute to the development of self-discipline and a strong work ethic.[30]

DIAGNOSING DISCIPLINARY PROBLEMS

Disciplinary problems can be caused by a number of reasons that are not equally serious. Understanding the causes of problems is essential because the causes suggest significantly different implications for managerial action. It makes a big difference, for example, to know whether a machine was damaged by willful destructiveness, simple carelessness, or an unwitting error caused by a lack of training. The cost of fixing the machine will not change in relation to the severity or lightness of the cause, but the appropriate disciplinary action should be different depending on the cause. A careful diagnosis of the nature and cause of each wrongdoing should precede any disciplinary action.

Most employee problems can be placed into one of the following categories: (1) rule violations, (2) unsatisfactory performance, (3) illegal acts, (4) personal problems, or (5) substance abuse.

RULE VIOLATIONS

The first category of disciplinary problems consists of violations of company rules. Some companies have general rules that are informally communicated to employees, while others have specific rules that prohibit such things as possession of weapons, use of alcohol or narcotics, abusive or threatening language, insubordination, sleeping on the job, carelessness, smoking in unauthorized places, fighting, gambling, abuse of sick leave, habitual tardiness, and horseplay.

Nonunion employers are free to make and enforce whatever rules they want, providing the rules are consistent with other laws. Employers who bargain with a union, however, do not have as much liberty in making and enforcing company rules. Unless the agreement says otherwise, the company has the right to make new rules without consulting the union. However, union members who think that the rules are unfair or that they have been falsely accused of breaking a rule can seek redress through arbitration. As noted earlier, arbitrators are not bound by precedent, but a fairly consistent set of guidelines has accumulated that describe what arbitrators are likely to uphold.[31]

An employee who refuses to follow a supervisor's instruction is guilty of insubordination. Arbitrators rarely reverse disciplinary actions for insubordination, provided that the instructions were clear, that the supervisor was the appropriately designated representative of management, and that the supervisor provided an explicit warning of the consequences of failure to comply with the instruction. However, employees are not required to follow orders that would endanger their health or safety.

Abusive language usually is considered a legitimate basis for disciplinary action. Arbitrators generally uphold disciplinary actions involving verbal abuse of supervisors, especially if such language was used to embarrass, ridicule, or degrade a supervisor and if other employees were present to hear it. All profane and obscene language will not necessarily lead to dismissal, however. Disciplinary discharges are usually overturned or reduced if the obscene language was a customary part of "shop talk," if it was not directed as a personal attack against the supervisor, or if the employee was provoked by the supervisor.

Horseplay is a common occurrence in almost any work group. Since it usually adds an element of humor and social interaction, it is not necessarily bad unless it gets out of hand. In determining how to handle incidents of horseplay at work, a distinction must be made between joking that involves only a remote possibility of injury or disruption and acts that seriously disrupt the flow of work or involve a high risk of injury. Conduct of the latter type warrants a serious penalty even if disastrous consequences do not occur. A line has to be drawn by management and arbitrators between simply "kidding around" and dangerous or vicious acts.

Gambling of some type is prevalent in many companies, such as a football pool or a lunch-hour poker game. Company rules sometimes prohibit all gambling because it infringes on company time and leads to occasional fights. If the company prohibits gambling at work, arbitrators generally uphold disciplinary actions, providing that good evidence exists. Discharge, however, is normally considered too severe a penalty for a first offense of gambling. But if the employees have been warned previously about gambling and they are caught gambling again during working hours, discharge is an appropriate action. Discharge is also an appropriate measure when employees are involved in an organized gambling racket.

Fights with coworkers or supervisors usually result in some form of disciplinary action, even if fighting is not expressly prohibited in the company rules. Most managers and arbitrators assume that prohibitions against fighting on the job are generally understood. In determining the appropriate discipline for fighting and aggressive behavior, many mitigating circumstances need to be considered. Arbitrators usually consider these factors:

The employee's length of service and overall work record.

Whether the misconduct was a single, thoughtless blow or a series of deliberate acts.

Whether the blow was struck with a dangerous weapon, a clenched fist, or an open hand.

The effect of the altercation on the safety and morale of other employees.

The presence of mitigating circumstances such as provocation, discrimination, or management's failure to take corrective action.

Whether the incident indicated that the employee has vicious tendencies, serious emotional instability, or propensities for such conduct.

A sensitive question is whether employees should be disciplined or terminated for off-the-job behavior. As a general rule, arbitrators uphold disciplinary actions for off-duty conduct if there is a link between the off-duty conduct and on-the-job activities. Disciplinary action is considered warranted when the off-duty conduct renders workers unable to perform their work satisfactorily, or when the behavior has a negative impact on the performance of coworkers or on management efficiency. Also relevant are the organization's reputation and the effects of adverse publicity. Many arbitrators apply higher standards for judging the propriety of the behavior of public employees, especially police, firefighters, and teachers.[32]

UNSATISFACTORY PERFORMANCE

Some employees are extremely frustrating to supervise because they fail to do their assigned work. It may take them twice as long to do a job as their supervisor expected and perhaps three times as long as its should have taken. Even worse, their work has so many mistakes the entire job has to be redone. Employees who have just entered the work force are the ones most frequently criticized for poor work habits. Some supervisors have estimated that about one-third of the new workers do not know how to work and do not want to learn. It is not unusual for the fastest employees to produce three to four times as much as the slowest employees.

A useful model for diagnosing the causes of unsatisfactory performance is presented in Figure 14.3. This model shows how unsatisfactory performance may be due to several causes that ought to be carefully assessed. If performance is low because employees do not have the appropriate skills and ability, the problem relates to job placement rather than to discipline. If unsatisfactory performance is caused by inadequate job knowledge, the problem relates to training. And if the unsatisfactory performance is caused by an inefficient organizational structure, the problem concerns job redesign and organizational structure.[33]

Unsatisfactory performance should only be viewed as a discipline problem when it is caused by inadequate motivation. Motivation problems are usually solved by rearranging the reinforcement contingencies. Positive rewards should be used to reinforce high-

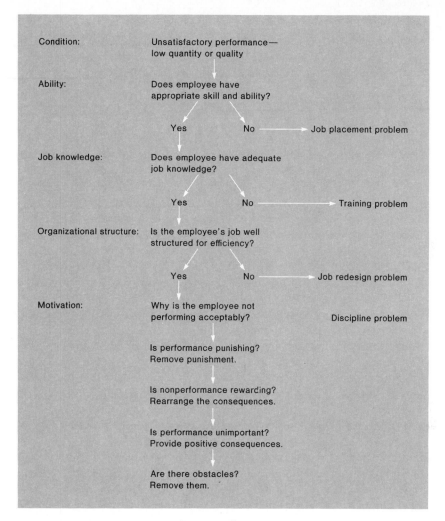

Condition: Unsatisfactory performance—
low quantity or quality

Ability: Does employee have
appropriate skill and ability?

Yes   No ──────▶ Job placement problem

Job knowledge: Does employee have adequate
job knowledge?

Yes   No ──────▶ Training problem

Organizational structure: Is the employee's job well
structured for efficiency?

Yes   No ──────▶ Job redesign problem

Motivation: Why is the employee not
performing acceptably?   Discipline problem

Is performance punishing?
Remove punishment.

Is nonperformance rewarding?
Rearrange the consequences.

Is performance unimportant?
Provide positive consequences.

Are there obstacles?
Remove them.

FIGURE 14.3 Diagnosing unsatisfactory performance.

quantity and high-quality performance. Progressively severe punishment, leading ultimately to discharge, should be provided for individuals who do not respond to the positive
reinforcement.

When disciplinary actions for unsatisfactory performance go to arbitration, the
decision of an arbitrator is greatly influenced by the cause of poor work. If the cause is
due to carelessness and willful misconduct, an arbitrator usually will uphold the disciplinary action, providing that the employee had been adequately warned and given an
opportunity to improve. But if poor performance is due to incompetence or a lack of
ability, an arbitrator is inclined to recommend transfer, demotion, or retraining as an
alternative to discharge.

ILLEGAL OR DISHONEST ACTS

A serious disciplinary problem for all organizations concerns any form of illegal or dishonest behavior, such as theft, embezzlement, misuse of company facilities, or falsifying records. Statistics show that such dishonest acts have increased dramatically in recent years. White-collar crime is not always in the form of employees stealing from the company. Many white-collar crimes are committed by the top corporate officers on behalf of a company.[34]

A model explaining the causes of fraud suggests that the decision to commit fraud is determined by an interaction of three forces: situational pressures, opportunities to commit fraud, and personal integrity. Situational pressures refer to the immediate pressures that individuals experience in their environment, such as high personal debts and financial losses. Opportunities to commit fraud refer to those that individuals create for themselves, such as gaining control of critical financial operations, and those that are created by an organization, such as having poor internal accounting procedures or allowing related-party transactions. Personal integrity refers to the personal code of ethical behavior adopted by an employee. According to the model, companies can reduce illegal and dishonest acts by reducing the situational pressures and convenient opportunities and by increasing personal integrity.[35]

When its employees are caught stealing, a company faces an uncomfortable dilemma. Prosecution usually consumes time and money and creates adverse publicity. But if theft continually goes unpunished, employees are more inclined to steal. Most companies prefer to quietly dismiss a dishonest employee rather than to prosecute the theft. This leaves the dishonest person free to find another job and to continue stealing. Many companies are surprised to discover when they begin to prosecute a crime that an accused employee has an extensive history of dishonest conduct that they had overlooked.

Even if an illegal act is not prosecuted, the employee committing the act is usually discharged. The official basis for the discharge is sometimes listed as a violation of a company rule rather than as criminal theft. Discharges for theft are almost always upheld by an arbitrator unless a company does not have sufficient evidence. Occasionally, an arbitrator will overturn falsification of a job application if the employee has a history of good performance. But falsification of work or time records, of expense accounts, and of medical records to obtain insurance benefits are usually automatic grounds for discharge if proof exists beyond a reasonable doubt.

PERSONAL PROBLEMS

Employees are normally expected to handle personal problems on their own without letting them interfere with work performance. Most employees succeed in handling day-to-day problems without a drastic reduction in their productivity, but problems occasionally arise that may temporarily overwhelm employees and render them essentially worthless. Temporary difficulties due to family problems are not uncommon. Falling in love, getting married, having children, and getting a divorce are potentially unsettling experiences that may affect performance on the job. Since most managers realize that such events are understandably more important than work, they do not become overly concerned about an employee's personal problems unless the employee's inadequate performance continues for a long time. Many large organizations provide personal counseling services for their employees.

SUBSTANCE ABUSE

The most serious personal problems are alcoholism and drug abuse. These problems are not temporary, and therefore, the worst response the employer can make is to be sympathetic, patient, and understanding. These problems are not solved by ignoring them or by assuming they will be corrected on their own.

The abuse of alcohol is a serious problem affecting employees at all levels in almost every company. Alcoholism increases the rates of absenteeism and tardiness, contributes significantly to accidents at work, and greatly reduces productivity. The National Council on Alcoholism estimates that about 10 percent of the work force are alcoholics and that another 10 percent are borderline alcoholics. The financial costs to industry alone are staggering. At least 25 percent of an alcoholic's annual income is pay for work not performed.[36]

For many years, companies ignored problems of alcoholism. Corporate attitudes ranged from denial ("We don't have alcoholics on our payroll") to disregard ("If they really wanted to quit drinking, they could; it's their decision") to self-justification ("We're a business organization set up to make money, not to spend it nursing along alcoholics"). Most organizations have been slow to respond to alcoholism problems because people generally do not like facing the problem.

Alcoholism is now viewed as a disease—a treatable disease. It is not a disease that will go away by itself; it requires treatment, usually a very confrontive form of treatment. The common signs of alcoholism are consistent tardiness—usually on Monday mornings; excessive absenteeism accompanied by excuses of minor illnesses; hangover symptoms such as headaches, thirst, shaking, and procrastination; deterioration in quality of work; and off-the-job problems such as debts and family discord. Most alcoholics have an endless ability to rationalize their poor performance. Usually, their jobs are the last pillars they cling to as their lives crumb e around them due to problems with finances, families, and friends.

The most effective approach to alcoholism is a very confrontive attack on the problem. An employee should be approached as soon as a problem is indicated. The deterioration in the employee's work should be described, and the employee should be told that discharge will result if no improvement is shown. Since an employee normally will deny having a problem, some companies require a suspected alcoholic to obtain a medical report concerning his or her alcohol dependence. If the report confirms the suspicion, the employee is required to obtain immediate help or be discharged. This hard-line position appears to be the best approach to handling alcoholism problems.

When an alcoholism case goes to arbitration, the disciplinary action is usually upheld by the arbitrator. Discharge is considered an appropriate penalty when drinking results in frequent absenteeism, when it contributes to other misconduct, or when it leads to an inability to perform the work, especially when the employee shows no sign of seeking rehabilitation.

The problems created by drug abuse are similar to those created by alcoholism: high rates of absenteeism and tardiness, frequent accidents, and reduced productivity. An additional problem related to drug abuse is theft, since most drug users need help supporting their expensive habits. In addition to the direct consequences that drug abuse creates for companies, it presents an additional complication—it is illegal. Most companies have rules against drug abuse, which they aggressively enforce. Employees hoping to avoid disciplinary action by arguing that their drug usage does not interfere with their work are usually disappointed. Most companies will initiate disciplinary action against drug abusers regardless of their performance simply because what they are doing is illegal.

DRUG TESTING

The statistics associated with drug use document how serious the problem is and why companies need to be involved in curtailing the use of illegal drugs. The financial costs to employers of drug-related illnesses, absences, health care premiums, lost productivity, and theft were estimated in 1986 to exceed $100 billion.[37] Other significant costs of concern to employers include the safety hazards created by employees working under diminished capacity, the damage to the company's credibility and image, and the loss of credibility to the customers. Worldwide, more money is spent on illegal drugs than is spent on food, and the United States leads other nations in the consumption of illegal drugs.[38] Numerous homicides are attributed to drug use and drug trafficking.

Employees who are caught selling illegal drugs are usually terminated. If employees are caught possessing or using illegal drugs, and it is the first time they have been caught, they may be asked to accept help to overcome the habit. If they accept help, most companies will work with them by providing counseling and professional assistance. But if they refuse help, they are usually terminated.

When a disciplinary action for drug abuse goes to arbitration, it is usually upheld, providing that evidence exists to support the allegation. The evidence does not necessarily have to be "beyond a reasonable doubt" as in a criminal court, but a "preponderance of evidence" should support the action. Since discharge for drug abuse is a serious threat to a worker's future career, most arbitrators require competent evidence, as distinguished from mere suspicion, assumption, and conjecture. If the evidence is sufficient, a disciplinary action is normally upheld for the possession, use, or sale of illegal drugs while at work.

Employees also can be disciplined for drug use away from work, even though what employees do on their own time and off the employer's premises is generally not the employer's concern. An arbitrator is likely to sustain discipline for drug-related conduct away from work if an employer can show that the employee's conduct created an adverse effect on the employer-employee relationship, adversely affected the employer's business, or created a legitimate fear for the safety of other employees or property.[39]

In an effort to reduce drug use in the workplace many employers, including about one-third of the Fortune 500 companies, are using drug testing to screen job applicants and, in some cases, current employees.[40] Drug-testing programs have been controversial, however, and employers must use caution in designing legal and defensible programs. Opinion surveys indicate that a majority of employees support drug-testing programs and do not want to work in an unsafe environment where coworkers use drugs.[41]

The legality of drug testing has been challenged by individuals who claim that it violates their rights of privacy. At the same time, employers may be liable for the acts of their employees if they knew or should have know that an employee's condition, propensity, or history created a serious risk and they failed to take precautions. Therefore, an employer's decision can be challenged for either acting or failing to act against drug users. Doing nothing is not a safe strategy for employers who suspect illegal drug use.[42]

The legal status of drug testing is not universally and precisely clear. Nevertheless, it appears that in all jurisdictions in the United States employers are free to institute *some* form of drug testing as part of a substance-abuse program. The great majority of private employers are relatively unrestricted in the type of testing program they may lawfully adopt, as long as it is nondiscriminatory. Public employers, however, have some restrictions regarding the type of test used, the reason for its use, and how they respond to a positive result.

As a general rule, all employers, both public and private, can legally require job applicants to pass a drug test as a condition of employment if the testing program is nondiscriminatory. According to the courts, applicants do not have a vested right to a job that warrants protection. Therefore, employers are not obliged to hire applicants who use illegal drugs.

In the case of *Wilkinson* v. *Times Mirror Corporation* (1989) a California Court of Appeal upheld a testing program for job applicants that included the following elements:

1. The samples were collected in a medical environment by persons unrelated to the employer.
2. Applicants furnished the samples unobserved by others.
3. The results were kept confidential.
4. The medical lab informed the employer if the applicant passed or failed the entire exam.
5. The applicants were notified of the portions of the test they failed.
6. Applicants could question and challenge the test results.
7. The applicant could reapply for employment in six months.[43]

The legality of testing current employees, however, is not as clear. Public employees have successfully argued that the Fourth Amendment to the federal Constitution, which protects them from unreasonable searches and seizures by the government (their employer), limits the kind of testing that can be performed. Some random testing and routine testing programs have been suspended, while mandatory testing for "reasonable suspicion" has been upheld. In specific court decisions, for example, prison guards, fire fighters, and police officers can be required to submit to a drug test on the basis of a reasonable suspicion where objective facts and reasonable inferences suggest that they are under the influence of alcohol or drugs.[44] The U.S. Supreme Court has approved drug testing as part of the periodic physical exams required of railroad and airline employees every three years, or if they have been off duty more than thirty days, or if they are involved in an accident.[45] Likewise, the high court upheld the constitutionality of regular drug testing for Customs Service employees involved in narcotics enforcement.[46]

Private employers have greater freedom than public employers to conduct random drug tests without reasonable suspicion because the constitutional "right of privacy," the Fourth Amendment's protection from unreasonable searches and seizures, and the Fifth Amendments right to due process do not apply to testing private employees. Nevertheless,

▌ **HRM in Action**

Which Law Applies?

Labor relations problems that cross national boundaries can be very complex and difficult to resolve. Two Americans contracted with Arabian American Oil Company, with offices in California, to perform work in Saudi Arabia. The contracts were signed in Texas and provided that Texas law would govern. However, the contracts also contained provisions of Saudi Arabian law, including a rule that workers cannot be fired without a valid reason.

As a side business, these two men operated a video-rental business without a business license in the American compound where they lived. Saudi Arabia, which has strict laws and social customs prohibiting pornography and sexual permissiveness, makes it difficult, if not impossible, for foreigners to obtain business licenses. In response to an anonymous letter complaining about the video rentals, the two men were apprehended and could have been severely punished. However, the oil company persuaded Saudi law enforcement officials to let the company handle the matter internally. The Saudi officials agreed and instructed the oil company to confiscate all videotapes, fire the employees, and order them to leave the country.

Back in the United States, the men claimed they had been unjustly terminated and sued the oil company for wrongful discharge. In a jury trial, the jury concluded that the oil company wrongfully terminated them because the employees were not given clear notice that their video-rental activities were illegal, as required by Saudi law. The trial judge threw out the jury's verdict, but a court of appeals reinstated it. The jury's verdict was consistent with Saudi law, but not with either California or Texas law. The appeals court reasoned that Saudi law should apply since it had the greatest "interest" in the matter.

Although the men won the case under Saudi Arabian law, their award was much less than they had hoped to recover. They attempted to recover tort damages for defamation, intentional infliction of emotional distress, and fraud. Under Saudi law, however, no such claims exist and the court held that they could not even recover damages for over 5,000 videotapes that were confiscated and destroyed. Furthermore, the company provided expert testimony that typical damages for breach of an employment contract in Saudi Arabia do not exceed three months' wages.

Source: *McGhee* v. *Arabian American Oil Co.*, Daily Journal D.A.R. 3937 (9th Cir. 1989).

to retain positive employee support, employers would do well to follow a systematic drug-testing program that has been announced to employees and that is not used as a pretext for discriminatory discharges.[47]

ADMINISTRATIVE JUSTICE

The protection of individual rights is not as well established in industrial matters as it is in civil and criminal matters. Nevertheless, a system of administrative justice has evolved over time that is generally accepted in most organizations and formally adopted by collective agreement in many union contracts. The two basic concepts supporting administrative justice are due process and just cause.

The concept of **due process** means that disciplinary actions must follow an accepted procedure that protects an employee from arbitrary, capricious, and unfair treatment. Due process normally involves providing individuals with written statements of the charges against them as well as the reasons for the penalties. The charged employees must have full opportunity to defend themselves and to utilize the formal grievance procedure if one exists or an impartial hearing if a formal grievance procedure does not exist. The employer is normally expected to bear the burden of proof to show both the evidence of wrongdoing and the need for discipline.[48]

A basic principle surrounding all disciplinary actions is that management should have just cause for imposing a discipline. The concept of **just cause** means that disciplinary action is taken for good and sufficient reason. This standard is written into most labor agreements or read into them by arbitrators.[49] Most agreements merely state that management has the right to discipline, suspend, or discharge for just cause and that employees have the right to submit grievances. Even in the absence of a labor agreement, the conditions defining just cause should be used to judge whether management acted fairly in enforcing company rules.

Administrative justice in the workplace through due process procedures and for reasons of just cause has steadily advanced. Employees enjoy greater protection of their individual rights now than in earlier years. In fact, many managers fear that the advances in administrative justice have been made at the expense of organizational efficiency. Some argue that excessive concern for individual rights threatens the smooth functioning and possibly even the survival of many organizations.[50]

One of the major forces behind the growth in administrative justice is the bureaucratization of modern organizations. As organizations increase in size and complexity, they tend to adopt formal and elaborate discipline and grievance procedures. The trend toward humanism in the workplace also has contributed to the growth in administrative justice. Human relations programs, quality of work-life projects, and other recent changes have emphasized employee rights and the need for protection against arbitrary management actions.

DISCIPLINARY PROCESS

The disciplinary process should follow a sequence of increasingly severe penalties for wrongdoing. The final step in the disciplinary process is discharge. This process is called **progressive discipline** because the disciplinary actions become increasingly severe. The following five steps illustrate progressive discipline:

1. *Verbal warning.* The first step in the disciplinary process is a simple comment by a supervisor to warn employees that certain acts are not acceptable. The purpose of the warning is to ensure that employees know what is expected of them and that what they are doing is wrong. Nothing is usually recorded, although the supervisor may refer to these discussions in performance appraisals. A verbal warning is frequently used for minor offenses such as infrequent tardiness, discourtesy to customers, horseplay, and obscene language.

2. *Verbal reprimand.* The second step is a verbal reprimand in which the supervisor informs the employee that the situation is not acceptable and that improvement is required. The reprimand should be given in private and should not be an emotional harangue. The supervisor should avoid sarcasm and belittling comments, and should not try to humiliate the employee. Instead, the focus of the reprimand should be a firm explanation of the rules and expectations. The supervisor should make certain that the employee understands the problem and knows how to correct it. Since the purpose of the reprimand is to correct the problem, the employee should leave the discussion feeling encouraged and committed to improve. The supervisor should make a written note of the conversation in case further discipline becomes necessary.

3. *Written reprimand.* The third step in the disciplinary process is a written description of the problem and the disciplinary action. This step is more formal than the first two steps, and the way it should be handled is carefully detailed in some labor agreements. The supervisor discusses the problem with the employee once more, reviewing the previous discussions and outlining the history of the problem. This time, however, the supervisor prepares a written record that summarizes what has been said and decided. A course of action should be established for the employee to correct the problem, and the written reprimand should set a target date for the completion of that action. The supervisor should sign the reprimand and ask the employee to sign it as an indication that the employee has read and understood it. If the employee refuses to sign the reprimand, the supervisor should sign it and note that the employee received a copy but refused to sign it. Copies of the reprimand are usually given to the employee, to the union steward, and to the human resource office, and a copy is placed in the supervisor's files. Although threats were not appropriate in the first two steps, they are at this step. The employee should be warned about the consequences if he or she does not change.

4. *Suspension.* If an employee fails to respond to the written reprimand and persists in wrongdoing, the next step is a suspension. A suspended employee is not allowed to work for a period of time and his or her compensation may be reduced accordingly. The purpose of the suspension is to demonstrate the seriousness of the offense and to reinforce the idea that appropriate behavior is a prerequisite for maintaining a job. The length of the suspension should be considered in light of the seriousness and type of offense. An indefinite suspension leaves the date for returning to work open and is normally used on second or third suspensions. Under certain circumstances, second and third suspensions are considered appropriate, such as when an employee seems to be making some progress or has a repentant attitude. However, repeated suspensions for violations are not considered very useful. Before an employee is suspended, the employee should know exactly why he or she is being disciplined. The conditions for the employee's return to work need to be carefully explained. Sometimes it is useful to have the employee determine the length of the suspension by telling the employee that the suspension is in effect so many days and not to return after that unless he or she is committed to improvement. Careful records describing the reasons for suspension need to be maintained in the event that the disciplinary action results in a grievance or goes to civil court as a discrimination charge.

5. *Discharge.* Employees who persist in wrongdoing and who fail to respond to previous disciplinary actions should be terminated. Discharge represents the final step in the disciplinary process. Some managers make the mistake of being too prone to fire employees; they respond as if discharge were the only solution to disciplinary problems. Employees should never be fired on the spot, although they may be ordered to leave the premises for flagrant violations. The final discharge should not be issued until all facts have been gathered and carefully considered and emotions are under control. Other managers make the mistake of waiting too long to terminate a problem employee. Discharge may be the best solution for both the employee and the company. Sometimes discharge forces an employee to face reality and to find a new job, and the employee frequently responds better in the new environment. At least one study has shown that discharged managers were better off after being terminated because they liked their new jobs better, their salaries were better, and they felt more successful.[51]

An alternative method of terminating an employee is **dehiring**, or getting the employee to quit. If the work environment is made sufficiently unpleasant, most employees will quit. Supervisors who want to get rid of unwanted employees sometimes try to make the employees' lives at work so uncomfortable that they choose to leave. If the employees leave voluntarily, the supervisor is spared the unpleasant chore of discharging them. Dehiring is usually not a forthright approach to discipline. Supervisors use dehiring as an unethical way of getting rid of employees that they do not like but have no legitimate basis for terminating through the established discipline system. Occasionally, however, dehiring is a supervisor's only recourse for handling an unproductive employee. In education, for example, incompetent teachers may be protected by tenure policies and therefore cannot be terminated easily. Sometimes department heads have told incompetent teachers that if they do not improve and if they refuse to leave, their lives will become very unpleasant: they will be assigned to teach more classes; they will have to teach the classes with the largest enrollments; they will be given smaller offices; and they will not receive any more pay increases.

Dehiring violates the law when it is used to discriminate on the basis of age, race, religion, sex, or national origin, and employees who quit can be reinstated and receive back pay on the legal theory of **constructive discharge**. When working conditions become so unpleasant that a reasonable person would find them intolerable, the courts have "constructed" from the facts of the case that the person was actually terminated even though the company claims the employee quit.

Demotions and transfers are two other alternatives for taking disciplinary action. Demoting employees to lower-level jobs or transferring them to a less desirable job are sometimes viewed as forms of punishment for wrongdoing. Some organizations, especially the military, use demotions as a routine form of punishment. Most of these organizations have a negative view of discipline that focuses more on punishment for past errors than on correcting future behavior. Whether problem employees should be demoted or transferred should depend on the nature of their problems. Personal problems, drug abuse, embezzlement, and habitual tardiness are seldom corrected by demotions or transfers. Demotions and transfers are usually recommended only for problems of unsatisfactory performance, such as when an employee has been promoted to a job that is too demanding. Some employees have difficulty handling the stigma of being demoted, even when it is in their best interests. In the United States, demotions are especially difficult for older employees to accept because of the social norms. The stigma attached to demotions is not as strong in Japan, where older employees often accept job changes that are more compatible with their declining strength and endurance.

PRINCIPLES OF EFFECTIVE DISCIPLINE

A highly recommended procedure for administering punishment is called the "hot-stove rule." A hot stove with its radiating heat provides a warning that it should not be touched.

Those who ignore the warning and touch it, like employees who violate a rule, are assured of being burned. The punishment, in this case the burn, is immediate and directly associated with violating the rule. Like the hot stove that immediately burns anyone who touches it, an established rule for employees to follow should be consistently enforced and should apply to all employees. The pain of a hot stove is administered in a rigid and impersonal way to everyone who touches it.[52]

Most arbitrators do not accept the rigidity of the hot-stove rule because they think personal motives and mitigating circumstances ought to be considered. A good disciplinary system must balance the dual objectives of protecting the rights of employees and preserving the interests of the organization. It must be flexible enough to provide problem employees with sufficient time and opportunities to correct their behavior if they have the proper inclination, and it must be rigorous enough to allow the discharge of unresponsive problem employees who have been warned about the consequences of their actions.

The following principles describe some of the most important elements of an effective disciplinary system.

DEFINITE POLICY AND PROCEDURE

Disciplinary procedures should follow a prescribed course of action rather than vary from day to day and from supervisor to supervisor. Consistency of action should be maintained throughout the organization. A well-designed and consistently applied disciplinary system is in the best interests of both management and the union. The disciplinary system should be carefully designed either by management alone or by a joint effort of management and union representatives.

SUPERVISORY RESPONSIBILITY

Supervisors are usually responsible for initiating disciplinary action. Most organizations rely upon supervisors to evaluate subordinates and to take the first action when problems arise. Supervisors generally have the authority to issue verbal warnings and verbal reprimands on their own. However, if a written reprimand is called for, a supervisor usually prepares the reprimand in consultation with the next level of management. If there is a labor agreement, the supervisor also should consult with the human resource office to make certain that the written reprimand is consistent with the procedures described in the agreement.

COMMUNICATION OF RULES

Employees must know and understand rules before they can be held accountable for them. Typically, employees are informed about company rules through an employee handbook and new-employee orientation programs. For the first offense, an employee should be given the benefit of the doubt and should be adequately warned about the consequences of his or her conduct but not punished. An exception may be made for misconduct so serious that the employee can be expected to know it is a punishable offense, such as drinking on the job, stealing from the company, or willful destruction of company property.

BURDEN OF PROOF

A basic principle underlying both English common law and United States constitutional law is that an individual is presumed innocent until proven guilty. This principle has been generally adopted in industrial relations; an employer must prove an employee's guilt before administering discipline. A common mistake made by an employer is to discipline an employee on the first hint of wrongdoing and then to collect information supporting the action. The appropriate procedure is to investigate the problem before making a decision to discipline. Where immediate action may be required, such as in the case of fraud or willful destruction of company property, the best course is to suspend the suspected employee with the understanding that he or she will be restored to the job and paid for time lost if an investigation proves the employee is innocent. An investigation should produce substantial evidence of guilt to justify disciplinary action. However, the evidence does not have to be conclusive or "beyond a reasonable doubt" except where the alleged misconduct is of such a criminal or reprehensible nature as to stigmatize the employee and to seriously impair his or her chances of future employment.

CONSISTENT TREATMENT

Rules and penalties must be applied evenhandedly and without discrimination. In a situation where one employee was disciplined for an offense while another who committed the same offense escaped punishment, an arbitrator very likely would overturn or at least reduce the punishment. Uneven application of discipline not only can destroy the effectiveness of a disciplinary system but also can create a feeling among employees that favoritism and discrimination exist. For example, if management has been lax about enforcing rules and then suddenly decides to crack down, most employees will charge that they are being treated unfairly. Renewed efforts to enforce rules should be preceded by warnings from management. Otherwise, disciplined employees will complain about discrimination, and arbitrators will probably overturn disciplinary actions.

CONSIDERATION OF THE CIRCUMSTANCES

Violations of company rules and other offenses should not be considered in isolation. The circumstances of each case should always be considered as well as the facts describing the offense. The appropriateness of disciplinary action and an arbitrator's willingness to uphold it are often determined by the surrounding circumstances. In fights between employees, for example, the employee who provoked the fight has sometimes received a harsher penalty than the employee who threw the first punch.

It has been suggested that a uniform scale of penalties for each offense would make discipline more consistent. Some labor agreements even specify the penalties that result from each offense. Published scales of penalties appear to eliminate the possibility that personal feelings and favoritism will affect disciplinary action, and they also remove some of the uncertainty about the consequences of an error. However, these apparent benefits of uniform penalties seem to disappear in actual practice. Uniform penalties generally are not perceived as fair or impartial because employees think the circumstances of each case should be considered, such as the reasons for an offense, the offending employee's previous record, and the employee's willingness to change.

Arbitrators generally overturn or reduce disciplinary actions when it can be shown that an employee was provoked by coworkers or a supervisor. Arbitrators and managers agree that an employee with a long history of good performance should not be disciplined as severely as a frequent offender. And most people believe that an employee who is remorseful about an error and willing to improve should be treated more leniently than an employee who is belligerent and defiant.

REASONABLE RULES AND PENALTIES

Even though a company is free to make whatever rules it wants, the rules should be reasonable. Most people are willing to accept company regulations as legitimate if the regulations are reasonably related to efficient and safe operations and are consistent with the conventions of society. The penalties also should be reasonable. Extremely harsh penalties for minor offenses are not perceived as fair by employees. Arbitrators are not inclined to uphold rules or penalties that are overly restrictive, unnecessary, and unreasonable. Rules and penalties that seem unreasonable create a negative attitude about discipline and foster an uncooperative attitude among employees.

STATUTE OF LIMITATIONS

Some people believe that written reprimands should not remain in an employee's file permanently because they may destroy the individual's opportunity to advance. Some companies actually remove written reprimands from an employee's file after the employee has had a three- to five-year period of good performance. Other companies do not remove written notices but counter them with descriptions of the employee's progress following the reprimands. Regardless of how written reprimands are handled, they should be placed in an employee's personal file with an understanding that there is a statute of limitations regarding the length of time that they can remain there untouched.

LEGAL PROTECTIONS

Specific legislation protects employees from being treated unfairly. Experience has demonstrated that in the absence of legislation many employers tend to discriminate against disadvantaged workers to the detriment of both these individuals and society. The interests of society are advanced when everyone has an opportunity to participate and contribute without unfair discrimination. The legal protections discussed here are concerned with age discrimination, sexual harassment, handicap discrimination, religious discrimination, and wrongful discharge.

AGE DISCRIMINATION

The Age Discrimination in Employment Act (ADEA) is designed to protect employees over age 40 from arbitrary and age-biased discrimination in hiring, promotion, training, benefits, compensation, discipline, and terminations. Employers are not even allowed to provide different health or medical benefits to older workers than younger workers, nor can they stop making contributions to an employee's pension plan just because that employee has reached retirement age but chooses to continue working. Early retirement programs are allowed under ADEA, but employers must be very careful to avoid using early retirement incentives as a means of forcing older workers to quit.

The ADEA applies to all private employers with twenty or more employees, governmental employers, employment agencies, and labor unions with twenty-five or more members. Since 1979 the regulatory and enforcement authority for this law has been delegated to the Equal Employment Opportunity Commission (EEOC), which was given broad authority to receive, investigate, and either conciliate settlements or initiate court actions. Each year thousands of age-discrimination cases are filed with the EEOC.

In 1987 the EEOC issued a new policy statement regarding **age harassment**.[53] This policy defines the kinds of demeaning acts that are considered age harassment and includes (1) age-inferred remarks having a derogatory connotation; (2) comments that attribute a person's health, attendance, performance, or attitudes to their age; (3) age-related jokes and sarcasm; and (4) the derisive use of age-related terms such as "pops," "the old man," "the old goat," and "dead wood."

Employers who try to induce older workers to quit by making their jobs unpleasant also violate the ADEA. By requiring them to perform difficult, degrading, or boring jobs, older workers can be forced to quit. This action is called "constructive discharge," because the court constructs from the facts of the situation evidence that the employee was actually discharged. A constructive discharge is deemed to have occurred if a reasonable person would have found the conditions of employment to be intolerable.[54]

Occasionally, however, there are legitimate reasons why a business decision should be based on age. The act itself states that it shall not be an unlawful employment act for employers to base certain decisions on age "where age is a bona fide occupational qualification (BFOQ) reasonably necessary to the normal operation of the particular business." It should be noted, however, that the BFOQ defenses have been very narrowly defined by the courts. The burden of proof is on the employers to show that their business survival depends on employing younger workers in specific jobs, such as youth councilor, fashion model, teen sales clerk, or actor/actress. If older workers are unable to perform a job because of reduced physical abilities or stamina, they should be removed from that job only after an individual assessment has been made showing they were unable to perform the job satisfactorily.[55] Only a few mandatory retirement policies have survived the scrutiny of the courts, including an age-55 retirement policy for police officers and an age-60 limit for airline captains. Although airline captains are not permitted to continue beyond age 60, as imposed by FAA regulations, flight engineers are allowed to continue until it is demonstrated that their performance is inadequate.

As a general rule, an employee can successfully claim age discrimination if:

1. the employee is over age 40;
2. the employee was fired, demoted, or adversely affected;
3. the employee had been performing the job well enough to meet the employer's legitimate expectations;
4. the employee was qualified to assume an available position at the time of the action; and
5. the employer made an intentional decision on the basis of age by showing preference for a younger worker.

A review of the relevant court cases indicates that employers facing age-discrimination charges have very little reason to be optimistic, since the court decisions have generally been against them.[56] Employers who are charged with age discrimination have basically three legal justifications for their decisions:

1. **Business necessity**. The decision was reasonably necessary to the normal operation of the business, or the decision was a bona fide occupational qualification.
2. **Good cause**. The decision was based on legitimate factors other than age, such as a violation of company policy, misconduct, absenteeism, or a lack of cooperation.
3. **Bona fide seniority system**. The decision was based on a bona fide seniority system as part of a collective bargaining agreement, and all employees are treated consistently with this policy regardless of their age.

SEXUAL HARASSMENT

Title VII of the Civil Rights Act prohibits **sexual harassment**. The EEOC has issued guidelines defining sexual harassment and outlining the employer's responsibility to prevent it.

> Unwelcome sexual advances, requests for sexual favors, and other verbal or physical conduct of a sexual nature constitutes sexual harassment when (1) submission to such conduct is made either explicitly or implicitly a term or condition of an individual's employment; (2) submission to or rejection of such conduct by an individual is used as the basis for employment decisions affecting such individual; or (3) such conduct has the purpose or effect of unreasonably interfering with an individual's work performance or creating an intimidating, hostile, or offensive working environment.[57]

The EEOC guidelines declare that the employer is responsible for the acts of its agents and supervisory employees with respect to sexual harassment, regardless of whether the employer knew or should have known of their occurrence. The employer is also responsible for conduct between coworkers, and even responsible for the acts of nonemployees, such as vendors or customers. It is the employer's responsibility to take all steps necessary to prevent sexual harassment, such as discussing the subject, expressing strong disapproval, and taking strong, appropriate sanctions when it occurs.

Recognizing how serious and how unacceptable it is, most companies have established formal policies banning sexual harassment and providing formal grievance procedures for reporting it. One survey of 156 companies found that 74 percent of them had a formal policy and 60 percent of them discuss the problem in formal education programs for managers and supervisors. Sexual harassment complaints were filed by 37 percent of the companies, the vast majority of which were by female workers complaining of a hostile or offensive work environment.[58]

The EEOC guidelines have forced employers to become involved in the romantic entanglements of their employees and the potentially discriminatory impact of these entanglements on employment decisions. The EEOC guidelines state "where employment opportunities or benefits are granted because of an individual's submission to the employer's sexual advances or requests for sexual favors, the employer may be held liable for unlawful sexual discrimination against other persons who were qualified for but denied that employment opportunity or benefit." According to this guideline, if two people are romantically involved and one partner promotes or gives preferential treatment to the other partner, then other members of the work group who did not get promoted can claim that they were the victims of unlawful sex discrimination. Because of the difficulty of knowing when a sexual advance is unwanted or the possibility that it may suddenly become unwanted, employers find that it is wise to have rules similar to their nepotism policies that prevent members of a work group from becoming romantically involved.[59]

HANDICAP DISCRIMINATION

A handicapped person is defined as any person who has a physical or mental impairment that substantially limits one or more major life activities, such as caring for themselves, performing manual tasks, walking, seeing, hearing, speaking, learning, and working. As with other forms of discrimination, handicapped individuals should not be discriminated against in hiring, promotions, transfers, training opportunities, termination, or compensation. A physical or mental impairment refers to a condition that weakens, diminishes, or restricts an individual's physical or mental ability. According to the Vocational Rehabilitation Act (1973) and the Americans with Disabilities Act (1990), an impairment could be a physiological disorder or condition, such as the loss of a limb or eyesight; a mental or psychological disorder, such as mental retardation or a learning disability; or a disabling or debilitating disease, such as drug addiction or alcoholism.

Employers are expected to make reasonable changes in order to accommodate "qualified handicapped" individuals. These individuals, who are called **otherwise qualified**, are people who could perform the essential functions of a job with reasonable accommodation. Employers are not expected to abandon legitimate job requirements or suffer burdensome sacrifices, however, to make accommodation. Although no specific guidelines define what constitutes a **reasonable accommodation**, the federal guidelines provide some suggestions, such as making facilities accessible to and usable by handicapped persons, restructuring jobs, instituting part-time or modified work schedules, acquiring or modifying equipment to be used by handicapped persons, and providing readers or interpreters. All employers are expected to examine each job and each handicapped person on a case-by-case basis and make reasonable accommodations to the extent that they are practical.[60]

The Supreme Court has ruled that at least two forms of communicable diseases, tuberculosis (TB) and acquired immune deficiency syndrome (AIDS), must be classified as physical handicaps. Furthermore, in the Civil Rights Restoration Act of 1988, Congress declared that AIDS should be treated as a physical handicap on a national level, even though this law affects only federal contractors and recipients of federal assistance. In a related move, the U.S. Office of Personnel Management issued a 1988 policy prohibiting discrimination against federal workers who have AIDS.

Although alcoholism and drug use are classified as addictive disabilities, employers are free to terminate employees if their alcohol or drug use affects their performance. The question of whether alcoholism or drug use is a "protected handicap" focuses on whether it is a past or present addiction. For example, in the case of *Davis* v. *Bucher* (1978) a district court held that persons with histories of drug use are considered handicapped individuals under the Rehabilitation Act, and therefore employers cannot absolutely refuse to consider hiring such persons because of their former drug abuse.[61] Instead, the requirements of the job and whether the applicants are now rehabilitated and capable of performing the job should be considered in an employment decision. Employees who have a present drug addiction, however, may be considered unfit for employment. In *Heron* v. *McGuire* (1986) the Second Circuit Court of appeals determined that a police officer with a heroin addiction could be terminated because he was not protected by a handicap-discrimination law.[62] In this case it was held that the officer's dependence on an illegal substance diminished his ability to perform and his use of an illegal substance was inconsistent with the laws he was entrusted to enforce.

Court decisions have indicated that epilepsy, cancer, heart conditions, and sometimes being overweight may be considered as protected handicaps. However, being too short or left-handed has not been considered a handicap.[63]

RELIGIOUS DISCRIMINATION

Similar to other protected groups under Title VII of the Civil Rights Act, employers are not allowed to hire, promote, train, compensate, discipline, lay off, or terminate on the basis of an individual's religious beliefs or observances. This provision is intended to protect employees from any adverse employment decisions caused by their religious beliefs and how they choose to observe them. A review of religious-discrimination court cases indicates that the most frequent type of accommodation requested is adjustments in an employee's work schedule.[64] Since most organizations have a Monday through Friday workweek and employees are free to practice their religious beliefs on the weekends, very few employers have had difficulty accommodating an employee's religious beliefs. Consequently, this provision has not attracted much attention and relatively few cases involving religious discrimination have been litigated in the courts.

Religious-discrimination charges typically arise after employees are asked to work overtime or when they are assigned to perform an unpleasant task. It may be difficult to know when the charges are frivolous claims based on resistance to change as opposed to legitimate religious conflicts requiring accommodation. In 1970 the Supreme Court defined religion as "a sincere and meaningful belief which occupies in the life of its possessor a place parallel to that filled by God." The EEOC guidelines say that religious beliefs are protected if they are "deeply and sincerely held as more conventional religious convictions." The sincerity of an employee's belief is suspect if the employee knew what the work schedule was before accepting the job or if the employee had previously worked that schedule without any objection. However, most religious-discrimination claims focus on whether the employer has made adequate accommodation rather than on whether the employee has a sincere belief. Therefore, if an employee has a legitimate request for time off for religious observances (for Sabbath or holy days), an employer should try to accommodate the request.

The amount of accommodation employers are expected to make was partially clarified by the Supreme Court in *Hardison* v. *Trans World Airlines* (1974).[65] In this case, an employee claimed that TWA did not satisfactorily accommodate his need to observe a Saturday Sabbath. TWA provided evidence showing that it had made several attempts, including possible job reassignments and schedule trades, but none of these alternatives was acceptable to the employee. The court concluded that TWA had made reasonable efforts to accommodate the employee and established four guiding principles for sufficient accommodation. Accommodation for religious observances, according to the Supreme Court, should not require an employer to: (1) sacrifice the rights of other workers to accommodate another employee; (2) breach a collective bargaining agreement to provide benefits or special needs that would not be equally enjoyed by others; (3) suffer a loss in work unit efficiency in their efforts to accommodate; and (4) provide more than "*de minimus*" action (in other words, the employer should not have to pay overtime for another worker or for a replacement worker).

WRONGFUL DISCHARGE

Historically, American employers have been free to dismiss employees for a good cause, for no cause, and even for causes that are morally wrong without violating the law. This condition, called "employment at-will," is based on a centuries-old common-law rule that claims employment relationships of indefinite length can be terminated at the whim of either party. This means that at any time and without notice, at-will employees may quit work or may be dismissed at the will of their employers. At-will employees are those whose employment depends almost entirely on the continued goodwill of their employers, which excludes public employees protected by civil service rules and union members protected by an agreement.[66]

With very few exceptions, the rule of employment at-will has survived in the United States. In most states today, an at-will employee can still be dismissed for good reason, for no reason, or even for an unfair or malicious reason as long as that reason is not specifically prohibited by statute. In recent years, however, a few exceptions to this policy have been created as direct expressions of public policy. Limits on an employer's ability to fire at-will stem from specific legislative protections and judicial decisions.

1. Many federal statutes prohibit employers from dismissing employees in retaliation for their helping to enforce the statute. For example, the National Labor Relations Act (1935) prohibits firing employees for organizing a union, striking, or testifying before the NLRB. The Occupational Safety and Health Act (1970), the Coal Mine Health and Safety Act (1969), and the Railroad Safety Act (1975) prohibit dismissing employees who file complaints, give testimony, or participate in a proceeding to enforce the statutes.[67] Likewise, many state statutes protect employees from retaliation for filing claims or participating in proceedings under workers' compensation laws, disability laws, and unemployment insurance laws.

2. Employers may be prevented from firing employees if they have an **implied contract** for employment. An example of an implied contract is a salary memo promising to pay employees an annual salary spread over the next twelve months.[68] Some courts have declared that terminating employees before the end of the year was a violation of this implied contract. Another example of an implied contract is a statement in an employee handbook that the policy of the company is that nonprobationary employees will not be released except for just cause.[69] Employee handbooks can also create an implied agreement by referring to employees as "permanent" employees or to jobs as "steady jobs." However, such interpretations by the courts are rare.

3. An employer may be guilty of improper discharge and liable for punitive damages if its breach of an employment agreement is fraudulent, oppressive, or malicious. An example of a fraudulent promise was an offer to give an employee a favorable recommendation if she agreed to quit. The employer had no intention of giving a recommendation; he only wanted to avoid unemployment compensation payments.[70]

4. Employers have been sued by employees and subjected to tort liability because they dismissed employees for reasons that violated public policy. These improper dismissals have been labeled "wrongful discharges," "abusive discharges," or "retaliatory discharges." Some examples of public policy violations include: (a) firing an employee for choosing to serve on a jury when she could have been excused because of her job[71] and (b) firing an agent for refusing to give false testimony before a legislative committee.[72]

Again, however, most courts are reluctant to decide what constitutes a public policy violation since this is a legislative responsibility. Therefore, they usually adhere to the doctrine of employment at-will. Thus, for example, courts have decided that at-will employees were properly dismissed for uncovering and reporting criminal activity by a supervisor, for resisting management's staffing instructions, even though they violated a nurse's ethical and professional duties, or for questioning the safety of a company's products.

In 1987 Montana enacted the first wrongful-discharge law in the United States. This law represents an uneasy compromise between the purposes of providing statutory protection for employees against wrongful discharge and protecting employers by restricting the available tort liabilities identified above.[73] One desirable outcome of this law was a reduction in the exorbitant jury awards that employees were winning for wrongful discharge. In 1989 the California Supreme Court acted to reduce these exorbitant awards by eliminating the availability of punitive damages in most discharge cases. The possibility of large punitive damages was the major financial incentive for attorneys to bring such suits.[74]

INTERNATIONAL HRM

The American doctrine of employment at-will, which allows layoffs and terminations for a multitude of reasons, is very unusual. In many other countries workers have legal protections against being terminated. When American managers are transferred abroad, they are often surprised to find how difficult it is to terminate an employee for any reason. Sizable termination awards are often required, not only when terminated employees show that the action is illegal, but even when terminations are necessitated by economic downturns. Foreign workers are protected by a combination of union rules and labor laws and the penalties for violating them can be costly to uninformed employers.

The labor laws in some countries provide almost complete protection against wrongful or unjust dismissal. In Mexico, for example, employees are regarded as permanent employees after they have passed a thirty-day trial period. The employees can quit if they want to, but they almost have to be convicted of a crime to be terminated. In Indonesia the process of firing an employee is very lengthy and bureaucratic. An incompetent worker must receive three written warnings from the employer documenting the problem and written copies must be sent to the appropriate government officials. Indonesian managers are also required to meet with the offending employee as part of the process and tactfully suggest how the employee can improve his or her performance.[75]

In China most factories are owned and controlled by the government and the managers who operate them are essentially prohibited from firing employees. However, the managers wield an enormous amount of power over the employees through a combination of punishments and social sanctions. Chinese employees can be fined for incompetence and carelessness on the job and they can even be imprisoned if their carelessness contributes to accidents that cause damage. Public criticism, however, is more powerful than civil penalties in disciplining problem employees. These public criticisms are particularly effective because they create embarrassment and a loss of face for family members in the cohesive Chinese communities. Chinese employees are allowed to form an industrial union and the union is often responsible for handling labor insurance for the workers. The union members are now allowed to strike.[76]

A high proportion of European workers belong to trade unions and are protected from unjust terminations by due-process provisions in the labor agreement. European countries also have laws that protect employees from plant closings. West Germany, England, Sweden, and The Netherlands all have plant-closing laws that go far beyond just notifying employees in advance of a shutdown. Government permission is required before a company can close a plant or lay off employees. (In France the law doesn't apply to companies with fewer than fifty employees, but in Sweden it applies to a layoff of even one worker.) Companies must also provide severance pay of up to two years' salary plus employer-paid training.[77]

Prior to Stalin's death in 1953, Soviet workers were subject to strict and severe penalties for minor work-rule infractions, such as tardiness or leaving the job site without permission. During the next three decades, work discipline was much more lax, which contributed to severe problems of inefficiency, alcoholism, and absenteeism. The lack of motivation was aptly illustrated by the popular Soviet saying, "You pretend to pay us and we pretend to work." As part of Gorbachev's economic reforms in the mid-1980s, Soviet managers were given greater authority to reward and punish workers with monetary incentives, and uncooperative workers could be fired and replaced more quickly. Thus worker discipline among Soviet workers is moving toward stronger expectations regarding productivity and accountability and less security. Employees are expected to produce and problem employees can be fired. Similar trends also seem to be occurring in other Eastern European countries and Cuba.[78]

SUMMARY

A. Every organization should have both a grievance procedure and a disciplinary procedure to maintain effective employee relations. A well-defined grievance procedure protects individual employees from arbitrary and unfair treatment and provides a process for them to seek redress of their grievances without fear of reprisal. A well-defined disciplinary procedure protects the organization from problem employees and provides a legitimate process for discharging unresponsive employees and rehabilitating responsive employees.

B. Grievances are generally caused by unsatisfactory work environments, inconsiderate supervisors, inequitable wages, unfair work assignments, and violations of the labor agreement.

C. Most grievances are submitted by problem employees, but some are submitted by employees attempting to improve conditions at work.

D. Grievance procedures in union companies generally contain three to five steps, depending on the size of the company. Most complaints are resolved between the supervisor and the employee—the first step of the grievance procedure. Complaints that are not settled satisfactorily at one level are appealed to the next level for a decision. The final step is usually binding arbitration.

E. Grievance procedures in nonunion organizations are more informal than those in union organizations and usually appear in the form of a grievance committee, an ombudsman, a grievance appeal procedure (similar to a union procedure), an open-door policy, or an investigative officer.

F. Labor disputes that cannot be resolved through the normal grievance process may be referred to arbitration. Both the federal courts and the NLRB have endorsed arbitration procedures for resolving disputes.

G. Arbitration procedures have been criticized for their costliness, lengthiness, and formality. Some groups are successfully using informal grievance procedures to reduce the cost and time delays associated with arbitration procedures.

H. Two major approaches to employee discipline are used. The negative approach emphasizes punishment for past errors and instills fear in all employees by making public examples of rule violators. The positive approach emphasizes correcting problems to obtain good performance in the future.

I. Disciplinary problems need to be diagnosed before disciplinary actions can be taken. The major categories of disciplinary problems are rule violations, unsatisfactory performance, personal problems, and illegal or dishonest acts.

J. To initiate disciplinary actions against employees without fear that an arbitrator or civil court judge will overturn the actions, two important principles of administrative justice should be followed: "due process" and "just cause." Due process means that the charges against an employee are stated explicitly, that evidence of the wrong is presented, that the employee is given an opportunity to present a defense, and that the case is decided by an impartial judge. Just cause means that the disciplinary action

is taken for good and sufficient reason after reasonable rules have been made and communicated to all employees.

K. Disciplinary actions should follow a procedure of progressive discipline whereby increasingly severe penalties are administered for serious or repeated wrongdoing, such as verbal warning, verbal reprimand, written reprimand, suspension, and, finally, discharge.

L. Dehiring, demotion, and transfer are alternatives to discharge, but they should only be used when appropriate.

M. An effective discipline procedure should exhibit these characteristics:
1. It should be based on definite policies.
2. The responsibility for administering disciplinary action should be determined, with the initial responsibility normally being placed on the immediate supervisors.
3. The rules must be communicated to all employees.
4. The burden of proof should rest on the organization.
5. Disciplinary action should be administered consistently among all employees.
6. Situational pressures and individual circumstances should be considered when the appropriate disciplinary action is being determined.
7. The rules and penalties should be reasonable and related to effective and safe operations.
8. Written reprimands should not remain in an employee's file indefinitely; instead, a statute of limitations should be imposed to change or remove such information.

N. Specific federal laws protect employees from unfair treatment. For example, the Age Discrimination in Employment Act protects workers over age 40 from discrimination in hiring, promotion, training, compensation, discipline, and termination. Employees have three legal justifications for making an unfavorable decision against someone over age 40: business necessity, good cause, or a bona fide seniority system.

O. Sexual harassment is defined as any unwelcome sexual advances, and it is the employer's responsibility to prevent sexual harassment in the workplace.

P. Legislation protecting handicapped individuals

requires employers to make reasonable accommodations that would allow people who are otherwise qualified to obtain employment. Handicaps include physical and psychological impairments and disabling or debilitating diseases, such as drug addiction, alcoholism, and AIDS.

Q. Employers are not allowed to discriminate against employees because of their religious beliefs. To the extent that it is reasonable, employers are expected to accommodate the religious observances of their employees.

R. The concept of employment at-will means that at any time and without notice an employment relationship can be terminated—employees can decide to quit, and employers can decide to dismiss employees. Only limited protections are available to prevent wrongful discharge: when it violates a federal statute such as OSH Act, when employees have an implied contract, when the firing is fraudulent or malicious, or when it is a clear violation of public policy.

QUESTIONS

1. Why do organizations need both grievance and discipline procedures? What is the purpose of each?

2. What is the profile of the typical person who submits a grievance?

3. What are the typical grievance procedures found in union and nonunion companies?

4. How might a nonunion grievance procedure be inferior to a union grievance procedure?

5. What can be done to make arbitration less costly and time consuming?

6. What are the differences between the positive and negative approaches to discipline?

7. What is a progressive discipline procedure? Why is such a procedure called progressive?

8. Explain the concepts of due process and just cause.

9. Why is dehiring not a forthright way to terminate an employee?

10. What are the advantages and disadvantages of developing a detailed list of rules regarding employee misconduct?

KEY TERMS

Age harassment: Demeaning comments and actions directed toward older workers, such as age-related jokes, sarcasm, and derisive labels.

Arbitration: The process of submitting a labor dispute to a third party for resolution. The third party is called an arbitrator. Both parties agree beforehand to accept the arbitrator's decision.

Business necessity: A BFOQ justifying a discriminatory decision because the action was necessary for the effective functioning of the organization.

Complaint system: A nonunion company grievance procedure designed to hear and respond to employees' complaints.

Constructive discharge: A decision constructed by a court that an employee who quit was actually discharged because of intolerable working conditions.

Dehiring: The process of getting an employee to quit, usually by making the work environment unpleasant and hostile. This form of pressuring employees to leave voluntarily is an alternative to discharge.

Demotion: Changing an employee's job to a lower-status position; the opposite of promotion.

Due process: A major concept of administrative justice that requires disciplinary actions to follow a process providing fair and unbiased treatment. For example, such a process might prescribe that specific charges of wrongdoing be stated, that evidence of wrongs be presented, that employees be allowed to defend themselves, and that cases be decided by an impartial judge.

Good cause: Where an adverse employment decision is based on misconduct, absenteeism, inadequate performance or other objective performance-related criteria.

Implied contract: A statement, usually in an employee handbook, that creates the expectation that an employee will not be terminated except for good cause.

Just cause: A major concept of administrative justice in which disciplinary actions are taken for good and sufficient reasons. For good and sufficient reasons to be established, company rules must be related to safe and efficient operations and must be clearly communicated to employees. Moreover, employers must show that rules have actually been violated.

Ombudsman: An impartial person designated by an organization to hear complaints from members who feel powerless and unable to obtain a fair hearing on their own.

Otherwise qualified: A handicapped individual who is capable of performing a job if unnecessary barriers created by their handicap are eliminated.

Progressive discipline: A sequence of disciplinary actions that specify increasingly severe penalties for repeated violations, such as verbal warning, verbal

reprimand, written reprimand, suspension, and discharge.

Reasonable accommodation: Efforts by an employer to facilitate the employment of a handicapped person that are not excessively expensive and do not interfere with normal operations.

Sexual harassment: Any unwelcome sexual advance, requests for sexual favors, or physical contact of a sexual nature, including conduct that interferes with a person's performance or that creates an intimidating or hostile environment.

Submission agreement: The opening statement of an arbitration hearing. It outlines the issues to be resolved and the authority granted to the arbitrator by both the union and the employer.

Tripartite board: An arbitration board consisting of three arbitrators rather than one. Usually one arbitrator represents the employer's interests, another represents the union's interests, and the third is impartial.

Whistle blower: An individual who observes an illegal or immoral action and makes the information public.

C O N C L U D I N G   C A S E

Treating Alcoholism

An employee was switching a boiler from oil to gas when the boiler backfired, resulting in a minor eye injury to the employee. When the employee reported to the plant nurse for treatment, the nurse noticed that the employee appeared to be intoxicated. Upon the advice of the company doctor, the nurse took the employee to a hospital for treatment of his eyes. At the hospital, the employee gave permission to have blood drawn for a blood alcohol test. The test showed that the employee was in a state of intoxication.

Two days later, the plant manager and plant superintendent told the employee that if he

chose to get some help for his drinking problem, he could remain on the payroll; if not, he would be terminated. The two plant officials reminded the employee that they had previously counseled him about his drinking habits on several occasions. The employee said that he was controlling his drinking and that he would not undergo treatment for alcoholism. As a result of his refusal to obtain help, the employee was terminated.

At an arbitration hearing on the employee's discharge, the union claimed that the employee had been unjustly terminated because he refused to undergo treatment for alcoholism, not because he drank on the job or was under the influence of alcohol. The union said it would not grieve a termination based on the latter reasons. The company replied that the employee had been treated with compassion and had been given an opportunity to rehabilitate himself. Most companies discharge an intoxicated person immediately. The company said it would have been derelict in its responsibilities if the employee had been allowed to remain in

a job where he would be a danger to himself, to his fellow workers, and to equipment.

Questions:

1. If you were the arbitrator, would you reinstate the employee?
2. If you terminate him, is it for drinking on the job or for refusing treatment?
3. If you reinstate him, do you recommend any special conditions he must follow?

NOTES

1. BNA Editorial Staff, *Grievance Guide*, 5th ed. (Washington D.C: Bureau of National Affairs, 1978), p. 53, p. 216.

2. Richard R. Cerbone and Joseph Walsh, "Management Judgment vs. Seniority—Grist for the Arbitration Mill," *Employee Relations Law Journal* 14 (Winter 1988/1989): 429–37.

3. E. A. Fleishman and E. F. Harris, "Patterns of Leadership Behavior Related to Employee Grievances and Turnover," *Personnel Psychology* 15, no. 1 (Spring 1962): 45–53.

4. Robert L. Walker and James W. Robinson, "The First-line Supervisor's Role in the Grievance Procedure," *Arbitration Journal* 32 (1977): 279–92.

5. Dan R. Dalton and William D. Todor, "Antecedents of Grievance Filing Behavior: Attitude/Behavioral Consistency and Union Steward," *Academy of Management Journal* 25, no. 1 (1982): 158–69.

6. See, for example, Clyde Scott and Trevor Bain, "How Arbitrators Interpret Ambiguous Contract Language," *Personnel* 64 (August 1987): 10–14.

7. Philip Ash, "The Parties to the Grievance," *Personnel Psychology* 23 (1970): 13–38.

8. H. A. Sulkin and R. W. Pranis, "Comparison of Grievants in a Heavy Machine Company," *Personnel Psychology* 20 (1967): 111–19.

9. John Price et. al., "Three Studies of Grievances," *Personnel Journal* 5, no. 1 (January 1976): 33–37; Chalmer E. Labig and Charles R. Greer, "Grievance Initiation: A Literature Survey and Suggestions for Future Research," *Journal of Labor Research* 9 (Winter 1988): 1–27.

10. D. Keith Denton, "Handling Employee Complaints Effectively," *Administrative Management* 48 (December

1987): 14–17; Michael E. Gordon and Roger L. Bowlby, "Propositions About Grievance Settlements: Finally, Consultation with Grievants," *Personnel Psychology* 41 (Spring 1988): 107–23.

11. Benjamin J. Taylor and Fred Whitney, *Labor Relations Law*, 5th ed. (Englewood Cliffs, N. J.: Prentice-Hall, 1987), Chapter 15.

12. Audrey Freedman, *Managing Labor Relations* (New York: The Conference Board, Report No. 765, 1979).

13. W. Steve Albrecht, Marshall B. Romney, David J. Cherrington, I. Reed Payne, and Allan J. Roe, *How to Detect and Prevent Business Fraud* (Englewood Cliffs, N. J.: Prentice Hall, 1982), p. 193; "Loyalty—the Whistle Blower," *Across the Board* (Conference Board Publications, November 1978).

14. George W. Bohlander and Harold C. White, "Building Bridges: Nonunion Employee Grievance Systems," *Personnel* 65 (July 1988): 62–66; Robert Coulson, "How Fair Are Your Grievance Procedures?" *Association Management* 37 (February 1985): 117, 119; Peter Florey, "A Growing Fringe Benefit: Arbitration of Nonunion Employee Grievances," *Personnel Administrator* 30 (July 1989): 14–18.

15. Jonathan Tansini and Patrick Houston, "Letting Workers Help Handle Workers' Gripes," *Business Week* (September 15, 1986): 82, 88; Steve Ventura and Eric Harvey, "Peer Review: Trusting Employees to Solve Problems," *Management Review* 77 (January 1988): 48–51.

16. James T. Ziegenfuss, Mary Rowe, Lee Robbins, and Robert Munzenrider, "Corporate Ombudsmen," *Personnel Journal* 68 (March 1989): 76–79.

17. "Non-union Approaches to Dispute Resolution," *Work Life Report* 6, no. 1 (1988): 3–4, 13; Edmund M. Diaz and

John W. Minton and David M. Saunders, "A Fair Non-union Grievance Procedure," *Personnel* 64 (April 1987): 13–18.

18. Charles R. McConnell, "Making Upward Communication Work for Your Employees: The One and the Many," *Health Care Supervisor* 5 (October 1988): 81–91.

19. Henry J. Pratt, "Employee Complaints: Act Early and Be Concerned," *ARMA Records Management Quarterly* 23 (January 1989): 26–28.

20. Patricia A. Greenfield, "The NLRB's Deferral to Arbitration Before and After Olin: An Empirical Analysis," *Industrial and Labor Relations Review* 42 (October 1988): 34–49; Betty Southard Murphy, Wayne E. Barlow, and D. Diane Hatch, "Federal Courts' Jurisdiction on Arbitration Awards," *Personnel Journal* 67 (February 1988): 30; Theodore St. Antoine, "Deferral to Arbitration and Use of External Law in Arbitration," *Industrial Relations Law Journal* 10, no. 1 (1988): 19–26.

21. *Friday* v. *Hughes Aircraft Company*, 236 Cal. Rptr. 290, 735 P.2d 117 (1987).

22. *United Paperworkers International Union* v. *Misco Inc.* 108 S.Ct. 364 (1987).

23. BNA Editorial Staff, *Grievance Guide*.

24. Peter A. Veglahn, "Grievance Arbitration by Arbitration Boards: A Survey of the Parties," *Arbitration Journal* 42 (June 1987): 47–54.

25. Brian Bemmels, "The Effect of Grievants' Gender on Arbitrators' Decisions," *Industrial and Labor Relations Review* (January 1988): 251–62; Brian Bemmels, "Gender Effects in Discipline Arbitration: Evidence from British Columbia," *Academy of Management Journal* 31 (September 1988): 699–706; Brian Bemmels, "Gender Effects in Discharge Arbitration," *Industrial and Labor Relations Review* 42 (October 1988): 63–76.

26. Christine D. Ver Ploeg, "Labor Arbitration: The Participants' Perspective," *Arbitration Journal* 43 (March 1988): 36–43.

27. James Power, "Improving Arbitration: Roles of Parties and Agencies," *Monthly Labor Review* 95 (November 1972): 15–22.

28. Richard N. Block and Jack Stieber, "The Impact of Attorneys and Arbitrators on Arbitration Awards," *Industrial and Labor Relations Review* 40 (July 1987): 543–55.

29. Ben Fischer, "Arbitration: The Steel Industry Experiment," *Monthly Labor Review* 95, (November 1972): 7.

30. David J. Cherrington, *The Work Ethic: Working Values and Values that Work* (New York: AMACOM 1980), Chapter 8.

31. The arbitration guidelines described in this chapter come from BNA Editorial Staff, *Grievance Guide*, 2nd ed. (Washington D.C.: Bureau of National Affairs, 1988).

32. Michael Marmo, "Public Employees: On-the-Job Discipline for Off-the-Job Behavior," *Arbitration Journal* 40 (June 1985): 3–23.

33. Dorri Jacobs, "Exploring Causes of Problem Performance," *Management Solutions* 33 (December 1988): 10–17.

34. W. Steve Albrecht et. al., *Business Fraud*.

35. W. Steve Albrecht et al., *Business Fraud*, Chapter 2.

36. Information supplied by the National Council on Alcoholism, 733 Third Avenue, New York City, NY.

37. BNA Special Report, *Alcohol and Drugs in the Workplace: Costs, Controls and Controversies* (1986), Chapter 8.

38. James Mills, *The Underground Empire: Where Crime and Governments Embrace* (Garden City, NY: Doubleday, 1986).

39. Pat Wynns, "Arbitration Standards in Drug Discharge Cases," *The Arbitration Journal* 34, no. 2 (June 1979): 19–27.

40. Lawrence Z. Lorber and J. Robert Kirk, *Fear Itself: A Legal and Personnel Analysis of Drug Testing, AIDS, Secondary Smoke, and VDTs* (Alexandria, Va.: ASPA Foundation, 1987).

41. Jack Hayes, "Poll: Sixty Percent Favor Drug Testing," *Hayes Report on Loss Prevention* 5 (Winter 1990): 3, 7.

42. Joseph D. Levesque, *People in Organizations: A Guide to Solving Critical Human Resource Problems* (Sacramento, Calif.: American Chamber of Commerce Publishers, 1989), II.1.18–23

43. *Wilkinson* v. *Times Mirror Corp.*, 215 Cal. App. 3rd 1034, 264 Cal. Rptr. 194 (1989).

44. Lorber and Kirk, *Fear Itself*, p. 18.

45. *Skinner* v. *Railway Labor Executives' Association*, 109 S.Ct. 1402 (1989).

46. *National Treasury Employees Union* v. *Von Raab*, 109 S.Ct. 1384 (1989).

47. "Special Report: Employee Drug Testing and the Law Update" (Spain and Spain, Pittsburgh, Pa., February 29, 1988).

48. Richard Wallace, "Union Waiver of Public Employees' Due Process Rights," *Industrial Relations Law Journal* 8, no. 4 (1986): 583–600.

49. Perry A. Zirkel, "Labor Arbitrators' Inference of 'Progressive Discipline' in Just Cause Clauses: The Court's View," *Journal of Collective Negotiations in the Public Sector* 17, no. 1 (1988): 27–34.

50. David W. Ewing, "What Business Thinks About Employee Rights," *Harvard Business Review* (September–October 1977): 81–94.

51. Lawrence Steinmetz, *Managing the Marginal and Unsatisfactory Performer* (Reading, Mass.: Addison-Wesley, 1969).

52. This principle is attributed to Douglas McGregor. See George Strauss and Leonard Sayles, *Personnel: The Human Problems of Management* (Englewood Cliffs, N.J.: Prentice-Hall, 1967).

53. 29 Code of Federal Regulations, Part 1604.25.

54. Sheila Finnegan, "Constructive Discharge Under Title VII and the ADEA," *University of Chicago Law Review* 53 (Spring 1986): 561–80.

55. Robert L. Richman, "The BFOQ Defense in ADEA Suits: The Scope of 'Duties of the Job',"*Michigan Law Review* 85 (November 1986): 330–51.

56. Alan M. Koral, "Age Discrimination Cases Continue Pro-Plaintiff Trend," *Employee Relations Today* 13 (Summer 1986): 105–13. It should be noted that technically there are five basic defense rationales employers may use to oppose age discrimination rather than just the three listed here: (1) bona fide occupational qualification, (2) business necessity, (3) factor other than age, (4) bona fide seniority system, and (5) good cause.

57. 29 Code of Federal Regulations, Part 1604.11.

58. Bureau of National Affairs, "Sexual Harassment: Employer Policies and Problems," PPF Survey, No. 144 (June 1987).

59. John Horty, "Hospitals Can Be Liable When Supervisors are Linked to Sexual Harassment Incidents" *Modern Healthcare* 17 (November 6, 1987): 142; William S. Rule, "Arbitral Standards in Sexual Harassment Cases," *Industrial Relations Law Journal* 10, no. 1 (1988): 12–18.

60. Michael J. Album, "Affirmative Action and the Handicapped," *Employment Relations Today* 15 (Summer 1988): 99–106.

61. *Davis* v. *Bucher*, 451 F. Supp. 791 (E.D.PA. 1988).

62. *Heron* v. *McGuire*, 803 F.2d. 67 (2nd Cir 1986).

63. Much of the information for this section has come from Joseph D. Levesque, *People in Organizations* (Sacramento, Calif.: American Chamber of Commerce Publishers, 1989).

64. William E. Lissy, "Labor Law for Supervisors: Accommodating Employees' Religious Practices" *Supervision* 49 (November 1988): 22–23, 27.

65. *Hardison* v. *Trans World Airlines*, 375 F. Supp. 877 (W.D. Mo. 1974).

66. Lawrence Z. Lorber, J. Robert Kirk, Kenneth H. Kirschner, and Charlene R. Handorf, *Fear of Firing: A Legal and Personnel Analysis of Employment At-Will* (Washington, D.C.: ASPA Foundation, 1984); Marianne Moody Jennings, "The Abolition of the Right to Fire—No-Fault Is In Divorce Only," *Business and Society* 27 (Spring 1988): 23–88.

67. Terry Collingsworth, "ERISA Section 510—A Further Limitation on Arbitrary Discharges," *Industrial Relations Law Journal* 10, no. 3 (1988): 319–49; Roslyn Corenzwit Lieb, "Constructive Discharge Under Section 8 (a)(3) of the National Labor Relations Act: A Study in Undue Concern Over Motives," *Industrial Relations Law Journal* 7, no. 2 (1985): 143–77.

68. *Greuer* v. *Valve & Primer Corp.*, 361 N.E. 2d 863 (Ill. App.2d 1977).

69. *Toussaint* v. *Blue Cross & Blue Shield of Michigan*, 292 NW 2d 880, 884 (Mich. 1980); Gerard Panaro, "Don't Let Your Personnel Manual Become a Contract," *Association Management* 40 (August 1988): 81–84; Gerard P. Panaro, "The Legal Tentacles of Wrongful Discharge Suits," *Security Management* 31 (July 1987): 98–106.

70. *Gates* v. *Life of Montana Insurance Co.*, 668 P. 2d 213 (Mont. 1983).

71. *Nees* v. *Hocks*, 536 P.2d 512, 516 (Ore. 1975).

72. *Petermann* v. *International Brotherhood of Teamsters*, 344 P. 2d (Cal. Appl. 1959).

73. Jonathan Tompkins, "Legislating the Employment Relationship: Montana's Wrongful-Discharge Law," *Employee Relations Law Journal* 14 (Winter 1988/1989): 387–98.

74. Richard B. Schmitt, "California Court Further Restricts Right of Fired Workers to Sue Ex-Employers," *Wall Street Journal* (May 26, 1989).

75. Daniel W. Kendall, "Rights Across the Waters," *Personnel Administrator* 33 (March 1988): 58–61.

76. James A. Nelson and John A. Reeder, "Labor Relations in China," *California Management Review* 27 (Summer 1985): 13–32.

77. Bureau of National Affairs, *Plant Closings* (Washington, D.C.: BNA, 1988): 26.

78. Paul R. Gregory and Janet E. Kohlhase, "The Earnings of Soviet Workers: Evidence from the Soviet Interview Project," *Review of Economics and Statistics* 70 (November 1, 1988): 23–32: Robin Pringle, "Mr. Gorbachev's Economic Reforms," *Banker* 137 (February 1987): 15–17.

CHAPTER 15

Employee Safety and Health

Learning Objectives

After studying this chapter, you should be able to:

1. List the sources of accident statistics, and compare the costs and incidences of industrial accidents with those of accidents away from work.
2. Explain the provisions of the Occupational Safety and Health Act and the enforcement activities of this act.
3. Describe the components of a good company safety program.
4. Discuss the problem of environmental health hazards.
5. Explain the concepts of anxiety, depression, burnout, and stress.
6. Describe the three stages of the stress syndrome and the physiological responses of the alarm reaction.
7. Describe the major techniques that can be used to reduce and manage stress.
8. Describe the characteristics of an effective employee assistance program.

Chapter Outline

Role of Safety and Health Programs

Accident Statistics
Accidental Deaths and Injuries / Costs of Accidents / Incidence Rates by Industry

Occupational Safety and Health Act
Provisions of the Act / Impact of OSHA

Safety Programs
Management Leadership / Assignment of Responsibility / Identification and Control of Hazards / Employee and Supervisor Training / Safety and Health Record Keeping / First Aid and Medical Assistance / Employee Awareness, Acceptance, and Participation

Employee Health Problems

Environmental Health Programs / Health Problems Affecting the Workplace / Mental Health Programs / Physical Health Programs / Employee Assistance Programs

I N T R O D U C T O R Y   C A S E

A Bad Day

January 23 was a bad day for the safety record of Andrew's Cabinet Company. Two serious accidents occurred within the same hour, and the company was cited for having a serious environmental health hazard.

The most serious accident meant the loss of a leg to Craig Williams, a twenty-four-year-old journeyman cabinetmaker. Craig had jumped on the back of a forklift to avoid having to walk to the end of the warehouse. The driver, who had been concentrating on the load he was carrying, had not realized that Craig was sitting behind him. As the forklift rounded a corner, the back end had brushed against a wall, crushing Craig's right leg. The leg had to be amputated just below the knee.

The second accident resulted in Cindy Jones being hospitalized with serious electrical burns. Melvin Harris, one of the office workers, had been using a vacuum cleaner with a badly damaged electrical cord. Cindy, a bookkeeper, noticed the exposed wires and decided to wrap them with some electrical tape. She unplugged the vacuum to avoid being shocked while fixing the cord. However, when Melvin returned and saw the plug out of the wall, he plugged it back in. As a result, Cindy was seriously shocked and burned.

The environmental health hazard consisted of an excessive buildup of organic vapors

and carbon monoxide in the assembly area. Because January 23 was an extremely cold day, the employees in the assembly area turned off the exhaust fans and kept the doors and windows closed. The lack of ventilation created a serious accumulation of carbon monoxide from the space heaters and organic vapors from the glue and adhesives used in the assembly process.

Before the day was over, Andrew's Cabinet Company was visited by two safety inspectors who told the company to either correct its environmental health hazards immediately or suspend operations. Andrew Flake, the president and manager of the company, and Marie Weston, the personnel manager responsible for safety, were stunned by the events of that day. When they met to discuss the situation, they wondered what had gone wrong.

Questions:

1. Should Andrew Flake and Marie Weston view the events of the day as unpredictable accidents or symptoms of a serious disregard for safety?
2. How should they diagnose their safety practices?
3. What administrative actions should be taken now?
4. Should the company be responsible for the careless acts of its employees?

ROLE OF SAFETY AND HEALTH PROGRAMS

Employee safety and health programs are typically under the jurisdiction of a human resource department. Although a small company may assign safety responsibilities to the production department and a large corporation may have a separate safety department, employee safety and health activities are usually considered human resource functions. A Bureau of National Affairs survey in 1988 found that the responsibility of safety programs and Occupational Safety and Health Administration compliance was assigned to the human resource department in 79 percent of the 685 companies surveyed.[1] But regardless of how the responsibility for safety is assigned, every organization is required by law "to assure so far as possible every working man and woman in the nation safe and healthful working conditions and to preserve our human resources."[2]

Industrial accidents are extremely costly, whether measured in terms of medical expenses and disability compensation, lost production and wages, or damage to plant and equipment. The human cost in death and suffering is beyond calculation. The frequency of industrial accidents is alarming; accident statistics have occasionally aroused public sentiment to the point that safety laws have been passed. State workers' compensation laws were the earliest laws to provide relief for occupational accidents. These laws are designed to compensate injured workers regardless of who caused an accident. In 1970 the Occupational Safety and Health Act was passed. The purpose of this act is to prevent the occurrence of injury and illness. Many companies have gone beyond what is legally required and have developed programs to protect and improve the health of their employees. This chapter explains the major safety laws and describes some of the most common safety and health programs.

In recent years the costs of accidents have increased dramatically because of civil litigation. Lawyers have succeeded in winning large awards for clients who were injured through accidents or by faulty products. Lawsuits thus have contributed greatly to the importance of studying occupational safety and health. Unfortunately, some jury awards have appeared unreasonable and exorbitant, such as a $1 million award to a bodybuilder who entered a footrace with a refrigerator strapped to his back and was injured when a strap broke. Another example is Bendectin, the only effective antinausea drug for pregnancy, the production of which was discontinued because of mounting lawsuits, even though medical research indicated that it was safe. In the case of Agent Orange, a defoliant used by the military in Vietnam, its manufacturers agreed to an out-of-court settlement of $160 million even though the weight of medical evidence was on their side and the judge declared that the suit had no basis in fact. The cost of a lengthy trial, the adverse publicity, and the uncertainty of knowing how the case would be decided by a typical jury, which lacked the technical expertise to evaluate the evidence scientifically, made an out-of-court settlement more attractive than going to court.

Because of the growing costs of accidents and product liability suits, OSHA, the National Safety Management Society, and the National Institute of Occupational Safety and Health (NIOSH) launched project Minerva in 1983. This project is designed to increase the amount of training in occupational safety and health that is offered in schools of business. NIOSH hopes to create greater safety awareness in future managers by teaching more safety in all business courses—personnel, economics, accounting, finance, marketing, and policy.

ACCIDENT STATISTICS

Industrial accident statistics in the United States are compiled and published by three major organizations: the U.S. Public Health Service, the National Safety Council, and the Bureau of Labor Statistics. The U.S. Public Health Service publishes the National Health Survey, a summary of data collected from a continuous sample of households. Of the nation's 84 million households, 39,000 are interviewed annually. Health data and injuries experienced by members of the households during the two weeks prior to the interview are published in the National Health Survey.

The National Safety Council was created in 1913 as a nonprofit public service organization furnishing leadership in safety. Although the council was chartered by an act of Congress in 1954, it is not a governmental agency. It provides safety services and materials to industries, homes, schools, governments, and farms. The accident statistics published by the National Safety Council are collected from a large assortment of agencies and are published annually in a booklet entitled *Accident Facts*.[3]

The Bureau of Labor Statistics of the Department of Labor publishes workplace injury and illness statistics based on a survey of representative companies in an annual report entitled *Occupational Injuries and Illnesses*. The survey is based on the reports that employers who have eleven or more employees are required to submit under OSHA regulations.

ACCIDENTAL DEATHS AND INJURIES

In 1988 industrial accidents resulted in about 10,600 deaths and approximately 1.8 million disabling injuries.[4] A disabling injury is defined by the National Safety Council as one that results in some degree of permanent impairment or renders an injured person unable to perform regular activities for a full day beyond the day of injury. Most disabilities in 1989 were temporary, and the injured workers were able to return to work. However, 60,000 workers suffered permanent impairments that created either partial or total disability. Permanent impairments include injuries ranging from the permanent stiffening of a joint to permanent, complete crippling.

Statistics indicate that industrial accidents cause many deaths and disabilities every year and that too many employees are killed or injured by accidents that might have been prevented. The goals of safety programs are to eliminate accidents, and the statistics indicate that industrial safety practices need to be greatly improved. New employees are especially prone to accidents, usually because of inadequate training, as are employees over age 65 because of slower reactions and the effects of aging.[5]

On the positive side, statistics indicate that fewer accidents occur at work than on the highways, at home, or in other public activities. Table 15.1 shows that almost five times as many deaths occurred as a result of motor vehicle accidents than as a result of accidents at work in 1988. Even the home appears to be more prone to accidents than the workplace: about 70 percent more deaths and 60 percent more disabling injuries occurred in the home than at work.[6]

Historical records also indicate that life at work is considerably safer now than in earlier years. From 1930 to 1988, the number of deaths from industrial accidents dropped 40 percent, from 19,000 to 10,600. The death rate (deaths per 100,000) declined even

TABLE 15.1   Accidental deaths and injuries (1988)

	Deaths	Temporary Total Disabilities	Permanent Impairments
Work	10,600	1,700,000	60,000
Public (except Motor Vehicles)	18,000	2,200,000	50,000
Home	22,500	3,300,000	90,000
Motor Vehicles	49,000	1,700,000	150,000
Total	96,000*	8,700,000*	340,000*

*The totals are not equal to the sum of the four categories due to rounding and because some deaths and injuries are included in more than one category.
Source: Accident Facts, 1989 Edition (Chicago: National Safety Council), p. 2.

more because the work force was larger in 1988 than in 1930. The death rate dropped from 50 in 1930 to 9 in 1988. The statistics show that both the number of deaths and the death rate have steadily declined over the past sixty years. The data for selected years are shown in Table 15.2. These data indicate that even though accidents continue to be a serious problem, significant progress has been achieved in making the workplace safer.

COSTS OF ACCIDENTS

The National Safety Council estimated that accidents involving death or disabling injuries from all causes cost the nation about $143.4 billion in 1988.[7] Motor vehicle accidents were the most costly at a total of $70.2 billion. At $47.1 billion, work accidents were just about as costly as those involving motor vehicles. The bill for industrial accidents is itemized in Table 15.3. The largest costs were indirect ones that included the money value of time lost by workers who were involved in giving first aid to injured workers and those costs associated with investigating accidents, writing reports, and other indirect activities. The total financial loss due to accidents at work is conservatively estimated as equal to the sum of lost wages, medical expenses, and insurance administration costs. When the total cost is divided by 114.3 million workers, the average cost per worker is $412.

The costs shown in Table 15.3, however, do not include all of the relevant costs. Accidents *away from work* are also expensive to society, employers, and employees. Three out of four deaths and more than half of the injuries suffered by workers in 1988 occurred off the job. The ratio of off-the-job deaths to on-the-job deaths was 3.52

TABLE 15.2   Accidental deaths at work (1930–1988)

Year	Deaths	Death Rate[a]	Year	Deaths	Death Rate[a]
1930	19,000	50	1965	14,100	20
1935	16,500	40	1970	13,800	18
1940	17,000	37	1975	13,000	15
1950	15,500	27	1980	13,200	13
1955	14,200	24	1985	11,500	11
1960	13,800	21	1988	10,600	9

[a]Deaths per 100,000 workers
Source: Accident Facts, 1989 Edition (Chicago: National Safety Council) p. 35.

to 1, and the ratio of off-the-job injuries to on-the-job injuries was 1.52 to 1. Production time lost due to off-the-job accidents totaled about 60 million days in 1988, compared with 35 million days lost by workers injured at work. Off-the-job accidents to workers cost the nation at least $44 billion in 1989, of which about one-third was borne by employers. In addition, injured workers received about $25 billion in workers' compensation payments.

The most significant costs of accidents, however, are not the financial costs. The human costs are always the most important, and they should not be overlooked even if they cannot be measured precisely. Industrial accidents, like other accidents, frequently involve high human costs, such as the physical pain and suffering caused by a disabling injury, the loss of self-esteem from being unable to live a normal life, the personal degradation of being dependent on others because of a permanent disability, the heartache of losing a friend or loved one, and the disruption to a family when the breadwinner is killed. These human costs make safety a vital concern both at work and off the job.

INCIDENCE RATES BY INDUSTRY

The Bureau of Labor Statistics compiles **incidence rates** for occupational injuries and illnesses from employer reports required by the Occupational Safety and Health Administration. An *incident* refers to a **recordable case** of occupational injury, illness, or death. The incidence rates are based on cases per 100 worker years using 200,000 employee

TABLE 15.3   Costs of accidents at work in 1988

	Costs in Billions
Indirect loss from work accidents	22.0
Insurance administrative costs	6.0
Wage losses	7.9
Medical and hospital costs	8.1
Fire losses	3.1
Total costs	47.1

Source: Accident Facts, 1989 Edition (Chicago: National Safety Council), p. 3

hours as the base (2,000 hours per year times 100 workers). The formula used to calculate incidence rates is:

$$\text{Incidence rate} \ = \ \frac{N}{EH} \times 200{,}000$$

$$N \ = \ \text{number of injuries and/or illness or lost workdays}$$
$$EH \ = \ \text{total employee hours worked by all employees during the calendar year}$$
$$200{,}000 \ = \ \text{equivalent of 100 full-time employees, each working fifty weeks of forty hours per week}$$

Using this formula, the BLS computes several incidence rates for each industry. Four of these rates for various industries are presented in Table 15.4.

1. *Total recordable cases* is a measure of accident frequency, that is, how often accidents occur. A *recordable case* is defined by OSHA as one that involves an occupational injury or illness, including death. Not recordable are first-aid cases that involve one-time treatment and subsequent observation, or minor scratches, cuts, splinters, or burns that do not ordinarily require medical care, even though such treatment may be provided by a physician or registered nurse.
2. *Cases involving days away from work and deaths* is a measure of accident frequency whereby only the more serious accidents are counted. *Lost workdays* are those days that the employee would have worked but could not because of occupational injury or illness.
3. *Days away from work* is a measure of accident severity. Serious accidents usually cause more lost workdays than less serious accidents. The number of lost workdays does not include the day on which an injury occurs or an illness begins.
4. *Total lost workdays* includes both days away from work and restricted activity days. Restricted activity days include all days (consecutive or not) on which, because of illness or injury: (1) the employee would have worked but could not, or (2) the employee was assigned to a temporary job, or (3) the employee worked at a perma-

nent job less than full time, or (4) the employee worked a permanent job but could not perform all duties normally connected with it.

The incidence rates shown in Table 15.4 indicate that dramatic differences exist among the safety records of different industries. In some industries, such as office and computing machines, guided missiles, industrial chemicals, and communications, the number of injuries and illnesses are significantly below average. Other industries, such as trucking, railroad-equipment manufacturing, sawmills, paperboard container manufacturing, and meatpacking, have remarkably high incidence rates, indicating serious safety problems.[8]

The incidence rates published by the BLS provide useful information for human resource administrators and safety directors. Incidence rates can be calculated for each organization and compared with rates for the entire industry. Safety directors, surprised to discover that their rates are considerably above the industry average, may decide to launch aggressive safety campaigns. By calculating an organization's incidence rates, safety directors also are able to analyze trends in accidents, spot weaknesses, and evaluate

TABLE 15.4   Occupational injury and illness rates for selected industries

Industry	Total Recordable Cases	Cases Involving Days Away from Work and Deaths	Days Away from Work	Total Lost Workdays
All industries	7.59	1.86	41	60
Agriculture	14.67	4.10	78	111
Mining	6.06	1.18	38	49
Construction	8.02	2.93	63	71
Manufacturing	8.05	1.59	37	58
Sawmills	12.27	5.02	105	128
Office and computing machines	1.85	.58	6	16
Railroad equipment	13.33	4.74	120	122
Guided missiles	2.41	.35	6	12
Paperboard containers	11.05	4.00	97	119
Industrial chemicals	3.97	.44	10	26
Transportation	6.28	2.45	48	67
Trucking	22.30	17.55	246	247
Communication	2.11	.72	13	17
Wholesale and Retail Trade	5.38	1.85	38	51
Services	5.09	2.03	28	35
Public Administration	13.85	3.83	89	103

the effectiveness of safety training. Incidence rates can be calculated for separate departments as well as for an entire organization.[9]

OCCUPATIONAL SAFETY AND HEALTH ACT

The Occupational Safety and Health Act, which was passed in 1970, is administered by the **Occupational Safety and Health Administration (OSHA)**. Before 1970 many states had enacted and were enforcing their own occupational safety and health laws. Most of these state laws provided acceptable protection against occupational hazards and disease and were subsequently approved by OSHA. Nevertheless, criticism that the state laws were weak and ineffectively enforced led to the passage of the federal safety law.

PROVISIONS OF THE ACT

A detailed presentation of the Occupational Safety and Health Act and its interpretation is available from the Bureau of National Affairs. However, OSHA has prepared materials that explain the act in simpler terms than the BNA materials. Two booklets written especially for employers—*All about OSHA* and *OSHA Handbook for Small Business*—can be obtained from OSHA's regional offices.

PURPOSE

The basic purposes of the act are to reduce hazards in the workplace and to encourage employers and employees to implement improved safety and health programs. To create a safe and healthy work environment, mandatory safety and health standards are developed and enforced by OSHA. OSHA also requires employers to maintain reporting and record-keeping systems that monitor job-related injuries and illnesses.

The act covers all employers and employees, with only a few exceptions, such as:

Self-employed persons

Family farms where only family members work

Workplaces already protected by other federal statues

State and local governments

STANDARDS

The general standard stated in the act is that each employer "must furnish . . . a place of employment which is free from recognized hazards that cause or are likely to cause death or serious physical harm to employees." In addition, employers are required to comply with any specific standards promulgated by OSHA.

Federal agencies that assist OSHA in the development of safety standards include the Department of Health and Human Services, the National Institute for Occupational Safety and Health (NIOSH), and various professional organizations. In addition, OSHA has two standing advisory committees that aid it in developing safety and health standards and OSHA occasionally appoints special ad hoc advisory committees to provide expertise. All OSHA standards are published in the *Federal Register*, which is available in most public libraries or may be purchased through the Superintendent of Documents, U.S. Government Printing Office, Washington, D.C. 20402.[10]

Some of OSHA's standards are extremely complex and appear to require interpretation by a highly trained, skilled expert. Nevertheless, it is the employer's responsibility to become familiar with the standards that apply to her or his establishment and to ensure that employees follow safe working practices and use personal protective equipment for safety. Even where OSHA has not developed specific standards, an employer is held responsible for following the intent of the act's general requirement to provide a safe workplace.

Employers may ask OSHA for a variance from a standard if they can prove that their facilities or methods of operation provide employee protection "at least as effective" as that required by OSHA. Employers also can request a one-time temporary variance for as long as one year if they cannot immediately comply with a standard and it does not pose an imminent danger.

RECORD KEEPING AND REPORTING

Employers with eleven or more employees must maintain records of occupational injuries and illnesses. One purpose of these records is to provide data from which the BLS can compile accident statistics identifying the most hazardous industries. Another purpose is to inform employees about the status of their employer's safety record.

All occupational illnesses must be recorded regardless of their severity. All occupational injuries must be recorded if they result in

Death (regardless of the length of time between injury and death)

One or more lost workdays

Restriction of work or motion

Loss of consciousness

Transfer to another job

Medical treatment other than first aid

Employers must keep separate injury and illness records for each establishment and report them on a calendar-year basis. However, if an accident occurs that results in the death or hospitalization of five or more employees, an employer is required to report the accident in detail to the nearest OSHA office within forty-eight hours.

KEEPING EMPLOYEES INFORMED

Employers are responsible for keeping employees informed about OSHA and other relevant safety and health matters. OSHA requires employers to post these materials in a prominent place at work during the month of February:

OSHA Report No. 200, the Log and Summary of Occupational Injuries and Illnesses

A *Job Safety and Health Protection* poster informing employees of their rights and responsibilities under the act

Copies of OSHA citations for violations of standards

INSPECTIONS

To enforce its standards, OSHA is authorized to conduct workplace inspections. Every establishment covered by the act is subject to an inspection by a compliance officer. With few exceptions, these inspections are conducted without advance notice. In fact, alerting an employer in advance of an OSHA inspection could result in a $1,000 fine and/or six months in jail.

When a compliance officer presents the appropriate credentials, the employer is required to allow the officer to "enter without delay" to "inspect and investigate." In 1978 the Supreme Court ruled that OSHA may not conduct warrantless inspections without an employer's consent.[11] This ruling does little to curtail OSHA inspections, however, because OSHA can acquire an authorized search warrant or its equivalent based on administrative probable cause.

Since OSHA cannot conduct annual inspections of every workplace, it has established a list of inspection priorities. The highest priority situations are those involving imminent danger. An imminent danger is any condition where a high probability exists that an accident may occur that will result in death or serious physical harm. If such a condition is found and not corrected, OSHA can apply to the nearest federal district court for a temporary restraining order, and the operation may be immediately shut down.

OSHA's second priority is to investigate fatalities and catastrophes that hospitalize five or more employees. Such an investigation is designed to determine whether OSHA standards have been violated and whether immediate changes are needed. OSHA's third priority is to investigate employee complaints of alleged violations. The act gives employees the right to request an inspection when they believe that an imminent danger exists or that OSHA standards are being violated. Employees can submit complaints anonymously, and employers are forbidden from discriminating against employees who request inspections. OSHA's next priority is to investigate industries with high incidence rates. Firms with the highest lost workday injury rates in high-hazard industries are targeted for inspection.

Inspections consist of an opening conference between the compliance officer and employer, an inspection tour, and a closing conference. The employer is asked to select an employer representative to accompany the compliance officer on the inspection tour.

CITATIONS AND PENALTIES

After compliance officers report their findings to the OSHA office, the area director determines what citations and penalties will be issued. The citations indicate which standards have been violated and set a time limit for correcting each problem. Citations are usually sent via registered mail, but they can be issued "on the spot" during the closing conference if warranted by the situation and if the area director is contacted.

Penalties of up to $10,000 may be imposed for a willful violation or up to $1,000 for a serious violation. If an employer is convicted of a willful violation (a violation the employer knowingly commits) that results in the death of an employee, the penalty could be $10,000 and/or six months in prison. A second conviction could double these maximum penalties. Falsifying records or reports can bring a fine of $10,000 and six months in jail. Assaulting a compliance officer or resisting, interfering, or intimidating an officer could bring a $5,000 fine and up to three years in prison. Failure to post the citations could bring a $1,000 penalty. And an employer who fails to correct a safety violation can be fined $1,000 for each day the violation continues. The penalties can be very costly, although they can be adjusted downward by as much as 80 percent, depending on an employer's good-faith efforts and history of previous conduct.

APPEALS

If an employer feels that a citation or penalty is unfair or incorrect, an appeal can be made. The employer is allowed fifteen working days after receiving a citation to file a Notice of Contest. There is no specific format for the Notice of Contest, but it should clearly explain the employer's reasons for filing an appeal.

The notice is forwarded to the Occupational Safety and Health Review Commission, which in turn assigns the case to an administrative law judge. The judge investigates the case and either throws it out or holds a hearing with the employer and employees before making a ruling. After the administrative law judge has ruled, any party to the case may request a further review by the commission. Commission rulings may be appealed to a federal court of appeals.

STATE PROGRAMS

When the Occupational Safety and Health Act was passed in 1970, many states already had their own state safety laws. Some of these laws were criticized for their weak standards, ineffective administration, and lax enforcement. Others were considered acceptable. The federal safety law offered states the opportunity to develop and administer their own safety and health programs, provided that the states could demonstrate that their programs were "at least as effective" as the federal program. State safety and health programs have to be approved by OSHA, and if they are approved, OSHA will pay up to 50 percent of their operating costs.

To obtain approval from OSHA, a state must demonstrate that its standards for safety and health are adequate and that it is capable of enforcing them. A state is given a three-year probationary period to demonstrate that it has adequate standards, enforcement, appeal procedures, protection for public employees, and trained safety inspectors. About half of the states have developed and are administering their own safety and health programs. OSHA continues to evaluate the state programs to ensure that they meet acceptable standards. If a state program fails to meet the standards, OSHA has the authority to withdraw approval of the program.

ON-SITE CONSULTATION

During the first few years after the act was passed, employers were very outspoken in their criticism of the new law. Some of the standards required expensive changes that employers considered unnecessary. Other changes seemed ridiculous, such as specifying a particular height for guardrails and installing U-shaped toilet seats in restrooms— regulations since revoked or modified by the agency. Small businesses were especially burdened by the new regulations because employers did not understand all the requirements and could not afford private consultation.

To provide greater help to employers, especially small businesses, OSHA developed a free, on-site consultation service that is available to employers upon request. A consultant visits the establishment, meets with the employer, and walks through the company's facilities. During the walk-through, the employer is told which OSHA standards are applicable and what they mean. If violations are found, they are explained to the employer, along with suggestions for correcting them. OSHA encourages employers to include employees in these on-site consultation visits to make them more aware of safety practices.

No citations or penalties are issued for violations during a consultation visit. The consultation staff is separate from the enforcement staff. However, in accepting a consultation visit, an employer must agree to immediately eliminate serious hazards that present an "imminent danger" of death or serious physical harm. Other hazards have to be eliminated within a reasonable period of time. When employers fail to eliminate imminent dangers or make no efforts to reduce other hazards, the consultation officer is required to notify OSHA to investigate and begin enforcement action. This onsite consultation program is a valuable service for employers who are seriously interested in creating a safe workplace.

Companies can be exempted from further inspections for one year if an on-site consultation indicates that they have a safe work environment and have an ongoing safety and health program.

IMPACT OF OSHA

Creating a safe and healthy workplace is a worthy social goal. People should not be asked to sacrifice their safety or health for any job. The intent of Congress in passing the Occupational Safety and Health Act was to require employers to provide safe workplaces. But how well has the law succeeded in creating safer workplaces?

In 1980 the United States Senate Committee on Labor and Human Resources conducted an evaluation on the impact of OSHA during its first ten years.[12] OSHA representatives acknowledged that during the early years the agency was justly criticized for haphazardly selecting companies to inspect and for enforcing insignificant rules that did not threaten health or safety. To improve its image and strengthen its effectiveness OSHA dropped almost 1,000 rules, clarified the remaining standards, and developed an improved targeting formula that focused its enforcement efforts on high-hazard industries with high employment. During the 1980s OSHA focused much of its efforts on education through on-site consultation. Employers appreciated the shift toward greater cooperation and education; however, OSHA was criticized for emphasizing education rather than punishment. This shift was blamed for the slight increase in injury and illness rates during the latter years of the 1980s. From 1973 to 1983 the overall injury rate declined from 10.6 to 7.6, but then increased slightly to 8.3 by 1987. Nevertheless, OSHA is proud of its success as evidenced by the improved safety records in hazardous industrial segments where it concentrates most of its inspections.

An independent study by Robert Smith at Cornell University also concluded that OSHA inspections tend to reduce accidents. Smith indicated that OSHA inspections may reduce injury rates by as much as 16 percent and that the time lag between an inspection and a noticeable reduction in injury rates is only about three months.[13]

A nagging question about all of the evidence supporting OSHA's existence concerns what would have happened without OSHA. It is not clear whether the decline in accidents should be entirely attributed to OSHA. As noted at the beginning of this chapter, occupational death rates had been declining for many years, long before OSHA was established. Data compiled by the National Safety Council show that the drop in the death rates from 1928 to 1970 was about the same as after 1970. Therefore, OSHA does not appear to have had a significant effect on reducing the number of deaths. Opinions about whether OSHA has had an impact on reducing injuries and illnesses are mixed. Since 1971, when the BLS started compiling the statistics submitted to OSHA, the incidence rates show that the total recordable cases have decreased slightly but that the lost workdays have increased. Therefore, the evidence to date does not indicate that OSHA has greatly decreased the number of accidents at work.[14]

One of the reasons OSHA has not been more successful in reducing accidents is because many accidents are caused by employee carelessness. Neither OSHA nor employers can force employees to work safely. An employer can be required to provide a safe workplace, but a safe environment does not ensure that employees will work safely. An employer can be required to train employees in safe work practices and to enforce safety rules, but employees often violate these rules, even when their own well-being is at stake.

SAFETY PROGRAMS

OSHA encourages every organization to maintain an ongoing safety program. Most large organizations can afford to hire a safety officer and to staff a separate safety department to develop and monitor a safety program. Establishing a safety program is a problem for small organizations, however, because they cannot afford to hire additional personnel. Consequently, safety responsibilities usually are added to the other responsibilities of the present staff in a small company. Many small proprietors are overwhelmed by what they believe are added burdens imposed by OSHA.

To help organizations, especially small businesses, comply with its regulations, OSHA recommends a seven-point safety program. These seven points include: (1) management leadership; (2) assignment of responsibility; (3) identification and control of hazards; (4) employee and supervisor training; (5) safety and health record keeping; (6) first aid and medical assistance, and (7) employee awareness, acceptance, and participation. OSHA claims that this approach does not require additional employees or large costs and that it can be easily integrated into other business functions.[15]

MANAGEMENT LEADERSHIP

Safety programs need the support of top management to be effective. When managers are not interested in safety and health, no one else is likely to show much interest either, and the safety program will remain inactive. To stimulate interest in safety and health programs, managers should demonstrate a sincere interest in them by following these procedures:

1. Post the OSHA workplace poster *Job Safety and Health Protection* where all employees can see it.
2. Hold periodic meetings with employees to discuss job safety and health matters.

3. Show employees a copy of the Occupational Safety and Health Act and explain the OSHA standards that apply to them.
4. Prepare a policy statement that clearly declares management's concern about safety and health. An example of a policy statement is presented in Table 15.5.
5. Include job safety and health topics in conversations with employees.
6. Review all inspection and accident reports and check to make certain that hazards are eliminated.
7. Participate actively in labor-management safety committees.

ASSIGNMENT OF RESPONSIBILITY

OSHA recommends that the responsibility for safety and health activities be clearly and expressly assigned to one individual. The job of this individual should be to ensure that an effective safety program is developed and implemented. However, safety and health need to concern more than just top management. The responsibility for safety and health activities needs to be shared by everyone. OSHA recommends that these responsibilities be considered a basic part of every supervisor's and employee's job. Employees should be responsible for following the prescribed safety and health procedures and for recognizing and reporting hazards in their areas. Supervisors should be responsible for making certain that safe practices are understood and followed. Avoiding accidents requires the cooperation of everyone. All employees should know that carelessness and willful disregard for safe practices may result in discipline and termination.

IDENTIFICATION AND CONTROL OF HAZARDS

OSHA requires employers to know what hazards exist in their workplaces and which standards apply to them. Employers may request on-site consultations from OSHA to help them know which standards apply and what changes are needed. They also may

---

TABLE 15.5   Model safety policy statement

The personal safety and health of each employee of this company is of primary importance. The prevention of injuries and illnesses is of such consequence that it will take precedence over operating productivity whenever necessary.

We will maintain a safety and health program conforming to the best practices available. To be successful, such a program must embody the proper attitudes toward injury and illness prevention on the part of supervisors and employees. It also requires cooperation in all safety and health matters, not only between supervisors and employees but also between employees. Only through a cooperative effort can a safety program in the best interests of all be established and preserved.

Our objective is a safety and health program that will reduce the number of injuries and illnesses to an absolute minimum. Our goal is zero accidents and injuries.

obtain technical assistance from their insurance carrier, the local safety council, professional societies, and many state and local government agencies. In some situations private consultants may be needed to provide technical scientific information.

More is needed than just identifying the hazards, however. Organizations need to periodically conduct their own self-inspections. New hazards need to be identified, and a thorough check should be made to ensure that safety rules are being followed.

Some organizations have found that the best way to identify and control hazards is to use a safety committee. The members of this committee may be trained safety experts who are permanently assigned to inspect the workplace on a systematic basis. There are advantages, however, to having at least some members of the committee selected from the various departments on a temporary basis. By giving many employees the opportunity to serve on the safety committee, new ideas and different perspectives are contributed. One of the best reasons for having a rotating membership is that more employees have an opportunity to serve and thus become committed to safety. A helpful procedure for identifying and controlling hazards is to develop a checklist of safety practices. This checklist could be used by the safety committee as it conducts periodic inspections. Supervisors and employees also could be asked to complete the checklist on a weekly or monthly basis so that they become more aware of the need for safety.

Some hazards can be significantly reduced by safeguards, protective clothing, and restraints. Two steel producers, for example, have found that mandatory safety footwear has dropped their incidence rates to less than half the industry average. Many accidents that would have resulted in permanent disability or amputation are only minor accidents because of the required protective footwear.[16] Physical safety devices should be used when possible to reduce accidents, but they are not always effective. Mechanical power presses, for example, are extremely hazardous and seem to cause many accidents in spite of the barrier guards, pull-back devices, two-hand controls,and other devices intended to reduce accidents. There is no substitute for vigilance and care on the part of employees.[17]

EMPLOYEE AND SUPERVISOR TRAINING

For a safety program to be effective, all employees and supervisors must receive adequate safety training. Employees should never perform a job until they have been authorized to do it and have received adequate job instruction. Accident statistics indicate that new employees are much more likely to be involved in an accident. Workers who have been employed between one and three months suffer three times as many injuries as workers with one to three years of work experience, and eight times as many injuries as workers with twenty or more years of experience. Furthermore, new employees are not as likely as long-term employees to recognize and report hazardous conditions.[18]

Specific safety training should inform employees about safe operating procedures and specific hazards. All employees should know about the materials and equipment they use and the potential hazards in their environment. They should be instructed to look for unsafe conditions, to report hazards immediately, and to always put safety first. If a job appears unsafe or if dangerous conditions arise, employees should know that they are not expected to do the job. Particular emphasis should be placed on safety rules that are a condition of employment, such as those concerning safety shoes, eye protection, and dangerous chemicals.

SAFETY AND HEALTH RECORD KEEPING

OSHA requires employers with eleven or more employees to maintain accurate records on accidents and illnesses. Employers are required to keep a running log of all accidents (OSHA Form No. 200, "Log and Summary of Occupational Injuries and Illnesses"), plus a detailed record of each recordable case (OSHA Form No. 101, "Supplementary Record of Occupational Injuries and Illness"). Every year a company's annual summary must be posted no later than February 1 for at least one month, preferably next to the required OSHA workplace poster. The various records must be maintained on the premises for OSHA review during an inspection, and the information from which they were compiled must be retained for five years.

The information provided by safety records also can be used in managing a safety program and in conducting accident research. Records make it feasible to examine areas with high incidence rates, to determine the causes of accidents, to compare rates with similar organizations, and to examine trends in accidents to judge the success of a new safety program. Carefully compiled safety records also can be used as evidence of "good faith" in applying for reductions in proposed penalties from OSHA. Safety records should not only contain a list of the injuries and illnesses but also a complete record of all safety training programs and self-inspections.

Many companies fail to maintain accurate and current safety records, prompting OSHA to issue numerous citations for improper record keeping. Some of these citations have resulted from conscious attempts to misrepresent the facts. However, a survey of 200 manufacturing firms suggested that the reporting problem is largely caused by carelessness rather than willful misrepresentation. A thorough examination of 4,000 cases found almost as many cases of overrecording (15 percent) as underrecording (20 percent). Some safety directors are apparently unclear about the definition of a recordable incident.[19]

FIRST AID AND MEDICAL ASSISTANCE

Although the goal of a safety program should be to eliminate accidents, a good safety program also must be prepared to handle injuries and illness. Large organizations often have their own medical personnel. Since small businesses usually cannot afford to have a medical staff and extensive first-aid supplies, they are not expected to have them unless there are no nearby medical facilities. However, when a job involves possible exposure to injurious corrosive materials, employers are required to provide suitable equipment for quick drenching or flushing with water the exposed part of the body.

EMPLOYEE AWARENESS, ACCEPTANCE, AND PARTICIPATION

The success of a safety program largely depends on whether the employees support it. Safety training and job instructions are useless if employees disregard them. Employees need to be motivated to follow safe working practices. They must be made aware of the requirements, accept them in their work, and participate actively in the safety program.[20]

Several strategies have been used to motivate employees to work safely. One of the most common methods of increasing employee awareness is a large billboard advertising

HRM in Action

Improving Safety at Pizzagalli Construction

According to Paul King, safety manager of Pizzagalli Construction, a safe job site is only possible when management demonstrates a sincere interest in safety. Pizzagalli specializes in one of America's most dangerous industries, heavy construction, such as high-rise office buildings and hydro power plants. Nevertheless, the company has significantly improved its safety record through a combination of training, inspections, and awards. Since 1986 the recordable injury rate has been cut in half, worker compensation costs have dropped 76 percent, general liability insurance has been reduced by an amazing 96 percent, and the lost-workday rate has dropped from 7.9 in 1986 to 5.2 in 1988. Obviously, management has communicated their concerns about safety.

The company decided to emphasize safety training because the statistics indicated that one in four construction workers was injured the first month on the job and new employees were responsible for more than half of the injuries. The first major training occurs in the new-employee orientation, which includes a thorough reading of the company's twelve-page rule book, a guided tour of the construction site, and a review by the foremen to ensure that safety procedures and issues are understood. This initial training is followed by weekly training meetings that include talks, videos, and demonstrations.

On-site inspections are routinely made on all sites. On large jobs, safety officers with medical training monitor compliance to the safety rules and procedures. Failure to comply with safety standards produces first a verbal warning and then a written warning; a third warning results in termination. All employees involved in accidents must provide urine and blood samples to test for substance abuse. Those who test positive are suspended for ninety days while they attend an employee assistance program.

The employees are very supportive of the safety program, in part because of the financial awards. To communicate their concern about safety the company gives monthly awards for the safest job sites. Furthermore, incentives in the form of cash bonuses are given to hourly employees who do not receive reportable injuries. For instance, 1,000 injury-free hours equals a $50 savings bond, and 6,000 injury-free hours equals a $1,000 bond.

Pizzagalli's safety record demonstrates how top management's commitment can reduce the occurrence of accidents, and the benefits are obvious. The employees spend more time in training and less in health care facilities. And rather than paying worker compensation insurance, the company gives safety awards to its employees.

Source: John C. Bruening, "Pizzagalli Construction: Performance-Oriented Safety Pays Off," *Occupational Hazards* 51 (June 1989): 4–48.

how many accidents occurred in the previous year, how many have occurred in the year to date, and how many days have elapsed since the last lost-time injury. Some organizations have safety contests in which departments compete against each other for the best safety records. Another method is to have work groups compete against their own previous accident records.

The incentive for most of the contests is some form of recognition on a bulletin board, in a company newsletter, or in a personal letter. Specific feedback and comments by superiors about safe practices are also valuable incentives. Reinforcement theories suggest that rewards for working safely should decrease the number of accidents, and some studies have demonstrated the effectiveness of safety incentives. The results of one study indicated that safety training and positive reinforcement in the form of verbal praise and feedback significantly increased the safety record in a food manufacturing plant. When the safety program was implemented, accidents were reduced. When the program was terminated, the number of accidents returned to its former level.[21]

Financial incentives and other extrinsic rewards apparently can be used to reduce the number of accidents, but when the rewards become large, informal pressure not to report accidents may develop among employees. Some employees suffer serious injuries and never report them because they do not want to ruin their department's safety record. Safety incentives need to be large enough to increase employee awareness, acceptance, and participation but not so large that employees become motivated to misrepresent what actually happens. More research is needed on the effects of safety incentives.

EMPLOYEE HEALTH PROGRAMS

The Occupational Safety and Health Act requires employers to provide both a safe *and healthy* workplace. Some of the major health hazards caused by toxic and hazardous substances are regulated by OSHA standards. In some companies, however, the concern for employee health has gone far beyond just controlling toxic materials. Many organizations have developed extensive programs to improve both the physical and mental health of their employees.

The motives for these programs are partially altruistic; employers are genuinely concerned about the health and well-being of their employees. However, these programs also are self-serving since managers are primarily concerned about their own health. Some health programs are designed exclusively for managers, while other programs are open to all employees.

Regardless of management's motives, health programs can be justified economically. Poor health represents an enormous cost to employers. An estimated $10 to $20 billion is lost through absence, hospitalization, and early deaths among executives. Alcoholism is a serious problem that costs industry about $15.6 billion annually due to absenteeism and medical costs. About 32 million workdays and $8.6 billion in wages are lost annually because of heart-related diseases.[22] The costs of health care insurance also are very high. In 1983 the average cost of health care insurance was $1,460 per employee and as high as $2,436 per employee in the primary metals industry.[23]

Employee health programs recently have moved in the holistic direction, an approach to health care that considers the total set of forces influencing health. These forces include toxic chemicals in the environment, food and nutrition, physical exercise, emotional stress, and personal problems.

ENVIRONMENTAL HEALTH PROGRAMS

The environment has always contained materials that contribute to illness and disease. In recent years, however, concern has grown over the harmful effects of toxic substances and the need for a concerted effort to control them. Part of this concern stems from discoveries that some of the materials once considered safe are not so safe after all. Before germs were discovered, a public drinking cup was typically provided near water fountains for the convenience of thirsty travelers. As people learned how diseases were transmitted, however, the public drinking cups were gradually replaced with more sanitary methods for obtaining a drink.

The history of asbestos illustrates how costly and destructive an environmental health hazard can be when the effects of a toxic substance are not recognized. Before the carcinogenic properties of asbestos were recognized, it was used extensively in insulation and other products. Unfortunately, now that we know how widespread and dangerous asbestos is, we are also learning that the removal of asbestos is an expensive process requiring skilled experts. A similar process is occurring in many other areas: more is becoming known about the kinds of substances that cause illnesses and death, the kinds of lifestyles that create stress, and the kinds of personal problems that damage mental health. Gradually, these problems are being corrected. Safety managers play an important role in identifying health hazards and in educating employees about the dangers of such hazards.

TOXIC AND HAZARDOUS SUBSTANCES

Toxic substances are chemicals and other materials that are poisonous to the body, such as lead, carbon monoxide, and benzene. In small doses, these substances cause minor illness, and in large doses, they may be fatal. Some substances, such as cotton and coal, are not highly poisonous in themselves, but when cotton dust and coal dust are inhaled in sufficient concentrations over an extended period of time, they can cause severe respiratory illnesses.

OSHA has identified several toxic and hazardous substances and has issued regulations governing their use. These regulations require an employer to follow explicit work practices and to train employees in the safety and health aspects of their jobs. When certain substances are present in the workplace, OSHA standards make the employer responsible for limiting certain job assignments to employees who are "certified," "competent," or "qualified"—meaning that these employees must have completed a special training course. Table 15.6 illustrates the training requirements for employees who work where cotton dust is present.

When evidence indicates that a substance poses a significant occupational risk to health, OSHA begins its rule-making process to develop standards for regulating use of the substance. Through the public rule-making process, OSHA seeks information about the substance and about how people will be affected by the rule. After this information is examined, the standards are established by OSHA and published in the *Federal Register* and employers are expected to comply with them.

OSHA points to the development of its vinyl chloride standard as an example of a successful regulation. In 1974 research indicated that workers exposed to vinyl chloride had a high risk of contracting angiosarcoma, a rare and fatal form of cancer. Based on this research, OSHA proposed a vinyl chloride standard in 1974. The vinyl chloride industry, consisting of twenty-seven firms, argued that the proposed standard would be impossible to comply with and would result in losses of $65 to $90 billion per year in lost production and the elimination of 1.7 to 2.2 million jobs. Nevertheless, the permanent standard went into effect in 1975. The disastrous predictions of the vinyl chloride indus-

---

TABLE 15.6   OSHA's training requirements for toxic or hazardous substances: cotton dust

Employees who work where cotton dust is present must be informed about:

The hazards of cotton dust

The specific operations that could result in exposure to cotton dust

The work practices specified by OSHA to protect them from excessive exposure

The proper use and limitations of the respirators which OSHA requires them to wear

The purpose for the medical surveillance program required by OSHA

The contents of OSHA's cotton dust standard, including the appendixes

Source: Training Requirements in OSHA Standards. U.S. Department of Labor, OSHA 2254, Revised 1979, p. 21.

---

try were never realized. With a sense of satisfaction, OSHA claims that compliance with the new standard forced the development of new technology that increased both the safety and efficiency of vinyl chloride production methods.[24]

OSHA's inspection of toxic and hazardous substances is determined by a health targeting model. This model is based on an inventory of which chemicals are used by which industries, an estimate of the number of persons exposed to each chemical, and the relative severity of each chemical. The industries with the highest risks are inspected first. OSHA has hired and trained a staff of nearly 500 industrial hygienists to conduct health inspections.

TOXICOLOGY

Most research into toxic substances is done in the **toxicology** research laboratories of major chemical and drug companies. Dow Chemical Company, for example, spends $20 million annually for research on health, safety, and the environment.[25] The science of toxicology is based on determining the toxic thresholds of chemicals. There is no such thing as a nontoxic material. Even common minerals and vitamins that are essential to human health are toxic in high doses. However, a basic concept of toxicology is that there is a **no-adverse-effect level** for virtually every material. This level is the highest dose or exposure that causes no ill effects. The **toxicity threshold** is the lowest dose level at which toxic effects can be demonstrated.

New chemicals and synthetic materials are carefully examined in toxicology research laboratories, mostly by testing them on rats, mice, guinea pigs, and rabbits. The tests determine the substance's toxicity threshold by assessing the acute effects of inhaling or swallowing it, or letting it come into contact with the eyes or skin. Special studies examine the effects of the substance on pregnancy, reproduction, and genetic mutations.

An understanding of toxicology helps dispel some of the popular myths about hazardous chemicals feared to cause cancer and other illnesses. The risks of using new chemicals and synthetic materials are often misunderstood. The toxic properties and cancer-risk factors of new materials are examined by extensive research. Many people object to using a chemical with a cancer risk of 1 in 1,000,000. Yet these people would not hesitate to accept a cancer risk of 1 in 10,000 by using peanut butter, which contains a powerful carcinogen, aflatoxin, or a cancer risk of 1 in 500 when they use alcohol and tobacco in combination.[26] *Any* substance is potentially harmful when there is too much of it. The solution is to know what is an acceptable dose and what the risks are of using each substance.

The most important line of defense against toxic substances is the liver. As blood passes through the liver, it detoxifies the poisons and keeps them from circulating through the body. If the liver is called upon to detoxify a larger quantity of materials than it can handle in a short time, the entire organism suffers. Long-lasting and possibly permanent damage may result when the body's defenses are overloaded with repeated exposure. Overindulgence in alcohol, for example, can cause severe, even permanent, injury to the liver.

Some chemicals that are considered safe for the average employee to handle are not considered safe for pregnant women. Consequently, some companies reassign women who become pregnant to other jobs. Other companies refuse to hire women still in their childbearing years for certain jobs. In some instances, women have decided to be sterilized to obtain one of these high-risk, high-paying jobs.[27]

An area of scientific research related to toxicology is epidemiology. **Epidemiology** is the study of diseases in the environment and of conditions that may cause health problems. Epidemiologists are medical specialists who study the causes of human disease. They typically examine the work environment and try to discover whether a rash of illnesses or deaths at a particular workplace was caused by a health hazard. Epidemiology is a relatively new field but one that has attracted attention because of society's growing concern over occupational health.

The work of epidemiologists is illustrated by Dow Chemical Company's team of a dozen epidemiologists who spent over two years trying to discover whether the deaths of twenty-four men at one of its plants were caused by toxic substances in the workplace. All twenty-four had died from brain cancer. Although the statistics indicated that this rate of brain cancer was unusually high, the epidemiologists were unable to find anything in the workplace that could have caused the cancer. The disturbing question that they could not answer definitively was whether it was toxic materials that caused the brain cancer or whether the high death rate was just a chance event.[28]

HEALTH PROBLEMS AFFECTING THE WORKPLACE

In recent years employers have been required to respond to three sensitive health concerns affecting employees in the workplace: smoking, video display terminals, and AIDS.

SMOKING

During the 1980s a significant change occurred in Americans' attitudes toward smoking. Whereas smoking had once been considered socially acceptable and even fashionable in some quarters, during the 1980s, it became unacceptable and even illegal in many designated areas.[29] This reversal of attitudes was caused by several factors, including mounting medical evidence demonstrating the debilitating health consequences to smokers, cost accounting data showing the incremental costs to companies of hiring smokers, and medical studies showing the harmful effects to nonsmokers who inhale passive smoke.[30] During the 1980s the number of companies with policies limiting smoking in the workplace increased from less than 10 percent to about 90 percent. A survey asking why companies developed their smoking policies found that the three most important reasons were a concern for the health and comfort of their employees, complaints from nonsmoking employees, and the need to comply with state or local law.[31]

Although some company policies ban smoking in all company buildings, most policies allow smoking in private offices and restrict it only in hallways, conference rooms, rest rooms, and open work areas. The Environmental Protection Agency published a recommendation that smoking be allowed only in designated smoking rooms that ventilate directly to the outside.

While the number of companies that limit their hiring to nonsmokers is small, the percentage is growing, particularly among health care organizations and high-tech companies with sensitive computer equipment. Smoking policies have generally been accepted and successfully implemented (1) when companies explain why they are important, (2) when they provide advance notice giving several months for employees to accept the policy, and (3) when they provide assistance to help employees quit smoking.[32] Some of the measures taken to encourage workers to quit smoking include distributing literature on how and why to quit smoking, sponsoring employee wellness programs, sponsoring quit-smoking programs on company time, reimbursing employees for attending quit-smoking programs, and other rewards to workers who quit. An ambulance company that paid nonsmokers a bonus of five dollars per month and an additional sixty-dollar bonus at the end of each full year of nonsmoking reported that over half of its smokers had quit by the end of the first year.[33]

For the most part, smoking in the workplace has been unregulated by legislation; however, nonsmokers have been granted certain specific rights by at least ten state statutes and some local ordinances. The most aggressive local measure is a San Francisco ordinance that bans smoking in a nonsmoker's work area if an informal compromise to settle the smoking dispute cannot be reached. In general, neither smokers nor nonsmokers have succeeded in promulgating federal or constitutional laws to establish their rights either to smoke or to avoid smoke. The resolution of such disputes is left to company policies or informal arrangements.[34]

VIDEO DISPLAY TERMINALS

With the ever-increasing application of computers, video display terminals (VDTs) have become an indispensable part of the modern workplace. Their popularity, however, has stimulated nagging concerns about their safety. They are new and not yet fully understood, and fears have been raised that prolonged exposure to VDTs contributes to reproductive hazards to pregnant women or their fetuses and to eye damage, especially a greater incidence of cataracts.

These fears were fueled by anecdotal evidence during the early years of VDT use. In one incident, fourteen babies were born in one year to women who used VDTs in the classified ads department of the *Toronto Star*, and four of these fourteen babies had birth defects. Suspicion that the defects were caused by VDTs was sparked by news reports of this occurrence. Concern that cataracts could be caused by VDTs became widespread after two young employees who worked at VDTs at the *New York Times* developed cataracts.[35]

The epidemiology of VDTs was carefully investigated in these and numerous other clusters of related incidences that seemed to attribute health problems to VDTs. The results of study after study concluded that VDTs were safe to use; the health problems were no greater among VDT users than among nonusers. It should be noted, however, that epidemiological studies are not very conclusive unless they have extremely large sample sizes and even then they cannot be definitive about causation.

Two potential hazards are attributed to the use of VDTs: (1) working for prolonged periods with eye strain, pressure to perform, and restricted movement; and (2) low-level radiation.[36] The physical problems caused by prolonged work on VDTs are real, and recommendations to reduce these problems include work breaks and frequent job changes. Fears about radiation are completely unfounded, however, since the radiation produced by VDTs is the nonionizing type, or radiation similar to that found in light, radio, and television signals. Furthermore, the amount of radiation from VDTs is trivial relative to the radiation that comes from other appliances, including hair dryers, baseboard heaters, and the electric typewriters that VDTs have replaced.

Legislative efforts to regulate VDTs have failed at the federal and state levels because the laws appear to be unnecessary. Nevertheless, several groups, including the National Institute for Occupational Safety and Health (NIOSH) have adopted guidelines for VDT use calling for maximum flexibility in (1) workstation design, (2) improved lighting to reduce glare, (3) periodic work breaks, and (4) vision testing.

AIDS

Acquired Immune Deficiency Syndrome (AIDS) is probably the most challenging health problem for employers in the workplace. Although the disease itself may not be contagious through casual contact, the fear of AIDS is very contagious for a good reason: AIDS has proven to be universally fatal. Consequently, employers are caught in the middle of a highly emotional conflict between protecting the rights of employees who have AIDS and accommodating those who fear they will become infected by working with AIDS victims.

AIDS is caused by a virus that kills the specialized blood cells that serve as the master control for the body's immune system. Once infected with the AIDS virus, the victim probably remains infected for life. The virus is usually latent for two to five years or more before it advances to the active stage characterized by a group of maladies known as AIDS-Related Complex, or ARC. The symptoms of ARC may include fever, sudden weight loss, fatigue, chronic diarrhea, and swollen glands. ARC can also be diagnosed with a blood test showing the presence of antibodies to the AIDS virus. Eventually, the immune system fails, leaving the victim susceptible to a host of opportunistic and deadly diseases.

Employees naturally worry about their safety when working with an AIDS victim. Every person who has the AIDS virus in his or her blood is capable of transmitting the disease to others, even during the latency period before any symptoms have appeared. Transmission occurs by a transference of body fluids, especially blood, and typically happens in one of three ways: blood transfusions, sharing drug needles, and sexual contact, especially homosexual contact. Health organizations have repeatedly claimed that AIDS is not spread by casual social contact unless the blood, semen, sweat, or saliva of a carrier come into physical contact with the bloodstream of another person. Therefore, the transmission of AIDS should not be a concern in the workplace except in specific industries, such as health care, where special precautions are necessary. Telling people not to be afraid, however, only serves to remind them of the potential hazards. For this reason, companies are not encouraged to publish an "AIDS Policy."

Blood tests to detect the presence of the AIDS antibody are very unreliable in the early stages of AIDS. At least five states and several cities prohibit the use of the AIDS antibody test for purposes of insurability and employment. But even if the test were reliable, employers probably could not justify using it because it invades personal privacy and is seldom job related. Employers should not reassign or terminate AIDS victims until the disease prevents them from performing adequately.[37]

Legal protections in AIDS cases favor those who have the disease rather than those who fear getting it. A group of nurses who insisted on wearing special protective clothing when treating AIDS patients claimed they were unfairly forced to transfer to a different shift. However, the California Labor Commission was not sympathetic to their fears of contagion and denied their claim of retaliation.[38]

Several court decisions, including the Supreme Court's ruling in *The School Board of Nassau County, Florida* v. *Arline* (1987), have held that victims of illnesses such as tuberculosis and AIDS are covered by handicapped discrimination laws. Consequently, victims who are otherwise qualified are protected against adverse employment decisions and employers are required to make reasonable accommodations for their disease.[39]

The Supreme Court outlined the general principles of reasonable accommodation when dealing with contagious diseases:

1. A person who poses a significant risk of communicating an infectious disease to others is not "otherwise qualified" if reasonable accommodation will not eliminate the risk.
2. Accommodation is not reasonable if it would impose undue financial or administrative burdens on the employer or require a fundamental alteration in the way of doing business.
3. Employers are not required to find another job for employees who are no longer qualified for their previous jobs, but they cannot deny them an alternative job if it is reasonably available.
4. "Reasonable accommodation" of employees with communicable diseases must be considered in light of reasonable medical judgments about the nature, duration, and severity of the risk, and the probability of transmitting the disease.

These guidelines require employers to base their employment decisions regarding AIDS victims on a case-by-case analysis using good medical advice.

MENTAL HEALTH PROGRAMS

The mental health of employees is just as important as their physical health. A highly stressful working environment can be just as destructive to mental health as toxic substances are to physical health. Unlike physical health, mental health is not protected by the Occupational Safety and Health Act. In some instances, however, employees can receive workers' compensation benefits for physical or mental breakdowns caused by the *cumulative trauma* of an excessively stressful job.

MENTAL ILLNESS

Mental illnesses are caused by many factors both on and off the job, including child abuse and other traumatic childhood experiences, marital conflicts and an unhappy family life, peer pressure and social ridicule, and a stressful work environment. Everyone occasionally feels frustrated, depressed, and a bit insecure, but most individuals are able to cope with temporary setbacks. Four of the most common challenges to good mental health are boredom, burnout, anxiety, and depression.

1. *Boredom*: Repetitive jobs that have short work cycles and require doing the same thing again and again are usually described as boring. Assembly-line jobs are frequently considered the most boring jobs. However, every job—even a glamorous one—probably has some boring aspects. Airline pilots, for example, have to cope with cockpit boredom.[40] All repetitive activities are not necessarily boring, however. Playing a slot machine is an example of a repetitive activity that some people find continually interesting.

2. *Burnout*: The demoralization, frustration, and reduced efficiency that result from an inability to handle continued stress on the job is called **burnout**. Burnout has been observed most frequently among people who work in the helping professions, especially psychiatrists, social workers, and counselors, who are constantly asked to give of themselves and eventually feel emotionally drained. Occupations that require a large investment of personal commitment and involvement are particularly prone to cause burnout.[41]

3. *Anxiety*: Anxiety refers to a state of tension associated with worry, apprehension, guilt, and a constant need for reassurance. It is more than the ordinary fear and apprehension associated with a specific event. Instead it refers to a general state of fear and apprehension that is abnormally high and not associated with a specific cause.

4. *Depression*: Depression is a mood characterized by dejection and gloom that usually contains feelings of worthlessness, guilt, and futility. Depression is more than just being unhappy or sad because of a specific unpleasant event. It is an intense sadness that has lost its relationship to a specific event.

Reactions of burnout and boredom are not universal, nor are they automatically caused by a particular situation. Conditions that are boring or that cause burnout for some continue to be meaningful and exciting to others. Boredom and burnout are individual reactions.[42] Job burnout and boredom are caused primarily by a lack of meaning in work. Burnout occurs on jobs that usually require a considerable amount of variety, significance, skill, and responsibility. At first employees feel excited about their work and their opportunities to make a significant contribution. They invest themselves in their jobs and often work extra hours. After a while, however, the excitement wears off, but the jobs still demand much in the way of effort and commitment. However, the jobs are no longer meaningful to the employees and they feel unwilling to exert the effort needed. Periodic vacations are usually recommended to allow professionals to take time to reassess the meaning and importance of their work. Occasionally, however, individuals suffering boredom or burnout feel that the only solution to their problem is to find different jobs. Burnout is considerably reduced by a supportive and considerate supervisor.[43]

Anxiety and depression are accompanied by a host of physiological effects. Anxiety usually leads to profuse perspiration, difficulty in breathing, gastric disturbances, rapid heartbeat, frequent urination, muscle tension, diarrhea, or high blood pressure. Depression is usually associated with a series of biochemical disturbances that may be linked to a genetic predisposition. Both anxiety and depression have been treated with drugs. However, recent reports discourage the use of drugs, especially as a long-term solution. Drug treatments often have undesirable side effects and they usually do not solve emotional problems in the long run. Various forms of psychiatric counseling are recommended for severe cases. For mild forms, a good book, a vacation, or talks with close friends are recommended. Some organizations have employee assistance programs that provide counseling and other activities to help employees maintain good mental health.[44]

STRESS

Occupational **stress** has received considerable attention in recent years because of the serious threat it poses to both physical and mental health. Our understanding of stress stems from the pioneering research of Dr. Hans Selye, a famous endocrinologist. In 1936 Selye described what he called a General Adaptation Syndrome (GAS), which was a major discovery in understanding the stress response. Selye made a clear distinction between *stress* and a *stressor*. Stress was defined as the nonspecific response of the body to any demand. A stressor was the object or event that caused the stress. Selye also made a distinction between positive stress, which he called **eustress**, and negative harmful stress, which he called **distress**. Some examples of eustress are falling in love, winning a contest, and receiving an award. Since stress is the nonspecific response of the body to any demand, the physiological responses of distress and eustress are virtually the same. However, eustress causes much less damage to the body because the person is more inclined to adapt to it successfully.[45]

When a stressor is present, a sequence of biological events occurs. The same sequence of biological events can be triggered by many different situations, both pleasant and unpleasant. Because the same syndrome of physiological responses is elicited by many different situations, Selye called it the General Adaptation Syndrome. The GAS consists of three stages: alarm, resistance, and exhaustion.

1. *The alarm reaction*: When a stressor is recognized, the **alarm reaction** occurs and a biological message is sent from the brain to the pituitary gland, a small gland just below the brain. The pituitary gland, the master control of the endocrine system, secretes a hormone (called ACTH) that causes the adrenal glands to secrete corticoids, such as adrenalin. Immediately the entire endocrine system is engaged in the secretion of complex hormones and a general alarm is sent to all systems of the body.
2. *Resistance stage*: Once the immediate threat has passed, the body tries to return to a state of equilibrium. The physiological changes of this stage are mostly the exact opposite of those that characterize the alarm reaction. The body tries to regain a state of balance, even if the stressor is still present.

3. *Exhaustion stage*: If the stressor continues, the body exhausts its ability to adapt. When the physiological responses of the alarm reaction persist unduly, severe wear and tear will occur, resulting in damage to a local area or death to the organism as a whole.

The alarm reaction has also been called the *fight or flight response*. In this stage the autonomic nervous system makes dozens of immediate responses to prepare the body for a physical action. When pedestrians are crossing the street and suddenly see a car speeding toward them, the alarm reaction prepares their bodies to get quickly out of the way. Some of the major responses that the body makes during the alarm reaction are listed in Table 15.7.

The alarm reaction is useful when a physical threat demands an immediate physical response. The alarm reactions most people face, however, do not call for an immediate physical response. Typical alarm reactions result from such things as taking exams, being called on in class, speaking before an executive committee, or seeing another motorist cut in front of you. A strenuous physical response is not appropriate in such situations.

The alarm reaction is a major source of distress when it is constantly turned on without being used for its intended purpose. When the alarm reaction is fired too often or too long, the body may remain in a constant state of mobilization, or in a state of chronic tension with high blood pressure, rapid heartbeat, and disrupted digestion. The consequences are usually serious. Damage can occur to the nervous system itself or to many vital organs. Possible results range from simple hypertension to fatal heart disease.

Some occupations are especially prone to tension and stress. For many years, the work of air traffic controllers has been recognized as a highly stressful activity. Studies

---

TABLE 15.7   Physiological responses to an alarm reaction

1. The breath rate increases to provide more oxygen.
2. Red blood cells flood the bloodsteam to carry more oxygen to the muscles.
3. The heart beats faster and blood pressure soars to provide blood to needed areas.
4. Stored sugar and fats are converted to blood glucose to provide fuel for quick energy.
5. Blood-clotting mechanisms are activated to protect against possible bleeding.
6. Digestion ceases so that blood may be diverted to muscles and brain.
7. Perspiration and saliva increase.
8. Bowel and bladder muscles loosen.
9. Muscles tense in preparation for strenuous activity.
10. The pupils dilate, allowing more light to enter the eye.
11. The endocrine system increases the production of hormones.

comparing the physical and psychological health of air traffic controllers and those in other jobs find no differences during the first three years of service. But after three years, air traffic controllers begin to report a significantly higher incidence of headaches, indigestion, chest pain, and ulcers. As their years of service increase, air traffic controllers report disproportionately higher levels of stress-related problems, including hypertension, peptic ulcers, and coronary heart disease.[46]

A common assumption is that top executives experience the most stressors. Stress-related illnesses, however, do not increase at higher organizational levels. A study of 270,000 male employees at a major corporation showed that the rate of coronary disease was lower at successively higher levels of the organization.[47] Top-level executives probably experience less stress than might be expected because they have greater control and predictability over their own situations than those in lower levels. Higher-level executives probably cause the stress felt by lower-level executives.

The adverse effects of a highly pressured work environment are largely a function of the inability to understand, predict, and control events at work. A study of 206 physicians, dentists, and nurses found that their ability to understand, predict, and control work situations was inversely related to perceived stress and positively related to job satisfaction. Employees feel a need to know what is going to happen and they want to have some control over the situation.[48]

STRESS MANAGEMENT PROGRAMS

Since stress cannot be eliminated from daily life, nor should it be, the solution is to manage it effectively. If it is managed effectively, stress can enhance rather than diminish individual productivity, interpersonal relationships, and a general zest for living. Numerous sources recommend how to benefit from stress and how to use it to improve the quality of life.[49]

The basic principle involved in managing stress is to terminate the stress response when it is fired inappropriately. The alarm reaction needs to be extinguished when it occurs at the wrong time. For pedestrians who see a car speeding toward them, the alarm reaction is appropriate, but the alarm reaction is not appropriate for motorists caught in heavy traffic. Several techniques have been proposed for controlling the stress response.

1. *Eliminate the stressor.* Sometimes the easiest way to manage stress is to avoid it either physically or psychologically. Some executives avoid the stress of traffic jams by being driven in chauffered cars. Supervisors avoid the stress of criticizing employees face-to-face by writing the criticism in a memo. Employees avoid stress by refusing promotions. Students avoid the stress of difficult exams by taking easy classes and not applying to graduate school. Some people avoid the stress of marital conflict by getting a divorce. Sometimes the stressor can be eliminated psychologically by changing the meaning of the situation. The objective here is to reassess the seriousness of the situation. Sometimes this is done by asking individuals to think about the worst consequences that could possibly occur and then decide how serious they really are. "If I don't get my research paper done, will I fail? No. Will my family abandon me? No. Will I flunk out of school? No. Will I fail this class? No, but I might get a poor grade. So how bad is that really? Well, I really want to go to graduate school and I need a good GPA. If I keep trying though, maybe I can redeem myself."

2. *Relaxation techniques*: Several techniques for managing stress involve some form of physical or mental relaxation. Some of these techniques have been advocated with the zeal and enthusiasm of new fads; however, the research evaluating their effectiveness is impressive. Two simple **relaxation techniques**, muscle massage and abdominal breathing, can effectively calm a person, yet go unnoticed during an angry phone call or a tense committee meeting. A muscle massage consists of slowly massaging the muscles of the neck, arms, back, legs, or feet, depending on the surroundings. Abdominal breathing means taking long, deep breaths, which causes the body to relax and counteracts the stress responses associated with an alarm reaction.

A third technique, transcendental meditation, uses a meaningless sound called a mantra to condition the subject to reduce the level of excitation and disorderly activity of the nervous system and to quiet the mind while maintaining alertness. Evidence evaluating transcendental meditation indicates that metabolic changes occur during meditation that move the body toward a deep state of rest.[50]

Biofeedback is another relaxation technique. It uses sophisticated equipment to observe some internal body processes and report this information in observable ways. Biofeedback equipment can monitor such events as muscular tension, skin temperature, heartbeat, blood pressure, and brain waves. This information is reported in the form of sounds, lights, or wavy lines on a graph, which helps the person to eventually control the stress responses.[51]

3. *Social support*: A social-support system refers to an interlocking network of people with whom an individual is able to interact to satisfy important human needs. A social-support system may include a wide variety of people, such as a spouse, family members, other relatives, friends, neighbors, a work supervisor, coworkers, members of self-help groups, religious or civic group associates, and health and welfare professionals. The most important form of social support is emotional support, which consists of providing empathy, love, caring, and trust. Research evidence indicates that the most important source of social support comes from the family unit, especially from one's spouse.[52] The death of a spouse is usually a traumatic experience that influences both the physical and mental health of the surviving partner. The trauma is much less severe, however, if individuals have other social supports that can help them, such as an understanding supervisor, coworkers who are willing to listen and empathize, and a counselor who can provide supportive, nondirective counseling.

4. *Physical exercise*: A carefully designed physical exercise program is not only an effective stress management technique, but also an important element in maintaining good mental and physical health. During a vigorous physical exercise routine, internal chemical changes occur that eliminate the tension that causes stress. At the same time, it improves physical conditioning, thereby making individuals better prepared to endure future stress. The benefits of physical exercise have encouraged companies to adopt a variety of physical exercise programs.

PHYSICAL HEALTH PROGRAMS

Rather than waiting for employees to get sick and then offering assistance, many companies are taking a preventive posture by trying to help employees avoid illness and accidents. These programs are referred to as **employee wellness programs** because they focus on trying to keep employees well. Some employee wellness programs include physical exams to assess employee health, and health education to teach proper dietary habits. Other wellness programs are designed to help employees stop smoking and to eliminate alcohol and drug use. Efforts to get employees to stop smoking have included both incentives in the form of sizable financial rewards and punishments in the form of threats of being fired for violating a no-smoking rule. The most important element in employee wellness programs, however, is a physical exercise program.

Exercise enthusiasts argue that the best technique for managing stress and maintaining good health is a regular program of physical exercise. Although these claims may be overstated, an enormous number of studies have shown that a well-designed physical exercise program can significantly improve both physical and emotional health.[53] Some of the major benefits are listed in Table 15.8.

Almost any form of physical activity can provide good exercise if it is done properly. Basketball, football, and tennis are good activities for staying in shape, but they are not recommended for getting into shape because of the potential harm from jarring and abrupt movements. A common mistake in exercising is overdoing and tearing the body down rather than building it up. Exercise should be systematic and regular and never too much at one time. People who have been inactive for several years need to start slowly when they begin exercising again.

Since 1970 **aerobic exercises** have gained in popularity.[54] Aerobic exercises refer to those that raise the heart and breathing rate to a training range and keep them within

---

TABLE 15.8   Benefits of regular exercise

General benefits to overall health

1. Increased strength and endurance
2. More efficient use of energy, even in mental tasks
3. Proper circulation is maintained
4. Improved grace, poise, and appearance
5. Improved posture and muscle tone
6. Reduction of chronic tiredness and tension
7. Improved weight control
8. Reduced aches, pains, and stiffness
9. Reduction in degenerative risk factors

Specific benefits to the heart

1. Resting heart rate is lowered, meaning that the heart does not have to work as hard to circulate blood to the body
2. Cardiac output is increased, meaning that under stress the heart is better able to distribute blood
3. Number of red blood cells is increased, meaning that more oxygen can be carried per pint of blood
4. Elasticity of the arteries is increased
5. Blood cholesterol level and triglyceride levels are lowered
6. Adrenal secretions in response to emotional stress are lowered
7. Lactic acid causing fatigue is more efficiently eliminated
8. Heart muscle is strengthened and additional blood vessels within it are formed

that range for a period of time. Some of the best aerobic exercises are jogging, cycling, swimming, and brisk walking, because they involve a constant level of activity. Aerobic exercise is recommended a minimum of three times each week for at least twelve to fifteen minutes each time. More exercise is better, but the gains are not large for exercise beyond forty-five minutes daily. One of the major arguments for aerobic exercise is that it reduces stress and prevents heart disease. Although some debate exists over the conclusiveness of the evidence, it is generally believed that regular vigorous exercise contributes to the prevention of heart disease and the reduction of stress for the reasons listed in Table 15.8.

Many executives recognize the value of physical exercise programs, and many large corporations have some form of in-house fitness facilities. The use of these facilities is sometimes limited to managers and executives, but increasingly the facilities are available to all members of the organization. A growing number of organizations encourage everyone to participate, and some organizations even offer financial incentives to participating employees. The Hospital Corporation of America gives its employees four cents a mile for cycling, sixteen cents per mile for walking or jogging, and sixty-four cents per mile for swimming.[55]

The American Foundation of Fitness Directors for Business and Industry is a professional society encouraging organizations to provide fitness centers. It collects information on the costs and benefits of fitness centers to show executives that such centers represent a wise financial decision. The costs are sometimes quite high. Kimberly Clark, for example, built a $2.3 million complex, complete with special health monitoring equipment and a staff of fifteen full-time health care personnel. Many organizations spend an average of $500 to $800 per year on each person who participates in a fitness program.[56]

Although the costs seem high, companies generally find that the benefits of an exercise program far outweigh the costs. Employees who participate in regular exercise programs are usually more productive, have less absenteeism, and have fewer medical expenses and disability claims than those employees who do not participate in a program. For example, a random sample of 900 employees of General Electric were assigned to participate in either an employee recreation program or an employee fitness program. The employees who participated in either program reported greater job satisfaction and averaged four fewer days of absenteeism per person.[57]

EMPLOYEE ASSISTANCE PROGRAMS

The performance of employees can be seriously impaired by personal problems. Fortunately, most personal problems are only temporary, and employees can solve them with their own resources and a little time. When problems get too big to handle, however, a sufferer usually needs professional help. The most difficult personal problems include alcoholism, drug abuse, marital conflict, and financial difficulties.

Many informal sources of help in the form of friends and acquaintances are usually available. However, well-meaning friends may do more harm than good. Supervisors and coworkers may be able to help with small problems by being sympathetic, listening, and providing emotional support. However, supervisors are not encouraged to get involved in counseling about serious personal problems.

▌ **HRM in Action**

J & J's Wellness Program Contributes to Profitability

Since 1979 Johnson & Johnson Company has provided voluntary corporate wellness programs for employees at selected locations. For example, at its headquarters office in New Bruswick, New Jersey, a well-equipped gymnasium is available to employees for regular workouts, healthy "heart foods" are served in the company cafeteria, and scales are available in the restrooms for employees to monitor their weight. The program, called Live for Life, is based on rather simple goals: to help employees stop smoking, eat more fruit and fewer fatty foods, exercise regularly, and buckle their seatbelts.

Most corporations believe wellness programs contribute to healthier employees although some of them question whether the benefits outweigh the costs. Johnson & Johnson decided to evaluate the financial impact of their program with the same rigor they use to test their products.

Johnson & Johnson's evaluation took three years and involved 8,000 employees. The experimental group consisted of 5,000 workers at three subsidiaries where the voluntary program was in operation. The control group consisted of workers at other facilities who did not have access to such a program. The company collected data on medical costs and productivity and compared the costs of operating the wellness program with the savings in reduced medical expenses.

During the first year, the wellness program cost more than it saved, but by the second year, the program broke even. In the third year, the program saved enough money to more than offset the losses of the first year. In 1989 Johnson & Johnson estimated that the cost of the program was about $200 per employee, while the savings were $378 per employee.

Although the program is voluntary, participating employees actively encourage the nonparticipants to become involved. The participants are expressly encouraged to drop hints to nonparticipants about losing weight, getting in shape, and giving up smoking. The encouragement is clearly not subtle, but the results of participation are too impressive to treat lightly. Health-care costs at Johnson & Johnson, which is self-insured, have increased about 310 percent over the past decade, but the same costs have increased about 460 percent in thirty similar companies. At least sixty other companies have modeled their wellness programs after Johnson & Johnson's program, which has been highly praised by outside experts.

Source: Neal Templin, "Johnson & Johnson 'Wellness' Program for Workers Shows Healthy Bottom Line," *Wall Street Journal*, May 21, 1990, p. B1.

Many organizations recognize the need for special programs to help employees with personal problems. These programs are typically called **employee assistance programs**. Earlier labels, such as "troubled employee program" or "alcohol rehabilitation program," were not very successful because of their negative implications. Troubled employees do not like to be called troubled employees. Over 65 percent of the *Fortune* 500 companies have employee assistance programs (EAPs) and the average annual cost is about $22 to $25 per employee for this benefit.[58]

Employee assistance programs are designed to provide professional assistance for employees with virtually any conceivable problem, even a small problem if it persists longer than it should. Some problems are handled by members of the employee assistance program staff. Problems that the staff is not equipped to handle are referred to professional services in the community. When an employee requests help, the person handling the case must be able to diagnose the real problem, decide whether it needs to be referred to an outside agency, and know which services are available in the community and how to make contact with them. Helping employees use community services is a simple process for a professional counselor who is familiar with the services. But getting personal help can be a bewildering nightmare for other individuals, especially those who are dependent on alcohol or drugs. Therefore, when employees know they can call one number for any kind of problem at any time of the day or night and receive professional, confidential help, they often are encouraged to request help before a situation becomes desperate. The characteristics of an effective employee assistance program are listed in Table 15.9.

Two methods are used to provide professional assistance. Many organizations operate their own employee assistance programs as part of their personnel services. Large organizations are able to afford a professional staff with counselors and psychiatric social workers. However, some organizations, both large and small, prefer to pay for the services of an outside professional organization of counselors to provide a program. The largest professional organization is Human Affairs, Inc., which was developed at Kennecott Copper Corporation in Utah and then offered to other companies. In 1990 the professional assistance of Human Affairs was available to 2.7 million employees in the United States and thirteen foreign countries.[59]

Employee assistance programs need to follow careful guidelines to avoid legal risks regarding privacy, malpractice, or coercion. The privacy of employees must be protected,

---

TABLE 15.9   Characteristics of an effective employee assistance program

1. The program must be staffed with competent people who know what services are available both in the company and in the community. The people must be sensitive to personal problems and able to relate empathetically.

2. The program must be accessible twenty-four hours a day, seven days a week, since behavioral problems do not fit a nine-to-five schedule.

3. The program should be advertised to all employees *and* their families so that everyone is aware of the program and knows an easy-to-remember telephone number that they can call. Problems are sometimes referred by family members, especially alcohol and drug-abuse problems.

4. The program should be open to all employees and family members. Some problems, such as marital conflicts or runaway children, require the involvement of other family members to solve them effectively.

5. Complete confidentiality must be maintained if an employee wants it that way. Knowing that their problems will be kept confidential, even from their families and supervisors, is important to many employees, especially those with drug and alcohol-abuse problems.

6. A staff member should be willing to meet wherever the employee or dependent would be most comfortable. Some people feel threatened by having to come to an office. Family counseling sometimes works best if it is done in the home.

including the confidentiality of information revealed to an EAP counselor. An EAP program also has a potential liability for malpractice if an employee sustains harm through an EAP counselor's negligence. Finally, a variety of unfair charges could be made if EAP services are used as an alternative to disciplinary action or as a step in the disciplinary process. Enrolling in an EAP may be part of the solution to an employee's problem, but an employee's misconduct should not be automatically excused because the employee agrees to accept help.[60]

Many companies using EAPs often wonder if their programs are cost-benefit effective. The value of EAPs was demonstrated in an evaluation of the Employee Counseling Services Program of the U.S. Department of Health and Human Services. Data from the program at several major sites were analyzed to determine the impact on job performance and where there was a reduction in the agency's administrative expenses. The analysis found that the program produced a 1:7 return after subtracting the actual costs of the program.[61] Other companies have also achieved significant financial returns from EAP programs. For example, Kimberly-Clark documented a 70 percent reduction in accidents among a sample of employees who participated in an EAP, and Phillips Petroleum calculated that its EAP netted more than $8 million per year in reduced accidents and sick leave and in higher productivity.[62]

An essential component for successful treatment is the desire to be helped. If employees are unwilling to admit they have a problem and resist help, efforts to assist are wasted. The futility of unwanted help is especially obvious with problems of alcohol and drug dependence. Alcoholics generally are unwilling to admit they have a drinking problem, and they tend to rationalize their conduct endlessly. For this reason, most organizations have learned that a very tough-minded approach is necessary to help alcoholic employees. If employees refuse to admit they have a drinking problem and claim they are only heavy social drinkers, the company insists that the employees undergo medical evaluations assessing their degree of dependence. If the reports confirm alcoholism, the employees are required to accept help in changing their lives or they are terminated. The company usually pays the cost of rehabilitation, which normally involves a two- to four-week stay in a hospital or special rehabilitation center. Supervisors are instructed to be encouraging and supportive of employees who are trying to reform but also to be strict and demanding in evaluating the performance of these employees.[63]

SUMMARY

A. Safety statistics are compiled and reported by three major organizations: the U.S. Public Health Service, the National Safety Council, and the Bureau of Labor Statistics.

B. Accidental deaths from industrial accidents have declined from 19,000 in 1930 to 10,600 in 1988.

C. In 1988, 1.8 million people were injured at work. However, there were fewer accidents at work than on the highways, at home, or at public activi-

ties. The cost of work accidents in 1988, $47.1 billion, was less than the $70.2 billion cost of motor vehicle accidents.

D. The standard measure used by the BLS to record accidents is the "incidence rate," which is based on recordable accidents per 100 worker years.

E. The Occupational Safety and Health Act of 1970 was designed to reduce hazards in the workplace by creating the Occupational Safety and

Health Administration (OSHA) and empowering it to establish safety and health standards, conduct inspections, issue citations, and propose penalties.

F. The evidence seems to suggest that OSHA has had some influence in reducing the number of accidents, but the reduction is somewhat disappointing relative to the money, time, and effort that have gone into it.

G. Effective safety programs require active leadership by top management, clearly assigned safety responsibilities, the identification and control of hazards, employee and supervisor training, accurate record keeping of safety and health activities, provisions for first aid and medical assistance, and active awareness and participation by employees.

H. Toxic substances are poisonous materials. OSHA has developed strict standards regulating the use of certain substances such as lead, carbon monoxide, and benzene. However, all substances, even water and vitamins necessary for health, can be toxic if too much of them is taken into the body. Toxicology, the study of toxic substances, attempts to identify the levels at which there are no adverse effects. The upper limit of a toxic substance at which there is still no adverse effect is called the toxicity threshold.

I. Anxiety and depression are two of the major mental illnesses observed in the workplace. Anxiety refers to an excessive state of tension or fear that is general and not associated with a specific problem. Depression refers to a mood of gloom and dejection that creates a general state of unhappiness and may lead to suicide.

J. Burnout is the inability to handle continued stress on the job and is usually associated with people in the helping professions, such as nurses, counselors, psychiatrists, and social workers. Burnout is similar to the boredom of blue-collar workers who do not find their work meaningful.

K. Stress is a physiological reaction to stressors in the environment. Stress can result from *both* pleasant and unpleasant experiences. The three stages of stress are the alarm stage, the resistance stage, and the exhaustion stage. During the alarm stage, the body's endocrine system prepares it for fight or flight reactions. If there is a physical danger, this reaction is desirable. But most stress situations do not call for a vigorous physical effort, and the body therefore responds to a false alarm. If too many false alarms occur, the body stays in a chronic state of alarm, and vital organs may be damaged.

L. The recommended methods for managing stress include eliminating the stressors, relaxation techniques, social support, and physical exercise.

M. Studies show that physical exercise not only helps to reduce stress, but also improves physical health and increases job satisfaction and productivity. Consequently, many companies have developed physical exercise programs for their employees. The evidence indicates that these exercise programs are cost-benefit effective.

N. Employee assistance programs provide a source of help for employees with personal problems. Typical problems are alcoholism, drug use, financial indebtedness, and marital conflict. Effective programs should be staffed with competent professionals who can provide counsel or refer employees to community services. Such programs should be available to all employees and family members at all times of the day or night, and the programs must be confidential.

QUESTIONS

1. In 1985 the number of occupational fatalities was 11,500 according to the National Safety Council, but only 3,750 according to the Bureau of Labor Statistics. Between these two extremes is the National Institute for Occupational Safety and Health's report of 6,442 occupational fatalities. The National Safety Council estimates (rounded) are based on data obtained from the National Center for Health Statistics, state industrial commissions, state departments of health, actual death certificates, and other reputable sources. The BLS data come from the safety reports of companies with eleven or more employees and a random probability sample of 280,000 employers nationally. The NIOSH data come from the coded death certificates. What factors could cause such large discrepancies between these statistics?

2. Since off-the-job accidents are so costly to employers, should employers try to reduce such accidents or influence what employees do on their own time? Why or why not?

3. Should OSHA focus more of its efforts on enforcement—inspections, citations, and fines—or on consultation? Why?

4. What would you say to an employer who claims that the OSHA regulations for the use of chemicals are too complex to understand and therefore is unwilling to comply with the act?

5. Should OSHA have the power to issue citations and propose fines, or should all penalties be handled by the Justice Department and the civil courts? Provide reasons for your opinion.

6. How much of a reduction in illnesses and injuries should be expected before the time, effort, and money spent by OSHA are considered justified?

7. Some companies, such as du Pont, offer incentives for safety. What would likely happen as the incentives for safety increased from minimal to very substantial rewards?

8. Do you think restricting women who are in their childbearing years from certain jobs, such as handling chemicals, is legitimate? Why or why not?

9. What are the typical situations in a student's life that can create alarm reactions?

10. What are the advantages and disadvantages of different stress management techniques?

11. Do you think it is legitimate for a company to become involved in employees' personal lives if the purpose is to help them solve their personal problems or to improve their mental health? Why or why not?

12. What would you do if one of your subordinates had a serious drinking problem but refused to admit it, even though it strongly influenced his or her performance on the job?

KEY TERMS

Aerobic exercise: Physical exercise that raises the heart rate to a training level and keeps it there for a period of time—preferably at least twelve to fifteen minutes daily.

Alarm reaction: The first stage of stress in which the body prepares for a fight or flight response by activating the endocrine system.

Biofeedback: The use of electronic monitoring equipment to measure internal body functions of which individuals are normally unaware, such as blood pressure and muscle tension. Being able to observe these functions helps individuals to control them.

Burnout: The inability to handle continued stress on the job and the feelings of psychological exhaustion.

Distress: Unpleasant or disease-producing stress that is destructive to physical and mental well-being.

Employee assistance program: A program usually operated by the human resource department with the h of social service agencies in the community that is designed to help employees with their personal problems, particularly alcoholism, drug abuse, financial indebtedness, and marital conflict.

Employee wellness programs: Programs aimed at helping employees stay healthy by encouraging them to obtain the proper rest, exercise, and nutrition, and to avoid smoking, alcohol, and drug abuse.

Epidemiology: The study of diseases in the environment and of conditions that may cause widespread health problems.

Eustress: Pleasant or curative stress that contributes to interest, enthusiasm, and a zest for living.

Incidence rate: Refers to a recordable case of occupational injury or illness based on cases per 100 worker years.

$$\text{Incidence rate} = \frac{N}{EH} \times 200,000$$

N = a) Total recordable cases
b) Cases involving days away from work and deaths
c) Days away from work
d) Total lost workdays

EH = Total employee hours

200,000 = Equivalent of 100 full-time employees, each working fifty weeks of forty hours per week

No-adverse-effect level: The highest dose of a material or exposure to it that causes no ill effects.

OSHA (Occupational Safety and Health Administration): Enforces the Occupational Safety and Health Act of 1970.

Recordable cases: Cases in which there was an occupational injury or illness, including death, but not including first-aid cases consisting of one-time treatment and subsequent observation of minor scratches, cuts, burns, or splinters.

Relaxation techniques: Techniques that use relaxation to reverse the alarm reaction and avoid stress, such as abdominal breathing, transcendental meditation, and biofeedback.

Stress: The physiological response of the body to a stressor. The initial stage is the alarm reaction, which readies the body to make an immediate response. The second stage attempts to return the body to a state of balance. The third stage, exhaustion, occurs when the body experiences repeated alarm reactions.

Toxicity threshold: The lowest dose level at which toxic effects can be demonstrated.

Toxicology: The study of poisonous materials and the exposure thresholds of each.

C O N C L U D I N G   C A S E

Loyalty or Carelessness?

Part I: The Accident

The Mecca Company was in the middle of a contest to boost production. Don Miner's and Sal Scott's departments had been running nip and tuck, with Don's in the lead. However, last week Don had some machine downtime, and it looked as though his department might finish behind schedule and be pushed out of first place. There was some good-natured heckling about it between departments, and the machine operators in Don's department decided they were not going to give up without a struggle. In fact, that was obvious when Don arrived at the plant on Monday morning. He was about fifteen minutes early, but most of his people were already at their machines waiting for the starting bell.

That's the way it went all week. Don's people worked at peak performance, and by

Thursday, it looked as if they had a good chance of being on top again.

Then, Thursday afternoon, one of the machines jammed. The operator, Tim Hurley, one of Don's best workers, tried to save time by fixing it himself. He reached in to free the jammed part, and one of his fingers was severely gashed. Another worker got the first-aid kit and fixed a temporary bandage. Then Don rushed Tim to the infirmary.

"How is he?" the others asked when Don returned.

"The nurse did what he could and sent Tim to the hospital," Don answered.

"Tim really meant it when he said we'd lose over his dead body," one of the workers said admiringly. Several others made similar comments, and Don realized that Tim was being regarded as some kind of hero by his coworkers.

What Tim did was stupid, Don thought, and a violation of a basic safety rule. What troubled Don the most, however, was the admiration shown by other members of the group for Tim's actions.

What should Don do to change the workers' attitudes about Tim's injury? Think about it, and then compare your answer to what actually happened.

Part II: The Action Taken

Don realized that Tim had taken the chance of reaching into the machine out of loyalty to the department. And, of course, the other workers realized this too. But Don felt that he couldn't condone letting a man risk his hands to get the work done. Don believed that if he didn't take some action, the department members might feel that he approved of taking a chance now and then.

When Tim came back to work, his hand still bandaged, Don waited until the other machinists had gathered to welcome him back. Don then walked over and said, "Glad to see you up and around."

"This is nothing," Tim said, obviously proud of his wound. "It won't keep me from doing my job."

"It's more serious than you think," said Don. "And I'm afraid it *is* going to keep you from doing your job because I'm suspending you for two days for violating safety rules."

The department members were stunned for a second, and then began to protest loudly.

"Knock it off," Don ordered. "You had all better get one thing straight. No one in this department can violate safety rules and get away with it, no matter what the reason. Everybody knows it's against the rules to reach into a jammed machine while the power is on."

Then Don turned to Tim. "Maybe you thought you could save some time so we could keep producing and get ahead again. But look what really happened. I lost you and the use of your machine for several days. As a result, we not only failed to get back on schedule, we'll end up behind for a second month. So, you see, you could have lost your entire hand for nothing."

Questions:

1. Do you think Don handled this situation properly?
2. What would you have done differently?

NOTES

1. ASPA-BNA Survey No. 52. "Personnel Activities, Budgets, and Staffs: 1987–88 " (September 1, 1988).

2. The Occupational Safety and Health Act of 1970, Section (2)(b).

3. *Accident Facts* is published annually by the National Safety Council, 444 North Michigan, Chicago, Ill. 60611.

4. The statistics in this section are from *Accident Facts, 1989 Edition* (Chicago: National Safety Council, 1989).

5. Olivia S. Mitchell, "The Relation of Age to Workplace Injuries," *Monthly Labor Review* 11 (July 1988): 8–13.

6. When death and injury rates of workers are examined both on the job and off the job, the rates are higher at home than at work. See *Accident Facts, 1989 Edition*, p. 36.

7. The statistics in this section are from *Accident Facts, 1989 Edition*.

8. Martin E. Personick and Katherine Taylor-Shirley, "Profiles in Safety and Health: Occupational Hazards of Meatpacking," Monthly Labor Review 112 (January 1989): 3–9.

9. Amy Hancock Boyd and Gary D. Herrin, "A Minimum Cost Sequential Test to Monitor Injury Incidents on an Operation," *IIE Transactions* 20 (September 1988): 269–79.

10. Each year the Office of the Federal Register publishes all current regulations and standards in the Code of Federal Regulations (CFR). OSHA's regulations are collected in Title 29 of the CFR, Part 1900–1999.

11. *Marshall* v. *Barlow's Inc.* (1978).

12. Statements of Ray Marshall, secretary of labor (April 1, 1980) and Basil Whiting, deputy assistant secretary of labor for occupational safety and health (March 21, 1980) before the Committee on Labor and Human Resources, U.S. Senate; statement of Eula Bingham, assistant secretary of labor for occupational safety and health before the Subcommittee on Health and Safety, House of Representatives (September 16, 1980).

13. Robert S. Smith, "The Impact of OSHA Inspections on Manufacturing Injury Rates," *Journal of Human Resources* 14, no. 2 (Spring 1979): 145–70.

14. W. Kip Viscusi, "The Impact of Occupational Safety and Health Regulation, 1973–1983," *Rand Journal of Economics* 17 (Winter 1986): 567–80.

15. *OSHA Handbook for Small Businesses* (Washington, D.C.: U.S. Department of Labor, OSHA 2209, rev. 1979).

16. Robert Reid, "Steel Producers—Standouts in Foot Protection," *Occupational Hazards* 48 (February 1986): 45–48.

17. Joseph P. Ryan, "Power Press Safeguarding: A Human Factors Perspective," *Professional Safety* 32 (August 1987): 23–26.

18. William W. Allison, "Safety Statistics," *Professional Safety* 33 (October 1988): 18–20.

19. William W. Eisenberg and Helen McDonald, "Evaluating Workplace Injury and Illness Records: Testing a Procedure," *Monthly Labor Review* 111 (April 1988): 58–60.

20. Nicole Dedobbeleer and Pearl German, "Safety Practices in Construction Industry," *Professional Safety* 34 (January 1989): 33–38.

21. J. Komski, K. D. Barwick, and L. R. Scott, "A Behavioral Approach to Occupational Safety: Pinpointing and Reinforcing Safe Performance in a Food Manufacturing Plant," *Journal of Applied Psychology* 63 (1978): 434–45.

22. Philip Goldberg, *Executive Health* (New York: McGraw-Hill, 1978).

23. *Employee Benefits 1983* (Washington D.C.: United States Chamber of Commerce, 1984), p. 13.

24. Statement of Basil Whiting, 30.

25. *Who Protects our Health and Environment?* (Dow Chemical Company, 1980).

26. Ibid., p. 8.

27. D. Roose, "Asia's Silicon Valley: Women in Hazardous Occupations," *Nation* 229 (August 25, 1979): 142–43; J. W. Singer, "Fertility and the Workplace," *Environment* 22 (December 1980), 5ff; A Rosenfeld, "Fertility May Be Hazardous to Your Job," *Saturday Review* 6 (April 28, 1979): 12–13; P. Carlyle-Gordge, "Jobs that Are Rated PG: Refusal to Employ Women of Childbearing Age," *Macleans* 92 (April 2, 1979): 16–18.

28. "Medical Sleuths: Fear of Toxic Materials Creates More Demand for Epidemiologists," *Wall Street Journal*, April 14, 1981, p. 1.

29. For a summary and state-by-state comparison, see *USA Today*, February 1990; A6.

30. W. L. Weiss, "Can You Afford to Hire Smokers?" *The Personnel Administrator* 26 (May 1981): 71–78; W. L. Weiss, "Profits up in Smoke," *Personnel Journal* (March 1981): 60; Wayne F. Cascio, *Costing Human Resources: The Financial Impact of Behavior in Organizations* (Boston: Kent, 1982), Chapter 4; U.S. Department of Health and Human Services, *The Health Consequences of Involuntary Smoking: A Report of the Surgeon General*, Public Health Service Centers for Disease Control, 1986.

31. ASPA-BNA Survey No. 50, "Smoking in the Workplace" (June 12, 1986); ASPA-BNA Survey No. 51, "Smoking in the Workplace: 1987 Update" (November 26, 1987).

32. George Munchus III, "An Update on Smoking: Employees' Rights and Employers' Responsibilities," *Personnel* 64 (August 1987): 46–50.

33. Cited by Lawrence Z. Lorber and J. Robert Kirk, *Fear Itself: A Legal and Personnel Analysis of Drug Testing, AIDS, Secondary Smoke and VDT's* (Alexandria, Va.: ASPA Foundation, 1987), p. 41.

34. *BNA Special Report: Where There's Smoke: Problems and Policies Concerning Smoking in the Workplace*, 2nd edition (Bureau of National Affairs, 1987); David S. Hames, "Key Concerns in Shaping a Company Smoking Policy," *Employee Relations Law Journal* 14 (Autumn 1988): 223–37.

35. Cited by Lawrence Z. Lorber and J. Robert Kirk, *Fear Itself: A Legal and Personnel Analysis of Drug Testing, AIDS, Secondary Smoke, VTDs* (op. cit.): 43–47.

36. Ella P. Gardner, Stephen R. Ruth, and Barry Render, "Job Stress and the VTD Clerical Worker," *Human Systems Management* 7, no. 4 (1988): 359–65; David Kirkpatrick, "How Safe Are Video Terminals?" *Fortune* 118 (August 29, 1988): 66–71.

37. Ibid., 27.

38. *Bonales, et al v. City and County of San Francisco, Department of Public Health, California Labor Commissioner* (September 9, 1985); *BNA Daily Labor Report* (September 23, 1985, at A-6).

39. *The Schoolboard of Nassau County, Florida v. Arline*, 94 L.E.d.2d 307 (March 3, 1987).

40. Vernin L. Grose, "Coping with Boredom in the Cockpit Before it's too Late," *Risk Management* 36 (August 1988): 30–35.

41. Amos Drory and Boas Shamir, "Effects of Organizational and Life Variables on Job Satisfaction and Burnout," *Group and Organization Studies* 13 (December 1988): 441–55; Roger R. Hock, "Professional Burnout Among Public School Teachers," *Public Personnel Management* 17 (Summer 1988): 167–89.

42. Anna-Maria Garden, "Depersonalization: A Valid Dimension of Burnout?" *Human Relations* 40 (September 1987): 545–55; Jocelyn A. Handy, "Theoretical and Methodological Problems within Occupation Stress and Burnout Research," *Human Relations* 41 (May 1988): 351–69.

43. Mary A. Kiely, "Theory A May Reduce Turnover," *Nursing Management* 20 (March 1989): 15–20; Michael P. Leiter and Christina Maslach, "The Impact of Interpersonal Environment on Burnout and Organizational Commitment," *Journal of Organizational Behavior* (October 1988): 297–308; Joseph Seltzer and Rita E. Numerof, "Supervisory Leadership and Subordinate Burnout," *Academy of Management Journal* 31 (June 1988): 439–46.

44. Philip Goldberg, *Executive Health* 43; Brent Q. Hafen, *Alcohol: The Crutch that Cripples* (St. Paul, Minn.: West, 1977); Brent Q. Hafen and Brenda Peterson, *Medicines and Drugs: Problems and Risks, Use and Abuse, 2nd ed.* (Philadelphia: Lea and Febiger, 1978).

45. Hans Selye, *The Stress of Life* (New York: McGraw-Hill, 1956, 1976); Hans Selye, *Stress Without Distress* (New York: Lippincott, 1974).

46. J. D. Dougherty, D. K. Trites, and J. R. Dille, "Self-reported Stress-related Symptoms among Air Traffic Control Specialists (ATCS) and Non-ATCS Personnel," *Aerospace Medicine* 36 (1966): 956–60; J. H. Crump, "Review of Stress in Air Traffic Control: Its Measurement and Effects," *Aviation, Space, and Environmental Medicine* 50 (March 1979): 243–48.

47. Goldberg, *Executive Health* 29; Stanley J. Modic, "Surviving Burnout: The Malady of Our Age," *Industry Week* 238 (February 20, 1989): 28–34.

48. Susan Ashford, "Individual Strategies for Coping with Stress during Organizational Transitions," *Journal of Applied Behavioral Science* 24 (1988): 19–36; Eli Glogow, "Burnout and Locus of Control," *Public Personnel Management* 15 (Spring 1986): 79–83; Lois E. Tetrick and James M. LaRocco, "Understanding, Prediction, and Control as Moderators of the Relationship between Perceived Stress, Satisfaction, and Psychological Well-being," *Journal of Applied Psychology* 72 (November 1987): 538–43.

49. Michael T. Matteson and John M. Ivancevich, "Individual Stress Management Interventions: Evaluation of Techniques," *Journal of Managerial Psychology* 2 (1987): 24–30; Lawrence R. Murphy, "A Review of Organizational Stress Management Research: Methodological Considerations," *Journal of Organizational Behavior Management* 8 (Fall/Winter 1986): 215–227.

50. Robert Schneider, Wendy Cavanaugh, and Shirley Boncheff, "Cost Reductions through Better Health," *Business and Health* 4 (November 1986): 39–42.

51. Barbara B. Brown, *Stress and the Art of Biofeedback* (New York: Harper, 1977).

52. James S. House, *Work Stress and Social Support* (Reading, Mass.: Addison-Wesley, 1981); Marcelline R. Fusilier, Daniel C. Ganster, and Bronston T. Mayes, "Effects of Social Support, Role Stress, and Locus of Control on Health," *Journal of Management* 13 (Fall 1987): 517–28; Srinika Jayaratne, David Himle, and Wayne A. Chess, "Dealing with Work Stress and Strain: Is the Perception of Support More Important than its Use?" *Journal of Applied Behavioral Science* 24 (1988): 191–202.

53. Nealia S. Bruning and David R. Frew, "Effects of Exercise, Relaxation, and Management Skills Training on Physiological Stress Indicators: A Field Experiment," *Journal of Applied Psychology* 72 (November 1987): 515–21; Loren E. Falkenberg, "Employee Fitness Programs: Their Impact on the Employee and the Organization," *Academy of Management Review* 12 (July 1987): 511–22.

54. Kenneth H. Cooper, *The Aerobics Way* (New York: Lippincott, 1977).

55. David Clutterbuck, "Executive Fitness Aids Corporate Health," *International Management* 35 (February 1980): 18–22; Geoffrey Broad, "Shaping Up Under Japanese Management," *Personnel Management* 19 (August 1987): 26–29.

56. Dale Feuer, "Wellness Programs: How do they shape up?" *Training* (April 1986): 25–28; Jack Martin, "The New Business Boom—Employee Fitness," *Nation's Business* 66 (February 1978): 68–73.

57. Kimberly J. Shinew and John C. Crossley, "A Comparison of Employee Recreation and Fitness Program Benefits," *Employee Benefits Journal* 13 (December 1988): 20–23.

58. Rick Lee, "The Evolution of Managed Mental Health Care," *Compensation and Benefits Management* 5 (Autumn 1988): 61–66; Patti Watts, "Effective Employee Assistance Hinges on Trained Managers," *Management Review* 77 (January 1988): 11–12.

59. "He Cures Kennecott's People Problems," *Business Week* (April 15, 1972); personal correspondence from Otto F. Jones, president of Human Affairs, Inc., 5801 Hillside Drive, Murray, UT 84107.

60. John L. Monroe, Jr., "Employee Assistance Programs—The Legal Issues," *Employment Relations Today* 15 (Autumn 1988): 239–43.

61. Dale A. Masi and Michelle E. Goff, "The Evaluation of Employee Assistance Programs," *Public Personnel Management* 16 (Winter 1987): 323–27.

62. James T. Wrich, "Beyond Testing: Coping with Drugs at Work," *Harvard Business Review* 66 (January/February 1988): 120–30.

63. Jerry Bell and Pat Bell, "Alcohol in the Workplace," *Professional Safety* 34 (February 1989): 11–15; Dale A. Masi and Seymour J. Friedland, "EAP Actions and Options," *Personnel Journal* 67 (June 1988): 61–67; Rich Walters, "Chemical Abuse and the Employer," *Management Quarterly* 28 (Fall 1987): 19–26.

APPENDIX A: PERSONNEL RESEARCH

Personnel Research

Students and managers are often frightened by the thought of personnel research because it raises the specter of statistics, hypothesis testing, and difficult reading. Although it is true that some personnel research involves theory building, hypothesis testing, and statistical analysis, most personnel research tries to answer simple questions that managers often face.

> What are the best schools for recruiting engineers?
>
> Is our selection process identifying the best applicants?
>
> Why are we losing our best people?
>
> Is our new employee orientation program better than the old one?

Because it collects extensive data, the human resource department can contribute to better management decisions through an effective personnel research program. Most human resource departments maintain extensive files of information on attendance, job satisfaction, job descriptions, compensation programs, training needs, and performance evaluations. A careful analysis of this information can help managers identify the strengths and weaknesses of the organization and assess the effectiveness of a variety of organizational problems. By analyzing this information, managers can diagnose organizational problems, such as the effectiveness of a recruiting strategy, the validity of a selection procedure, the value of an incentive compensation program, the cause of increased grievance rates, or whether safety training is reducing accidents.

SOURCES OF INFORMATION An important part of effective personnel research is having good data to analyze. The ideal circumstance is to have data that specifically measure each variable being considered. For example, to know how something influences job satisfaction, direct measures of job satisfaction would yield the most specific data. Unfortunately, direct job-satisfaction measures are often not available, so researchers may be forced to

rely on indirect measures, such as absenteeism, turnover, or grievance rates. These variables are related to job satisfaction but only indirectly. In conducting personnel research, four kinds of data may be available: archive data, observations, interviews, and questionnaires.

1. *Archive data*: Archive data refer to the kinds of information contained in the personnel files. Every organization is required by law to accurately record certain information, and this record-keeping responsibility is typically delegated to the human resource department. For example, the EEOC says human resource managers have the responsibility to assure nondiscrimination in employment. The Uniform Guidelines on Employee Selection Procedures require employers to maintain and have available for inspection data showing whether their recruitment and placement practices are fair. Likewise, the Fair Labor Standards Act requires employers to maintain accurate records of the hours worked by employees. Employers have a legal responsibility to maintain accurate archival data.

Sometimes this information is referred to as *unobtrusive measures*, because the nature of the data and the way they are obtained do not influence how employees behave. The advantages of using archive data are that they already exist without having to be collected and they may cover a fairly lengthy historical period, thereby providing a long-term perspective. Some of the types of information that are frequently available as archive data are shown in Table A.1.

2. *Observations*: Some research questions can be answered only by observing the behavior of employees. For example, the best method of assessing a job-redesign program is to observe a work group and determine whether the work flows smoothly, with cooperative effort. The disadvantage of observations is that they are an intrusive type of measure—the process of observing an employee's performance often causes the employee to behave differently. (This phenomenon is called the "Hawthorne Effect" after the Hawthorne studies, 1924–1934.) Most employees tend to work faster when they know they are being observed and their productivity is

TABLE A.1	Sources of archival data in personnel files	
Accident records		Interview records
Affirmative action records		Job descriptions
Application forms		Job specifications
Arbitration awards		Medical records
Attitude surveys		Payroll records
Disciplinary records		Performance evaluations
Exit interviews		Salary-increase records
Grievance reports		Test scores
Human resource information system		Training records
Insurance records		

being measured. However, other employees intentionally alter their performance to create meaningless data.

3. *Interviews:* Interviews are an effective way to learn how employees feel about an issue and to understand their personal opinions. The advantage of an interview is that it is a rich source of data collection in the sense that it provides information about a broad range of topics, rather than just the narrow agenda of an interviewer. The major disadvantage of interviews is that they are time consuming and only a limited number of people can be interviewed.

A method for making interviews more useful is through focus groups, which are group interviews with a moderator and eight to twelve people who share a common interest. Effective focus groups require the moderator to present a precise problem statement and then listen unobtrusively to the group discussion. These group discussions can provide qualitatively different information than individual interviews because the presence of other group members creates greater anonymity, candor, insight, and breadth of analysis.

4. *Questionnaires:* A carefully developed questionnaire can be administered to a large sample of employees, and the information can be conveniently analyzed and interpreted. The popularity of questionnaire data for research purposes is largely attributed to the ease of administration and convenience of analysis. However, the disadvantages of questionnaires are that they are time consuming

to develop and the data can only answer the specific questions in the questionnaire. If all the relevant issues are not covered in the questionnaire, the information obtained will be inadequate and possibly even misleading. The best solution to this dilemma is to interview a sample of workers to identify the relevant issues and then to use the information from these interviews to construct a questionnaire.

RESEARCH METHODS   A variety of research methods are available for diagnosing problems and answering research questions. The choice of a research method is sometimes dictated by the constraints of the situation. However, some methods are clearly superior to others and should be preferred when the circumstances allow. Four of the most popular research methods are case study, field survey, field experiment, and laboratory experiment.

1. *Case study:* A case study is often referred to as an observational research method since it involves observing an event and then trying to assess and interpret what happened. Researchers who utilize case studies attempt to keep a careful, ongoing record of the events they observe, either as they occur or as soon as possible thereafter, to minimize reliance on memory. While they are observing, researchers need to be careful to avoid influencing the event they are observing or allowing their personal biases to guide their observations.

651

Although the case study is a popular method of analyzing a wide variety of problems, it is a poor research design because of inadequate experimental controls. A case study does not eliminate competing explanations of the results; the conclusions of the researcher depend entirely upon the researcher's ability to make careful observations.

2. *Field survey:* A field survey consists of gathering information from employees who are working in their natural, everyday environment. A field survey is sometimes called a correlational research method since most field surveys attempt to identify variables that are related. For example, a study of the relationship between age and accidents would be a correlational study in which the age of employees is correlated with the frequency of recordable accidents. A positive correlation coefficient would indicate that older workers tend to have more accidents, while a negative correlation coefficient would imply just the opposite. A correlation coefficient close to zero would indicate that age was not related to accidents. Although correlational studies are useful for showing relationships, they do not demonstrate causality. A significant correlation coefficient between age and accidents, for example, does not necessarily mean that age causes people to have more accidents or that having more accidents causes people to grow older.

3. *Field experiment:* A field experiment is similar to a field survey to the extent that the data are collected from employees working in their natural environment. However, a field experiment involves manipulating or altering one variable (the independent variable) and analyzing its effects on other variables (the dependent variables). The advantage of a field experiment over a field survey is that it allows researchers to infer causality. For example, a field experiment would be an appropriate methodology for testing whether financial incentives cause employees to work more safely. To illustrate, a group of workers could be randomly divided into three groups and offered incentives of one dollar, twenty-five cents, or nothing for every day without a recordable accident. If the group that received no incentive had the most accidents and the group receiving one dollar per day had the fewest accidents, a researcher could conclude that financial incentives influence safety behavior.

4. *Laboratory experiments:* The most tightly controlled research design is the laboratory experiment, in which individuals are brought into a research laboratory and asked to participate in a standardized test. Some assessment-center activities are essentially laboratory experiments, since the participants are placed in an artificial situation where the activities and the environment are standardized for all participants. Although laboratory experiments are the most rigorous research design and allow researchers to make more precise statements of causality, they are not always the best research design. An organizational environment cannot be accurately reproduced in an experimental laboratory; therefore, the artificial nature of the environment and the difficulty of using this method to study certain problems do not make it universally superior.

RESEARCH DESIGN   Four of the most popular research designs were described at the end of Chapter 9 (see Figure 9.2). Two of these designs, the case study (or posttest-only design) and the pretest-posttest comparison, are not good experimental designs because they fail to control for competing explanations of the results. However, the other two designs, the pretest-posttest control group design and the Solomon four-group design, are considered excellent research designs not only for evaluating the effectiveness of a training program but also for answering other research questions. In addition to these two designs, there are other good designs available to personnel researchers, such as the posttest-only control group design, the time-series design, and the separate-sample pretest-posttest control group design. These designs are illustrated in Figure A.1.

1. *Posttest-only control group design:* The posttest-only control group design is an excellent experimental design because it allows a researcher to eliminate most competing explanations for the experimental results. This design involves randomly dividing the sample of people into two groups and giving the experimental treatment to only one group. Neither of the groups receives a pretest, which explains why this design is called the posttest-only design. After one group receives the ex-

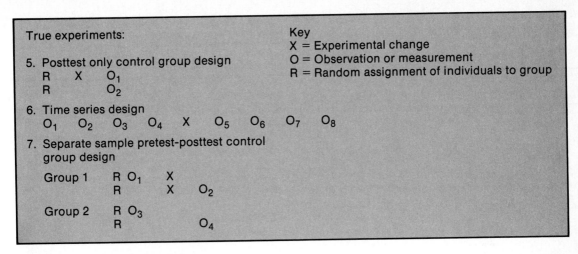

FIGURE A.1 Additional research designs.

perimental treatment, both groups are evaluated to see if the treatment had a significant impact.

This design is ideal when the experimental treatment and the posttest measurement can be administered to employees as a single, natural package or where a pretest would be awkward. Suppose you wanted to know whether a different set of instructions would motivate employees to provide more thorough data on a health survey. A random sample of employees could be identified and given a modified form with the revised instructions. If the data they provided were significantly more complete than the group that randomly received the original form, then a researcher could safely conclude that the revised instructions had a significant impact.

2. *Time-series design:* A time-series design consists of periodically measuring something and introducing an experimental change during this series of measures. If the measures that are taken after the experimental change are significantly different than the earlier measures, there is some reason to believe that the experimental change had a significant impact. For example, if the average absenteeism has fluctuated between 7 and 10 percent for the past six months, but immediately drops to a range of 2 to 4 percent for a three-month period during which a special attendance-award program is operating, then it is reasonable to conclude that the

award program probably reduced absenteeism. The major disadvantage of a time-series design is that in the absence of a control group it is not possible to know for certain that the change did not result from some outside historical factor that occurred at the same time. For example, the reduced absenteeism could have resulted from the threat of a layoff rumored about the same time the attendance program was initiated. Greater certainty can be attached to the impact of the attendance-award program if it can be systematically started and stopped two or three times to see if absenteeism is lower when the program is operating and higher when it is not.

3. *Separate sample pretest-posttest control group design:* Sometimes employees work together in groups and it is not possible to introduce an experimental change only to a randomly selected part of a group. Employees can be measured or observed individually, but the experimental change must be administered to the entire group. In this situation, the separate sample pretest-posttest control group design is an effective and convenient research design. This design utilizes two existing groups that may not be equivalent. Only one group receives the experimental change. A randomly selected part of each group is pretested and the others are posttested. If the pretest/posttest differences for the group that received the experimental treatment are different than the pretest/posttest change in the other group, there is some reason to believe that the experimental change had a significant effect. This design would be useful for studying such things as the effects of music on productivity, the effects of a safety-training film on attitudes toward OSHA, or the effects of a new communication system on productivity.

The time-series design and the separate sample pretest-posttest control group design are called quasi-experimental designs because they occur in a natural setting where you can introduce an experi-mental change and collect data, but you do not have complete control over the experimental setting. Quasi-experimental designs are recommended when better designs are not feasible, such as when subjects cannot be randomly assigned to groups or when you have difficulty scheduling when and to whom the experimental change will be adminis-tered. Although quasi-experimental designs are not as conclusive as other experimental designs, they are, nevertheless, capable of indicating whether an experimental change has a significant impact.

APPENDIX B: PROFESSIONAL PERSONNEL ASSOCIATIONS

Date founded	1990 Membership	Name
1923	75,000	American Management Association (AMA) 135 W. 50th Street New York, NY 10020
1948	40,000	Society for Human Resource Management (SHRM) 606 N. Washington Street Alexandria, VA 22314
1913	26,000	International Association of Personnel in Employment Security (IAPES) 1801 Louisville Road Frankfort, KY 40601
1944	23,000	American Society for Training and Development (ASTD) 1630 Duke Street Alexandria, VA 22314
1924	7,500	American College Personnel Association 5999 Stevenson Avenue Alexandria, VA 22314
1936	7,200	Academy of Management P.O. Drawer KZ Mississippi State University Mississippi St, MS 39762
1973	5,122	International Personnel Management Association (IPMA) 1637 Duke Street Alexandria, VA 22314
1975	5,000	Human Resource Certification Institute (HRCI) 606 N. Washington Street Alexandria, VA 22314
1946	4,000	College and University Personnel Association (CUPA) 1233 20th Street N.W., Suite 503 Washington, D.C. 20036
1964	2,550	American Society for Hospital Personnel Administration (ASHPA) 840 N. Lake Shore Drive Chicago, IL 60611
1950	1,900	International Association for Personnel Women (IAPW) 5820 Wilshire Boulevard, Suite 500 Los Angeles, CA 90036
1940	1,250	American Association of School Personnel Administrators 825 Lurline Drive Foster City, CA 94404

Source: Gayle Research Company, *Encyclopedia of Associations* (Detroit, Mich.: Booktower Publishing Company, 1990).

APPENDIX C: ORGANIZATIONS RELATED TO PERSONNEL AND HUMAN RESOURCE MANAGEMENT

Administrative Management Society
2360 Maryland Rd.
Willow Grove, PA 19090
(215) 659-4300

AFL-CIO
815 16th St. NW
Washington, DC 20006
(202) 637-5010

American Arbitration Association
140 W. 51st St.
New York, NY 10020
(212) 484-4800

American Compensation Association
P.O. Box 1176
Scottsdale, AZ 85252
(602) 951-9191

American Management Association
135 W. 50th St.
New York, NY 10020
(212) 586-8100

American Society for Hospital Personnel
Administration
840 N. Lake Shore Dr.
Chicago, IL 60611
(312) 280-6428

American Society for Industrial Security
1655 N. Fort Meyer Dr., Suite 1200
Arlington, VA 22209
(703) 522-5800

American Society for Public Administration
1120 G St. NW, Suite 500
Washington, DC 20005
(205) 393-7878

American Society for Training and Development
600 Maryland Ave. SW, Suite 305
Washington, DC 20024
(202) 484-2390

American Society of Pension Actuaries
1700 K St. NW, Suite 404

Washington, DC 20006
(202) 737-4360

American Society of Safety Engineers
850 Busse Highway
Park Ridge, IL 60068
(312) 692-4121

Association for Fitness in Business
1312 Washington Blvd.
Stamford, CT 06902
(203) 359-2188

Association for Workplace Democracy
1747 Connecticut Ave. NW
Washington, DC 20009
(202) 265-7727

Association of Executive Search Consultants, Inc.
151 Railroad Ave.
Greenwich, CT 06830
(203) 661-6606

Association of Outplacement Consulting Firms
c/o Sage Gray Todd & Sims
Two World Trade Center
New York, NY 10048
(212) 677-4040

Association of Part-time Professionals
Flow General Bldg.
7655 Old Springhouse Rd.
McLean, VA 22102
(703) 734-7975

Bureau of Industrial Relations
University of Michigan
Ann Arbor, MI 48104

Bureau of Labor Statistics (BLS)
Department of Labor
3rd Street & Constitution Ave. NW
Washington, DC 20210

Bureau of National Affairs (BNA)
1231 25th Street, NW
Washington, DC 20037
(202) 452-4320

Canadian Public Personnel Management
Association
220 Laurier Ave. West, Suite 720
Ottawa, Ontario
Canada KIP 5Z9
(613) 233-1742

Council on Employee Benefits
1144 E. Market St.
Akron, OH 44316
(216) 796-4008

Council on Multiemployer Pension Security
1000 Potomac St. NW, #103
Washington, DC 20007
(202) 337-0203

Department of Labor
3rd Street & Constitution Ave. NW
Washington, DC 20210

Employee Benefit & Research Institute
2121 K St. NW, Suite 860
Washington, DC 20037
(202) 659-0670

Employee Relocation Council
1627 K St. NW
Washington, DC 20006
(202) 857-0857

Employers Council on Flexible Compensation
1700 Pennsylvania Ave. NW
Washington, DC 20006
(202) 393-1728

Employment Management Association
20 William St.
Wellesley, MA 02181
(617) 235-8878

Equal Employment Opportunity Commission
(EEOC)
2401 E Street, NW
Washington, DC 20506

ESOP Association
1725 De Sales St. NW, Suite 400
Washington, DC 20036
(202) 293-2971

Hewitt Associates
100 Half Day Road
Lincolnshire, IL 60015
(312) 295-5000

Human Resource Systems Professionals, Inc.
3051 Adeline St., 2nd Floor
Berkeley, CA 94703
(415) 548-1364

Human Resources Planning Society
P.O. Box 2553
Grand Central Station
New York, NY 10163
(212) 837-0630

Industrial Cooperative Association
249 Elm St.
Somerville, MA 02144
(617) 628-7330

Industrial Relations Research Association
7226 Social Science Bldg.
Madison, WI 53706
(608) 262-2762

Internal Revenue Service (IRS)
111 Constitution Ave., NW
Washington, DC 20224

International Association for Personnel Women
211 E. 43rd St., Suite 1601
New York, NY 10017
(212) 867-4194

International Foundation of Employee Benefit
Plans
18700 Blue Mound Rd.
Brookfield, WI 53005
(414) 786-6700

International Personnel Management Association
1850 K St. NW, Suite 870
Washington, DC 20006
(202) 833-5860

International Society of Pre-Retirement Planners
3500 Clayton Rd., Suite B
Concord, CA 94519
(415) 676-0397

Labor Management Mediation Service
1620 I St. NW, Suite 616
Washington, DC 20006

National Association for the Advancement of Col-
ored People (NAACP)
1790 Broadway
New York, NY 10019

National Association of Manufacturers (NAM)
1776 F. St. NW
Washington, DC 20006

National Association of Personnel Consultants
1432 Duke St.
Alexandria, VA 22314
(703) 684-0180

National Association of Pension Consultants and
Administrators
Three Piedmont Center Bldg., Suite 300
Atlanta, GA 30305
(404) 231-0100

National Association of Suggestion Systems
230 N. Michigan Ave., Suite 1200
Chicago, IL 60601
(312) 372-1700

National Association of Temporary Services
119 S. St. Asaph St.
Alexandria, VA 22314
(703) 549-6287

National Center for Employee Ownership
927 S. Walter Reed, #6
Arlington, VA 22204
(703) 979-2375

National Employee Benefits Institute
1341 G Street NW, Suite 610
Washington, DC 20005
(202) 638-1984

National Employee Services & Recreation
Association
2400 S. Downing Ave.
Westchester, IL 60153
(312) 562-8130

National Public Employer Labor Relations
Association
55 E. Monroe St.
Chicago, IL 60603
(312) 782-1752

Occupational Safety and Health Administration
(OSHA)
200 Constitution Ave., NW
Washington, DC 20210

Office of Federal Contract Compliance Programs
(OFCCP)
200 Constitution Ave., NW
Washington, DC 20210

Pension Benefit Guaranty Corporation
P.O. Box 7119
Washington, DC 20044

Profit Sharing Council of America
200 N. Wacker Drive, Suite 722
Chicago, IL 60606
(312) 372-3411

Profit Sharing Research Foundation
1718 Sherman Ave.
Evanston, IL 60201
(312) 869-8787

Psychological Corporation
555 Academic Court
San Antonio, TX 78204-0952
(512) 299-1061

Society for Human Resource Management
606 N. Washington St.
Alexandria, VA 22314
(703) 548-3440

Society of Professional Benefit Administrators
2033 M St. NW, #605
Washington, DC 20036
(202) 223-6413

U.S. Chamber of Commerce
1615 H St., NW
Washington, DC 20062

Work in America Institute
700 White Plains Rd.
Scarsdale, NY 10583
(912) 472-9600

APPENDIX D: PERSONNEL MANAGEMENT LITERATURE

Research-oriented Journals

These journals contain articles that report original research. These journals typically contain a literature review, a statement of the hypotheses being tested, a description of the research method, a presentation of the results, a discussion of the research implications, and supporting references.

Academy of Management Journal

Academy of Management Review

Administrative Science Quarterly

Advances in Experimental Social Psychology

American Journal of Sociology

American Psychologist

American Sociological Review

Annual Review of Psychology

Behavioral Science

British Journal of Industrial Relations

Decision Sciences

Group and Organizational Studies

Human Organization

Human Relations

Industrial & Labor Relations Review

Industrial Relations

Interfaces

Journal of Abnormal Psychology

Journal of Applied Behavioral Science

Journal of Applied Psychology

Journal of Business

Journal of Business Communications

Journal of Business Research

Journal of Communications

Journal of Experimental Social Psychology

Journal of Consulting and Clinical Psychology

Journal of Counseling Psychology

Journal of Industrial Relations

Journal of Management

Journal of Management Studies

Journal of Personality and Social Psychology

Journal of Social Psychology

Journal of Social Issues

Journal of Vocational Behavior

Management Science

Occupational Psychology

Organization and Administrative Sciences

Organizational Behavior and Human Performance

Pacific Sociological Review

Personnel Psychology

Psychological Monographs

Psychological Review

Psychological Reports

Psychology of Women Quarterly

Social Forces

Social Science Research

Sociology of Work and Occupations

Sociology and Social Research

Sociometry

Management-oriented Journals

These journals generally cover a wide range of subjects. Articles in these publications are normally written for practitioners and are written to interpret, summarize, or discuss research and administrative applications. The ideas presented in some of these articles are not always supported by research and may simply express the opinions of an author.

Administrative Management

Advanced Management Journal

American Journal of Small Business

Arbitration Journal

Australian Journal of Management

Business

Business and Society Review

Business Horizons

Business Management

California Management Review

Canadian Manager

Columbia Journal of World Business

Compensation Review

Dun's Business Month

Employee Benefit Plan Review

Employee Benefits Journal

Employee Law Journal

Employment Relations Today

Forbes

Fortune

Harvard Business Review

Hospital & Health Services Administration

HRMagazine

Human Behavior

Human Resource Management

Human Resource Planning

Human Systems Management

Industry Week

Labor Law Journal

Long-Range Planning

Manage

Management Advisor

Management Planning

Management Review

Management World

Michigan State University Business Topics

Monthly Labor Review

National Productivity Review

Nation's Business

OD Practitioner

Organizational Behavior Teaching Review

Organizational Dynamics

Pension World

Personnel

Personnel Journal

Personnel Management

Public Administration Review

Public Opinion Quarterly

Public Personnel Management

Psychology Today

Research Management

Sloan Management Review

Sociology Today

Supervision

Supervisory Management

Training

Training and Development Journal

Working Woman

Yale Review

Abstracts and Indices

The following indices and abstracts are helpful in locating articles. Many university libraries also have computer-assisted reference resources.

Applied Science and Technology Index

Business Periodicals

Dissertation Abstracts

Employee Relations Index

Index to Legal Periodicals

Index to Social Sciences and Humanities

Management Abstracts

Management Contents

Personnel Management Abstracts

Psychological Abstracts

Reader's Guide to Periodical Literature

Social Science Index

Sociological Abstracts

Wall Street Journal Index

NAME INDEX